THE
STRATEGY
READER

SECOND EDITION

EDITOR

SUSAN SEGAL-HORN

The Open University

Blackwell Publishing

BLACKWELL PUBLISHING
350 Main Street, Malden, MA 02148-5020, USA
108 Cowley Road, Oxford OX4 1JF, UK
550 Swanston Street, Carlton, Victoria 3053, Australia

First edition published 1998 by Blackwell Publishers Ltd in association with
The Open University
Second edition published 2004 by Blackwell Publishing Ltd in association with
The Open University

Library of Congress Cataloging-in-Publication Data

The strategy reader / edited by Susan Segal-Horn.–2nd ed.
     p. cm.
   Includes bibliographical references and index.
   ISBN 1-4051-2687-6
  1. Strategic planning. I. Segal-Horn, Susan.
   HD30.28.S73969 2004
   658.4'012–dc22

                                                                                              2004008397

A catalogue record for this title is available from the British Library.

Set in 10/12 Dante
by Kolam Information Services Pvt. Ltd, Pondicherry, India
Printed and bound in the United Kingdom
by TJ International, Padstow, Cornwall

The publisher's policy is to use permanent paper from mills that operate a sustainable forestry policy, and which has been manufactured from pulp processed using acid-free and elementary chlorine-free practices. Furthermore, the publisher ensures that the text paper and cover board used have met acceptable environmental accreditation standards.

For further information on
Blackwell Publishing, visit our website:
www.blackwellpublishing.com

CONTENTS

PART III   THE RESOURCE-BASED VIEW OF STRATEGY   161

PART IV   CONNECTIONS BETWEEN STRATEGY, STRUCTURE AND PROCESS   241

PART V   ISSUES IN CORPORATE STRATEGY   319

PART VI   DEVELOPING INTERNATIONAL STRATEGY   371

FIGURES

TABLES

FOREWORD

The past decade-and-a-half has been a remarkable period for strategic management. The field has been energized and transformed by a number of new concepts, techniques, and theories. Even over the lifetime of my own book, *Contemporary Strategy Analysis,* which was first published in 1991, the field has developed at a blistering pace. This rapid development is partly a consequence of the challenges presented by the business environment. Companies have had to adjust their strategies to internationalization, disruptive technological change, fast changing consumer preferences, deregulation and privatization, and pressures for social and environmental responsibility. The pace of development is also a tribute to the creativity and intellectual dynamism of those involved in the field, not just business school academics, but also consultants and company executives.

Important areas of progress have included:

- The nature of strategy and alternative approaches to strategy making. Despite a growing consensus about what strategy is, there is much less agreement over how companies should determine their strategies. The long running debate between the advocates of rationally designed strategies and supporters of "emergent strategies" shows signs of resolution. In fast-changing business environments, strategic planning is more likely to be about setting direction in terms of statements of mission and vision rather than detailed plans while the growing complexity of organizations and their environments points to the strategic leadership as more about guiding organizational evolution rather than providing top-down direction.
- The analysis of industry and competition has developed way beyond Porter's 'five forces' analysis to embrace game theory, Schumpeterian 'creative destruction,' winner-take-all markets where technical standards rule, and ecological and evolutionary approaches.
- Most important, strategic analysis has shifted from its previous focus on the external environment of the firm to consider more closely firms' internal environment. The major feature of this shift has been the attention given to the resources and capabilities of the firm. Since Hamel and Prahalad's hugely influential article on 'core competences' there has been rapid development in resource-based approaches to the analysis of competitive advantage, exploration of the origins and development of organizational capabilities, and examination of dynamic capabilities.
- Interest in the internal environment of firms has also stimulated interest in organizational structure, management systems, corporate governance, and patterns of cooperation and coordination that form the foundations of organizational capability.
- Much of the pioneering work in understanding the internal aspects of the corporation in the process of strategy implementation has been driven by work in international strategy. The challenges faced by multinational corporations in adapting to and exploiting national differ-

ences while pursuing global strategies has resulted in pioneering work on organizational structure, management systems and corporate leadership notably by Chris Bartlett and Sumantra Ghoshal.

In addressing these issues, strategic management has been forced to be inclusive and eclectic with regard to the concepts, ideas and theories upon which it draws. During recent years, strategy has looked beyond economics and organization theory to draw inspiration from biology, ecology, systems theory, and the mathematics of chaos and complexity. This eclecticism of strategic management is an important reason for its vitality. While some areas of management are dominated by a single discipline – finance by economics, organization theory by sociology, consumer marketing by psychology – strategic management has felt free to plunder the intellectual heritage of numerous disciplines. The reason is that strategic management is driven primarily by practical issues: What technological standards will be set in mobile telephony over the next five years? Who will be the world leader in digital imaging: Kodak, Canon, HP or Sony? Can networks of cooperating individuals as represented by the Linux and Apache communities really challenge the market dominance of software giants like Microsoft? Can established corporations adapt to disruptive technologies?

One consequence of its intellectual dynamism has been a continuous expansion of the boundaries of strategic management. Thirty years ago the field was preoccupied with techniques of strategic planning. Twenty years ago it was dominated by questions of industry selection, competitive positioning and diversification. Now, strategic management is interested in all aspects of the development and long-term performance of company – including areas of interest that were once the preserve of other fields of study: organization theory and design, the management of technology, marketing, and operations management.

The readings in this book mark milestones in the development of strategic management over the past decade and a half and point towards issues and ideas that will mark the future of the field. The readings represent the contributions of some of the most influential thinkers in the field and reflect both the power of the ideas which have shaped thinking about strategy, and the rich variety of its intellectual heritage. Behind the readings are events and trends which shaped the ideas expressed in the papers. For example, the idea that strategy emerges from complex organizational processes was a consequence of the failure of so many of the carefully planned strategies of leading corporations. Interest in the role of standards in driving competitive advantage in technology-based industries was stimulated by the classic battles of the 1980s between VHS and Betamax in VCRs and between Mac and Wintel in PCs. New thinking about global strategies and multinational organization reflects the struggles of companies such as P&G, Toyota, IKEA, and HSBC to adapt to a world of competition and national differences.

In putting together this book of readings, Susan Segal-Horn has done a remarkable job not just of identifying the key recent developments in strategic management thinking, but also in capturing the vigor and excitement of this dynamic field of management. *The Strategy Reader* is a uniquely stimulating, wide-ranging, and useful set of key readings for anyone wishing to get to grips with the central ideas shaping current thinking in strategy.

Robert M. Grant

Georgetown University
Washington DC
August 2004

ACKNOWLEDGEMENTS

The editor and publisher would like to thank the following for permission to include copyright material:

R. Amit and P. J. H. Schoemaker (1993) 'Strategic Assets and Organizational Rent' from *Strategic Management Journal*, Vol. 14: 33–46. Copyright © 1993 John Wiley.

Christopher A. Bartlett, Sumantra Ghoshal and Julian Birkinshaw (2004) 'Preparing for the Future: Evolution of the Transnational' in Christopher A. Bartlett, Sumantra Ghoshal and Julian Birkinshaw *Transnational Management: Text, Cases and Readings in Cross-border Management* (New York: McGraw-Hill/Irwin), 8, pp. 756–73. Copyright © 2004 McGraw-Hill.

Nicole Woolsey Biggart and Gary G. Hamilton (1992) 'On the Limits of a Firm-based Theory' from *Networks and Organisation: Structure, Form and Action* by Nitin Nohria and Robert G. Eccles (Boston, MA: Harvard Business School Press, 1992), pp. 471–91. Copyright © 1992 President and Fellows of Harvard College.

Julian M. Birkinshaw (1997) 'Entrepreneurship in Multinational Corporations: The Characteristics of Subsidiary Initiatives' from *Strategic Management Journal*, Vol. 18, No. 3: 207–29. Copyright © 1997 John Wiley.

A. Campbell and S. Yeung (1991) 'Creating a Sense of Mission' from *Long Range Planning*, 24(4): 10–20. Copyright © 1991 Elsevier Science.

Michael Goold, Andrew Campbell and Marcus Alexander (1998) 'Corporate Strategy and Parenting Theory' from *Long Range Planning*, Vol. 31, No. 2: 308–14. Copyright © 1998 Elsevier Science.

Robert M. Grant (1991) 'The Resource-based Theory of Competitive Advantage: Implications for Strategy Formulation' from *California Management Review*, Vol. 33, No. 3. Copyright © 1991 Regents of the University of California.

G. Hamel and C. K. Prahalad (1993) 'Strategy as Stretch and Leverage' from *Harvard Business Review*, March–April 1993. Copyright © 1993 President and Fellows of Harvard College.

Michael A. Hitt, R. Duane Ireland and Michael D. Santoro (2004) 'Developing and Managing Strategic Alliances, Building Social Capital and Creating Value,', in A. Ghobadian, N. O'Regan, D. Gallear and H. Viney (eds.) *Strategy and Performance: Achieving Competitive Advantage in the Global Marketplace* (London: Palgrave Macmillan, 2004), pp. 13–34. Copyright © 2004 Michael A. Hitt, R. Duane Ireland and Michael D. Santoro.

Larue T. Hosmer (1994) 'Strategic Planning as if Ethics Mattered' from *Strategic Management Journal*, Vol. 15, Special Issue, Summer: 17–34. Copyright © 1994 John Wiley.

Gerry Johnson (1992) 'Managing Strategic Change – Strategy, Culture and Action' from *Long Range Planning*, Vol. 25 (1): 28–36. Copyright © 1992 Elsevier Science.

Constantinos C. Markides and Peter J. Williamson (1994) 'Related Diversification, Core Competences and Corporate Performance' from *Strategic Management Journal*, Vol. 15, Special Issue, Summer: 149–65. Copyright © 1994 John Wiley.

Danny Miller (1992) 'The Icarus Paradox' from *Business Horizons*, Vol. 35, Issue 1: 24–36. Copyright © 1992 by the Trustees at Indiana University, Kelley School of Business.

H. Mintzberg and J. A. Waters (1985) 'Of Strategies, Deliberate and Emergent' from *Strategic Management Journal*, 6: 257–72. Copyright © 1985 by John Wiley.

H. Mintzberg (1979) extract from *The Structuring of Organizations* (Englewood Cliffs, N.J.: Prentice-Hall Inc.).

Richard T. Pascale (1999) 'Surfing the Edge of Chaos' from *Sloan Management Review*, Spring: 83–94. Copyright © 1999 Tribune Media Services.

Michael E. Porter and Claas van der Linde, 1995, 'Green and Competitive: Ending the Stalemate' from *Harvard Business Review* September–October: 120–34. Copyright © 1995 President and Fellows of Harvard College.

Michael E. Porter (1996) 'What is Strategy?' from *Harvard Business Review*, November–December 1996: 61–78. Copyright © 1996 President and Fellows of Harvard College.

C. K. Prahalad and G. Hamel (1990) 'The Core Competence of the Corporation' from *Harvard Business Review*, May–June 1990: 79–91. Copyright © 1990 President and Fellows of Harvard College.

R. P. Rumelt (1991) 'How Much Does Industry Matter?' from *Strategic Management Journal*, 12: 167–85. Copyright © 1991 John Wiley.

Ron Sanchez (1996) 'Strategic Product Creation: Managing New Interactions of Technology, Markets and Organisations' from *European Management Journal*, Vol. 14, No. 2: 121–38. Copyright © 1996 Elsevier Science.

Susan Segal-Horn (1993) 'The Internationalisation of Service Firms' from *Advances in Strategic Management*, Vol. 9: 31–55. Copyright © 1993 by JAI Press Inc.

Carl Shapiro and Hal R. Varian (1999) 'The Art of Standards Wars' from *California Management Review*, Vol. 14, No. 2: 8–32. Copyright © 1999, by The Regents of the University of California. By permission of The Regents.

Sumantra Ghoshal (1987) 'Global Strategy: An Organising Framework' from *Strategic Management Journal*, Vol. 8: 425–40. Copyright © 1987 John Wiley.

David J. Teece, Gary Pisano and Amy Shuen (1997) 'Dynamic Capabilities and Strategic Management' from *Strategic Management Journal*, Vol. 18, No. 7: 509–33. Copyright © 1997 John Wiley.

Every effort has been made to trace copyright holders and to obtain their permission for the use of copyright material. The editor and publisher will gladly receive any information enabling them to rectify in subsequent editions any error or omission.

INTRODUCTION
THE DEVELOPMENT OF STRATEGIC MANAGEMENT THOUGHT

Susan Segal-Horn

Before we pursue the ideas contained in these readings, it may be useful to review some of the background and history of strategy and so begin to enter the strategist's way of thinking. The idea of strategy is very ancient indeed. It has been around for thousands of years as a way of thinking about survival and of achieving success through leadership in war or politics. In the time of the ancient Greek civilization, the term 'strategy' was used to describe a senior military commander or a chief magistrate. Political and military rulers or leaders have always had to make choices: about direction and policy; about the resources at their disposal; about how best to distribute those resources in pursuit of objectives, just as managers of modern organizations do. However, the use of the concept of 'strategy' in relation to organizations, and the application of the subject of strategic management, most typically to business firms and corporations, have only occurred since the twentieth century. The term 'strategic management' only began to be popularized in the 1960s via the American business schools. Nevertheless, activities which most modern managers would now think of as 'strategic' have been understood and acted upon in all the world's great civilizations over the centuries. Classic texts such as Sun Tzu's *The Art of War*, written in China 2,500 years ago, the political strategy of Machiavelli who wrote *The Prince* in 1513, or German military strategists such as von Clausewitz in the nineteenth century, are still well known and highly influential.

What I will try to explain in this Introduction is how the subject that we now call 'strategic management' has developed rapidly during the past sixty years. It began with assumptions of top-down planning seen as the responsibility of senior management, to more recent approaches based on assumptions of chaos and complexity in a world of rapid change. From 'planning' to 'chaos' in just over half a century needs explaining.

THE ORIGIN OF THE BASIC FRAMEWORKS

In the 1960s, strategic management was more likely to be called 'business policy'. The theory and practice of strategic management, as we know it today, have their roots in the work of a number of academics, industrialists and consultants from the 1960s and 1970s. The historical development of the field of strategy from the 1960s had its roots in the ideas of Alfred Chandler, a business historian; Igor Ansoff, a management theorist; Kenneth Andrews, a Harvard Business School business policy professor; and Alfred Sloan, a businessman and renowned industrialist who was the founder of the (then) giant American car firm General Motors. The 1960s and 1970s also saw the rise of a number of consulting practices specializing in strategy. The most influential of these were the Boston Consulting Group (BCG), founded in 1963, and McKinsey, whose founder, James McKinsey, was already operating as one of the first ever management consultants in the 1930s in the USA, before the company emerged in its present form as McKinsey & Co. in 1946. We will return later to the contribution made to the development of strategic management by these two management consulting firms.

Ansoff was originally a professor at the Carnegie Institute of Technology in the USA. His job title is instructive. He was professor of 'Industrial Administration'. His best-known and most influential book published in 1965 was called *Corporate Strategy* and subtitled 'An analytic approach to business policy for growth and expansion'. This gives a clear feel for the approach to management he espoused and which was one of the first coherent statements of this relatively new field of business strategy. Together with Chandler (1962, 1977) and Sloan (1963), they established a perspective which Whittington (2001) in his very helpful summary calls the 'Classical' school of strategic thinking and which is more commonly called the 'planning' approach to strategic management. The focus within the 'planning' school of strategy was on strategy as deliberate and rational, directed towards profit maximization, and very much the restricted domain of top management. It drew heavily on notions of military leadership and viewed corporations as hierarchies to be directed from the top. For a more modern example of this genre, see Ohmae (1983) and Porter (1980, 1985). The definition Chandler gave of strategy was:

> the determination of the basic long-term goals and objectives of an enterprise, and the adoption of courses of action and the allocation of resources necessary for those goals. (1962: 13)

This represented a view of strategy as planning. The focus of Chandler's work then, not surprisingly, was the organizational structures that would enable these managerial hierarchies to work efficiently by allowing top managers to allocate resources as they saw fit to achieve their strategic objectives. Companies and organizations were seen as efficient and rational resource-allocating mechanisms. Strategy in the Classical planning school is thus seen as a rational process of analysis which is designed to achieve (in the phrase popularized by Porter, 1985) 'competitive advantage' of one organization over another in the long term.

The need for a formal approach to corporate strategy was first identified by senior managers within what Chandler (1962, 1990) called M-Form (i.e. multi-business and multidivisional) organizations. These were firms that began to emerge in the late nineteenth century, first in the United States and then in Europe. They made large-scale investments to exploit new potential economies of scale in production, and economies of scope in distribution, to address the first newly emerging mass markets in the industrializing nations. Chandler used the term the 'visible hand' (1977) to describe the guiding role of a new breed of professional managers who actively designed and administered these new M-Form or multidivisional organizations. Multidivisional (M-Form) organizations made large investments in manufacturing and marketing and designed managerial hierarchies of control and decision-making to co-ordinate these various important functions. Management was therefore a co-ordinated functional hierarchy steered by the 'visible hand' of a cadre of professional managers, who controlled but did not own the organizations they managed. Ghemawat (2002) provides an excellent extended discussion of this period and the various building blocks of strategic management to which it contributed.

Further key contributions were made in this period by the work of Igor Ansoff (1965) and Kenneth Andrews (1971). Andrews argued that:

> every business organisation, every sub-unit of organisation, and even every individual ought to have a clearly defined set of purposes or goals which keeps it moving in a deliberately chosen direction and prevents it drifting in undesired directions. (1971: 23)

By the 1960s, the business policy course at Harvard Business School was emphasizing the need to match a company's 'strengths' and 'weaknesses' (i.e. its internal capabilities or distinctive competence) against perceived 'opportunities' and 'threats' (i.e. the risks arising from the competitive marketplace). This approach has become very well known indeed as the SWOT framework, which could first be found presented in the way that has become familiar to modern students of management by Andrews (1971: 69). Most importantly, Andrews also argued (as had Chandler) that 'the strategic decision is concerned with the long-term development of the enterprise'. Therefore, which of the firm's distinctive competences ('strengths') were enduring over the longer term and which were likely to need to change in line with changes in the marketplace, was, and indeed remains, one of the most difficult issues for strategic management.

Ansoff argued that companies should first ask whether new products had a 'common thread' with its existing products, both in order to reduce unnecessary risk and to build first on a fit with the firm's distinctive competence. He argued that the 'common thread' should arise from the firm's mission and current market position and should enable the firm to retain its strategic focus. This is the origin of the famous Ansoff 'Product/Mission Matrix' (1965: 128) which is part of an attempt to translate the SWOT framework into the basis for the further development of strategies.

By 1963, the majority of large US corporations had formal planning departments, as did many large European corporations. Although they made considerable use of the ideas and frameworks developed by management academics, they increasingly turned also to management consulting firms. The contribution of these consulting firms to the development of strategic thinking throughout the 1960s and 1970s was considerable. I will confine this Introduction just to the contribution of the two best-known strategy consulting firms: BCG and McKinsey.

BCG was itself an offshoot of the academic business policy faculty of Harvard Business School through its founder Bruce Henderson and many of its early associates. Similarly, later on in the 1980s and 1990s the Monitor Consultancy was an offshoot founded by Michael Porter, also of Harvard. BCG's success as a strategy consulting firm was largely based on its development and application of the concept of the Experience Curve (or learning curve). This was derived from their analysis of the impact of accumulated experience on competitors' costs and industry prices. BCG claimed that for each doubling of 'experience', total costs would decline by about 20–30 per cent as a result of economies of scale, organizational learning and technical innovation. This has strong strategic implications. If correct, it meant that both the value of market share and market share growth could be calculated, as could the effect of rates of growth. This led directly to another framework that was very well known and extremely influential on strategic thinking: the BCG Growth–Share Matrix. The BCG Growth–Share Matrix was the founding father of 'portfolio analysis', which mapped the relative potential of a corporation's various business units and their relative potential as areas for future investment. The BCG four-box (two-by-two) Matrix was the grid on which these assessments were plotted and the terms coined, such as 'Dog', 'Star' and 'Cash Cow', permanently entered the language and thinking of strategy and business. Other consulting firms came up with their versions of matrices for portfolio analysis.

McKinsey & Co. by 1971 had developed a nine-box (three-by-three) matrix known as the GE/McKinsey Matrix, developed jointly with the US company GE, having judged the two criteria used by the BCG grid as insufficiently detailed. Both these approaches required the separation of diversified corporations into Strategic Business Units (SBUs), to allow performance analysis and appraisal to be applied to the individual SBU. By the mid-1970s many large corporations had corporate planning departments and had introduced some form of portfolio analysis and portfolio planning techniques as a basic part of their strategic management of the firm.

Everything described so far is part of the planning approach to strategic management. Indeed, you may have noticed that I have spent a large part of this introduction to strategic management thought so far discussing writers, ideas and frameworks that do not appear in the Reader articles at all. Although they have been largely overtaken by later writers and ideas that I shall now be moving on to, it is very important to understand their role as part of the building blocks of modern strategic management. The contribution made by these earlier thinkers and practitioners is enormous, especially since the frameworks I have described are still part of almost every standard strategy textbook and part of the knowledge base of the subject of strategic management.

I will now briefly introduce the later stages of strategic management thought.

DEVELOPMENT IN THE 1980S AND 1990S

During the 1970s a shift occurred. What had been an emphasis on strategy as planning, dominated by corporate planning departments that focused on long-range planning and using mainly quantitative analysis techniques as the basis for strategic decision-making, suddenly began to break down. Their focus on cost-reduction and minimizing financial risk was inadequate and inappropriate as a more complex reality started to break through. It challenged the increasingly mechanical and formulaic application of the same analytical techniques by many firms across many industries. Ghemawat (2002: 50) describes this period in the late 1970s as 'leading to stalemates as more than one competitor pursued the same generic success factor'. In 1980, Hayes and Abernathy wrote a devastating and very influential critique of the effect of the spread of these analytical techniques, particularly within US firms (less so in Europe and almost absent in Japan) on the ability and willingness of managers to innovate and invest for future opportunities. At the same time, not only did the external business environment change utterly with the oil crises of 1974 and 1979, which ushered in a period of (permanent?) economic and geopolitical instability, but also international competition suddenly blossomed as Japanese, European and South-East Asian firms grew strong. The concepts of competition and competitiveness, both between firms, within industries, and between nations, grew in importance. Corporate planning was out; strategic thinking and strategic management, with their emphasis on the competitive environment and sources of competitive advantage, were in. Strategy became focused on performance and the search for profitability.

At first in the 1980s the explanation for differences in performance and profitability followed the strong influence of the industrial organization (IO) economists led by Michael Porter (1980, 1985) of Harvard Business School. His universally successful books emphasized the external environment of the firm and, most particularly, the analysis of industry structures to determine levels of industry attractiveness and comparative levels of potential industry profitability. However, after a decade of strategic management focus on industry structure and market positioning as the key drivers of performance and potential profitability of firms, a new perspective on strategy emerged in the 1990s. That is the approach known as the 'resource-based' view (RBV) of strategy

(Prahalad and Hamel, 1990; Grant, 1991). In contrast to the search for optimal market positioning, and market share leadership within attractive industries or segments, from 1990 onwards, and arising from the RBV perspective, the emphasis for strategic management shifted once again. Interest shifted from the external competitive environment to the internal analysis of the firm, as the basis for building strategies and finding sources of competitive advantage.

In a way, RBV marks a return to Andrews (1971) idea of 'distinctive competence' within firms. RBV takes the view that organizations are bundles of resources which managers have to develop and build towards achieving their strategic objectives. These basic resources constitute inputs into more complex resource clusters built up within each organization. How effectively these complex resource clusters are built and managed is determined by managerial capabilities. Since such managerial capabilities will vary, this suggests that two firms with the same physical resources but with different managerial or organizational talent will generate different levels and types of performance. In the same industry, therefore, firms may pursue different strategies and achieve different (heterogeneous) performance levels, as a result of similar resources but differing competences or capabilities. Thus, the RBV provides a convincing explanation for *heterogeneity* (i.e. performance differences between firms in the same industry), even where they face the same industry structure and the same wider competitive environment and are pursuing similar strategies, and even when they may possess broadly similar resources. This therefore places a premium on the role of management in creating relevant processes for capability-building within their organizations. As Porter (1996: 64; see Chapter 3 in the Reader) points out: 'Competitive strategy is about being different. It means deliberately choosing a different set of activities to deliver a unique mix of value.'

PARALLEL PERSPECTIVES

In his excellent and distinctive overview of the field of strategy, Whittington (2001) has chosen to summarize the development of strategic management thought into four perspectives: the Classical (which I have discussed at some length as the rational planning approach to strategy), the Evolutionary, the Processual (process) and the Systemic perspectives.

The Evolutionary approach to strategy (Nelson and Winter, 1982; Henderson, 1989) sees rational planning as frequently irrelevant, due to permanent environmental turbulence. Markets are seen as dynamic and businesses (and their strategies) must evolve or die. In this school of thought, it is markets not managers, which force choices. Successful strategies emerge in response to environmental turbulence and the role of managers is to fit their strategies as well as possible to the turbulence. A more recent, and much tougher, child of this approach to strategy is the Population Ecology approach to strategy which claims that the structure, character and resource endowment of an organization are fixed shortly after its birth. Its survival then depends upon its ability to acquire an adequate amount of the resources available within its relevant population of firms. The struggle for resources will then drive out the less 'fit' organization (as in Darwinian 'survival of the fittest'). A more useful version of this approach is to be found in Barnett and Hansen (1996) where they extend the idea of the 'Red Queen' to the evolution of organizations. The term the 'Red Queen' comes from the story by Lewis Carroll, *Alice Through the Looking Glass*, where the young girl Alice notices that she seems to be standing still even though she is running in a race. The Red Queen replies that in a fast world one must run just to stand still. Barnett and Hansen found that organizations learn over time as a response to competition, which in turn itself helped to create, and benefit from, stronger competitors.

Organizations were less likely to fail if they had recent competitive experience, and were more likely to get stuck in a 'competence trap' if their experience of competition was in the distant past. The Red Queen effect means that as organizations struggle to adapt to competitive pressures, they become stronger competitors themselves. However, it also means that over time, the general overall level of competitiveness of firms will rise and that therefore, no source of competitive advantage is likely to be sustainable over the longer term.

The Processual (process) approach to strategy, like the Evolutionary approach, sees strategy-making as a *process* within which strategy emerges from a combination of influences within the organisation. From this perspective, whose best-known exponent is Henry Mintzberg (1987), strategy is emergent (i.e. 'emerges' gradually in response to a range of views within the organization in addition to those from the top management), rather than deliberate, rational and top-down as the Classical planning school would argue. Strategy as process not only reflects the views of top management, but represents a set of pragmatic compromises between various stakeholders in the organization (Pettigrew, 1985). The implication of this process view of strategy is that those strategies which are imposed top-down, without incorporating other organizational constituencies, are unlikely, in practice, to be effective, fully implemented and realized strategies. Another equally important implication of the view of strategy as a process is that it means that strategic management is not seen as a linear sequence of one-off activities of analysis, evaluation and implementation which are carried out in a logical sequence every few years. Instead, it must be understood and practised as continuous and iterative, which more realistically reflects the internal and external complexity with which it has to deal.

Systems thinkers (Granovetter, 1985; Shrivastava, 1986) see strategy as the child of context: social context, geographic context, political context, cultural context, etc. This derives initially from Granovetter's (1985) use of the sociological concept of the 'social embeddedness' of all economic activity. By 'embeddedness' he means that strategies will reflect the social, political or cultural systems within which the strategist is embedded. It then follows that strategy must always be *contingent* on that context rather than absolute. The practice of strategy will differ in different social, political, economic or religious contexts. Profit maximization may be a (or the) key driver of strategic objectives in Anglo-Saxon systems (although that is often less the case now than in the past), whereas efficiency and performance may be considerably less important than family, social or national welfare in other cultures. Therefore, Asian or Middle Eastern strategic thinking may vary considerably from Western European or Eastern European strategic thinking. Viable strategies will therefore be context-specific. More recent application of this concept of 'embeddedness' can be found in social network theory applied within strategy. Network perspectives build on the view that 'economic actions are influenced by the social context in which they are embedded and that actions can be influenced by the position of actors in social networks' (Gulati, 1998: 295). An excellent example of the application of social network theory may be found in Gulati's (1998) research on the impact of social networks on strategic alliances. He shows how social networks of pre-existing social ties such as family, friendship or overlapping organizational membership lead to more shared information and knowledge, which in turn affect the dynamics of alliance formation and the ability to understand the complexities of managing a portfolio of alliances.

As the previous discussion illustrates, the great questions in strategy are continually being revisited in the light of current needs and current knowledge. The relationship between strategy and structure is one such endless debate. For example, the ground-breaking work carried out originally by Chandler (1962, 1977, 1990) on the relationship between strategy and organizational structure has been taken forward from quite different perspectives by Bartlett and Ghoshal (1993) and Hedlund (1994). Chandler's work explained the logic behind the shape, size and purpose of the growth of large M-Form corporations as industrialization expanded from country to country, driven by the search for scale and scope efficiencies. As the title of their 1993 article 'Beyond the M-Form' indicated, Bartlett and Ghoshal argued for a newer type of large corporation, one that could deal more flexibly with current managerial requirements for initiative, creativity, collaboration and learning than the traditional M-Form structure that had been designed to deliver cost efficiencies. Hedlund (1994) went further and talked about the rise of 'N-Form' organizations, by which he meant 'network' organizations and other kinds of virtual organizational types which have emerged as collaborative networking between organizations, and the sharing of resources for specific purposes and projects, became more viable and necessary. As co-operative strategies have become almost as significant for the strategic manager as competitive strategies, it is not surprising that new structures will emerge to meet the needs of the new strategies. As Mintzberg (1979) has long argued (see Chapter 13 in this Reader), types of organization structure will vary according to the strategic needs and purposes of the organization, so that strategy and structure must always walk in step with each other and take each other into account.

CURRENT DEVELOPMENTS

In the past decade there has been a profusion of further developments within the field of strategic management. Probably the most significant element within all areas of the subject is the predominance of the concept of strategy *dynamics*. Most managers feel that they are coping with accelerating rates of evolutionary change in their industry and are searching for guidance within this context of what D'Aveni has popularly called 'hypercompetition' (1994). Whether we are talking about competitive dynamics, dynamic capabilities, systems dynamics or change management, the common thread is the search for theory and practice which are able to cope with balancing the conflicting requirements of strategy formulation for the longer term, combined with immediate short-term pressures. Given this sense of an ever-increasing push of competitive pressures, it is not surprising that strategy has shifted in the late 1990s and early twenty-first century, to a search for dynamic theories of competition. Ghemawat (2002: 64) has expressed this particularly wryly as

> the dynamic question of how businesses might create and sustain competitive advantage in the presence of competitors who could not be counted on to remain inert all the time.

Game theory is a strategy perspective derived from mathematics. It studies the interactions between players whose payoffs for their decisions depend on each other's choices. 'Zero-sum' games (i.e. if you win, I lose, and vice versa) allow only one winner and the winner's gains will be exactly balanced by the losses of the other players. There are also 'non-zero-sum' games in which there are opportunities for co-operation as well as competition. It is these non-zero-sum games that are seen as particularly relevant to strategic thinking in the modern world where so many firms depend on contributions from, and alliances with, other firms to implement their strategies, since the resources of one firm alone are insufficient. Although the empirical base of game theory is limited, it does provide both a language and a logical way of approaching strategic analysis that is especially helpful in competitive versus co-operative relationships (Brandenburger and Nalebuff, 1996).

As well as game theory, other new types of approaches have also been emerging. Chaos theory (Stacey, 1993), complexity theory (Brown and Eisenhardt, 1998), the strategic use of knowledge (von Krogh *et al.*, 2000), evolutionary biology, cognitive psychology and real options theory derived from finance (Schwartz and Trigeorgis, 2001), are all being applied to strategic analysis and strategic choice. The common factor within all these newer approaches is the view that the degree of turbulence facing the modern organization is such that traditional approaches to strategic management will not do. Conflicting ideas and views within organizations need to be encouraged to surface within teams and networks so that experimentation and learning can take place. This is an exciting and challenging time to be studying and practising strategy.

Overall in developmental terms, there has been a gradual evolution in strategic management as a subject away from a rational planning view of strategy and towards an emergent, incremental, process view of strategy. In these more recent schools of thought, industry type does not of itself determine strategic possibilities. Innovation and learning are as relevant in mature industries as in growth industries, and possibly more so. Strategic management now offers many differing views on how to compete for resources and for customers. This suggests, rightly, that strategic decision-making is complex and difficult and has to take place in contexts that are continuously dynamic. The gradual development of theories of learning and complexity within strategy shows a vibrant subject continuously responding to organizational changes and managerial needs.

Having discussed some of the history and development of strategic management as a subject, let us consider the reasons why such a subject should have arisen at all.

WHAT IS STRATEGY FOR?

At some time in the life-cycle of virtually every organization, its ability
to succeed in spite of itself runs out. (Brier's First Law)

I am indebted to my colleague Professor John Constable for introducing me to Brier's First Law. Neither he nor I were ever sure of Brier's identity or if there ever was a second 'Law', but he deserves his fifteen minutes of fame just for the First. It is saying something essential about the purpose of strategy. The existence of a clear strategy is what gives drive and strategic intent to an organization (Hamel and Prahalad, 1989). It defines a target for where the organization wants to be in the future. There can be only a very poor second place for an organization that addresses operational processes in isolation from strategic intent, as Porter has forcibly argued (1996).

Strategy is a practical subject. That does not mean that it contains no concepts, frameworks or methodologies to provide pathways for analysis and implementation. It means that it has emerged as an academic subject because a practical need exists to better understand processes of strategy-making and strategy implementation. That is because in modern societies strategy is most strongly associated with economic life and business organizations and is thus closely identified with economic growth and job and wealth creation. On that basis, effective (and ineffective) strategies have social, political and economic consequences for the societies in which we live and for our daily lives. As Rumelt *et al.* (1994) have said:

> Strategic management as a field of enquiry is firmly grounded in practice and exists because of the importance of its subject.

Strategy is about choices, which affect outcomes. Organizations can often survive, and indeed do well, for periods of time in conditions of relative stability, low environmental turbulence and little competition for resources. Virtually none of these conditions prevail in the modern world for any organization or sector, public or private. Hence the rationale for strategic management: to enable an organization to identify, build and deploy resources most effectively towards the attainment of its objectives. To achieve this, Henderson (1984) suggested the following were necessary:

- a critical mass of knowledge concerning the competitive process
- the ability to integrate this knowledge and understand cause and effect
- imagination to foresee alternative actions and logic to analyse their consequences
- availability of resources beyond current needs in order to invest in future potential.

Although this list of factors emphasizes the analytical part of strategic thinking and seems to ignore the process of strategy-making, the view taken in this book is that the purpose of analysis is to help understand the issues. It does not of itself provide the answers. Managers must discover these for themselves. I would agree with Henderson that it is in their use of their 'imagination to foresee alternative actions', and deciding in which possible futures to invest, that the true test of their strategic thinking will emerge. Although there are many reliable frameworks for carrying out strategic analysis, there are no recipes for good strategy. Analysis is a necessary but not a sufficient condition for strategic thinking. Strategic thinking is about managers making judgements, which they then translate into decisions. Judgements are not context-free and neither is strategic decision-making. Ultimately it depends on exercising judgement in the light of your own deep understanding of your organization and your context.

THE STRUCTURE OF THIS BOOK

The readings in this book are organized into seven parts. Each part contains a mixture of articles: some develop the conceptual ideas and frameworks of strategic management; others describe broad empirical research findings or particular industry or company practice. All are part of the continuous critical debate within strategy.

The collection of papers in Part I, 'What Is Strategy?', explores the nature and the purpose of strategy, how it is generated within an organization and who 'owns' or controls it. Are strategies used to further the aspirations of an organization or to limit them? These articles were chosen because they support the view that organizations make their own strategy: that strategic thinking is at least as important, and may be more important, than the industry or external environment in which the organization is placed. In Part II, 'The Context of Strategy', the theme of strategic thinking is continued, in examining the nature of external influences on strategy. How influential is industry context on strategy? Are strategic thinking and strategic management ethical? What, if any, values do they reflect and how do these influence strategic decisions? How should managers respond to wider stakeholder interests in their organization? How do differences in national culture and belief systems affect the strategic thinking of managers? If environmental context is important for strategy, then which are the most important environmental domains and why? Part III of the book, 'The Resource-Based View of Strategy', balances the focus upon external environmental and context of Part II. It treats in some depth the internal analysis of the organization's resources and capabilities. It is an approach to strategy that complements the externally focused industry-and-market-positioning strategy paradigm popularized by Michael Porter in the 1980s which regarded strategy as driven by differences in market structure. By contrast, the resource-based view looks at the organization in terms of internal features and the resources that it owns or controls as the key to strategy. The articles in Part IV, 'Connections Between Strategy, Structure and Process', address strategy implementation. They seek to reflect both the creativity and the difficulties of strategy implementation. In particular, these articles present the relationship between strategy and organization structure, between strategy and organizational culture, and the continuous inter-relationship in all organizations between all three elements of strategy, structure and culture. The readings emphasize strategy as a *process* within a structural and cultural context.

All of the issues discussed in the previous sections of the book will reappear in both Part V, 'Issues in Corporate Strategy', and Part VI, 'Developing International Strategy'. That reflects the fact that corporate strategy and international strategy both have to deal with all the standard strategy issues of structure, culture, resources, design and process as well as a further range of problems arising from how to manage the co-ordination and integration of multidivisional and cross-border organizations. Managing the relationship between a portfolio of businesses owned, or controlled, by the same corporate parent, adds additional layers of complexity to the strategic thinking required of corporate, as opposed to business unit (SBU) managers. What is the strategic logic that justifies the mix of businesses in the portfolio or the set of alliances within which the firm is placed? Part VI, 'Developing International Strategy', tries to explain both what drives organizations towards internationalization in terms of the potential commercial benefits available (i.e. sources of potential strategic advantage) as well as the difficulties arising from being a multinational corporation (MNC). However, it also shows where future sources of advantage available to international organizations pursuing international strategies are likely to be found, and more recent approaches to strategy and structure for MNCs.

The book ends with the 'Postscript' in Part VII that attempts to capture both the present complexities and the future directions for strategic management. Strategic decision-making has to cope with continuous uncertainty and unpredictability and is a reflection of the context both inside and outside the organization. Strategic management as a practical guide to managers and as a field of enquiry has to find ways of helping managers manage within this dynamic context. Therefore, the book ends by returning to the overview of different types of approaches to strategy, where such future perspectives in the further development of strategic management might come from and what ideas they might contain. This final section is not designed to neatly close issues down but instead to open them wide to the complexity, diversity and paradox that make up organizational life.

THE PURPOSE OF THIS BOOK

If this book has a message, it is that management matters and that organizations are heterogeneous and that these two factors are intimately related. The book has been designed to stimulate the imagination and inform the judgement of all those engaged in strategic decision-making, either currently or in the future, since it is assumed that the quality of their judgement matters. All of the contributions in their separate ways are challenging strategic thinking. Some are already regarded as classics in the field and others are more unusual or less well-known contributions, which have been chosen for their additional insight and perspective. It is a collection that provides an overview of where the field of strategy is going and what the emerging issues are for strategic thinking for the next decade. Strategy in the future must be able to deal with complexity, learning and flexibility. Managers must be prepared and able to change their thinking and aspirations accordingly:

... .if the times and conditions change, he will be ruined because he does not change his methods of procedure ... because he cannot be persuaded to depart from a path, having always prospered by following it. (Machiavelli, 1513)

The book has been designed to present both the past and the future of strategy. It has done this by selecting topics that, in the view of the editor, are substantive rather than merely fashionable or transitory and from which the reader should emerge with an excitement about what it means to practise strategy.

REFERENCES

Andrews, K.R. (1971) *The Concept of Corporate Strategy*, Homewood, IL: Irwin.

Ansoff, I. (1965) *Corporate Strategy*, Harmondsworth: Penguin.

Barnett, W.P. and Hansen M.T. (1996) 'The Red Queen in Organisational Evolution', *Strategic Management Journal*, Vol. 17, Special Issue: 139–57.

Bartlett, C.A. and Ghoshal, G. (1993) 'Beyond the M-Form: Toward a Managerial Theory of the Firm', *Strategic Management Journal*, Vol. 14: 23–46.

Brandenburger, A.M. and Nalebuff, B.J. (1996) *Co-opetition*, New York: HarperCollins.

Brown, S. and Eisenhardt, K. (1998) *Competing on the Edge: Strategy as Structured Chaos*, Boston: Harvard Business School Press.

Chandler, A.D. (1962) *Strategy and Structure*, Cambridge, MA: MIT Press.

Chandler, A.D. (1977) *The Visible Hand*, Cambridge, MA: Harvard University Press.

Chandler, A.D. (1990) *Scale and Scope*, Cambridge, MA: Harvard University Press/Belknap.

D'Aveni, R. (1994) *Hypercompetition: Managing the Dynamics of Strategic Maneuvering*, New York: Free Press.

Ghemawat, P. (2002) 'Competition and Business Strategy in Historical Perspective', *Business History Review*, Vol. 76, Spring: 37–74.

Granovetter, M. (1985) 'Economic Action and Social Structure: The Problem of Embeddedness', *American Journal of Sociology*, Vol. 91, No. 3: 481–510.

Grant, R.M. (1991) 'The Resource-Based Theory of Competitive Advantage: Implications for Strategy Formulation', *California Management Review*, Spring: 114–35.

Gulati, R. (1998) 'Alliances and Networks', *Strategic Management Journal*, Vol. 19: 293–317.

Hamel, G. and Prahalad, C.K. (1989) 'Strategic Intent', *Harvard Business Review*, May–June: 63–76.

Hayes, R.H. and Abernathy, W.J. (1980) 'Managing Our Way to Economic Decline', *Harvard Business Review*, July–August: 67–75.

Hedlund, G. (1994). 'A Model of Knowledge Management and the N-Form Corporation', *Strategic Management Journal*, Vol. 15, Special Issue: 73–90.

Henderson, B.D. (1984) *The Logic of Business Strategy*, Cambridge, MA: Ballinger.

Henderson, B.D. (1989) 'The Origin of Strategy', *Harvard Business Review*, November–December, 139–43.

Machiavelli, N. (1984) *The Prince*, Oxford: Oxford University Press.

Mintzberg, H. (1979) *The Structuring of Organizations*, Englewood Cliffs, NJ: Prentice-Hall.

Mintzberg, H. (1987) 'Crafting Strategy', *Harvard Business Review*, July–August: 65–75.

Nelson, R. and Winter, S. (1982) *An Evolutionary Theory of Economic Change*, Cambridge, MA: Harvard University Press.

Ohmae, K. (1983) *The Mind of the Strategist*, Harmondsworth: Penguin.

Pettigrew, A. (1985) *The Awakening Giant: Continuity and Change in ICI*, Oxford: Blackwell.

Porter, M.E. (1980) *Competitive Strategy*, New York: Free Press.

Porter, M.E. (1985) *Competitive Advantage*, New York: Free Press.

Porter, M.E. (1996) 'What is Strategy?' *Harvard Business Review*, November–December: 61–78.

Prahalad, C.K. and Hamel, G. (1990) 'The Core Competence of the Corporation', *Harvard Business Review*, May–June: 71–91.

Quinn, J.B. (1992) *Intelligent Enterprise*, New York: Free Press.

Rumelt, R.P., Schendel, D.E. and Teece, D.J. (1994) *Fundamental Issues in Strategy: A Research Agenda*, Boston: Harvard Business School Press.

Schwartz, E.S. and Trigeorgis, L. (2001) *Real Options and Investment under Uncertainty: Classical Readings and Recent Contributions*, Cambridge, MA: MIT Press.

Shrivastava, P. (1986) 'Is Strategic Management Ideological?', *Journal of Management*, Vol. 12, No. 3: 363–77.

Sloan, A.P. (1963) *My Years with General Motors*, London: Sedgwick & Jackson.

Stacey, R. (1993) 'Strategy as Order Emerging from Chaos', *Long Range Planning*, Vol. 26, No. 1: 10–17.

Sun Tzu (1983) *The Art of War*, New York: Dell Publishing.

von Krogh, G., Ichijo, K. and Nonaka, I. (2000). *Enabling Knowledge Creation*, New York: Oxford University Press.

Whittington, R. (2001) *What is Strategy – and Does It Matter?* 2nd edition, London: Thomson Learning.

PART I

WHAT IS STRATEGY?

INTRODUCTION

The article by Mintzberg and Waters that opens Part I, asks the fundamental question: 'How do strategies form in organizations?' Is strategy-making controlled solely by the senior management of the organization? They draw the important distinction between the plans and intentions of organizational leaders (*intended* strategy) and what the organization actually did (*realized* strategy). By comparing the two they are able to provide a basic framework of types of strategy-making processes, in the form of a continuum. At one end of the continuum is planned strategy, where intentions are clearly formulated and subsequently translated into actions. The further the authors move along the continuum away from planned to entrepreneurial, ideological and umbrella strategies, the less precisely articulated is the strategy and the looser the central control. At the far end of the continuum are the 'emergent' strategies, such as the consensus strategy arrived at through mutual adjustment, which may frequently attract wider support and speedier implementation within an organization since it has been arrived at ('emerged') from a wider array of views. Using the continuum as their framework, Mintzberg and Waters are able to show powerfully that there is no 'one best way' of formulating strategy. The process appropriate for one type of organization may be wholly inappropriate for another facing a different environmental context, different tasks and different stakeholder expectations. Theirs, then, is a 'contingency' view of strategy. However, Mintzberg and Waters do stress that emergent strategies do not imply that the organization is no longer being managed, only that the management is able to listen and learn; just as they similarly recognize that managers do sometimes need to impose a clear sense of (intended) direction on their organizations. The gap that they reveal between intended and realized strategy will be returned to later in Part IV.

The article by Prahalad and Hamel broke new ground for strategic thinking in the 1990s. It is one of a series of six articles published by Hamel and Prahalad in the *Harvard Business Review* from the mid-1980s to the mid-1990s. In those articles a distinct body of work has been set out which has acquired a wide readership amongst both academics and practitioners. Their perspective on strategy extends the traditional conceptual strategy frameworks as follows:

Traditional approach	*Hamel and Prahalad*
Strategy as fit	Strategy as stretch
Resource allocation	Resource leverage
Portfolio of businesses	Portfolio of competences
Competition as confrontation	Competition as collaboration

Their work asks: 'why do some companies redefine the industries in which they compete, while others take the existing structure as given?' Hamel and Prahalad answer their own question about the aspirations and objectives of companies in terms of what they call 'managerial frames of reference' – the assumptions and received wisdom which 'frame' a company's understanding of itself and its industry and which drive its managers' competitive strategy. They argue that existing frames of reference can only deliver existing types of strategies, those that fit the existing industry recipes about how to compete. They specifically emphasize the role of senior management in setting ambitious targets and being creative in their internal and external view of resources. In the development of their idea of 'stretch' in this article, Hamel and Prahalad are their own best illustration of how the concept of 'stretch' can impact on strategic thinking. Their stance on strategy is that managerial aspirations should drive resources, rather than vice versa. They should 'design a chasm between ambition and resources'. The concept of 'leveraging' (i.e. getting the most out of the resources one has) is critical to this vision because it is saying that managers should not be constrained by the level of resources they have but should instead be seeking greater resource productivity. They see leveraging as the opposite of resource downsizing and delayering which are inherently demoralizing, whereas leveraging is creative and energizing. Their ideas will be returned to in Part III.

The final chapter in Part I is a powerful restatement and development by Michael Porter of the 'positioning' school of strategy. Porter stresses his anxiety that managers are no longer distinguishing between operational effectiveness and strategy and that as a result, 'bit by bit, almost imperceptibly, management tools have taken the place of strategy'. Porter argues that *both* are essential to superior performance but that they work in very different ways. In Porter's terms, having a strategy means deliberately choosing, exercising choice: 'choosing a particular set of activities to deliver a unique mix of value'. He considers this to be the reason why Japanese corporations have become less successful. Their success was based predominantly on operational efficiency and their lead has been narrowed and in some sectors wiped out. Porter argues that they will now 'have to learn strategy', by which he means making hard choices about which markets, which customers, which service levels, etc. Imitating each other's improvements in quality, outsourcing or partnerships leads to a convergence of strategies and 'a series of races down identical paths no one can win'. Continuous improvement in operational effectiveness alone is not the basis of advantage. Porter argues that choices and trade-offs are essential in strategy. It is important to choose and deliberately limit what an organization offers. Operational effectiveness is critical but it is not a substitute for strategic thinking or a substitute for choosing a strategy.

In this article Porter is dismissive of the Evolutionary school of strategy and the current popular view of 'hypercompetition' (i.e. extreme environmental turbulence) as driving strategy. He regards this as an excuse for poor management and a lack of clear strategic thinking: 'what some call hypercompetition is a self-inflicted wound, not the inevitable outcome of a changing paradigm of competition'. He also sees Hamel and Prahalad's ideas as, at best difficult to implement, at worst, unrealistic, and overall certainly focused on operational rather than strategic objectives. Hamel and Prahalad are more concerned to enrich the strategy process, the way in which organizations can renovate their strategic thinking, while Porter is concerned that organizations should make strategic choices and then focus coherently on the consequences of that choice for the way the organization is managed.

1

Of Strategies, Deliberate and Emergent

Henry Mintzberg and James A. Waters

Introduction

How do strategies form in organizations? Research into the question is necessarily shaped by the underlying conception of the term. Since strategy has almost inevitably been conceived in terms of what the leaders of an organization 'plan' to do in the future, strategy formation has, not surprisingly, tended to be treated as an analytic process for establishing long-range tools and action plans for an organization; that is, as one of formulation followed by implementation. As important as this emphasis may be, we would argue that it is seriously limited, that the process needs to be viewed from a wider perspective so that the variety of ways in which strategies actually take shape can be considered.

For over 10 years now, we have been researching the process of strategy formation based on the definition of strategy as 'a pattern in a stream of decisions' (Mintzberg, 1972, 1978; Mintzberg and Waters, 1982, 1984; Mintzberg *et al.*, 1986; Mintzberg and McHugh, 1985; Brunet, Mintzberg and Waters, 1986). This definition was developed to 'operationalize' the concept of strategy, namely to provide a tangible basis on which to conduct research into how it forms in organizations. Streams of behaviour could be isolated and strategies identified as patterns or consistencies in such streams. The origins of these strategies could then be investigated, with particular attention paid to exploring the relationship between leadership plans and intentions and what the organizations actually did. Using the label strategy for both of these phenomena – one called *intended*, the other *realized* – encouraged that exploration.
[. . .]

Comparing intended strategy with realized strategy, as shown in Figure 1.1, has allowed us to distinguish *deliberate* strategies – realized as intended – from *emergent* strategies – patterns or consistencies realized despite, or in the absence of, intentions.
[. . .]

This paper sets out to explore the complexity and variety of strategy formation processes by refining and elaborating the concepts of deliberate and emergent strategy. We begin by specifying more precisely what pure deliberate and pure emergent strategies might mean in the context of organization, describing the conditions under which each can be said to exist. What does it mean for an 'organization' – a collection of people joined together to pursue some mission in common – to act deliberately? What does it mean for a strategy to emerge in an organization, not guided by intentions? We then identify various types of strategies that have appeared in our

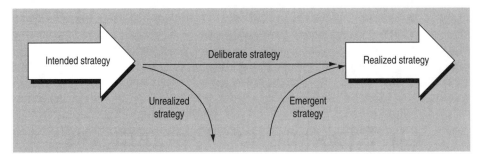

Figure 1.1 Types of strategies

empirical studies, each embodying differing degrees of what might be called deliberateness or emergentness. The paper concludes with a discussion of the implications of this perspective on strategy formation for research and practice.

PURE DELIBERATE AND PURE EMERGENT STRATEGIES

For a strategy to be perfectly deliberate – that is, for the realized strategy (pattern in actions) to form exactly as intended – at least three conditions would seem to have to be satisfied. First, there must have existed precise intentions in the organization, articulated in a relatively concrete level of detail, so that there can be no doubt about what was desired before any actions were taken. Secondly, because organization means collective action, to dispel any possible doubt about whether or not the intentions were organizational, they must have been common to virtually all the actors: either shared as their own or else accepted from leaders, probably in response to some sort of controls. Thirdly, these collective intentions must have been realized exactly as intended, which means that no external force (market, technological, political, etc.) could have interfered with them. The environment, in other words, must have been either perfectly predictable, totally benign, or else under the full control of the organization. These three conditions constitute a tall order, so that we are unlikely to find any perfectly deliberate strategies in organizations. Nevertheless, some strategies do come rather close, in some dimensions if not all.

For a strategy to be perfectly emergent, there must be order – consistency in action over time – in the absence of intentions about it. (No consistency means no strategy or at least unrealized strategy – intentions not met.) It is difficult to imagine action in the *total* absence of intention – in some pocket of the organization if not from the leadership itself – such that we would expect the purely emergent strategy to be as rare as the purely deliberate one. But again, our research suggests that some patterns come rather close, as when an environment directly imposes a pattern of action on an organization.

Thus, we would expect to find tendencies in the directions of deliberate and emergent strategies rather than perfect forms of either. In effect, these two form the poles of a continuum along which we would expect real-world strategies to fall. Such strategies would combine various states of the dimensions we have discussed above: leadership intentions would be more or less precise, concrete and explicit, and more or less shared, as would intentions existing elsewhere in the organization; central control over organizational actions would be more or less firm and more or less pervasive; and the environment would be more or less benign, more or less controllable and more or less predictable.

Below we introduce a variety of types of strategies that fall along this continuum, beginning with those closest to the deliberate pole and ending with those most reflective of the characteristics of emergent strategy. We present these types, not as any firm or exhaustive typology (although one may eventually emerge), but simply to explore this continuum of emergentness of strategy and to try to gain some insights into the notions of intention, choice and pattern formation in the collective context we call organization.

The Planned Strategy

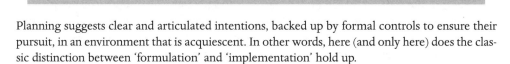

Planning suggests clear and articulated intentions, backed up by formal controls to ensure their pursuit, in an environment that is acquiescent. In other words, here (and only here) does the classic distinction between 'formulation' and 'implementation' hold up.

In this first type, called *planned strategy*, leaders at the centre of authority formulate their intentions as precisely as possible and then strive for their implementation – their translation into collective action – with a minimum of distortion, 'surprise-free'. To ensure this, the leaders must first articulate their intentions in the form of a plan, to minimize confusion, and then elaborate this plan in as much detail as possible, in the form of budgets, schedules and so on, to pre-empt discretion that might impede its realization. Those outside the planning process may act, but to the extent possible they are not allowed to decide. Programmes that guide their behaviour are built into the plan, and formal controls are instituted to ensure pursuit of the plan and the programmes.

But the plan is of no use if it cannot be applied as formulated in the environment surrounding the organization so the planned strategy is found in an environment that is, if not benign or controllable, then at least rather predictable. Some organizations, as Galbraith (1967) describes the 'new industrial states', are powerful enough to impose their plans on their environments. Others are able to predict their environments with enough accuracy to pursue rather deliberate, planned strategies. We suspect, however, that many planned strategies are found in organizations that simply extrapolate established patterns in environments that they assume will remain stable. In fact, we have argued elsewhere (Mintzberg and Waters, 1982) that strategies appear not to be *conceived* in planning processes so much as elaborated from existing visions or copied from standard industry recipes (see Grinyer and Spender, 1979); planning thus becomes programming, and the planned strategy finds its origins in one of the other types of strategies described below.

Although few strategies can be planned to the degree described above, some do come rather close, particularly in organizations that must commit large quantities of resources to particular missions and so cannot tolerate unstable environments. They may spend years considering their actions, but once they decide to act, they commit themselves firmly. In effect, they deliberate so that their strategies can be rather deliberate. Thus, we studied a mining company that had to engage in a most detailed form of planning to exploit a new ore body in an extremely remote part of Quebec. Likewise, we found a very strong planning orientation in our study of Air Canada, necessary to coordinate the purchase of new, expensive jet aircraft with a relatively fixed route structure. [. . .]

The Entrepreneurial Strategy

In this second type of strategy, we relax the condition of precise, articulated intentions. Here, one individual in personal control of an organization is able to impose his or her vision of direction

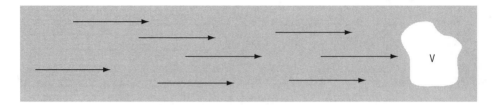

on it. Because such strategies are rather common in entrepreneurial firms, tightly controlled by their owners, they can be called *entrepreneurial strategies*.

In this case, the force for pattern or consistency in action is individual vision, the central actor's *concept* of his or her organization's place in its world. This is coupled with an ability to impose that vision on the organization through his or her personal control of its actions (e.g. through giving direct orders to its operating personnel). Of course, the environment must again be co-operative. But entrepreneurial strategies most commonly appear in young and / or small organizations (where personal control is feasible), which are able to find relatively safe niches in their environments. Indeed, the selection of such niches is an integral part of the vision. These strategies can, however, sometimes be found in larger organizations as well, particularly under conditions of crisis where all the actors are willing to follow the direction of a single leader who has vision and will.

Is the entrepreneurial strategy deliberate? Intentions do exist. But they derive from one individual who need not articulate or elaborate them. Indeed, for reasons discussed below, he or she is typically unlikely to want to do so. Thus, the intentions are both more difficult to identify and less specific than those of the planned strategy. Moreover, there is less overt acceptance of these intentions on the part of other actors in the organization. Nevertheless, so long as those actors respond to the personal will of the leader, the strategy would appear to be rather deliberate.

In two important respects, however, that strategy can have emergent characteristics as well. First, as indicated in the previous diagram, vision provides only a general sense of direction. Within it, there is room for adaptation: the details of the vision can emerge *en route*. Secondly, because the leader's vision is personal, it can also be changed completely. To put this another way, since here the formulator is the implementor, step by step, that person can react quickly to feedback on past actions or to new opportunities or threats in the environment. He or she can thus reformulate vision, as shown in the figure below.

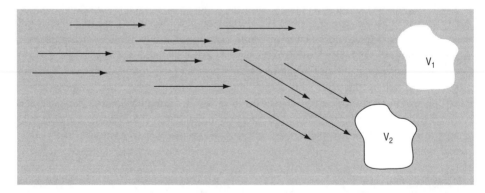

It is this adaptability that distinguishes the entrepreneurial strategy from the planned one. Visions contained in single brains would appear to be more flexible, assuming the individual's

willingness to learn, than plans articulated through hierarchies, which are composed of many brains. Adaptation (and emergentness) of planned strategies are discouraged by the articulation of intentions and by the separation between formulation and implementation. Psychologists have shown that the articulation of a strategy locks it into place, impeding willingness to change it (e.g. Kiesler, 1971). The separation of implementation from formulation gives rise to a whole system of commitments and procedures, in the form of plans, programmes and controls elaborated down a hierarchy. Instead of one individual being able to change his or her mind, the whole system must be redesigned. Thus, despite the claims of flexible planning, the fact is that organizations plan not to be flexible but to realize specific intentions. It is the entrepreneurial strategy that provides flexibility, at the expense of the specificity and articulation of intentions.

[. . .]

THE IDEOLOGICAL STRATEGY

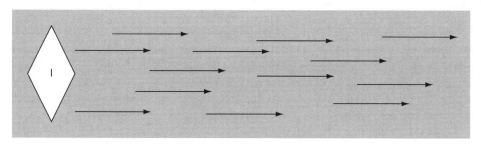

Vision can be collective as well as individual. When the members of an organization share a vision and identify so strongly with it that they pursue it as an ideology, then they are bound to exhibit patterns in their behaviour, so that clear realized strategies can be identified. These may be called *ideological strategies*.

Can an ideological strategy be considered deliberate? Since the ideology is likely to be somewhat overt (e.g. in programmes of indoctrination), and perhaps even articulated (in rough, inspirational form, such as a credo), intentions can usually be identified. The question thus revolves around whether these intentions can be considered organizational and whether they are likely to be realized as intended. In an important sense, these intentions would seem to be most clearly organizational. Whereas the intentions of the planned and entrepreneurial strategies emanate from one centre and are accepted passively by everyone else, those of the ideological strategy are positively embraced by the members of the organization.

As for their realization, because the intentions exist as a rough vision, they can presumably be adapted or changed. But collective vision is far more immutable than individual vision. All who share it must agree to change their 'collective mind'. Moreover, ideology is rooted in the past, in traditions and precedents (often the institutionalization of the vision of a departed, charismatic leader: one person's vision has become everyone's ideology). People, therefore, resist changing it. The object is to interpret 'the word', not defy it. Finally, the environment is unlikely to impose change: the purpose of ideology, after all, is to change the environment or else to insulate the organization from it. For all these reasons, therefore, ideological strategy would normally be highly deliberate, perhaps more so than any type of strategy except the planned one.

[. . .]

21

THE UMBRELLA STRATEGY

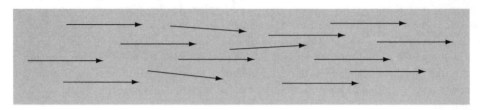

Now we begin to relax the condition of tight control (whether bureaucratic, personal or ideological) over the mass of actors in the organization and, in some cases, the condition of tight control over the environment as well. Leaders who have only partial control over other actors in an organization may design what can be called *umbrella strategies*. They set general guidelines for behaviour – define the boundaries – and then let other actors manoeuvre within them. In effect, these leaders establish kinds of umbrellas under which organizational actions are expected to fall – for example that all products should be designed for the high-priced end of the market (no matter what those products might be).

When an environment is complex, and perhaps somewhat uncontrollable and unpredictable as well, a variety of actors in the organization must be able to respond to it. In other words, the patterns in organizational actions cannot be set deliberately in one central place, although the boundaries may be established there to constrain them. From the perspective of the leadership (if not, perhaps, the individual actors), therefore, strategies are allowed to emerge, at least within these boundaries. In fact, we can label the umbrella strategy not only deliberate and emergent (intended at the centre in its broad outlines but not in its specific details), but also 'deliberately emergent' (in the sense that the central leadership intentionally creates the conditions under which strategies can emerge).

[. . .]

We have so far described the umbrella strategy as one among a number of types that are possible. But, in some sense, virtually all real-world strategies have umbrella characteristics. That is to say, in no organization can the central leadership totally pre-empt the discretion of others (as was assumed in the planned and entrepreneurial strategies) and, by the same token, in none does a central leadership defer totally to others (unless it has ceased to lead). Almost all strategy making behaviour involves, therefore, to some degree at least, a central leadership with some sort of intentions trying to direct, guide, cajole or nudge others with ideas of their own. When the leadership is able to direct, we move towards the realm of the planned or entrepreneurial strategies, when it can hardly nudge, we move towards the realm of the more emergent strategies. But in the broad range between these two can always be found strategies with umbrella characteristics.

In its pursuit of an umbrella strategy – which means, in essence, defining general direction subject to varied interpretation – the central leadership must monitor the behaviour of other actors to assess whether or not the boundaries are being respected. In essence, like us, it searches for patterns in streams of actions. When actors are found to stray outside the boundaries (whether inadvertently or intentionally), the central leadership has three choices: to stop them, ignore them (perhaps for a time, to see what will happen), or adjust to them. In other words, when an arm pokes outside the umbrella, you either pull it in, leave it there (although it might get wet), or move the umbrella over to cover it.

In this last case, the leadership exercises the option of altering its own vision in response to the behaviour of others. Indeed, this would appear to be the place where much effective strategic learning takes place – through leadership response to the initiatives of others. The leadership that is never willing to alter its vision in such a way forgoes important opportunities and tends to lose touch with its environment (although, of course, the one too willing to do so may be unable to sustain any central direction). The umbrella strategy thus requires a light touch, maintaining a subtle balance between proaction and reaction.

THE PROCESS STRATEGY

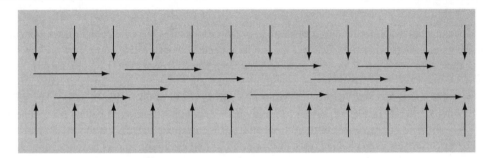

Similar to the umbrella strategy is what can be called the *process strategy*. Again, the leadership functions in an organization in which other actors must have considerable discretion to determine outcomes, because of an environment that is complex and perhaps also unpredictable and uncontrollable. But instead of trying to control strategy content at a general level, through boundaries or targets, the leadership instead needs to exercise influence indirectly. Specifically, it controls the *process* of strategy making while leaving the *content* of strategy to other actors. Again, the resulting behaviour would be deliberate in one respect and emergent in others: the central leadership designs the system that allows others the flexibility to evolve patterns within it.

The leadership may, for example, control the staffing of the organization, thereby determining who gets to make strategy if not what that strategy will be (all the while knowing that control of the former constitutes considerable influence over the latter). Or it may design the structure of the organization to determine the working context of those who get to make strategy.
[. . .]

Divisionalized organizations of a conglomerate nature commonly use process strategies: the central headquarters creates the basic structure, establishes the control systems and appoints the division managers, who are then expected to develop strategies for their own businesses (typically planned ones for reasons outlined by Mintzberg, 1979: 384–92); note that techniques such as those introduced by the Boston Consulting Group to manage the business portfolios of divisionalized companies, by involving headquarters in the business strategies to some extent, bring their strategies back into the realm of umbrella ones.

THE UNCONNECTED STRATEGIES

The *unconnected strategy* is perhaps the most straightforward one of all. One part of the organization with considerable discretion – a sub-unit, sometimes even a single individual – because it is only loosely coupled to the rest, is able to realize its own pattern in its stream of actions.
[. . .]

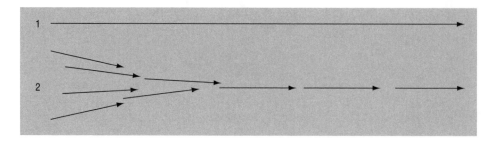

Unconnected strategies tend to proliferate in organizations of experts, reflecting the complexity of the environments that they face and the resulting need for considerable control by the experts over their own work, providing freedom not only from administrators but sometimes from their own peers as well. Thus, many hospitals and universities appear to be little more than collections of personal strategies, with hardly any discernible central vision or umbrella, let alone plan, linking them together. Each expert pursues his or her own strategies – method of patient care, subject of research, style of teaching. On the other hand, in organizations that do pursue central, rather deliberate strategies, even planned ones, unconnected strategies can sometimes be found in remote enclaves, either tolerated by the system or lost within it.

[. . .]

THE CONSENSUS STRATEGY

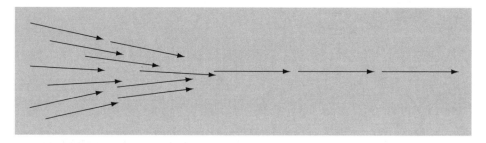

In no strategy so far discussed have we totally dropped the condition of prior intention. The next type is rather more clearly emergent. Here many different actors naturally converge on the same theme, or pattern, so that it becomes pervasive in the organization, without the need for any central direction or control. We call it the *consensus strategy*. Unlike the ideological strategy, in which a consensus forms around a system of beliefs (thus reflecting intentions widely accepted in the organization), the consensus strategy grows out of the mutual adjustment among different actors, as they learn from each other and from their various responses to the environment and thereby find a common, and probably unexpected, pattern that works for them.

In other words, the convergence is not driven by any intentions of a central management, nor even by prior intentions widely shared among the other actors. It just evolves through the results of a host of individual actions. Of course, certain actors may actively promote the consensus, perhaps even negotiate with their colleagues to attain it (as in the congressional form of government). But the point is that it derives more from collective action than from collective intention.

[. . .]

THE IMPOSED STRATEGIES

All the strategies so far discussed have derived in part at least from the will (if not the intentions) of actors within the organization. The environment has been considered, if not benign, then at least acquiescent. But strategies can be *imposed* from outside as well; that is, the environment can directly force the organization into a pattern in its stream of actions, regardless of the presence of central controls. The clearest case of this occurs when an external individual or group with a great deal of influence over the organization imposes a strategy on it. We saw this in our study of the state-owned Air Canada, when the minister who created and controlled the airline in its early years forced it to buy and fly a particular type of aircraft. Here the imposed strategy was clearly deliberate, but not by anyone in the organization. However, given its inability to resist, the organization had to resign itself to the pursuit of the strategy, so that it became, in effect, deliberate.

Sometimes, the 'environment' rather than people *per se* imposes strategies on organizations, simply by severely restricting the options open to them. Air Canada chose to fly jet aeroplanes and later wide-body aeroplanes. But did it? Could any 'world class' airline have decided otherwise? Again the organization has internalized the imperative so that strategic choice becomes a moot point.
[. . .]

Reality, however, seems to bring organizations closer to a compromise position between determinism and free choice. Environments seldom pre-empt all choice, just as they seldom offer unlimited choice. That is why purely determined strategies are probably as rare as purely planned ones. Alternatively, just as the umbrella strategy may be the most realistic reflection of leadership intention, so too might the partially imposed strategy be the most realistic reflection of environmental influence. As shown in the figure below, the environment bounds what the organization can do, in this illustration determining under what part of the umbrella the organization can feasibly operate.
[. . .]

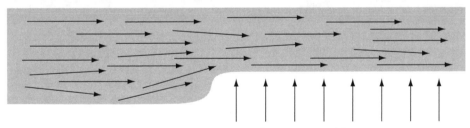

This completes our discussion of various types of strategies. Table 1.1 summarizes some of their major features.

EMERGING CONCLUSIONS

This article has been written to open up thinking about strategy formation, to broaden perspectives that may remain framed in the image of it as an *a priori*, analytic process or even as a

Table 1.1   Summary description of types of strategies

Strategy	Major features
Planned	Strategies originate in formal plans: precise intentions exist, formulated and articulated by central leadership, backed up by formal controls to ensure surprise-free implementation in benign, controllable or predictable environment; strategies most deliberate
Entrepreneurial	Strategies originate in central vision: intentions exist as personal, unarticulated vision of single leader, and so adaptable to new opportunities; organization under personal control of leader and located in protected niche in environment; strategies relatively deliberate but can emerge
Ideological	Strategies originate in shared beliefs: intentions exist as collective vision of all actors, in inspirational form and relatively immutable, controlled normatively through indoctrination and/or socialization; organization often proactive *vis-à-vis* environment; strategies rather deliberate
Umbrella	Strategies originate in constraints: leadership, in partial control of organizational actions, defines strategic boundaries or targets within which other actors respond to own forces or to complex, perhaps also unpredictable environment; strategies partly deliberate, partly emergent and deliberately emergent
Process	Strategies originate in process: leadership controls process aspects of strategy (hiring, structure, etc.), leaving content aspects to other actors; strategies partly deliberate, partly emergent (and, again, deliberately emergent)
Unconnected	Strategies originate in enclaves: actor(s) loosely coupled to rest of organization produce(s) patterns in own actions in absence of, or in direct contradiction to, central or common intentions; strategies organizationally emergent whether or not deliberate for actor(s)
Consensus	Strategies originate in consensus: through mutual adjustment, actors converge on patterns that become pervasive in absence of central or common intentions; strategies rather emergent
Imposed	Strategies originate in environment: environment dictates patterns in actions either through direct imposition or through implicitly re-empting or bounding organizational choice; strategies most emergent, although may be internalized by organization and made deliberate

sharp dichotomy between strategies as either deliberate or emergent. We believe that more research is required on the process of strategy formation to complement the extensive work currently taking place on the content of strategies; indeed, we believe that research on the former can significantly influence the direction taken by research on the latter (and vice versa).

One promising line of research is investigation of the strategy formation process and of the types of strategies realized as a function of the structure and context of organizations. Do the various propositions suggested in this article, based on our own limited research, in fact hold up in broader samples, for example, that strategies will tend to be more deliberate in tightly coupled, centrally controlled organizations and more emergent in decentralized, loosely coupled ones?

It would also be interesting to know how different types of strategies perform in various contexts and also how these strategies relate to those defined in terms of specific content. Using Porter's (1980) categories, for example, will cost leadership strategies prove more deliberate (specifically, more often planned), differentiation strategies more emergent (perhaps umbrella in nature), or perhaps entrepreneurial? Or using Miles and Snow's (1978) typology, will defenders prove more deliberate in orientation and inclined to use planned strategies, whereas prospectors tend to be more emergent and more prone to rely on umbrella or process or even unconnected, strategies? It may even be possible that highly deliberate strategy-making processes will be found to drive organizations away from prospecting activities and towards cost leadership strategies whereas emergent ones may encourage the opposite postures.

The interplay of the different types of strategies we have described can be another avenue of inquiry: the nesting of personal strategies within umbrella ones or their departure in clandestine form from centrally imposed umbrellas; the capacity of unconnected strategies to evoke organizational ones of a consensus or even a planned nature as peripheral patterns that succeed pervade the organization; the conversion of entrepreneurial strategies into ideological or planned ones as vision becomes institutionalized one way or another; the possible propensity of imposed strategies to become deliberate as they are internalized within the organization; and so on. An understanding of how these different types of strategies blend into each other and tend to sequence themselves over time in different contexts could reveal a good deal about the strategy formation process.

At a more general level, the whole question of how managers learn from the experiences of their own organizations seems to be fertile ground for research. In our view, the fundamental difference between deliberate and emergent strategy is that whereas the former focuses on direction and control – getting desired things done – the latter opens up this notion of 'strategic learning'. Defining strategy as intended and conceiving it as deliberate, as has traditionally been done, effectively precludes the notion of strategic learning. Once the intentions have been set, attention is riveted on realizing them, not on adapting them. Messages from the environment tend to get blocked out. Adding the concept of emergent strategy, based on the definition of strategy as realized, opens the process of strategy making up to the notion of learning.

Emergent strategy itself implies learning what works – taking one action at a time in search for that viable pattern or consistency. It is important to remember that emergent strategy means, not chaos, but, in essence, *unintended order*. It is also frequently the means by which deliberate strategies change. As shown in Figure 1.2, in the feedback loop added to our basic diagram, it is often through the identification of emergent strategies – its patterns never intended – that managers and others in the organization come to change their intentions. This is another way of saying that not a few deliberate strategies are simply emergent ones that have been uncovered and subsequently formalized. Of course, unrealized strategies are also a source of learning, as managers find out which of their intentions do not work, rejected either by their organizations themselves or else by environments that are less than acquiescent.

We wish to emphasize that emergent strategy does not have to mean that management is out of control, only – in some cases at least – that it is open, flexible and responsive, in other words, willing to learn. Such behaviour is especially important when an environment is too unstable or complex to comprehend, or too imposing to defy. Openness to such emergent strategy enables management to act before everything is fully understood – to respond to an evolving reality rather than having to

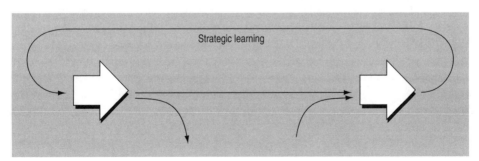

Strategic learning

Figure 1.2 Strategic learning

focus on a stable fantasy. For example, distinctive competence cannot always be assessed on paper *a priori*; often, perhaps usually, it has to be discovered empirically, by taking actions that test where strengths and weaknesses really lie. Emergent strategy also enables a management that cannot be close enough to a situation, or to know enough about the varied activities of its organization, to surrender control to those who have the information current and detailed enough to shape realistic strategies. Whereas the more deliberate strategies tend to emphasize central direction and hierarchy, the more emergent ones open the way for collective action and convergent behaviour.

Of course, by the same token, deliberate strategy is hardly dysfunctional either. Managers need to manage too, sometimes to impose intentions on their organizations – to provide a sense of direction. That can be partial, as in the cases of umbrella and process strategies, or it can be rather comprehensive, as in the cases of planned and entrepreneurial strategies. When the necessary information can be brought to a central place and environments can be largely understood and predicted (or at least controlled), then it may be appropriate to suspend strategic learning for a time to pursue intentions with as much determination as possible (see Mintzberg and Waters, 1984).

Our conclusion is that strategy formation walks on two feet, one deliberate, the other emergent. As noted earlier, managing requires a light deft touch – to direct in order to realize intentions while at the same time responding to an unfolding pattern of action. The relative emphasis may shift from time to time but not the requirement to attend to both sides of this phenomenon.

REFERENCES

Brunet, J.P., Mintzberg, H. and Waters, J. (1986) 'Does planning impede strategic thinking? the strategy of Air Canada, 1937–1976', in Lamb, R. (ed.) *Advances in Strategic Management*, Vol. 4, Prentice-Hall, Englewood Cliffs, NJ.

Galbraith, J.K. (1967) *The New Industrial State*, Houghton Mifflin, Boston.

Grinyer, P.H. and Spender, J.C. (1979) *Turnaround: the fall and rise of the Newton Chambers Group*, Associated Business Press, London.

Kiesler, C.H. (1971) *The Psychology of Commitment: experiments linking behaviour to belief*, Academic Press, New York.

Miles, R. and Snow, C. (1978) *Organizational Strategy, Structure and Process*, McGraw-Hill, New York.

Mintzberg, H. (1972) 'Research on strategy-making', *Proceedings of the 32nd Annual Meeting of the Academy of Management*, Minneapolis.

Mintzberg, H. (1978) 'Patterns in strategy formation', *Management Science*, Vol. 24, pp. 934–48.

Mintzberg, H. (1979) *The Structuring of Organizations*, Prentice-Hall, Englewood Cliffs, NJ.

Mintzberg, H. and McHugh, A. (1985) 'Strategy formation in adhocracy', *Administrative Science Quarterly*.

Mintzberg, H., Otis, S., Shamsie, J. and Waters, J.A. (1986) 'Strategy of design: a study of "architects in co-partnership"', in Grant, J. (ed.) *Strategic Management Frontiers*, JAI Press, Greenwich, CT.

Mintzberg, J. and Waters, J.A. (1982) 'Tracking strategy in an entrepreneurial firm', *Academy of Management Journal*, pp. 465–99.

Mintzberg, H. and Waters, J.A. (1984) 'Researching the formation of strategies: the history of Canadian Lady, 1939–1976', in Lamb, R. (ed.) *Competitive Strategic Management*, Prentice-Hall, Englewood Cliffs, NJ.

Porter, M.E. (1980) *Competitive Strategy: techniques for analyzing industries and competitors*, The Free Press, New York.

2

STRATEGY AS STRETCH AND LEVERAGE

Gary Hamel and C. K. Prahalad

General Motors versus Toyota. CBS versus CNN. Pan Am versus British Airways. RCA versus Sony. Suppose you had been asked, 10 or 20 years ago, to choose the victor in each of these battles. Where would you have placed your bets? With hindsight, the choice is easy. But at the time, GM, CBS, Pan Am, and RCA all had stronger reputations, deeper pockets, greater technological riches, bigger market shares, and more powerful distribution channels. Only a dreamer could have predicted that each would be displaced by a competitor with far fewer resources – but far greater aspirations.

Driven by the need to understand the dynamics of battles like these, we have turned competitiveness into a growth industry. Companies and industries have been analysed in mind-numbing detail, autopsies performed, and verdicts rendered. Yet when it comes to understanding where competitiveness comes from and where it goes, we are like doctors who have diagnosed a problem – and have even found ways to treat some of its symptoms – but who still don't know how to keep people from getting sick in the first place.

Consider the analogy. The first step in understanding competitiveness is to observe competitive outcomes: some companies gaining market share, others losing it, some companies in the black, others bleeding red ink. Like doctors taking a patient's blood pressure or temperature, we can say whether the patient is well or ill, but little more.

The next step is to move from observation to diagnosis. To diagnose competitive problems, we rely on industry structure analysis. A company's market position – the particular market segments in which the company participates – broadly determines the potential for profitability and growth. Within any particular market segment, it is the company's relative competitive advantage that determines actual profitability and growth.

Industry structure analysis points us to the *what* of competitiveness: *what* makes one company more profitable than another. As new whats have been discovered, companies have been exhorted to strive for six sigma quality, compete on time, become customer led, and pursue a host of other desirable advantages. In diagnosing a specific competitive disease, we may conclude that a company is in an unattractive industry segment with a cost disadvantage and sub-par quality. This is a bit like determining that a patient has Parkinson's disease: the diagnosis may point to a cure, but it isn't the cure itself and certainly won't prevent disease.

To find a cure, the medical researcher must unravel the workings of disease. The competitive analogy lies in studying organizational structure and process: for example, what are the administrative attributes of a speedy product-development process or a successful total quality management programme? But however deeply we understand the various elements of a company's competitive advantage, we are still addressing the what of competitiveness, not the *why*.

Understanding the what of competitiveness is a prerequisite for catching up. Understanding the why is a prerequisite for getting out in front. Why do some companies continually create new forms of competitive advantage, while others watch and follow? Why do some companies redefine the industries in which they compete, while others take the existing industry structure as a given?

To answer these questions, another layer of understanding must be peeled back. If the goal of medicine is to prevent rather than simply cure disease, a doctor must search for the reason some people fall ill while others do not. Differences in life style and diet, for instance, predispose some to sickness and others to wellness. A company's institutional environment is the industrial corollary here. Monetary and fiscal policy, trade and industrial policy, national levels of education, the structure of corporate ownership, and the social norms and values of a particular nation all have an impact on how well that nation's industries will compete.

But often too much attention is paid to these factors, especially by managers eager to externalize the causes of competitive decline – and the responsibility for it. After all, we regularly see companies that fail to benefit from the inherent advantages of their institutional context and others that manage to escape the disadvantages. Why hasn't Japan, with more snow skiers than any country on earth, produced a world-class manufacturer of ski equipment? Conversely, why did Yamaha, a Japanese company, become the world's largest producer of high-quality grand pianos, which are not suited to the homes or traditional musical tastes of Japanese customers? And why do US computer manufacturers, competing in an industry targeted by Japan's industrial policy-makers, thrive around the world when US automakers often wilt in the face of Japanese competition? Institutional factors are only part of the story.

Breaking the Managerial Frame

To understand why some people contract a disease while others do not, a medical researcher must finally confront genetics. Just as genetic heritage manifests itself as a susceptibility to some diseases and an ability to resist others, managerial frames of reference – the assumptions, premises, and accepted wisdom that bound or 'frame' a company's understanding of itself and its industry and drive its competitive strategy – determine in large part which diseases a company will fall prey to and which it will avoid.

Managers acquire their frames of reference invisibly from business school and other educational experiences, from peers, consultants, and the business press, and, above all, from their own career experiences. But invisible as the frames themselves may be, their consequences are visible at every turn in how a company's senior managers understand what it means to be 'strategic', in their choice of competitive stratagems, in their relationships with subordinates. In this sense, managerial frames, perhaps more than anything else, bound a company's approach to competitive warfare and thus determine competitive outcomes.

Failure to reckon with managerial frames was understandable as long as competition took place mostly between companies whose managers graduated from the same universities, hired the same consultants, subscribed to the same trade journals, and job-hopped among the same few companies. After all, it wasn't Ford that challenged GM's long-held managerial precepts, nor Thomson that compelled Philips to discard once-sacrosanct organizational tenets. Today such blindness is inexcusable. Just as the health of biological species depends, over time, on genetic variety, so it is with global companies: long-term competitiveness depends on managers' willingness to challenge continually their managerial frames.

The term 'head-to-head competition' is literal. Global competition is not just product versus product, company versus company, or trading bloc versus trading bloc. It is mind-set versus mind-set, managerial frame versus managerial frame.

FROM FIT TO STRETCH

A good place to begin deconstructing our managerial frames is with the question, 'What is strategy?' For a great many managers in large Western companies, the answer centres on three elements: the concept of fit, or the relationship between the company and its competitive environment; the allocation of resources among competing investment opportunities; and a long-term perspective in which 'patient money' figures prominently. From this perspective, 'being strategic' implies a willingness to take the long view, and 'strategic' investments are those that require a large and pre-emptive commitment of resources – betting bigger and betting earlier – as well as a distant return and substantial risk.

This dominant strategy frame is not wrong, only unbalanced. That every company must ultimately effect a fit between its resources and the opportunities it pursues, that resource allocation is a strategic task, and that managers must often countenance risk and uncertainty in the pursuit of strategic objectives all go without saying. But the predominance of these planks in corporate strategy platforms has obscured the merits of an alternative frame in which the concept of stretch supplements the idea of fit, leveraging resources is as important as allocating them, and the long term has as much to do with consistency of effort and purpose as it does with patient money and an appetite for risk.

To illustrate the effects of these opposing frames, imagine two companies competing in the same industry. Alpha, the industry leader, has accumulated a wealth of resources of every kind – human talent, technical skills, distribution access, well-known brands, manufacturing facilities, and cash flow – and it can fund just about any initiative it considers strategic. But its aspirations to remain atop its present perch, to grow as fast as its industry, and to achieve a 15 per cent return on equity are modest. 'Where do you go,' Alpha's managers ask themselves, 'when you're already number one?'

Beta, its rival, is a relative latecomer to the industry. It is much smaller than Alpha and has no choice but to make do with fewer people, a smaller capital budget, more modest facilities, and a fraction of Alpha's R&D budget. Nevertheless, its ambitions belie its meagre resource base. Beta's managers have every intention of knocking Alpha off its leadership perch. To reach this goal, they know that they must grow faster than Alpha, and build a worldwide brand franchise and a presence in every major market, all while expending fewer resources. The misfit between Beta's resources and its aspirations would lead most observers to challenge the feasibility of its goals, if not the sanity of its managers.

But consider the likely effects of Alpha's abundance and Beta's ambition on how the two companies frame their competitive strategies and marshal their resources.

Clearly, Alpha is much better placed to behave 'strategically': to pre-empt Beta in building new plant capacity, to outspend Beta on R&D, to buy market share through aggressive pricing, and so on. Alpha's managers are likely to rest easily, confident that they can overpower their smaller rival in any confrontation. They are also likely to approach their battles with a mind-set reminiscent of World War I trench warfare – 'Whoever runs out of ammunition first is the loser' – however resource-inefficient this approach may be.

Beta, on the other hand, is likely to adopt the tactics of guerrilla warfare in hopes of exploiting the orthodoxies of its more powerful enemy. It will search for undefended niches rather than confront its competitor in well-defended market segments. It will focus investments on a relatively small number of core competencies where management feels it has the potential to become a world leader. It might even find itself compelled to invent lean manufacturing with an emphasis on doing more with less.

The argument here is substantially more subtle than the oft-made point that small companies are more nimble. What distinguishes Beta from Alpha is not Beta's smaller resource base but the greater gap that exists between Beta's resources and its aspirations. In contrast, Alpha's problem is not that it is large – there's no inherent virtue in being small – but that it has insufficient stretch in its aspirations. Alpha's managers will not think and behave as if they were in a small, resource-restrained company. What bedevils Alpha is not a surfeit of resources but a scarcity of ambition.

The products of stretch – a view of competition as encirclement rather than confrontation, an accelerated product-development cycle, tightly knit cross-functional teams, a focus on a few core competencies, strategic alliances with suppliers, programmes of employee involvement, consensus – all are elements of a managerial approach typically labelled 'Japanese'. But as the less than sterling performance of Japan's well-endowed banks and brokerage houses reminds us, there is no magic simply in being Japanese. Indeed, so-called Japanese management may have less to do with social harmony and personal discipline than it does with the strategic discipline of stretch. Companies like NEC, CNN, Sony, Glaxo, and Honda were united more by the unreasonableness of their ambitions and their creativity in getting the most from the least than by any cultural or institutional heritage. Material advantages are as poor a substitute for the creativity stretch engenders in Japan as they are in the United States or Europe. Creating stretch, a misfit between resources and aspirations, is the single most important task senior management faces.

FROM ALLOCATION TO LEVERAGE

'If only we had more resources, we could be more strategic.' Every experienced manager will recognize that lament. Yet it is clear that copious resources cannot guarantee continued industry leadership. Tens of billions of dollars later, no one can accuse GM of not being 'strategic' in its pursuit of factory automation. If anything, GM was *too* strategic. The company's ability to invest outpaced its ability to absorb new technology, retrain workers, re-engineer work flows, rejuvenate supplier relationships, and discard managerial orthodoxies.

Conversely, if modest resources were an insurmountable deterrent to future leadership, GM, Philips and IBM would not have found themselves on the defensive with Honda, Sony and Compaq. NEC succeeded in gaining market share against AT&T, Texas Instruments and IBM despite an R&D budget that for most of its history was more modest in both absolute and relative terms than those of its rivals. Toyota developed a new luxury car for a fraction of the resources required by Detroit. IBM challenged Xerox in the copier business and failed, while Canon, a company only 10 per cent the size of Xerox in the mid-1970s, eventually displaced Xerox as the world's most prolific copier manufacturer. CNN in its adolescence managed to provide 24 hours of news a day with a budget estimated at one-fifth that required by CBS to turn out one hour of evening news. Performance like this isn't just lean manufacturing; it's lean everything.

Allocating resources across businesses and geographies is an important part of top management's strategic role. But leveraging what a company already has rather than simply allocating it is a more creative response to scarcity. In the continual search for less resource-intensive ways to achieve ambitious objectives, leveraging resources provides a very different approach from the downsizing and delayering, the restructuring and retrenchment that have become common as managers contend with rivals around the world who have mastered the art of resource leverage.

There are two basic approaches to gathering greater resource productivity, whether those resources be capital or human. The first is downsizing, cutting investment and head count in hopes of becoming lean and mean – in essence, reducing the buck paid for the bang. The second approach, resource leveraging, seeks to get the most out of the resources one has – to get a much bigger bang for the buck. Resource leverage is essentially energizing, while downsizing is essentially demoralizing. Both approaches will yield gains in productivity, but a company that continually ratchets down its resource base without improving its capacity for resource leverage will soon find that downsizing and restructuring become a way of life – until investors locate a new owner or demand a management team with a better track record. Indeed, this is happening in the United States and in Europe as an increasing share of human and physical capital falls through acquisition, joint venture and surrender of market share to competitors who are better at getting more from less.

THE ARENAS OF RESOURCE LEVERAGE

Management can leverage its resources, financial and non-financial, in five basic ways: by *concentrating* them more effectively on key strategic goals; by *accumulating* them more efficiently; by *complementing* one kind of resource with another to create higher order value; by *conserving* resources wherever possible; and by *recovering* them from the market-place in the shortest possible time. Let us look, one by one, at some of the components that make up these broad categories and ask the questions that managers must ask to assess the scope within their company for further resource leverage.

Convergence – Have we created a chasm between resources and aspirations that will compel creative resource leverage? Have we been loyal to our strategic goals and consistent in their pursuit?

Concentrating resources: convergence and focus. Leverage requires a strategic focal point, or what we have called a strategic intent, on which the efforts of individuals, functions, and businesses can converge over time. Komatsu's goal of 'encircling Caterpillar', President Kennedy's challenge to 'put a man on the moon by the end of the decade', British Airways' quest to become the 'world's favourite airline', and Ted Turner's dream of global news all provided a strategic intent.

Yet in many, probably most, companies there is neither a strategic focal point nor any deep agreement on the company's growth trajectory. As a result, priorities shift constantly. Resources are squandered on competing projects. Potentially great ideas are abandoned prematurely. And the very definition of core business changes often enough to confuse both investors and employees. It is hardly surprising then that in many companies there is little cumulativeness to month-by-month and year-by-year strategic decisions.

Compare NEC's relentless pursuit of 'computers and communication' with IBM's on-again, off-again affair with telecommunications. While NEC was first a telecommunications equipment manufacturer and IBM first a computer maker, both have long recognized that the two industries are converging. Yet IBM's Satellite Business Systems, dalliances with MCI and Mitel, and the acquisition of Rolm have come and, for the most part, gone, while its communications business remains a poor relation to its computer business. NEC, on the other hand, is the only company in the world that is a top-five producer of both computer and communications equipment. NEC achieved this not by outspending IBM but rather through its strategic focus. In the mid-1970s, management established the goal of becoming a leader in both computers and communications; next it elaborated

33

the implications of that goal in terms of the skills and capabilities it would require; and finally, it pursued its ambition unswervingly for the next decade and a half.

As NEC's experience suggests, convergence requires an intent that is sufficiently precise to guide decisions. Converging resources around an amorphous goal – becoming a $100 billion company, growing as fast as the industry, achieving a 15 per cent return on equity – is difficult if not impossible.

Resource convergence is also unlikely if strategic goals fail to outlive the tenures of senior executives. Even with a high degree of resource leverage, the attainment of worldwide industry leadership may be a ten-year quest. Recasting the company's ambition every few years virtually guarantees that leadership will remain elusive. The target has to sit still long enough for all members of the organization to calibrate their sights, take a bead on the target, fire, adjust their aim, and fire again.

> *Focus* – Have we clearly identified the next competitive advantage that we must build? Is top management's attention focused firmly on the task until it is accomplished?

If convergence prevents the diversion of resources over time, focus prevents the dilution of resources at any given time. Just as a general with limited forces must pick his targets carefully, so a company must specify and prioritize the improvements it will pursue. Too many managers, finding their companies behind on cost, quality, cycle time, customer service, and other competitive metrics, have tried to put everything right at the same time and then wondered why progress was so painfully slow. No single business, functional team, or department can give adequate attention to all these goals at once. Without focused attention on a few key operating goals at any one time, improvement efforts are likely to be so diluted that the company ends up as a perpetual laggard in every critical performance area.

Consider Komatsu. Starting with products that were judged only half the quality of Caterpillar's, Komatsu won Japan's highest quality award, the Deming Prize, in three years. Many other companies have been wrestling with quality for a decade or more and still cannot lay claim to world-class standards. What accounts for this difference? When Komatsu initiated its total quality control programme, every manager was given explicit instructions to vote quality in a choice between cost and quality. Although quality may be free in the long run, Komatsu's managers recognized that the pursuit of quality is anything but free in the short run. Thus Komatsu focused almost exclusively on quality until it had achieved world standards. Then, and only then, did it turn successively to value engineering, manufacturing rationalization, product-development speed, and the attainment of variety at low cost. Each new layer of advantage provided the foundation for the next.

Dividing meagre resources across a host of medium-term operational goals creates mediocrity on a broad scale. Middle managers are regularly blamed for failing to translate top-management initiatives into action. Yet middle management often finds itself attempting to compensate for top management's failure to sort out priorities, with the result that mixed messages and goals that are conflicting prevent a sufficient head of steam from developing behind any task.

> *Extraction* – Are we willing to apply lessons learned on the front line, even when they conflict with long-held orthodoxies? Have we found a way to tap the best ideas of every employee?

Accumulating resources: extracting and borrowing. Every company is a reservoir of experiences. Every day, employees come in contact with new customers, learn more about competitors, confront and solve technical problems, and discover better ways of doing things. But some companies are better than others at extracting knowledge from those experiences. Thus what differentiates companies over time may be less the relative quality or depth of their stockpile of experiences than their capacity to draw from that stockpile. Because experience comes at a cost, the ability to maximize the insights gained from every experience is a critical component of resource leverage. Being a 'learning organization' is not enough; a company must also be capable of learning more efficiently than its competitors.

Take Mazda, for example. The Japanese automaker has launched a fraction of the new models created by Ford or GM, yet it seems capable of developing new products in a fraction of the time it takes the other two and at a fraction of the cost. Mazda's experience mocks the experience curve because it suggests that the rate of improvement in a company's capabilities is determined not by some lockstep relationship with accumulated volume but by the relative efficiency with which the company learns from experience. The smaller a company's relative experience base, the more systematic its managers must be in searching for clues to where and how improvements might be made.

The capacity to learn from experience depends on many things: employees who are both reflective and well schooled in the art of problem solving; forums (such as quality circles) where employees can identify common problems and search for higher order solutions; an environment in which every employee feels responsible for the company's competitiveness; the willingness to fix things before they're broken; continuous benchmarking against the world's best practice. But learning takes more than the right tools and attitudes. It also requires a corporate climate in which the people who are closest to customers and competitors feel free to challenge long-standing practices. Unless top management declares open season on precedent and orthodoxy, learning and the unlearning that must precede it cannot begin to take place.

> *Borrowing* – Are we willing to learn from outsiders as well as from insiders? Have we established borrowing processes and learning goals for employees working within alliances and joint ventures?

'Borrowing' the resources of other companies is another way to accumulate and leverage resources. The philosophy of borrowing is summed up in the remark of a Japanese manager that 'you [in the West] chop down the trees, and we [in Japan] build the houses.' In other words, you do the hard work of discovery, and we exploit those discoveries to create new markets. It is instructive to remember that Sony was one of the first companies to commercialize the transistor and the charge-coupled device, technologies pioneered by AT&T's Bell Laboratories. Increasingly, technology is stateless. It crosses borders in the form of scientific papers, foreign sponsorship of university research, international licensing, cross-border equity stakes in high-tech start-ups, and international academic conferences. Tapping into the global market for technology is a potentially important source of resource leverage.

At the extreme, borrowing involves not only gaining access to the skills of a partner but also internalizing those skills. Internalization is often a more efficient way to acquire new skills than acquiring an entire company. In making an acquisition, the acquirer must pay both for the critical skills it wants and for skills it may already have. Likewise, the costs and problems of integrating cultures and harmonizing policy loom much larger in an acquisition than they do in an alliance.

NEC relied on hundreds of alliances, licensing deals, and joint ventures to bolster its product-development efforts and to gain access to foreign markets. Alliances with Intel, General Electric, Varian, and Honeywell, to name a few, multiplied NEC's internal resources. Indeed, NEC managers have been forthright in admitting that without the capacity to learn from their partners, their progress towards the goal of computers and communication would have been much slower.

Borrowing can multiply more than technical resources. Companies such as Canon, Matsushita, and Sharp sell components and finished products on an OEM basis to Hewlett-Packard, Kodak, Thomson, Philips and others to finance their leading-edge research in imaging, video technology and flat-screen displays. Almost every Japanese company we have studied had a bigger share of world development spending in core competence areas and a bigger share of world manufacturing in core components than its brand share in end-product markets. The goal is to capture investment initiative from companies either unwilling or unable to invest in core competence leadership, in order to gain control of critical core competencies. Think of this as borrowing distribution channels and market share from downstream partners to leverage internal development efforts and reduce market risks.

In leveraging resources through borrowing, absorptive capacity is as important as inventive capacity. Some companies are systematically better at borrowing than others are, not least because they approach alliances and joint ventures as students, not teachers. Suffice it to say, arrogance and a full stomach are not as conducive to borrowing as humility and hunger. Captives of their own success, some companies are more likely to surrender their skills inadvertently than to internalize their partners' skills. We might call this negative leverage!

Borrowing can take a myriad of forms: welding tight links with suppliers to exploit their innovations; sharing development risks with critical customers; borrowing resources from more attractive factor markets (as, for example, when Texas Instruments employs relatively low-cost software programmers in India via a satellite hook-up); participating in international research consortia to borrow foreign taxpayers' money. Whatever the form, the motive is the same, to supplement internal resources with resources that lie outside a company's boundaries.

> *Blending* – Have we created a class of technology generalists who can multiply our resources? Have we created an environment in which employees explore new skill combinations?

Complementing resources: blending and balancing. By blending different types of resources in ways that multiply the value of each, management transforms its resources while leveraging them. The ability to blend resources involves several skills: technological integration, functional integration, and new-product imagination.

It is possible that GM or Ford could outspend Honda in developing engine-related technologies like combustion engineering, electronic controls, and lean burn – and perhaps even attain scientific leadership in each area – but still lag Honda in terms of all-around engine performance because the US companies were able to blend fewer technologies. Blending requires technology generalists, systems thinking, and the capacity to optimize complex technological trade-offs. Leadership in a range of technologies may count for little and the resources expended in such a quest may remain under-leveraged if a company is not as good at the subtle art of blending as it is at brute-force pioneering.

Successfully integrating diverse functional skills like R&D, production, marketing and sales is a second form of blending. Where narrow specialization and organizational chimneys exist, functional excellence is rarely translated into product excellence. In such cases, a company may outinvest its competitors in every functional area but reap much smaller rewards in the marketplace. Again, what is required is a class of generalists who understand the interplay of skills, technologies, and functions.

The third form of blending involves a company's ingenuity in dreaming up new-product permutations. Sony and 3M, for example, have demonstrated great imagination in combining core technologies in novel ways. Sony's 'Walkman' brought together well-known functional components – headphones and an audiotape playback device – and created a huge market if not a new life style.

Yamaha combined a small keyboard, a microphone and magnetically encoded cards to create a play-along karaoke piano for children. In these cases, the leverage comes not only from better amortizing past investments in core competencies but also from combining functional elements to create new markets.

Balancing – Have we pursued high standards across the board so that our ability to exploit excellence in one area is never imperilled by mediocrity in another? Can we correct our imbalances?

Balancing is another approach to complementing resources. To be balanced, a company, like a stool, must have at least three legs: a strong product-development capability; the capacity to produce its products or deliver its services at world-class levels of cost and quality; and a sufficiently widespread distribution, marketing and service infrastructure. If any leg is much shorter than the others, the company will be unable to exploit the investments it has made in its areas of strength. By gaining control over the missing resources, however, management can multiply the profits extracted from the company's unique assets.

To illustrate, consider the situation EMI faced in the early 1970s when it invented computerized axial tomography, or the CAT scanner. Although the British company had a ground-breaking product, it lacked a strong international sales and service network and adequate manufacturing skills. As a result, EMI found it impossible to capture and hold onto its fair share of the market. Companies like GE and Siemens, with stronger distribution and manufacturing capabilities, imitated the concept and captured much of the financial bonanza. As for EMI, it ultimately abandoned the business.

Today many small, high-tech companies are unbalanced the way EMI was. While they can enter partnerships with companies that have complementary resources, the innovators are likely to find themselves in a poor bargaining position when it comes to divvying up profits. This imbalance explains why so many Japanese companies worked throughout the 1980s to set up their own worldwide distribution and manufacturing infrastructures rather than continue to borrow from their downstream partners. They realized they could fully capture the economic benefits of their innovations only if they owned all complementary resources. Today, in contrast, Japanese companies are acquiring innovators to complement their strong brand and manufacturing skills. Of the more than 500 small, high-tech US companies sold to foreign interests between 1988 and 1991, Japanese companies bought about two-thirds.

Whatever the nature of the imbalance, the logic is the same. A company cannot fully leverage its accumulated investment in any one dimension if it does not control the other two in some meaningful way. Rebalancing leads to leverage when profits captured by gaining control over critical complementary assets more than cover acquisition costs.

> *Recycling* – Do we view core competencies as corporate resources rather than the property of individual businesses? Have we created lateral communication to ensure that ideas aren't trapped?

Conserving resources: recycling, co-opting, and shielding. The more often a given skill or competence is used, the greater the resource leverage. Sharp exploits its liquid-crystal-display competence in calculators, electronic pocket calendars, mini-TVs, large-screen-projection TVs and laptop computers. Honda has recycled engine-related innovations across motorcycles, cars, outboard motors, generators, and garden tractors. It is little wonder that these companies have unmatched R&D efficiency. The common saying in Japan is, 'No technology is ever abandoned, it's just reserved for future use.' Honda and Sharp are proof of that maxim.

Recycling isn't limited to technology-based competencies. Brands can be recycled too. Familiarity with a high-quality 'banner' brand can predispose customers at least to consider purchasing new products that bear the 'maker's mark.' Think of the leverage Sony gets when it launches a new product, thanks to the relatively modest incremental cost of building credibility with retailers and consumers and the implicit goodwill with which the product is imbued simply because it carries the Sony brand.

Banner branding cannot turn a loser into a winner. In fact, a lousy product will undermine the most respected brand. And in companies such as Unilever and Procter & Gamble, with a long history of product branding, it would be foolish to abandon well-loved brands for an unknown corporate banner. Yet even these companies are more and more apt to use their corporate monikers along with well-known product brands. For example, in working to build a strong presence in Japan, P&G recognized the added oomph its efforts would receive from a judicious use of its corporate name. Building brand leadership in a new market is always a slow and expensive process. But it becomes even more so when advertising budgets and customer awareness are fragmented across multiple brands.

Walk through an international airport and note the billboards bearing the corporate logos of Japan's and Korea's industrial giants. For these companies, brand building is a corporate responsibility. No one expects each business to bear the costs of building global share of mind. A few years ago, a major US company took what, for it, was an unusual step. It erected an illuminated billboard at Heathrow with its logo and a slogan. The billboard didn't stay up long, however; none of the business units was willing to pay for the sign. A few days later, that piece of English sky belonged to a Japanese competitor.

Opportunities for recycling hard-won knowledge and resources are manifold. The ability to switch a production line quickly from making widgets to making gadgets, known as flexible manufacturing, is one. Others include sharing merchandising ideas across national sales subsidiaries, transferring operating improvements from one plant to another, using the same subsystem across a range of products, quickly disseminating ideas for better customer service, and lending experienced executives to key suppliers. But recycling will not occur without a strong organizational foundation. It requires a view of the corporation as a pool of widely accessible skills and resources rather than a series of fiefdoms.

> *Co-option* – Have we identified the industry players who are dependent on us for some critical skill or for their very livelihood? Do we understand how to enroll others in the pursuit of our goals?

Co-option provides another route to conserving resources. Enticing a potential competitor into a fight against a common enemy, working collectively to establish a new standard or develop a new technology, building a coalition around a particular legislative issue – in these and other cases, the goal is to co-opt the resources of other companies and thereby extend one's own influence. In borrowing resources, management seeks to absorb its partners' skills and make them its own; in co-opting resources, the goal is to enroll others in the pursuit of a common objective.

The process of co-option begins with a question: 'How can I convince other companies that they have a stake in my success?' The logic is often, 'My enemy's enemy is my friend.' Philips has a knack for playing Sony and Matsushita against each other, enrolling one as a partner to block the other. Being slightly Machiavellian is no disadvantage when it comes to co-opting resources.

Sometimes co-option requires a stick as well as a carrot of common purpose. Typically, the stick is control over some critical resource, and the unstated logic here is, 'Unless you play the game my way, I'll take my ball and go home.' Fujitsu's relationship with its partners in the computer business is a good example. Each of these partners – ICL in Britain, Siemens in Germany, and Amdahl in the United States – shares a common objective to challenge the dominance of IBM. That is the carrot. The stick is the substantial, in some cases almost total, dependence of these companies on Fujitsu's semi-conductors, central processors, disk drives, printers, terminals, and components.

> *Shielding* – Do we understand competitors' blind spots and orthodoxies? Can we attack without asking retaliation? Do we know how to explore markets through low-cost, low-risk incursions?

To understand shielding, the third form of resource conservation, think about military tactics. Wise generals ensure that their troops are never exposed to unnecessary risks. They disguise their true intentions. They reconnoitre enemy territory before advancing. They don't attack heavily fortified positions. They feint to draw the enemy's forces away from the intended point of attack. The greater the enemy's numerical advantage, the greater the incentive to avoid a full frontal confrontation. The goal is to maximize enemy losses while minimizing the risk to one's own forces. This is the basis for 'resource shielding.'

Attacking a competitor in its home market, attempting to match a larger competitor strength-for-strength, accepting the industry leader's definition of market structure or 'accepted industry practice' are strategies akin to John Wayne taking on all the bad guys single-handedly – and they work better in Hollywood than they do in global competition. In business, judo is more useful than a two-fisted brawl. The first principle in judo is to use your opponent's weight and strength to your own advantage: deflect the energy of your opponent's attack; get him off balance; then let momentum and gravity do the rest.

Dell Computer, America's fastest growing personal computer company, could never have matched Compaq's dealer network or IBM's direct sales force, so the company chose to sell its computers by mail. Computer industry incumbents have found it almost impossible to match Dell, not because they don't have the resources but because these companies face powerful constituents who have a big stake in the status quo. Critical success factors become orthodoxies when a competitor successfully changes the rules of engagement. Such competitive innovation is an important way of shielding resources.

Searching for underdefended territory is another way to shield resources. Honda's success with small motorbikes, Komatsu's early forays into Eastern Europe and Canon's entry into the 'convenience' copier segment all failed to alert incumbents whose attention was focused elsewhere. Understanding a competitor's definition of its 'served market' is the first step in the search for underdefended competitive space. The goal is to build up forces just out of sight of stronger competitors. This may be one reason why Toyota chose to launch the Lexus, its challenge to Mercedes Benz, not in Germany but in California, where buyers are technologically sophisticated, value conscious and not overly swayed by brand loyalty.

> *Recovery* – Have we shortened product-development, order-processing, and product-launch times? Have we built global brands and distribution positions that allow us to pre-empt slower rivals?

Recovering resources: expediting success.   The time between the expenditure of resources and their recovery through revenues is yet another source of leverage – the more rapid the recovery process, the higher the resource multiplier. A company that can do anything twice as fast as its competitors, with a similar resource commitment, enjoys a twofold leverage advantage. This rudimentary arithmetic explains, in part, why Japanese companies have been so intent on accelerating product-development times. Consider the effects of the two-to-one development-time advantage Japanese automakers traditionally held over their US and European rivals. This lead not only allowed them to recoup investments more quickly but also gave them more up-to-date products and gave customers more excuses to abandon their brand loyalties.

But fast-paced product development is only one way of expediting recovery time. A company that has built a highly esteemed global brand will find customers eager to try out new products. This predisposition to buy can expedite recovery dramatically, since recovery time is measured not from product concept to product launch but from product concept to some significant level of world-market penetration.

STRETCH WITHOUT RISK

The essential element of the new strategy frame is an aspiration that creates by design a chasm between ambition and resources. For many managers great ambition equals big risk. If managers at Ford, for instance, were simply to extrapolate past practices, they might believe that developing a car five times as good as the Escort (a potential Lexus beater, say) would require five times the resources. But stretch implies risk only when orthodox notions dictate how the ambition is to be achieved.

Stretch can beget risk when an arbitrarily short time horizon is set for long-term leadership goals. Impatience brings the risk of rushing into markets not fully understood, ramping up R&D spending faster than it can be managed, acquiring companies that cannot be digested easily, or rushing into alliances with partners whose motives and capabilities are poorly understood. Trouble inevitably ensues if resource commitments outpace the accumulation of customer and competitor insights. The job of top management is not so much to stake out the future as it is to help accelerate the acquisition of market and industry knowledge. Risk recedes as knowledge grows, and as knowledge grows, so does the company's capacity to advance.

The notion of strategy as stretch helps to bridge the gap between those who see strategy as a grand plan thought up by great minds and those who see strategy as no more than a pattern in a stream of incremental decisions. On the one hand, strategy as stretch is strategy by design, in that top management has a clear view of the goal line. On the other hand, strategy as stretch is strategy by incrementalism, in that top management must clear the path for leadership metre by metre. In short, strategy as stretch recognizes the essential paradox of competition: leadership cannot be planned for, but neither can it happen without a grand and well-considered aspiration.

<table>
<tr><td>3</td></tr>
</table>

WHAT IS STRATEGY?

Michael E. Porter

OPERATIONAL EFFECTIVENESS IS NOT STRATEGY

For almost two decades, managers have been learning to play by a new set of rules. Companies must be flexible to respond rapidly to competitive and market changes. They must benchmark continuously to achieve best practice. They must outsource aggressively to gain efficiencies. And they must nurture a few core competencies in the race to stay ahead of rivals.

Positioning – once the heart of strategy – is rejected as too static for today's dynamic markets and changing technologies. According to the new dogma, rivals can quickly copy any market position, and competitive advantage is, at best, temporary.

But those beliefs are dangerous half-truths, and they are leading more and more companies down the path of mutually destructive competition. True, some barriers to competition are falling as regulation eases and markets become global. True, companies have properly invested energy in becoming leaner and more nimble. In many industries, however, what some call *hypercompetition* is a self-inflicted wound, not the inevitable outcome of a changing paradigm of competition.

The root of the problem is the failure to distinguish between operational effectiveness and strategy. The quest for productivity, quality and speed has spawned a remarkable number of management tools and techniques: total quality management, benchmarking, time-based competition, outsourcing, partnering, reengineering, change management. Although the resulting operational improvements have often been dramatic, many companies have been frustrated by their inability to translate those gains into sustainable profitability. And bit by bit, almost imperceptibly, management tools have taken the place of strategy. As managers push to improve on all fronts, they move further away from viable competitive positions.

Operational effectiveness: necessary but not sufficient

Operational effectiveness and strategy are both essential to superior performance, which, after all, is the primary goal of any enterprise. But they work in very different ways.

A company can outperform rivals only if it can establish a difference that it can preserve. It must deliver greater value to customers or create comparable value at a lower cost, or do both. The arithmetic of superior profitability then follows: delivering greater value allows a company to charge higher average unit prices; greater efficiency results in lower average unit costs.

Ultimately, all differences between companies in cost or price derive from the hundreds of activities required to create, produce, sell, and deliver their products or services, such as calling on customers, assembling final products, and training employees. Cost is generated by performing activities, and cost advantage arises from performing particular activities more efficiently than competitors. Similarly, differentiation arises from both the choice of activities and how they are performed. Activities, then, are the basic units of competitive advantage. Overall advantage or disadvantage results from all a company's activities, not only a few.[1]

Operational effectiveness (OE) means performing similar activities *better* than rivals perform them. Operational effectiveness includes but is not limited to efficiency. It refers to any number of practices that allow a company to better utilize its inputs by, for example, reducing defects in products or developing better products faster. In contrast, strategic positioning means performing *different* activities from rivals' or performing similar activities in *different ways*.

Differences in operational effectiveness among companies are pervasive. Some companies are able to get more out of their inputs than others because they eliminate wasted effort, employ more advanced technology, motivate employees better, or have greater insight into managing particular activities or sets of activities. Such differences in operational effectiveness are an important source of differences in profitability among competitors because they directly affect relative cost positions and levels of differentiation.

Differences in operational effectiveness were at the heart of the Japanese challenge to Western companies in the 1980s. The Japanese were so far ahead of rivals in operational effectiveness that they could offer lower cost and superior quality at the same time. It is worth dwelling on this point, because so much recent thinking about competition depends on it. Imagine for a moment a *productivity frontier* that constitutes the sum of all existing best practices at any given time. Think of it as the maximum value that a company delivering a particular product or service can create at a given cost, using the best available technologies, skills, management techniques and purchased inputs. The productivity frontier can apply to individual activities, to groups of linked activities such as order processing and manufacturing, and to an entire company's activities. When a company improves its operational effectiveness, it moves towards the frontier. Doing so may require capital investment, different personnel, or simply new ways of managing.

The productivity frontier is constantly shifting outward as new technologies and management approaches are developed and as new inputs become available. Laptop computers, mobile communications, the Internet, and software such as Lotus Notes, for example, have redefined the productivity frontier for sales-force operations and created rich possibilities for linking sales with such activities as order processing and after-sales support. Similarly, lean production, which involves a family of activities, has allowed substantial improvements in manufacturing productivity and asset utilization.

For at least the past decade, managers have been preoccupied with improving operational effectiveness. Through programmes such as TQM, time-based competition, and benchmarking, they have changed how they perform activities in order to eliminate inefficiencies, improve customer satisfaction and achieve best practice. Hoping to keep up with shifts in the productivity frontier, managers have embraced continuous improvement, empowerment, change management, and the so-called learning organization. The popularity of outsourcing and the virtual corporation reflect the growing recognition that it is difficult to perform all activities as productively as specialists.

As companies move to the frontier, they can often improve on multiple dimensions of performance at the same time. For example, manufacturers that adopted the Japanese practice of rapid changeovers in the 1980s were able to lower cost and improve differentiation simultaneously. What were once believed to be real trade-offs between defects and costs, for example turned out to be illusions created by poor operational effectiveness. Managers have learned to reject such false trade-offs.

Constant improvement in operational effectiveness is necessary to achieve superior profitability. However, it is not usually sufficient. Few companies have competed successfully on the basis of operational effectiveness over an extended period, and staying ahead of rivals gets harder every day. The most obvious reason for that is the rapid diffusion of best practices. Competitors

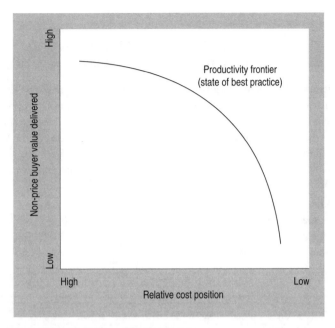

Figure 3.1 Operational effectiveness v. strategic planning

can quickly imitate management techniques, new technologies, input improvements, and superior ways of meeting customers' needs. The most generic solutions – those that can be used in multiple settings – diffuse the fastest. Witness the proliferation of OE techniques accelerated by support from consultants.

OE competition shifts the productivity frontier outward, effectively raising the bar for everyone. But although such competition produces absolute improvement in operational effectiveness, it leads to relative improvement for no one. Consider the $5 billion-plus US commercial printing industry. The major players – R.R. Donnelley & Sons Company, Quebecor, World Color Press, and Big Flower Press – are competing head to head, serving all types of customers, offering the same array of printing technologies (gravure and web offset), investing heavily in the same new equipment, running their presses faster, and reducing crew sizes. But the resulting major productivity gains are being captured by customers and equipment suppliers, not retained in superior profitability. Even industry leader Donnelley's profit margin, consistently higher than 7% in the 1980s, fell to less than 4.6% in 1995. This pattern is playing itself out in industry after industry. Even the Japanese, pioneers of the new competition, suffer from persistently low profits. (See the insert 'Japanese Companies Rarely Have Strategies.')

The second reason that improved operational effectiveness is insufficient – competitive convergence – is more subtle and insidious. The more benchmarking companies do, the more they look alike. The more that rivals outsource activities to efficient third parties, often the same ones, the more generic those activities become. As rivals imitate one another's improvements in quality, cycle times, or supplier partnerships, strategies converge and competition becomes a series of races down identical paths that no one can win. Competition based on operational effectiveness alone is mutually destructive, leading to wars of attrition that can be arrested only by limiting competition.

The recent wave of industry consolidation through mergers makes sense in the context of OE competition. Driven by performance pressures but lacking strategic vision, company after company has had no better idea than to buy up its rivals. The competitors left standing are often those that outlasted others, not companies with real advantage.

JAPANESE COMPANIES RARELY HAVE STRATEGIES

The Japanese triggered a global revolution in operational effectiveness in the 1970s and 1980s, pioneering practices such as total quality management and continuous improvement. As a result, Japanese manufacturers enjoyed substantial cost and quality advantages for many years.

But Japanese companies rarely developed distinct strategic positions of the kind discussed in this article. Those that did – Sony, Canon and Sega, for example – were the exception rather than the rule. Most Japanese companies imitate and emulate one another. All rivals offer most if not all product varieties, features and services; they employ all channels and match one another's plant configurations.

The dangers of Japanese style competition are now becoming easier to recognize. In the 1980s, with rivals operating far from the productivity frontier, it seemed possible to win on both cost and quality indefinitely. Japanese companies were all able to grow in an expanding domestic economy and by penetrating global markets. They appeared unstoppable. But as the gap in operational effectiveness narrows, Japanese companies are increasingly caught in a trap of their own making. If they are to escape the mutually destructive battles now ravaging their performance, Japanese companies will have to learn strategy.

To do so they may have to overcome strong cultural barriers. Japan is notoriously consensus oriented, and companies have a strong tendency to mediate differences among individuals rather than accentuate them. Strategy, on the other hand, requires hard choices. The Japanese also have a deeply ingrained service tradition that predisposes them to go to great lengths to satisfy any need a customer expresses. Companies that compete in that way end up blurring their distinct positioning, becoming all things to all customers.

(This discussion of Japan is drawn from the author's research with Hirotaka Takeuchi, with help from Mariko Sakakibara.)

After a decade of impressive gains in operational effectiveness, many companies are facing diminishing returns. Continuous improvement has been etched on managers' brains. But its tools unwittingly draw companies toward imitation and homogeneity. Gradually, managers have let operational effectiveness supplant strategy. The result is zero-sum competition, static or declining prices, and pressures on costs that compromise companies' ability to invest in the business for the long term.

STRATEGY RESTS ON UNIQUE ACTIVITIES

Competitive strategy is about being different. It means deliberately choosing a different set of activities to deliver a unique mix of value.

Southwest Airlines Company, for example, offers short-haul, low-cost, point-to-point service between midsize cities and secondary airports in large cities. Southwest avoids large airports and does not fly great distances. Its customers include business travellers, families and students. Southwest's frequent departures and low fares attract price-sensitive customers who otherwise would travel by bus or car, and convenience-oriented travellers who would choose a full-service airline on other routes.

Most managers describe strategic positioning in terms of their customers: 'Southwest Airlines serves price- and convenience-sensitive travellers', for example. But the essence of strategy is in the activities – choosing to perform activities differently or to perform different activities than rivals. Otherwise, a strategy is nothing more than a marketing slogan that will not withstand competition.

A full-service airline is configured to get passengers from almost any point A to any point B. To reach a large number of destinations and serve passengers with connecting flights, full-service airlines employ a hub-and-spoke system centred on major airports. To attract passengers who desire more comfort, they offer first-class or business-class service. To accommodate passengers who must change planes, they co-ordinate schedules and check and transfer baggage. Because some passengers will be travelling for many hours, full-service airlines serve meals.

Southwest, in contrast, tailors all its activities to deliver low-cost, convenient service on its particular type of route. Through fast turnarounds at the gate of only 15 minutes, Southwest is able to keep planes flying longer hours than rivals and provide frequent departures with fewer aircraft. Southwest does not offer meals, assigned seats, interline baggage checking, or premium classes of service. Automated ticketing at the gate encourages customers to bypass travel agents, allowing Southwest to avoid their commissions. A standardized fleet of 737 aircraft boosts the efficiency of maintenance.

Southwest has staked out a unique and valuable strategic position based on a tailored set of activities. On the routes served by Southwest, a full-service airline could never be as convenient or as low cost.

Ikea, the global furniture retailer based in Sweden, also has a clear strategic positioning. Ikea targets young furniture buyers who want style at low cost. What turns this marketing concept into a strategic positioning is the tailored set of activities that make it work. Like Southwest, Ikea has chosen to perform activities differently from its rivals.

Consider the typical furniture store. Showrooms display samples of the merchandise. One area might contain 25 sofas; another will display five dining tables. But those items represent only a fraction of the choices available to customers. Dozens of books displaying fabric swatches or wood samples or alternative styles offer customers thousands of product varieties to choose from. Salespeople often escort customers through the store, answering questions and helping them navigate this maze of choices. Once a customer makes a selection, the order is relayed to a third-party manufacturer. With luck, the furniture will be delivered to the customer's home within six to eight weeks. This is a value chain that maximizes customization and service but does so at high cost.

In contrast, Ikea serves customers who are happy to trade off service for cost. Instead of having a sales associate trail customers around the store, Ikea uses a self-service model based on clear, instore displays. Rather than rely solely on third-party manufacturers, Ikea designs its own low-cost, modular, ready-to-assemble furniture to fit its positioning. In huge stores, Ikea displays every product it sells in roomlike settings, so customers don't need a decorator to help them imagine how to put the pieces together. Adjacent to the furnished showrooms is a warehouse section with the products in boxes on pallets. Customers are expected to do their own pickup and delivery, and Ikea will even sell you a roof rack for your car that you can return for a refund on your next visit.

Although much of its low-cost position comes from having customers 'do it themselves', Ikea offers a number of extra services that its competitors do not. Instore child care is one. Extended hours are another. Those services are uniquely aligned with the needs of its customers, who are young, not wealthy, likely to have children (but no nanny), and, because they work for a living, have a need to shop at odd hours.

The origins of strategic positions

Strategic positions emerge from three distinct sources, which are not mutually exclusive and often overlap. First, positioning can be based on producing a subset of an industry's products or services. I call this *variety-based positioning* because it is based on the choice of product or service varieties rather than customer segments. Variety-based positioning makes economic sense when a company can best produce particular products or services using distinctive sets of activities.

Jiffy Lube International, for instance, specializes in automotive lubricants and does not offer other car repair or maintenance services. Its value chain produces faster service at a lower cost than broader line repair shops, a combination so attractive that many customers subdivide their purchases, buying oil changes from the focused competitor, Jiffy Lube, and going to rivals for other services.

The Vanguard Group, a leader in the mutual fund industry, is another example of variety-based positioning. Vanguard provides an array of common stock, bond and money market funds that offer predictable performance and rock-bottom expenses. The company's investment approach deliberately sacrifices the possibility of extraordinary performance in any one year for good relative performance in every year. Vanguard is known, for example, for its index funds. It avoids making bets on interest rates and steers clear of narrow stock groups. Fund managers keep trading levels low, which holds expenses down; in addition, the company discourages customers from rapid buying and selling because doing so drives up costs and can force a fund man-

FINDING NEW POSITIONS: THE ENTREPRENEURIAL EDGE

Strategic competition can be thought of as the process of perceiving new positions that woo customers from established positions or draw new customers into the market. For example, superstores offering depth of merchandise in a single product category take market share from broad-line department stores offering a more limited selection in many categories. Mail-order catalogues pick off customers who crave convenience. In principle, incumbents and entrepreneurs face the same challenges in finding new strategic positions. In practice, new entrants often have the edge.

Strategic positionings are often not obvious, and finding them requires creativity and insight. New entrants often discover unique positions that have been available but simply overlooked by established competitors. Ikea, for example, recognized a customer group that had been ignored or served poorly. Circuit City Stores' entry into used cars, CarMax, is based on a new way of performing activities – extensive refurbishing of cars, product guarantees, no-haggle pricing, sophisticated use of in-house customer financing – that has long been open to incumbents.

New entrants can prosper by occupying a position that a competitor once held but has ceded through years of imitation and straddling. And entrants coming from other industries can create new positions because of distinctive activities drawn from their other businesses. CarMax borrows heavily from Circuit City's expertise in inventory management, credit and other activities in consumer electronics retailing.

Most commonly, however, new positions open up because of change. New customer groups or purchase occasions arise; new needs emerge as societies evolve; new distribution channels appear; new technologies are developed; new machinery or information systems become available. When such changes happen, new entrants, unencumbered by a long history in the industry, can often more easily perceive the potential for a new way of competing. Unlike incumbents, newcomers can be more flexible because they face no trade-offs with their existing activities.

ager to trade in order to deploy new capital and raise cash for redemptions. Vanguard also takes a consistent low-cost approach to managing distribution, customer service and marketing. Many investors include one or more Vanguard funds in their portfolio, while buying aggressively managed or specialized funds from competitors.

The people who use Vanguard or Jiffy Lube are responding to a superior value chain for a particular type of service. A variety-based positioning can serve a wide array of customers, but for most it will meet only a subset of their needs.

A second basis for positioning is that of serving most or all the needs of a particular group of customers. I call this *needs-based positioning*, which comes closer to traditional thinking about targeting a segment of customers. It arises when there are groups of customers with differing needs, and when a tailored set of activities can serve those needs best. Some groups of customers are more price-sensitive than others, demand different product features, and need varying amounts of information, support and services. Ikea's customers are a good example of such a group. Ikea seeks to meet all the home furnishing needs of its target customers, not just a subset of them.

A variant of needs-based positioning arises when the same customer has different needs on different occasions or for different types of transactions. The same person, for example, may have different needs when travelling on business than when travelling for pleasure with the family. Buyers of cans – beverage companies, for example – will likely have different needs from their primary supplier than from their secondary source.

It is intuitive for most managers to conceive of their business in terms of the customers' needs they are meeting. But a critical element of needs-based positioning is not at all intuitive and is often overlooked. Differences in needs will not translate into meaningful positions unless the best set of activities to satisfy them *also* differs. If that were not the case, every competitor could meet those same needs, and there would be nothing unique or valuable about the positioning.

In private banking, for example, Bessemer Trust Company targets families with a minimum of $5 million in investable assets who want capital preservation combined with wealth accumulation. By assigning one sophisticated account officer for every 14 families, Bessemer has configured its activities for personalized service. Meetings, for example, are more likely to be held at a client's ranch or yacht than in the office. Bessemer offers a wide array of customized services, including investment management and estate administration, oversight of oil and gas investments, and accounting for racehorses and aircraft. Loans, a staple of most private banks, are rarely needed by Bessemer's clients and make up a tiny fraction of its client balances and income. Despite the most generous compensation of account officers and the highest personnel cost as a percentage of operating expenses, Bessemer's differentiation with its target families produces a return on equity estimated to be the highest of any private banking competitor.

Citibank's private bank, on the other hand, serves clients with minimum assets of about $250,000 who, in contrast to Bessemer's clients, want convenient access to loans from jumbo mortgages to deal financing. Citibank's account managers are primarily lenders. When clients need other services, their account manager refers them to other Citibank specialists, each of whom handles pre-packaged products. Citibank's system is less customized than Bessemer's and allows it to have a lower manager to client ratio of 1:125. Biannual office meetings are offered only for the largest clients. Both Bessemer and Citibank have tailored their activities to meet the needs of a different group of private banking customers. The same value chain cannot profitably meet the needs of both groups.

The third basis for positioning is that of segmenting customers who are accessible in different ways. Although their needs are similar to those of other customers, the best configuration of activities to reach them is different. I call this *access-based positioning*. Access can be a function of customer geography or customer scale, or of anything that requires a different set of activities to reach customers in the best way.

Segmenting by access is less common and less well understood than the other two bases. Carmike Cinemas, for example, operates movie theatres exclusively in cities and towns with populations under 200,000. How does Carmike make money in markets that are not only small but also won't support big-city ticket prices? It does so through a set of activities that result in a lean cost structure. Carmike's small-town customers can be served through standardized, low-cost theatre complexes requiring fewer screens and less sophisticated projection technology than big-city theatres. The company's proprietary information system and management process eliminate the need for local administrative staff beyond a single theatre manager. Carmike also reaps advantages from centralized purchasing, lower rent and payroll costs (because of its locations), and rock-bottom corporate overhead of 2% (the industry average is 5%). Operating in small communities also allows Carmike to practice a highly personal form of marketing in which the theatre manager knows patrons and promotes attendance through personal contacts. By being the dominant if not the only theatre in its markets – the main competition is often the high school football team – Carmike is also able to get its pick of films and negotiate better terms with distributors.

Rural versus urban-based customers are one example of access driving differences in activities. Serving small rather than large customers or densely rather than sparsely situated customers are other examples in which the best way to configure marketing, order processing, logistics, and after-sale service activities to meet the similar needs of distinct groups will often differ.

Positioning is not only about carving out a niche. A position emerging from any of the sources can be broad or narrow. A focused competitor, such as Ikea, targets the special needs of a subset of customers and designs its activities accordingly. Focused competitors thrive on groups of customers who are overserved (and hence overpriced) by more broadly targeted competitors, or underserved (and hence underpriced). A broadly targeted competitor – for example, Vanguard or Delta Air Lines – serves a wide array of customers, performing a set of activities designed to meet their common needs. It ignores or meets only partially the more idiosyncratic needs of particular customer groups.

Whatever the basis – variety, needs, access, or some combination of the three – positioning requires a tailored set of activities because it is always a function of differences on the supply side; that is, of differences in activities. However, positioning is not always a function of differences on the demand, or customer, side. Variety and access positioning, in particular, do not rely on *any* customer differences. In practice, however, variety or access differences often accompany needs differences. The tastes that is, the needs of Carmike's small-town customers, for instance, run more towards comedies, Westerns, action films and family entertainment. Carmike does not run any films rated NC-17.

Having defined positioning, we can now begin to answer the question, 'What is strategy?' Strategy is the creation of a unique and valuable position, involving a different set of activities. If there were only one ideal position, there would be no need for strategy. Companies would face a simple imperative: win the race to discover and pre-empt it. The essence of strategic positioning is to choose activities that are different from rivals'. If the same set of activities were best to produce all varieties, meet all needs, and access all customers, companies could easily shift among them and operational effectiveness would determine performance.

A SUSTAINABLE STRATEGIC POSITION REQUIRES TRADE-OFFS

Choosing a unique position, however, is not enough to guarantee a sustainable advantage. A valuable position will attract imitation by incumbents, who are likely to copy it in one of two ways.

First, a competitor can reposition itself to match the superior performer. J.C. Penney, for instance, has been repositioning itself from a Sears clone to a more upscale, fashion-oriented, soft-goods retailer. A second and far more common type of imitation is straddling. The straddler

THE CONNECTION WITH GENERIC STRATEGIES

In *Competitive Strategy* (The Free Press, 1985), I introduced the concept of generic strategies – cost leadership, differentiation, and focus – to represent the alternative strategic positions in an industry. The generic strategies remain useful to characterize strategic positions at the simplest and broadest level. Vanguard, for instance, is an example of a cost leadership strategy, whereas Ikea, with its narrow customer group, is an example of cost-based focus. Neutrogena is a focused differentiator. The bases for positioning – varieties, needs, and access – carry the understanding of those generic strategies to a greater level of specificity. Ikea and Southwest are both cost-based focusers, for example, but Ikea's focus is based on the needs of a customer group, and Southwest's is based on offering a particular service variety.

The generic strategies framework introduced the need to choose in order to avoid becoming caught between what I then described as the inherent contradictions of different strategies. Trade-offs between the activities of incompatible positions explain those contradictions. Witness Continental Lite, which tried and failed to compete in two ways at once.

seeks to match the benefits of a successful position while maintaining its existing position. It grafts new features, services, or technologies onto the activities it already performs.

For those who argue that competitors can copy any market position, the airline industry is a perfect test case. It would seem that nearly any competitor could imitate any other airline's activities. Any airline can buy the same planes, lease the gates, and match the menus and ticketing and baggage handling services offered by other airlines.

Continental Airlines saw how well Southwest was doing and decided to straddle. While maintaining its position as a full-service airline, Continental also set out to match Southwest on a number of point-to-point routes. The airline dubbed the new service Continental Lite. It eliminated meals and first-class service, increased departure frequency, lowered fares, and shortened turnaround time at the gate. Because Continental remained a full-service airline on other routes, it continued to use travel agents and its mixed fleet of planes and to provide baggage checking and seat assignments.

But a strategic position is not sustainable unless there are trade-offs with other positions. Trade-offs occur when activities are incompatible. Simply put, a trade-off means that more of one thing necessitates less of another. An airline can choose to serve meals adding cost and slowing turnaround time at the gate or it can choose not to, but it cannot do both without bearing major inefficiencies.

Trade-offs create the need for choice and protect against repositioners and straddlers. Consider Neutrogena soap. Neutrogena Corporation's variety-based positioning is built on a 'kind to the skin,' residue-free soap formulated for pH balance. With a large retail force calling on dermatologists, Neutrogena's marketing strategy looks more like a drug company's than a soap maker's. It advertises in medical journals, sends direct mail to doctors, attends medical conferences, and performs research at its own Skincare Institute. To reinforce its positioning, Neutrogena originally focused its distribution on drugstores and avoided price promotions. Neutrogena uses a slow, more expensive manufacturing process to mould its fragile soap.

In choosing this position, Neutrogena said no to the deodorants and skin softeners that many customers desire in their soap. It gave up the large volume potential of selling through supermarkets and using price promotions. It sacrificed manufacturing efficiencies to achieve the soap's desired attributes. In its original positioning, Neutrogena made a whole raft of trade-offs like those, trade-offs that protected the company from imitators.

Trade-offs arise for three reasons. The first is inconsistencies in image or reputation. A company known for delivering one kind of value may lack credibility and confuse customers – or even undermine its reputation – if it delivers another kind of value or attempts to deliver two inconsistent things at the same time. For example, Ivory soap, with its position as a basic, inexpensive everyday soap would have a hard time reshaping its image to match Neutrogena's premium 'medical' reputation. Efforts to create a new image typically cost tens or even hundreds of millions of dollars in a major industry – a powerful barrier to imitation.

Second, and more important, trade-offs arise from activities themselves. Different positions (with their tailored activities) require different product configurations, different equipment, different employee behaviour, different skills and different management systems. Many trade-offs reflect inflexibilities in machinery, people, or systems. The more Ikea has configured its activities to lower costs by having its customers do their own assembly and delivery, the less able it is to satisfy customers who require higher levels of service.

However, trade-offs can be even more basic. In general, value is destroyed if an activity is overdesigned or underdesigned for its use. For example, even if a given salesperson were capable of providing a high level of assistance to one customer and none to another, the salesperson's talent (and some of his or her cost) would be wasted on the second customer. Moreover, productivity can improve when variation of an activity is limited. By providing a high level of assistance all the time, the salesperson and the entire sales activity can often achieve efficiencies of learning and scale.

Finally, trade-offs arise from limits on internal co-ordination and control. By clearly choosing to compete in one way and not another, senior management makes organizational priorities clear. Companies that try to be all things to all customers, in contrast, risk confusion in the trenches as employees attempt to make day-to-day operating decisions without a clear framework.

Positioning trade-offs are pervasive in competition and essential to strategy. They create the need for choice and purposefully limit what a company offers. They deter straddling or repositioning, because competitors that engage in those approaches undermine their strategies and degrade the value of their existing activities.

Trade-offs ultimately grounded Continental Lite. The airline lost hundreds of millions of dollars, and the CEO lost his job. Its planes were delayed leaving congested hub cities or slowed at the gate by baggage transfers. Late flights and cancellations generated a thousand complaints a day. Continental Lite could not afford to compete on price and still pay standard travel agent commissions, but neither could it do without agents for its full-service business. The airline compromised by cutting commissions for all Continental flights across the board. Similarly, it could not afford to offer the same frequent-flier benefits to travellers paying the much lower ticket prices for Lite service. It compromised again by lowering the rewards of Continental's entire frequent-flier program. The results: angry travel agents and full-service customers.

Continental tried to compete in two ways at once. In trying to be low cost on some routes and full service on others, Continental paid an enormous straddling penalty. If there were no trade-offs between the two positions, Continental could have succeeded. But the absence of trade-offs is a dangerous half-truth that managers must unlearn. Quality is not always free. Southwest's convenience, one kind of high quality, happens to be consistent with low costs because its frequent departures are facilitated by a number of low-cost practices – fast gate turnarounds and automated ticketing, for example. However, other dimensions of airline quality – an assigned seat, a meal, or baggage transfer – require costs to provide.

In general, false trade-offs between cost and quality occur primarily when there is redundant or wasted effort, poor control or accuracy, or weak co-ordination. Simultaneous improvement of cost and differentiation is possible only when a company begins far behind the productivity frontier or when the frontier shifts outward. At the frontier, where companies have achieved current best practice, the trade-off between cost and differentiation is very real indeed.

After a decade of enjoying productivity advantages, Honda Motor Company and Toyota Motor Corporation recently bumped up against the frontier. In 1995, faced with increasing customer resistance to higher automobile prices, Honda found that the only way to produce a less expensive car was to skimp on features. In the United States, it replaced the rear disc brakes on the Civic with lower cost drum brakes and used cheaper fabric for the back seat, hoping customers would not notice. Toyota tried to sell a version of its best-selling Corolla in Japan with unpainted bumpers and cheaper seats. In Toyota's case, customers rebelled, and the company quickly dropped the new model.

For the past decade, as managers have improved operational effectiveness greatly, they have internalized the idea that eliminating trade-offs is a good thing. But if there are no trade-offs companies will never achieve a sustainable advantage. They will have to run faster and faster just to stay in place.

As we return to the question, What is strategy? we see that trade-offs add a new dimension to the answer. Strategy is making trade-offs in competing. The essence of strategy is choosing what *not* to do. Without trade-offs, there would be no need for choice and thus no need for strategy. Any good idea could and would be quickly imitated. Again, performance would once again depend wholly on operational effectiveness.

FIT DRIVES BOTH COMPETITIVE ADVANTAGE AND SUSTAINABILITY

Positioning choices determine not only which activities a company will perform and how it will configure individual activities but also how activities relate to one another. While operational effectiveness is about achieving excellence in individual activities, or functions, strategy is about *combining* activities.

Southwest's rapid gate turnaround, which allows frequent departures and greater use of aircraft, is essential to its high-convenience, low-cost positioning. But how does Southwest achieve it? Part of the answer lies in the company's well-paid gate and ground crews, whose productivity in turnarounds is enhanced by flexible union rules. But the bigger part of the answer lies in how Southwest performs other activities. With no meals, no seat assignment, and no interline baggage transfers, Southwest avoids having to perform activities that slow down other airlines. It selects airports and routes to avoid congestion that introduces delays. Southwest's strict limits on the type and length of routes make standardized aircraft possible: every aircraft Southwest turns is a Boeing 737.

What is Southwest's core competence? Its key success factors? The correct answer is that everything matters. Southwest's strategy involves a whole system of activities, not a collection of parts. Its competitive advantage comes from the way its activities fit and reinforce one another.

Fit locks out imitators by creating a chain that is as strong as its *strongest* link. As in most companies with good strategies, Southwest's activities complement one another in ways that create real economic value. One activity's cost, for example, is lowered because of the way other activities are performed. Similarly, one activity's value to customers can be enhanced by a company's other activities. That is the way strategic fit creates competitive advantage and superior profitability.

Types of fit

The importance of fit among functional policies is one of the oldest ideas in strategy. Gradually, however, it has been supplanted on the manage merit agenda. Rather than seeing the company as a whole, managers have turned to 'core' competencies, 'critical' resources, and 'key' success factors. In fact, fit is a far more central component of competitive advantage than most realize.

Fit is important because discrete activities often affect one another. A sophisticated sales force, for example, confers a greater advantage when the company's product embodies premium technology and its marketing approach emphasizes customer assistance and support. A production line with high levels of model variety is more valuable when combined with an inventory and order processing system that minimizes the need for stocking finished goods, a sales process equipped to explain and encourage customization, and an advertising theme that stresses the benefits of product variations that meet a customer's special needs. Such complementarities are pervasive in strategy. Although some fit among activities is generic and applies to many companies, the most valuable fit is strategy-specific because it enhances a position's uniqueness and amplifies trade-offs.[2]

There are three types of fit, although they are not mutually exclusive. First-order fit is *simple consistency* between each activity (function) and the overall strategy. Vanguard, for example, aligns all activities with its low-cost strategy. It minimizes portfolio turnover and does not need highly compensated money managers. The company distributes its funds directly, avoiding commissions to brokers. It also limits advertising, relying instead on public relations and word-of-mouth recommendations. Vanguard ties its employees' bonuses to cost savings.

Consistency ensures that the competitive advantages of activities cumulate and do not erode or cancel themselves out. It makes the strategy easier to communicate to customers, employees, and shareholders, and improves implementation through single-mindedness in the corporation.

Second-order fit occurs when *activities are reinforcing*. Neutrogena, for example, markets to upscale hotels eager to offer their guests a soap recommended by dermatologists. Hotels grant Neutrogena the privilege of using its customary packaging while requiring other soaps to feature the hotel's name. Once guests have tried Neutrogena in a luxury hotel, they are more likely to purchase it at the drugstore or ask their doctor about it. Thus Neutrogena's medical and hotel marketing activities reinforce one another, lowering total marketing costs.

In another example, Bic Corporation sells a narrow line of standard, low-priced pens to virtually all major customer markets (retail, commercial, promotional, and give-away) through virtually all available channels. As with any variety-based positioning serving a broad group of customers, Bic emphasizes a common need (low price for an acceptable pen) and uses marketing approaches with a broad reach (a large sales force and heavy television advertising). Bic gains the benefits of consistency across nearly all activities, including product design that emphasizes ease of manufacturing, plants configured for low cost, aggressive purchasing to minimize material costs, and in-house parts production whenever the economics dictate

Yet Bic goes beyond simple consistency because its activities are reinforcing. For example, the company uses point-of-sale displays and frequent packaging changes to stimulate impulse buying. To handle point-of-sale tasks, a company needs a large sales force. Bic's is the largest in its industry, and it handles point-of-sale activities better than its rivals do. Moreover, the combination of point-of-sale activity, heavy television advertising, and packaging changes yields far more impulse buying than any activity in isolation could.

Third-order fit goes beyond activity reinforcement to what I call *optimization of effort*. The Gap, a retailer of casual clothes, considers product availability in its stores a critical element of its strategy. The Gap could keep products either by holding store inventory or by restocking from warehouses. The Gap has optimized its effort across these activities by restocking its selection of basic clothing almost daily out of three warehouses, thereby minimizing the need to carry large instore inventories. The emphasis is on restocking because the Gap's merchandising strategy sticks to basic items in relatively few colours. While comparable retailers achieve turns of three to four times per year, the Gap turns its inventory seven and a half times per year. Rapid restocking, moreover, reduces the cost of implementing the Gap's short model cycle, which is six to eight weeks long.[3]

Co-ordination and information exchange across activities to eliminate redundancy and minimize wasted effort are the most basic types of effort optimization. But there are higher levels as well. Product design choices, for example, can eliminate the need for after-sale service or make it possible for customers to perform service activities themselves. Similarly, co-ordination with suppliers or distribution channels can eliminate the need for some in-house activities, such as end-user training.

In all three types of fit, the whole matters more than any individual part. Competitive advantage grows out of the *entire system* of activities. The fit among activities substantially reduces cost or increases differentiation. Beyond that, the competitive value of individual activities or the associated skills, competencies, or resources cannot be decoupled from the system or the strategy. Thus in competitive companies it can be misleading to explain success by specifying individual strengths, core competencies, or critical resources. The list of strengths cuts across many functions, and one strength blends into others. It is more useful to think in terms of themes that pervade many activities, such as low cost, a particular notion of customer service, or a particular conception of the value delivered. These themes are embodied in nests of tightly linked activities.

Fit and sustainability

Strategic fit among many activities is fundamental not only to competitive advantage but also to the sustainability of that advantage. It is harder for a rival to match an array of interlocked activities than it is merely to imitate a particular sales-force approach, match a process technology, or replicate a set of product features. Positions built on systems of activities are far more sustainable than those built on individual activities.

Consider this simple exercise. The probability that competitors can match any activity is often less than one. The probabilities then quickly compound to make matching the entire system highly unlikely $(0.9 \times 0.9 = 0.81; 0.9 \times 0.9 \times 0.9 \times 0.9 = 0.66,$ and so on). Existing companies that try to reposition or straddle will be forced to reconfigure many activities. And even new entrants, though they do not confront the trade-offs facing established rivals, still face formidable barriers to imitation.

The more a company's positioning rests on activity systems with second- and third-order fit, the more sustainable its advantage will be. Such systems, by their very nature, are usually difficult to untangle from outside the company and therefore hard to imitate. And even if rivals can identify the relevant interconnections, they will have difficulty replicating them. Achieving fit is difficult because it requires the integration of decisions and actions across many independent sub-units.

A competitor seeking to match an activity system gains little by imitating only some activities and not matching the whole. Performance does not improve; it can decline. Recall Continental Lite's disastrous attempt to imitate Southwest.

Finally, fit among a company's activities creates pressures and incentives to improve operational effectiveness, which makes imitation even harder. Fit means that poor performance in one activity will degrade the performance in others, so that weaknesses are exposed and more prone to get attention. Conversely, improvements in one activity will pay dividends in others. Companies with strong fit among their activities are rarely inviting targets. Their superiority in strategy and in execution only compounds their advantages and raises the hurdle for imitators.

When activities complement one another, rivals will get little benefit from imitation unless they successfully match the whole system. Such situations tend to promote winner-take-all competition. The company that builds the best activity system – Toys R Us, for instance – wins, while rivals with similar strategies – Child World and Lionel Leisure – fall behind. Thus finding a new strategic position is often preferable to being the second or third imitator of an occupied position.

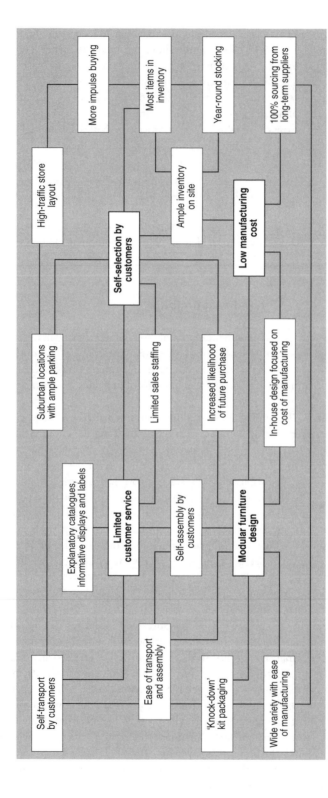

Figure 3.2 Activity-system maps, such as this one for Ikea, show how a company's strategic position is contained in a set of tailored activities designed to deliver it. In companies with a clear strategic position, a number of higher-order strategic themes (in darker tint) can be identified and implemented through clusters of tightly linked activities (in lighter tint).

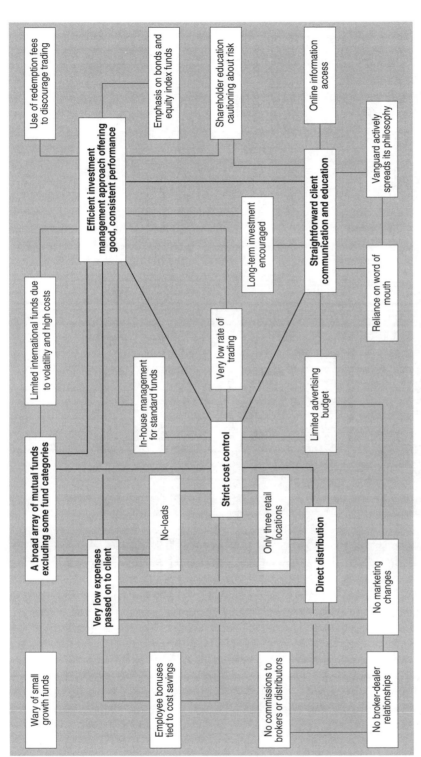

Figure 3.3 Activity-system maps can be useful for examining and strengthening strategic fit. A set of basic questions should guide the process. First, is each activity consistent with the overall positioning the varieties produced, the needs served, and the type of customers accessed? Ask those responsible for each activity to identify how other activities within the company improve or detract from their performance. Second, are there ways to strengthen how activities and groups of activities reinforce one another? Finally, could changes in one activity eliminate the need to perform others?

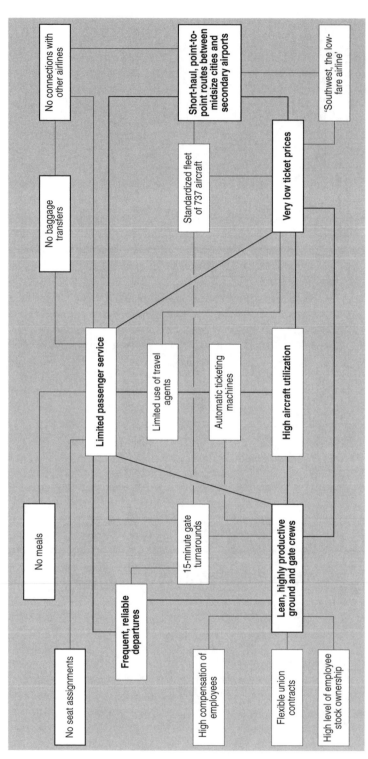

Figure 3.4 Southwest Airlines' activity-system

The most viable positions are those whose activity systems are incompatible because of trade-offs. Strategic positioning sets the trade-off rules that define how individual activities will be configured and integrated. Seeing strategy in terms of activity systems only makes it clearer why organizational structure, systems and processes need to be strategy-specific. Tailoring organization to strategy, in turn, makes complementarities more achievable and contributes to sustainability.

One implication is that strategic positions should have a horizon of a decade or more, not of a single planning cycle. Continuity fosters improvements in individual activities and the fit across activities, allowing an organization to build unique capabilities and skills tailored to its strategy. Continuity also reinforces a company's identity.

Conversely, frequent shifts in positioning are costly. Not only must a company reconfigure individual activities, but it must also realign entire systems. Some activities may never catch up to the vacillating strategy. The inevitable result of frequent shifts in strategy, or of failure to choose a distinct position in the first place, is 'me-too' or hedged activity configurations, inconsistencies across functions, and organizational dissonance.

What is strategy? We can now complete the answer to this question. Strategy is creating fit among a company's activities. The success of a strategy depends on doing many things well – not just a few – and integrating among them. If there is no fit among activities, there is no distinctive strategy and little sustainability. Management reverts to the simpler task of overseeing independent functions, and operational effectiveness determines an organization's relative performance.

REDISCOVERING STRATEGY

The failure to choose

Why do so many companies fail to have a strategy? Why do managers avoid making strategic choices? Or, having made them in the past, why do managers so often let strategies decay and blur?

Commonly, the threats to strategy are seen to emanate from outside a company because of changes in technology or the behaviour of competitors. Although external changes can be the problem,

ALTERNATIVE VIEWS OF STRATEGY

The implicit strategy model of the past decade	Sustainable competitive advantage
One ideal competitive position in the market	Unique competitive position for the company
Benchmarking of all activities and achieving best practice	Activities tailored to strategy
Aggressive outsourcing and partnering to gain efficiencies	Clear trade-offs and choice vis-à-vis competitors
Advantages rest on a few key success factors, critical resources, core competencies	Competitive advantage arises from fit across activities
Flexibility and rapid responses to all competitive and market changes	Sustainability comes from activity system, not the parts
	Operational effectiveness a given

the greater threat to strategy often comes from within. A sound strategy is undermined by a misguided view of competition, by organizational failures, and, especially, by the desire to grow.

Managers have become confused about the necessity of making choices. When many companies operate far from the productivity frontier, trade-offs appear unnecessary. It can seem that a well-run company should be able to beat its ineffective rivals on all dimensions simultaneously. Taught by popular management thinkers that they do not have to make trade-offs, managers have acquired a macho sense that to do so is a sign of weakness.

Unnerved by forecasts of hypercompetition, managers increase its likelihood by imitating everything about their competitors. Exhorted to think in terms of revolution, managers chase every new technology for its own sake.

The pursuit of operational effectiveness is seductive because it is concrete and actionable. Over the past decade, managers have been under increasing pressure to deliver tangible, measurable performance improvements. Programs in operational effectiveness produce reassuring progress, although superior profitability may remain elusive. Business publications and consultants flood the market with information about what other companies are doing, reinforcing the best-practice mentality. Caught up in the race for operational effectiveness, many managers simply do not understand the need to have a strategy.

Companies avoid or blur strategic choices for other reasons as well. Conventional wisdom within an industry is often strong, homogenizing competition. Some managers mistake 'customer focus' to mean they must serve all customer needs or respond to every request from distribution channels. Others cite the desire to preserve flexibility.

Organizational realities also work against strategy. Trade-offs are frightening, and making no choice is sometimes preferred to risking blame for a bad choice. Companies imitate one another in a type of herd behaviour, each assuming rivals know something they do not. Newly empowered employees, who are urged to seek every possible source of improvement, often lack a vision of the whole and the perspective to recognize trade-offs. The failure to choose sometimes comes down to the reluctance to disappoint valued managers or employees.

The growth trap

Among all other influences, the desire to grow has perhaps the most perverse effect on strategy. Trade-offs and limits appear to constrain growth. Serving one group of customers and excluding others, for instance, places a real or imagined limit on revenue growth. Broadly targeted strategies emphasizing low price result in lost sales with customers sensitive to features or service. Differentiators lose sales to price-sensitive customers.

Managers are constantly tempted to take incremental steps that surpass those limits but blur a company's strategic position. Eventually, pressures to grow or apparent saturation of the target market lead managers to broaden the position by extending product lines, adding new features, imitating competitors' popular services, matching processes, and even making acquisitions. For years, Maytag Corporation's success was based on its focus on reliable, durable washers and dryers, later extended to include dishwashers. However, conventional wisdom emerging within the industry supported the notion of selling a full line of products. Concerned with slow industry growth and competition from broad-line appliance makers, Maytag was pressured by dealers and encouraged by customers to extend its line. Maytag expanded into refrigerators and cooking products under the Maytag brand and acquired other brands – Jenn-Air, Hardwick Stove, Hoover, Admiral, and Magic Chef – with disparate positions. Maytag has grown substantially from $684 million in 1985 to a peak of $3.4 billion in 1994, but return on sales has declined from 8–12%

in the 1970s and 1980s to an average of less than 1% between 1989 and 1995. Cost cutting will improve this performance, but laundry and dishwasher products still anchor Maytag's profitability.

Neutrogena may have fallen into the same trap. In the early 1990s, its US distribution broadened to include mass merchandisers such as Wal-Mart Stores.

Under the Neutrogena name, the company expanded into a wide variety of products – eye make-up remover and shampoo, for example – in which it was not unique and which diluted its image, and it began turning to price promotions.

Compromises and inconsistencies in the pursuit of growth will erode the competitive advantage a company had with its original varieties or target customers. Attempts to compete in several ways at once create confusion and undermine organizational motivation and focus. Profits fall, but more revenue is seen as the answer. Managers are unable to make choices, so the company embarks on a new round of broadening and compromises. Often, rivals continue to match each other until desperation breaks the cycle, resulting in a merger or downsizing to the original positioning.

Profitable growth

Many companies, after a decade of restructuring and cost-cutting, are turning their attention to growth. Too often, efforts to grow blur uniqueness, create compromises, reduce fit, and ultimately undermine competitive advantage. In fact, the growth imperative is hazardous to strategy.

What approaches to growth preserve and reinforce strategy? Broadly, the prescription is to concentrate on deepening a strategic position rather than broadening and compromising it. One approach is to look for extensions of the strategy that leverage the existing activity system by offering features or services that rivals would find impossible or costly to match on a stand-alone basis. In other words, managers can ask themselves which activities, features or forms of competition are feasible or less costly to them because of complementary activities that their company performs.

Deepening a position involves making the company's activities more distinctive, strengthening fit, and communicating the strategy better to those customers who should value it. But many companies succumb to the temptation to chase 'easy' growth by adding hot features, products or services without screening them or adapting them to their strategy. Or they target new customers or markets in which the company has little special to offer. A company can often grow faster and far more profitably by better penetrating needs and varieties where it is distinctive than by slugging it out in potentially higher growth arenas in which the company lacks uniqueness. Carmike, now the largest theatre chain in the United States, owes its rapid growth to its disciplined concentration on small markets. The company quickly sells any big-city theatres that come to it as part of an acquisition.

Globalization often allows growth that is consistent with strategy, opening up larger markets for a focused strategy. Unlike broadening domestically, expanding globally is likely to leverage and reinforce a company's unique position and identity.

Companies seeking growth through broadening within their industry can best contain the risks to strategy by creating stand-alone units, each with its own brand name and tailored activities. Maytag has clearly struggled with this issue. On the one hand, it has organized its premium and value brands into separate units with different strategic positions. On the other, it has created an umbrella appliance company for all its brands to gain critical mass. With shared design, manufacturing, distribution, and customer service, it will be hard to avoid homogenization. If a given business unit attempts to compete with different positions for different products or customers, avoiding compromise is nearly impossible.

RECONNECTING WITH STRATEGY

Most companies owe their initial success to a unique strategic position involving clear trade-offs. Activities once were aligned with that position. The passage of time and the pressures of growth, however, led to compromises that were, at first, almost imperceptible. Through a succession of incremental changes that each seemed sensible at the time, many established companies have compromised their way to homogeneity with their rivals.

The issue here is not with the companies whose historical position is no longer viable; their challenge is to start over, just as a new entrant would. At issue is a far more common phenomenon: the established company achieving mediocre returns and lacking a clear strategy. Through incremental additions of product varieties, incremental efforts to serve new customer groups, and emulation of rivals' activities, the existing company loses its clear competitive position. Typically, the company has matched many of its competitors' offerings and practices and attempts to sell to most customer groups.

A number of approaches can help a company reconnect with strategy. The first is a careful look at what it already does. Within most well-established companies is a core of uniqueness. It is identified by answering questions such as the following:

- Which of our product or service varieties are the most distinctive?
- Which of our product or service varieties are the most profitable?
- Which of our customers are the most satisfied?
- Which customers, channels or purchase occasions are the most profitable?
- Which of the activities in our value chain are the most different and effective?

Around this core of uniqueness are encrustations added incrementally over time. Like barnacles, they must be removed to reveal the underlying strategic positioning. A small percentage of varieties or customers may well account for most of a company's sales and especially its profits. The challenge, then, is to refocus on the unique core and realign the company's activities with it. Customers and product varieties at the periphery can be sold or allowed through inattention or price increases to fade away.

A company's history can also be instructive. What was the vision of the founder? What were the products and customers that made the company? Looking backwards, one can re-examine the original strategy to see if it is still valid. Can the historical positioning be implemented in a modern way, one consistent with today's technologies and practices? This sort of thinking may lead to a commitment to renew the strategy and may challenge the organization to recover its distinctiveness. Such a challenge can be galvanizing and can instil the confidence to make the needed trade-offs.

The role of leadership

The challenge of developing or re-establishing a clear strategy is often primarily an organizational one and depends on leadership. With so many forces at work against making choices and trade-offs in organizations, a clear intellectual framework to guide strategy is a necessary counterweight. Moreover, strong leaders willing to make choices are essential.

In many companies, leadership has degenerated into orchestrating operational improvements and making deals. But the leader's role is broader and far more important. General management is more than the stewardship of individual functions. Its core is strategy: defining and communicating the company's unique position, making trade-offs, and forging fit among activities. The leader must provide the discipline to decide which industry changes and customer needs the company will respond to, while avoiding organizational distractions and maintaining the company's distinctiveness. Managers at lower levels lack the perspective and the confidence to maintain a strategy. There will be constant pressures to compromise, relax trade-offs, and emulate rivals. One of the leader's jobs is to teach others in the organization about strategy – and to say no.

Strategy renders choices about what not to do as important as choices about what to do. Indeed, setting limits is another function of leadership. Deciding which target group of customers, varieties, and needs the company should serve is fundamental to developing a strategy. But so is deciding not to serve other customers or needs and not to offer certain features or services. Thus strategy requires constant discipline and clear communication. Indeed, one of the most important functions of an explicit, communicated strategy is to guide employees in making choices that arise because of trade-offs in their individual activities and in day-to-day decisions.

Improving operational effectiveness is a necessary part of management, but it is *not* strategy. In confusing the two, managers have unintentionally backed into a way of thinking about competition that is driving many industries toward competitive convergence, which is in no one's best interest and is not inevitable.

EMERGING INDUSTRIES AND TECHNOLOGIES

Developing a strategy in a newly emerging industry or in a business undergoing revolutionary technological changes is a daunting proposition. In such cases, managers face a high level of uncertainty about the needs of customers, the products and services that will prove to be the most desired, and the best configuration of activities and technologies to deliver them. Because of all this uncertainty, imitation and hedging are rampant: unable to risk being wrong or left behind, companies match all features, offer all new services, and explore all technologies.

During such periods in an industry's development, its basic productivity frontier is being established or re-established. Explosive growth can make such times profitable for many companies, but profits will be temporary because imitation and strategic convergence will ultimately destroy industry profitability. The companies that are enduringly successful will be those that begin as early as possible to define and embody in their activities a unique competitive position. A period of imitation may be inevitable in emerging industries, but that period reflects the level of uncertainty rather than a desired state of affairs.

In high-tech industries, this imitation phase often continues much longer than it should. Enraptured by technological change itself, companies pack more features – most of which are never used – into their products while slashing prices across the board. Rarely are trade-offs even considered. The drive for growth to satisfy market pressures leads companies into every product area. Although a few companies with fundamental advantages prosper, the majority are doomed to a rat race no one can win.

Ironically, the popular business press, focused on hot, emerging industries, is prone to presenting these special cases as proof that we have entered a new era of competition in which none of the old rules are valid. In fact the opposite is true.

Managers must clearly distinguish operational effectiveness from strategy. Both are essential, but the two agendas are different.

The operational agenda involves continual improvement everywhere there are no trade-offs. Failure to do this creates vulnerability even for companies with a good strategy. The operational agenda is the proper place for constant change, flexibility, and relentless efforts to achieve best practice. In contrast, the strategic agenda is the right place for defining a unique position, making clear trade-offs, and tightening fit. It involves the continual search for ways to reinforce and extend the company's position. The strategic agenda demands discipline and continuity; its enemies are distraction and compromise.

Strategic continuity does not imply a static view of competition. A company must continually improve its operational effectiveness and actively try to shift the productivity frontier; at the same time, there needs to be ongoing effort to extend its uniqueness while strengthening the fit among its activities. Strategic continuity, in fact, should make an organization's continual improvement more effective.

A company may have to change its strategy if there are major structural changes in its industry. In fact, new strategic positions often arise because of industry changes, and new entrants unencumbered by history often can exploit them more easily. However, a company's choice of a new position must be driven by the ability to find new trade-offs and leverage a new system of complementary activities into a sustainable advantage.

NOTES

1 I first described the concept of activities and its use in understanding competitive advantage in *Competitive Advantage* (New York: The Free Press, 1985). The ideas in this article build on and extend that thinking.

2 Paul Milgrom and John Roberts have begun to explore the economics of systems of complementary functions, activities and functions. Their focus is on the emergence of 'modern manufacturing' as a new set of complementary activities, on the tendency of companies to react to external changes with coherent bundles of internal responses, and on the need for central coordination – a strategy – to align functional managers. In the latter case, they model what has long been a bedrock principle of strategy. See Paul Milgrom and John Roberts, 'The economics of modern manufacturing: technology, strategy, and organization,' *American Economic Review* 80 (1990): 511–28; Paul Milgrom, Yingyi Qian and John Roberts, 'Complementarities, momentum, and evolution of modern manufacturing,' *American Economic Review* 81 (1991) 84–8; and Paul Milgrom and John Roberts, 'Complementarities and fit: strategy, structure, and organizational changes in manufacturing,' *Journal of Accounting and Economics*, vol. 19 (March–May 1995): 179–208.

3 Material on retail strategies is drawn in part from Jan Rivkin, 'the rise of retail category killers,' unpublished working paper, January 1995. Nicolaj Siggelkow prepared the case study on the Gap.

Part II

THE CONTEXT OF STRATEGY

INTRODUCTION

We begin Part II with one of the big controversies in strategy. Is a firm's performance driven primarily by industry characteristics or by firm-specific factors? In other words, how important is the industry in which your organization is placed (i.e. industry context) in influencing the overall performance of the firm? Or do the quality of strategy and the effective harnessing of organizational resources outweigh industry context and industry characteristics as determinants of the firm performance? The article included here by Rumelt (Chapter 4) is seminal in its treatment of this issue and must therefore be seen as strategy classic. However, there is still widespread disagreement about his conclusions, as explained below.

In Part I, we focused on the impact of idiosyncratic organizational styles and purposes on strategy. Part I ended with a strong restatement from Michael Porter of the 'positioning' school of strategy where differences in market positioning are seen as governing differences in profit potential. One of the early consequences of the positioning school was that much academic research and much managerial effort went into analyses of the relative 'attractiveness' of various industries. Since it is usually unrealistic (due to various combinations of entry, exit and mobility barriers) for firms to move easily out of one industry sector and into another, most firms must make do with the sector they are in. Indeed, had they all attempted to move into attractive industries, certain sectors were likely to be overcrowded and profitability (and their attractiveness) would be affected.

Rumelt's research and data (Chapter 4) return to the question of the relative emphasis to be placed in strategy on the characteristics of the organization, or the characteristics of the industry: which has the more powerful impact on performance? He argues that 'long-term rates of return are not associated with industry, but with the unique endowments, positions and strategies of individual businesseses'. He shows that businesses differ from one another in their performance and profitability a great deal more than industries differ from one another. Industries are not homogeneous; they are heterogeneous. Performance is more homogeneous *between* industries than *within* industries. He thus provides evidence that managerial action greatly outweighs the importance of industry structure on long-term organizational returns. Therefore, the quality of strategic thinking and the actions of managers do matter.

The implications of Rumelt's findings are exciting, significant and controversial. They have generated much argument and a lot of further research. Two of the most recent contributions to this continuing debate about industry versus firm are from recent editions of the *Strategic Management Journal*, the leading strategy research journal. Adner and Helfat (2003), strongly dispute Rumelt's conclusion that corporate-level effects 'exhibit little or no (differential) ability to affect business unit returns'. They found instead that corporate-level managers in different firms in the same industry made different decisions in response to changes in the external environment and that these had a measurable impact on firm performance. Of the three levels examined by Rumelt (industry, corporate and business/firm), he found corporate effects to be negligible whereas Adner and Helfat found them to be significant, based on a different style of data. Hawawini, Subramanian and Verdin (2003) argue that Rumelt's conclusions apply only to 'leader' and 'loser' firms within an industry, but that for average firms, the industry effect is stronger than the firm effect. The debate continues.

The next two articles are new to this second edition of the *Strategy Reader*. They represent a significant development within the field of strategic management in that both are part of a resurgence of awareness about corporate social responsibility (CSR), representing wider stake-holder influences on strategy-making within firms. Hosmer's article (Chapter 5) on the urgent need for a central role for ethics within the strategy process, has acquired great resonance since its publication, as a result of the many corporate scandals of the late 1990s involving manifestly unethical managerial behaviour. Hosmer is making a general case rather than a specific one. He argues that as corporate strategy in the 1980s 'adopted the language and logic of economics', corporate social responsibility slipped down the agenda almost to invisibility. More recently, however, both managers and business academics have been forced to deal with competitive issues in a global context. This has led to recognition that greater consideration must be given to 'how to maintain a competitive posture and an ethical stance jointly'. International and global strategies for firms are particularly in need of guiding principles since such enormous cultural, economic, political and regulatory differences are evident. We are given a revealing discussion of the nature and true cost of *moral hazard* for businesses, especially in the context of principal–agent agent relationships.

> The ethical principles of analysis, of course, do address what is 'right', what is 'just', and what is 'fair' in the critical relationships between the firm and its various stakeholder groups, and were designed to eliminate short-term self-interest as a decision criteria by the representatives of the firm.

However, Hosmer does not appear to be arguing for principles of social justice and CSR in, and for, themselves. He is arguing for them as an integral part of strategic thinking, strategy formulation and strategy implementation because ethical principles are an essential precondition of commitment by all stakeholders to specific strategies, since they generate trust, and commitment to what is necessarily a co-operative effort.

Porter and van der Linde (Chapter 6) reinforce Porter and Rumelt's arguments regarding the importance of the quality of strategic thinking in firm performance. Their article concentrates on one particular type of CSR issue: that of environmental regulation and its relation to the competitiveness of firms and industries. The stakeholder relationship between firms and the environment has acquired great political and economic significance in the past decade, including a largely adversarial relationship between issues concerning environmental quality and resource sustainability, compared to the costs borne by industry in achieving these social benefits. Porter and van der Linde examine the relationship between environmental regulation, legislation, innovation and competitiveness. They make the strong case for pollution to be recognized as inefficient use of resources. If that is seen to be so, then rather than both managers and regulators fighting over the actual costs of eliminating or reducing pollution and who should bear those costs, the opportunity costs of pollution (in wasted resources) becomes clearer. They make the comparison with the historic relationship between innovation and cost-reduction. Whereas initially the assumption was that there was a trade-off between improving quality and cost, so that higher quality inevitably meant higher costs: 'today we have little trouble grasping the idea that innovation can improve quality while actually lowering cost'. Their argument is that companies are now at roughly the same stage in their attitudes towards pollution and the sense that higher environmental standards will inevitably erode industry and firm competitiveness. This is especially assumed to be so as far as international competitiveness is concerned, since only some countries will be adopting high environmental standards and enforcing them through legislation. Other countries will not; at least not yet. Firms therefore perceive themselves to be at a potential disadvantage in bearing costs imposed on them that are not imposed on competitor firms from other economies. Rather than environmental legislation being something lawyers fight over, the costs of environmental regulation can be reduced to a minimum 'through innovation that delivers other competitive benefits'. Thus, environmental protection and competitiveness can move forward together.

The remaining two chapters in Part II deal with the effect of the organization's cultural, institutional and regulatory contexts on strategic decision-making. Biggart and Hamilton take the period of the Asian 'economic miracle' of the 1960s to the 1990s during which Japan and the other 'tiger' economies achieved such spectacular growth. They review and challenge Western attitudes and assumptions about the underlying social, cultural, business and economic structure of the Asian economies. In particular, they explore the differences between the Western and the Asian versions of capitalism and competition. Since the 1990s when the massive growth phase came to an end and these same Asian economies have been undergoing problems associated instead with stagnation, this analysis of underlying Asian differences from the West is possibly even more relevant.

Markets and industries are the operational contexts for firms. All firms have to determine the industries and markets they wish to address. The importance of Biggart and Hamilton's analysis is in showing the gulf between Asian and Western notions of industries and markets and therefore the contrasting organizations, values, social relations and ultimately strategies, that each generates. The assumptions of Western economic individualism, and the social, legal and institutional structures to which it gives rise, are that social relations in a market lead only to such uncompetitive practices as price-fixing and various other forms of collusion. In other words, 'keeping economic actors apart is a crucial condition of capitalism' in the neo-classical ('Western') view. Individual competence is seen as the just way of selecting and rewarding people and organizations. Personal relations in the workplace or between organizational members are seen as collusion, nepotism and favouritism. Asian economies, by contrast, are organized through networks. Just as Western economies have legal and regulatory frameworks for maintaining autonomy, so Asian economies have institutions that encourage and maintain ties between actors. In other words, Asian nations have built economic policies around the presence of social relations among market actors. What Western governments, organizations or managers regard as impediments to free trade express an ethnocentric view of the economic institutions of capitalism. Asian history and experience have led to the institutionalization of social networks in governments and organizations. The beliefs and institutions of individual autonomy are deeply Western in origin and history. The pervasiveness of networks (social, economic, organizational and institutional) is equally deeply Asian. The implications for managerial practice and strategic thinking and decision-making are profound. They also have a broader impact on the economic and social policies of Asian nations and how they are implemented. This also explains many of the problems faced by Western firms in their operations within Asian markets.

From this sweeping comparative overview of Western and Asian cultural and institutional contexts affecting markets and the behaviour of firms, we now move to a completely different type of context issue: the setting of technology standards in an industry. The process for setting compatible international standards for anything from electric plugs and railway gauges, to satellite broadcasting and telecommunication links, to computer hardware and software, is of outstanding strategic significance. Within some industries, particularly those with strong network effects, products will converge around a common configuration of uniform technical standards that determine all further product development. The competitive position of individual firms stands or falls on the result of what Shapiro and Varian call these 'standards wars' that determine the choice of what that uniform technical standard is to be and which company controls it. Shapiro and Varian have written a classic competitive strategy article which contains a 'battle manual' derived from analysis of famous historical battles for control of an industry standard, such as the battle to determine the standard for railway gauges in the nineteenth century when the railways were first being built. They show that first-mover advantage is not always decisive; that victory almost always requires alliance-building with customers, suppliers and (some) other competitors; that dominant position does not necessarily survive into the next generation, and so on. They explain the particularly devastating impact of standards wars on markets where *network effects* (i.e. when the value of a product to a customer depends on the number of other users of the same product, such as a fax machine) are strong. Shapiro and Varian are describing a competitive, rather than a regulatory, battle for technical standards that will in turn drive market share. Technical standards are hard to set, and when a governmental regulating authority is involved, the results are frequently worse than when the market is left alone to fight it out (Grindley, 1995). What drives such battles over technology and the strategies involved in surviving them are what is addressed here.

In so far as context drives strategy and performance, we have discussed the most significant contextual factors: cultural (both national and corporate), technical, ethical, environmental and regulatory. Industry context should not (and Rumelt and others strongly argue, does not) determine the profitability of firms, but it is undoubtedly one of the key elements in formulating effective strategies.

REFERENCES

Adner, R. and Helfat, C.E. (2003) 'Corporate Effects and Dynamic Managerial Capabilities', *Strategic Management Journal*, Vol. 24, Special Issue: 1011–26.

Grindley, P. (1995) 'Regulation and Standards Policy: Setting Standards by Committees and Markets' in Bishop, M., Kay, J. and Mayer, C. (eds) *The Regulatory Challenge*, Oxford: Oxford University Press.

Hawawini, G., Subramanian, V. and Verdin, P. (2003) 'Is Performance Driven by Industry or by Firm-Specific Factors? A New Look at the Evidence', *Strategic Management Journal*, Vol. 24, No. 1: 1–16.

4

How Much Does Industry Matter?

Richard P. Rumelt

This study partitions the total variance in rate of return among FTC Line of Business reporting units into industry factors (whatever their nature), time factors, factors associated with the corporate parent, and business-specific factors. Whereas Schmalensee (1985) reported that industry factors were the strongest, corporate and market share effects being extremely weak, this study distinguishes between stable and fluctuating effects and reaches markedly different conclusions. The data reveal negligible corporate effects, small stable industry effects, and very large stable business-unit effects. These results imply that the most important sources of economic rents are business-specific; industry membership is a much less important source and corporate parentage is quite unimportant.

Because competition acts to direct resources towards uses offering the highest returns, persistently unequal returns mark the presence of either natural or contrived impediments to resource flows. The study of such impediments is a principal concern of industrial organization economics and the dominant unit of analysis in that field has been the *industry*. The implicit assumption has been that the most important market imperfections arise out of the collective circumstances and behaviour of firms. However, the field of business strategy offers a contrary view: it holds that the most important impediments are not the common property of collections of firms, but arise instead from the unique endowments and actions of individual corporations or business-units. If this is true, then industry may not be the most useful unit of analysis. Consequently, there should be considerable interest in the relative sizes of inter-industry and intra-industry dispersions in long-term profit rates.

Despite these arguments for this issue's salience, surprisingly little work addressed it until Schmalensee's (1985) estimation of the variance components of profit rates in the FTC Line of Business (LB) data. Schmalensee decomposed the total variance of rates of return on assets in the 1975 LB data into industry, corporate, and market-share components. He reported that: (1) corporate effects did not exist; (2) market-share effects accounted for a negligible fraction of the variance in business-unit rates of return; (3) industry effects accounted for 20 per cent of the variance in business-unit returns; (4) industry effects accounted for at least 75 per cent of the variance in industry returns.[1] He concluded, 'the finding that industry effects are important supports the classical focus on industry-level analysis as against the revisionist tendency to downplay industry differences' (1985: 349).

Schmalensee's study was innovative and technically sophisticated. Nevertheless, there are difficulties with it traceable to the use of a single year of data. In this article I perform a new variance components analysis of the FTC LB data that corrects this weakness. I analyse the four years (1974–1977) of data available and include components for overall business cycle effects, stable and transient industry effects, as well as stable and transient business-unit effects.[2] Like Schmalensee, I find that corporate effects are negligible. However, I draw dramatically different conclusions about the importance of industry effects, the existence and importance of business-level effects, and the validity of industry-level analysis.

The most straightforward way to review my analysis is to start with what Schmalensee's results left undecided. The first major incertitude is that, although 20 per cent of business-unit returns are explained by 'industry effects', we do not know how much of this 20 per cent is due to stable industry effects rather than to transient phenomena. For example, in 1975 the return on assets of the passenger automobile industry was 6.9 per cent and that of the corn wet milling industry was 35 per cent. But this difference was far from stable: in the following year the industries virtually reversed positions, auto's return rising to 22.1 per cent and corn wet milling's return falling to 11.5 per cent (Federal Trade Commission, 1975, 1976). The presence of industry-specific fluctuations like these adds to the variance in industry returns observed in any *one* year. Thus, Schmalensee's snapshot estimate of the variance of 'industry effects' is the variance among stable industry effects *plus* the variance of annual fluctuations. But the 'classical focus' is surely on the stable differences among industries, rather than on random year-to-year variations in those differences.

My analysis of the FTC LB data shows that stable industry effects account for only 8 per cent of the variance in business-unit returns. Furthermore, only about 40 per cent of the dispersion in industry returns is due to stable industry effects.

The second incertitude concerns the variance not explained by industry effects. Schmalensee noted (p. 350) 'it is important to recognize that 80 per cent of the variance in business-unit profitability is unrelated to industry or share effects. While industry differences matter, they are clearly not all that matters.' If this intra-industry variance is due to transient disequilibrium phenomena, then the 'classical focus on industry' would still be a contender; although it explains only 8 per cent of the variance, it would be the only stable pattern in the data. But, if a large portion of the intra-industry variance is due to stable differences among business-units within industries, then the 'classical focus on industry' may be misplaced.

The conceptual conclusions are straightforward. The 'classical focus on industry analysis' is mistaken because these industries are too heterogeneous to support classical theory. It is also mistaken because the most important impediments to the equilibration of long-term rates of return are not associated with industry, but with the unique endowments, positions, and strategies of individual businesses.

In this study, I find that the majority of this 'residual' variance is due to stable long-term differences among business-units rather than to transient phenomena. Using Schmalensee's sample, I find that stable business-unit effects account for 46 per cent of the variance. Indeed, the stable business-unit effects are six times more important than stable industry effects in explaining the dispersion of returns. Business-units differ from one another within industries a great deal more than industries differ from one another.

The empirical warning is equally striking. Most of the observed differences among industry returns have nothing to do with long-term industry effects; they are due to the random distribution of especially high- and low-performing business-units across industries. As will be shown, an FTC industry return must be at least 15.21 percentage points above the mean to warrant a conclusion (95 per cent confidence) that the true stable industry effect is positive. Fewer than one in forty industry returns are high enough to pass this test.

BACKGROUND

Most industrial organization research on business, corporate, and industry profitability tests propositions about the causes of differential performance. The primary tradition made industry the unit of analysis and sought a link between industry concentration (and entry barriers) and industry profitability (usually measured with pooled data).[3] A second tradition focused on inter-firm differences in performance, seeking explanation first in terms of firm size and later in terms of market share.[4] The early reaction against the mainline tradition viewed the concentration–profitability correlation as an artefact induced by the deeper share-profitability link.[5] Finally, the *stochastic* and *efficiency* views explain both firm profitability and market-share, and thus concentration, in terms of exogenous differential firm efficiencies.[6]

In contrast to economics, business strategy research began with the presumption of heterogeneity within industries and has only recently come to grips with the question of how differences in efficiency are sustained in the face of competition. Thus, the earliest case research informed by the 'strategy' concept focused on the different approaches to competition adopted by firms within the same industry. As the field matured, attention turned towards developing quantitative measures of this diversity[7] and, more recently, to its explanation in economic terms.[8] Each of these streams of work presumes different causal mechanisms and employs different units of analysis. Claims about whether profit-rate dispersion reflects collusion, share-based market power, or difficult-to-imitate resources are coupled with claims that the more aggregate phenomena are spurious or counter-claims that less aggregate phenomena are noise. My intention here is to suppress concern with *causal* mechanisms and focus instead on the question of *locus*. Put differently, my concern here is with the existence and relative importance of time, corporate, industry, and business-unit effects, *however generated*, on the total dispersion of reported rates of return.

Most prior work touching on the issue of *locus* has done so tangentially, rough measures of intra-industry dispersions in return being mentioned in passing within a study on a different topic. Stigler, for example, studying the convergence of profit rates over time, used the relative proportions of positive-profit and loss corporations to construct rough estimates of intra-industry variances in the rate of return by IRS size class (his estimates unavoidably confound inter-period and inter-firm variances). He remarked in passing (1963: 48) that these values were much larger than inter-industry variances, but drew no implications. Fisher and Hall (1969) measured the long-term (1950–1964) dispersion in rates of return about industry averages in order to obtain a measure of risk that could be regressed against industry profitability. Although they did not remark the fact, they obtained estimates that were approximately double their reported standard deviation in inter-industry rates of return.

McEnally (1976), in an analysis of results obtained by Conrad and Plotkin (1968), showed that industries with larger average return tend also to have larger dispersions in long-term inter-firm rates of return. His figures[9] show inter-firm variances that are two to five times as large as inter-industry variances.

As part of a re-examination of the concentration–profitability relationship, Gort and Singamsetti (1976) were apparently the first to explicitly ask whether or not 'the profit rates of firms cluster around industry means.' Assigning firms to 3-digit and 4-digit industries, they found to their surprise that the data failed to support the hypothesis that industries have different characteristic levels of profitability. Furthermore, they noted that the proportion of the total variance explained by industry was low (approximately 11 per cent, adjusted), did not increase as they moved from 3-digit to 4-digit industry definitions, and did not increase as the sample was restricted to more specialized firms.

In an unpublished working paper I performed a variance components analysis of corporate returns using 20 years of Compustat data (Rumelt, 1982). Although problems of industry definition and firm diversification prevented definitive results, here again the intra-industry effect dominated the inter-industry effect: the measured intra-industry variance in long-term firm effects was three to ten times as large as the variance due to industry-specific effects.

Schmalensee's (1985) study was the first published work aimed squarely at these issues and is the direct ancestor of the work presented here. Looking at the 1975 FTC LB data, Schmalensee estimated the following random-effects model:[10]

$$r_{ik} = \mu + \alpha_i + \beta_k + \eta S_{ik} + \epsilon_{ik} \tag{1}$$

where r_{ik} is the rate of return of corporation k's activity in industry i, S_{ik} is the corresponding market share, α_i and β_k are industry and corporate effects respectively, and ϵ_{ik} is a disturbance. Schmalensee used regression to conclude that corporate effects were non-existent ($\beta_k = 0$), and variance components estimation to show that industry effects were significant and substantial ($\sigma_\alpha^2 > 0$), and that share effects were significant but not substantial ($\eta > 0$ and $s_a^2 \geq h^2 \sigma_S^2$).

Kessides (1987) re-analysed Schmalensee's data, excluding corporations active in less than three industries. He found statistically significant corporate effects in the restricted sample, suggesting that inclusion of the less-diversified corporations had lowered the power of Schmalensee's test. In a related vein, Wernerfelt and Montgomery (1988) estimated a model patterned after Schmalensee's, replacing return on assets with Tobin's q and replacing the numerous corporate dummy variables with a single continuous measure of 'focus' (the inverse of diversification). They found industry effects and share effects of about the same magnitudes as Schmalensee found, and also found a small, but statistically significant, positive association between corporate focus and performance.

Cubbin and Geroski (1987) attacked the question of the relative strength of industry and firm effects with a different methodology. Using a sample of 217 large UK firms, they measured how much of firms' profitability *movements* over time were unique, how much were related to other firms' movements, and how much were related to common industry movements. Nearly one-half of the companies in their sample exhibited no common industry-wide response to dynamic factors.

Hansen and Wernerfelt (1989) studied the relative importance of economic and organizational factors in explaining inter-firm differences in profit rates. They found that industry explained 19 per cent of the variance in profit rates, but that organizational characteristics were roughly twice as important.

Data

Because the impetus for this study comes from the existence of the unique FTC LB data, and because the statistical work performed is fundamentally descriptive rather than hypothesis testing, I break with convention and discuss the data before introducing the model.

Data on the operations of large US Corporations are available from a variety of sources. However, there is only one source of disaggregate data on the profits of corporations by industry – the FTC's Line of Business Program. The FTC collected data on the domestic operations of large corporations in each of 261 4-digit FTC manufacturing industry categories. Information on a total of 588 different corporations was collected for the years 1974–1977; because of late additions, deletions, acquisitions, and mergers, the number of corporations reporting in any one year ranged from 432 to 471. The average corporation reported on about eight business-units.

Schmalensee's sample was constructed by starting with Ravenscraft's (1983) data-set of 3,186 stable and meaningful business-units – those which were not in miscellaneous categories and which were neither newly created nor terminated during the 1974–1976 period. He then dropped business-units in 16 FTC industries judged to be primarily residual classifications, dropped business-units with sales less than 1 per cent of 1975 FTC industry total sales, and excluded one outlier.

Two data sets were used in this research, labelled A and B. Sample A was constructed by starting with Schmalensee's sample of 1,775 business-units from the 1975 file and appending data on the same business-units from the 1974, 1976 and 1977 files. After this expansion, one business-unit was judged to have unreliable asset measures (in 1976–77) and was dropped. Eight other observations were eliminated because assets were reported as zero. Sample A then contained 6,932 observations provided by 457 corporations on 1,774 business-units operating in a total of 242 4-digit FTC industries.

Sample B was constructed by adding to Sample A the 1,070 'small' business-units which had failed Schmalensee's size criterion. After adjoining the 1974, 1976 and 1977 data for these business-units, 34 were excluded due to (apparent) measurement problems: negative or zero assets, sales-to-assets ratios over 30, and extreme year-to-year variations in assets that were unconnected to changes in sales. Sample B then contained 10,866 observations provided by 463 corporations on 2,810 business-units operating in a total of 242 4-digit FTC industries.

The rate of return was taken to be the ratio of profit before interest and taxes to total assets, expressed as a percentage. In sample A the average return was 13.92 and the sample variance was 279.35. In sample B, the average and sample variance of return were 13.17 and 410.73 respectively.

The FTC defined operating income as total revenues (including transfers from other units) less cost of goods sold, less selling, advertising, and general and administrative expenses. Both expenses and assets were further divided into 'traceable' and 'untraceable' components, the traceable component being directly attributable to the line of business and the untraceable component being allocated by the reporting firm among lines of business using 'reasonable procedures'. In 1975, 15.8 per cent of the total expenses and 13.6 per cent of total assets of the average business-unit were allocated.

A number of scholars have advanced arguments that accounting rates of return are systematically biased measures of true internal rates of return.[11] Whatever the merits of this position, the purpose of this study is to partition the variance in reported business-unit rates of return. If different industry practices or corporate policies do induce systematic biases in reported returns, the estimated variance components will reflect these facts and, therefore, help in estimating their importance.

A Variance Components Model

In discussing the heterogeneity within industries the term 'firm' has an ambiguity that easily leads to confusion. In economics a 'firm' is usually an autonomous competitive unit within an industry, but the term is also often used to indicate a legal entity: a 'company' or 'corporation'. Because most empirical studies are of large corporations, and because most large corporations are substantially diversified, legal or corporate 'firms' are, at best, amalgams of individual theoretical competitive units. Confusion can arise if one author uses the term 'firm effects' to indicate intra-industry dispersion among theoretical 'firms', and another author uses the same term to denote differences among corporations which are not explained by their patterns of industry activities.

To reduce the ambiguity in what follows I avoid the term 'firm'. Instead, I use the term *business-unit* to denote that portion of a company's operations which are wholly contained within a single industry.[12] I use the term *corporation* to denote a legal company which owns and operates one or more business-units. Thus, both industries and corporations are considered to be sets of business-units.

In this regard, note that Schmalensee (1985) used the term 'firm-effects' to denote what I call corporate effects. Thus, his first proposition, 'firm effects do not exist' (p. 349), refers to what are here termed corporate effects. Consequently, as he noted, finding insignificant corporate effects does not rule out the presence of substantial intra-industry effects. However, unless more than one year of data are analysed, intra-industry effects pool with the error and cannot be detected.

Taking the unit of analysis to be the business-unit, assume that each business-unit is observed over time and is classified according to its industry membership and its corporate ownership. Let r_{ikt} denote the rate of return reported in time period t by the business-unit owned by corporation k and active in industry i. A particular business-unit is labelled ik, highlighting the fact that it is simultaneously a member of an industry and a corporation. Working with this notation, I posit the following descriptive model:

$$r_{ikt} = \mu + \alpha_i + \beta_k + \gamma_t + \delta_{it} + \phi_{ik} + \epsilon_{ikt} \qquad (2)$$

where the α_i are industry effects ($i = 1, ..., l_\alpha$), the β_k are corporate effects ($k = 1, ..., l_\beta$), the γ_i are year effects ($t = 1, ..., l_\gamma$) the δ_{it} are industry–year interaction effects (l_δ distinct it combinations), and the ϕ_{ik} are business-unit effects (l_ϕ distinct ik combinations). The ϵ_{ik} are random disturbances (one for each of the N observations). Each corporation is only active in a few industries, so $l_\phi < l_\alpha l_\beta$. Because a few industries may not be observed over all years, $l_\delta \le l_\alpha l_\gamma$. The model takes the assignment of business-units to corporations and industries as given and is essentially descriptive. In particular, it offers no causal or structural explanation for profitability differences across industries, years, corporations, or business-units – it simply posits the existence of differences in return associated with these categories.

There are two key differences between this model and Schmalensee's. First, the terms γ_t, and δ_{it} have been added to deal with year-to-year variations in overall returns and year-to-year variations in industry-specific returns. Second, the market-share term has been replaced by ϕ_{ik}. In this regard, it is useful to recall Schmalensee's persuasive reasons for turning to a nominal measure of industry. He argued (1985: 343) that conventional market-level variables (e.g. concentration) are very imperfect measures of the theoretical constructs (perceived interdependence) they are supposed to represent. Therefore, the fact that these variables perform poorly, relative to market-share, in cross-sectional regressions may not mean that 'industry' is unimportant. Hence, Schmalensee sought to measure the importance of *all* industry effects, using nominal industry categories, and compare it to the importance of market-share. But, just as concentration is an imperfect measure of industry structure, so market-share is an imperfect measure of resource heterogeneity among businesses. Comparing *all* industry effects to market-share effects may unfairly load the dice in favour of industry. Consequently, in this study I extend Schmalensee's argument to the business-unit and, rather than give special attention to market-share, I measure the importance of *all* stable industry effects, and *all* stable business-unit effects.

Were this a *fixed-effects* model, the usual assumption would be that the ϵ_{ikt} are random disturbances, drawn independently from a distribution with mean zero and unknown variance σ_ϵ. In this model I make the additional assumption that all of the other effects, like the error term, are realizations of random processes with zero means and constant, but unknown variances σ_α^2, σ_β^2, σ_γ^2, σ_δ^2, and σ_ϕ.

Note that this *random effects* assumption does not mean that the various effects are inconstant. Instead, for example, each business-unit effect ϕ_{ik} is seen as having been independently generated by a random process with variance σ_ϕ^2, and, having once been set, remaining fixed thereafter.

The random-effects assumption says nothing about why effects differ from one another – effects may differ from one another in either fixed-effects or random-effects models. The real substance of the random-effects assumption is that the differences among effects, whatever their source, are 'natural', not having been controlled or contrived by the research design, and are independent of other effects. That is, the effects in the data represent a *random* sample of the effects in the population. Independence implies that knowing the value of a particular ϕ_{ik}, for example, is of no help in predicting the values of other business-unit effects or the values of any industry, corporate, or year effects. An important exception to this assumption, involving an association between industry and corporate effects, is discussed below.

Readers familiar with fixed-effects regression models may be concerned that the effects posited in this model are not estimable. Such a concern is well placed – the individual effects cannot be estimated. Furthermore, regression methods cannot deliver unambiguous estimates of the relative importance of classes of effects. However, the statistical problem is not to estimate the thousands of effects, but to estimate the six variances. Despite the nesting in the model, the variance components are estimable. Note that it is the assumption that the underlying effects are realizations of random processes that allows a measure of their relative 'importance'. Were they assumed to be 'fixed', one could test for statistical significance, but there would be no reliable way of assessing importance. *It is only by estimating the variances of effects that relative importance can be assessed.*

The α_i represent all persistent industry-specific impacts on observed rates of return. Differences among the α_i reflect differing competitive behaviour, conditions of entry, rates of growth, demand-capacity conditions, differing levels of risk, differing asset utilization rates, differing accounting practices, and any other industry-specific impacts on the rate of return. The fundamentally descriptive model used here offers no hypotheses as to the nature of these industry differences – the α_i represent their total collective impact.

Corporate effects β_k should arise from differences in the quality of monitoring and control, differences in resource sharing and other types of synergy, and differences in accounting policy. Total corporate returns will, of course, also be affected by the industry memberships of their constituent businesses. However, the unit of analysis here is the business-unit, not the corporation.

The ϕ_{ik} represent persistent differences among business-unit returns other than those due to industry and corporate membership. That is, they are due to the presence of business-specific skills, resources, reputations, learning, patents, and other intangible contributions to stable differences among business-unit returns. Such differences may also arise from persistent errors in the allocation of costs or assets among a corporation's business-units. (Note, however, that corporate-wide or industry-wide biases in accounting will appear as corporate or industry effects.) The section on Empirical Results presents the results of a test for the presence of allocation errors.

Are the differences among business-unit returns within industries simply disequilibrium phenomena? Until recently, rates of return were thought to converge fairly rapidly to 'normal' levels. Consequently, the idea of business-unit effects had little currency. If they surfaced empirically, they were treated as an autocorrelation problem. However, researchers using more disaggregate data have discovered that abnormal profit rates do not rapidly fade away; Mueller (1977, 1985) and Jacobson (1988) have found them to be extraordinarily persistent. This consideration, and the fact that the FTC LB data covers only four years, leads to modelling the business-unit effects as fixed. If this assumption is incorrect, and the business-unit effects decay over time, then the estimated residuals will display positive autocorrelation. Such a finding would signal the need for a more complex autoregressive model. As will be seen, no such autocorrelation was found in the data studied here.

The γ_t represent year-to-year fluctuations in macroeconomic conditions that influence all business-units equally. The δ_{it} represent industry-specific year-to-year fluctuations in return. Finally, there is an ε_{ikt} associated with each observation. Although these effects have been named 'error', they may equally well be thought of as year-to-year variations that are specific to each business-unit.

In an important exception to the independence assumption, Schmalensee (1985: 344) argued that corporations which are more skilful at operating businesses might also be more skilled at having identified and entered more profitable industries, thereby inducing a dependence between the values of β and α observed across business-units. Incorporating this presumption, and maintaining elsewhere the assumption of independence, the total variance σ_r of returns may be decomposed into these variance–covariance components:

$$\sigma_r^2 = \sigma_\alpha^2 + \sigma_\beta^2 + \sigma_\gamma^2 + \sigma_\delta^2 + \sigma_\phi^2 + \sigma_\varepsilon^2 + 2C_{\alpha\beta} \qquad (3)$$

where $C_{\alpha\beta}$ is the covariance between α_i and β_k, given that corporation k is active in industry i (i.e., $E(\alpha_i \beta_k) = C_{\alpha\beta}$ if business-unit ik exists, and 0 otherwise). [...]

Empirical Results

Table 4.1 displays the estimated variance-covariance components for the full model. The procedure used does not prohibit negative estimates. The normal practice is to replace small negative estimates with zero and take large negative estimates as an indication of specification error. In sample A, $\sigma_\gamma^2 = -2.82$, and in sample B, $2C_{\alpha\beta} = -0.01$, results surely indistinguishable from zero.

Treating the model as one with fixed, rather than random, effects provides additional information on its adequacy. Table 4.2 shows sequential analyses of variance with business-unit effects entering last and then again with industry-year effects entering last. The R^2 for the sample A regression is 0.765 (0.632 corrected) and for the sample B regression it is 0.696 (0.549 corrected). Both regressions are highly significant overall. Additionally, in both samples the estimates of σ_ϵ^2 obtained from the fixed-effect regressions are quite close to those obtained from the variance components procedure. This confirmatory test provides an indication that the model is adequately specified.

The fixed-effects estimations provide residuals that can be examined for autocorrelation. The correlation between the residuals and their lagged values was −0.018 in sample A and 0.001 in sample B. Thus, there is no evidence in these data that business-unit effects decay. The lack of autocorrelation confirms the decision to model business-unit effects as fixed over the 4-year sample period.

It is important to note that with fixed-effects estimation, strict tests for the presence of effects are possible only for the last effects fitted. Thus, Table 4.2 shows that business-unit effects and industry-year effects are quite significant. However, because of the nesting in the model, it is not possible to fit industry or corporate effects *after* fitting business-unit effects. Put differently, in analysis-of-variance one cannot hold business-unit effects 'constant' and then estimate industry or corporate effects. Thus, the significance attaching to the entry of 'corporation' in Table 4.2 (F-value $= 6.13$) does not necessarily mean that corporate effects are significantly different from zero.[13] Thus, analysis of variance or regression cannot reveal whether the apparent explanatory power of corporation is due to real corporate effects or whether it reflects differences among corporate returns induced by large uncontrolled business-unit effects. The same problem arises in interpreting the results on industry effects.

This ambiguity is a central reason for turning to variance components estimation; unlike regression, variance components procedures can assess the independent importance of nested business-unit, corporate and industry effects. Indeed, as Table 4.1 shows, corporate effects are essentially nil (in Sample A). Thus, the apparent significance attached to the introduction of corporate effects in the fixed-effect estimation is wholly due to the dispersion among corporate returns induced by the deeper business-unit effects. This case is an excellent illustration of the problem associated with using R^2 or 'incremental' R^2 as a measure of a factor's importance. In Sample A (Table 4.2) the marginal R^2 of the industry and corporate effects are roughly comparable at 18 and 15 per cent respectively (the adjusted marginal R^2s are about 14 and 10 per cent). Yet Table 4.1 shows that the corporate variance component is only one-hundredth as large as the industry variance component.

The results strongly suggest that $\sigma_\gamma^2 = 0$ and $C_{\alpha\beta} = 0$ in both samples. Accordingly, the model was re-estimated with these restrictions. The results are shown in Table 4.3. The restrictions produce only slight changes in the estimates of the remaining variance components.[14]

Table 4.1 Variance–covariance components estimates: full model

Component	Sample A	Sample B
Year	−2.82	0.20
Industry-year	24.74	21.89
Industry	20.49	16.62
Corporation	0.19	6.75
Business-unit	131.69	181.49
$2C_{\alpha\beta}$	2.13	−0.01
Error	102.51	184.06

Table 4.2   Fixed-effects ANOVA results

Business-Unit Entering Last

		Sample A			Sample B	
Source	df	Incr. R^2	F-Value	df	Incr. R^2	F-Value
Year	3	0.0003	1.78	3	0.0008	6.09[b]
Industry	241	0.179	14.03[a]	241	0.103	10.28[a]
Industry-Year	721	0.098	2.57[a]	721	0.071	2.36[a]
Corporation	456	0.148	6.13[a]	462	0.109	5.70[a]
Business-unit	1076	0.339	5.94[a]	2106	0.413	4.72[a]
Total Model	2497	0.765	5.78[a]	3533	0.696	4.75[a]
Error	4434	0.235		7332	0.304	
Total	6931			10865		

Industry-Year Entering Last

		Sample A			Sample B	
Source	df	Incr. R^2	F-Value	df	Incr. R^2	F-Value
Year	3	0.0003	1.78	3	0.0008	6.09[b]
Corporation	456	0.176	7.27[a]	462	0.116	6.05[a]
Industry	241	0.153	11.98[a]	241	0.098	9.76[a]
Business-unit	1076	0.340	5.95[a]	2106	0.414	4.74[a]
Industry-Year	721	0.096	2.52[a]	721	0.068	2.26[a]
Total Model	2497	0.765	5.78[a]	3533	0.696	4.75[a]
Error	4434	0.235		7332	0.304	
Total	6931			10865		

[a]Significant at 0.0001 level.
[b]Significant at 0.0005 level.

Table 4.3   Variance components estimates: restricted model (year effects and $C_{\alpha\beta}$ removed)

	Sample A			Sample B		
Component	Est.	Std. Error	Per cent	Est.	Std. Error	Per cent
Industry-Year	21.92	2.04	7.84	22.09	2.31	5.38
Industry	23.26	4.72	8.32	16.55	4.26	4.03
Corporation	2.25	3.84	0.80	6.74	3.31	1.64
Business-unit	129.63	6.91	46.37	181.50	7.04	44.17
Error	102.51	2.18	36.87	184.06	3.04	44.79
Total	279.56		100.00	410.95		100.00

Since σ_ϵ^2 was also obtained by fixed-effects regression, the variance of this estimate is available from standard regression theory and is reported in Table 4.3. However, the sampling distributions of the other variance components estimators are not known and, even under normality assumptions, usable expressions for the variances of the estimates are not available. To provide some guidance on this matter I provide standard errors of the estimates that would be observed were the true variance components equal to their estimated values and were the underlying distributions normal. These estimates were obtained by simulation: taking the variance components at their estimated values, a realization of each effect in the model was generated by a draw from the appropriate normal distribution, these effects were then combined according to the original data structure, and the variance components estimation procedure was then re-applied to the simulated data set. The standard errors shown are based on 1000 such trials. The values obtained offer convincing evidence that the estimates of the larger variance components are not overly noisy. With regard to the corporate effect, I conclude that there is no evidence of non-zero corporate effects in sample A, whereas the inclusion of the smaller business-units (sample B) provides some evidence of (small) corporate effects.

As has been noted, the estimate of the variance among business-unit effects reflects both 'real' differences in return and any persistent errors in the corporate allocation of costs and assets among business-units. If allocation error is an important phenomenon in these data it should be detectable through the induced statistical dependence among business-unit returns within corporations. That is, an allocation error which increases one business-unit's return must also decrease the returns of other business-units in the same corporation.

More formally, assume that errors in a corporation's allocation policy add u_i to the ith business-unit's return and that these allocations are constrained such that $\sum w_i u_i = 0$, where the w_i are positive constants. If the *unconditional* distribution of each u_i is normal with mean zero and variance σ_u^2, it is not hard to show that the distribution of the ui, *conditional* on the constraint, is joint (singular) normal such that

$$cov(u_i, u_j) = Eu_i u_j = -k_{ij}\sigma_u^2,$$

where $k = w_i w_j / \sum_m w_m^2$. Thus, instead of independence, allocation error implies that $E\,\phi_{ik}\,\phi_{jk} < 0$.

To examine this question, it is useful to first 'adjust' returns for industry-year effects so that attention may be focused on business-unit phenomena. Accordingly, the deviation in return d_{ikt} from the average for that industry in that year was defined:

$$d_{ikt} = r_{ikt} - r_{i.t}/n_{i.t},$$

one pair of these measures was randomly selected from each corporation (in each year) with two or more business-units. To a first approximation, $d_{ikt} \approx \phi_{ik} + \epsilon_{ikt}$. If, within corporations, ϕ_{ik} is independent of ϕ_{jk} and ϵ_{ikt} is independent of ϵ_{jkt}, the covariance between the 1,321 paired measures should be zero. The calculated covariance was 0.007, providing no reason to doubt independence. Looking further, and taking the weight w_i to be the fraction of a corporation's assets utilized in the ith business, the regression of the products of the paired measures ($d_{ikt} d_{jkt}$) on the kij (defined above) was then computed: the coefficient of k_{ij} is a direct estimate of σ_u^2. Neither the constrained ($m = 0$) nor the unconstrained regression was significant ($t = -0.43$ and $t = -0.6$). These results do not support the view that allocation errors are an important source of heterogeneity in the FTC LB data.

Discussion and Implications

The variance in business-unit profitability in sample A (B) may be partitioned approximately as follows: 8 (4) per cent industry effects, 1 (2) per cent corporate effects, 46 (44) per cent business-unit effects, 8 (5) per cent industry-year effects, and 37 (45) per cent residual error.

The fundamental difference between the two samples is that in sample B the non-industry variances are substantially larger, making industry relatively less important. Whereas the indus-

Table 4.4 Comparison with Schmalensee's results (percentage of total variance by source)

Source	This Study Sample A	Schmalensee (1985)
CORPORATE	0.80	×
Industry	8.28	×
Industry-Year	7.84	×
ALL INDUSTRY	16.12	19.46
Share	×	0.63
Share-Industry Covariance	×	−0.62
Business-Unit	46.38	×
Business-Unit-Year	36.70	×
ALL INTRA-INDUSTRY	83.08	80.54
TOTAL	100.00	100.00

× Component not estimated

try and industry-year components are comparable in both samples, in sample B business-unit variance component is 40 per cent larger than in sample A and the residual error is 80 per cent larger. (The corporate variance component is three times as large but its magnitude is small in both samples.) If the components are expressed as percentages, the opposite pattern emerges: the contribution of industry falls from 8.29 per cent in sample A to 4.01 per cent in sample B, whereas the percentage contribution of the business-unit component is virtually unchanged.

Table 4.4 compares the variance partition for sample A with that reported by Schmalensee (1985). Schmalensee estimated that 19.59 per cent of the total variance was due to industry effects. In this study, I find that somewhat less, 16.12 per cent, is due to all industry effects (stable plus year-to-year fluctuations). The difference between the estimates arises mainly because 1975 was an abnormal year – repeating Schmalensee's one-year analysis in 1976 and 1977 yields smaller industry components. More importantly, I find that only one-half of this variance is due to stable effects. Long-term industry effects account for only 8.28 per cent of the observed variance among sample A business-unit returns.

Turning to the intra-industry variance, Schmalensee reported that 80.41 per cent of the variance was unexplained by industry; the comparable figure in this study is 83.08 per cent. However, my partition of this intra-industry variance into stable and year-to-year components reveals that over one-half is due to stable business-unit effects. Indeed, the variance among stable business-unit effects is six times as large as the variance among stable industry effects – business-units differ from one another within industries much more than industries differ from one another.

Despite the fact that this is a descriptive study, some strong general results can be reported:

1   There are significant business-unit effects in US manufacturing activities that strongly outweigh industry and corporate membership as predictors of profitability. The variance among business-unit effects is much larger than the variance among industry effects (six times larger in sample A and eleven times larger in sample B).
2   Corporate effects, although present in sample B, are not important in explaining the dispersion in observed rates of return among business-units.

Business-unit effects

The large observed variance component for business-unit effects overshadows the other variance components. Although this model cannot reveal the sources of this dispersion, some insight can be gained by examining Schmalensee's results on the importance of market share. His study of sample A for 1975 measured a variance component due to share of 2.2. This amounts to 1.7 per cent of the business-unit variance component estimated for sample A data in this study. Hence, it seems safe to conclude that only a very small part of the large business-unit effects can be associated with differences in the relative sizes of business-units.

The large business-unit effects indicate that there is more intra-industry heterogeneity than has been commonly recognized. Whereas economists are quick to refer to *inframarginal rents* when this issue arises, the unspoken presumption is that these effects are small, or related to scale. The results are otherwise. The business-unit effects are large and owe only a small fraction of their strength to market share. Some portion of these effects may, of course, be due to measurement biases. But the most obvious sources of bias, differences in industry accounting and differences in corporate policy, should appear as industry or corporate effects.

The presence of strong business-unit effects is consonant with the presumptions in portions of the *business strategy* literature. Beginning with Caves and Porter's mobility barriers concept, based on the hypothesis that 'sellers within an industry are likely to differ systematically in traits other than size' (1977: 250), ideas in this area have evolved in the direction of recognizing increasingly disaggregate sources of resource immobility or specificity.[15] According to this view, product-specific reputation, team-specific learning, a variety of first-mover advantages, causal ambiguity that limits effective imitation, and other special conditions permit equilibria in which competitors earn dramatically different rates of return. Although this study cannot discriminate among the various theories regarding the sources of intra-industry heterogeneity, it necessarily gives broad support to this class of theory and should encourage further work in this vein.

What do industry returns measure?

If business-units within industries have large and persistent differences in return, it becomes necessary to ask what the 'industry returns' measures used in many industrial organization studies actually represent. That is, when industries exhibit differing levels of overall return, to what extent are such differences due to systematic industry effects and to what extent are such differences the veiled result of differences in individual business-unit performance? I undertake a very simple exploration of this question by examining the variance of $\gamma_i = \sum_{k \cdot t} r_{i \cdot \cdot} / n_{i \cdot \cdot}$, the average return observed for industry i over all four years, so that

$$y_i = \mu + \alpha_i + \sum_t \frac{n_{i \cdot t}}{n_{i \cdot \cdot}} \delta_{it} + \sum_k \frac{n_{ik \cdot}}{n_{i \cdot \cdot}} \phi_{ik} + \sum_{k \cdot t} \frac{n_{ikt}}{n_{i \cdot \cdot}} \epsilon_{ikt}. \tag{4}$$

The sample variance s_γ^2 of industry returns was 61.9 in sample A and 58.1 in sample B. Extending the development of (10) to cover industry-year effects, the expected value of this measure can be written

$$E\left(s_y^2\right) = s_a^2 + \left(\sum_{i \cdot t} \frac{n_{i \cdot t}^2}{l_a n_{i \cdot \cdot}^2}\right) s_d^2 + \left(\sum_{i \cdot k} \frac{n_{ik \cdot}^2}{l_a n_{i \cdot \cdot}^2}\right) s_f^2 + \left(\sum_i \frac{1}{l_a n_{i \cdot \cdot}}\right) s_\epsilon^2.$$

This equation, and the Table 4.3 estimates of σ_α^2, σ_δ^2, σ_ϕ^2 and σ_ϵ^2 allow the construction of a partitioned estimate of $E(s_y^2)$; the result is shown in Table 4.5. The agreement between the sample values and the total expected values appears to be good.

This partition reveals that only 40 per cent of the variance among industry returns is actually due to stable industry effects. In sample A an additional 40 per cent of s_y^2 is due to business-unit effects which randomly combine to affect industry averages; in sample B the corresponding proportion is close to one-half. The remaining variance (one-fifth in sample A, one-eighth in sample B) is due to various industry-year and business-unit-year fluctuations. (This portion would be smaller had the averages been taken over more than 4 years.) Because only 40 per cent of the variance in industry returns is due to industry effects, industry returns are noisy estimates of the true industry effects.

How large does an industry return have to be in order to justify a conclusion that the corresponding industry effect is positive? From (14), it should be clear that

$$y_i = \mu + \alpha_i + e_i$$

where e_i is a weighted average of industry-year, business-unit, and error effects, and where α_i and e_i are independent. To simplify matters, assume that μ is known. Then $E\,(y_i) = \mu$, $E\,(\alpha_i) = 0$, and cov $(y_i,\, \alpha_i) = E\,(\alpha_i^2) = \sigma_\alpha^2$

Let $x = [\alpha_i,\, y_i]$, so that $Ex = [0\ \mu]$, and

$$\text{var}\,(x) = \begin{bmatrix} V_{11} & V_{12} \\ V_{21} & V_{22} \end{bmatrix} = \begin{bmatrix} s_\alpha^2 & s_\alpha^2 \\ s_\alpha^2 & s_y^2 \end{bmatrix}.$$

Now consider the conditional distribution of α_i given y_i. Assuming that x is bivariate normal, the desired conditional distribution is normal with these parameters:

$$E(\alpha_i | y_i) = V_{11}(y_i - \mu)/V_{22} = \zeta\,(y_i - \mu)$$
$$\text{Var}(\alpha_i | y_i) = V_{11} - V_{12}^2/V_{22} = (1 - \zeta)\sigma_\alpha^2,$$

where $\zeta = \sigma_\alpha^2 / \sigma_y^2$. Table 4.3 indicates that $\sigma_\alpha^2 \approx 23$ and Table 4.5 shows that $\zeta \approx 0.4$. Therefore, $\sigma_{\alpha i\,|\,yi} = \sqrt{0.6 \cdot 23} = 3.71$.

Thus, if y_i is 10 percentage points above the mean, the expectation is that $\alpha_i = 0.4 \cdot 10 = 4$. But the conditional distribution of α_i has a standard deviation of 3.71 – although the expectation is of a 4-point industry effect, this estimate is only 1.08 standard deviations above zero. Using the normal distribution, $F_N(-1.08) = 0.14$. That is, although industry i has an average return that is 10 percentage points above the mean, there remains a 0.14 probability that α_i is actually negative.

To reduce the chance of this type of error to 0.05 or less, the conditional estimate of α_i must be at least 1.64 standard deviations above zero ($F_N\,(1.64) = 0.95$). That is, if one is to conclude $\alpha_i > 0$ with 95 per cent confidence, the inequality

Table 4.5 Estimated components of sample variance among industry average returns

Source	Sample A		Sample B	
	Component	Per cent	Component	Per cent
Industry	23.3	39.3	16.6	29.8
Industry-Year	5.5	9.3	5.6	10.0
Business-Unit	25.3	42.7	26.6	47.7
Error	5.2	8.7	7.0	12.5
Total	59.27	100.0	55.8	100.0
Actual Sample Variance	61.9		58.1	

$$0.4(y_i - \mu) > 1.64 \cdot 3.71$$

must be satisfied. It follows that $\gamma_i - \mu > 13.21$ is required.

Thus, in order to have 95 per cent confidence that $\alpha_i > 0$, the observed industry average must be at least 15.21 percentage points above the mean. How often will this happen? The standard deviation σ_y of industry returns has the approximate value $\sqrt{23/0.4} = 7.58$. Obviously, the 'typical' industry returns does not pass the 15.21 point criterion. Indeed, the 15.21 point cut-off lies two standard deviations above the mean! Hence, only one in forty industries ($F_N(2) = 0.977$) will exhibit a return large enough to warrant a conclusion that the true industry effects is positive. Put differently, industry returns are such noisy measures of industry effects that only about six of the 242 FTC industries studied could be judged (95 per cent confidence) to have positive industry effects.

Corporate effects

Turning to the issue of corporate effects, corporations exhibit little or no (differential) ability to affect business-unit returns. It is not that corporate effects do not exist – it appears that $s_\beta^2 > 0$ in sample B – but rather that corporate effects are astonishingly small. Put differently, if one business-unit within a corporation is very profitable, there is little reason to expect that any of the corporation's other business-units will be performing at other than the norms set by industry, year, and industry-year effects.

Corporate returns will, of course, differ from one another for reasons other than corporate effects. Corporate returns will differ because of their differing patterns of participation in industries. More importantly, corporate returns will differ because their portfolios of business-units differ. But the results indicate that the dispersion among corporate returns can be fully explained by the dispersions of industry and business-unit effects; there is no evidence of 'synergy'.

Given the extent of the literature on corporate strategy, corporate culture, the number of consulting firms that specialize in corporate management, and the focus on senior corporate leaders in the business world, it is surprising to find only vanishingly small corporate effects on these data. This result, first obtained by Schmalensee, remains a puzzle and deserves further investigation.

Implications

To the extent that accounting returns measure the presence of economic rents, the results obtained here imply that by far the most important sources of rents in US manufacturing businesses are due to resources or market positions that are specific to particular business-units rather than to corporate resources or to membership in an industry. Put simply, business-units within industries differ from one another a great deal more than industries differ from one another.

Empirical results are rarely definitive and there are a number of issues left unresolved in this study. It may be, for example, that the FTC 4-digit industries are simply too broad to reveal the true strength of industry effects. Or, it may be that the assumption of a constant σ_ϕ is unjustified, some industries being much more heterogeneous than others. Nevertheless, most empirical work within the industrial organization paradigm has been conducted on data at this or higher levels of aggregation and persistent intra-industry heterogeneity has been generally assumed away rather than measured. Consequently, it seems worthwhile to sharply and clearly state the implications of this study:

1   The neoclassical model of industry as composed of firms that are homogeneous (but for scale) does not describe 4-digit industries: these data show real industries to be extremely heterogeneous.

2   The simple revisionist model in which business-units differ in size due to differences in manufacturing efficiency is incorrect – only a small portion of the large observed variance among business-unit effects can be associated with differences in relative size.

3   Theoretical or statistical explanations of business-unit performance that use industry as the unit of analysis can, at best, explain only about 8 per cent of the observed dispersion among business-unit profit rates.

4   Theoretical or statistical explanations of business-unit performance that use the corporation as the unit of analysis can, at best, explain only about 2 per cent of the observed dispersion among business-unit profit rates.

5   Theoretical or statistical work seeking to explain an important portion of the observed dispersion in business-unit profit rates must use the business-unit (or even less aggregate entities) as the unit of analysis and must focus on sources of heterogeneity within industries other than relative size.

NOTES

1   Industry and corporate 'effects' are (unobserved) components of business-unit returns that are associated with membership in each particular industry and corporation. An 'Industry return' is the calculated average return of the business-units in that industry.

2   'Stable' industry effects are the (unobserved) time-invariant components of business-unit returns associated with membership in each industry. 'Stable' business-unit effects are the (unobserved) time-invariant components of business-unit returns that are not due to industry or corporate membership.

3   See Weiss' (1974) survey of this line of work.

4   See Scherer's (1980) review of prior work on this topic.

5   Ravenscraft (1980, 1983) is the best example of this line.

6   See Demsetz (1973) and Mancke (1974), as well as Lippman and Rumelt (1982).

7   Hatten and Schendel (1977) provided early contributions; see McGee and Thomas (1986) for a review of the strategic groups literature.

8   See Teece (1982), Rumelt (1984) and Wernerfelt (1984).

9   Conrad and Plotkin computed intra-industry variances directly from deviations about industry averages. Because they are not based on true variance components estimation, their results may over estimate intra-industry variances and produce substantially upwards biased estimates of inter-industry variances (although the latter was not of direct interest to them or to McEnally).

10 I have altered his notation to preserve consistency within this paper.

11 In particular, see Fisher and McGowan (1983).

12 It is common practice among FTC LB researchers to refer to a business-unit as an 'LB'. I avoid this usage because many others naturally, but erroneously, believe that the term 'Line of Business' refers to an industry group rather than to an individual business-unit within a larger firm.

13 Formally, neither β, nor $\beta_i - \beta_j$, $i \neq j$, is estimable. A common practice is to force estimability by imposing the 'usual' restrictions – in this case an assumption that the average business-unit effect in each industry is zero. The problem with that approach is that it 'deals' with the potential distortions caused by the unobserved business-unit effects by simply assuming them away.

14 Because the sample variance s_r^2 is computed about the sample average, rather than about the true mean μ, the sum of the variance components is not the sample variance. However, it is very close in both cases and the difference will be ignored in what follows.

15 See Rumelt (1987) for a summary of the *isolating mechanisms* viewpoint.

REFERENCES

Caves, R.E. and Porter, M.E. (1977) 'From entry barriers to mobility barriers: conjectural decisions and contrived deterrence to new competition', *Quarterly Journal of Economics*, Vol. 91, pp. 241–61.

Conrad, G.R. and Plotkin, I.H. (1968) 'Risk/return: U.S. industry pattern', *Harvard Business Review*, March–April, pp. 90–9.

Cubbin, J. and Geroski, P. (1987) 'The convergence of profits in the long run: inter-firm and inter-industry comparisons', *Journal of Industrial Economics*, Vol. 35, pp. 427–42.

Demsetz, H. (1973) 'Industry structure, market rivalry, and public policy', *Journal of Law and Economics*, Vol. 16, pp. 1–9.

Federal Trade Commission, *Statistical Report: Annual Line of Business Reports, 1975, 1976.* Published in 1981 and 1982.

Fisher, F. and McGowan, J. (1983) 'On the misuse of accounting rates of return to infer monopoly profits', *American Economic Review*, Vol. 73, pp. 82–97.

Fisher, I.N. and Hall, G.R. (1969) 'Risk and corporate rates of return', *Quarterly Journal of Economics*, Vol. 83, pp. 79–92.

Gort, M. and Singamsetti, R. (1976) 'Concentration and profit rates: new evidence on an old issue', *Occasional Papers of the National Bureau of Economic Research: Explorations in Economic Research*, Vol. 3, Winter, pp. 1–20.

Hansen, G.S. and Wernerfelt, B. (1989) 'Determinants of firm performance: the relative importance of economic and organizational factors', *Strategic Management Journal*, Vol. 10, pp. 399–411.

Hatten, K.J. and Schendel, D.E. (1977) 'Heterogeneity within an industry', *Journal of Industrial Economics*, Vol. 26, pp. 97–113.

Jacobson, R. (1988) 'The persistence of abnormal returns', *Strategic Management Journal*, Vol. 9, pp. 415–30.

Kessides, I.N. (1987) 'Do firms differ much? Some additional evidence', Working Paper, Department of Economics, University of Maryland.

Lippman, S.A. and Rumelt, R.P. (1982) 'Uncertain imitability: an analysis of inter-firm differences in efficiency under competition', *Bell Journal of Economics*, Vol. 13, pp. 418–38.

Mancke, R.B. (1974) 'Causes of interfirm profitability differences: a new interpretation of the evidence', *Quarterly Journal of Economics*, Vol. 88, pp. 181–93.

McEnally, R.W. (1976) 'Competition and dispersion in rates of return: a note', *Journal of Industrial Organization*, Vol. 25, pp. 69–75.

McGee, J. and Thomas, H. (1986) 'Strategic groups: theory, research and taxonomy', *Strategic Management Journal*, Vol. 7, pp. 141–60.

Mueller, D.C. (1977) 'The persistence of profits above the norm', *Economica*, Vol. 44, pp. 369–80.

Mueller, D.C. (1985) *Profits in the Long Run*, Cambridge University Press, Cambridge.

Ravenscraft, D.J. (1980) 'Price-raising and cost reducing effects in profit-concentration studies: a Monte-Carlo simulation analysis', PhD thesis, Northwestern University.

Ravenscraft, D.J. (1983) 'Structure–profit relationships at the line of business and industry level', *Review of Economics and Statistics*, Vol. 65, pp. 22–31.

Rumelt, R.P. (1982) 'How important is industry in explaining firm profitability?' unpublished working paper, UCLA.

Rumelt, R.P. (1984) 'Toward a strategic theory of the firm', in R.B. Lamb (ed.) *Competitive Strategic Management*, Prentice-Hall, Englewood Cliffs, NJ, pp. 557–70.

Rumelt, R.P. (1987) 'Theory, strategy and entrepreneurship', in D. Teece (ed.) *The Competitive Challenge: strategies for industrial innovation and renewal*, Ballinger, Cambridge, MA, pp. 137–58.

Scherer, F.M. (1980) *Industrial Market Structure and Economic Performance* (2nd edn), Rand-McNally, Chicago, IL.

Schmalensee, R. (1985) 'Do markets differ much?' *American Economic Review*, Vol. 75, pp. 341–51.

Searle, S.R. (1971) *Linear Models*, Wiley & Sons, New York.

Stigler, G.J. (1963) *Capital and Rates of Return in Manufacturing Industries*, National Bureau of Economic Research, New York.

Teece, D.J. (1982) 'Toward an economic theory of the multi-product firm', *Journal of Economic Behaviour and Organization*, Vol. 3, pp. 39–63.

Weiss, L.W. (1974) 'The concentration-profits relationship and antitrust', in H.J. Goldschmid *et al.* (eds), *Industrial Concentration: The New Learning*, Little, Brown, Boston.

Wernerfelt, B. (1984) 'A resource-based view of the firm', *Strategic Management Journal*, April–June, pp. 171–80.

Wernerfelt, B. and Montgomery, C.A. (1988) 'Tobin's *q* and the importance of focus in firm performance', *American Economic Review*, Vol. 78, pp. 246–51.

5

STRATEGIC PLANNING AS IF ETHICS MATTERED

Larue Tone Hosmer

Ethics and the moral obligations of management were an accepted component in the planning process during the early development of Corporate Strategy as a field of study. It is proposed that ethics must be brought back into that planning process in order to build trust on the part of all of the stake-holders of the firm. Trust generates commitment. Commitment ensures effort, and effort that is cooperative, innovative and strategically directed is essential for success in a competitive global economy. Ethics should be central, not peripheral, to the overall management of the firm.

Ethics and the moral obligations of management were an accepted component in the strategic planning process during the early development of Corporate Strategy as a field of study. Barnard led the way here, as he did in so many other conceptual segments of the discipline. He described the functions of the executive as the need to: (1) maintain communication channels (2) ensure individual contributions and (3) formulate organizational goals. He then continued with the statement that this executive process 'is not intellectual; it is aesthetic and moral, involving a sense of fitness, of appropriateness, of responsibility (1938: 257). Further, in a quotation that is too little remembered, he talked of the need for the executive to 'inspire cooperative personal decisions by creating faith in common understanding, faith in the probability of success, faith in the ultimate satisfaction of personal motives, and faith in the integrity of common purpose' (Barnard, 1938: 259).

The integrity of common purpose was a common theme during much of the early work in corporate strategy. Simon certainly shared that view; he explained in his most famous work (1947: 47) that administrative decisions in an organizational context always had an 'ethical as well as factual content.' Learned, Christensen, Andrews and Guth (1965: 520) devoted a chapter to the 'the moral aspects of choice; the impact on the public good of the strategic alternatives.' Schendel and Hofer (1979) followed with a proposal for an enterprise strategy that would relate the organization to its social and political environment in much the same way that corporate strategy interfaced with the industry structure and the economic environment.

An excellent beginning, but where do we stand now? The *Strategic Management Journal* is certainly acknowledged as publishing the most advanced work in the discipline, yet over the past 3 years the term 'ethics' has never burdened the readers' understanding. Three articles with a semisocial benefit or stakeholder theme have been published. Bromiley and Marcus (1989) found that the equity market did not punish companies for product recalls in the American automobile industry during the 1970s. Weigelt and Camerer (1988) observed that a firm's reputation is an asset which can generate future rents, but stopped short of considering means of building that reputation beyond fulfilling industrial supply contracts. Kim and Mauborgne (1991) looked at the procedural justice of the strategic planning process, though justice in this instance was defined only as the openness of the communications between the head office and subsidary units in a global firm.

The recent book publications in our field have paid equally little attention to ethics and the moral obligations of management. An examination of the indexes in Lorange (1980), Porter (1980), Quinn (1980), Ohmae (1982), Porter (1985), Hamermesh (1986), Prahalad and Doz (1987), Burgelman and Maidique (1988), Ghemawat (1991) and Mintzberg and Quinn (1992) omit any mention of the ethical and moral terms.

We certainly have to recognize Freeman (1984) who recommended negotiating with the various stakeholders as a part of the strategic management process. And certainly we should not forget Miles (1982) who studied the strategic adaptation of organizations to externally imposed stress in the tobacco industry. But, these recommendations and studies have remained peripheral to the main thrust of the conceptual development of the field. No one has followed through on the advice of Freeman and Gilbert (1988: xiii) that we learn to build corporate strategy on a foundation of ethical reasoning, rather than pretending any longer that strategy and ethics are separate and distinct and unrelated fields of study.

Freeman and Gilbert (1988), of course, took a major step in that direction with their admonition that if corporate strategy did not recognize the individual values and goals (or 'projects') of the members, both internal and external to the firm, then those members could not be expected to cooperate to achieve organizational goals. Ethical analysis, in the view of the authors, is the only means available to resolve conflicts in values, goals, and 'projects,' and consequently essential in the processes of corporate strategy. This same argument was expanded and then compared to 12 alternative strategic processes in Gilbert (1992) who concluded that all 12 neglected the essential concept of justice if one looked at the firm as a 'joint enterprise advancing the individual purposes of people inside and outside the organization' (Bauerschmidt, 1993: 398). Both books are major works, but their impact has been, from an ethicist's point of view, less than might be desired. Let us try a somewhat different approach.

PURPOSE OF THE ARTICLE

This article will consider firstly whether it is possible to build corporate strategy on a 'foundation of ethical reasoning,' and secondly whether it is worthwhile in any sense beyond that of moral sensitivity and/or ethical smugness to do so. In short, this article will question whether the 'integrity of common purpose' should be included as an integral rather than a peripheral component in the strategic planning process.

The article will start with a definition of moral problems, which are the harms caused to other people in ways outside their own control. It will then move on to the ethical principles, which are the means by which the decisions and actions leading towards those harms to others can be objectively judged to be 'right' or 'wrong,' 'just' or 'unjust,' 'fair' or 'unfair.' The 10 most basic or most widely accepted ethical principles will be described in some detail. The article will next discuss briefly the methods by which the ethical principles can be included in the strategic management process. The major discussion will be on the basic reasons they should be included. Ethics do pay, it will be the conclusion of that section, but in a much longer time frame and with a much wider organizational impact than previously considered. The article will then end with a specific proposal for a major change in the strategic management paradigm, and a very brief discussion of the research problems that will be encountered in any empirical effort to provide support for that proposed change.

Before moving on to the nature of moral problems, it may be worthwhile to consider why there has been so little work at the juncture between corporate strategy and managerial ethics since the early efforts by Barnard, Simon, Andrews, and others. There are, it would appear, two very basic causes and one very recent change.

Divergent conceptual frameworks

As long as corporate strategy was based upon a strengths-weaknesses-opportunities-threats approach (Andrews, 1971), and as long as managerial ethics was primarily concerned with the social responsibilities of successful corporations (Ackerman, 1976) there was at the least the possibility of an understanding on both sides. Both used simple analytical procedures. Both had generally similar terminologies. Both assumed benign competitive conditions. But, corporate strategy in the 1980s 'adopted the language and logic of economics' (Rumelt, Schendel, and Teece, 1991: 5). And, managerial ethics during the same time period moved from corporate social responsibilities to organizational decision processes (Epstein, 1987). Now, the analytical procedures were very different. The basic terminologies were very different. And, the benign competitive conditions no longer existed. The gap had become too large to bridge easily, while the attention of scholars in both disciplines was being focused on the special problems created by global competition.

Inherent conceptual misunderstandings

The two approaches to general management separated during the 1980s, but in addition there have always been misunderstandings between the two fields. Many persons active in the research and teaching of business management view managerial ethics as a matter of personal virtue, not corporate strategy. They believe that ethics is concerned with issues of insider trades, bribery payments, untruthful statements and dishonest acts. These are the ones who often claim that, 'you can't teach ethics because the morals of the students are fully formed by the time they reach college or graduate school.' See for example Kristol (1987), Vogel (1987), or Levin (1989). Conversely, many of the people active in the research and teaching of normative ethics have a deep distrust of business management, and accept a very basic microeconomic view of the firm that stresses profit maximization at the cost of human values. See Crisp (1987), Newton (1988), or Hoffman (1990). To elaborate on the previous analogy of the 'gap too large to bridge,' perhaps the foundations do not exist for the bridge supports.

Recent conceptual clarification

Why then is there beginning to be an effort now to connect managerial ethics and corporate strategy? This effort has been epitomized by the call of Freeman and Gilbert mentioned above to stop pretending that 'strategy and ethics are separate and distinct and unrelated fields of study,' and by the concern of Brady (1990: v) that, 'Unless we connect ethical theory more closely with management practice we may be dressing our business curriculum windows with philosophical finery but failing to meet the urgent need for clarity of thought in management ethics.'

Perhaps it is the need for 'clarity of thought in management ethics' that has made the difference. The normative ethicists who previously were members of philosophy departments have now become applied ethicists teaching at business schools. They have been forced to deal with competitive issues in a global context. They have had to recognize that business management within that context is more than simply a matter of profit maximization under market, legal, and ethical constraints, and in which their only function was to stress those latter constraints. They have had to consider how to maintain a competitive posture and an ethical stance jointly.

There are some interesting things to be said and to be studied in combining competitiveness and ethics. In short, to continue the simple and by now perhaps annoying analogy, the foundations appear presently to exist for the proposed bridge on the side of the ethicists. Let us move on, then, to a discussion of the nature of moral problems, the principles of ethical analysis, and the benefits of integrating corporate strategy and managerial ethics, and see if equivalent foundations can be justified on the side of the strategists.

THE NATURE OF MORAL PROBLEMS

Moral problems are concerned with the harms caused or brought to others, and particularly with the harms caused or brought to others in ways that are outside their own control. A decision is made to move manufacturing operations to Mexico in search of lower wage rates, and x thousand people lose their jobs. A decision is made to eliminate emergency response teams at oil refineries and terminals, and y million gallons of crude are spread across the fishing grounds and recreational areas of Alaskan residents. Harms to specific individuals and groups in ways outside of their own control are the focal points of moral problems.

Moral problems in corporate management are particularly complex because the harms to some individuals and groups are inevitably associated with benefits to other individuals and groups. The movement of manufacturing operations to low wage rate areas in Mexico obviously harms the displaced workers in the United States, but equally obviously benefits the new employees in Mexico and the existing shareholders in the U.S. and may benefit the suppliers, distributors, creditors, managers, and other workers in both countries through improved competitiveness. The spillage of crude oil in Prince William Sound obviously harms the local population as well as the regional environment, but the elimination of the emergency response team – which had not been needed nor used for more than 18 years – doubtless reduced product costs for customers and increased dividend payments for owners.

'Harms to others in ways outside their own control' is a new though generally accepted definition in managerial ethics. See for example Velasquez (1992). It has supplanted the earlier definition that moral problems were decisions and actions that contravened the legal or moral standards of the community for exactly the reason mentioned previously: the need for greater clarity of thought. 'Harms to some and benefits to others' is a new and partially accepted extension of that definition. See for example Hosmer (1992). It has been adopted to increase realism and to recognize competition: some managerial actions have to be taken, despite the harms to some, in order to maintain or enlarge the benefits to others.

THE PRINCIPLES OF ETHICAL ANALYSIS

The principles of ethical analysis are the means by which a person can objectively determine whether the decisions or actions that either have led or will lead to an expected mixture of benefits and harms are 'right' or 'wrong,' 'just' or 'unjust,' 'fair' or 'unfair.' Ethical principles are not subjective measures that vary with cultural, social, and economic conditions; they are objective statements that transcend countries, religions, and times. They are the basic rules or first principles that have been proposed to ensure a 'good' society. A 'good' society is one in which people willingly cooperate for the benefit of all. See Rawls (1971) or Nozick (1974). I would hope that readers remember this definition; it is central to the latter argument.

'Normative ethics' is the study of these basic rules or first principles; the objective of that study until recently was to select the one principle that all could agree to be logically the most compelling. This is a goal that has never been satisfactorily achieved. Normative ethicists are still debating the relative merits of the various principles after 2,400 years, following the earliest considerations by Protagoras and Socrates.

'Applied ethics' is the use of these basic rules or first principles to gain insight and under-standing. It must be admitted that this new approach – termed 'ecumenical' by Dunfey (1991: 33) and a 'practitioner model (that) is philosophically suspect' by Lippke (1991: 367) – is not as thoroughly accepted as are the modern definitions of moral problems described earlier. The new applied approach on ethical principles is currently more popular in instruction than in research, but the advantages are rapidly becoming more obvious. Even normative philosophers such as Hoffman (1984: 263) have admitted that 'no one theory provides a complete answer to the question, what should I do?'

Multiple theories used to gain insight and understanding do provide an answer to that ques-tion, though at the expense of some rigor in the underlying concepts. It is no longer necessary, for example, to recognize all of the distinctions such as those between act utilitarianism and rule utilitarianism. Normative philosophers such as Lippke and Hoffman who have spent their work-ing lives studying those distinctions *and* advancing the clarity of the principles are obviously hesitant to abandon the rigor though they acknowledge the usefulness of the applied approach.

Here is a summary of 10 of the most cited principles expressed in applied ethics terms; for fur-ther explanation see any current text in business ethics such as DeGeorge (1989), Velasquez (1992), or Hosmer (1992). They are described in some detail in order to avoid any of the conceptual misunderstandings that have prevented joint work in the past.

Self-interests (ethical egoism)

The argument here is that if we would all look after our own self-interests, without forcefully interfering with the rights of others, then society as a whole will be better off for the members of society will be as free and productive as possible. Over the short term this seems to be a sim-ple recipe for selfishness; over the long term, however, it creates a much more meaningful guide for action for our long-term interests are usually very different from our short-term desires. The principle, then, can be expressed as 'never take any action that is not in the *long-term* self-interests of yourself and/or of the organization to which you belong.'

Personal virtues (Aristotle)

The argument in this instance is that the lack of forceful interference is not enough. As we each pursue our own self-interests, even those that are good only over the long term, we have to adopt a set of standards for our 'fair' and courteous treatment of one another. We have to be honest, open and truthful, for example, to eliminate distrust, and we should live temperately so as not to incite envy. In short, we should be proud of our actions and of our lives. The principle, then, can be expressed as 'never take any action which is not honest, open and truthful, and which you would not be proud to see reported widely in national newspapers and on network news programs.'

Religious injunctions (St. Augustine and St. Thomas Aquinas)

Honesty, truthfulness and temperance are not enough; we also have to have some degree of compassion and kindness towards others to form a truly 'good' society. That compassion and kindness is best expressed in the Golden Rule, which is not limited to the Judeo Christian tradition but is part of almost all of the world's religions. Reciprocity – do unto others as you would have them do unto you – and compassion together build a sense of community. The principle, then, can be expressed as 'never take any action that is not kind and compassionate, and that does not build a sense of community, a sense of all of us working together for a commonly accepted goal.'

Government requirements (Hobbes and Locke)

Compassion and kindness would be ideal if everyone would be compassionate and kind, but everyone won't be. People compete for property and for position, and some people will always take advantage of others. In order to restrain that competition and maintain peace within our society, we all have to obey some basic rules from a central authority that has the power to enforce those rules. In a democratic nation we think of that authority as the government, and of those rules as the law. The principle, then, can be expressed as 'never take any action that violates the law, for the law represents the minimal moral standards of our society.'

Utilitarian benefits (Bentham and Mill)

Common obedience to basic rules would work if the people associated with the central authority did not have self-interests of their own. They do. Consequently we need a means of evaluating the laws of the government, and that same means can be used to evaluate the justice of our own actions. A law or an act is 'right' if it leads to greater net social benefits than social harms. This is the principle that is often summarized as the *greatest good for the greatest number*. A more accurate way of expressing the principles is, 'never take any action that does not result in greater good than harm for the society of which you are a part.'

Universal rules (Kant)

Net social benefit is elegant in theory, but the theory does not say anything about how we should measure either the benefits or the harms – what is your life or health or well-being worth? – nor how we should distribute those benefits and allocate those harms. What we need is a rule to eliminate the self-interest of the person who decides, and that rule has to be applicable to everyone. This principle, then, can be expressed as 'never take any action that you would not be willing to see others, faced with the same or a closely similar situation, also be free or even encouraged to take.'

Individual rights (Jefferson and King)

Eliminating self-interest on the part of the decision maker isn't really possible, given what people actually are like. They are self-interested. Consequently we need a list of agreed-upon rights for everyone that will be upheld by everyone. These rights would certainly include guarantees against arbitrary actions of the government and would ensure freedom of speech, of assembly, of religion, etc. and would provide security against seizure of property, interference with privacy, or deprivation of liberty without due process. The principle, then, can be expressed as 'never take any action that abridges the agreed-upon and accepted rights of others.'

Economic efficiency (Smith, Friedman and Blinder)

Basic rights are meaningless without the essentials of food, clothing and shelter. Therefore we should maximize the output of the needed goods and services at minimal usage of resources by setting marginal revenues equal to marginal costs. At this point the economic system will be operating as efficiently as possible, and we can reach a condition known as Pareto Optimality in which it is impossible to make any one person better off without harming someone else. The principle, then, is 'always act to maximize profits subject to legal and market constraints, for maximum profits are evidence of the most efficient production.'

Distributive justice (Rawls)

The problem with the economic efficiency argument is that the market distributes the output of needed goods and services unjustly, for it excludes those who are poor, uneducated, or unemployed. We need a rule to ensure that those people are not left out. If we did not know who among us would be rich and who poor, who educated and who uneducated, then any rule that we made for the distribution of the output goods and services could be considered just. It can be argued that under those conditions – known as the Social Contract – the only agreement we could make would be that the poor and uneducated and unemployed should not be made worse off. The principle, then, is 'never take any action in which the least among us are harmed in some way.'

Contributive liberty (Nozick)

Perhaps liberty – the freedom to follow one's own self-interests within the constraints of the law and the market – is more important than justice – the right to be included in the overall distribution of goods and services. If so, then the only agreement that would be made under the conditions of the Social Contract – in which people do not know who would be rich and who poor, who active and who slothful – would be that no law should interfere with the right of self-development, for self-development will eventually contribute to the welfare of society. The principle, then, is 'never take any action that will interfere with the right of all of us for our self-development and self-fulfillment to the limit of our abilities.'

Let me stress, once again, that these ethical principles of analysis are objective, not subjective. Let me state, as clearly as I can, that they do not vary by culture, by country, or by time. The rule of Rawls, for example, that we not harm the least among us, those with the least education, the least income and wealth, the least ability to influence the events which affect them, means exactly the same thing in Uzbekistan, India, Japan, and New York City. We can certainly disagree on exactly who qualifies as the 'least among us' on a global scale. We can certainly ask whether peasant farmers in Uzbekistan are better or worse off than homeless residents of New York City. But the rule does not require either selectivity or precision. It is in fact very straightforward: we should not harm either of those groups for our own benefit. We do not have to help them; we should merely avoid harming them in order to help ourselves. A simple and, to my mind, decent ethical principle of analysis that is objective consistent, and timeless.

JUSTIFICATION OF THE OBJECTIVITY OF ETHICAL PRINCIPLES

Many people confuse morals, values and ethics and this has led to a belief – widely accepted among both the theorists and practitioners of management – that the ethical principles of analysis are not and cannot be objective, consistent, and timeless. Let me digress for a moment here, to explain the ethicist's view of the important distinctions between morals, values, and ethics, and the consequent reasons for the reliance that can be placed upon the objectivity; consistency; and timelessness of ethical principles.

Most people, when they encounter a moral problem in which some individuals or groups are going to be hurt or harmed in some way while others are to be benefited, turn first to their moral standards of behavior. Moral standards do vary by culture, by country, and by time. They are subjective gauges of conduct. They are the way we human beings intuitively feel about the rightness or goodness of various actions.

Moral standards have been more formally defined as 'the means by which we judge our actions, and those of our neighbors' (Hosmer 1987: 96). Moral standards are 'the expectations of society relative to the conduct of an individual that affects the interests of other people' (Beauchamp and Bowie, 1979: 3). These 'means by which we judge our actions' and those 'expectations of society' will obviously vary with the background of the individual and the culture of the society. Moral standards, most ethicists readily admit, are not objective, consistent, nor timeless. They are personal, and vary with the individual.

Value judgments are the second means most people use to decide what is 'right' and 'just' and 'fair' when confronting a moral problem in which some individuals or groups are to be hurt or harmed in some way while others are to be benefited. For simple moral temptations, particularly those involving such basic issues as insider trading or bribe paying where the harms are obvious and widespread and the benefits are limited and focused, there is no need for most of us to go beyond our personal moral standards. But, for the more complex managerial dilemmas, where the outcomes are mixed as in the coal-fired generation of electricity which results in low costs for the consumer and acid emissions for the environment, or where the duties are unclear as in corporate downsizing where the harms for a small group are offset by benefits for a much larger number of individuals, most people move from their moral standards of behavior to their value judgments of purpose.

Value judgments of purpose also vary by culture, by country, and by time. They are subjective evaluations of what we think is important. They are the way we human beings intuitively feel about the rightness and goodness of various goals.

Value judgments in more formal definitions are thought of as priorities by Hosmer (1994) and as preferences by Hofstede (1984). 'A shorthand definition of a value is a broad preference for one state of affairs over others' (1994: 389). Rokeach in his truly basic work (1973) identifies instrumental values as desirable modes of conduct and terminal values as desirable end states of existence. The desirable end states of existence or value judgements clearly dominate the desirable modes of conduct or moral standards.

McCoy adopts this priority or preference among end states view of values when he states that it is necessary to take more than profit into account in business management, and that 'values beyond the short-term bottom line are a necessity, not an option, to be considered' (1985: 6). He continues with the statement that making decisions and setting policies in a business firm involves choosing between competing purposes, and that choosing involves having a clear listing of priorities or values. The paramount task of senior executives, McCoy concludes, is the setting of priorities, or the management of values.

McCoy does not state, however, how those values to be managed should be selected for it seems clear to most of us that the values of the senior executives will doubtless differ from the values of the hourly employees, and it seems even more obvious to those who have had global experience that the differences between the values of those two groups will either narrow or widen once we reach India, Japan, or Europe. Value judgments are similar to moral standards in the view of most ethicists: they are variable. They are not objective, consistent, and timeless. Again, they are personal, and vary with the individual.

Moral standards and value judgements differ between people. There have been numerous studies in anthropology, sociology, and a new subfield now known as descriptive ethics confirming these differences between social groups, national states, and historical periods. It is not, in my opinion, necessary to cite those studies. We all have experience of these differences, and accept their existence.

The reasons for these moral and value differences between groups, countries and times are not as clearly known, nor as widely accepted. Kohlberg (1981) provided a definitive study of the moral development of individuals, through stages. It now seems apparent, however, that there are religious/cultural and economic/social influences upon that development. See, for example, Likona (1976) or Gilligan (1982). These influences have not been as definitely studied, but it is certainly possible to cite Inkles and Smith's (1974) discussions of the changes in personal values and behavior patterns as a result of economic development; Matasugu's (1982) description of the influence of national culture on the development of moral standards; and Haney's (1983) study of the impact of economic and social variables upon the norms of acceptable behavior as examples of the needed work in this area.

Ethical principles, however, do not differ between people. They remain exactly the same across cultural groups, national states, and historical periods. They form the bedrock of moral philosophy. They are, to repeat the earlier definition that I peremptorily asked readers to remember, the first principles of what constitutes a 'good' society; and a 'good' society has been further

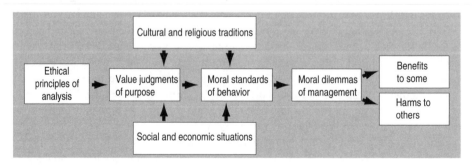

94 **Figure 5.1** Relationships between morals, values and ethics

defined as one in which people willingly cooperate for the benefit of all (Hobbes, 1986, Rawls 1971, or Nozick 1974).

Ethical principles are the fundamental rules by which an individual can, if he or she chooses and has the necessary knowledge of the principles, examine his or her moral standards and verify his or her value judgments. Ethical principles are, finally, the topic of Socrates' most impassioned plea: 'The unexamined life is not worth living' (Plato, 1955: 43). This was his final statement in his defense at the trial that led to his death in 399 BC. It has been taken by generations of scholars to mean that we should all examine our standards of behavior and our choice of goals using the fundamental logic of the ethical principles of analysis.

Ethics has been more formally defined as thinking about moral standards in a logical and structured manner (Frankena, 1963). It is the study of what is good or right for human beings (Hoffman and Moore, 1984). It is the search for the general character that makes right acts right (Ross, 1930). Ethics, finally, has been defined by DeGeorge in a sentence that almost exactly follows the conceptual framework expressed here as 'a systematic attempt through the use of reason to make sense of our individual and social moral experience in such a way as to determine the rules which ought to govern human conduct and the values worth pursuing in life' (1982: 12).

In summary, we can legitimately justify the conception of ethical principles as objective, consistent, and timeless if we accept the proposed distinctions between morals, values, and ethics, and if we understand that only our moral standards and value judgements are subject to cultural, religious, social and economic influences. The ethical principles are not subject to those influences. This is the accepted view, as was cited in the discussion, of most normative ethicists.

Ethical Principles Applied to Strategic Management: The Method

What does all this mean? What possible connection can the closing statements at a trial in 399 BC have with the managerial practices of the late 20th Century? Let us say that you accept, for now, the proposal that the ethical principles of analysis are objective, not subjective, and that they do provide collectively a way of deciding what is 'right' and 'just' and 'fair' in human actions and goals. How can they be used in management, and – particularly – how can they be used in strategic management which determines firstly the goals, policies, and character (Andrews, 1971) and secondly the competitive posture and position (Porter, 1980) of the firm?

These 10 ethical principles of analysis provide different perspectives, different ways of looking at either the content or the process of strategic management decisions and actions. The more usual perspectives are those of (1) neoclassical economics which uses accounting measures of return and/or stock price changes, (2) industry organization economics which uses sustainable competitive advantages and/or market share improvements, and (3) population ecology, which uses organizational survival, growth and/or development.

Currently changes in corporate or divisional strategies are examined using those measures from neoclassical economics, industry organizational economics, and population ecology. What effect will this proposed change have upon our return on investment and our stock price? Upon our competitive advantage and our market share? Upon our organizational potential for survival, growth, and development?

If we wish to add ethical considerations to strategic planning, then we must begin to look at those proposed changes using the perspectives and the measures of the applied ethical principles. What effect will this proposed change have upon our long-term, rather than merely our short-term, self interests? Is this proposed change open and honest and truthful; and something of which we could all be proud if it were to become widely known? Does it build a sense of community among all of our stakeholders, or does it tend to destroy – or even worse, to exploit – that sense of community?

It is assumed that any company adding these ethical considerations to the strategic planning process currently uses some approximation of the iterative planning system originally described in Chandler (1966) and then further detailed by Lorange and Vancil (1977) for multidivisional firms. A statement of planning objectives is first prepared by the central office, and then strategic plans (the method of competition), program plans (the allocation of resources), and budgetary plans (the estimation of revenues and expenses) to meet those objectives are prepared by the divisions and approved by the headquarters, in sequence. It is clear that ethical considerations can be part of the approval process at all three stages. The important issue, however, is not whether ethical principles *can be included* in the planning process; it is whether they *should be included*.

Ethical Principles Applied to Strategic Management: The Reason

Now we come to the critical issue. Granted that ethical principles are objective, and do provide different perspectives that can help in determining whether a given decision or action can be considered to be 'right' and 'just' and 'fair.' Granted that it is possible to include these ethical principles in the strategic management process so that given decisions or actions that impact the welfare of stakeholder groups can be considered to be 'right' and 'just' and 'fair.' The critical question is whether we are under any compunction to do so.

It may make us feel good to be moral. It may make us feel superior to be moral. It may even make us feel less susceptible to legal claims from unfairly discharged employees and/or badly misinformed customers to be moral. Why should we do so?

The argument of this article is that it may or may not be nice to be moral, it may or may not be better to be moral, it may or may not be prudent to be moral, but that *it is essential in any competitive sense to be moral.* Let me make this argument in a series of propositions:

> *Proposition 1 Companies operating in a competitive global economy are dependent upon a wide range of stakeholders.*

Stakeholders have been defined (Freeman 1984: 46) as those groups that 'are affected by and can in turn affect the achievement of the organizational objectives' of the firm. There has been little debate about that concept. The ability of stakeholders to affect the achievement of objectives, both negatively and positively, is widely accepted though seldom explicitly mentioned in the literature.

Which individuals and groups should be included among the stakeholders? There is less agreement here, but hourly workers, administrative staff, functional and technical managers, senior executives and the other groups that fit within the hierarchical boundaries of the firm are almost always included. Material and component suppliers, and wholesale and retail distributors, outside of the hierarchical boundaries but within the industry limits, are generally included following the examples of the Japanese keiretsu. Customers often are included, following the precepts of the total quality approach. Creditors, investors, and the organizations that supply advanced technologies and trained personnel are equally necessary to the firm though less subject to their direction and control, and may or may not be included. Industry associations, interest groups, joint ventures, and strategic alliances are even further out on the periphery of the organization, but able to interact with domestic and foreign governmental agencies which obviously can affect the operations of the firm, and again may or may not be included.

The issue, however, is not whether or not these groups have been included at some point in the past in a definition of an extended organization. The issue is whether or not these groups at some point in the future can affect the achievement of the objectives of the firm. It seems reasonable to make the assumption that they can. Figure 5.2 provides a graphic depiction of the full range of stakeholder groups following that assumption.

> *Proposition 2 Companies are dependent upon their stakeholder groups not only for cooperative actions but also for innovative developments.*

The need for cooperation among the stakeholder groups is obvious; indeed, this need is inherent in the definition of stakeholders previously cited as the individuals and groups who 'are affected by and can in turn affect the achievement of the organizational objectives'.

The question, however, is whether cooperation in the sense of 'you tell us what to do and we'll do it' is enough. Perhaps innovation is also required for meaningful technology advances, product and process developments, cost reductions, and quality improvements. Certainly many of the popular management books of the 1980s such as Peters and Waterman (1982) and Pinchot (1985) stressed the need for innovation and entrepreneurship. The problem was that the focus seemed to be on new products rather than on new strategies, and that the entrepreneur or – more properly – the intrapreneur often seemed to be a loose cannon, paying little attention to the directions or intentions of the management.

The recent work of Hamel and Prahalad (1989) seems much more relevant to strategic rather than product innovation, though it continues to focus within the hierarchy of the firm. They start by deriding organizations so 'hidebound, so orthodox ridden that the only way to innovate is to put a few bright people in a small dark room, pour in some money, and hope that something wonderful will happen' (1989: 66). They then stress the need for improvisation, creativity, and innovation. 'While strategic intent is clear about ends, it is flexible as to means – it leaves room for improvisation. Achieving strategic intent requires enormous creativity with respect to means ... The goal is not competitive imitation but competitive innovation' (1989: 67).

> *Proposition 3 It is difficult to motivate behavior that is both cooperative and innovative by all of the stakeholders of the firm.*

Does 'competitive innovation' come only from lower level employees, as seems to be implied in Hamel and Prahalad? Or, can this key to competitive success come from any and all of the stakeholders, including employees, suppliers, distributors, customers, creditors, owners, technology centers, educational institutions, industry associations, and all of the other groups

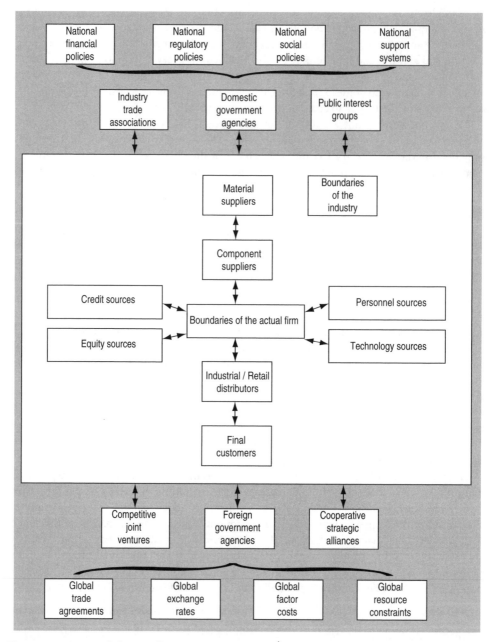

Figure 5.2   An extended view of business organizations

shown in Figure 5.2? Innovations reducing the cost of health care or increasing the supply of trained workers would certainly improve the competitive position of companies in a global economy, for example, so it would seem clear that creativity and improvisation can and should come from any and all of the stakeholders. At all events, it seems reasonable once again to make that assumption.

If we accept the first assumption that companies operating in a competitive global environment are dependent upon their stakeholders, both those within the firm and those outside the formal authority structure, and if we accept the second assumption that this dependency extends beyond simple cooperative acts to the much more complex innovative developments, then we are faced with the need to motivate creativity and improvisation.

Motivation has been the topic of extensive work in the behavioral sciences. See, for example, Steers and Porter (1987). Most of this work however has focused on cooperation, not innovation, by persons within the formal, not the extended, organization. The usual recommendation starts with a proposal that goals be set, either by joint agreement or by administrative fiat. Actual results are then measured against these planned outcomes, the divergences are analyzed, and positive or negative performance evaluations are computed. Incentives are then paid to reward the positive performance evaluations.

The incentives can be financial (commissions or bonuses), positional (promotions or 'perks' in lieu of promotions), or perceptual (widespread recognition and approval by members of the organization). The effectiveness of these incentives is said to vary depending upon the nature of the task, the needs of the individual, and the cohesion of the group. The process obviously focuses on cooperative acts for which measurable goals can be set, and is primarily designed for individuals and groups within the formal hierarchy who can legitimately be given commissions, bonuses, promotions, or 'perks.'

Incentives to motivate creativity and improvisation by individuals and groups outside the formal hierarchy of the firm seems seldom to have been considered in behavioral theory. Here we have to move to the more general approach of agency theory which can be applied to any principal–agent relationship, including those outside the hierarchical boundaries (Harris and Raviv 1978, quoted in Eisenhardt, 1989). Agency theory is not limited to the special case of the owner/manager relationship. It can be and has been used to design governance mechanisms that will limit any agent's self-serving behavior given goal conflicts and varying levels of risk aversion, task programmability, and outcome uncertainty, exactly the issues we wish to address.

Principal–agent contracts can be based upon either behaviors or outcomes. *Behaviors* in the nonprogrammable tasks – i.e., those that involve a substantial degree of improvisation and creativity – cannot be accurately measured, and therefore investments in information systems or management structures to detect self serving acts and lack of effort (the joint moral hazards) cannot be justified (Demski and Feltham, 1978, again quoted in Eisenhardt, 1989).

Outcomes in some of these nonprogrammable tasks can be measured, but then the risk is transferred to the agent. The risk is transferred because the outcome is only partially a function of the behavior; technological feasibilities, competitive actions, government policies, economic and social changes all 'cause uncontrollable variations in outcomes' (Eisenhardt, 1989: 61). Outcomes in other nonprogrammable tasks – i.e., those that 'take a long time to complete, involve joint or team effort, or produce soft outcomes' (1989: 62) cannot easily be measured.

Proposition 4 It is possible to build trust, commitment and effort on the part of all of the stakeholders by including the ethical principles in the strategic decision processes of the firm.

What can be done when it becomes overly expensive to transfer risk to the agent in the event of measurable but uncertain outcomes, or when it becomes overly difficult to measure those outcomes? The only solution is to overcome the moral hazards by building trust, commitment, and effort among the agents who are, of course, the stakeholders of the firm.

Trust is 'confidence in the honesty, integrity, reliability, justice of another person or thing' (Websters, 1953: 1565). Trust in managerial terms is confidence that the self-interests of the principal will not necessarily take total precedence over the self-interests of the agent. Trust, again in managerial terms, is reliance upon the belief that when agents or stakeholders of the firm are to be hurt or harmed in some way outside of their own control, while others, often including the owners and managers, are to be benefited, the decision will be made by applying the ethical principles of analysis in addition to the more common microeconomic, industry organization, and population ecology standards. The ethical principles of analysis, of course, do address what is 'right,' what is 'just,' and what is 'fair' in the critical relationships between the firm and its various stakeholder groups, and were designed to eliminate short-term self-interest as a decision criteria by the representatives of the firm.

The basic argument of this article is that decisions and actions by the managers of extended firms that (1) recognize the moral problems that occur when one or more of the stakeholders groups will be hurt or harmed in some way outside of their own control that; (2) resolve those moral problems by applying the ethical principles of analysis in addition to the more common strategic concepts of industry position, competitive advantage, and organizational development; and that (3) have the moral courage to insist upon the recognition and resolution of those problems, will result in trust amongst all of the stakeholder groups. Trust generates commitment. Commitment builds effort. Effort that is cooperative, innovative and strategically directed results in success whether measured by stock price, market share, or organizational development.

In brief, an ethical approach to strategic management does not penalize the extended firm in a competitive global economy. It benefits that company by ensuring a cooperative, innovative, and directed effort on the part of all of the stakeholders of the firm.

JUSTIFICATION OF THE ETHICS-TRUST-COMMITMENT-EFFORT SEQUENCE

Why should this be so? Why should we accept the proposal that the application of ethical principles to strategic decisions builds stakeholder trust, that stakeholder trust generates organizational commitment, and that organizational commitment results in the cooperative and innovative effort that is so essential for success given the intensely competitive nature of the global economy?

Certainly there is very limited empirical support for this proposal. This lack of existent studies, however, should not surprise us. The divergent conceptual frameworks and the inherent conceptual misunderstandings of corporate strategy and managerial ethics – both described earlier, in the introduction to this article – have precluded the joint work that might have been so useful. And managerial ethics, despite its applied nature, has remained normative, not descriptive, in most of its research and cannot provide the needed support by itself.

We all know of anecdotal examples that seem to support the proposal that trust builds commitment, particularly when the affected stakeholders are customers and/or employees. Johnson and Johnson removed Tylenol from store shelves nationwide at a cost of $80,000,000 when it was feared that the product poisoning might have spread beyond the original boundaries of Chicago, and the company has benefited extensively from consumer goodwill. Herman Miller offered all employees a silver parachute when it was feared that the company might be the subject of a hostile take-over attempt, and worker morale has remained exceedingly high. But, anecdotal evidence is not very compelling. Given the lack of large-scale studies and the unsatisfactory nature

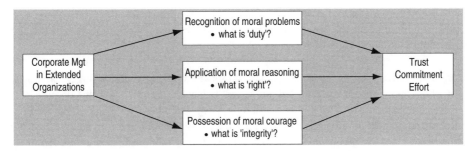

Figure 5.3 Building trust, commitment, and effort

of most case examples, let us adopt a more conceptual approach. Let us return to agency theory, and the accepted economic rationale of the principal–agent relationship.

The economic rationale of the principal–agent relationship looks at each exchange as a new event, unemcumbered by feelings of gratitude, indifference, disloyalty, or revenge. Any notion of intended reciprocity for past benefits and/or harms on the part of the agent is sternly excluded. Indeed, moral hazards – the lack of enthusiastic adherence to contractural agreements – are felt to be a problem only for the agent, never for the principal, and consequently acts on the part of the principal that might induce feelings of ingratitude, indifference, or 'getting even' on the part of the agent are thought not to occur.

What happens if we relax this requirement? What happens if we accept the belief that contractural agreements between companies and stakeholders have both explicit and implicit terms, and that companies may only occasionally violate the explicit obligations but frequently compromise the implicit understandings? An energetic marketing manager who has maintained sales for a mature product line is legally subject to employment 'at will,' but I think it is safe to assume that was not the impression given by the corporate recruiter 5 years previously. An innovative component supplier who has developed a successful product feature for their customer has no guarantee of future orders, but I doubt that was clearly explained at the award ceremony honoring the supplier.

What happens if the marketing manager sees her friends and associates within the firm unjustly battered by corporate restructurings? What happens if the component supplier sees other suppliers unfairly given its drawings for the new product feature and asked to bid competitively? Agency theory assumes that both will continue to work for the advantage of the principal, without any slackening of their energy and/or innovation, because it is in their short-term self-interest to do so *as long as their behavior can be measured or their output can be evaluated.* The problem is seen to be in the measurement and evaluation procedures, and the need to make these more precise for unprogramed tasks and extended time frames. The problem is not thought to be in the microeconomic behavioral assumptions of short-term advantage and self-interest maximization, which may be misleading given the lack of trust, commitment, and effort that often come from acts that are felt by agents to be 'unjust' or 'unfair.'

Numerous economists and sociologists have questioned the microeconomic behavioral assumptions of short-term advantage and self-interest maximization for either descriptive or predictive use. See, for example, the lengthy source listing in Sen (1991: 16f) that follows his classic statement, 'To try to use the demands of rationality in going to battle on behalf of the standard behavioral assumption of economic theory (to wit, actual self-interest maximization) is like leading a cavalry charge on a lame donkey'.

None of us want to lead such a cavalry charge. What other behavioral assumptions are possible, then, following an overall belief in economic rationality; that could be seen as including knowledge by the agent about *prior benefits and harms* of the principal in the principal–agent contract that might influence the degree of cooperation and the amount of innovation by the agent? There would seem to be three alternatives:

1. *Multiple utilities.* Etzioni (1988) is well known for his amusing attacks upon the assumption of short-term rationality and self-interested behavior. 'People typically do not render rational decisions. They brush their teeth but do not fasten their seat belts' (1988: xi). Etzioni instead suggests that decisions are based upon an I/We dichotomy, with equal concerns for the person and for the group. He terms the group half of this dichotomy a deontological commitment, or moral sense of duty to others, and he recommends the use of dual utilities to encompass both the personal and the moral sources of motivation.

   Etzioni has directly applied this concept of dual personal and moral interests to the issue with which we are concerned here, that of the principal–agent relationship, and finds that concern for the good of the group and trust in the reliability of the principle are both essential. 'Moral commitments reduce what economists have come to call *moral hazards*. Specifically, the stronger the moral underwriting of implicit contracts, the lower the administrative costs resulting in less of a need to buy hedge protection' (1986: 175). It has to be admitted, however, that the I/We paradigm proposed by Prof. Etzioni has not gained wide support. Dual utilities are computationally complex, and the continual question arises: why stop at two? Why not add affection, anger, conformity, homogeneity, or others? Etzioni provides some support for the importance of trust in principal–agent relationships with his concept of multiple utilities, but perhaps we can go further.

2. *Interdependent utilities.* Sen (1991) addresses the same personal vs. group concerns, and also writes with an amusing, elegant style, but he has less bite and more compassion for the problem of developing an economic theory that is both parsimonious and complete. He is a very distinguished economist, which makes his beliefs more acceptable to that large part of the academic spectrum, and he bases his arguments on rights rather than duties which certainly appeals to many if not most of the ethicists.

   It is difficult to summarize this argument on rights, but let me make the attempt. Sen starts by rejecting utility as a motivational means. 'It is ... arguable that since the claim of utility to be the only source of value rests allegedly on identifying utility with well-being, it can be criticized both on the ground that well-being is not the only thing that is valuable, and on the ground that utility does not adequately represent well-being' (1991: 46).

   Well-being is not the only thing that is valuable because people value the promotion of both causes (rights, liberties, and opportunities) and groups (families, communities, and classes). Utility does not adequately represent well-being because of the interpersonal comparisons that are possible. You may have more than I do, or your group may have more than my group, in either advantage or freedom, and that affects my conception of my goal, and my means of achieving that goal. I may, however, recognize that my achieving my complex goal is interdependent with you achieving your complex goal and therefore cooperation is essential. 'Behavior is ultimately a social matter as well, and thinking in terms of what "we" should do, or what should be "our" strategy, may reflect a sense of identity involving recognition of other people's goals, and the mutual interdependencies involved' (1991: 85).

   If we accept Sen's argument that behavior is socially motivated by a comparison of personal utilities and a recognition of mutual interdependencies, then we have a new and more compelling reason to accept the proposal that the actions of the principal affect the behavior of the agent, and that trust in the mutual beneficiency of the principal is essential for the cooperation and innovation by the agent. However, we may be able to find an even simpler economic rationale.

3. *Extended utilities.* The standard economic rationale for the motivation of the agent in principal–agent transactions is short-term advantage or personal utility. Both Etzioni and Sen object to the monolithic nature of this concept, but let us accept it for now with the proviso that we extend the time frame through a series of infinite exchanges. That would seem to be a reasonable proviso. Energetic employees expect to be employed not 'at will' but over time with some sense of gratitude by the company for the past market share achievements that were so beneficial. Innovative suppliers expect to receive additional orders not 'at cost,' but over time with some sense of appreciation for the past product feature developments that were so helpful. These expectations of future benefits can obviously be discounted back by the agent to be added to his or her sense of current advantage or utility.

    What happens if the actions of the principal, in distributing the benefits and allocating the harms of company operations, destroys those expectations? The motivations of the agent towards cooperation and innovation will clearly be decreased. Stakeholders expect 'right,' 'just' and 'fair' treatment, and those expectations can be destroyed by actions that are arbitrary or capricious, and that do not follow the known principles of ethical analysis that tend to give the same consideration to the self-interests of the agent as to the self-interests of the principal. Actions of the principal that give total weight to their own short-term self-interests, and neglect those of the agent, would seem to destroy the trust, commitment, and effort of the agent through reducing the long-term utility of his or her future cooperation and innovation.

    In short, we can rationally justify the ethics-trust-commitment-effort sequence if we first assume that principals in any principal/agent exchange occasionally act in ways that can be seen by the agents to be 'unjust' or 'unfair' and if we are willing to conceive of either multiple utilities, interdependent utilities, or extended utilities. The latter, in my view, is computationally most simple and logically follows most directly from the accepted economic rationale of agency theory.

CONCLUSION

The basic argument of this article – which is that the trust, commitment and effort on the part of all of the stakeholders of a firm are as essential to the success of that firm as are the competitive advantages and strategic positions of its planning process – can be summarized in a series of five statements:

1. The strategic decisions of any large-scale economic enterprise in a competitive global environment result in both benefits and harms. The harms, which include the discharge of employees, the termination of suppliers, the deterioration of environments, etc. cannot be avoided though until recently they have been ignored.
2. It is the responsibility of the senior executives of the firm to distribute those benefits and allocate those harms among the stakeholders of the company. This can be done arbitrarily or thoughtfully. If it is done thoughtfully, then the ethical principles offer the only form of analysis that is relevant.
3. The ethical principles offer the only form of analysis that is relevant for the distribution of benefits and the allocation of harms because they provide the only means of recognizing the

interests and rights of each of the stakeholders and comparing those interests and rights through the use of known principles.

4. Stakeholders who believe that the benefits have been distributed and the names allocated through a process that recognizes their interests and rights, and that compares those interests and rights with those of other stakeholders through the use of known principles, will develop trust in the direction of the firm.

5. Stakeholders who develop trust in the direction of the firm will show commitment to its future. Commitment to the future of a firm will ensure efforts that are both cooperative and innovative. Cooperative, innovative, and directed efforts on the part of all of the stakeholder groups will lead to competitive and economic success, however measured, for that firm over time.

This is a considerable departure from the existing paradigm of the field, which is that the selection of a strategic posture within an industry (Porter, 1980) and the leveraging of strategic resources across industries (Prahalad and Hamel, 1990) lead towards competitive and economic success. The argument here is that the selection of the posture and the leveraging of the resources are not enough in a competitive global economy. Trust, commitment, and effort must be added to ensure cooperative and innovative acts on the part of all of the stakeholders. The argument here is that strategic planning must be both analytical and ethical, which brings us back to the original views of Barnard, Simon, and Andrews.

ADDENDUM

A traditional objection by normative philosophers to the use of simplified ethical principles in the analysis of pragmatic moral problems is that these principles, while ostensibly leading towards the betterment of society over the short-term, in reality lead towards the betterment of the decision maker over the long-term. No one, to my knowledge, has ever used the term 'heuristic' in describing this view of the simplified ethical principles, but that meaning is implied. 'You are unable,' the traditionalist philosopher would state, 'to think through the full consequences of your actions because you are unable to anticipate the full range of possible actions by others, and therefore you are attempting to ensure their future cooperation in your endeavors by recognizing their self-interests now.' This, in the view of the traditional ethicist, negates those principles for it substitutes personal betterment for the common good. Perhaps, for the nontraditional strategist, this verifies those principles for it makes them heuristics, and very useful heuristics, for strategic planning in an increasingly competitive global economy.

REFERENCES

Ackerman, R. W. (1976). *Corporate Social Responsiveness*. Reston Publishing, Reston, VA.

Andrews, K. R. (1971). *The Concept of Corporate Strategy*. Irwin, Homewood, IL.

Aristotle, (1947). 'Nicomachean Ethics'. In R. McKeon (ed.), *Introduction to Aristotle*. Modern Library, New York.

Barnard, C. I. (1938). *The Functions of the Executive*. Harvard University Press, Cambridge, MA.

Bauerschmidt, A. (1993). 'A Comment on Gilbert's "The Twilight of Corporate Strategy" ', *Strategic Management Journal*, 14(5), pp. 397–99.

Beauchamp, T. L. and N. E. Bowie (1979). *Ethical Theory and Business*. Prentice-Hall, Englewood Cliffs, NJ.

Bentham, J. (1948). *Introduction to the Principles of Morals and Legislation*, J. Lafler (ed.). Hafner, New York.

Blinder, A. (1987). *Hard Heads, Soft Hearts: Tough Minded Economics for a Just Society*. Addison-Wesley, Reading, MA.

Brady, N. (1990). *Ethical Managing: Rules and Results*. Macmillan, New York.

Bromiley, P. and A. Marcus (1989). 'The deterrent to dubious corporate behavior: Profitabily, probability and safety recalls', *Strategic Management Journal*, 10(3), pp. 251–70.

Burgelman, R. and M. Maidique (1988). *Strategic Management of Technology and Innovation*. Richard D. Irwin, Homewood, IL.

Chandler, A. (1966). *Strategy and Structure*. MIT Press, Cambridge, MA.

Crisp, R. (1987). Pervasive advertising, autonomy and the creation of desire', *Journal of Business Ethics*, 6, pp. 413–18.

DeGeorge, R. (1982). *Business Ethics* (1st ed). Macmillan, New York.

DeGeorge, R. (1989). *Business Ethics* (2nd ed). Macmillan, New York.

Dunfey, T. (1991). 'Business ethics and extant social contracts', *Business Ethics Quarterly*, I, pp. 23–51.

Eisenhardt, K. (1989). 'Agency theory: An assessment and review', *Academy of Management Review*, 14, pp. 57–72.

Epstein, E. (1987). 'The corporate social policy process', *California Management Review*, 29, pp. 99–114.

Etzioni, A. (1986). The case for a multiple-utility conception', *Economics and Philosophy*, 2, pp. 159–83.

Etzioni, A. (1988). *The Moral Dimension: Toward a New Economics*. Free Press, New York.

Frankena, W. K. (1963). *Ethics*. Prentice-Hall, Englewood Cliffs, NJ.

Freeman, R. (1984). *Strategic Management: A Stakeholder Approach*. Pitman, Marshfield, MA.

Freeman, R. and D. Gilbert (1988). *Corporate Strategy and the Search for Ethics*. Prentice-Hall, Englewood Cliffs, NJ.

Friedman, M. (1962). *Capitalism and Freedom*. University of Chicago Press, Chicago, IL.

Ghemawat, P. (1991). *Commitment: The Dynamic of Strategy*. Free Press, New York.

Gilbert, D. (1992). *The Twilight of Corporate Strategy*. Oxford University Press, Oxford.

Gilligan, C. (1982). *In a Different Voice: Psychological Theory and Women's Development*. Harvard University Press, Cambridge, MA.

Hamel, G. and C. K. Prahalad (May–June 1989). 'Strategic intent', *Harvard Business Review*, pp. 73–83.

Hamermesh, R. G. (1986). *Making Strategy Work*. Wiley, New York.

Haney, C. W. (1983). 'The good, the bad, and the lawful: An essay on psychological injustice'. In W. Laufer and J. Day (eds.), *Personality Theory, Moral Development and Criminal Behavior*. Lexington Books, Toronto, pp. 107–17.

Hobbes, T. (1986). *Leviathan*. Macmillan, New York.

Hoffman, W. M. (1990). 'The Ford Pinto'. In W. M. Hoffman and J. M. Moore (eds.), *Business Ethics* (2nd ed). McGraw-Hill, New York, pp. 585–91.

Hoffman, W. M. and J. M. Moore (1984). *Business Ethics* (1st ed). McGraw-Hill, New York.

Hofstede, G. (1984). 'The cultural relativity of the quality of life concept'. *Academy of Management Review*, 9, pp. 389–98.

Hosmer, L. (1987). *The Ethics of Management* (1st ed). Richard D. Irwin, Homewood, IL.

Hosmer, L. (1992). *The Ethics of Management* (2nd ed). Richard D. Irwin, Homewood, IL.

Hosmer, L. (1994). *Moral Leadership in Business*. Richard D. Irwin, Homewood, IL.

Inkles, A. and D. H. Smith (1974). *Becoming Modern: Individual Change in Six Developing Countries*. Harvard University Press, Cambridge, MA.

Jefferson, T. (1964). 'Declaration of Independence'. In M. Petters (ed.), *Portable Thomas Jefferson*. Penguin, New York.

Kant, I. (1964). *Groundwork of the Metaphysics of Morals*. J. Peter (trans). Harper & Row, New York.

Kim, W. C. and R. A. Mauborgne (1991). 'Implementing global strategies: The role of procedural justice', *Strategic Management Journal*, 12, Summer Special Issue, pp. 125–45.

King, M. L. (1972). 'I have a dream', from R. and B. Hofstsadter, *Great Issues in American History*, Vol. 3 (2nd ed). Vintage Press, New York, pp. 449–53.

Kohlberg, L. (1981). *The Philosophy of Moral Development: Essays in Moral Development*. Harper & Row, New York.

Kristol, I. (September 25, 1987). 'Ethics Anyone? Or Morals?', *The Wall Street Journal*, p. 16.

Learned, E., C. R. Christensen, K. R. Andrews, and W. D. Guth (1965). *Business Policy: Text and Cases*. Richard D. Irwin, Homewood, IL.

Levin, M. (November 25, 1989). 'Ethics courses: Useless', *The New York Times*, p. 14.

Likona, T. (ed.) (1976). *Moral Development and Behavior: Theory, Research, and Social Issues*. Holt, Rinehart and Winston, New York.

Lippke, R. (1991). 'A critique of business ethics', *Business Ethics Quarterly*, I, pp. 367–84.

Locke, J. (1952). *The Second Treatise of Government*. Bobbs-Merrill, Indianapolis, IN.

Lorange, P. (1980). *Corporate Planning: An Executive Viewpoint*. Prentice-Hall, Englewood Cliffs, NJ.

Lorange, P. and R. Vancil (1977). *Strategic Planning Systems*. Prentice-Hall, Englewood Cliffs, NJ.

Matasugu, M. (1982). *The Modern Samurai Society*. AMACOM, New York.

McCoy, C. (1985). *Management of Values: The Ethical Difference in Corporate Policy and Performance*. Pitman, Marshfield, MA.

Miles, R. H. (1982). *Coffin Nails and Corporate Strategies*. Prentice-Hall, Englewood Cliffs, NJ.

Mill, J. S. (1957). *Utilitarianism*. P. Osker (ed.). Macmillan, New York.

Mintzberg, H. and J. B. Quinn (1992). *The Strategy Process: Concepts and Contexts*. Prentice-Hall; Englewood Cliffs, NJ.

Newton, L. H. (1988). 'The hostile takeover: An opposition view'. In T. L. Beauchamp and N. E. Bowie (eds.), *Ethical Theory and Business* (3rd ed). Prentice-Hall, Englewood Cliffs, NJ, pp. 501–10.

Nozick, R. (1974). *Anarchy, State, and Utopia*. Basic Books, New York.

Ohmae, K. (1982). *The Mind of the Strategist*. McGraw-Hill, New York.

Peters, T. J. and R. H. Waterman (1982). *In Search of Excellence*. Harper & Row, New York.

Pinchot, G. (1985). *Intrapreneuring*. Harper & Row, New York.

Plato (1955). 'Apologia'. In R. Demos (ed.) *Plato Selections*. Charles Scribner's Sons, New York, pp. 206–10.

Porter, M. E. (1980). *Competitive Strategy: Techniques for Analyzing Industries and Competitors*. Free Press, New York.

Porter, M. E. (1985). *Competitive Advantage: Creating and Sustaining Superior Performance*. Free Press, New York.

Prahalad, C. K. and Y. Doz (1987). *The Multinational Mission: Balancing Local Demands and Global Views*. Free Press, New York.

Prahalad, C. K. and G. Hamel (May–June 1990). 'The core competence of the corporation', *Harvard Business Review*, pp. 71–91.

Protagoras (1968). 'Man is the measure'. In J. Robinson, *An Introduction to Early Greek Philosophy*. Houghton-Mifflin, New York.

Quinn, J. B. (1980): *Strategies for Change: Logical Incrementalism*. Richard D. Irwin, Homewood, IL.

Rawls, J. A. (1971). *Theory of Justice*. Harvard University Press, Cambridge, MA.

Rokeach, M. (1973). *The Nature of Human Values*. Free Press, New York.

Ross, W. D. (1930). *The Right and the Good*. Clarendon Press, Oxford.

Rumelt, R. P., D. Schendel, and D. J. Teece (1991). 'Strategic management and economics', *Strategic Management Journal*, Winter Special Issue, 12, pp. 5–29.

Schendel, D. and C. Hofer (1979). *Strategic Management: A New View of Business Policy and Planning*. Little, Brown, Boston, MA.

Sen, A. (1991). *On Ethics and Economics*. Basil Blackwell, Oxford.

Simon, H. (1947). *Administrative Behavior*. Free Press, New York.

Smith, A. (1962). *An Inquiry into the Nature and Causes of the Wealth of Nations*. R. Campbell (ed.). Oxford University Press, Oxford.

St. Augustine (1934). *The City of God*. D. Knowles (ed.). Norton, New York.

St. Thomas Aquinas (1988). 'Summa Theologica', In P. Sigmund (ed.), *St. Thomas Aquinas on Politics and Ethics*. Norton, New York.

Steers, R. M. and L. Porter (1987). *Motivation and Work Behavior* (4th ed). McGraw-Hill, New York.

Velasquez, M. (1992). *Business Ethics: Concepts and Cases* (3rd ed). Prentice-Hall, Englewood Cliffs, NJ.

Vogel, D. (April 17, 1987). 'Could an ethics course have kept Ivan from going bad?', *Wall Street Journal*, p. 24.

Websters' *New World Dictionary* (1953). World Publishing Company, Cleveland, OH.

Weigelt, K. and C. Camerer (1988). 'Reputation and corporate strategy: A review of recent theory and applications', *Strategic Management Journal*, 9(5), pp. 443–54.

6

GREEN AND COMPETITIVE: ENDING THE STALEMATE

Michael E. Porter and Claas van der Linde

The need for regulation to protect the environment gets widespread but grudging acceptance: widespread because everyone wants a livable planet, grudging because of the lingering belief that environmental regulations erode competitiveness. The prevailing view is that there is an inherent and fixed trade-off: ecology versus the economy. On one side of the trade-off are the *social* benefits that arise from strict environmental standards. On the other are industry's *private* costs for prevention and cleanup – costs that lead to higher prices and reduced competitiveness. With the argument framed this way, progress on environmental quality has become a kind of arm-wrestling match. One side pushes for tougher standards; the other tries to roll them back. The balance of power shifts one way or the other depending on the prevailing political winds.

This static view of environmental regulation, in which everything except regulation is held constant, is incorrect. If technology, products, processes, and customer needs were all fixed, the conclusion that regulation must raise costs would be inevitable. But companies operate in the real world of dynamic competition, not in the static world of much economic theory. They are constantly finding innovative solutions to pressures of all sorts – from competitors, customers, and regulators.

Properly designed environmental standards can trigger innovations that lower the total cost of a product or improve its value. Such innovations allow companies to use a range of inputs more productively – from raw materials to energy to labor – thus offsetting the costs of improving environmental impact and ending the stalemate. Ultimately, this enhanced *resource productivity* makes companies more competitive, not less.

Consider how the Dutch flower industry has responded to its environmental problems. Intense cultivation of flowers in small areas was contaminating the soil and groundwater with pesticides, herbicides, and fertilizers. Facing increasingly strict regulation on the release of chemicals, the Dutch understood that the only effective way to address the problem would be to develop a closed-loop system. In advanced Dutch greenhouses, flowers now grow in water and rock wool, not in soil. This lowers the risk of infestation, reducing the need for fertilizers and pesticides, which are delivered in water that circulates and is reused.

The tightly monitored closed-loop system also reduces variation in growing conditions, thus improving product quality. Handling costs have gone down because the flowers are cultivated on specially designed platforms. In addressing the environmental problem, then, the Dutch have innovated in ways that have raised the productivity with which they use many of the resources involved in growing flowers. The net result is not only dramatically lower environmental impact but also lower costs, better product quality, and enhanced global competitiveness. (See the insert 'Innovating to Be Competitive: The Dutch Flower Industry.')

This example illustrates why the debate about the relationship between competitiveness and the environment has been framed incorrectly. Policy makers, business leaders, and environmentalists have focused on the static cost impacts of environmental regulation and have ignored the more important offsetting productivity benefits from innovation. As a result, they have acted too often in ways that unnecessarily drive up costs and slow down progress on environmental issues. This static mind-set has thus created a self-fulfilling prophecy leading to ever more costly environmental regulation. Regulators tend to set regulations in ways that deter innovation. Companies, in turn, oppose and delay regulations instead of innovating to address them. The whole process has spawned an industry of litigators and consultants that drains resources away from real solutions.

POLLUTION = INEFFICIENCY

Are cases like the Dutch flower industry the exception rather than the rule? Is it naïve to expect that reducing pollution will often enhance competitiveness? We think not, and the reason is that pollution often is a form of economic waste. When scrap, harmful substances, or energy forms are discharged into the environment as pollution, it is a sign that resources have been used incompletely, inefficiently, or ineffectively. Moreover, companies then have to perform additional activities that add cost but create no value for customers: for example, handling, storage, and disposal of discharges.

The concept of resource productivity opens up a new way of looking at both the full systems costs and the value associated with any product. Resource inefficiencies are most obvious within a company in the form of incomplete material utilization and poor process controls, which result in unnecessary waste, defects, and stored materials. But there also are many other hidden costs buried in the life cycle of the product. Packaging discarded by distributors or customers, for example, wastes resources and adds costs. Customers bear additional costs when they use products that pollute or waste energy. Resources are lost when products that contain usable materials are discarded and when customers pay – directly or indirectly – for product disposal.

Environmental improvement efforts have traditionally overlooked these systems costs. Instead, they have focused on pollution control through better identification, processing, and disposal of discharges or waste – costly approaches. In recent years, more advanced companies and regulators have embraced the concept of pollution prevention, sometimes called source reduction, which uses such methods as material substitution and closed-loop processes to limit pollution before it occurs.

But, although pollution prevention is an important step in the right direction, ultimately companies must learn to frame environmental improvement in terms of resource productivity.[1] Today managers and regulators focus on the actual costs of eliminating or treating pollution. They must shift their attention to include the opportunity costs of pollution – wasted resources, wasted effort, and diminished product value to the customer. At the level of resource productivity, environmental improvement and competitiveness come together.

This new view of pollution as resource inefficiency evokes the quality revolution of the 1980s and its most powerful lessons. Today we have little trouble grasping the idea that innovation can improve quality while actually lowering cost. But as recently as 15 years ago, managers believed there was a fixed trade-off. Improving quality was expensive because it could be achieved only through inspection and rework of the 'inevitable' defects that came off the line. What lay behind the old view was the assumption that both product design and production processes were fixed. As managers have rethought the quality issue, however, they have abandoned that old mind-set. Viewing defects as a sign of inefficient product and process design – not as an inevitable by-product of manufacturing – was a breakthrough. Companies now strive to build quality into the entire process. The new mind-set unleashed the power of innovation to relax or eliminate what companies had previously accepted as fixed trade-offs.

Like defects, pollution often reveals flaws in the product design or production process. Efforts to eliminate pollution can therefore follow the same basic principles widely used in quality programs: Use inputs more efficiently, eliminate the need for hazardous, hard-to-handle materials, and eliminate unneeded activities. In a recent study of major process changes at ten manufacturers of printed circuit boards, for example, pollution-control personnel initiated 13 of 33 major changes. Of the 13 changes, 12 resulted in cost reduction, 8 in quality improvements, and 5 in extension of production capabilities.[2] It is not surprising that total quality management (TQM) has become a source of ideas for pollution reduction that can create offsetting benefits. The Dow Chemical Company, for example, explicitly identified the link between quality improvement and environmental performance by using statistical-process control to reduce the variance in processes and to lower waste.

INNOVATION AND RESOURCE PRODUCTIVITY

To explore the central role of innovation and the connection between environmental improvement and resource productivity, we have been collaborating since 1991 with the Management Institute for Environment and Business (MEB) on a series of international case studies of industries and sectors significantly affected by environmental regulation: pulp and paper, paint and coatings, electronics manufacturing, refrigerators, dry cell batteries, and printing inks. (See the table 'Environmental Regulation Has Competitive Implications.') The data clearly show that the costs of addressing environmental regulations can be minimized, if not eliminated, through innovation that delivers other competitive benefits. We first observed the phenomenon in the course of our research for a study of national competitiveness, *The Competitive Advantage of Nations* (The Free Press, 1990).

Consider the chemical sector, where many believe that the ecology-economy trade-off is particularly steep. A study of activities to prevent waste generation at 29 chemical plants found innovation offsets that enhanced resource productivity. Of 181 of these waste prevention activities, only one resulted in a net cost increase. Of the 70 activities with documented changes in product yield, 68 reported increases; the average for 20 initiatives documented with specific data was 7%. These innovation offsets were achieved with surprisingly low investments and very short payback times. One-quarter of the 48 initiatives with detailed capital cost information required *no* capital investment at all; of the 38 initiatives with data on the payback period, nearly two-thirds recouped their initial investments in six months or less. The annual savings per dollar spent on source reduction averaged $3.49 for the 27 activities for which this information could be calculated. The study also found that the two main motivating factors for source reduction activities were waste disposal costs and environmental regulation.

ENVIRONMENTAL REGULATION HAS COMPETITIVE IMPLICATIONS

Sector/Industry	Environmental Issues	Innovative Solutions	Innovation Offsets
Pulp and paper	Dioxin released by bleaching with chlorine	Improved cooking and washing processes Elimination of chlorine by using oxygen, ozone, or peroxide for bleaching Closed-loop processes (still problematic)	Lower operating costs though greater use of by product energy sources 25% initial price premium for chlorine-free paper
Paint and coatings	Volatile organic compounds (VOCs) in solvents	New paint formulations (low-solvent-content paints, water-borne paints) Improved application techniques Powder or radiation-cured coatings	Price premium for solvent free paints Improved coatings quality in some segments Worker safety benefits Higher coatings-transfer efficiency Reduced coating costs through materials savings
Electronics manufacturing	Volatile organic compounds (VOCs) in cleaning agents	Semiaqueous, terpene-based cleaning agents Closed-loop systems No-clean soldering where possible	Increase in cleaning quality and thus in product quality 30% to 80% reduction in cleaning costs, often for one-year payback periods Elimination of an unnecessary production step
Refrigerators	Chlorofluorocarbons (CFCs) used as refrigerants Energy usage Disposal	Alternative refrigerants (propane-isobutane mix) Thicker insulation Better gaskets Improved compressors	10% better energy efficiency at same cost 5% to 10% initial price premium for 'green' refrigerator

Sector/Industry	Environmental Issues	Innovative Solutions	Innovation Offsets
Dry cell batteries	Cadmium, mercury, lead, nickel, cobalt, lithium, and zinc releases in landfills or to the air (after incineration)	Rechargeable batteries of nickel-hydride (for some applications) Rechargeable lithium batteries (now being developed)	Nearly twice as efficient at same cost Higher energy efficiency Expected to be price competitive in the near future
Printing inks	VOCs in petroleum inks	Water-based inks, and soy inks	Higher efficiency, brighter colors, and better printability (depending on application)

Sources: Benjamin C. Bonifant, Ian Ratcliffe, and Claas van der Linde.

INNOVATION-FRIENDLY REGULATION

Regulation, properly conceived, need not drive up costs. The following principles of regulatory design will promote innovation, resource productivity, and competitiveness:

Focus on outcomes, not technologies. Past regulations have often prescribed particular remediation technologies, such as catalysts or scrubbers for air pollution. The phrases 'best available technology' (BAT) and 'best available control technology' (BACT) are deeply rooted in U.S. practice and imply that one technology is best, discouraging innovation.

Enact strict rather than lax regulation. Companies can handle lax regulation incrementally, often with end-of-pipe or secondary treatment solutions. Regulation, therefore, needs to be stringent enough to promote real innovation.

Regulate as close to the end user as practical, while encouraging upstream solutions. This will normally allow more flexibility for innovation in the end product and in all the production and distribution stages. Avoiding pollution entirely or, second best, mitigating it early in the value chain is almost always less costly than late-stage remediation or cleanup.

Employ phase-in periods. Ample but well-defined phase-in periods tied to industry-capital-investment cycles will allow companies to develop innovative resource-saving technologies rather than force them to implement expensive solutions hastily, merely patching over problems. California imposed such short compliance deadlines on its wood-furniture industry that many manufacturers chose to leave the state rather than add costly control equipment.

Use market incentives. Market incentives such as pollution charges and deposit-refund schemes draw attention to resource inefficiencies. In addition, tradable permits provide continuing incentives for innovation and encourage creative use of technologies that exceed current standards.

111

Continued

INNOVATION-FRIENDLY REGULATION—cont'd

Harmonize or converge regulations in associated fields. Liability exposure in the United States leads companies to stick to safe, BAT approaches, and inconsistent regulation on alternative technologies deters beneficial innovation. For example, one way to eliminate refrigerator cooling agents suspected of damaging the ozone layer involves replacing them with small amounts of propane and butane. But narrowly conceived safety regulations covering these gases seem to have impeded development of the new technology in the United States, while several leading European companies are already marketing the new products.

Develop regulations in sync with other countries or slightly ahead of them. It is important to minimize possible competitive disadvantages relative to foreign companies that are not yet subject to the same standard. Developing regulations slightly ahead of other countries will also maximize export potential in the pollution-control sector by raising incentives for innovation. When standards in the United States lead world developments, domestic companies get opportunities for valuable early-mover advantages. However, if standards are too far ahead or too different in character from those that are likely to apply to foreign competitors, industry may innovate in the wrong directions.

Make the regulatory process more stable and predictable. The regulatory process is as important as the standards. If standards and phase-in periods are set and accepted early enough and if regulators commit to keeping standards in place for, say, five years, industry can lock in and tackle root-cause solutions instead of hedging against the next twist or turn in government philosophy.

Require industry participation in setting standards from the beginning. U.S. regulation differs sharply from European in its adversarial approach. Industry should help in designing phase-in periods, the content of regulations, and the most effective regulatory process. A predetermined set of information requests and interactions with industry representatives should be a mandatory part of the regulatory process. Both industry and regulators must work toward a climate of trust because industry needs to provide genuinely useful information and regulators need to take industry input seriously.

Develop strong technical capabilities among regulators. Regulators must understand an industry's economics and what drives its competitiveness. Better information exchange will help avoid costly gaming in which ill-informed companies use an array of lawyers and consultants to try to stall the poorly designed regulations of ill-informed regulators.

Minimize the time and resources consumed in the regulatory process itself. Time delays in granting permits are usually costly for companies. Self-regulation with periodic inspections would be more efficient than requiring formal approvals. Potential and actual litigation creates uncertainty and consumes resources. Mandatory arbitration procedures or rigid arbitration steps before litigation would lower costs and encourage innovation.

For an extended discussion of the ways in which environmental regulation should change, see Michael E. Porter and Claas van der Linde, 'Toward a New Conception of the Environment-Competitiveness Relationship,' *Journal of Economic Perspectives* 9, no. 4 (fall 1995).

Innovation in response to environmental regulation can fall into two broad categories. The first is new technologies and approaches that minimize the cost of dealing with pollution once it occurs. The key to these approaches often lies in taking the resources embodied in the pollution and converting them into something of value. Companies get smarter about how to process toxic materials and emissions into usable forms, recycle scrap, and improve secondary treatment. For example, at a Rhône-Poulenc plant in Chalampe, France, nylon by-products known as diacids used to be incinerated. Rhône-Poulenc invested 76 million francs and installed new equipment to recover and sell these diacids as additives for dyes and tanning and as coagulation agents. The new recovery process has generated annual revenues of about 20.1 million francs. New de-inking technologies developed by Massachusetts-based Thermo Electron Corporation, among others, are allowing more extensive use of recycled paper. Molten Metal Technology of Waltham, Massachusetts, has developed a cost-saving catalytic extraction method to process many types of hazardous waste.

The second and far more interesting and important type of innovation addresses the root causes of pollution by improving resource productivity in the first place. Innovation offsets can take many forms, including more efficient utilization of particular inputs, better product yields, and better products. (See the insert 'Environmental Improvement Can Benefit Resource Productivity.') Consider the following examples.

Resource productivity improves when less costly materials are substituted or when existing ones are better utilized. Dow Chemical's California complex scrubs hydrochloric gas with caustic to produce a wide range of chemicals. The company used to store the wastewater in evaporation ponds. Regulation called for Dow to close the evaporation ponds by 1988. In 1987, under pressure to comply with the new law, the company redesigned its production process. It reduced the use of caustic soda, decreasing caustic waste by 6,000 tons per year and hydrochloric acid waste by 80 tons per year. Dow also found that it could capture a portion of the waste stream for reuse as a raw material in other parts of the plant. Although it cost only $250,000 to implement, the process gave Dow an annual savings of $2.4 million.[3]

3M also improved resource productivity. Forced to comply with new regulations to reduce solvent emissions by 90%, 3M found a way to avoid the use of solvents altogether by coating products with safer, water-based solutions. The company gained an early-mover advantage in product development over competitors, many of whom switched significantly later. The company also shortened its time to market because its water-based product did not have to go through the approval process for solvent-based coatings.[4]

3M found that innovations can improve process consistency, reduce downtime, and lower costs substantially. The company used to produce adhesives in batches that were then transferred to storage tanks. One bad batch could spoil the entire contents of a tank. Lost product, downtime, and expensive hazardous-waste disposal were the result. 3M developed a new technique to run rapid quality tests on new batches. It reduced hazardous wastes by 110 tons per year at almost no cost, yielding an annual savings of more than $200,000.[5]

Many chemical-production processes require an initial start-up period after production interruptions in order to stabilize output and bring it within specifications. During that time, only scrap material is produced. When regulations raised the cost of waste disposal, Du Pont was motivated to install higher-quality monitoring equipment, which in turn reduced production interruptions and the associated production start-ups. Du Pont lowered not only its waste generation but also cut the amount of time it wasn't producing anything.[6]

Process changes to reduce emissions and use resources more productively often result in higher yields. As a result of new environmental standards, Ciba-Geigy Corporation reexamined the waste-water streams at its dye plant in Tom's River, New Jersey. Engineers made two

ENVIRONMENTAL IMPROVEMENT CAN BENEFIT
RESOURCE PRODUCTIVITY

Process Benefits
- □ materials savings resulting from more complete processing, substitution, reuse, or recycling of production inputs
- □ increases in process yields
- □ less downtime through more careful monitoring and maintenance
- □ better utilization of by-products
- □ conversion of waste into valuable forms
- □ lower energy consumption during the production process
- □ reduced material storage and handling costs
- □ savings from safer workplace conditions
- □ elimination or reduction of the cost of activities involved in discharges or waste handling, transportation, and disposal
- □ improvements in the product as a by-product of process changes (such as better process control)

Product Benefits
- □ higher quality, more consistent products
- □ lower product costs (for instance, from material substitution)
- □ lower packaging costs
- □ more efficient resource use by products
- □ safer products
- □ lower net costs of product disposal to customers
- □ higher product resale and scrap value

changes to the production process. First, they replaced sludge-creating iron with a less harmful chemical conversion agent. Second, they eliminated the release of a potentially toxic product into the wastewater stream. They not only reduced pollution but also increased process yields by 40%, realizing an annual cost savings of $740,000. Although that part of the plant was ultimately closed, the example illustrates the role of regulatory pressure in process innovation.

Process innovations to comply with environmental regulation can even improve product consistency and quality. In 1990, the Montreal Protocol and the U.S. Clean Air Act required electronics companies to eliminate ozone-depleting chlorofluorocarbons (CFCs). Many companies used them as cleaning agents to remove residues that occur in the manufacture of printed circuit boards. Scientists at Raytheon confronted the regulatory challenge. Initially, they thought that complete elimination of CFCs would be impossible. After research, however, they found an alternate cleaning agent that could be reused in a closed-loop system. The new method improved average product quality – which the old CFC-based cleaning agent had occasionally compromised – while also lowering operating costs. Responding to the same regulation, other researchers identified applications that did not require any cleaning at all and developed so-called no-clean soldering technologies, which lowered operating costs without compromising quality. Without environmental regulation, that innovation would not have happened.

Innovations to address environmental regulations can also lower product costs and boost resource productivity by reducing unnecessary packaging or simplifying designs. A 1991 law in Japan set standards to make products easier to recycle. Hitachi, along with other Japanese appliance producers, responded by redesigning products to reduce disassembly time. In the process, it cut back the number of parts in a washing machine by 16% and the number of parts in a vacuum cleaner by 30%. Fewer components made the products easier not only to disassemble but also to assemble in the first place. Regulation that requires such recyclable products can lower the user's disposal costs and lead to designs that allow a company to recover valuable materials more easily. Either the customer or the manufacturer who takes back used products reaps greater value.

Although such product innovations have been prompted by regulators instead of by customers, world demand is putting a higher value on resource-efficient products. Many companies are using innovations to command price premiums for "green" products and to open up new market segments. Because Germany adopted recycling standards earlier than most other countries, German companies have first-mover advantages in developing less packaging-intensive products, which are both lower in cost and sought after in the marketplace. In the United States, Cummins Engine Company's development of low-emissions diesel engines for such applications as trucks and buses – innovation that U.S. environmental regulations spurred – is allowing it to gain position in international markets where similar needs are growing.

These examples and many others like them do not prove that companies always can innovate to reduce environmental impact at low cost. However, they show that there are considerable opportunities to reduce pollution through innovations that redesign products, processes, and methods of operation. Such examples are common in spite of companies' resistance to environmental regulation and in spite of regulatory standards that often are hostile to innovative, resource-productive solutions. The fact that such examples are common carries an important message: Today a new frame of reference for thinking about environmental improvement is urgently needed.

DO WE REALLY NEED REGULATION?

If innovation in response to environmental regulation can be profitable – if a company can actually offset the cost of compliance through improving resource productivity – why is regulation necessary at all? If such opportunities exist, wouldn't companies pursue them naturally and would't regulation be unnecessary? That is like saying there will rarely be ten-dollar bills to be found on the ground because someone already will have picked them up.

Certainly, some companies do pursue such innovations without, or in advance of, regulation. In Germany and Scandinavia, where both companies and consumers are very attuned to environmental concerns, innovation is not uncommon. As companies and their customers adopt the resource productivity mind-set and as knowledge about innovative technologies grows, there may well be less need for regulation over time in the United States.

But the belief that companies will pick up on profitable opportunities without a regulatory push makes a false assumption about competitive reality – namely, that all profitable opportunities for innovation have already been discovered, that all managers have perfect information about them, and that organizational incentives are aligned with innovating. In fact, in the real world, managers often have highly incomplete information and limited time and attention. Barriers to change are numerous. The Environmental Protection Agency's Green Lights program, which works with companies to promote energy-saving lighting, shows that many ten-dollar bills are still waiting to be picked up. In one audit, nearly 80% of the projects offered paybacks within two years or less, and yet the companies considering them had not taken action.[7] Only after companies joined the program and benefited from the EPA's information and cajoling were such highly profitable projects implemented.

We are now in a transitional phase of industrial history in which companies are still inexperienced in handling environmental issues creatively. Customers, too, are unaware that resource inefficiency means that they must pay for the cost of pollution. For example, they tend to see discarded packaging as free because there is no separate charge for it and no current lower-cost alternative. Because there is no direct way to recapture the value of the wasted resources that customers already have paid for, they imagine that discarding used products carries no cost penalty for them.

Regulation, although a different type than is currently practiced, is needed for six major reasons:

- To create pressure that motivates companies to innovate. Our broader research on competitiveness highlights the important role of outside pressure in overcoming organizational inertia and fostering creative thinking.
- To improve environmental quality in cases in which innovation and the resulting improvements in resource productivity do not completely offset the cost of compliance; or in which it takes time for learning effects to reduce the overall cost of innovative solutions.
- To alert and educate companies about likely resource inefficiencies and potential areas for technological improvement (although government cannot know better than companies how to address them).
- To raise the likelihood that product innovations and process innovations in general will be environmentally friendly.
- To create demand for environmental improvement until companies and customers are able to perceive and measure the resource inefficiencies of pollution better.
- To level the playing field during the transition period to innovation-based environmental solutions, ensuring that one company cannot gain position by avoiding environmental investments. Regulation provides a buffer for innovative companies until new technologies are proven and the effects of learning can reduce technological costs.

Those who believe that market forces alone will spur innovation may argue that total quality management programs were initiated without regulatory intervention. However, TQM came to the United States and Europe through a different kind of pressure. Decades earlier, TQM had been widely diffused in Japan – the result of a whole host of government efforts to make product quality a national goal, including the creation of the Deming Prize. Only after Japanese companies had devastated them in the marketplace did Americans and Europeans embrace TQM.

THE COST OF THE STATIC MIND-SET

Regulators and companies should focus, then, on relaxing the trade-off between environmental protection and competitiveness by encouraging innovation and resource productivity. Yet the current adversarial climate drives up the costs of meeting environmental standards and circumscribes the innovation benefits, making the trade-off far steeper than it needs to be.

To begin with, the power struggle involved in setting and enforcing environmental regulations consumes enormous amounts of resources. A 1992 study by the Rand Institute for Civil Justice, for example, found that 88% of the money that insurers paid out between 1986 and 1989 on Superfund claims went to pay for legal and administrative costs, whereas only 12% was used for actual site cleanups.[8] The Superfund law may well be the most inefficient environmental law in the United States, but it is not the only cause of inefficiency. We believe that a substantial fraction of environmental spending as well as of the revenues of environmental products and services companies relates to the regulatory struggle itself and not to improving the environment.

One problem with the adversarial process is that it locks companies into static thinking and systematically pushes industry estimates of the costs of regulation upward. A classic example occurred during the debate in the United States on the 1970 Clean Air Act. Lee Iacocca, then executive vice president of the Ford Motor Company, predicted that compliance with the new regulations would require huge price increases for automobiles, force U.S. production to a halt by 1975, and severely damage the U.S. economy. The 1970 Clean Air Act was subsequently enacted, and Iacocca's dire predictions turned out to be wrong. Similar stories are common.

Static thinking causes companies to fight environmental standards that actually could enhance their competitiveness. Most distillers of coal tar in the United States, for example, opposed 1991 regulations requiring substantial reductions in benzene emissions. At the time, the only solution was to cover the tar storage tanks with costly gas blankets. But the regulation spurred Aristech Chemical Corporation of Pittsburgh, Pennsylvania, to develop a way to remove benzene from tar in the first processing step, thereby eliminating the need for gas blankets. Instead of suffering a cost increase, Aristech saved itself $3.3 million.

Moreover, company mind-sets make the costs of addressing environmental regulations appear higher than they actually are. Many companies do not account for a learning curve, although the actual costs of compliance are likely to decline over time. A recent study in the pulp-and-paper sector, for example, found the actual costs of compliance to be $4 to $5.50 per ton, whereas original industry estimates had been as high as $16.40.[9] Similarly, the cost of compliance with a 1990 regulation controlling sulfur dioxide emissions is today only about half of what analysts initially predicted, and it is heading lower. With a focus on innovation and resource productivity, today's compliance costs represent an upper limit.

There is legitimate controversy over the benefits to society of specific environmental standards. Measuring the health and safety effects of cleaner air, for example, is the subject of ongoing scientific debate. Some believe that the risks of polution have been overstated. But whatever the level of *social* benefits proves to be, the *private* costs to companies are still far higher than necessary.

GOOD REGULATION VERSUS BAD

In addition to being high-cost, the current system of environmental regulation in the United States often deters innovative solutions or renders them impossible. The problem with regulation is not its strictness. It is the way in which standards are written and the sheer inefficiency with which regulations are administered. Strict standards can and should promote resource productivity. The United States' regulatory process has squandered this potential, however, by concentrating on cleanup instead of prevention, mandating specific technologies, setting compliance deadlines that are unrealistically short, and subjecting companies to unnecessarily high levels of uncertainty.

The current system discourages risk taking and experimentation. Liability exposure and the government's inflexibility in enforcement, among other things, contribute to the problem. For example, a company that innovates and achieves 95% of target emissions reduction while also registering substantial offsetting cost reductions is still 5% out of compliance and subject to liability. On the other hand, regulators would reward it for adopting safe but expensive secondary treatment. (See the insert 'Innovation-Friendly Regulation.')

Just as bad regulation can damage competitiveness, good regulation can enhance it. Consider the differences between the U.S. pulp-and-paper sector and the Scandinavian. Strict early U.S. regulations in the 1970s were imposed without adequate phase-in periods, forcing companies to adopt best available technologies quickly. At that time, the requirements invariably meant installing proven but costly end-of-pipe treatment systems. In Scandinavia, on the other hand, regulation permitted more flexible approaches, enabling companies to focus on the production process itself, not just on secondary treatment of wastes. Scandinavian companies developed innovative pulping and bleaching technologies that not only met emission requirements but also lowered operating costs. Even though the United States was the first to regulate, U.S. companies were unable to realize any first-mover advantages because U.S. regulations ignored a critical principle of good environmental regulation: Create maximum opportunity for innovation by letting industries discover how to solve their own problems.

Unfortunately for the U.S. pulp-and-paper industry, a second principle of good regulation was also ignored: Foster continuous improvement; do not lock in on a particular technology or the status quo. The Swedish regulatory agency took a more effective approach. Whereas the United States mandated strict emissions goals and established very tight compliance deadlines, Sweden started out with looser standards but clearly communicated that tougher ones would follow. The results were predictable. U.S. companies installed secondary treatment systems and stopped there. Swedish producers, anticipating stricter standards, continually incorporated innovative environmental technologies into their normal cycles of capacity replacement and innovation.

The innovation-friendly approach produced the residual effect of raising the competitiveness of the local equipment industry. Spurred by Scandinavian demand for sophisticated process improvements, local pulp-and-paper-equipment suppliers, such as Sunds Defibrator and Kamyr, ultimately made major international gains in selling innovative pulping and bleaching equipment.

INNOVATING TO BE COMPETITIVE: THE DUTCH FLOWER INDUSTRY

The Dutch flower industry is responsible for about 65% of world exports of cut flowers – an astonishing figure given that the most important production inputs in the flower business would seem to be land and climate. Anyone who has been to the Netherlands knows its disadvantages on both counts. The Dutch have to reclaim land from the sea, and the weather is notoriously problematic.

How can the Dutch be the world's leaders in the flower business when they lack comparative advantage in the traditional sense? The answer, among other reasons, is that they have innovated at every step in the value chain, creating technology and highly specialized inputs that enhance resource productivity and offset the country's natural disadvantages.

In selling and distribution, for example, the Netherlands has five auction houses custom designed for the flower business. Carts of flowers are automatically towed on computer-guided paths into the auction room. The buying process occurs in a few seconds. Buyers sit in an amphitheater, and the price on the auction clock moves down until the first buyer signals electronically. That buyer's code is attached to the cart, which is routed to the company's shipping and handling area. Within a few minutes, the flowers are on a truck to regional markets or in a specialized, pre-cooled container on their way to nearby Schiphol airport. Good airports and highway systems may be plentiful elsewhere, too. But the Netherlands' innovative, specialized infrastructure is a competitive advantage. It leads to very high productivity. It is so successful that growers from other countries actually fly flowers there to be processed, sold, and reexported.

Paradoxically, having a *shortage* of general-purpose or more basic inputs can sometimes be turned into an advantage. If land were readily available and the climate more favorable, the Dutch would have competed the same way other countries did. Instead they were forced to innovate, developing a high-tech system of year-round greenhouse cultivation. The Dutch continually improve the unique, specialized technology that creates high resource productivity and underpins their competitiveness.

In contrast, an abundance of labor and natural resources or a lack of environmental pressure may lead a country's companies to spend the national resources unproductively. Competing based on cheap inputs, which could be used with less productivity, was sufficient in a more insular, less global economy. Today, when emerging nations with even cheaper labor and raw materials are part of the global economy, the old strategy is unsustainable.

Eventually, the Scandinavian pulp-and-paper industry was able to reap innovation offsets that went beyond those directly stemming from regulatory pressures. By the early 1990s, producers realized that growing public awareness of the environmental problems associated with pulp-mill effluents was creating a niche market. For a time, Scandinavian companies with totally chlorine-free paper were able to command significant price premiums and serve a rapidly growing market segment of environmentally informed customers.

IMPLICATIONS FOR COMPANIES

Certainly, misguided regulatory approaches have imposed a heavy burden on companies. But managers who have responded by digging in their heels to oppose all regulation have been shortsighted as well. It is no secret that Japanese and German automobile makers developed lighter and more fuel-efficient cars in response to new fuel consumption standards, while the less competitive U.S. car industry fought such standards and hoped they would go away. The U.S. car industry eventually realized that it would face extinction if it did not learn to compete through innovation. But clinging to the static mind-set too long cost billions of dollars and many thousands of jobs.

To avoid making the same mistakes, managers must start to recognize environmental improvement as an economic and competitive opportunity, not as an annoying cost or an inevitable threat. Instead of clinging to a perspective focused on regulatory compliance, companies need to ask questions such as What are we wasting? and How could we enhance customer value? The early movers – the companies that can see the opportunity first and embrace inno-vation-based solutions – will reap major competitive benefits, just as the German and Japanese car makers did. (See the insert 'The New Environmentalists.')

At this stage, for most companies, environmental issues are still the province of outsiders and specialists. That is not surprising. Any new management issue tends to go through a predictable life cycle. When it first arises, companies hire outside experts to help them navigate. When prac-tice becomes more developed, internal specialists take over. Only after a field becomes mature do companies integrate it into the ongoing role of line management.

Many companies have delegated the analysis of environmental problems and the develop-ment of solutions to outside lawyers and environmental consultants. Such experts in the adver-sarial regulatory process, who are not deeply familiar with the company's overall technology and operations, inevitably focus on compliance rather than innovation. They invariably favor end-of-pipe solutions. Many consultants, in fact, are associated with vendors who sell such technologies. Some companies are in the second phase, in which environmental issues are assigned to internal specialists. But these specialists – for example, legal, governmental-affairs, or environmental departments – lack full profit responsibility and are separate from the line organization. Again, the result is almost always narrow, incremental solutions.

If the sorts of process and product redesigns needed for true innovation are even to be con-sidered, much less implemented, environmental strategies must become an issue for general management. Environmental impact must be embedded in the overall process of improving productivity and competitiveness. The resource-productivity model, rather than the pollution-control model, must govern decision making.

How can managers accelerate their companies' progress toward a more competitive environ-mental approach? First, they can measure their direct and indirect environmental impacts. One of the major reasons that companies are not very innovative about environmental problems is igno-rance. A large producer of organic chemicals, for example, hired a consultant to explore waste reduction opportunities in its 40 waste streams. A careful audit uncovered 497 different waste streams – the company had been wrong by a factor of more than ten.[10] Our research indi-cates that the act of measurement alone leads to enormous opportunities to improve productivity.

Companies that adopt the resource-productivity framework and go beyond currently regulated areas will reap the greatest benefits. Companies should inventory all unused, emitted, or discarded resources or packaging. Within the company, some poorly utilized resources will be held within plants, some discharged, and some put in dumpsters. Indirect resource inefficiencies will occur at the level of suppliers, channels, and customers. At the customer level, resource inefficiencies show up in the use of the product, in discarded packaging, and in resources left in the used-up product.

Second, managers can learn to recognize the opportunity cost of underutilized resources. Few companies have analyzed the true cost of toxicity, waste, and what they discard, much less the second-order impacts that waste and discharges have on other activities. Fewer still look beyond the out-of-pocket costs of dealing with pollution to the opportunity cost of the resources they waste or the productivity they forgo. There are scarcely any companies that think about cus-tomer value and the opportunity cost of wasted resources at the customer level.

Many companies do not even track environmental spending carefully, and conventional accounting systems are ill equipped to measure underutilized resources. Companies evaluate environmental projects as discrete, stand-alone investments. Straightforward waste- or dis-charge-reduction investments are screened using high hurdle rates that presume the investments are risky – leaving ten-dollar bills on the ground. Better information and evaluation methods will help managers reduce environmental impact while improving resource productivity.

Third, companies should create a bias in favor of innovation-based, productivity-enhancing solutions. They should trace their own and their customers' discharges, scrap, emissions, and disposal activities back into company activities to gain insight about beneficial product design, packaging, raw material, or process changes. We have been struck by the power of certain systems solutions: Groups of activities may be reconfigured, or substitutions in inputs or packaging may enhance utilization and potential for recovery. Approaches that focus on treatment of discrete discharges should be sent back to the organization for rethinking.

Current reward systems are as anti-innovation as regulatory policies. At the plant level, companies reward output but ignore environmental costs and wasted resources. The punishment for an innovative, economically efficient solution that falls short of expectations is often far greater than the reward for a costly but 'successful' one.

Finally, companies must become more proactive in defining new types of relationships with both regulators and environmentalists. Businesses need a new mind-set. How can companies argue shrilly that regulations harm competitiveness and then expect regulators and environmentalists to be flexible and trusting as those same companies request time to pursue innovative solutions?

THE WORLD ECONOMY IN TRANSITION

It is time for the reality of modern competition to inform our thinking about the relationship between competitiveness and the environment. Traditionally, nations were competitive if their companies had access to the lowest cost inputs – capital, labor, energy, and raw materials. In industries relying on natural resources, for example, the competitive companies and countries were those with abundant local supplies. Because technology changed slowly, a comparative advantage in inputs was enough for success.

Today globalization is making the notion of comparative advantage obsolete. Companies can source low-cost inputs anywhere, and new, rapidly emerging technologies can offset disadvantages in the cost of inputs. Facing high labor costs at home, for example, a company can automate away the need for unskilled labor. Facing a shortage of a raw material, a company can find an alternative raw material or create a synthetic one. To overcome high space costs, Japanese companies pioneered just-in-time production and avoided storing inventory on the factory floor.

It is no longer enough simply to have resources. Using resources productively is what makes for competitiveness today. Companies can improve resource productivity by producing existing products more efficiently or by making products that are more valuable to customers – products customers are willing to pay more for. Increasingly, the nations and companies that are most competitive are not those with access to the lowest-cost inputs but those that employ the most advanced technology and methods in using their inputs. Because technology is constantly changing, the new paradigm of global competitiveness requires the ability to innovate rapidly.

This new paradigm has profound implications for the debate about environmental policy – about how to approach it, how to regulate, and how strict regulation should be. The new paradigm has brought environmental improvement and competitiveness together. It is important to use resources productively, whether those resources are natural and physical or human and capital. Environmental progress demands that companies innovate to raise resource productivity – and that is precisely what the new challenges of global competition demand. Resisting innovation that reduces pollution, as the U.S. car industry did in the 1970s, will lead not only to environmental damage but also to the loss of competitiveness in the global economy. Developing

THE NEW ENVIRONMENTALISTS

Environmentalists can foster innovation and resource productivity by speaking out for the right kind of regulatory standards and by educating the public to demand innovative environmental solutions. The German section of Greenpeace, for example, noted in 1992 that a mixture of propane and butane was safer for cooling refrigerators than the then-prevalent cooling agents – hydrofluorocarbons or hydrochlorofluorocarbons – that were proposed as replacements for chlorofluorocarbons. Greenpeace for the first time in its history began endorsing a commercial product. It actually ran an advertising campaign for a refrigerator designed by Foron, a small refrigerator maker on the verge of bankruptcy. The action was greatly leveraged by extensive media coverage and has been a major reason behind the ensuing demand for Foron-built propane-butane refrigerators and the switch that the established refrigerator producers in Germany later made to the same technology.

Environmental organizations can support industry by becoming sources of information about best practices that may not be well known outside of a few pioneering companies. When it realized that German magazine publishers and readers alike were unaware of the much improved quality of chlorine-free paper, Greenpeace Germany issued a magazine printed on chlorine-free paper. It closely resembled the leading German political weekly, *Der Spiegel*, and it encouraged readers to demand that publishers switch to chlorine-free paper. Shortly after, *Der Spiegel* and several other large magazines did indeed switch. Other environmental organizations could shift some resources away from litigation to focus instead on funding and disseminating research on innovations that address environmental problems.

Among U.S. environmental groups, the Environmental Defense Fund (EDF) has been an innovator in its willingness to promote market-based regulatory systems and to work directly with industry. It supported the sulfur-dioxide trading system that allows companies either to reduce their own emissions or to buy emissions allowances from companies that have managed to exceed their reduction quotas at lower cost. The EDF-McDonald's Waste Reduction Task Force, formed in 1990, led to a substantial redesign of McDonald's packaging, including the elimination of the polystyrene-foam clamshell. EDF is now working with General Motors on plans to remove heavily polluting cars from the road and with Johnson & Johnson, McDonald's, NationsBank, The Prudential Insurance Company of America, Time Warner, and Duke University to promote the use of recycled paper.

Source: Benjamin C. Bonifant and Ian Ratcliffe, 'Competitive Implications of Environmental Regulation in the Pulp and Paper Industry,' working paper, Management Institute for Environment and Business, Washington, D.C., 1994.

countries that stick with resource-wasting methods and forgo environmental standards because they are 'too expensive' will remain uncompetitive, relegating themselves to poverty.

How an industry responds to environmental problems may, in fact, be a leading indicator of its overall competitiveness. Environmental regulation does not lead inevitably to innovation and competitiveness or to higher productivity for all companies. Only those companies that innovate successfully will win. A truly competitive industry is more likely to take up a new standard as a challenge and respond to it with innovation. An uncompetitive industry, on the other hand, may not be oriented toward innovation and thus may be tempted to fight all regulation.

It is not at all surprising that the debate pitting the environment against competitiveness has developed as it has. Indeed, economically destructive struggles over redistribution are the norm in many areas of public policy. But now is the time for a paradigm shift to carry us forward into the next century. International competition has changed dramatically over the last few decades. Senior managers who grew up at a time when environmental regulation was synonymous with litigation will see increasing evidence that environmental improvement is good business. Successful environmentalists, regulatory agencies, and companies will reject old trade-offs and build on the underlying economic logic that links the environment, resource productivity, innovation, and competitiveness.

NOTES

1 One of the pioneering efforts to see environmental improvement this way is Joel Makower's *The E-Factor: The Bottom-Line Approach to Environmentally Responsible Business,* New York: Times Books, 1993.

2 Andrew King, 'Improved Manufacturing Resulting from Learning from Waste: Causes, Importance, and Enabling Conditions,' working paper, Stern School of Business, New York University, New York, 1994.

3 Mark H. Dorfman, Warren R. Muir, and Catherine G. Miller, *Environmental Dividends: Cutting More Chemical Wastes* (New York: INFORM 1992).

4 Don L. Boroughs and Betsy Carpenter, 'Helping the Planet and the Economy,' *U.S. News and World Report* 110, no. 11, March 25, 1991, p. 46.

5 John H. Sheridan, 'Attacking Wastes and Saving Money ... Some of the Time,' *Industry Week,* February 17, 1992, p. 43.

6 Gerald Parkinson, 'Reducing Wastes Can Be Cost-Effective,' *Chemical Engineering* 97, no. 7, July 1990, p. 30.

7 Stephen J. DeCanio. 'Why Do Profitable Energy-Saving Projects Languish?' working paper, Second International Research Conference of the Greening of Industry Network, Cambridge, Massachusetts, 1993.

8 Jan Paul Acton and Lloyd S. Dixon, 'Superfund and Transaction Costs: The Experiences of Insurers and Very Large Industrial Firms,' working paper, Rand Institute for Civil Justice, Santa Monica, California, 1992.

9 Norman Bonson, Neil McCubbin, and John B. Sprague, 'Kraft Mill Effluents in Ontario,' report prepared for the Technical Advisory Committee, Pulp and Paper Sector of MISA, Ontario Ministry of the Environment, Toronto, March 29, 1988, p. 166.

10 Parkinson, p. 30.

7

On the Limits of a Firm-Based Theory to Explain Business Networks: The Western Bias of Neo-Classical Economics

Nicole Woolsey Biggart and Gary G. Hamilton

INTRODUCTION

The leading business success story of the last two decades cannot be disputed: the tremendous growth and economic development of the East Asian economies. During the fifteen-year period from 1965 to 1980, Japan and the newly industrialized countries (NICs) of South Korea, Taiwan, Hong Kong, and Singapore grew at an average annual rate of 8.8%. At the same time, the US economy grew 2.9%. In the period from 1980 to 1985, a time of world recession, Japan grew 3.8%, while the Asian NICs 'slowed' to 6.6%. The comparable figure for all industrial market economies for that five-year period was 2.5%.

Both the popular and the scholarly press have lauded the economic development of Asia using such hyperbole as 'miracle' and 'astounding' to describe nations whose economies were little more than rubble after World War II and the Korean War. Observers have marvelled at the ability of countries with poor resources not only to grow, but also to become world-class competitors in the most advanced industrial sectors, including automobiles, steel, shipbuilding, electronics, and pharmaceuticals.

It is no small irony that precisely those countries that Westerners have marvelled at have come under severe attack for their patterns of economic development and international trade practices. Analysts and trade negotiators describe Japan and her neighbours as being 'unfair' in bilateral trading relations, and suffering 'imperfections' that 'distort' their domestic economies. These criticisms are most often levelled at the dense networks of ties between firms in Asia, ties that look like cartels to Westerners. Network ties link major industrial firms into groups, such as Sumitomo in Japan and Samsung in Korea, as well as the myriad small manufacturers in the Taiwanese economy.

Why the paradox? Why should Asian economies that have been extraordinarily successful by every economic measure at the same time be described as unprincipled and distorted? Is it merely a reflection of Westerners' sense of fair play or perhaps even their own inadequacy in the face of vigorous economic competition? Or is it a fundamental misunderstanding of the patterns of Asian capitalism?

While it is no doubt frightening to have one's economic well-being challenged by other nations' competitive success, we do not believe that this is the primary reason for the strong American critique of Asian economies. For example, the United States has had substantial trade deficits with its second-largest trading partner, Canada, for years with little public outcry. The recent heavy investment by the Japanese in the United States has met with far more invective than has US investment by the British or the Dutch, two economies that have higher levels of American investment than Japan does.

We believe, rather, that the response to Asian capitalism as unfair and distorted is primarily the result of ethnocentrism, a Western-based view of the proper organization and functioning of a market economy. American economic thinking is largely grounded in the neo-classical economic tradition. This perspective views competition between autonomous economic actors, both individual capitalists and firms acting as fictive individuals, as a necessity of mature capitalism. In numerous ways the United States has institutionalized competitive individualism in its market structure. Asian economies, in contrast, are organized through networks of economic actors that are believed to be natural and appropriate to economic development. Likewise, Asian nations have institutionalized policies and practices that flow from a network vision of correct market relations.

We argue two points in this chapter. First, Western academic and popular conceptualizations of Asia, particularly those based on the neo-classical model, are biased portrayals of Asian economic dynamics. A Western perspective leads analysts to conclude that Asia's network capitalism rests on market imperfections, and therefore that the vibrant capitalism of the region has been artificially induced and maintained. Second, and more important, the successful network structure of Asian capitalism reveals the neo-classical model to be not a general theory of capitalism, but rather an ethnocentric model developed from Western experience and applicable only to Western economies. We will not argue that neo-classical economics is wrong, merely that its utility is limited to settings where its institutional assumptions are in force.

Markets Are Not All Alike

The neo-classical economic paradigm conceives of ideal conditions for perfect competition: a large number of firms making substitutable products so that buyers have no reason to prefer one firm's output over another, independent and dispersed firms, and complete knowledge of all offers to buy and sell (Stigler 1968).

This model of competitive economic relations conceives of actors as isolated units. Capitalists, both buyers and sellers, ideally are independent and mindless of one another and indifferent as to the parties from whom they buy or whom they sell. Price is the only criterion for a transaction. This is an asocial conceptualization of economic action (Abolafia and Biggart 1990) in the sense that it believes meaningful social relations are unimportant to competitive outcomes under idealized conditions. Where social relations are recognized to occur, they are viewed pejoratively and called 'friction'. Social relations in a market can lead only to such anticompetitive practices as price-fixing, restriction of output, and other forms of collusion. Keeping economic actors apart is a crucial condition of capitalism in the neo-classical view.

Western markets, particularly the Anglo-American economies, attempt to approximate tenets of the neo-classical paradigm at the level of both firms and individuals. Laws, including corporate and employment regulations, stress individual rights and obligations. Contracts, for example, bind only on the parties involved and not on their families or communities. Employers for the most part hire, promote, and otherwise reward workers based on their personal efforts. Seniority, to many Americans, does not seem a just way of determining pay or promotion. Affirmative action laws similarly express a belief that employment decisions should be made regardless of social characteristics or connections; it is individual competence and effort that should be the basis of selection.

Americans are fearful of hiring spouses, blood relatives, and even friends into the same company. Many firms have antinepotism rules to limit the effects of personal relations in the workplace, effects assumed to be detrimental. Employers may require disclosure of stock ownership and other ties, even through relatives, to outside firms. Disclosure guards against favouritism in awarding contracts, something most Americans think is wrong.

An individualistic institutional structure exists at the corporate level as well. State regulatory agencies, such as the Federal Trade Commission, prevent firms from colluding with each other. Strong antitrust laws enforced by the Attorney General limit monopoly power and the formation of cartels, except under very unusual situations (such as public utilities, where there exists what economists call a 'natural' monopoly). The role of the US government in the economy is largely a regulatory one. Government does not have a co-ordinated planning role, and does not have a strategic management plan for the United States' place in the world economy. Its primary function is to maintain competitive – that is, autonomous – conditions between economic actors.

At both the level of individuals and the level of corporations, people in the United States act to maintain an 'open' market in which independent buyers, sellers, and workers can pursue their own interests in arm's-length transactions. In the United States 'open' means free from social relations between individuals and firms.

Market Conditions in Asia

The free market conditions Westerners think are crucial technical requisites for a successful capitalist economy are frequently not in evidence in Asia. In fact, they are often not even presumed to be necessary. Asian economies espouse different institutional logics from Western economies, ones rooted in connectedness and relationships: Asians believe that social relations between economic actors do not impede market functioning, but rather promote it. Just as Western economies have institutionalized ways of maintaining autonomy between actors, Asian economies are rooted in institutions that encourage and maintain ties.

For example, the crucial economic actor in Asian societies is typically not the individual, but rather the network in which the individual is embedded. In major Japanese firms, cohorts are often hired, compensated, and promoted, with individual performance differences having little import until late in a career (Clark 1979). Korean firms encourage workers to nominate their friends and relatives for vacant jobs; Koreans believe that social relations exert pressure on workers to perform well and to work hard for fear of embarrassing their nominators. The major source of venture capital in Taiwan, a country noted for its economy of small-scale entrepreneurial concerns, is friends and relatives (Biggs 1988). Impersonal sources of funds, such as banks and unknown investors, are far less important in Taiwan than in Western societies. In all three countries, buyers favour suppliers with whom they have an established relation, rather than the least-cost supplier. They routinely violate the neo-classical expectation that price is the critical factor in purchase decisions.

Although relationships are manifest in multiple ways at the interpersonal level in Asian business, they are seen dramatically and most importantly in business networks between Asian firms. It is impossible to underestimate the importance of business networks – sometimes called enterprise or business groups – to the development of Asian capitalism. The Japanese economy is dominated by *kigyo shudan*, modern-day descendants of pre-World War II *zaibatsu*, family-controlled conglomerates. Kigyo shudan are networks of firms in unrelated businesses that are joined together, no longer by family ties, but by central banks or trading companies. Michael Gerlach (1992) has recently argued that these inter-market networks constitute a form of capitalism that he calls 'alliance capitalism'. Many of the largest firms in Japan are members of these major business networks: Mitsubishi, Mitsui, Sumitomo, Fuji, Dai-Ichi, and Sanwa. Other forms of networks link Japanese businesses. For example, a major manufacturer and its affiliated subcontractors (e.g., the Toyota 'independent group'), and small neighbourhood retailers (*gai*) that may invest together (Orru, Hamilton, and Suzuki 1989).

The South Korean economy is dominated by networks that on the surface resemble Japan's, but in fact have substantial differences (Amsden 1989; Whitley 1990; Kim 1991; Biggart 1990; Orru, Biggart, and Hamilton 1991; Hamilton and Biggart 1988). South Korean *chaebol* are networks of firms owned and controlled by a single person or family and organized through a central staff, which may be a holding company or 'mother' firm. By far the most powerful actors in the Korean economy are the major chaebol networks, which include Samsung, Hyundai, Lucky-Goldstar, Daewoo.

The Japanese and Korean economies are ruled by networks of medium-sized to very large firms. Networks are important in Taiwan, too, but they link smaller numbers of smaller firms (Numazaki 1986; Hamilton and Kao 1990; Hamilton and Biggart 1988). The leading economic actor in Taiwan, although occupying a less central position than the kigyo shudan or chaebol, is the family firm and family-owned conglomerates, which are called *jituanqiye*. Chinese business networks are usually based on family and friendship ties between owners and partners who often cross-invest in businesses, hold multiple positions throughout the network, and act as suppliers or upstream producers to downstream firms.

What the American economy works so studiously to prevent – connections between individuals, links between firms – Asian economies accept as appropriate and inevitable. Moreover, Asian nations have institutionalized networks and built economic policies around the presence and presumption of social relations among market actors.

Explaining Differences

With the extraordinary success of Asian economies, both business people and scholars have attended to the apparent differences between Asian and Western business practices. Analysts hope to understand the differences in order to explain success, to project patterns of growth, and to predict likely competitive outcomes of Asian economic practices. There are diverse explanations for Asian economic differences from the west, but three types of theories are most influential: development theories, culture theories, and market imperfection theories.

Development theory

Development theories are concerned with the factors that aid or impede economies in their presumed march toward industrialization. In their earliest form, 'modernization' theories assumed a linear progression that all nations passed through on the path toward development into a modern capitalist economy, epitomised by the United States and industrialized Europe. There was the presumption that stages of development were more or less alike and that at some unspecified future moment there would be a convergence, with all market economies having similar market institutions – for example, a capitalist class, a freely accessible money and banking system, a rational orientation toward economic matters.

More recent versions of modernization theory argue that learning is possible; countries can skip stages by observing and emulating more advanced nations, or by having 'modern' economic practices imposed on them through colonial subjugation, for example, or as a precondition for development loans. Alice Amsden's *Asia's Next Giant: South Korea and Late Industrialization* (1989) is in this genre, arguing that South Korea was able to rapidly industrialize, leapfrogging early development stages, by appropriating technologies and processes formulated by more advanced nations.[1]

Alternatively, another set of development theories, conventionally labelled 'dependency' theories, argues that the more-developed industrial economies are systemically linked to and impede the development of the less-developed economies (Evans and Stephens 1988). Powerful advanced nations maintain the dependency of less-developed economies by enforcing, for example, unfavourable trading relations or lending policies. A web of political relations shapes nations' differential possibilities for advancement.

There are a number of criticisms of development theories (Evans and Stephens 1988). It is increasingly clear, for example that there is no convergence toward a single model of capitalism as exemplified by the West. It is also equally apparent that the world economy is neither a monolithic economic system nor easily divided into core and peripheral areas (Gereffi and Hamilton 1990). Moreover, Asia's differences, as well as those of some other industrializing nations, are not disappearing as they become more developed (Orru, Biggart, and Hamilton 1991). While it is certainly true that nations can learn from more developed economies, the learning thesis is not especially useful because it cannot predict which countries can or will learn, or indeed which models they will choose to emulate. For example, both Taiwan and South Korea were colonies of Japan, and both received substantial economic aid and policy directives from the United States. Neither economy looks very much like the United States or Japan, although Korea has adopted some elements of Japanese industrial organization.

One branch of development economics, the endogenous growth models, does ask why differences in the fact and rate of economic growth and well-being persist over time. Neo-classical economic models predict that capital, both labour and financial, flows to the most efficient locales, eventually limiting nation-state differences. In fact, there is great diversity in per capita economic well-being and national growth rates, and the differences endure. Endogenous growth models posit that variations are attributable to differences in trade policies and human capital differences – that is, the differential investment in learning by various labour forces. Labour forces are not all the same in their approach to hard work, learning, and productivity. Endogenous growth models go beyond an earlier individualistic approach to human capital, which focused on the returns on investment in learning by individuals, to posit that there are social returns on effects, at the level of groups such as families and firms, to the acquisition of new skills and orientations by labour. It seems to us that this perspective is important in raising the unit of observation from the individual to the group, showing the cumulative effects of individual economic decisions (for example, to invest in school rather than to take a low-skilled job). By focusing on effects, however, endogenous growth models do not seek answers as to why observably different patterns are pursued in different locales, whether they be trade policies or human capital decisions. R. E. Lucas, for example, dismisses the possibility of identifying the social impulse for human capital acquisition: 'We can no more directly measure the amount of human capital a society has, or the rate at which it is growing, than we can measure the degree to which a society is imbued with the Protestant Ethic' (1988: 35).

Culture theory

Culture theories do precisely what the endogenous growth models leave aside: attempt to account for the differential bases for economic action and organization. They are popular in journalistic accounts of Asian management practice, but also have academic standing (e.g., Berger and Hsiao 1988). Culture – the beliefs, values, symbols – of a society is understood to be the basis for economic practices and institutions. For example, the Japanese penchant for involving all members of a firm in decision making is seen to be an expression of a belief in the importance of consensus and harmony (*wa*) (Alston 1986). In contrast, the American CEO is expected to make independent decisions, probably after consulting subordinates, but ultimately to take individual responsibility. The two sets of decision-making practices, common in their respective economies, are explained by culture theory as respective expressions of the cultural values of communitarianism and individualism.

Cultural explanations have much truth in them; clearly, a preference for groupness or individualism will be reflected in commercial practices. Culture, though, is a problematic basis for comparative analysis (Hamilton and Biggart 1988: S69–S74). American culture, even if one could define it, cannot explain the differences in business practice one encounters in the United States. Is IBM's strong hierarchical management style the 'true' organizational expression of American culture? Or is Apple Computer's decentralized and team-based system the 'real' exemplar of American ideals? When comparing Japan with the West, which Western practices form the basis of comparison? Culture theories, by building up from rich and diverse data in a single society, make generalizations – and hence comparisons – difficult.

Market imperfection theory

Market imperfection theory is based on the logic of neo-classical economics and is the most important explanation of Asian distinctiveness. Under perfectly competitive market conditions, optimal firm size is a function of the demand for and the economies of scale to produce a product (Stigler 1968: 1). When markets are not fully competitive, that is, when they suffer from constraints, then firm size is influenced by the constraints as well as by production and demand requirements. For example, when there is no market, as in a socialist command economy, then decrees by the state will influence the size and structure of the firm. Although economists recognize that a fully competitive market is an ideal condition that does not exist anywhere in reality, they use this conception of the ideal market and the optimal firm as a model against which to assess real conditions. They can then compare actual markets and firms to see how well they conform to the ideal. Deviations are either more or less 'perfect'.

This conceptualization of the perfect market, with its conditions of autonomy and impersonality and its resultant 'optimal' firms, was developed as a means to understand the structure and functioning of Western societies, primarily the British and American economies. Economists, however, do not regard this model as an abstract, ethnocentric representation of these economies, but rather as a general model of capitalism that can be applied worldwide.

According to neo-classical theory there are only two forms of economic organization: markets and firms (also called hierarchies). Economists have difficulty applying this model of markets and firms to Asia with its developed interfirm networks (Aoki 1984, 1990; Goto 1982). Networks are neither independent market actors, nor hierarchically governed firms. Nonetheless, Western economists attempt to interpret Asian economic organization in terms of this dualistic neo-classical conceptualization. Alfred Chandler, for example, describes the Japanese zaibatsu, the historical precursor to the kigyo shudan, as an 'organization comparable to the M-form', or multidivisional firm that originated in the United States (1982, p. 22). Nathaniel Leff (1976, 1978) writes that Asian firms, as well as firms in other non-Western societies, actually constitute a single firm organized on a 'group principle'. 'The group is a multicompany firm which transacts in different markets but which does so under common entrepreneurial and financial control' (Leff 1978, p. 644). Others endorse the idea that despite some differences, the Asian business group is the functional equivalent of the Western firm. Like Western firms, some groups are large and monopolistic while others are small or operate in competitive markets in which the group principle allows economies of scale without actually expanding the size of firms.

Several Japanese economists (Aoki 1984; Goto 1982) have slightly qualified this view. Knowing Japan well, they argue that Japanese business groups are neither firms nor markets, but constitute an intermediate phenomenon that exists between the two. They argue that Japanese business groups do not operate like a single firm. They have neither a single set of owners, nor a tightly integrated system of financial controls. They are not independent, competitive firms, nor do they constitute a single megafirm. They are networks, according to Goto (1982), that buffer and channel market forces.

Despite some disagreement about how to categorize Asian business groups, economists do concur on how to explain their presence. Virtually all use a theory of market imperfections that to neo-classical economists seems self-evident. States Leff:

> The group pattern of industrial organization is readily understood as a micro-economic response to well-known conditions of market failure in the less-developed countries. In fact, the emergence of the group as an institutional mode might well have been predicted on the basis of familiar theory and a knowledge of the environment in these countries (1978: 666).

Chandler (1982) explains the differences between the Japanese zaibatsu and the M-form American and European conglomerates by citing 'undeveloped' capital markets in Japan. Even Goto explains Japanese business group networks the same way:

> The group is an institutional device designed to cope with market failure as well as internal organizational failure. Under certain circumstances, transactions within a group of firms are more efficient than transactions through the market or transactions through the internal organization of the firm (1982, p. 69).

More recently, but using the same logic, Jorgensen, Hafsi, and Kiggundu (1986) argue that in developing countries, a category in which they place Japan, market imperfections occur in the course of 'striving for self-sufficiency' and the absence of an adequate 'density of market transactions' (424). In promoting a 'rational', risk-controlling policy for industrialization, governments promote such market 'distortions' as tariffs to protect infant industries, exchange controls to create price advantages, and administrative hierarchies to co-ordinate resource allocation and other forms of market imperfections (426). They note four common 'aberrations' in developing economies: the entrepreneurial family firm, the industrial cluster, the multinational corporation subsidiary, and the state-owned enterprise (427–32). All four of these so-called aberrations are common in Asian economies, even the most developed, and are not disappearing.

There are other variants of the market imperfection thesis. Political economists emphasize the importance of the 'developmental state' in creating systemic distortions, both in the economy and in the society, that allow for concentrated capital accumulation and rapid development. Such theorists thus create a link between market imperfection and development theories. American trade negotiators likewise argue that Japan has created 'structural impediments' to 'free' trade that prevent American access to Japanese markets; most notable of the alleged impediments are business groups that limit competition. Although they focus more on political factors that create distortions, the logic of both political economists and trade negotiators is much the same as the market-imperfections thesis: Asian economies deviate from the Western ideal and therefore suffer imperfections.

We believe that market imperfection theories, like developmental and cultural theories, do not explain the Asian 'difference' very well. The neo-classical paradigm is a framework that assumes one fundamental 'perfect' economy against which real economies can be gauged. Although it does not exist anywhere in reality, the model is an approximation of the market economies that developed during Western industrialization. It is not a theory of Asian capitalism but a theory of Western capitalism applied to Asia, and its logic is akin to the logic of Henry Higgins' question in *My Fair Lady*: 'Why can't a woman be more like a man?' Answers to a question so framed can only detail the ways in which a woman deviates from a man; they cannot lead to discovery of what a woman is. A market imperfection theory can describe the ways in which Asian capitalism deviates from the neo-classical ideal, but it cannot discover the principles of Asian capitalism.

Evidence of the economic vitality of Asia leads us to advance two points. First, a model of Asian capitalism based on Asia's institutional foundations is overdue. It stretches credibility to describe Japan, the world's second-largest economy, as 'imperfect' or 'deviant', even for analytic purposes. Second, the poor fit of the neo-classical model to the Asian case, suggests to us not an imperfect economy, but rather an inappropriate theory. Asia calls into questions the presumption that this model is a general theory of capitalism. We will argue that the neo-classical model is more suited to the institutional arena that it was developed to explain: England and the United States. In fact, neo-classical economics rests on an institutional theory of firm autonomy that displays great power in explaining Western economic dynamics. It is not, however, a general theory of capitalism.

THE DEVELOPMENT OF MARKETS IN THE WEST

The neo-classical model is based on a central idea: the autonomy of economic actors, both individuals and firms, who seek their self-interest in economic matters. Actors go into the marketplace and, mindless of all social and moral considerations, rationally calculate exchanges based only on price. This portrait of economic actors as individuated, asocial, and rational is the useful fiction that economists have drawn to provide a parsimonious behaviourist model of economic action. While few economists would argue that any real person acts exactly this way, it is assumed that this is the ideal that most people, at least in the aggregate, approximate.

Homo economicus is a generic individual distinguished not by sex, ethnicity, religion, age, or any other social characteristic. The presumption is that any person, in any place, at any time would behave more or less the same way – that is, as a rational individual. In building on this central idea, neo-classical economics assumes that social relations and characteristics do not make significant differences in economic choice. To the extent that these assumptions have a universal reality, they support claims that the neo-classical paradigm is a general theory of capitalism.

Recently, a number of scholars have attempted to question tenets of the neo-classical paradigm. For example, the individual decision-making studies of psychologists Tversky and Kahneman (1974) suggest that people are not the hyperrational actors assumed by the model. Economic sociologist Amitai Etzioni (1988) has marshalled substantial evidence that people consider moral as well as economic factors in making economic choices. Anthropologist Richard Schweder's (1986) anthropological studies of a community in India demonstrate that economic rationality is based on substantive beliefs, not abstract calculus. Similarly, Mark Granovetter has argued that the economy is embedded in social relationships and is not the aggregate activity of isolated individuals (1985). Our own studies (Hamilton and Biggart 1988; Orru, Biggart, and Hamilton 1991) have suggested, as we do in this chapter, that Asian economic action is based on different principles of social action, principles developed through the historical experience of Asian nations.

While these and other studies question crucial elements of the neo-classical model, particularly as they apply to non-Western locales, it remains clear that the model does describe in important ways the aggregate dynamics of Western economies, especially those of the United States.

We believe that it is possible to reconcile the power of the neo-classical paradigm in understanding much of the West, with its limitations in explaining micro-economics phenomena, especially in non-Western settings: The neo-classical model assumes and tacitly incorporates many of the features of the Western societies it was developed to explain. Its 'ideal-typical' premises aptly characterize the institutional setting in which Anglo-American capitalism developed.[2]

The institutional foundations of Western markets

The rise of markets in Western Europe followed what Barrington Moore (1966) called the 'routes' that Western nations took in moving from feudalism to modernity. At the first of the period, sometime before the thirteenth century, markets were embedded in *oikos* economy dominated by aristocratic households. A market city either comprised a part of the manor and was actually owned by the lords of the land (Koebner, 1964), or existed as a free city, characterized by Weber (1968, pp. 1212–36) as a 'non-legitimate' enclave located at the margin of a manorial economy. Although it varied from region to region, the feudal economy was embedded in the political structure of Western Europe, and when that structure began to change decisively with the rise of absolutism, market economies also began to change.

Absolutism gradually moved the organizing locus of the economy from manors to cities, particularly national cities such as London and Paris that were dominated by kings. Mercantilism followed an economic policy designed to fill royal treasuries, which were used mainly to pay for navies and land armies needed to defend or expand territory. When European kings had difficulty gaining revenues from territory owned by their fellow aristocrats, they tried to compensate by creating royal companies, such as the East India Company, designed to generate royal surplus from overseas adventures. Mercantilistic policies created national urban-centred, consumer-oriented economies. Urban-centred consumption in turn fostered an integrated marketing system linking urban, rural, and overseas areas and nurtured rural industries that produced raw resources and handicraft items for urban consumption (Jones 1987). Although commercial markets were certainly growing and prospering, the mercantilistic economy rested on royal institutions, including the kings' courts and the kings' companies.

The revolutionary period, starting in the last half of the eighteenth century, entirely changed the institutional structure of Western economies and accelerated the growth of 'free market' capitalism. Social scientists have described the changes from a mercantilistic to a free market economy as a 'great transformation' (Polanyi 1957). The phrase is somewhat hyperbolic for economic activity but quite accurate for the institutional change that occurred after these revolutions, a period in which all the major economic institutions that we associate with capitalism first developed.

The change in government from absolutism to democracy marked a pivotal switch from an institutional environment based on centralized public spheres to one dispersed through decentralized private spheres. With great insight, Michel Foucault (1979) has described this shift in connection with the institutions for criminal justice, but an even larger and more profound shift occurred in the regulation and conduct of the economic activity. Isomorphic with the shift in other institutional spheres, the shift in the economic sphere in Western Europe and the United States moved from centrally instituted economies through royal banks, companies, courts, market taxes – all institutions against which Adam Smith (1991) inveighed in his *Wealth of Nations* – to a 'self-regulating' economy. The economic counterpart of Bentham's Panopticon that so intrigued Foucault (1979) was the commodity and equity markets created in the same period as circular Panopticon prisons. Both institutional structures embodied the principles of self-regulation: in the circular market pit, where all buyers and all sellers exchange simultaneously, everyone sees everything.

The institutionalization of firm autonomy

Underlying self-regulation in markets, as in prisons, was the notion of the autonomy of individual units. In the criminal justice system, as in society in general, rested the presumption that every individual was distinct and responsible for his or her own actions. The same principles applied in the economy: every firm was distinct and responsible for its own actions.

This belief in individual autonomy, as applied to both people and their businesses, arose out of an intellectual tradition that is characteristically Western. The strands of this tradition can be traced to antiquity, particularly to the Roman legal system, which had decisive effects on modern Western European state structure, citizenship, commercial law, and to Christianity, which conceptualized each individual as a distinct soul-bearing entity. Despite the many strands, however, the institutionalization of individual autonomy did not occur until after absolutism gave way to democracy.

The cornerstone of self-regulating markets based on firm autonomy came from the Enlightenment philosophers' reconceptualization of private property. In Western Europe, with the enactment of the constitutional state based on natural laws, ownership and control of property were not so much an economic issue as a political issue with economic implications. Property rights became a crucial principle in the articulation of democracy, an idea used by citizens to claim rights over jurisdictions that formerly had been held by absolutist monarchs. The writings of eighteenth-century philosophers, such as John Locke and slightly later Adam Smith, are rife with the notion of private property and its implications for individual political control vis-à-vis an authoritarian stage. Therefore, when constitutional states were enacted, the right to property was embodied in individualism, in the very conception of what an individual was.

The idea of individual autonomy in a society is the principle of nineteenth-century democracy, and the idea of firm autonomy in the economy is the principle of self-regulating markets in a democratic society. These ideas were not only abstract philosophies, but also working principles gradually instituted throughout society to conform to changing social and economic conditions. Such abstract ideas have a very technical dimension when they are used to order everyday reality.

The legal assignment of private rights requires a clear delineation of who claims ownership and what is owned. When non-state businesses in the West were subsumed under the legal definition of private property, business firms became in principle separate, distinct, and independent. They became conceptualized as a person – as autonomous, legally indivisible units that could form contractual links with people and with other firms. The clearest demonstration of this occurred in the United States, where under the Fourteenth Amendment corporations were held to be a person and could not be 'deprived of life, liberty, or property' without due process.

In the early nineteenth century, when businesses were small and individually or family owned, firms were equated with property and due process applied to their owners, and not to the firms as separate entities. With the growth of American capitalism and large firms with multiple owners, the firm itself took on the status of an individual. The test case in the US Supreme Court in 1882 was a conflict between a California county and the Southern Pacific Railway Company. The issue was who owed taxes to the government. The Court upheld the idea, already established, that 'incorporation' created a unified entity – literally, a body – that had an existence over and above the parts that made it up.

This legal formulation had far-reaching effects on the development of Western business practices. Importantly, the law required the individuation of firms. Each firm was conceptualized as a separate body, a single entity distinct from all others. Business practices conformed to this principle, not because it was efficient or necessary, but because it was the law and deeply rooted in Western political and social ideas. The principle of individual corporateness established an institutional environment that formed a basis for Western capitalism's organizational structure and dynamics.

As legislated by most Western countries, and independently by states in the United States, laws of incorporation require firm autonomy, require the specification of ownership and corporate assets. National and state laws of taxation demand accounting procedures that delineate ownership and income. Capital markets assume that firms are autonomous: the loan provisions of the banking system, the equity provisions of the stock markets, the insurance provisions of industry all have institutionalized the principle of firm autonomy. Antitrust legislation, in working to prevent cartels and monopolies, provides sanctions to sustain autonomous corporations.

Firm autonomy has been institutionalized in many ways. A part of this process has been to work out legally and procedurally modes of legitimate interfirm linkages. That firms are really autonomous from all other firms or that individuals are entirely independent of one another is, of course, a fiction. But it is a fiction that was created historically as a means to specify institutionally the interrelation among people in the creation of a democratic political order. The fiction of autonomy became true, with time, for firms as well as for people. Interrelationships between businesses and people in the West are specified in legal terms, through contracts – that is, through autonomous entities exercising their free will to make agreements. Firm autonomy and personal autonomy are not independent of the institutions that reinforce such autonomy.

Therefore, to see firm autonomy as a universal element of capitalism, as something inherent to it in all time and all places, is really a misreading of history and of economies. It is a profoundly ethnocentric point of view.

The Development of Markets in Asia

It is incorrect to think that Asian economies 'matured' only after being exposed to Western capitalism. While it is certainly the case that they changed considerably after the nineteenth century opening of Chinese and Japanese economies, it is not the case that the respective economies were undeveloped before the nineteenth century. The dazzling innovation in, and virtual explosion of, Western societies and economies after the seventeenth century have obscured the fact that Asian societies were economically quite advanced and quite complex. Although neither was heading toward industrial capitalism, both Japanese and Chinese economies were quite dynamic and quite old. They had been mature for a long time.

The organization of these economies, like the organization of society, rested on principles quite different from those found in the West. The great historian of Chinese science, Joseph Needham, has clarified these differences by contrasting Chinese 'associative thinking' with what he calls the Western 'billiard ball' conception of reality. Westerners, he says, see their world in terms of 'rational' cause and effect: like billiard balls bounding off each other, one motion causes another motion, which causes another motion in turn. Had he written later, he might have called this the 'rational choice' model of human behaviour: reduced to individual units, causative, and lawlike.

According to Needham (1956, pp. 279–91), a Chinese world-view is completely unlike a Western one. Although highly developed and more advanced than Western science until the seventeenth and eighteenth centuries, Chinese science did not rest on correlations based on cause and effect, on first principles, or on lawlike assertions. Instead, Chinese science rests on a conception of order. In the Chinese thinking, order rests on a stable relationship among things. There is order in a family when all the relationships in a family are obeyed; there is order in a country when all the reciprocal relationships between subjects and rulers are fulfilled; there is order in the universe when mankind fulfils its relationship with heaven and earth. Needham (1956, p. 286) compares this Chinese notion of order to a dance that has no beginning and no ending and in which all partners dance in time to the music: 'an extremely and precisely ordered universe, in which things "fitted" so exactly that you could not insert a hair between them.' Everything causes everything else. Therefore, what is essential in life is not the individual cause and effect, but the order in the group as a whole.

In Asian societies the principle informing human behaviour is not for people to obey the law, whether God's laws or natural laws or economic laws. Instead it is for people to create order by obeying the requirements of human relationships as these are manifest in a situational context. The person in Asia is always embedded in ongoing relationships and is not an abstract entity that exists outside society, not even for purposes of rational calculation.

Just as individualism is institutionalized in the Western societies, social relationships are institutionalized in Asian societies. Legal codes in Asia, as many have argued, are in fact codifications of morality embedded in social relationships. For instance, the Tang Dynasty legal codes, which influenced Japan's legal codes and were passed down more or less intact through all the remaining dynasties in China, made unfilial behaviour to one's parents one of the 'Ten Abominations', and a crime punishable by death. Other relationships, such as those outlined in the *wulun* (five relationships: parent/child, emperor/subject, husband/wife, older sibling/younger sibling, and friend), were upheld in the magistrate's courts as well as in quasi-legal settings such as the lineage, village, and merchant associations. Because everyone has a responsibility for order in a group, failure to uphold one's responsibility in a relationship could lead not only to personal punishment, but also to the punishment of others in one's group. In this way mutual surveillance has come to be an essential part of the institutionalization of social relationships in East Asian societies. The Western concept of an individual's 'right to privacy' has no meaning in an Eastern setting.

The eminent Chinese sociologist Fei Xiaotong (1992) shows that this relational logic produces a society that rests on social networks. Every person is a part of multiple networks: family, friends, neighbours, co-workers – the list goes on and on. Each person is not an independent, self-willed actor, but rather is responsible simultaneously for the order within multiple networks;

135

Fei shows that network ties are ranked, with family ties taking precedence over more distant kin-ship ties, which in turn may (or may not, depending on the context) have priority over ties with other types of people. Fei also shows that every institutional sphere, including the economy, is based on a structure of networks of relationships.

The institutional foundations of Asian markets

Using these insights, we can show that network organization is an institutional feature of Asian capitalism. These networks precede the modern era. For instance, in China during the Ming and Qing Dynasties (extending from the sixteenth to the twentieth centuries), commercial activities and handicraft industries were highly developed with a level of production and a volume of movement exceeding all other locations in the world until the eighteenth century. This level of complexity was achieved without support from the state, even in such matters as maintaining a currency, establishing weights and measures, and creating commercial laws. In short, creating order within the worlds of merchants and artisans was not a function undertaken by the impe-rial state, but one that remained in the hands of those actually engaged in business.

Through *huiguan*, associations of fellow regionals, merchants and artisans themselves estab-lished and enforced economic standards that created predictability and continuity in the mar-ketplace (Hamilton 1985). Huiguan were literally meeting halls, places where people from the same native place would congregate. As a number of researchers have shown (Fewsmith 1983; Golas 1977; Hamilton 1979; and Skinner 1977) all the main merchant groups in late imperial China were out-of-towners organized through huiguan. Within the huiguan, people with com-mon origins were pledged to a moral relationship (*tongxiang guanxi*) that generated sufficient trustworthiness for them to monopolize an area or areas of business for themselves. They would set and enforce standards for the trade as well as moral standards for fellow regionals in the trade.

Although the regional associations mediated the trading relationships, the actual firms engaged in business were always family firms. The family firms, through their ties with other firms, often owned by fellow regionals, stretched beyond any one locale. In fact, through using native place ties as the medium of organization, merchants were able to monopolize commerce in a commodity for an entire region, as the Swatow merchants did for the sugar trade for all of China. The success of the overseas Chinese in Southeast Asia in the nineteenth century was organizationally based on regional networks.

In the premodern era, Japanese merchants were organized quite differently from the Chinese merchants. Japanese merchants were organized as members of city-based guilds. Unlike Chinese firms, which would come and go, Japanese merchant and artisan firms were members of stable communities of firms, each one of which would be passed from father to eldest son or to a surrogate for him. Whereas Chinese firms would often be dissolved at the death of the owner because of partible inheritance, many Japanese firms continued intact for generations. Moreover, as members of stable networks of urban-based firms, Japanese merchants often devel-oped long-term creditor-debtor relationships with members of the samurai class.

In the modern era, the same general network configurations persist both in overseas Chinese communities, including Taiwan, Hong Kong and Southeast Asia, and in modern Japan. Continually changing patrilineal networks of small firms that connect near and distant kin, and frequently friends, into production-and-supply networks characterize modern Chinese economies. Likewise, relatively stable business networks of large firms dominate the modern Japanese economy. Neither Asian social sphere has ever had a legacy of autonomous firms comparable to those of the West, nor are they likely to develop. Recent scholarship confirms that the institutional environments that support associative network relationships remain strong in Asia at the interpersonal, business, and state levels.

Conclusion: The Neo-Classical Paradigm as an Institutional Theory

The fundamental assumptions of neo-classical economics include the idea that economic actors are rational and autonomous, and that they seek their self-interest independent of social relations or characteristics. Even a brief examination of the history of Western Europe demonstrates that these characteristics of individuals, to the extent that they are true now, were not always evident. In feudal society, people were not autonomous but were bound by traditional ties of fealty and homage. In absolutist Europe, people belonged to the 'body politic' that was personified by the king himself (Kantorowicz 1957). Kings 'embodied' nations, so that individuals within those jurisdictions were presumed to have no ultimate autonomy. Only after the institutionalization of the constitutional states in the West did an order arise in which the building blocks of societies and economies – people and firms – became rationally and systematically individuated.

The factors that neo-classical economics assumes are universal traits of the human condition are, in fact, part of the development of the modern West. Western institutions are embodiments of beliefs in individual autonomy and economic rationality. Now institutionalized, these principles are reproduced by individuals and firms who go about acting 'rationally' and 'autonomously'. Neo-classical economics captures, at least at some level, institutional characteristics of American and European societies, and it would be surprising if this theory did not work well in explaining important aspects of Western economic activity. Nonetheless, this paradigm cannot sustain a claim to universal status. It fits poorly the Asian economies that do not have the same institutional heritage. Asian societies have never had a Western-style legal system that treated each person as a separate entity, equal to all others. Asia has had no salvationist religion from which to derive a principle of individual rights. Individuals are not the basic social, economic, or political units in Asia. Rather, networks of people linked together through differentially categorized social relationships form the building blocks of Asian social orders and derive from Asia's institutional history. Individuals play roles in these networks, to be sure, but it is the networks that have stability. The presence of networks – of kin, of friends, of fellow regionals – is institutionalized in business and other social practices.

Persuasive explanations for the success of Asian business will ultimately come from an institutional analysis of Asian societies and the economies that are embedded in them. Explanations will not come – indeed, cannot come – from an attempt to apply a theory rooted in Western experience to an alien institutional arena. That can only result in explaining Asia as 'imperfect' and 'distorted'.

NOTES

1 Earlier versions of this theory include Marion Levy (1972) and the very sophisticated treatment of Ronald Dore (1973) as applied to Japan.
2 This point requires a short digression into what the methods of what Milton Friedman calls 'positive economics'. Friedman (1953) makes it clear that not even those economists who believe fully in the utility of models of perfect competition would argue for the universality and the validity

of these theories. Friedman argues for the utility of economic models, but at the same time says that they are not valid or universal in an absolute sense. In this regard, economic models resemble Weberian ideal types more than they resemble natural laws. Economic models represent a slice of reality from which a few causal factors or processes are reformulated at a more abstract plane and are made more precise and internally logical. The model is then applied back to the same or like contexts from which the main elements have been abstracted in order to see how well the model predicts the actual behaviour. 'The ideal types,' says Friedman (1953, p. 36), 'are not intended to be descriptive; they are designed to isolate the features that are crucial for a particular problem.' In this role economic models, logically, neither make a truth claim nor require an assumption of universality. The model merely has to meet the test of usefulness.

REFERENCES

Abolafia, M. and Biggart, N.W. (1990) 'Competition and markets', in Etzioni, A. and Lawrence, P. (eds) *Perspectives on Socio-Economics*, M.E. Sharpe, Armonk, NY.

Alston, J. (1986) *The American Samurai*, De Gruyter, Berlin.

Amsden, A. (1989) *Asia's Next Giant: South Korea and Late Industrialization*, Oxford University Press, Oxford.

Aoki, M. (1984) *The Economic Analysis of the Japanese Firm*, North-Holland, Amsterdam.

Aoki, M. (1990) 'Toward an economic model of the Japanese firm', *Journal of Economic Literature*, Vol. 28, pp. 1–27.

Berger, P.L. and Hsin-Huang Michael Hsiao (eds) (1988) *In Search of an East Asian Development Model*, Transaction Books, New Brunswick, NJ.

Biggart, N.W. (1990) 'Institutionalized patrimonialism in Korean business', in Calhoun, C. (ed.) *Comparative Social Research*, 12. Greenwich, CT: JAI Press, pp. 113–33.

Biggs, T.S. (1988) 'Financing the emergence of small and medium enterprises in Taiwan: financial mobilization and the flow of domestic credit to the private sector'. Working paper.

Chandler, A.D. and Daems, H. (1980) *Managerial Hierarchies: comparative perspectives on the rise of the modern industrial enterprise*, Harvard University Press, Cambridge, MA.

Clark, R. (1979) *The Japanese Company*, Yale University Press, New Haven, CT.

Dore, R. (1973) *British Factory–Japanese Factory: the origins of national diversity in industrial relations*, University of California Press, Berkeley.

Etzioni, A. (1988) *The Moral Dimension: toward a new economics*, The Free Press, New York.

Evans, P.B. and Stephens, J.D. (1988) 'Development and the world economy', in Smelser, N. (ed.) *Handbook of Sociology*, Sage, Newbury Park, CA.

Fei Xiaotong (1992) *Up From the Soil: the foundations of Chinese society*, Hamilton, G. and Wang Zheng (trans.) University of California Press, Berkeley.

Fewsmith, J. (1983) 'From guild to interest group: the transformation of public and private in late Qing China', *Comparative Studies in Society and History*, Vol. 25, pp. 617–40.

Foucault, M. (1979) *Discipline and Punish: the birth of the prison*, Vintage, New York.

Friedman, M. (1953) *Essays in Positive Economics*, University of Chicago Press, Chicago, IL.

Gereffi, G. and Hamilton, G. (1990) 'Modes of incorporation in an industrial world: the social economy of global capitalism'. Unpublished paper presented at the American Sociological Association meetings, Washington, DC, August.

Gerlach, M. (1992) *Alliance capitalism: the social oganization of Japanese business*, University of California Press, Berkeley.

Golas, P.J. (1977) 'Early Ch'ing guilds', in Skinner, W. (ed.) *The City in Late Imperial China*, Stanford University Press, Stanford, pp. 555–80.

Goto, A. (1982) 'Business groups in a market economy', *European Economic Review*, Vol. 19, pp. 53–70.

Granovetter, M. (1985) 'Economic action and social structure', *American Journal of Sociology*, Vol. 91, pp. 393–426.

Hamilton, G. and Biggart, N.W. (1988) 'Market, culture, and authority: a comparative analysis of management and organization in the Far East', *American Journal of Sociology*, Vol. 94, pp. S52–S94.

Hamilton, G. and Cheng-shu Kao (1990) 'The institutional foundations of Chinese business: the family firm in Taiwan', *Comparative Social Research*, Vol. 12, pp. 95–112.

Jones, E.L. (1987) *The European Miracle*, Cambridge University Press, Cambridge.

Jorgensen, J.J., Taieb Hafsi and Kiggundu, M.N. (1986) 'Towards a market imperfections theory of organizational structure in developing countries', *Journal of Management Studies*, Vol. 24, pp. 419–42.

Kantorowicz, E. (1957) *The King's Two Bodies*, Princeton University Press, Princeton.

Kim, Eun Mee (1991) 'The industrial organization and growth of the Korean chaebol: integrating development and organizational theories', in Hamilton, G. (ed.) *Business Networks and Economic Development in East and Southeast Asia*, Centre of Asian Studies, Hong Kong.

Koebner, R. (1964) 'German towns and Slav markets', in Thupp, S. (ed.) *Change in Medieval Society*, Appleton-Century-Crofts, New York.

Leff, N. (1976) 'Capital markets in the less developed countries: the group principle', in McKinnon, R.I. (ed.) *Money and Finance in Economic Growth and Development: essays in honor of Edward S. Shaw*, M. Decker, New York, pp. 97–122.

Leff, N. (1978) 'Industrial Organization and entrepreneurship in the developing countries: the economic groups', *Economic Development and Cultural Change*, Vol. 26, pp. 661–75.

Levy, M. (1972) *Modernization: latecomers and survivors*, Basic Books, New York.

Lucas, R.E. (1988) 'On the mechanics of economic development', *Journal of Monetary Economics*, Vol. 22, pp. 3–42.

Moore, B. (1966) *Social Origins of Dictatorship and Democracy: lord and peasant in the making of the modern world*, Beacon Press, Boston.

Needham, J. (1956) *The Grand Titration*, Toronto University Press, Toronto.

Numazaki, I. (1986) 'Networks of Taiwan big business', *Modern China*, Vol. 12, pp. 487–534.

Orru, M., Biggart, N.W. and Hamilton, G. (1991) 'Organizational isomorphism in East Asia', in Powell, W.W. and DiMaggio, P. (eds.) *The New Institutionalism in Organizational Analysis*, University of Chicago Press, Chicago.

Orru, M., Hamilton, G. and Suzuki, M. (1989) 'Patterns of inter-firm control in Japanese business', *Organization Studies*, Vol. 10, pp. 549–74.

Polanyi, K. (1957) *The Great Transformation*, Beacon Press, Boston.

Schweder, R. (1986) 'Divergent rationalities', in Fiske, R.W. and Schweder, R. (eds) *Metatheory in the Social Sciences: pluralisms and subjectivities*, Chicago University Press, Chicago.

Skinner, W.F. (1977) *The City in Late Imperial China*, Stanford University Press, Stanford.

Smith, A. (1991) *The Wealth of Nations*, Knopf, New York.

Stigler, G. (1968) *The Organization of Industry*, Irwin, Homewood, IL.

Tversky, A. and Kahneman, D. (1974) 'Judgement under uncertainty: heuristics and biases', *Science*, Vol. 185, pp. 1124–31.

Weber, M. (1968) *Economy and Society*, University of California Press, Berkeley.

Whitley, R.D. (1990) 'Eastern Asian enterprise structures and the comparative analysis of forms of business organization', *Organization Studies*, Vol. 11, pp. 47–74.

8

THE ART OF STANDARDS WARS

Carl Shapiro and Hal R. Varian

Standards wars – battles for market dominance between incompatible technologies – are a fixture of the information age. Based on our study of historical standards wars, we have identified several generic strategies, along with a number of winning tactics, to help companies fighting today's – and tomorrow's – battles.

There is no doubt about the significance of standards battles in today's economy. Public attention is currently focused on the Browser War between Microsoft and Netscape (oops, America On-Line). Even as Judge Jackson evaluates the legality of Microsoft's tactics in the Browser War, the Audio and Video Streaming Battle is heating up between Microsoft and RealNetworks over software to deliver audio and video over the Internet. The 56 k Modem War of 1997 pitted 3Com against Rockwell and Lucent. Microsoft's Word and Excel have vanquished WordPerfect and Lotus 1-2-3 respectively. Most everyone remembers the Video-Cassette Recorder Duel of the 1980s, in which Matsushita's VHS format triumphed over Sony's Betamax format. However, few recall how Philips's digital compact cassette and Sony's minidisk format both flopped in the early 1990s. Then it was DVD versus Divx in the battle to replace both VCRs and CDs.

Virtually every high-tech company has some role to play in these battles, perhaps as a primary combatant, more likely as a member of a coalition or alliance supporting one side, and certainly as a customer seeking to pick a winner when adopting new technology. The outcome of a standards war can determine the very survival of the companies involved. How do you win one?

HISTORICAL EXAMPLES

Happily, companies heading off to fight a standards war do not have to reinvent the wheel. The fact is, standards wars are *not* unique to the information age. Unlike technology, the economics underlying such battles changes little, if at all, over time. We begin with three instructive standards battles of old. From these and many more historical episodes we have distilled the battle manual for standards wars that follows.

North vs. South in railroad gauges[1]

As railroads began to be built in the early 19th century, tracks of varying widths (gauges) were employed in the United States. By 1860, seven different gauges were in use in America. Just over half of the total mileage was of the 4′ 8½″ standard. The next most popular was the 5′ gauge concentrated in the South. Despite clear benefits, railroad gauge standardization faced three major obstacles: it was costly to change the width of existing tracks; each group wanted the others to make the move; and workers whose livelihoods depended upon the incompatibilities resisted the proposed changes, in fact to the point of rioting. Nonetheless, standardization was gradually achieved between 1860 and 1890. How?

The Westward expansion provided part of the answer. The big eastern railroads wanted to move western grain to the East, and pushed for new lines to the West to be at standard gauge. Since the majority of the Eastbound traffic terminated on their lines, they got their way. The Civil War played a role, too. The Union military had pressing needs for efficient East-West transportation, giving further impetus for new western lines to be built at standard gauge. In 1862, when Congress specified the standard gauge for the transcontinental railroads, the Southern states had seceded, leaving no one to push for the 5′ gauge. After the war, the Southern railroads found themselves increasingly in the minority. For the next twenty years, they relied upon various imperfect interconnections with the North and West: cars with a sliding wheel base, hoists to lift cars from one wheel base to another, and, most commonly, building a third rail.

Southern railroad interests finally threw in the towel and adopted the standard gauge in 1886. On two days during the Spring of 1886, the gauges were changed, converting 5′ gauge into the now-standard 4′8½″ gauge on more than 11,000 miles of track in the South to match the Northern standard – a belated victory for the North.

Many of the lessons from this experience are very relevant today:

- Incompatibilities can arise almost by accident, yet persist for many years.
- Network markets tend to tip towards the leading player, unless the other players coordinate to act quickly and decisively.
- Seceding from the standard-setting process can leave you in a weak market position in the future.
- A large buyer (in this case the U.S. government) can have more influence than suppliers in tipping the balance.
- Those left with the less popular technology will find a way to cut their losses, either by employing adapters or by writing off existing assets and joining the bandwagon.

Edison vs. Westinghouse in electric power: the battle of the systems[2]

Another classic 19th century standards battle concerned the distribution of electricity. Thomas Edison promoted a direct current (DC) system of electrical power generation and distribution. Edison was the pioneer in building power systems, beginning in New York City in 1882. Edison's direct current system was challenged by the alternating current (AC) technology developed and deployed in the U.S. by George Westinghouse.

Thus was joined the 'Battle of the Systems.' Each technology had pros and cons. Direct current had, for practical purposes relating to voltage drop, a one-mile limit between the generating station and the user, but was more efficient at generating power. Direct current had also had two significant commercial advantages: a head start and Edison's imprimatur.

Unlike railroads, however, standardization was less of an imperative in electricity. Indeed, the two technologies initially did not compete directly, but were deployed in regions suited to their relative strengths. DC was most attractive in densely populated urban areas, while AC made inroads in small towns. Nonetheless, a battle royal ensued in the 1887–1892 period, a struggle that was by no means confined to competition in the marketplace, but rather extended to the courtroom, the political arena, public relations, and academia. We can learn much today from the tactics followed by the rival camps.

The Edison group moved first with infringement actions against the Westinghouse forces, which forced Westinghouse to invent around Edison patents, including patents involving the Edison lamp. Edison also went to great lengths to convince the public that the AC system was unsafe, going so far as to patent the electric chair. Edison first demonstrated the electric chair using alternating current to electrocute a large dog, and then persuaded the State of New York to execute condemned criminals 'by administration of an alternating current.' The Edison group even used the term 'to Westinghouse' to refer to electrocution by alternating current.

Ultimately, three factors ended the Battle of the Systems. First and foremost, advances in polyphase AC made it increasingly clear that AC was the superior alternative. Second, the rotary converter introduced in 1892 allowed existing DC stations to be integrated into AC systems, facilitating a graceful retreat for DC. Third, by 1890 Edison had sold his interests, leading to the formation of the General Electric Company in 1892, which was no longer a DC-only manufacturing entity.[3] By 1893, both General Electric and Westinghouse were offering AC systems and the battle was over.

The battle between Edison and Westinghouse illustrates several key aspects of strategy in standards wars:

- Edison fought hard to convince consumers that DC was safer, in no small part because consumer expectations can easily become self-fulfilling in standards battles.
- Technologies can seek well-suited niches if the forces towards standardization are not overwhelming.
- Ongoing innovation (here, polyphase AC) can lead to victory in a standards war.
- A first-mover advantage (of DC) can be overcome by a superior technology (of AC), if the performance advantage is sufficient and users are not overly entrenched.
- Adapters can be the salvation of the losing technology and can help to ultimately defuse a standards war.

RCA vs. CBS in color television[4]

Our third historical example is considerably more recent: the adoption of color television in the United States fifty years ago. Television is perhaps the biggest bandwagon of them all. Some 99% of American homes have at least one television, making TV sets more ubiquitous than telephones or flush toilets.

We begin our story with the inauguration of commercial black and white television transmission in the United States on July 1, 1941. At that time, RCA – the owner of NBC and a leading manufacturer of black and white sets – was a powerful force in the radio and television world. However, the future of television was clearly to be color, which had first been demonstrated in America by Bell Labs in 1929.

Throughout the 1940s, CBS, the leading television network, was pushing for the adoption of the mechanical color television system it was developing. During this time RCA was busy selling black and white sets, improving its technology, and, under the legendary leadership of David Sarnoff, working on its own all-electronic color television system. As the CBS system took the lead in performance, RCA urged the FCC to wait for an electronic system. A major obstacle for the CBS system was that it was not backward-compatible: color sets of the CBS-type would not be able to receive existing black and white broadcasts without a special attachment.

Despite this drawback, the FCC adopted the CBS system in October 1950, after a test between the two color systems. The RCA system was just not ready. As David Sarnoff himself said, 'The monkeys were green, the bananas were blue, and everyone had a good laugh.' This was a political triumph of major proportions for CBS.

The market outcome was another story. RCA and Sarnoff refused to throw in the towel. To the contrary, they re-doubled their efforts, on three fronts. First, RCA continued to criticize the CBS system in an attempt to slow its adoption. Second, RCA intensified its efforts to place black and white sets and thus build up an installed base of users whose equipment would be incompatible with the CBS technology. 'Every set we get out there makes it that much tougher on CBS,' said Sarnoff at the time. Third, Sarnoff intensified RCA's research and development on its color television system, with around-the-clock teams working in the lab.

CBS was poorly placed to take advantage of its political victory. To begin with, CBS had no manufacturing capability at the time, and had not readied a manufacturing ally to move promptly into production. As a result, the official premier of CBS color broadcasting, on June 25, 1951, featuring Ed Sullivan among others, was largely invisible, only seen at special studio parties. There were about 12 million TV sets in America at the time, but only a few dozen could receive CBS color. Luck, of a sort, entered into the picture, too. With the onset of the Korean War, the U.S. government said that the materials needed for production of color sets were critical instead for the war effort and ordered a suspension of the manufacture of color sets.

By the time the ban was modified in June 1952, the RCA system was ready for prime time. A consensus in support of the RCA system had formed at the National Television Systems Committee (NTSC). This became known as the NTSC system, despite the fact that RCA owned most of the hundreds of patents controlling it. This re-labeling was a face-saving device for the FCC, which could be seen to be following the industry consortium rather than RCA. In March 1953, Frank Stanton, the President of CBS, raised the white flag, noting that with 23 million black and white sets in place in American homes, compatibility was rather important. In December 1953, the FCC officially reversed its 1950 decision.

However, yet again, political victory did not lead so easily to success in the market. In 1954, Sarnoff predicted that that RCA would sell 75,000 sets. In fact, only 5,000 sets were purchased, perhaps because few customers were willing to pay $1000 for the 12½″ color set rather than $300 for a 21″ black-and-white set. With hindsight, this does not seem surprising, especially since color sets would offer little added value until broadcasters invested in color capability and color programming became widespread. All this takes time. The chicken-and-egg problem had to be settled before the NBC peacock could prevail.

As it turned out, NBC and CBS affiliates invested in color transmission equipment quite quickly: 106 of 158 stations in the top 40 cities had the ability to transmit color programs by 1957. This was of little import to viewers, since the networks were far slower in offering color programming. By 1965, NBC offered 4000 hours of color, but CBS still showed only 800 color hours, and ABC 600. The upshot: by 1963, only about 3% of TV households had color sets, which remained three to five times as expensive as black and white sets.

As brilliant as Sarnoff and RCA had been in getting their technology established as the standard, they, like CBS, were unable to put into place all the necessary components of the system to obtain profitability during the 1950s. As a result, by 1959, RCA had spent $130 million to develop color TV with no profit to show for it. The missing pieces were the creation and distribution of the programming itself: content. Then, as now, a 'killer app' was needed to get households to invest in color television sets. The killer app of 1960 was 'Walt Disney's Wonderful World of Color,' which Sarnoff obtained from ABC in 1960. RCA's first operating profit from color television sales came in 1960, and RCA started selling picture tubes to Zenith and others. The rest is history: color sets got better and cheaper, and the NBC peacock became famous.

We can all learn a great deal from this episode, ancient though it is by Internet time.

- Adoption of a new technology can be painfully slow if the price/performance ratio is unattractive and if it requires adoption by a number of different players.[5]
- First-mover advantages need not be decisive, even in markets strongly subject to tipping.
- Victory in a standards war often requires building an alliance.
- A dominant position in one generation of technology (such as RCA enjoyed in the sale of black-and-white sets) does not necessarily translate into dominance in the next generation of technology.

WAR OR PEACE?

Standards wars are especially bitter – and especially crucial to business success – in markets with strong *network effects* that cause consumers to play high value on compatibility.[6] We do not consider it a coincidence that there is a single worldwide standard for fax machines and for modems (for which compatibility is crucial), while multiple formats persist for cellular telephones and digital television (for which compatibility across regions is far less important).

We do not mean to suggest that every new information technology must endure a standards war. Take the compact disk (CD) technology, for instance.

Sony and Philips pooled together and openly licensed their CD patents as a means to establish their new CD technology. While CDs were completely incompatible with the existing audio technologies of phonographs, cassette players, and reel-to-reel tapes, Sony and Philips were not in a battle with another new technology. They 'merely' had to convince consumers to take a leap and invest in a CD player and compact disks.

What is distinct about standards wars is that there are *two* firms, or more commonly alliances, vying for dominance. In some cases, one of the combatants may be an incumbent that controls a significant base of customers who use an older technology, as when Nintendo battled Sony in the video game market in the mid-1990s. Nintendo had a large installed base from the previous generation when both companies introduced 64-bit systems. In other instances, both sides may be starting from scratch, as in the battle between Sony and Matsushita in videotape machines as well as in the browser war between Netscape and Microsoft.

Standards wars can end in: a *truce*, as happened in 56k modems and color television where a common standard was ultimately adopted; a *duopoly*, as we see in video games today with Nintendo and Sony battling toe-to-toe; or a *fight to the death*, as with railroad gauges, AC versus DC electric power, and videotape players. True fight-to-the-death standards wars are unique to markets with powerful positive feedback based on strong network effects. Thus, traditional principles of strategy, while helpful, need to be supplemented to account for the peculiar economics of networks.

Before entering into a standards battle, would-be combatants are well-advised to consider a peaceful solution.[7] Unlike many other aspects of competition, where coordination among rivals would be branded as illegal collusion, declaring an early truce in a standards war can benefit *consumers* as well as vendors, and thus pass antitrust muster.[8]

Even bitter enemies such as Microsoft and Netscape have repeatedly been able to cooperate to establish standards when compatibility is crucial for market growth. First, when it appeared that a battle might ensue over standards for protecting privacy on the Internet, Microsoft announced its support for Netscape's *Open Profiling Standard*, which subsequently became part of the *Platform for Privacy Preferences* being developed by the Word Wide Web Consortium. Second, Microsoft and Netscape were able to reach agreement on standards for viewing 3-D images over the Internet. In August 1997, they decided to support compatible versions of *Virtual Reality Modeling Language*, a 3-D viewing technology, in their browsers. Again, Microsoft was pragmatic rather than proud, adopting a language invented at Silicon Graphics. Third, Microsoft and Netscape teamed up (along with Visa and MasterCard as well as IBM) to support the *Secure Electronic Transactions* standard for protecting the security of electronic payments by encrypting credit card numbers sent to online merchants. Cooperative standard-setting often takes place through the auspices of formal standard-setting organizations such as the American National Standards Institute or the International Telecommunications Union.[9]

We must note, however, the clear analogy between technology battles and military battles: the more costly a battle is to both sides, the greater are the pressures to negotiate a truce; and one's strength in battle is an overriding consideration when meeting to conduct truce talks. Whether you are planning to negotiate a product standard or fight to the death, you will benefit from understanding the art (read: economics and strategy) of standards wars.

CLASSIFICATION OF STANDARDS WARS

Not all standards wars are alike. Standards battles come in three distinct flavors. The starting point for strategy in a standards battle is to understand which type of war you are fighting. The critical distinguishing feature of the battle is the magnitude of the switching costs, or more generally the adoption costs, for each rival technology. We classify standards wars depending on how compatible each player's proposed new technology is with the current technology.

When a company or alliance introduces new technology that is *compatible* with the old, we say that they have adopted an 'Evolution' strategy. Evolutionary strategies are based on offering superior performance with minimal consumer switching or adoption costs. The NTSC color television system selected by the FCC in 1953 was evolutionary: NTSC signals could be received by black-and-white sets, and the new color sets could receive black-and-white signals, making adoption of color far easier for both television stations and households. In contrast, the CBS system that the FCC had first endorsed in 1950 was not backward compatible.

When a company or alliance introduces new technology that is *incompatible* with the old, we say that they have adopted a 'Revolution' strategy. Revolutionary strategies are based on offering such compelling performance that consumers are willing to incur significant switching or adoption costs.

If both your technology and your rival's technology are compatible with the older, established technology, but incompatible with each other we say the battle is one of 'Rival Evolutions.' Competition between DVD and Divx (both of which will play CDs), the 56k modem battle (both types communicate with slower modems), and competition between various flavors of Unix (which can run programs written for older versions of plain vanilla Unix) all fit this pattern.

145

If your technology offers backward compatibility and your rival's does not, we have 'Evolution versus Revolution.' The 'Evolution versus Revolution' war is a contest between the backward compatibility of Evolution and the superior performance of Revolution. Evolution versus Revolution includes the important case of an upstart fighting against an established technology that is offering compatible upgrades. The struggle in the late 1980s between Ashton Tate's dBase IV and Paradox in the market for desktop database software fit this pattern. (The mirror image of this occurs if your rival offers backward compatibility but you do not: 'Revolution versus Evolution.')

Finally, if neither technology is backward compatible we have 'Rival Revolutions.' The contest between Nintendo 64 and the Sony Playstation, and the historical example of AC versus DC in electrical systems, follow this pattern.

These four types of standards battles are described in Table 8.1.

KEY ASSETS IN NETWORK MARKETS

In our view, successful strategy generally must harness a firm's resources in a manner that harmonizes with the underlying competitive environment. In a standards battle, the competitive environment is usefully characterized by locating the battle in Table 8.1. What about the firms' resources?

Your ability to successfully wage a standards war depends on your ownership of seven key assets:

- control over an installed base of users;
- intellectual property rights;
- ability to innovate;
- first-mover advantages;
- manufacturing capabilities;

Table 8.1 Types of standards wars

		Rival Technology	
		Compatible	**Incompatible**
Your Technology	**Compatible**	Rival Evolutions	Evolution *versus* Revolution
	Incompatible	Revolution *versus* Evolution	Rival Revolutions

- strength in complements; and
- brand name and reputation.

What these assets have in common in that they place you in a potentially unique position to contribute to the adoption of a new technology. If you own these assets, your value-added to other players is high. Some assets, however, such as the ability to innovate or manufacturing capabilities, may even be more valuable in peace than in war.

No one asset is decisive. For example, control over an older generation of technology does not necessarily confer the ability to pick the next generation. Sony and Philips controlled CDs but could not move unilaterally into DVDs. Atari had a huge installed base of first-generation video games in 1983, but Nintendo's superior technology and hot new games caught Atari flat-footed. The early leader in modems, Hayes, tried to buck the crowd when modems operating at 9600 kbps were introduced, and ended up in Chapter 11.

Don't forget that *customers* as well as technology suppliers can control key assets, too. A big customer is automatically in 'control' of at least part of the installed base. America Online recognized this in the recent 56k modem standards battle. Content providers played a key role in the DVD standards battle. IBM was pivotal in moving the industry from 5¼″ diskettes to 3½″ disks. Most recently, TCI has not been shy about flexing its muscle in the battle over the technology used in TV set-top boxes.

Control over an installed base of customers

An incumbent firm, like Microsoft, that has a large base of loyal or locked-in customers is uniquely placed to pursue an Evolution strategy offering backward compatibility. Control over an installed base can be used to block cooperative standard setting and force a standards war. Control can also be used to block rivals from offering compatible products, thus forcing them to play the more risky Revolution strategy.

Intellectual property rights

Firms with patents and copyrights controlling valuable new technology or interfaces are clearly in a strong position. Qualcomm's primary asset in the digital wireless telephone battle was its patent portfolio. The core assets of Sony and Philips in the CD and DVD areas were their respective patents. Usually, patents are stronger than copyrights, but computer software copyrights that can be used to block compatibility can be highly valuable. This is why Lotus fought Borland all the way to the Supreme Court to try to block Borland's use of the Lotus command structure (see below), and why Microsoft watched the trial intently to protect Excel's ability to read macros originally written for Lotus 1-2-3.

Ability to innovate

Beyond your existing intellectual property, the ability to make proprietary extensions in the future puts you in a strong position today. In the color TV battle, NBC's R&D capabilities were crucial after the FCC initially adopted the CBS color system. NBC's engineers quickly developed a color system that was compatible with the existing black-and-white sets, a system which the FCC then accepted. Hewlett-Packard's engineering skills are legendary in Silicon Valley; it is often in their interest to compromise on standards since they can out-engineer their competition once the standard has been defined, even if they have to play some initial catch up.

First-mover advantages

If you already have done a lot of product development work and are farther down the learning curve than the competition, you are in a strong position. Netscape obtained stunning market capitalization based on a their ability to bring new technology to market quickly. RealNetworks currently has a big lead on Microsoft in audio and video streaming.

Manufacturing capabilities

If you are a low-cost producer, due to either scale economies or manufacturing competence, you are in a strong position. Cost advantages can help you survive a standards war, or capture share competing to sell a standardized product. Compaq and Dell both have pushed hard on driving down their manufacturing costs, which gives them a strong competitive advantage in the PC market. Rockwell has lower costs than its competitors in making chipsets for modems. HP has long been a team player in Silicon Valley, welcoming standards because of their engineering and manufacturing skills. These companies benefit from open standards, which emphasize the importance of efficient production.

Strength in complements

If you produce a product that is a significant complement for the market in question, you will be strongly motivated to get the bandwagon rolling. This, too, puts you in a natural leadership position, since acceptance of the new technology will stimulate sales of the other products you produce. This force is stronger, the larger are your gross margins on your established products. Intel's thirst to sell more CPUs has been a key driver in their efforts to promote new standards for other PC components, including interfaces between motherboards and CPUs, busses, chipsets, and graphics controllers.

Reputation and brand name

A brand-name premium in any large market is highly valuable. But reputation and brand name are especially valuable in network markets, where expectations are pivotal. It's not enough to have the best product; you have to convince consumers that you will win. Previous victories and a recognized name count for a lot in this battle. Microsoft, HP, Intel, Sony, and Sun each have powerful reputations in their respective domains, giving them instant credibility.[10]

PREEMPTION

Preemption is one of two crucial marketplace tactics that arise over and over again in standards battles. The logic of preemption is straightforward: build an early lead, so positive feedback works for you and against your rival. The same principle applies in markets with strong learning-by-doing: the first firm to gain significant experience will have lower costs and can pull even further ahead. Either way, the trick is to exploit positive feedback. With learning-by-doing, the positive feedback is through lower costs. With network externalities, the positive feedback comes on the demand side; the leader offers a more valuable product or service.

One way to preempt is simply to be first to market. Product development and design skills can be critical to gaining a first-mover advantage. But watch out: early introduction also can entail compromises in quality and a greater risk of bugs, either of which can doom your product. This was the fate of the color television system promoted by CBS and of Japan's HDTV system. The race belongs to the swift, but speed must come from superior product design, not by marketing an inferior system.

In addition to launching your product early, you need to be aggressive early on to build an installed base of customers. Find the 'pioneers' (a.k.a. gadget freaks) who are most keen to try new technology and sign them up swiftly. Pricing below cost (i.e., *penetration pricing*) is a common tactic to build an installed base. Discounting to attract large, visible, or influential customers is virtually unavoidable in a standards war.

In some cases, especially for software with a zero marginal cost, you can go beyond free samples and actually *pay* people to take your product. As we see it, there is nothing special about zero as a price, as long as you have multiple revenue streams to recover costs. Some cable television programmers pay cable operators to distribute their programming, knowing that a larger audience will augment their advertising revenues. In the same fashion, Netscape is prepared to give away its browser for free, or even pay OEMs (original equipment manufacturers) to load it on new machines, in order to increase the usage of Navigator and thus direct more traffic to the Netscape Web site.

The big danger with negative prices is that someone will accept payment for 'using' your product and then not really use it. This problem is easily solved in the cable television context, because programmers simply insist that cable operators actually carry their programming once they are paid to do so. Likewise, Netscape can check that an OEM loads Navigator (in a specified way) on new machines, and can conduct surveys to see just how the OEM configuration affects usage of Navigator.[11]

Before you go overboard giving your product away, or paying customers to take it, you need to ask three questions. First, if you pay someone to take your product, will they really use it and generate network externalities for other, paying customers? Second, how much is it really worth to you to build up your installed base? Where is the offsetting revenue stream, and when will it arrive? Third, are you fooling yourself? Beware the well-known 'Winner's Curse': the tendency of the most optimistic participant to win in a bidding war, only to find that they were overly optimistic and other bidders were more realistic.

Penetration pricing may be difficult to implement if you are building a coalition around an 'open' standard. The sponsor of a proprietary standard can hope to recoup the losses incurred during penetration pricing once it controls an established technology. Without a sponsor, no single supplier will be willing to make the necessary investments to preempt using penetration pricing. For precisely this reason, penetration pricing can be particularly effective when used by a company with a proprietary system against a rival touting its openness.

Another implication is that the player in a standards battle with the largest profit streams from related products stands to win the war. We have seen this with smart cards in Europe. They were introduced with a single application – public telephone service – but soon were expanded to other transactions involving small purchases. Eventually, many more applications such as identification and authentication will be introduced. Visa, MasterCard, and American Express are already jockeying for position in the smart card wars. Whichever player can figure out the most effective way to generate multiple revenue streams from an installed base of smart card holders will be able to bid most aggressively, but still profitably, to build up the largest base of customers.

EXPECTATIONS MANAGEMENT

The second key tactic in standards wars is the management of expectations. Expectations are a major factor in consumer decisions about whether or not to purchase a new technology, so make sure that you do your best to manage those expectations. Just as incumbents will try to knock down the viability of new technologies that emerge, so will those very entrants strive to establish credibility.

Vaporware is a classic tactic aimed at influencing expectations: announce an upcoming product so as to freeze your rival's sales. In the 1994 antitrust case brought by the Justice Department against Microsoft, Judge Sporkin cited vaporware as one reason why he found the proposed consent decree insufficient. In an earlier era, IBM was accused of the same tactic. Of course, drawing the line between 'predatory product pre-announcements' and simply being late bringing a product to market is not so easy to draw, especially in the delay-prone software market. Look at what happened to Lotus in spreadsheets and Ashton-Tate and database software. After both of these companies repeatedly missed launch dates, industry wags said they should be merged and use the stock ticker symbol 'LATE.' We must note with some irony that Microsoft's stock took a 5.3% nose-dive in late 1997 after Microsoft announced a delay in the launch of Windows 98 from the first to the second quarter of 1998.

The most direct way to manage expectations is by assembling allies and by making grand claims about your product's current or future popularity. Sun has been highly visible in gathering allies in support of Java, including taking out full-page advertisements listing the companies in the Java coalition. Indicative of how important expectations management is in markets with strong network externalities, WordPerfect even filed a court complaint against Microsoft to block Microsoft from claiming that its word processing software was the most popular in the world. Barnes & Noble did the same thing to Amazon, arguing that their claim to being the 'world's largest bookstore' was misleading.

ONCE YOU'VE WON

Moving on from war to the spoils of victory, let's consider how best to proceed once you have actually *won* a standards war. Probably you made some concessions to achieve victory, such as promises of openness or deals with various allies. Of course, you have to live with those, but there is still a great deal of room for strategy. In today's high-tech world, the battle never really ends. So, take a deep breath and be ready to keep moving.

Staying on your guard

Technology marches forward. You have to keep looking out for the next generation of technology, which can come from unexpected directions. Microsoft, with all its foresight and savvy, has had to scurry to deal with the Internet phenomenon and try to defuse any threat to their core business.

You may be especially vulnerable if you were victorious in one generation of technology through a preemption strategy. Going early usually means making technical compromises, which gives that much more room for others to execute an incompatible Revolution strategy against you. Apple pioneered the market for personal digital assistants, but U.S. Robotics perfected the idea with their Palm Pilot. If your rivals attract the power users, your market position and the value of your network may begin to erode.

The hazards of moving early and then lacking flexibility can be seen in the case of the French Minitel system. Back in the 1980s, the French were world leaders in on-line transactions with the extensive Minitel computer network, which was sponsored and controlled by France Telecom. Before the Internet was widely known, much less used, million of French subscribers used the Minitel system to obtain information and conduct secure on-line transactions. Today, Minitel boasts more than 35 million French subscribers and 25,000 vendors. One reason Minitel has attracted so many suppliers is that users pay a fee to France Telecom each time they visit a commercial site, and a portion of these fees are passed along to vendors. Needless to say, this is quite a different business model than we see on the Web.

Now, however, the Minitel systems is seen as inflexible, and France is lagging behind in moving onto the Internet. Just as companies that invested in dedicated word processing systems in the 1970s were slow to move to more generalized personal computers in the 1980s, the French have been slow to invest in equipment that can access the Internet. Only about 3% of the French population uses the Internet, far short of the estimated 20% in the U.S. and 9% is the U.K. and Germany. Roughly 15% of French companies have a Web site, versus nearly 35% of U.S. businesses. Only in August 1997 did the French government admit that the Internet, not Minitel, was the way of the future rather than an instrument of American cultural imperialism. France Telecom is now in the planning stages to introduce next-generation Minitel terminals that will access the Internet as well as Minitel.

What is the lesson here? The French sluggishness to move to the Internet stems from two causes that are present in many other settings. First, France Telecom and the vendors had an incentive to preserve the revenue streams they were earning from Minitel. This is understandable, but it should be recognized as a choice to harvest an installed base, with adverse implications for the future. Milking the installed base is sometimes the right thing to do, but make this a calculated choice, not a default decision. Second, moving to the Internet presents substantial collective switching costs – and less incremental value – to French consumers in contrast with, say, American consumers. Precisely because Minitel was a success, it reduced the attractiveness of the Internet.

The strategic implication is that you need a migration path or roadmap for your technology. If you cannot improve your technology with time, while offering substantial compatibility with older versions, you will be overtaken sooner or later. Rigidity is death, unless you build a really big installed base, and even this will fade eventually without improvements.

Offer customers a migration path

To fend off challenges from upstarts, you need to make it hard for rivals to execute a revolution strategy. The key is to anticipate the next generation of technology and co-opt it. Look in all directions for the next threat and take advantage of the fact that consumers will not switch to a new incompatibility technology unless it offers a marked improvement in performance. Microsoft has been the master of this strategy with its 'Embrace and Extend' philosophy of anticipating or imitating improvements and incorporating them into its flagship products.[12] Avoid being frozen in place by your own success. If you cater too closely to your installed base by emphasizing backward compatibility, you open the door to a Revolution strategy by an upstart. This is precisely what happened to Ashton-Tate in databases, allowing Borland and later Microsoft to offer far superior performance with their Paradox and FoxPro products. Your product road map has to offer your customers a smooth migration path to ever-improving technology, and it must stay close to, if not on, the cutting edge.

One way to avoid being dragged down by the need to retain compatibility is to give older members of your installed base free or inexpensive upgrades to a recent but not current version of your product. This is worth doing for many reasons: users of much older versions have revealed that they do not need the latest bells and whistles and thus are less likely to actually buy the latest version; the free 'partial' upgrade can restore some lost customer loyalty; you can save on support costs by avoiding 'version-creep'; and you can avoid being hamstrung in designing your latest products by a customer-relations need to maintain compatibility with older and older versions. To compromise the performance of your latest version in the name of compatibility with ancient versions presents an opening for a rival to build an installed base among more demanding users. Happily, this 'lagged upgrade' approach is easier and easier with distribution so cheap over the Internet.

Microsoft did a good job with this problem with migration to Windows 95. Politely put, Windows 95 is a kludge, with all sorts of special workarounds to allow DOS programs to execute in the Windows environment, thereby maintaining compatibility with customers' earlier programs. Microsoft's plan with Windows 98 is to move the consumer version of Windows closer to the professional version, Windows NT, eventually ending up with only one product, or at least only one user interface.

Commoditize complementary products

Once you've won, you want to keep your network alive and healthy. This means that you've got to attend not only to your own products, but to the products produced by your complementors as well. Your goal should be to retain your franchise as the market leader, but have a vibrant and competitive market for complements to your product.

This can be tricky. Apple has flipped back and forth on its developer relations over the years. First they wanted to just be in the computer business, and let others develop applications. Then they established a subsidiary, Claris, to do applications development. When this soured relations with other developers they spun Claris off. And so it went – a back-and-forth dance.

Microsoft faced the same problem, but with a somewhat different strategy. If an applications developer became successful, Microsoft just bought them (or tried to – Microsoft's intended purchase of Intuit was blocked by the Department of Justice). Nowadays a lot of new business plans in the software industry have the same structure: 'Produce product, capture emerging market, be bought by Microsoft.'

Our view is that you should try to maintain a competitive market in complementary products and avoid the temptation to meddle. Enter into these markets only if integration of your core product with adjacent products adds value to consumers, or if you can inject significant additional competition to keep prices low. If you are truly successful, like Intel, you will need to spur innovation in complementary products to continue to grow, both by capturing revenues from new complementary products and by stimulating demand for your core product.

Competing against your own installed base

You may need to improve performance just to compete against your installed base, even without an external threat. How can you continue to grow when your information product or technology starts to reach market saturation? One answer is to drive innovation ever faster. Intel is pushing to improve hardware performance of complementary products (such as graphics chips and chipsets) and helping develop applications that crave processing power so as to drive the hardware upgrade cycle. Competition with one's own installed base is not a new problem for companies selling durable goods. The stiffest competition faced by Steinway in selling pianos is from used Steinways.

One way to grow even after you have a large installed base is to start discounting as a means of attracting the remaining customers who have demonstrated (by waiting) that they have a relatively low willingness-to-pay for your product. This is a good instinct, but be careful. First, discounting established products is at odds with a penetration pricing strategy to win a standards war. Second, if you regularly discount products once they are well established, consumers may learn to wait for the discounts. The key question: Can you expand the market and not spoil your margins for traditional customers?

Economists have long recognized this as the 'durable-goods monopoly' problem. Ronald Coase, recent winner of the Nobel Prize in Economics, wrote 35 years ago about the temptation of a company selling a durable product to offer lower and lower prices to expand the market once many consumers already purchased the durable good. He conjectured that consumers would come to anticipate these price reductions and hold off buying until prices fall. Since then, economists have studied a variety of strategies designed to prevent the resulting erosion of profits. The problem raised by Coase is especially severe for highly durable products such as information and software.

One of the prescriptions for solving the durable-goods monopoly problem is to *rent* your product rather than sell it. This will not work for a microprocessor or a printer, but rapid technological change can achieve the same end. If a product becomes obsolete in two or three years, used versions won't pose much of a threat to new sales down the line. This is a great spur for companies like Intel to rush ahead as fast as possible increasing the speed of their microprocessors. The same is true on the software side, where even vendors who are dominant in their category (such as Autodesk in computer-aided design) are forced to improve their programs to generate a steady stream of revenues.

Protecting your position

A variety of defensive tactics can help secure your position. This is where antitrust limits come in most sharply, however, since it is illegal to 'maintain a monopoly' by anticompetitive means.

One tactic is to offer ongoing attractive terms to important complementors. For example, Nintendo worked aggressively to attract developers of hit games and used its popularity to gain very strong distribution. This tactic can, however, cross the legal line if you insist that your suppliers, or distributors, deal with you to the exclusion of your rivals. For example, FTD, the floral network, under pressure from the Justice Department, had to cancel its program giving discounts to florists who used FTD exclusively. Since FTD had the lion's share of the floral delivery network business, this quasi-exclusivity provision was seen as protecting FTD's near-monopoly position. Ticketmaster was subjected to an extensive investigation for adopting exclusivity provisions in its contracts with stadiums, concert halls, and other venues. The Justice Department in 1994 attacked Microsoft's contracts with OEMs for having an effect similar to that of exclusive licenses.

A less controversial way to protect your position is to take steps to avoid being held up by others who claim that your product infringes their patents or copyrights. Obviously, there is no risk-free way to do this. However, it makes a great deal of sense to ask those seeking access to your network to agree not to bring the whole network down in an infringement action. Microsoft took steps along these lines when it launched Windows 95, including a provision in the Windows 95 license for OEMs that prevented Microsoft licensees from attempting to use certain software patents to block Microsoft from shipping Windows 95. Intel regularly asks companies taking licenses to its open specifications to agree to offer royalty-free licenses to other participants for any patents that would block the specified technology. This 'two-sided openness' strategy prevents *ex post* hold-up problems and helps safely launch a new specification.

Leveraging your installed base

Once you have a strong installed base, basic principles of competitive strategy dictate that you seek to leverage into adjacent product spaces, exploiting the key assets that give you a unique ability to create value for consumers in those spaces. In some cases, control over an interface can be used to extend leadership from one side of the interface to the other.

But don't get carried away. You may be better off encouraging healthy competition in complementary products, which stimulates demand for your core product, rather than trying to dominate adjacent spaces. Acquisitions of companies selling neighboring products should be driven by true synergies of bringing both products into the same company, not simply by a desire to expand your empire. Again, legal limits on both 'leveraging' and on vertical acquisitions can come into play. For example, the FTC forced Time Warner to agree to carry a rival news channel on its cable systems when Time Warner acquired CNN in its merger with Turner.

Geographic expansion is yet another way to leverage your installed base. This is true for traditional goods and services, but with a new twist for network products: when expanding the geographic scope of your network, make sure your installed base in one region becomes a competitive advantage in another region. But careful: don't build a two-way bridge to another region where you face an even stronger rival; in that case, more troops will come across the bridge attacking you than you can send to gain new territory.

Geographic effects were powerful in the FCC auctions of spectrum space for PCS services, the successor to the older cellular telephone technology. If you provide Personal Digital Assistance (PDA) wireless services in Minneapolis, you have a big advantage if you also provide such services in St. Paul. The market leader in one town would therefore be willing to outbid rivals in neighboring locations. In the PCS auctions, bidders allegedly 'signaled' their most-preferred territories by encoding them into their bids as an attempt to avoid a mutually unprofitable bidding war. The Department of Justice is investigating these complaints. Our point is not to offer bidding strategy, but to remind you that geographic expansion of a network can be highly profitable. Network growth generates new customers and offers more value to existing customers at the same time.

Staying a leader

How can you secure a competitive advantage for yourself short of maintaining direct control over the technology, e.g., through patent or copyright protection? Even without direct control over the installed base or ownership of key patents, you may be able to make the other factors work for you, while garnering enough external support to set the standards you want.

If you have a good development team, you can build a bandwagon using an 'openness' approach of ceding current control over the technology (e.g., through licenses at low or nominal royalties) while keeping tight control over improvements and extensions. If you know better than others how the technology is likely to evolve, you can use this informational advantage to preserve important future rights without losing the support of your allies. IBM chose to open up the PC, but then they lost control because they did not see what the key assets would be in the future. Besides the now-obvious ones (the design of the operating system and manufacturing of the underlying microprocessor), consider the example of interface standards between the PC and the monitor. During the 1980s, IBM set the first four standards: the Monochrome Graphics Adapters (MGA), the Color Graphics Adapter (CGA), the Enhanced Graphics Adapter (EGA), and the Video Graphics Adapter (VGA), the last in 1987. But by the time of the VGA, IBM was losing control, and the standard started to splinter with the Super VGA around 1988. Soon, with the arrival of the VESA interface, standard-setting passed out of IBM's hands altogether. By anticipating advances in the resolution of monitors, IBM could have done more to preserve its power to set these interface standards, without jeopardizing the initial launch of the PC.

Developing proprietary extensions is a valuable tactic to recapture at least partial control over your own technology. You may not be able to exert strong control at the outset, but you may gain some control later if you launch a technology that takes off and you can be first to market with valuable improvements and extensions.

One difficulty with such an approach is that your new technology may be *too* successful. If the demand for your product grows too fast, many of your resources may end up being devoted to meeting current demand rather than investing in R&D for the future. This happened to Cisco. All of their energies were devoted to the next generation of networking gear, leaving them little time for long-run research. If you are lucky enough to be in Cisco's position, do what they did: use all the profits you are making to identify and purchase firms that are producing the next-generation products. As Cisco's CEO, John Chambers, puts it: 'We don't do research – we buy research!'

Allow complementors, and even rivals, to participate in developing standards, but under *your* terms. Clones are fine, so long as you set the terms under which they can operate. Don't flip-flop in your policies, as Apple did with its clone manufacturers: stay open, but make sure that you charge enough for access to your network (e.g., in the form of licensing fees) that your bottom line does not suffer when rivals displace your own sales. Build the opportunity costs of lost sales into your access prices or licensing fees.

Rear-Guard Actions

What happens if you fall behind? Can you ever recover?

That depends upon what you mean by 'recover.' Usually it is not possible to wrest leadership from another technology that is equally good and more established, unless your rival slips up badly. However, if the network externalities are not crushing, you may be able to protect a niche in the market. And you can always position yourself to make a run at leadership in the next generation of technology.

Atari, Nintendo, Sega, and Sony present a good example. Atari was dominant in 8-bit systems, Nintendo in 16-bit systems, Sega made inroads by being first-to-market with 32-bit systems, and Sony is giving Nintendo a run for their money in 64-bit systems. Losing one round does not mean you should give up, especially if backward compatibility is not paramount.

This leaves a set of tricky issues of how to manage your customers if you have done poorly in one round of the competition. Stranding even a small installed base of customers can have lasting reputational effects. IBM was concerned about this when they dropped the PC Jr. in the mid-1980s. Apart from consumer goodwill, retaining a presence in the market can be vital to keeping up customer relations and brand identity, even if you have little prospect of making major sales until you introduce a new generation of products. Apple faces this problem with their new operating system, Rhapsody. How do they maintain compatibility with their loyal followers while still building a path to what they hope will be a dramatic improvement in the operating environment?

Adapters and interconnection

A tried and true tactic when falling behind is to add an adapter, or to somehow interconnect with the larger network. This can be a sign of weakness, but one worth bearing if the enhanced network externalities of plugging into a far larger network are substantial. We touched on this in our discussion of how to negotiate a truce; if you are negotiating from weakness, you may simply seek the right to interconnect with the larger network.

The first question to ask is whether you even have the right to build an adapter. Sometimes the large network can keep you out. Atari lacked the intellectual property rights to include an adapter in their machines to play Nintendo cartridges, because of Nintendo's lock-out chip. In other cases, you may be able to break down the door, or at least try. The dominant ATM network in Canada, Interac, was compelled to let non-member banks interconnect. In the telephone area, the FCC is implementing elaborate rules that will allow competitive local exchange carriers to interconnect with the incumbent monopoly telephone networks.

The most famous legal case of a less-popular network product maneuvering to achieve compatibility is the battle between Borland and Lotus in spread-sheets. To promote its Quattro-Pro spreadsheet as an alternative to the dominant spreadsheet of the day, Lotus 1-2-3, Borland not only made sure than Quattro-Pro could import Lotus files, but copied part of the menu structure used by Lotus. Lotus sued Borland for copyright infringement. The case went all the way to the Supreme Court; the vote was deadlocked so Borland prevailed based on its victory in the First Circuit Court of Appeals. This case highlights the presence of legal uncertainty over what degree of imitation is permissible; the courts are still working out the limits on how patents and copyrights can be used in network industries.

There are many diverse examples of 'adapters.' Conversion of data from another program is a type of adapter. Translators and emulators can serve the same function when more complex code is involved. Converters can be one-way or two-way, with very different strategic implications. Think about WordPerfect and Microsoft Word today. WordPerfect is small and unlikely to gain much share, so they benefit from two-way compatibility. Consumers will be more willing to buy or upgrade WordPerfect if they can import files in Word format and export files in a format that is readable by users of Word. So far, Word will import files in WordPerfect format, but if Microsoft ever eliminates this feature of Word, WordPerfect should attempt to offer an export capability that preserves as much information as possible.

The biggest problem with adapters, when they are technically and legally possible, is performance degradation. Early hopes that improved processing power would make emulation easy have proven false. Tasks become more complex.

Digital's efforts with its Alpha microprocessor illustrate some of the ways in which less popular technologies seek compatibility. The Alpha chip has been consistently faster than the fastest Intel chips on the market. Digital sells systems with Alpha chips into the server market, a far smaller market than the desktop and workstation markets. And Digital's systems are far more expensive than systems using Intel chips. As a result, despite its technical superiority, the Alpha sold only 300,000 chips in 1996 compared to 65 million sold by Intel. This leaves Digital in the frustrating position of having a superior product but suffering from a small network. Recognizing that Alpha is in a precarious position, Digital has been looking for ways to interconnect with the Intel (virtual) network. Digital offers an emulator to let its Alpha chip run like an Intel architecture chip, but most of the performance advantages that Alpha offers are neutralized by the emulator. Hoping to improve the performance of systems using the Alpha chip, Digital and Microsoft announced in January 1998 an enhanced Alliance for Enterprise Computing, under which Windows NT server-based products will be released concurrently for Alpha- and Intel-based systems. Digital also has secured a commitment from Microsoft that Microsoft will cooperate to provide source-code compatibility between Alpha-and Intel-based systems for Windows NT application developers, making it far easier for them to develop applications to run on Alpha-based systems in native mode.

Adapters and converters among software programs are also highly imperfect. Converting files from WordStar to WordPerfect, and now from WordPerfect to Word, is notoriously buggy. Whatever the example, consumers are rightly wary of translators and emulators, in part because of raw performance concerns and in part because of lurking concerns over just how compatible the conversion really is: consider the problems that users have faced with Intel to Motorola architectures, or dBase to Paradox databases.

Apple offers a good example of a company that responded to eroding market share by adding adapters. Apple put in disk drives that could read floppy disks formatted on DOS and Windows machines in the mid-eighties. In 1993, Apple introduced a machine that included an Intel 486 chip and could run DOS and Windows software along with Macintosh software. But Apple's case also exposes the deep tension underlying an adapter strategy: the adapter adds (some) value, but undermines confidence in the smaller network itself.

Finally, be careful about the large network changing interface specifications to avoid compatibility. IBM was accused of this in mainframe computers. Indeed, we suggested this very tactic in the section above on strategies for winners, so long as the new specifications are truly superior, not merely an attempt to exclude competitors.

Survival pricing

The marginal cost of producing information goods is close to zero. This means that you can cut your price very low and still cover (incremental) costs. Hence, when you find yourself falling behind in a network industry, it is tempting to cut price in order to spur sales, a tactic we call *survival pricing*.

However, the temptation should be resisted. Survival pricing is unlikely to work. It shows weakness, and it is hard to find examples where it made much difference. Computer Associates gave away 'Simply Money' (for a $6.95 shipping and handling fee), but this didn't matter. Simply Money still did not take off in its battle against Quicken and Money. On the other hand, Computer Associates got the name and vital statistics of each buyer, which was worth something in the mail list market, so it wasn't total loss. IBM offered OS/2 for as little as $50, but look where it got them. Borland priced QuattroPro very aggressively when squeezed between Lotus1-2-3 and Microsoft Excel back in 1993.

The problem is that the purchase price of software is minor in comparison with the costs of deployment, training, and support. Corporate purchasers, and even individual consumers, were much more worried about picking the winner of the spreadsheet wars than they were in whether their spreadsheet cost $49.95 or $99.95. At the time of the cut-throat pricing, Borland was a distant third in the spreadsheet market. Lotus and Microsoft both said they would not respond to the low price. Frank Ingari, Lotus's vice president for marketing, dismissed Borland as a 'fringe player' and said the $49 price was a 'last gasp move.'

Survival pricing – cutting your price after the tide has moved against you – should be distinguished from penetration pricing, which is offering a low price to invade another market. Borland used penetration pricing very cleverly in the early 1980s with its Turbo Pascal product. Microsoft, along with other compiler companies, ignored Turbo Pascal, much to their dismay later on.

Legal approaches

If all else fails, sue. No, really. If the dominant firm has promised to be open and has reneged on that promise, you should attack its bait-and-switch approach. The Supreme Court in the landmark *Kodak* case opened the door to antitrust attacks along these lines, and many companies have taken up the invitation. The key is that a company may be found to be a 'monopolist' over its own installed base of users, even if it faces strong competition to attract such users in the first place. Although the economics behind the *Kodak* case are murky and muddled, it can offer a valuable lever to gain compatibility or inter-connection with a dominant firm.

CONCLUSIONS AND LESSONS

Before you can craft standards strategy, you first need to understand what type of standards war you are waging. The single most important factor to track is the compatibility between the dueling new technologies and established products. Standards wars come in three types: Rival Evolutions, Rival Revolutions, and Revolution versus Evolution.

Strength in the standards game is determined by ownership of seven critical assets:

- control of an installed base
- intellectual property rights
- ability to innovate
- first-mover advantages
- manufacturing abilities
- presence in complementary products
- brand name and reputation.

Our main lessons for strategy and tactics, drawn from dozens of standards wars over the past century and more, are these:

- *Before you go to war, assemble allies.* You'll need the support of consumers, suppliers of complements, and even your competitors. Not even the strongest companies can afford to go it alone in a standards war.

- *Preemption is a critical tactic during a standards war.* Rapid design cycles, early deals with pivotal customers, and penetration pricing are the building blocks of a preemption strategy.
- *Managing consumer expectations is crucial in network markets.* Your goal is to convince customers – and your complementors – that you will emerge as the victor. Such expectations can easily become a self-fulfilling prophecy when network effects are strong. To manage expectations you should engage in aggressive marketing, make early announcements of new products, assemble allies, and make visible commitments to your technology.
- *When you've won your war, don't rest easy.* Cater to your own installed base and avoid complacency. Don't let the desire for backward compatibility hobble your ability to improve your product; doing so will leave you open to an entrant offering less compatibility but superior performance. Commoditize complementary products to make your systems more attractive for consumers.
- *If you fall behind, avoid survival pricing; it just signals weakness.* A better tactic is to establish a compelling performance advantage, or to interconnect with the prevailing standard using converters and adapters.

NOTES

1   For a lengthy discussion of railroad gauge standardization, see Amy Friedlander, *Emerging Infrastructure: The Growth of Railroads* (Reston, VA: Corporation for National Research Initiatives, 1995).

2   For further details on the Battle of the Systems, see Julie Ann Bunn and Paul David, 'The Economics of Gateway Technologies and Network Evolution: Lessons from Electricity Supply History.' *Information Economics and Policy*, 3/2 (1988).

3   In this context, Edison's efforts can be seen as an attempt to prevent or delay tipping towards AC, perhaps to obtain the most money in selling his DC interests.

4   A very nice recounting of the color television story can be found in David Fisher and Marshall Fisher, 'The Color War,' *Invention & Technology*, 3/3 (1997). See, also, Joseph Farrell and Carl Shapiro, 'Standard Setting in High-Definition Television,' *Brookings Papers on Economic Activity: Microeconomics* (1992).

5   For color TV to truly offer value to viewers, it was not enough to get set manufacturers and networks to agree on a standard; they had to produce sets that performed well at reasonable cost, they had to create compelling content, and they had to induce broadcasters to invest in transmission gear. The technology was just not ready for the mass market in 1953, much less 1950. Interestingly, the Europeans, by waiting another decade before the adoption of PAL and SECAM, ended up with a better system. The same leapfrogging is now taking place in reverse: the digital HDTV system being adopted in the U.S. is superior to the system selected years before by the Japanese.

6   For a fuller discussion of positive feedback, network effects, and network externalities, see Chapter 7 of Carl Shapiro and Hal R. Varian, *Information Rules: A Strategic Guide to the Network Economy* (Boston, MA: Harvard Business School Press, 1998). See, also, Michael Katz and Carl Shapiro, 'Systems Competition and Network Effects,' *Journal of Economic Perspectives*, 8/2 (1994); Brian Arthur, *Increasing Returns and Path Dependence in the Economy* (Ann Arbor MI: University of Michigan Press, 1994).

7   We recognize, indeed emphasize, that building an alliance of customers, suppliers, and complementors to support one technology over another in a standards battle can be the single most important tactic in such a struggle. We explore alliances and cooperative strategies to achieve compatibility separately in Chapter 8 of *Information Rules* [Shapiro and Varian, op. cit], See, also,

David B. Yoffie, 'Competing in the Age of Digital Convergence,' *California Management Review*, 38/4 (1996).

8   For a discussion of the antitrust treatment of standards, see the Federal Trade Commission Staff Report, *Competition Policy in the New High-Tech, Global Marketplace*, Chapter 9, 'Networks and Standards'; Joel Klein, 'Cross-Licensing and Antitrust Law,' 1997, available at www.usdoj.gov/atr/public/speeches/1123.htm; Carl Shapiro, 'Antitrust in Network Industries,' 1996, available at www.usdoj.gov/atr/public/speeches/shapir.mar; Carl Shapiro, 'Setting Compatibility Standards: Cooperation or Collusion?' Working Paper, University of California, Berkeley, 1998.

9   We cannot explore cooperation and compatibility tactics in any depth here. We discuss tactics for participation in formal standard setting in Chapter 8 of *Information Rules* [Shapiro and Varian, op. cit.].

10   Even these companies have had losers, too, such as Microsoft's Bob, Intel's original Celeron chip, and Sun's 386 platform. Credibility and brand name recognition without allies and a sound product are not enough.

11   Manufacturers do the same thing when they pay 'slotting allowances' to supermarkets for shelf space by checking that their products are actually displayed where they are supposed to be displayed.

12   Indeed, the strategy has been so successful that some have amended the name to 'Embrace, Extend and Eliminate.'

PART III

THE RESOURCE-BASED VIEW OF STRATEGY

Introduction

The four chapters in Part III present the resource-based view (RBV) of strategy. It is an approach that has a long provenance, but that came into prominence in strategic thinking as the dominant strategy paradigm of the 1990s. The most important emphasis in RBV is the issue of 'heterogeneity' (i.e. different performance by firms within the same industry). This assumes that each firm consists of a unique cluster of resources (both tangible and intangible) and capabilities. These will differ between firms in the same industry and will make possible different strategies and different performance. The RBV places the firm rather than the industry at the centre of strategy formulation and strategic decision-making. RBV is therefore able to explain some of the factors contributing to Rumelt's results described in Part II. It has an internal resource focus rather than an external industry or market focus for strategic thinking. It is most productive, however, not to place the RBV and the positioning schools in opposition to each other but rather to see them as complementary perspectives on strategy and how to compete.

We begin Part III with another of the series of ground-breaking *Harvard Business Review* articles by Prahalad and Hamel (Chapter 9). The reason I chose this article to begin Part III is that it is the one that, in 1990, kick-started the managerial debate about core competencies, although it was not the first to be published about RBV. That honour probably goes to Wernerfelt (1984). Nevertheless, it was the Hamel and Prahalad HBR article that helped to tilt the analysis and practice of strategic management to begin to look inside the organization once again for key drivers of strategy. In this article they argue that competitiveness for corporations is no longer about cost or quality issues, since these must by now be taken as given, rather than being sources of differentiation. Instead, competitiveness, in their view, derives from the core competencies from which new products or services emerge.

> The real sources of advantage are to be found in management's ability to consolidate corporate-wide technologies and production skills into competencies that empower individual businesses (within the corporation) to adapt quickly to changing opportunities.

They therefore set out to redefine the corporation to work *across* traditionally defined internal organizational boundaries. They see this as crucial to the practice of core competence-based strategy that involves many levels of people and all functions. Their concern is with managers 'trapped in the strategic business unit (SBU) mindset'. By definition, potential core competencies cannot be realized where top management is 'unable to conceive of the corporation as anything other than a collection of discrete businesses'. Their article thus constituted an attack on the SBU

163

system of management and its mindset, which concentrated on products rather than underlying core competencies. That may be why this article had such an impact on managers. Prahalad and Hamel urged managers to think of organizations as 'repositories of skills rather than portfolios of products'. They enlarge the concept of 'relatedness' in corporate strategy. Organizational coherence is to be found in corporate portfolios of competencies rather than just portfolios of related businesses. This should help to generate unconventional options for corporate direction. It has shifted the role of top management from resource allocation to building strategic architecture to map future core competencies, and their constituent technologies, to safeguard the future of the corporation.

While Prahalad and Hamel set out the general terrain, the two chapters by Grant, and Amit and Schoemaker both really start to explain in more detail this idea of the organization as bundles of resources and capabilities. Grant (Chapter 10) gives the simplest and best definition that I have read of the distinction between resources and capabilities. He argues:

> There is a key distinction between resources and capabilities. Resources are inputs into the production process – they are the basic units of analysis ... But, on their own, few resources are productive. Productive activity requires the co-operation and co-ordination of teams of resources. A capability is the capacity for a team of resources to perform some task or activity. While resources are the source of a firm's capabilities, capabilities are the main source of its competitive advantage.

Such teams of resources are certainly not just human teams. They are any cluster of tangible, intangible or human resources including buildings, ideas, systems, staff, equipment, technology, finance and managerial talent, the combining of which make different organizations different. Grant is arguing for strategies which 'exploit to maximum effect each firm's unique characteristics'. However, Grant also makes clear that achieving financial returns from a firm's resources and capabilities ('rent-earning potential') depends upon two key factors. The first is the sustainability of the competitive advantage which resources and capabilities confer upon the firm. The second is the ability of the firm to appropriate the rents from its resources and capabilities via such things as patents, copyrights, or brand names. *Appropriability* remains a difficult issue despite these types of protections, since much of what is contained in capabilities is represented by the human capital of the individual and the tacit knowledge they possess.

Amit and Schoemaker (Chapter 11) present the economist's view of resources. They agree with Grant that organizations differ in their ability to secure advantage from resources and capabilities. Furthermore, they argue that uncertainty, complexity and conflict, both inside and outside the organization, constitute the normal conditions under which managers have to manage. However, this leaves room for 'discretionary managerial decisions on strategy crafting'. In other words, it is precisely such uncertainties that create the opportunity for differences between firms to develop, often as a result of better or worse decision-making by managers about the external environment or the internal resource mix. Their chapter suggests that the challenge facing managers is to identify and nurture a set of 'strategic assets' directly arising from the firm's resources and capabilities. These strategic assets refer to the specific set of firm resources and capabilities developed by management as the basis for creating and protecting the firm's competitive advantage. They will have the following characteristics:

> they should be scarce, durable, not easily traded and difficult to imitate, thus enabling the firm to secure a revenue stream from them over time and generate superior economic returns from superior performance.

That is an important set of points about what makes certain resources and capabilities valuable. Both Grant and Amit and Shoemaker emphasize these same characteristics. We can understand therefore, how important within the RBV is the idea of the intrinsic inimitability of scarce, valuable resources. Resources and capabilities which are common, short-lived and easy to imitate must be less valuable to an organization than those which are scarce, durable and difficult to imitate. It is the latter which form the basis of sustainability in strategy.

The final article in Part III by Teece, Pisano and Shuen (Chapter 12), represents a further development within the RBV approach to strategy. Work on *dynamic capabilities* emerged in the mid-to-late 1990s. It extends the RBV by explaining how firm-specific capabilities (which enable them to perform some activities better than their competitors) could be built up and redeployed over long periods of time. The dynamic capabilities approach is therefore about capability-building and develops a dynamic, rather than a static, view of capabilities. Capabilities must be developed rather than taken as given. This article by Teece, Pisano and Shuen is recognized as the seminal work in this area. Indeed, it was awarded the *Strategic Management Journal (SMJ)* Best Paper prize for 2003, for its outstanding contribution to the field of strategy since its publication in 1997. The *SMJ* is the premier academic journal in the field of strategic management and its award winners are selected for their impact over a significant period of time. The key difference between RBV and the dynamic capabilities approach is the emphasis it places on patterns of current practice, skill acquisition and learning, since these are critical to 'capability accumulation'. The term used to describe these patterns of current practice and learning is 'organizational routines'. These organizational routines are at the heart of 'directed activities by firms which create differentiated capabilities, and ... managerial efforts to deploy these assets in co-ordinated ways'. Strategy implementation moves to the top of the strategy agenda as soon as managers begin thinking about capability-building. That is because the process of capability-building is path dependent (i.e. it is determined by the firm's previous investments and its existing routines) and it is also subject to long time lags. An additional issue is that existing routines may translate over time into *core rigidities* within the organization and therefore become sources of inertia rather than progression. So managers attempting to build future capabilities must pay great attention to the management of R&D, product and process development and all aspects of human resource management since it is their staff who are the repository of current routines and the pathway to future capabilities.

REFERENCE

Wernerfelt B. (1984) 'A Resource-based View of the Firm', *Strategic Management Journal*, Vol. 5: 171–80.

9

THE CORE COMPETENCE
OF THE CORPORATION

C. K. Prahalad and Gary Hamel

RETHINKING THE CORPORATION

Once, the diversified corporation could simply point its business units at particular end-product markets and admonish them to become world leaders. But with market boundaries changing ever more quickly, targets are elusive and capture is at best temporary. A few companies have proven themselves adept in inventing new markets, quickly entering emerging markets, and dramatically shifting patterns of customer choice in established markets. These are the ones to emulate. The critical task for management is to create an organization capable of infusing products with irresistible functionality or, better yet, creating products that customers need but have not yet even imagined.

This is a deceptively difficult task. Ultimately, it requires radical change in the management of major companies. It means, first of all, that top managements of Western companies must assume responsibility for competitive decline. Everyone knows about high interest rates, Japanese protectionism, outdated antitrust laws, obstreperous unions, and impatient investors. What is harder to see, or harder to acknowledge, is how little added momentum companies actually get from political or macro-economic 'relief'. Both the theory and practice of Western management have created a drag on our forward motion. It is the principles of management that are in need of reform.

THE ROOTS OF COMPETITIVE ADVANTAGE

In the short run, a company's competitiveness derives from the price/performance attributes of current products. But the survivors of the first wave of global competition, Western and Japanese alike, are all converging on similar and formidable standards for product cost and quality – minimum hurdles for continued competition, but less and less important as sources of differential advantage. In the long run, competitiveness derives from an ability to build, at lower cost and more speedily than competitors, the core competencies that spawn unanticipated products. The real sources of advantage are to be found in management's ability to consolidate corporate-wide technologies and production skills into competencies that empower individual businesses to adapt quickly to changing opportunities.

Senior executives who claim that they cannot build core competencies either because they feel the autonomy of business units is sacrosanct or because their feet are held to the quarterly budget fire should think again. The problem in many Western companies is not that their senior executives are any less capable than those in Japan or that Japanese companies possess greater technical capabilities. Instead, it is their adherence to a concept of the corporation that unnecessarily limits the ability of individual businesses to fully exploit the deep reservoir of technological capability that many American and European companies possess.

The diversified corporation is a large tree. The trunk and major limbs are core products, the smaller branches are business units; the leaves, flowers, and fruit are end products. The root system that provides nourishment, sustenance, and stability is the core competence. You can miss the strength of a tree if you look only at its leaves (see Figure 9.1).

Core competencies are the collective learning in the organization, especially how to co-ordinate diverse production skills and integrate multiple streams of technologies.

Consider Sony's capacity to miniaturize or Philips' optical-media expertise. The theoretical knowledge to put a radio on a chip does not in itself assure a company the skill to produce a miniature radio no bigger than a business card. To bring off this feat, Casio must harmonize know-how in miniaturization, microprocessor design, materials science, and ultrathin precision casing – the same skills it applies in its miniature card calculators, pocket TVs, and digital watches.

If core competence is about harmonizing streams of technology, it is also about the organization of work and the delivery of value. Among Sony's competencies is miniaturization. To bring miniaturization to its products, Sony must ensure that technologists, engineers, and marketers have a shared understanding of customer needs and of technological possibilities. The force of core competence is felt as decisively in services as in manufacturing. Citicorp was ahead of others investing in an operating system that allowed it to participate in world markets twenty-four hours a day. Its competence in systems has provided the company the means to differentiate itself from many financial service institutions.

Core competence is communication, involvement, and a deep commitment to working across organizational boundaries. It involves many levels of people and all functions. World-class

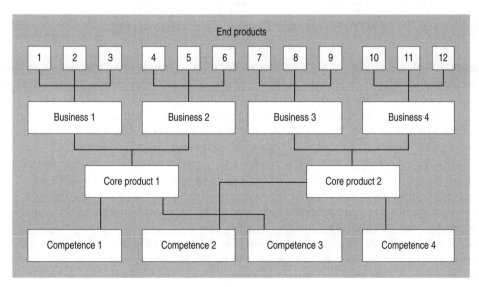

Figure 9.1 Competencies as the roots of competitiveness

research in, for example, lasers or ceramics can take place in corporate laboratories without having an impact on any of the businesses of the company. The skills that together constitute core competence must coalesce around individuals whose efforts are not so narrowly focused that they cannot recognise the opportunities for blending their functional expertise with those of others in new and interesting ways.

Core competence does not diminish with use. Unlike physical assets, which do deteriorate over time, competencies are enhanced as they are applied and shared. But competencies still need to be nurtured and protected; knowledge fades if it is not used. Competences are the glue that binds existing businesses. They are also the engine for new business development. Patterns of diversification and market entry may be guided by them, not just by the attractiveness of markets.

Consider 3M's competence with sticky tape. In dreaming up businesses as diverse as 'Post-it' note pads, magnetic tape, photographic film, pressure-sensitive tapes, and coated abrasives, the company has brought to bear widely shared competencies in substrates, coatings, and adhesives and devised various ways to combine them. Indeed, 3M has invested consistently in them. What seems to be an extremely diversified portfolio of businesses belies a few shared core competencies.

In contrast, there are major companies that have had the potential to build core competencies but failed to do so because top management was unable to conceive of the company as anything other than a collection of discrete businesses. General Electric sold much of its consumer electronics business to Thomson of France, arguing that it was becoming increasingly difficult to maintain its competitiveness in this sector. That was undoubtedly so, but it is ironic that it sold several key businesses to competitors who were already competence leaders – Black & Decker in small electrical motors, and Thomson, which was eager to build its competence in microelectronics and had learned from the Japanese that a position in consumer electronics was vital to this challenge.

Management trapped in the strategic business unit (SBU) mind-set almost inevitably finds its individual businesses dependent on external sources for critical components, such as motors or compressors. But these are not just components. They are core products that contribute to the competitiveness of a wide range of end products. They are the physical embodiments of core competencies.

HOW NOT TO THINK OF COMPETENCE

Since companies are in a race to build the competencies that determine global leadership, successful companies have stopped imagining themselves as bundles of businesses making products. Canon, Honda, Casio, or NEC may seem to preside over portfolios of businesses unrelated in terms of customers, distribution channels, and merchandising strategy. Indeed, they have portfolios that may seem idiosyncratic at times: NEC is the only global company to be among leaders in computing, telecommunications, and semiconductors *and* to have a thriving consumer electronics business.

But looks are deceiving. In NEC, digital technology, especially VLSI and systems integration skills, is fundamental. In the core competencies underlying them, disparate businesses become coherent. It is Honda's core competence in engines and power trains that gives it a distinctive advantage in car, motorcycle, lawn mower, and generator businesses. Canon's core competencies in optics, imaging, and microprocessor controls have enabled it to enter, even dominate, markets as seemingly diverse as copiers, laser printers, cameras, and image scanners. Philips worked for more than fifteen years to perfect its optical-media (laser disc) competence, as did JVC in building a leading position in video recording. Other examples of core competencies might include mechantronics (the ability to marry mechanical and electronic engineering), video displays, bioengineering, and microelectronics. In the early stages of its competence building, Philips could not have imagined all the products that would be spawned by its optical-media competence, nor could JVC have anticipated miniature camcorders when it first began exploring videotape technologies.

Unlike the battle for global brand dominance, which is visible in the world's broadcast and print media and is aimed at building global 'share of mind', the battle to build world-class competencies is invisible to people who aren't deliberately looking for it. Top management often tracks the cost and quality of competitors' products, yet how many managers untangle the web of alliances their Japanese competitors have constructed to acquire competencies at low cost? In how many Western boardrooms is there an explicit, shared understanding of the competencies the company must build for world leadership? Indeed, how many senior executives discuss the crucial distinction between competitive strategy at the level of a business and competitive strategy at the level of an entire company?

Let us be clear. Cultivating core competence does not mean outspending rivals on research and development. In 1983, when Canon surpassed Xerox in worldwide unit market share in the copier business, its R&D budget in reprographics was but a small fraction of Xerox's. Over the past twenty years NEC has spent less on R&D as a percentage of sales than almost all of its American and European competitors.

Nor does core competence mean shared costs, as when two or more SBUs use a common facility – a plant, service facility, or sales force – or share a common component. The gains of sharing may be substantial, but the search for shared costs is typically a *post hoc* effort to rationalize production across existing businesses, not a premeditated effort to build the competencies out of which the businesses themselves grow.

Building core competencies is more ambitious and different than integrating vertically, moreover. Managers deciding whether to make or buy will start with end products and look upstream to the efficiencies of the supply chain and downstream towards distribution and customers. They do not take inventory of skills and look forward to applying them in non-traditional ways. (Of course, decisions about competencies *do* provide a logic for vertical integration. Canon is not particularly integrated in its copier business, except in those aspects of the vertical chain that support the competencies it regards as critical.)

IDENTIFYING CORE COMPETENCIES – AND LOSING THEM

At least three tests can be applied to identify core competencies in a company. First, a core competence provides potential access to a wide variety of markets. Competence in display systems, for example, enables a company to participate in such diverse businesses as calculators, miniature TV sets, monitors for laptop computers, and automotive dashboards – which is why Casio's entry into the handheld TV market was predictable. Second, a core competence should make a significant contribution to the perceived customer benefits of the end product. Clearly, Honda's engine expertise fills this bill.

Finally, a core competence should be difficult for competitors to imitate. And it will be difficult if it is a complex harmonization of individual technologies and production skills. A rival might acquire some of the technologies that comprise the core competence, but it will find it more difficult to duplicate the more-or-less comprehensive pattern of internal co-ordination and learning. JVC's decision in the early 1960s to pursue the development of a videotape competence passed the three tests outlined here. RCA's decision in the late 1970s to develop a stylus-based video turntable system did not.

Few companies are likely to build world leadership in more than five or six fundamental competencies. A company that compiles a list of twenty to thirty capabilities has probably not produced a list of core competencies. Still, it is probably a good discipline to generate a list of this sort and to see aggregate capabilities as building blocks. This tends to prompt the search for licensing deals and alliances through which the company may acquire, at low cost, the missing pieces.

Most Western companies hardly think about competitiveness in these terms at all. It is time to take a tough-minded look at the risks they are running. Companies that judge competitiveness, their own and their competitors', primarily in terms of the price/performance of end products are courting the erosion of core competencies – or making too little effort to enhance them. The embedded skills that give rise to the next generation of competitive products cannot be 'rented in' by outsourcing and original equipment manufacturer (OEM) supply relationships. In our view, too many companies have unwittingly surrendered core competencies when they cut internal investment in what they mistakenly thought were just 'cost centres' in favour of outside suppliers.

Of course, it is perfectly possible for a company to have competitive product line up but be a laggard in developing core competencies – at least for a while. If a company wanted to enter the copier business today, it would find a dozen Japanese companies more than willing to supply copiers on the basis of an OEM private label. But when fundamental technologies changed or if its supplier decided to enter the market directly and become a competitor, that company's product line, along with all of its investments in marketing and distribution, could be vulnerable. Outsourcing can provide a shortcut to a more competitive product, but it typically contributes little to building the people-embodied skills that are needed to sustain product leadership.

Nor is it possible for a company to have an intelligent alliance or sourcing strategy if it has not made a choice about where it will build competence leadership. Clearly, Japanese companies have benefited from alliances. They've used them to learn from Western partners who were not fully committed to preserving core competencies of their own. Learning within an alliance takes a positive commitment of resources – travel, a pool of dedicated people, test-bed facilities, time to internalize and test what has been learned. A company may not make this effort if it doesn't have clear goals for competence building.

Another way of losing is forgoing opportunities to establish competencies that are evolving in existing businesses. In the 1970s and 1980s, many American and European companies – like General Electric, Motorola, GTE, Thorn, and General Electric Company (GEC) – chose to exit the colour television business, which they regarded as mature. If by 'mature' they meant that they had run out of new product ideas at precisely the moment global rivals had targeted the TV business for entry, then yes, the industry was mature. But it certainly wasn't mature in the sense that all opportunities to enhance and apply video-based competencies had been exhausted.

In ridding themselves of their television business, these companies failed to distinguish between divesting the business and destroying their video media-based competencies. They not only got out of the TV business but they also closed the door on a whole stream of future opportunities reliant on video-based competencies.

There are two clear lessons here. First, the costs of losing a core competence can be only partly calculated in advance. The baby may be thrown out with the bath water in divestment decisions. Second, since core competencies are built through a process of continuous improvement and enhancement that may span a decade or longer, a company that has failed to invest in core competence building will find it very difficult to enter an emerging market, unless, of course, it will be content simply to serve as a distribution channel.

American semiconductor companies like Motorola learned this painful lesson when they

elected to forgo direct participation in the 256k generation of DRAM chips. Having skipped this round, Motorola, like most of its American competitors, needed a large infusion of technical help from Japanese partners to rejoin the battle in the 1-megabyte generation. When it comes to core competencies, it is difficult to get off the train, walk to the next station, and then reboard.

FROM CORE COMPETENCIES TO CORE PRODUCTS

The tangible link between identified core competencies and end products is what we call the core products – the physical embodiments of one or more core competencies. Honda's engines, for example, are core products, linchpins between design and development skills that ultimately lead to a proliferation of end products. Core products are the components or sub-assemblies that actually contribute to the value of the end products. Thinking in terms of core products forces a company to distinguish between the brand share it achieves in end-product markets (for example, 40 per cent of the US refrigerator market) and the manufacturing share it achieves in any particular core product (for example, 5 per cent of the world share of compressor output).

It is essential to make this distinction between core competencies, core products, and end products because global competition is played out by different rules and for different stakes at each level. To build or defend leadership over the long term, a corporation will probably be a winner at each level. At the level of core competence, the goal is to build world leadership in the design and development of a particular class of product functionality – be it compact data storage and retrieval, as with Philips's optical-media competence, or compactness and ease of use, as with Sony's micromotors and microprocessor controls.

To sustain leadership in their chosen core competence areas, these companies *seek to maximize their world manufacturing share in core products*. The manufacture of core products for a wide variety of external (and internal) customers yields the revenue and market feedback that, at least partly, determines the pace at which core competencies can be enhanced and extended. This thinking was behind JVC's decision in the mid-1970s to establish VCR supply relationships with leading national consumer electronics companies in Europe and the United States. In supplying Thomson, Thorn, and Telefunken (all independent companies at that time) as well as US partners, JVC was able to gain the cash and the diversity of market experience that ultimately enabled it to outpace Philips and Sony. (Philips developed videotape competencies in parallel with JVC, but it failed to build a worldwide network of OEM relationships that would have allowed it to accelerate the refinement of its videotape competence through the sale of core products.)

JVC's success has not been lost on Korean companies like Goldstar, Samsung, Kia, and Daewoo, who are building core product leadership in areas as diverse as displays, semiconductors, and automotive engines through their OEM-supply contracts with Western companies. Their avowed goal is to capture investment initiative away from potential competitors, often US companies. In doing so, they accelerate their competence-building efforts while 'hollowing out' their competitors. By focusing on competence and embedding it in core products, Asian competitors have built up advantages in component markets first and have then leveraged off their superior products to move downstream to build brand share. And they are not likely to remain the low-cost suppliers forever. As their reputation for brand leadership is consolidated, they may well gain price leadership. Honda has proven this with its Acura line, and other Japanese carmakers are following suit.

Control over core products is critical for other reasons. A dominant position in core products allows a company to shape the evolution of applications and end markets. Such compact audio disc-related core products as data drives and lasers have enabled Sony and Philips to influence the evolution of the computer-peripheral business in optical-media storage. As a company multiplies the number of application arenas for its core products, it can consistently reduce the cost, time, and risk in new product development. In short, well-targeted core products can lead to economies of scale and scope.

THE TYRANNY OF THE SBU

The new terms of competitive engagement cannot be understood using analytical tools devised to manage the diversified corporation of twenty years ago, when competition was primarily domestic (GE versus Westinghouse, General Motors versus Ford) and all the key players were speaking the language of the same business schools and consultancies. Old prescriptions have potentially toxic side effects. The need for new principles is most obvious in companies organized exclusively according to the logic of SBUs. The implications of the two alternative concepts of the corporation are summarized in Table 9.1.

Obviously, diversified corporations have a portfolio of products and a portfolio of businesses. But we believe in a view of the company as a portfolio of competencies as well. United States companies do not lack the technical resources to build competencies, but their top management often lacks the vision to build them and the administrative means for assembling resources spread across multiple businesses. A shift in commitment will inevitably influence patterns of diversification, skill deployment, resource allocation priorities, and approaches to alliances and outsourcing.

We have described the three different planes on which battles for global leadership are waged: core competence, core products, and end products. A corporation has to know whether it is winning or losing on each plane. By sheer weight of investment, a company might be able to beat its rivals to blue-sky technologies yet still lose the race to build core competence leadership. If a company is winning the race to build core competencies (as opposed to building leadership in a few technologies), it will almost certainly outpace rivals in new business development. If a company is winning the race to capture world manufacturing

Table 9.1 Two concepts of the corporation

	SBU	*Core competence*
Basis for competition	Competitiveness of today's products	Interfirm competition to build competencies
Corporate structure	Portfolio of businesses related in product-market terms	Portfolio of competencies, core products, and business
Status of the business unit	Autonomy is sacrosanct; the SBU 'owns' all resources other than cash	SBU is a potential reservoir of core competencies
Resource allocation	Discrete businesses are the unit of analysis; capital is allocated business by business	Businesses and competencies are the unit analysis: top management allocates capital and talent
Value added of top management	Optimising corporate returns through capital allocation trade-offs among businesses	Enunciating strategic architecture and building competencies to secure the future

share in core products, it will probably outpace rivals in improving product features and the price/performance ratio.

Determining whether one is winning or losing end-product battles is more difficult because measures of product market share do not necessarily reflect various companies' underlying competitiveness. Indeed, companies that attempt to build market share by relying on the competitiveness of others, rather than investing in core competencies and world core-product leadership, may be treading on quicksand. In the race for global brand dominance, companies like 3M, Black & Decker, Canon, Honda, NEC, and Citicorp have built global brand umbrellas by proliferating products out of their core competencies. This has allowed their individual businesses to build image, customer loyalty, and access to distribution channels.

When you think about this reconceptualization of the corporation, the primacy of the SBU – an organizational dogma for a generation – is now clearly an anachronism. Where the SBU is an article of faith, resistance to the seductions of decentralization can seem heretical. In many companies, the SBU prism means that only one plane of the global competitive battle, the battle to put competitive products on the shelf *today*, is visible to top management. What are the costs of this distortion?

Underinvestment in developing core competencies and core products

When the organization is conceived of as a multiplicity of SBUs, no single business may feel responsible for maintaining a viable position in core products or be able to justify the investment required to build world leadership in some core competence. In the absence of a more comprehensive view imposed by corporate management, SBU managers will tend to underinvest. Recently, companies such as Kodak and Philips have recognized this as a potential problem and have begun searching for new organizational forms that will allow them to develop and manufacture core products for both internal and external customers.

SBU managers have traditionally conceived of competitors in the same way they've seen themselves. On the whole, they've failed to note the emphasis Asian competitors were placing on building leadership in core products or to understand the critical linkage between world manufacturing leadership and the ability to sustain development pace in core competence. They've failed to pursue OEM-supply opportunities or to look across their various product divisions in an attempt to identify opportunities for co-ordinated initiatives.

Imprisoned resources

As an SBU evolves, it often develops unique Competences. Typically, the people who embody this competence are seen as the sole property of the business in which they grow up. The manager of another SBU who asks to borrow talented people is likely to get a cold rebuff. SBU managers are not only unwilling to lend their competence carriers but they may actually hide talent to prevent its redeployment in the pursuit of new opportunities. This may be compared to residents of an underdeveloped country hiding most of their cash under their mattresses. The benefits of competencies, like the benefits of the money supply, depends on the velocity of their circulation as well as on the size of the stock the company holds.

Western companies have traditionally had an advantage in the stock of skills they possess. But have they been able to reconfigure them quickly to respond to new opportunities? Canon, NEC, and Honda have had a lesser stock of the people and technologies that compose core competencies but could move them much quicker from one business unit to another. Corporate R&D spending at Canon is not fully indicative of the size of Canon's core competence stock and tells the casual observer nothing about the velocity with which Canon is able to move core competencies to exploit opportunities.

When competencies become imprisoned, the people who carry the competencies do not get assigned to the most exciting opportunities, and their skills begin to atrophy. Only by fully leveraging core competencies can small companies like Canon afford to compete with industry giants like Xerox. How strange that SBU managers, who are perfectly willing to compete for cash in the capital budgeting process, are unwilling to compete for people – the company's most precious asset. We find it ironic that top management devotes so much attention to the capital budgeting process yet typically has no comparable mechanism for allocating the human skills that embody core competencies. Top managers are seldom able to look four or five levels down into the organization, identify the people who embody critical competencies, and move them across organizational boundaries.

Bounded innovation

If core competencies are not recognized, individual SBUs will pursue only those innovation opportunities that are close at hand – marginal product-line extensions or geographic expansions. Hybrid opportunities like fax machines, laptop computers, handheld televisions, or portable music keyboards will emerge only when managers take off their SBU blinkers. Remember, Canon appeared to be in the camera business at the time it was preparing to become a world leader in copiers. Conceiving of the corporation in terms of core competencies widens the domain of innovation.

DEVELOPING STRATEGIC ARCHITECTURE

The fragmentation of core competencies becomes inevitable when a diversified company's information systems, patterns of communication, career paths, managerial rewards, and processes of strategy development do not transcend SBU lines. We believe that senior management should spend a significant amount of its time developing a corporate-wide strategic architecture that establishes objectives for competence building. A strategic architecture that establishes objectives for competence building. A strategic architecture is a road map of the future that identifies which core competencies to build and their constituent technologies.

By providing an impetus for learning from alliances and a focus for internal development efforts, a strategic architecture like NEC's C&C (computers and communication) can dramatically reduce the investment needed to secure future market leadership. How can a company make partnerships intelligently without a clear understanding of the core competencies it is trying to build and those it is attempting to prevent from being unintentionally transferred?

Of course, all of this begs the question of what a strategic architecture should look like. The answer will be different for every company. But it is helpful to think again of that tree, of the corporation organized around core products and, ultimately, core competencies. To sink sufficiently strong roots, a company must answer some fundamental questions: How long could we preserve our competitiveness in this business if we did not control this particular core competence? How central is this core competence to perceived customer benefits? What future opportunities would be foreclosed if we were to lose this particular competence?

The architecture provides a logic for product and market diversification, moreover. An SBU manager would be asked: Does the new market opportunity add to the overall goal of becoming the best player in the world? Does it exploit or add to the core competence? At Vickers, for example, diversification options have been judged in the context of becoming the best power and motion control company in the world.

The strategic architecture should make resource allocation priorities transparent to the entire organization. It provides a template for allocation decisions by top management. It helps lower-level managers understand the logic of allocation priorities and disciplines senior management to maintain consistency. In short, it yields a definition of the company and the markets it serves. 3M, Vickers, NEC, Canon, and Honda all qualify on this score. Honda knew it was exploiting what it had learned from motorcycles – how to make high-revving, smooth-running, lightweight engines – when it entered the car business. The task of creating a strategic architecture forces the organization to identify and commit to the technical and production linkages across SBUs that will provide a distinct competitive advantage.

It is consistency of resource allocation and the development of an administrative infrastructure appropriate to it that breathes life into a strategic architecture and creates a managerial culture, teamwork, a capacity to change, and a willingness to share resources, to protect proprietary skills, and to think long term. That is also the reason the specific architecture cannot be copied easily or overnight by competitors. Strategic architecture is a tool for communicating with customers and other external constituents. It reveals the broad direction without giving away every step.

REDEPLOYING TO EXPLOIT COMPETENCIES

If the company's core competencies are its critical resource and if top management must ensure that competence carriers are not held hostage by some particular business, then it follows that SBUs should bid for core competencies in the same way they bid for capital. We've made this point glancingly. It is important enough to consider more deeply.

Once top management (with the help of divisional and SBU managers) has identified overarching competencies, it must ask businesses to identify the projects and people closely connected with them. Corporate officers should direct an audit of the location, number, and quality of the people who embody competence.

This sends an important signal to middle managers: core competencies are corporate resources and may be reallocated by *corporate* management. An individual business doesn't own anybody. SBUs are entitled to the services of individual employees so long as SBU management can demonstrate that the opportunity it is pursuing yields the highest possible payoff on the investment in their skills. This message is further underlined if each year in the strategic planning or budgeting process, unit managers must justify their hold on the people who carry the company's core competencies.

Also, reward systems that focus only on product-line results and career paths that seldom cross SBU boundaries engender patterns of behaviour among unit managers that are destructively competitive. At NEC, divisional managers come together to identify next-generation competencies. Together they decide how much investment needs to be made to build up each further competency and the contribution in capital and staff support that each division will need to make. There is also a sense of equitable exchange. One division may make a disproportionate contribution or may benefit less from the progress made, but such short-term inequalities will balance out over the long term.

Incidentally, the positive contribution of the SBU manager should be made visible across the company. An SBU manager is unlikely to surrender key people if only the other business (or the general manger of that business who may be a competitor for promotion) is going to benefit from the redeployment. Co-operative SBU managers should be celebrated as team players. Where priorities are clear, transfers are less likely to be seen as idiosyncratic and politically motivated.

Transfers for the sake of building core competence must be recorded and appreciated in the corporate memory. It is reasonable to expect a business that has surrendered core skills on behalf of corporate opportunities in other areas to lose, for a time, some of its competitiveness. If these losses in performance bring immediate censure, SBUs will be unlikely to assent to skills transfers next time.

Finally, there are ways to wean key employees off the idea that they belong in perpetuity to any particular business. Early in their careers, people may be exposed to a variety of businesses through a carefully planned rotation programme.

Competence carriers should be regularly brought together from across the corporation to trade notes and ideas. The goal is to build a strong feeling of community among those people. To a great extent, their loyalty should be to the integrity of the core competence area they represent and not just to particular businesses. In travelling regularly, talking frequently to customers, and meeting with peers, competence carriers may be encouraged to discover new market opportunities.

Core competencies are the wellspring of new business development. They should constitute the focus for strategy at the corporate level. Managers have to win manufacturing leadership in core products and capture global share though brand-building programmes aimed at exploiting economies of scope. Only if the company is conceived of as a hierarchy of core competencies, core products, and market-focused business units will it be fit to fight.

Nor can top management be just another layer of accounting consolidation, which it often is in a regime of radical decentralization. Top management must add value by enunciating the strategic architecture that guides the competence acquisition process. We believe an obsession with competence building will characterize the global winners of the 1990s. With the decade underway, the time for rethinking the concept of the *corporation is already overdue.*

10

THE RESOURCE-BASED THEORY OF COMPETITIVE ADVANTAGE: IMPLICATIONS FOR STRATEGY FORMULATION

Robert M. Grant

Strategy has been defined as 'the match an organization makes between its internal resources and skills . . . and the opportunities and risks created by its external environment.'[1] During the 1980s, the principal developments in strategy analysis focused upon the link between strategy and the external environment. Prominent examples of this focus are Michael Porter's analysis of industry structure and competitive positioning and the empirical studies undertaken by the PIMS project.[2] By contrast, the link between strategy and the firm's resources and skills has suffered comparative neglect. Most research into the strategic implications of the firm's internal environment has been concerned with issues of strategy implementation and analysis of the organizational processes through which strategies emerge.[3]

Recently there has been a resurgence of interest in the role of the firm's resources as the foundation for firm strategy. This interest reflects dissatisfaction with the static, equilibrium framework of industrial organization economics that has dominated much contemporary thinking about business strategy and has renewed interest in older theories of profit and competition associated with the writings of David Ricardo, Joseph Schumpeter, and Edith Penrose.[4] Advances have occurred on several fronts. At the corporate strategy level, theoretical interest in economies of scope and transaction costs have focused attention on the role of corporate resources in determining the industrial and geographical boundaries of the firm's activities.[5] At the business strategy level, explorations of the relationships between resources, competition, and profitability include the analysis of competitive imitation,[6] the appropriability of returns to innovations,[7] the role of imperfect information in creating profitability differences between competing firms,[8] and the means by which the process of resource accumulation can sustain competitive advantage.[9]

Together, these contributions amount to what has been termed 'the resource-based view of the firm'. As yet, however, the implications of this 'resource-based theory' for strategic management are unclear for two reasons. First, the various contributions lack a single integrating framework. Second, little effort has been made to develop the practical implications of this theory. The purpose of this article is to make progress on both these fronts by proposing a framework for a

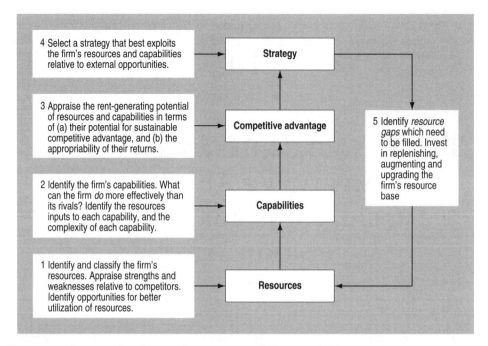

Figure 10.1   A resource-based approach to strategy analysis: a practical framework

resource-based approach to strategy formulation which integrates a number of the key themes arising from this stream of literature. The organizing framework for the article is a five-stage procedure for strategy formulation: analysing the firm's resource-base; appraising the firm's capabilities; analysing the profit-earning potential of firm's resources and capabilities; selecting a strategy; and extending and upgrading the firm's pool of resources and capabilities. Figure 10.1 outlines this framework.

RESOURCES AND CAPABILITIES AS THE FOUNDATION FOR STRATEGY

The case for making the resources and capabilities of the firm the foundation for its long-term strategy rests upon two premises: first, internal resources and capabilities provide the basic direction for a firm's strategy; second, resources and capabilities are the primary source of profit for the firm.

Resources and capabilities as a source of direction

The starting point for the formulation of strategy must be some statement of the firm's identity and purpose – conventionally this takes the form of a mission statement which answers the question: 'What is our business?' Typically the definition of the business is in terms of the served market of the firm: e.g., 'Who are our customers?' and 'Which of their needs are we seeking to serve?' But in a world where customer preferences are volatile, the identity of customers is changing, and the technologies for serving customer requirements are continually evolving, an externally focused orientation does not provide a secure foundation for formulating long-term strategy. When the external environment is in a state of flux, the firm's own resources and capabilities may be a much more stable basis on which to define its identity. Hence, a definition of a business in terms of what it is capable of doing may offer a more durable basis for strategy than a definition based upon the needs which the business seeks to satisfy.

Theodore Levitt's solution to the problem of external change was that companies should define their served markets broadly rather than narrowly: railroads should have perceived themselves to be in the transportation business, not the railroad business. But such broadening of the target market is of little value if the company cannot easily develop the capabilities required for serving customer requirements across a wide front. Was it feasible for the railroads to have developed successful trucking, airline, and car rental businesses? Perhaps the resources and capabilities of the railroad companies were better suited to real estate development, or the building and managing of oil and gas pipelines. Evidence suggests that serving broadly defined customer needs is a difficult task. The attempts by Merrill Lynch, American Express, Sears, Citicorp and, most recently, Prudential-Bache to 'serve the full range of our customers' financial needs' created serious management problems. Allegis Corporation's goal of 'serving the needs of the traveller' through combining United Airlines, Hertz car rental and Westin Hotels was a costly failure. By contrast, several companies whose strategies have been based upon developing and exploiting clearly defined internal capabilities have been adept at adjusting to and exploiting external change. Honda's focus upon the technical excellence of 4-cycle engines carried it successfully from motorcycles to automobiles to a broad range of gasoline-engine products. 3M Corporation's expertise in applying adhesive and coating technologies to new product development has permitted profitable growth over an ever-widening product range.

Resources as the basis for corporate profitability

A firm's ability to earn a rate of profit in excess of its cost of capital depends upon two factors: the attractiveness of the industry in which it is located, and its establishment of competitive advantage over rivals. Industrial organization economics emphasizes industry attractiveness as the primary basis for superior profitability, the implication being that strategic management is concerned primarily with seeking favourable industry environments, locating attractive segments and strategic groups within industries, and moderating competitive pressures by influencing industry structure and competitors' behaviour. Yet empirical investigation has failed to support the link between industry structure and profitability. Most studies show that differences in profitability within industries are much more important than differences in profitability between industries.[10] The reasons are not difficult to find: international competition, technological change, and diversification by firms across industry boundaries have meant that industries which were once cosy havens for making easy profits are now subject to vigorous competition.

The finding that competitive advantage rather than external environments is the primary source of inter-firm profit differentials between firms focuses attention upon the sources of competitive advantage. Although the competitive strategy literature has tended to emphasize issues of strategic positioning in terms of the choice between cost and differentiation advantage, and between broad and narrow market scope, fundamental to these choices is the resource position of the firm. For example, the ability to establish a cost advantage requires possession of scale-efficient plants, superior process technology, ownership of low-cost sources of raw materials, or access to low-wage labour. Similarly, differentiation advantage is conferred by brand reputation, proprietary technology, or an extensive sales and service network.

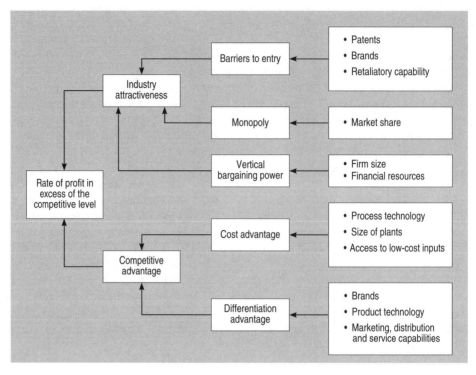

Figure 10.2   Resources as the basis for profitability

This may be summed up as follows: business strategy should be viewed less as a quest for monopoly rents (the returns to market power) and more as a quest for Ricardian rents (the returns to the resources which confer competitive advantage over and above the real costs of these resources). Once these resources depreciate, become obsolescent, or are replicated by other firms, so the rents they generate tend to disappear.[11]

We can go further. A closer look at market power and the monopoly rent it offers, suggests that it too has its basis in the resources of firms. The fundamental prerequisite for market power is the presence of barriers to entry.[12] Barriers to entry are based upon scale economies, patents, experience advantages, brand reputation, or some other resource which incumbent firms possess but which entrants can acquire only slowly or at disproportionate expense. Other structural sources of market power are similarly based upon firms' resources: monopolistic price-setting power depends upon market share which is a consequence of cost efficiency, financial strength, or some other resource. The resources which confer market power may be owned individually by firms, others may be owned jointly. An industry standard (which raises costs of entry), or a cartel, is a resource which is owned collectively by the industry members.[13] Figure 10.2 summarizes the relationships between resources and profitability.

TAKING STOCK OF THE FIRM'S RESOURCES

There is a key distinction between resources and capabilities. Resources are inputs into the production process – they are the basic units of analysis. The individual resources of the firm include items of capital equipment, skills of individual employees, patents, brand names, finance, and so on.

But, on their own, few resources are productive. Productive activity requires the co-operation and co-ordination of teams of resources. A capability is the capacity for a team of resources to perform some task or activity. While resources are the source of a firm's capabilities, capabilities are the main source of its competitive advantage.

Identifying resources

A major handicap in identifying and appraising a firm's resources is that management information systems typically provide only a fragmented and incomplete picture of the firm's resource base. Financial balance sheets are notoriously inadequate because they disregard intangible resources and people-based skills – probably the most strategically important resources of the firm.[14] Classification can provide a useful starting point. Six major categories of resource have been suggested: financial resources, physical resources, human resources, technological resources, reputation, and organizational resources.[15] The reluctance of accountants to extend the boundaries of corporate balance sheets beyond tangible assets partly reflects difficulties of valuation. The heterogeneity and imperfect transferability of most intangible resources preclude the use of market prices. One approach to valuing intangible resources is to take the difference between the stock market value of the firm and the replacement value of its tangible assets.[16] On a similar basis, valuation ratios provide some indication of the importance of firms' intangible resources. Table 10.1 shows that the highest valuation ratios are found among companies with valuable patents and technology assets (notably drug companies) and brand-rich consumer-product companies.

The primary task of a resource-based approach to strategy formulation is maximizing rents over time. For this purpose we need to investigate the relationship between resources and organizational capabilities. However, there are also direct links between resources and profitability which raise issues for the strategic management of resources:

- *What opportunities exist for economizing on the use of resources?* The ability to maximize productivity is particularly important in the case of tangible resources such as plant and machinery, finance, and people. It may involve using fewer resources to support a larger volume of business. The success of aggressive acquirors, such as ConAgra in the US and Hanson in Britain, is based upon expertise in rigorously pruning the financial, physical and human assets needed to support the volume of business in acquired companies.
- *What are the possibilities for using existing assets more intensely and in more profitable employment?* A large proportion of corporate acquisitions are motivated by the belief that the resources of the acquired company can be put to more profitable use. The returns from transferring existing assets into more productive employment can be substantial. The remarkable turnaround in the performance of the Walt Disney Company between 1985 and 1987 owed much to the vigorous exploitation of Disney's considerable and unique assets: accelerated development of Disney's vast landholdings (for residential development as well as entertainment purposes); exploitation of Disney's huge film library through cable TV, videos, and syndication; fuller utilization of Disney's studios through the formation of Touchstone Films; increased marketing to improve capacity utilization at Disney theme parks.

Table 10.1 Twenty companies among the US Top 100 companies with the highest ratios of stock price to book value on 16 March 1990

Company	Industry	Valuation Ratio
Coca-Cola	Beverages	8.77
Microsoft	Computer software	8.67
Merck	Pharmaceuticals	8.59
American Home Products	Pharmaceuticals	8.00
Wal Mart Stores	Retailing	7.51
Limited	Retailing	6.65
Warner Lambert	Pharmaceuticals	6.34
Waste Management	Pollution control	6.18
Marrion Merrell Dow	Pharmaceuticals	6.10
McGaw Cellular Communications	Telecom equipment	5.90
Bristol Myers Squibb	Pharmaceuticals	5.48
Toys R Us	Retailing	5.27
Abbot Laboratories	Pharmaceuticals	5.26
Walt Disney	Entertainment	4.90
Johnson & Johnson	Health care products	4.85
MCI Communications	Telecommunications	4.80
Eli Lilly	Pharmaceuticals	4.70
Kellogg	Food products	4.58
H.J. Heinz	Food products	4.38
Pepsico	Beverages	4.33

Source: The 1990 Business Week Top 1000

IDENTIFYING AND APPRAISING CAPABILITIES

The capabilities of a firm are what it can do as a result of teams of resources working together. A firm's capabilities can be identified and appraised using a standard functional classification of the firm's activities.

For example, Snow and Hrebiniak examined capabilities (in their terminology, 'distinctive competencies') in relation to ten functional areas.[17] For most firms, however, the most important capabilities are likely to be those which arise from an integration of individual functional capabilities. For example, McDonald's possesses outstanding functional capabilities within product development, market research, human resource management, financial control and operations management. However, critical to McDonald's success is the integration of these functional capabilities to create McDonald's remarkable consistency of products and services in thousands of restaurants spread across most of the globe. Hamel and Prahalad use the term 'core competencies' to describe these central, strategic capabilities. They are 'the collective learning in the organization, especially how to co-ordinate diverse production skills and integrate multiple streams of technology.'[18] Examples of core competencies include:

- NEC's integration of computer and telecommunication technology
- Philips' optical-media expertise
- Casio's harmonization of know-how in miniaturization, microprocessor design, material science, and ultrathin precision casting

- Canon's integration of optical, microelectronic, and precision-mechanical technologies which forms the basis of its success in cameras, copiers and facsimile machines
- Black and Decker's competence in the design and manufacture of small electric motors.

A key problem in appraising capabilities is maintaining objectivity. Howard Stevenson observed a wide variation in senior managers' perceptions of their organizations' distinctive competencies.[19] Organizations frequently fall victim to past glories, hopes for the future, and wishful thinking. Among the failed industrial companies of both America and Britain are many which believed themselves world leaders with superior products and customer loyalty. During the 1960s, the CEOs of both Harley-Davidson and BSA-Triumph scorned the idea that Honda threatened their supremacy in the market for 'serious motorcycles'.[20] The failure of the US steel companies to respond to increasing import competition during the 1970s was similarly founded upon misplaced confidence in their quality and technological leadership.[21]

The critical task is to assess capabilities relative to those of competitors. In the same way that national prosperity is enhanced through specialization on the basis of comparative advantages, so for the firm, a successful strategy is one which exploits relative strengths. Federal Express's primary capabilities are those which permit it to operate a national delivery system that can guarantee next day delivery; for the British retailer Marks and Spencer, it is the ability to manage supplier relations to ensure a high and consistent level of product quality; for General Electric, it is a system of corporate management that reconciles control, co-ordination, flexibility and innovation in one of the world's largest and most diversified corporations. Conversely, failure is often due to strategies which extend the firm's activities beyond the scope of its capabilities.

Capabilities as organizational routines

Creating capabilities is not simply a matter of assembling a team of resources: capabilities involve complex patterns of co-ordination between people and between people and other resources. Perfecting such co-ordination requires learning through repetition. To understand the anatomy of a firm's capabilities, Nelson and Winter's concept of 'organizational routine' is illuminating. Organizational routines are regular and predictable patterns of activity which are made up of a sequence of co-ordinated actions by individuals. A capability is, in essence, a routine, or a number of interacting routines. The organization itself is a huge network of routines. These include the sequence of routines which govern the passage of raw material and components through the production process, and top management routines which include routines for monitoring business unit performance, for capital budgeting and for strategy formulation.

The concept of organizational routines offers illuminating insights into the relationships between resources, capabilities and competitive advantage:

- *The relationship between resources and capabilities.* There is no predetermined functional relationship between the resources of a firm and its capabilities. The types, the amounts, and the qualities of the resources available to the firm have an important bearing on what the firm can do since they place constraints upon the range of organizational routines that can be performed and the standard to which they are performed. However, a key ingredient in the relationship between resources and capabilities is the ability of an organization to achieve co-operation and co-ordination within teams. This requires that an organization motivate and socialize its members in a manner conducive to the development of smooth-functioning routines. The organization's style, values, traditions and leadership are critical encouragements to the co-operation and commitment of its members. These can be viewed as intangible resources which are common ingredients of the whole range of corporation's organizational routines.

- *The trade-off between efficiency and flexibility.* Routines are to the organization what skills are to the individual. Just as the individual's skills are carried out semi-automatically, without conscious co-ordination, so organizational routines involve a large component of tacit knowledge, which implies limits on the extent to which the organization's capabilities can be articulated. Just as individual skills become rusty when not exercised, so it is difficult for organizations to retain co-ordinated responses to contingencies that arise only rarely. Hence there may be a trade-off between efficiency and flexibility. A limited repertoire of routines can be performed highly efficiently with near-perfect co-ordination – all in the absence of significant intervention by top management. The same organization may find it extremely difficult to respond to novel situations.

- *Economies of experience.* Just as individual skills are acquired through practice over time, so the skills of an organization are developed and sustained only through experience. The advantage of an established firm over a newcomer is primarily in the organizational routines that it has perfected over time. The Boston Consulting Group's 'experience curve' represents a naive, yet valuable attempt to relate the experience of the firm to its performance. However, in industries where technological change is rapid, new firms may possess an advantage over established firms through their potential for faster learning of new routines because they are less committed to old routines.

- *The complexity of capabilities.* Organizational capabilities differ in their complexity. Some capabilities may derive from the contribution of a single resource. Du Pont's successful development of several cardiovascular drugs during the late 1980s owed much to the research leadership of its leading pharmacologist Pieter Timmermans.[22] Drexel Burnham Lambert's capability in junk bond underwriting during the 1980s resided almost entirely in the skills of Michael Milken. Other routines require highly complex interactions involving the co-operation of many different resources. Walt Disney's 'imagineering' capability involves the integration of ideas, skills, and knowledge drawn from movie making, engineering, psychology, and a wide variety of technical disciplines. As we shall see, complexity is particularly relevant to the sustainability of competitive advantage.

EVALUATING THE RENT-EARNING POTENTIAL: SUSTAINABILITY

The returns to a firm's resources and capabilities depend upon two key factors: first, the sustainability of the competitive advantage which resources and capabilities confer upon the firm; and, second, the ability of the firm to appropriate the rents earned from its resources and capabilities.

Over the long term, competitive advantage and the returns associated with it are eroded both through the depreciation of the advantaged firm's resources and capabilities and through imitation by rivals. The speed of erosion depends critically upon the characteristics of the resources and capabilities. Consider markets where competitive advantage is unsustainable: in 'efficient' markets (most closely approximated by the markets for securities, commodities, and foreign exchange) competitive advantage is absent; market prices reflect all available information, prices adjust instantaneously to new information, and traders can only expect normal returns. The absence of competitive advantage is a consequence of the resources required to compete in these markets. To trade in financial markets, the basic requirements are finance and information. If both are available on equal terms to all participants, competitive advantage cannot exist. Even if privileged information is assumed to exist ('weakly efficient' markets), competitive advantage is not sustainable. Once a trader acts upon privileged information, transactions volume and price movements signal insider activity, and other traders are likely to rush in seeking a piece of the action.

The essential difference between industrial markets and financial markets lies in the resource requirements of each. In industrial markets, resources are specialized, immobile, and long-lasting. As a result, according to Richard Caves, a key feature of industrial markets is the existence of 'committed competition – rivalrous moves among incumbent producers that involve resource commitments that are irrevocable for non-trivial periods of time.'[23] The difficulties involved in acquiring the resources required to compete and the need to commit resources long before a competitive move can be initiated also implies that competitive advantage is much more sustainable than it is in financial markets. Resource-based approaches to the theory of competitive advantage point towards four characteristics of resources and capabilities which are likely to be particularly important determinants of the sustainability of competitive advantage: *durability, transparency, transferability,* and *replicability*.

Durability

In the absence of competition, the longevity of a firm's competitive advantage depends upon the rate at which the underlying resources and capabilities depreciate or become obsolete. The durability of resources varies considerably: the increasing pace of technological change is shortening the useful life spans of most capital equipment and technological resources. On the other hand, reputation (both brand and corporate) appears to depreciate relatively slowly, and these assets can normally be maintained by modest rates of replacement investment. Many of the consumer brands which command the strongest loyalties today (e.g. Heinz sauces, Kellogg's cereals, Campbell's soup, Hoover vacuum cleaners) have been market leaders for close to a century. Corporate reputation displays similar longevity: the reputations of GE, IBM, Du Pont, and Proctor and Gamble as well-managed, socially responsible, financially sound companies which produce reliable products and treat their employees well has been established over several decades. While increasing environmental turbulence shortens the life spans of many resources, it is possible that it may have the effect of bolstering brand and corporate reputations.

Firm capabilities have the potential to be more durable than the resources upon which they are based because of the firm's ability to maintain capabilities through replacing individual resources (including people) as they wear out or move on. Rolls Royce's capability in the craft-based manufacture of luxury cars and 3M's capability in new product introduction have been maintained over several generations of employees. Such longevity depends critically upon the management of these capabilities to ensure their maintenance and renewal. One of the most important roles that organizational culture plays in sustaining competitive advantage may be through its maintenance support for capabilities through the socialization of new employees.[24]

Transparency

The firm's ability to sustain its competitive advantage over time depends upon the speed with which other firms can imitate its strategy. Imitation requires that a competitor overcomes two problems. First is the information problem: What is the competitive advantage of the successful rival, and how is it being achieved? Second is the strategy duplication problem: How can the would-be competitor amass the resources and capabilities required to imitate the successful strategy of the rival? The information problem is a consequence of imperfect information on two sets of relationships. If a firm wishes to imitate the strategy of a rival, it must first establish the capabilities which underlie the rival's competitive advantage, and then it must determine what resources are required to replicate these capabilities. I refer to this as the 'transparency' of competitive advantage. With regard to the first transparency problem, a competitive advantage which is the consequence of superior capability in relation to a single performance variable is more easy to identify and comprehend than a competitive advantage that involves multiple capabilities conferring superior performance across several variables. Cray Research's success in the computer industry rests primarily upon its technological capability in relation to large, ultra-powerful computers. IBM's superior performance is multi-dimensional and is more difficult to understand. It is extremely difficult to distinguish and appraise the relative contributions to IBM's success of research capability, scale economies in product development and manufacturing, self-sufficiency through backward integration, and superior customer service through excellence in sales, service, and technical support.

With regard to the second transparency problem, a capability which requires a complex pattern of co-ordination between large numbers of diverse resources is more difficult to comprehend than a capability which rests upon the exploitation of a single dominant resource. For example, Federal Express's next-day delivery capability requires close co-operation between numerous employees, aircraft, delivery vans, computerized tracking facilities and automated sorting equipment, all co-ordinated into a single system. By contrast, Atlantic Richfield's low-cost position in the supply of gasoline to the California market rests simply on its access to Alaskan crude oil. Imperfect transparency is the basis for Lippman and Rumelt's theory of 'uncertain imitability': the greater the uncertainty within a market over how successful companies 'do it', the more inhibited are potential entrants, and the higher the level of profit that established firms can maintain within that market.[25]

Transferability

Once an established firm or potential entrant has established the sources of the superior performance, imitation then requires amassing the resources and capabilities necessary for a competitive challenge. The primary source of resources and capabilities is likely to be the markets for these inputs. If firms can acquire (on similar terms) the resources required for imitating the competitive advantage of a successful rival, then that rival's competitive advantage will be short lived. As we have seen, in financial markets the easy access by traders to finance and information causes competitive advantage to be fleeting. However, most resources and capabilities are not freely transferable between firms; hence, would-be competitors are unable to acquire (on equal terms) the resources needed to replicate the competitive advantage of an incumbent firm. Imperfections in transferability arise from several sources:

- *Geographical immobility*. The costs of relocating large items of capital equipment and highly specialized employees put firms which are acquiring these resources at a disadvantage to firms which already possess them.
- *Imperfect information*. Assessing the value of a resource is made difficult by the heterogeneity of resources (particularly human resources) and by imperfect knowledge of the potential

productivity of individual resources.[26] The established firm's ability to build up information over time about the productivity of its resources gives it superior knowledge to that of any prospective purchaser of the resources in question.[27] The resulting imperfection of the markets for productive resources can then result in resources being either underpriced or overpriced, thus giving rise to differences in profitability between firms.[28]

- *Firm-specific resources.* Apart from the transactions costs arising from immobility and imperfect information, the value of a resource may fall on transfer due to a decline in its productivity. To the extent that brand reputation is associated with the company which created the brand reputation, a change in ownership of the brand name erodes its value. Once Rover, MG, Triumph and Jaguar were merged into British Leyland, the values of these brands in differentiating automobiles declined substantially. Employees can suffer a similar decline in productivity in the process of inter-firm transfer. To the extent that an employee's productivity is influenced by situational and motivational factors, then it is unreasonable to expect that a highly successful employee in one company can replicate his/her performance when hired away by another company. Some resources may be almost entirely firm-specific – corporate reputation can only be transferred by acquiring the company as a whole, and even then the reputation of the acquired company normally depreciates during the change in ownership.[29]

- *The immobility of capabilities.* Capabilities, because they require interactive teams of resources, are far more immobile than individual resources – they require the transfer of the whole team. Such transfers can occur (e.g. the defection of 16 of First Boston's managers and acquisitions staff to Wasserstein, Perella and Company).[30] However, even if the resources that constitute the team are transferred, the nature of organizational routines – in particular, the role of tacit knowledge and unconscious co-ordination – makes the recreation of capabilities within a new corporate environment uncertain.

Replicability

Imperfect transferability of resources and capabilities limits the ability of a firm to buy in the means to imitate success. The second route by which a firm can acquire a resource of capability is by internal investment. Some resources and capabilities can be easily imitated through replication. In retailing, competitive advantages which derive from electronic point-of-sale systems, retailer charge cards, and extended hours of opening can be copied fairly easily by competitors. In financial services, new product innovations (such as interest rate swaps, stripped bonds, money market accounts, and the like) are notorious for their easy imitation by competitors.

Much less easily replicable are capabilities based upon highly complex organizational routines. IBM's ability to motivate its people and Nucor's outstanding efficiency and flexibility in steel manufacture are combinations of complex routines that are based upon tacit rather than codified knowledge and are fused into the respective corporate cultures. Some capabilities appear simple but prove exceptionally difficult to replicate. Two of the simplest and best-known Japanese manufacturing practices are just-in-time scheduling and quality circles. Despite the fact that neither require sophisticated knowledge or complex operating systems, the co-operation and attitudinal changes required for their effective operation are such that few American and European firms have introduced either with the same degree of success as Japanese companies. If apparently simple practices such as these are deceptively difficult to imitate, it is easy to see how firms that develop highly complex capabilities can maintain their competitive advantage over very long periods of time. Xerox's commitment to customer service is a capability that is not located in any particular department, but it permeates the whole corporation and is built into the fabric and culture of the corporation.

Even where replication is possible, the dynamics of stock-flow relationships may still offer an advantage to incumbent firms. Competitive advantage depends upon the stock of resources and capabilities that a firm possesses. Dierickx and Cool show that firms which possess the initial stocks of the resources required for competitive advantage may be able to sustain their advantages over time.[31] Among the stock-flow relationships they identify as sustaining advantage are: 'asset mass efficiencies' – the initial amount of the resource which the firm possesses influences the pace at which the resource can be accumulated; and 'time compression diseconomies' – firms which rapidly accumulate a resource incur disproportionate costs ('crash programs' of R&D and 'blitz' advertising campaigns tend to be less productive than similar expenditures made over a longer period).

EVALUATING RENT-EARNING POTENTIAL: APPROPRIABILITY

The returns to a firm from its resources and capabilities depend not only on sustaining its competitive position over time, but also on the firm's ability to appropriate these returns. The issue of appropriability concerns the allocation of rents where property rights are not fully defined. Once we go beyond the financial and physical assets valued in a company's balance sheet, ownership becomes ambiguous. The firm owns intangible assets such as patents, copyrights, brand names, and trade secrets, but the scope of property rights may lack precise definition. In the case of employee skills, two major problems arise: the lack of clear distinction between the technology of the firm and the human capital of the individual; and the limited control which employment contracts offer over the services provided by employees. Employee mobility means that it is risky for a firm's strategy to be dependent upon the specific skills of a few key employees. Also, such employees can bargain with the firm to appropriate the major part of their contribution to value added.

The degree of control exercised by a firm and the balance of power between the firm and an individual employee depends crucially on the relationship between the individual's skills and organizational routines. The more deeply embedded are organizational routines within groups of individuals and the more they are supported by the contributions of other resources, then the greater is the control that the firm's management can exercise. The ability of IBM to utilize its advanced semiconductor research as an instrument of competitive advantage depends, in part, upon the extent to which the research capability is a team asset rather than a reflection of the contribution of brilliant individuals. A firm's dependence upon skills possessed by highly trained and highly mobile key employees is particularly important in the case of professional service companies where employee skills are the overwhelmingly important resource.[32] Many of the problems that have arisen in acquisitions of human-capital-intensive companies arise from conflicts over property rights between the acquiring company and employees of the acquired company. An interesting example is the protracted dispute which followed the acquisition of the New York advertising agency Lord, Geller, Fredrico, Einstein by WPP Group in 1988. Most of the senior executives of the acquired company left to form a new advertising agency taking several former clients with them.[33] Similar conflicts have arisen over technology ownership in high-tech start-ups founded by former employees of established companies.[34]

Where ownership is ambiguous, relative bargaining power is the primary determinant of the allocation of the rents between the firm and its employees. If the individual employee's contribution to productivity is clearly identifiable, if the employee is mobile, and the employee's skills offer similar productivity to other firms, then the employee is well placed to bargain for that contribution. If the increased gate receipts of the LA Kings ice hockey team can be attributed primarily to the presence of Wayne Gretzky on the team and if Gretzky can offer a similar performance enhancement to other teams, then he is in a strong position to appropriate (as salary and bonuses) most of the increased contribution. The less identifiable is the individual's contribution, and the more firm-specific are the skills being applied, the greater is the proportion of the return which accrues to the firm. Declining profitability among investment banks encouraged several to reassert their bargaining power vis-à-vis their individual stars and in-house gurus by engineering a transfer of reputation from these key employees to the company as a whole. At Citibank, Salomon Brothers, Merrill Lynch, and First Boston, this resulted in bitter conflicts between top management and some senior employees.[35]

FORMULATING STRATEGY

Although the foregoing discussion of the links between resources, capabilities, and profitability has been strongly theoretical in nature, the implications for strategy formulation are straightforward. The analysis of the rent-generating potential of resources and capabilities concludes that the firm's most important resources and capabilities are those which are durable, difficult to identify and understand, imperfectly transferable, not easily replicated, and in which the firm possesses clear ownership and control. These are the firm's 'crown jewels' and need to be protected; and they play a pivotal role in the competitive strategy which the firm pursues. The essence of strategy formulation, then, is to design a strategy that makes the most effective use of these core resources and capabilities. Consider, for example, the remarkable turnaround of Harley-Davidson between 1984 and 1988. Fundamental was top management's recognition that the company's sole durable, non-transferable, irreplicable asset was the Harley-Davidson image and the loyalty that accompanied that image. In virtually every other area of competitive performance – production costs, quality, product and process technology, and global market scope – Harley was greatly inferior to its Japanese rivals. Harley's only opportunity for survival was to pursue a strategy founded upon Harley's image advantage, while simultaneously minimising Harley's disadvantages in other capabilities. Harley-Davidson's new models introduced during this period were all based around traditional design features, while Harley's marketing strategy involved extending the appeal of the Harley image of individuality and toughness from its traditional customer group to more affluent professional types. Protection of the Harley-Davidson name by means of tougher controls over dealers was matched by wider exploitation of the Harley name through extensive licensing. While radical improvements in manufacturing efficiency and quality were essential components of the turnaround strategy, it was the enhancing and broadening of Harley's market appeal which was the primary driver of Harley's rise from 27 to 44 percent of the US heavyweight motorcycle market between 1984 and 1988, accompanied by an increase in net income from £6.5 million to $29.8 million.

Conversely, a failure to recognize and exploit the strategic importance of durable, untransferable, and irreplicable resources almost inevitably has dire consequences. The troubles of BankAmerica Corporation during the mid-1980s can be attributed to a strategy that became increasingly dissociated from the bank's most important assets: its reputation and market position in retail banking in the Western United States. The disastrous outcome of US Air Group's acquisition of the Californian carrier, PSA, is similarly attributable to US Air's disregard for PSA's most important asset – its reputation in the Californian market for a friendly, laid-back style of service.

Designing strategy around the most critically important resources and capabilities may imply that the firm limits its strategic scope to those activities where it possesses a clear competitive advantage. The principal capabilities of Lotus, the specialist manufacturer of sports cars, are in design and engineering development; it lacked both the manufacturing capabilities or the sales volume to compete effectively in the world's auto market. Lotus's turnaround during the 1980s followed its decision to specialize upon design and development consulting for other auto manufacturers, and to limit its own manufacturing primarily to formula one racing cars.

The ability of a firm's resources and capabilities to support a sustainable competitive advantage is essential to the time frame of a firm's strategic planning process. If a company's resources and capabilities lack durability or are easily transferred or replicated, then the company must either adopt a strategy of short-term harvesting or it must invest in developing new sources of competitive advantage. These considerations are critical for small technological start-ups where the speed of technological change may mean that innovations offer only temporary competitive advantage. The company must seek either to exploit its initial innovation before it is challenged by stronger, established rivals or other start-ups, or it must establish the technological capability for a continuing stream of innovations. A fundamental flaw in EMI's exploitation of its invention of the CT scanner was a strategy that failed to exploit EMI's five-year technical lead in the development and marketing of the X-ray scanner and failed to establish the breadth of technological and manufacturing capability required to establish a fully fledged medical electronics business.

Where a company's resources and capabilities are easily transferable or replicable, sustaining a competitive advantage is only feasible if the company's market is unattractively small or if it can obscure the existence of its competitive advantage. Filofax, the long-established British manufacturer of personal organizers, was able to dominate the market for its products so long as that market remained small. The boom in demand for Filofaxes during the mid-1980s was, paradoxically, a disaster for the company. Filofax's product was easily imitated and yuppie-driven demand growth spawned a host of imitators. By 1989, the company was suffering falling sales and mounting losses.[36] In industries where competitive advantages based upon differentiation and innovation can be imitated (such as financial services, retailing, fashion clothing, and toys), firms have a brief window of opportunity during which to exploit their advantage before imitators erode it away. Under such circumstances, firms must be concerned not with sustaining the existing advantages, but with creating the flexibility and responsiveness that permits them to create new advantages at a faster rate than the old advantages are being eroded by competition.

Transferability and replicability of resources and capabilities are also a key issue in the strategic management of joint ventures. Studies of the international joint ventures point to the transferability of each party's capabilities as a critical determinant of the allocation of benefits from the venture. For example, Western companies' strengths in distribution channels and product technology have been easily exploited by Japanese joint venture partners, while Japanese manufacturing excellence and new product development capabilities have proved exceptionally difficult for Western companies to learn.[37]

IDENTIFYING RESOURCE GAPS AND DEVELOPING THE RESOURCE BASE

The analysis so far has regarded the firm's resource base as predetermined, with the primary task of organizational strategy being the deployment of these resources so as to maximize rents over time. However, a resource-based approach to strategy is concerned not only with the deployment of existing resources, but also with the development of the firm's stock of resources and to augment resources in order to buttress and extend positions of competitive advantage as well as broaden the firm's strategic opportunity set. This task is known in the strategy literature as filling 'resource gaps'.[38]

Sustaining advantage in the face of competition and evolving customer requirements also requires that firms constantly develop their resource bases. Such 'upgrading' of competitive advantage occupies a central position in Michael Porter's analysis of the competitive advantage of nations.[39] Porter's analysis of the ability of firms and nations to establish and maintain international competitive success depends critically upon the ability to continually innovate and to shift the basis of competitive advantage from 'basic' to 'advanced' factors of production. An important feature of these 'advanced' factors of production is that they offer a more sustainable competitive advantage because they are more specialized (therefore less mobile through market transfer) and less easy to replicate.

Commitment to upgrading the firm's pool of resources and capabilities requires strategic direction in terms of the capabilities that will form the basis of the firm's future competitive advantage. Thus, Prahalad and Hamel's notion of 'core competencies' is less an identification of a company's current capabilities than a commitment to a path of future development. For example, NEC's strategic focus on computing and communications in the mid-1970s was not so much a statement of the core strengths of the company as it was a long-term commitment to a particular path of technological development.

Harmonizing the exploitation of existing resources with the development of the resources and capabilities for competitive advantage in the future is a subtle task. To the extent that capabilities are learned and perfected through repetition, capabilities develop automatically through the pursuit of a particular strategy. The essential task, then, is to ensure that strategy constantly pushes slightly beyond the limits of the firm's capabilities at any point of time. This ensures not only the perfection of capabilities required by the current strategy, but also the development of the capabilities required to meet the challenges of the future. The idea that, through pursuing its present strategy, a firm develops the expertise required for its future strategy is referred to by Hiroyuki Itami as 'dynamic resource fit':

> Effective strategy in the present builds invisible assets, and the expanded stock enables the firm to plan its future strategy to be carried out. And the future strategy must make effective use of the resources that have been amassed.[40]

Matsushita is a notable exponent of this principle of parallel and sequential development of strategy and capabilities. For example, in developing production in a foreign country, Matsushita typically began with the production of simple products, such as batteries, then moved on to the production of products requiring greater manufacturing and marketing sophistication:

> In every country batteries are a necessity, so they sell well. As long as we bring a few advanced automated pieces of equipment for the processes vital to final product quality, even unskilled labor can produce good products. As they work on this rather simple product, the workers get trained, and this increased skill level then permits us to gradually expand production to items with increasingly higher technology level, first radios, then televisions.[41]

The development of capabilities which can then be used as the basis for broadening a firm's product range is a common feature of successful strategies of related diversification. Sequential product addition to accompany the development of technological, manufacturing, and marketing expertise was a feature of Honda's diversification from motorcycles to cars, generators, lawn-mowers, and boat engines; and of 3M's expansion from abrasives to adhesives, video tape, and computer disks.

In order both to fully exploit a firm's existing stock of resources, and to develop competitive advantages for the future, the external acquisition of complementary resources may be necessary. Consider the Walt Disney Company's turnaround between 1984 and 1988. In order for the new management to exploit more effectively Disney's vast, under-utilized stock of unique resources, new resources were required. Achieving better utilization of Disney's film studios and expertise in animation required the acquisition of creative talent in the form of directors, actors, scriptwriters, and cartoonists. Putting Disney's vast real estate holdings to work was assisted by the acquisition of the property development expertise of the Arvida Corporation. Building a new marketing team was instrumental in increasing capacity utilization at Disneyland and Disney World.

CONCLUSION

The resources and capabilities of a firm are the central considerations in formulating its strategy: they are the primary constants upon which a firm can establish its identity and frame its strategy, and they are the primary sources of the firm's profitability. The key to a resource-based approach to strategy formulation is understanding the relationships between resources, capabilities, competitive advantage, and profitability – in particular, an understanding of the mechanisms through which competitive advantage can be sustained over time. This requires the design of strategies which exploit to maximum effect each firm's unique characteristics.

NOTES

1   Charles W. Hofer and Dan Schendel, *Strategy Formulation: Analytical Concepts* (St. Paul, MN: West, 1978), p. 12.

2   Robert D. Buzzell and Bradley T. Gale, *The PIMS Principles: Linking Strategy to Performance* (New York, NY: Free Press, 1987).

3   See, for example, Henry Mintzberg, 'Of Strategies, Deliberate and Emergent', *Strategic Management Journal*, 6 (1985): 257–72; Andrew M. Pettigrew, 'Strategy formulation as a political process', *International Studies of Management and Organization*, 7 (1977): 78–87; J.B. Quinn, *Strategies for Change: Logical Incrementalism* (Homewood, IL: Irwin, 1980).

4   David Ricardo, *Principles of Political Economy and Taxation* (London: G. Bell, 1891); Joseph A. Schumpeter, *The Theory of Economic Development* (Cambridge, MA: Harvard University Press, 1934); Edith Penrose, *The Theory of the Growth of the Firm* (New York, NY: John Wiley and Sons, 1959).

5   David J. Teece, 'Economies of scope and the scope of the enterprise', *Journal of Economic Behavior and Organization*, 1 (1980): 223–47; S. Chatterjee and B. Wernerfelt, 'The link between resources and types of diversification: theory and evidence', *Strategic Management Journal*, 12 (1991): 33–48.

6   R.P. Rumelt, 'Towards a Strategic Theory of the Firm', in R.B. Lamb, ed., *Competitive Strategic Management* (Englewood Cliffs, NJ: Prentice Hall, 1984); S.A. Lippman and R.P. Rumelt, 'Uncertain imitability: an analysis of interfirm differences in efficiency under competition', *Bell Journal of Economics*, 23 (1982): 418–38; Richard Reed and R.J. DeFillippi, 'Causal ambiguity, bar-

riers to imitation, and sustainable competitive advantage', *Academy of Management Review*, 15 (January 1990): 88–102.

7 David J. Teece, 'Capturing value from technological innovation: integration, strategic partnering and licensing decisions', *Interfaces*, 18/3 (1988): 46–61.

8 Jay B. Barney, 'Strategic factor markets: expectations, luck and business strategy', *Management Science*, 32/10 (October 1986): 1231–41.

9 Ingemar Dierickx and Karel Cool, 'Asset stock accumulation and the sustainability of competitive advantage', *Management Science*, 35/12 (December 1989): 1504–13.

10 R. Schmalensee, 'Industrial economics: an overview', *Economic Journal*, 98 (1988): 643–81; R.D. Buzzell and B.T. Gale, *The PIMS Principles* (New York, NY: Free Press, 1987).

11 Because of the ambiguity associated with accounting definitions of profit, the academic literature increasingly uses the term 'rent' to refer to 'economic profit'. 'Rent' is the surplus of revenue over the 'real' or 'opportunity' cost of the resources used in generating that revenue. The 'real' or 'opportunity' cost of a resource is the revenue it can generate when put to an alternative use in the firm or the price which it can be sold for.

12 W.J. Baumol, J.C. Panzer and R.D. Willig, *Contestable Markets and the Theory of Industrial Structure* (New York, NY: Harcourt Brace Jovanovitch, 1982).

13 In economist's jargon, such jointly owned resources are 'public goods' – their benefits can be extended to additional firms at negligible marginal cost.

14 Hiroyuki Itami (*Mobilizing Invisible Assets*, Cambridge, MA: Harvard University Press, 1986) refers to these as 'invisible assets'.

15 Based upon Hofer and Schendel, op. cit., pp. 145–8.

16 See, for example, Iain Cockburn and Zvi Griliches, 'Industry Effects and the Appropriability Measures in the Stock Market's Valuation of R&D and Patents', *American Economic Review*, 78 (1988): 419–23.

17 General management, financial management, marketing and selling, market research, product R&D, engineering, production, distribution, legal affairs, and personnel. See Charles C. Snow and Lawrence G. Hrebiniak, 'Strategy, Distinctive Competence, and Organizational Performance', *Administrative Science Quarterly*, 25 (1980): 317–36.

18 C.K. Prahalad and Gary Hamel, 'The core competence of the corporation', *Harvard Business Review* (May/June 1990), pp. 79–91.

19 Howard H. Stevenson, 'Defining corporate strengths and weaknesses', *Sloan Management Review* (Spring 1976), pp. 51–68.

20 Richard T. Pascale, 'Honda (A)', Harvard Business School, Case no. 9–384–049, 1983.

21 Paul R. Lawrence and Davis Dyer, *Renewing American Industry* (New York, NY: Free Press, 1983), pp. 60–83.

22 'Du Pont's "drug hunter" stalks his next big trophy', *Business Week*, November 27, 1989, pp. 174–82.

23 Richard E. Caves, 'Economic Analysis and the Quest for Competitive Advantage', *American Economic Review*, 74 (1984): 127–8.

24 Jay B. Barney, 'Organizational culture: can it be a source of sustained competitive advantage?' *Academy of Management Review*, 11 (1986): 656–65.

25 Lippman and Rumelt, op. cit.

26 This information problem is a consequence of the fact that resources work together in teams and their individual productivity is not observable. See A.A. Alchian and H. Demsetz, 'Production, Information costs and economic organization', *American Economic Review*, 62 (1972): 777–95.

27 Such asymmetric information gives rise to a 'lemons' problem. See G. Akerlof, 'The market for lemons: qualitative uncertainty and the market mechanism', *Quarterly Journal of Economics*, 84 (1970): 488–500.

28 Barney, op. cit.

29   The definition of resource specificity in this article corresponds to the definition of 'specific assets' by Richard Caves ('International corporations: the industrial economics of foreign investment', *Economica*, 38, 1971: 1–27); it differs from that used by O.E. Williamson (*The Economic Institutions of Capitalism*, New York, NY: Free Press, 1985, pp. 52–6). Williamson refers to assets which are specific to particular transactions rather than to particular firms.

30   'Catch a falling star', *The Economist*, April 23 1988, pp. 88–90.

31   Dierickx and Cool, op. cit.

32   The key advantage of partnerships as an organizational form for such businesses is in averting conflict over control and rent allocation between employees and owners.

33   'Ad world is abuzz as top brass leaves Lord Geller agency', *Wall Street Journal*, March 23, 1988, p. A1.

34   Charles Ferguson ('From the people who brought you voodoo economics', *Harvard Business Review*, May/June 1988, pp. 55–63) has claimed that these start-ups involve the individual exploitation of technical knowledge which rightfully belongs to the former employers of these new entrepreneurs.

35   'The decline of the superstar', *Business Week*, August 17, 1987, pp. 90–6.

36   'Faded fad', *The Economist*, September 30, 1989, p. 68.

37   Gary Hamel, Yves Doz, and C.K. Prahalad, 'Collaborate with your competitors – and win', *Harvard Business Review* (January/February 1989), pp. 133–9.

38   Stevenson (1985), op. cit.

39   Michael E. Porter, *The Competitive Advantage of Nations* (New York, NY: Free Press, 1990).

40   Itami, op. cit., p. 125.

41   Arataroh Takahashi, *What I Learned from Konosuke Matsushita* (Tokyo: Jitsugyo no Nihonsha, 1980 (in Japanese)). Quoted by Itami, op. cit., p. 25.

11

STRATEGIC ASSETS AND ORGANIZATIONAL RENT

Raphael Amit and Paul J. H. Schoemaker

We build on an emerging strategy literature that views the firm as a bundle of resources and capabilities, and examine conditions that contribute to the realization of sustainable economic rents. Because of (1) resource-market imperfections and (2) discretionary managerial decisions about resource development and deployment we expect firms to differ (in and out of equilibrium) in the resources and capabilities they control. This asymmetry in turn can be a source of sustainable economic rent. The paper focuses on the linkages between the industry analysis framework, the resource-based view of the firm, behavioural decision biases and organizational implementation issues. It connects the concept of Strategic Industry Factors at the market level with the notion of Strategic Assets at the firm level. Organizational rent is shown to stem from imperfect and discretionary decisions to develop and deploy selected resources and capabilities, made by boundedly rational managers facing high uncertainty, complexity, and intrafirm conflict.

INTRODUCTION

However they phrase them, executives often examine such questions as, 'What makes us distinctive or unique?' 'Why do some and not other customers buy from us?' 'Why are we profitable?' Typical answers might refer to the firm's 'technical know-how', 'responsiveness to market needs', 'design and engineering capability', or 'financial resources'. The common theme among these responses is that management deems some firm-specific resources and capabilities to be crucial in explaining a firm's performance.

While empirical models may, ex post, point to a limited set of resources and capabilities that explain some of the firm's past performance, *ex ante* such models offer limited insight into the dimensions of competition that will prevail in the future. For managers, the challenge is to identify, develop, protect, and deploy resources and capabilities in a way that provides the firm with a sustainable competitive advantage and, thereby, a superior return on capital.

Managerial decisions concerning such resources and capabilities are ordinarily made in a setting that is characterized by: (1) *Uncertainty* about (a) the economic, industry, regulatory, social, and technological environments, (b) competitors' behaviour, and (c) customers' preferences; (2) *Complexity* concerning (a) the interrelated causes that shape the firm's environments, (b) the competitive interactions ensuing from differing perceptions about these environments; and by (3) *Intraorganizational conflicts* among those who make managerial decisions and those affected by them. These conditions of uncertainty, complexity, and conflict are usually difficult to articulate or model. For example, the exact relationships between the firm's bundle of capabilities and its performance may be unclear in the present, let alone the future.[1]

By explicitly addressing these dimensions of the managerial challenge, our paper attempts to link the 'industry analysis framework' with the 'resource view of the firm' and highlight the human limitations in crafting firm strategy. We start by briefly reviewing the existing literature on the resource-based view and defining the terms we use. We proceed by articulating our view and contribution to the theory. We end by examining the theory in the context of multiple dimensions and emphasising the heuristic nature of organizational rent creation.

LITERATURE AND DEFINITIONS

A growing body of empirical literature points to the importance of firm-specific factors in explaining variations in economic rent[2] (Jacobson 1988; Hansen and Wernerfelt, 1989). For example, Cool and Schendel (1988) reported significant and systematic performance differences among firms belonging to the same strategic group within the US pharmaceutical industry. Additionally, Rumelt (1991) found that business units differ far more within than across industries. Theorists have long recognized the importance of firm differences and distinctive competencies (Selznick, 1957; Ansoff, 1965; Andrews, 1971; Hofer and Schendel, 1978). Current managerial writings such as Irvin and Michaels (1989), Wernerfelt (1989), Prahalad and Hamel (1990), Grant (1991), or Stalk, Evans, and Shulman (1992) further evidence a continuing interest in core skills and capabilities as a source of competitive advantage.

Vasconcellos and Hambrick (1989) recently conducted an empirical, ex post test of the long-standing strategy premise that an organization's success depends on the match between the strengths and the Key Success Factors (KSF)[3] in its environment. Using a range of mature industrial product industries, their empirical findings showed that organizations which rated highest on industry KSF clearly outperformed their rivals.

Although this analysis provides an important test of a core thesis in strategy, it also raises further questions. First, the Vasconcellos and Hambrick (1989) study considers the industry as the primary unit of analysis, whereas managers operate from a firm perspective. Second, the empirical analysis is ex post, whereas managers need to make resource deployment decisions exante, which involves uncertainty, complexity and organizational conflict. Third, it should be recognized that if all firms score high on the presumed KSF, these factors will cease to be KSF. Thus, we need to introduce sustainable asymmetry into the analysis, possibly stemming from mobility barriers, organizational inertia, heterogeneous expectations, failures in resource markets, and so forth.

The use of KSF as a core concept in strategy was recently critiqued by Ghemawat (1991a) as lacking: (1) identification (there may be many success factors, making it hard to decide which ones to focus on); (2) concentrates (ambiguity about the causal processes that tie the firm's success factors to its performance); (3) generality (to be success factors they must be undervalued; i.e., the cost benefit ratio associated with their development must be less than one); and (4) necessity (the failure of the success factor approach to account for dynamic aspects of strategy). Whereas we agree with Ghemawat (1991a) about these challenges, it should be pointed out that without uncertainty, complexity, and conflict, there would be no room for discretionary managerial decisions on strategy crafting. Only differences in initial endowments, or luck, could underlie asymmetric performance in that case.

Since KSF notions are commonly used by strategy scholars and managers alike, they need to be related more carefully to strategy theory. An emerging theoretical perspective – that of the firm as a collection of resources and capabilities required for product/market competition – provides one such underpinning. This Resource View of the firm (Coase, 1937; Penrose, 1959; Nelson and Winter, 1982; Teece, 1982; Rumelt, 1984; Wernerfelt, 1984; Barney, 1986a, 1986b, 1989, 1991; Dierickx and Cool, 1989a, 1989b, 1990; Teece, Pisano, and Shuen, 1990; Conner, 1991; Ghemawat, 1991b; Peteraf, 1991) focuses on factor market imperfections and highlights the heterogeneity of firms, their varying degrees of specialization, and the limited transferability of corporate resources. The resource perspective complements the industry analysis framework (Porter, 1980; Schmalensee, 1985). The latter focuses on product markets; it views the sources of profitability to be the characteristics of the industry as well as the firm's position within the industry. The resource view holds that the type, magnitude, and nature of a firm's resources and capabilities are important determinants of its profitability.

In developing the theoretical foundations, we shall build on both perspectives: The resource view of the firm and the industry analysis framework. In addition, we introduce a third perspective, that of Behavioural Decision Theory (BDT). This new field explicitly acknowledges that managers often make sub-optimal choices, be it in personnel selection or in crafting their firm's strategy. BDT can shed light on how boundedly rational managers cope with the kinds of uncertainty and complexity referred to above. Unlike the resource view, which focuses on failures in resource markets, the BDT perspective highlights cognitive imperfections that, while internal to the firm (e.g. internal conflict, cognitive biases of managers, etc.[4]), have a great impact on the firm's approach to its external environment. To date, few links have been drawn between the BDT literature, the industry analysis framework and the resource view of the firm (for an exception, see Zajac and Bazerman, 1991). Before proceeding to the theory section, where these perspectives are examined and integrated, we clarify below the key terms and concepts we use.

Definitions

The firm's *Resources* will be defined as stocks of available factors that are owned or controlled by the firm. *Resources* are converted into final products or services by using a wide range of other firm assets and bonding mechanisms such as technology, management information systems, incentive systems, trust between management and labour, and more. These *Resources* consist, *inter alia*, of know-how that can be traded (e.g., patents and licenses), financial or physical assets (e.g., property, plant and equipment), human capital, etc.[5]

Capabilities, in contrast, refer to a firm's capacity to deploy *Resources*, usually in combination, using organizational processes, to effect a desired end. They are information-based, tangible and intangible processes that are firm-specific and are developed over time through complex interactions among the firm's *Resources*. They can abstractly be thought of as 'intermediate goods' generated by the firm to provide enhanced productivity of its *Resources*, as well as strategic flexibility and protection for its final product or service. Unlike *Resources*, *Capabilities* are based on developing, caring, and exchanging information through the firm's human capital. Itami (1987) refers to information-based Capabilities as 'invisible assets'. He notes that some of the firm's invisible assets are not carried by its employees but rather depend on the perceptions of the firm's customer base (as brand names may do). *Capabilities* are often developed in functional areas (e.g., brand management in marketing) or by combining physical, human, and technological Resources at the corporate level. As a result, firms may build such corporate *Capabilities* as highly reliable service, repeated process or product innovations, manufacturing flexibility, responsiveness to market trends, and short product development cycles.

Some of the firm's *Resources*, but especially its *Capabilities*, may be subject to market failure; that is, an inability to trade these factors in perfect markets. Multiple sources of market failure have been suggested: Williamson (1975) points to small numbers, opportunism, and information impactedness; Klein, Crawford and Alchian (1978) focus on factor specialization in terms of use or location; Caves (1984) highlights sunk costs, and suggests that a factor's value is inversely related to the extent of its specialization for a particular [SMT1] industry or setting.[6] We thus define the firm's *Strategic Assets* as the set of difficult to trade and imitate, scarce, appropriable and specialized *Resources and Capabilities* that bestow the firm's competitive advantage.

When the industry (or product market) is the unit of analysis, one may observe that, at a given time, certain *Resources* and *Capabilities* which are subject to market failures, have become the prime determinants of economic rents. These will be referred to as *Strategic Industry Factors* (SIF). For instance, Ghemawat (1991b) suggests that one may classify industries in terms of the 'strategic factors that drive competition in them by virtue of dominating the structure of sunk costs incurred in the course of competition'. *Strategic Industry Factors*, in this context, are characterized by their proneness to market failures and subsequent asymmetric distribution over firms. By definition, *Strategic Industry Factors* are determined at the market level through complex interactions among the firm's competitors, customers, regulators, innovators external to the industry, and other stakeholders. Their main characteristics are articulated in Table 11.1. It is

Table 11.1 General characteristics of strategic industry factors (SIF)

a	Stock type *Resources* and *Capabilities* that ex post are shown to be key determinants of firm profitability in an industry:
b	Determined at the market level through complex interactions among industry rivals, new entrants, customers, regulators, innovators, suppliers, and other stakeholders:
c	Strategic in that they are subject to market failures and may be the basis for competition among rivals:
d	The bundle of SIF changes over time and is not known ex ante:
e	Their development takes time, skill, and capital; they may be specialized to particular uses:
f	Investments in them are largely irreversible (i.e., entail sunk costs):
g	Their values deteriorate or appreciate, over time, at varying rates of change:
h	Their pace of accumulation may be affected by a range of managerial actions (policy levers) and by the magnitude of other *Resources* and *Capabilities* that are controlled by industry rivals. One cannot easily speed up their development (e.g. doubling the investment will not usually halve the time);
i	Their value to any particular firm may depend on its control of other factors – the complementarity property. For instance, the value of a firm's product design capability may depend upon the effectiveness of its distribution network;
j	Not all aspects of their development and interactions will be known or controllable.

This table synthesizes notions from Penrose, 1959; Nelson and Winter, 1982; Teece, 1982; Rumelt, 1984; Wernerfelt, 1984; Barney, 1989, 1991; Dierickx and Cool, 1989a, 1989b; Teece *et al.*, 1990; Conner, 1991; Ghemawat, 1991b; Peteraf, 1991.

important to recognize that the relevant set of *Strategic Industry Factors* changes and cannot be predicted with certainty ex ante.[7]

The challenge facing a firm's managers is to identify, ex ante, a set of *Strategic Assets* (SA) as grounds for establishing the firm's sustainable competitive advantage, and thereby generate *Organizational Rents*. These are economic rent that stem from the organization's *Resources and Capabilities*, and that can be appropriated by the organization (rather than any single factor). This requires managers to identify the present set of *Strategic Industry Factors* (SIF) as well as to assess the possible sets of SIF that may prevail in the future. Also, decisions on the further development of existing and new *Strategic Assets* – those that are most likely to contribute to the creation and protection of economic rents – need to be made. Not every firm will succeed with its targeted set of SA, as their applicability and relevance ultimately hinges on the complex interaction referred to above. Examples of possible SA include: Technological capability; fast product development cycles; brand management; control of, or superior access to, distribution channels; a favourable cost structure; buyer-seller relationships; the firm's installed user base; its R&D capability; the firm's service organization; its reputation and so forth. The relationships between industry determined *Strategic Industry Factors*, and firm level *Resources, Capabilities*, and *Strategic Assets*, are depicted in Figure 11.1.[8]

A RESOURCE VIEW OF STRATEGIC ASSETS

By focusing on the firm as the relevant unit of analysis, managers are concerned with the creation of a bundle of tangible as well as intangible *Resources and Capabilities* (R&C), whose economic returns are appropriable by the firm. The basic idea that underlies this perspective, cited earlier as the *Resource-Based View Of The Firm*, is that marshalling a set of complementary and specialized *Resources and Capabilities* which are scarce, durable, not easily graded, and difficult to imitate, may enable the firm to earn economic rents. Thus, according to the resource perspective, the value of a firm's *Strategic Assets* extends beyond their contribution to the production process. It depends on a wide range of characteristics (see Figure 11.2), and varies with changes in the relevant set of *Strategic Industry Factors*, as depicted by Figure 11.1. The supposition is that, even in equilibrium, firms may differ in terms of the *Resources and Capabilities* they control, and that such asymmetric firms may coexist until some exogenous change or Schumpeterian shock occurs (Schumpeter, 1934).[9]

Economic rents, in this setting, derive from asymmetry in initial resource endowments, resource scarcity, limited transferability of *Resources*, imperfect substitutability, and appropriability.[10] Barney (1986a, 1986b, 1989, 1991), Dierickx and Cool (1989a, 1989b, 1990), and Ghemawat (1991b) provide incisive discussions of desired attributes of such firm *Resources*. Figure 11.2 summarizes the primary determinants of the rent producing capacity of a firm's Strategic Assets.

In general, the strategic value of a firm's *Resources and Capabilities* is enhanced the more difficult they are to buy, sell, imitate or substitute. For example, invisible assets such as tacit organizational knowledge or trust between management and labour cannot be traded or easily replicated by competitors since they are deeply rooted in the organization's history. Such firm-specific and often tacit assets accumulate slowly over a period of time (i.e., they are history-dependent state variables. See Dierickx and Cool 1989a, 1989b, 1990). The focus here is not just on the material aspects of Resources and Capabilities, but especially on their transformational characteristics. These are often specific to a firm and/or to a particular industry at a given point in time. This idiosyncrasy makes them difficult to imitate and their development time cannot be easily compressed.

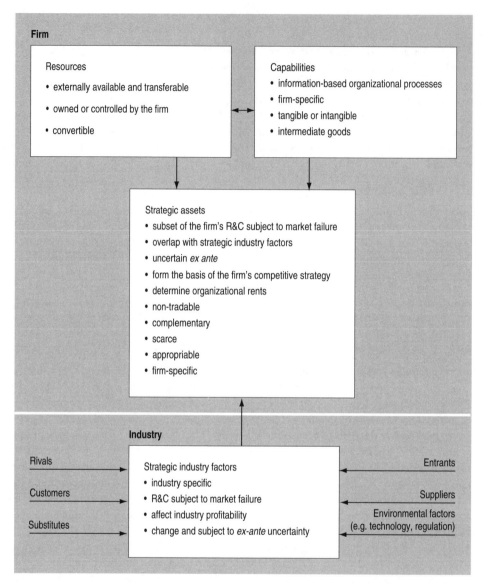

Figure 11.1 Key constructs

In addition, the applicability of the firm's bundle of *Resources and Capabilities* to a particular industry setting (i.e., the overlap with the set of *Strategic Industry Factors*), will determine the available rent. Managers influence the development and deployment of *Strategic Assets* by adopting a process perspective (in contrast to an input-output model). This perspective recognizes distinct phases of development, the importance of feedback, and the need for vision. It also entails careful scripting of how *Resources*, information and people are combined and sequenced over time in order to evolve specific *Capabilities*. In this sense, the viewpoint is essentially an institutional one (de Gregori, 1987). Dierickx and Cool (1989a, 1989b) especially highlight the importance of processes for asset accumulation and their impact on inimitability of the firm's *Resources*.

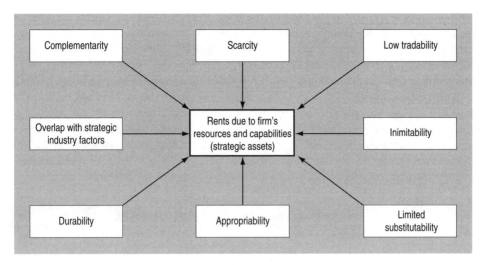

Figure 11.2   Desired characteristics of the firm's resources and capabilities

The firm's *Strategic Assets* may further exhibit *complementarity* in deployment or application (Barnard, 1938); that is, the strategic value of each asset's relative magnitude may increase with an increase in the relative magnitude of other *Strategic Assets* (also known as positive externalities; see Dierickx and Cool, 1990). An example is Teece's (1986) notion of co-specialized assets – those for which there is a bilateral dependence in application. Under complementarity, the combined value of the firm's *Resources and Capabilities* may be higher than the cost of developing or deploying each asset individually. Conversely, the strategic value of the firm's *Resources and Capabilities* declines to the extent that they are substitutes.[11]

The more *firm-specific, durable and scarce Strategic Assets* are, the more valuable to the firm can be their deployment, for at least three reasons. First, if few other firms have R&C that are in high demand and are difficult to imitate, fewer firms will pursue market strategies based thereon, since others would find these strategies too costly and time consuming.[12] Second, firm-specificity and the presence of transaction costs suggest that the value of some *Resources and Capabilities* will be lower for certain firms. Third, the more durable they are, the smaller will be the investment required to offset their depreciation, if any.[13]

These characteristics of the firm's assets emphasize the trade-off between the specialization of assets (a necessary condition for rent) and the robustness of these assets across alternative futures (see Schoemaker, 1992a). The trade-off between specialization and robustness is only partial, as specialization can be of two kinds: (1) limited use or (2) unique use. Limited use entails reduced robustness in that the asset is of little value in particular states of nature. Uniqueness, in contrast, is defined relative to other players (rather than to states of nature) and need not be restricted in scope or by circumstance. Due to competitive pressures, the kinds of specialization that can yield positive rents tend to entail limited use (and hence, risk). Uniqueness, in contrast, may reflect historical accident or heterogeneous expectations as the primary reasons for non-imitation.

In essence, firms develop specialized assets to enhance profits at the price of reduced flexibility in the face of Schumpeterian shocks. This trade-off is, in our view, a core issue in deciding which R&C to develop. Sustainable advantage is obtained when existing and potential competitors (new entrants) lack either the ability or desire to imitate the rent-producing R&C. A firm's managers can lessen the incentives of competitors to imitate or develop close substitutes by, for example, erecting entry or mobility barriers or by building 'isolating mechanisms' (Rumelt, 1984). Like Ghemawat (1986), we focus here on aspects that relate to the firm's superior *access* to *Resources*. (Of course, competitive advantage may also arise from size and scope, as well as legal or other restrictions on competition.)

Given the competitive and changing context in which managers must decide which R&C to develop as their firm's basis for competition, it is doubtful that decisions about which SA to develop and deploy can be optimally deduced from a general normative theory. More likely, continually changing heuristics will emerge that strive to better incorporate the uncertainty, complexity and organizational conflicts confronting managers.[14] As such, our view extends that of Porter's (1980) by emphasizing not only the industry environment in determining future profit but especially the importance of managerial discretion and innovation in SA decisions. The latter are by no means foregone conclusions; the external environment is only one part of the economic rent story.

DECISIONS ABOUT STRATEGIC ASSETS

In making investment decisions about *Strategic Assets*, managers face the daunting tasks of (1) anticipating possible futures, (2) assessing competitive interactions within each projected future, and (3) overcoming organizational inertia and internal dispute in order to realign the firm's bundle of SA. Recent psychological literature (Kahneman, Slovic, and Tversky, 1982) suggests that managers will approach this uncertainty, complexity, and conflict with considerable bias, illusion, and suboptimality. Even if highly simplified and abstracted, the associated SA decisions may not be solvable in close-form equilibrium terms (although, see Camerer, 1991).[15]

Uncertainty

Under rational expectations, the SA challenge will largely vanish as managers will hold the same expectations about the set of SIF that will prevail in the future. Since they will maximize the expected value of returns, their initial SA endowments are the only source of variance regarding their behaviour. In reality, however, managers face considerable uncertainty and ambiguity, stemming from new proprietary technologies, economic and political trends, competitive actions, changes in societal values, and corresponding shifts in consumer preferences. Pervasive uncertainty and ambiguity make it probable that mangers will hold diverse expectations about such key variables as demand growth, price levels, costs, and consumer tastes. Further, their judgements and choices are likely to exhibit idiosyncratic aversions to risk and ambiguity (Kahneman, Slovic and Tversky, 1979; Einhorn and Hogarth, 1986).[16] The joint effects of heterogeneous beliefs and manager-specific decision processes (and biases) make equilibrium analyses hard to conduct for both managers and researchers. Coupled with overconfidence (Lichtenstein, Fischhoff, and Phillips, 1982) and a penchant for confirming over disconfirming evidence (Klayman and Ha, 1987), Strategic Assets choices under uncertainty may entail opposing biases whose net effects are hard to assess. For example, ambiguity aversion and underweighting of medium and high probabilities will normally lead to risk aversion. However, this tendency may be countered or mitigated by overconfidence and ambitious targets, either of which can induce strong risk-seeking.[17] Consequently, the final SA investment decisions are hard to predict without detailed micro-level knowledge of managers' reference points, problem framing, degrees of overconfidence, non-linear weighting of probabilities, etc. (see Schoemaker, 1992b).

A bounded rationality view (Simon, 1979) may nonetheless predict some overriding biases. For example, managers will probably over-emphasize past *Strategic Industry Factors*, and the SA associated therewith. People generally tend to repeat what was rewarded before. Consequently, managers might be too focused on past competitors and pay too much attention to recent experience. The latter is known as the recency effect which is closely linked to the more general notion of the availability heuristic (Tversky and Kahneman, 1974). If perceptions about strategy are unduly anchored on past SA, rent opportunities arise for firms that approach the future more flexibly and imaginatively. These may be new firms or incumbent ones that vigorously challenge their own beliefs. Past success may especially bias managers toward an illusion of control (Langer, 1975). Recent emphasis on the strategic importance of continual organizational learning (de Geus, 1988; Senge, 1990) underscore the special challenges posed by uncertainty and complexity, whether the firm has been successful or not.

Complexity

To keep SA decisions within cognitive bounds, managers must often and extensively simplify (Russo and Schoemaker, 1989). The kinds of simplification they engage in may lead to additional biases. Tversky and Kahneman (1981) offer persuasive examples of how simplified framing (such as isolating alternatives or expressing outcomes relatively) can lead to inconsistent decisions. Specifically, frames may (1) bound out important futures, competitors, or new technologies; (2) dictate the reference point relative to which SAs are measured (e.g., Chrysler comparing its quality control capability to GM's rather than to Japan's Honda); and, (3) specify the yardsticks or metric used to measure SA (e.g., measuring quality in terms of defective parts per thousand vs. number and type of consumer complaints).

In hindsight, chance and skill are often confused (Fischhof and Beyth, 1975). Judgements about correlation or relative importance frequently miss important cues and interactions (Jennings, Amabile, and Ross, 1982; Hammond, 1955; Hogarth, 1987), especially if not driven by a causal theory. Imputations about causality, in turn, may be overly sensitive to temporal and spatial contiguity, covariation, and similarity of cause and effect (Einhorn and Hogarth, 1986). Unless aided by formal analyses, managers may easily misconstrue the industry's success factors and persist in erroneous beliefs about their firm's SA until proven wrong by competitors.

Lindblom (1959) and Quinn (1980), among others, have highlighted the incremental way in which managers usually deal with complexity. Writers on policy formation have, in general, emphasized the contextual and labile nature of organizational decision making (Mintzberg, 1978; Isenberg, 1987, MacCrimmon and Wehrung, 1986). An example is Cohen, March, and Olsen's (1972) garbage can model, in which problems, solutions, hidden agendas, coalitions and so on mesh in complex ways to yield decisions. Mintzberg (1978) and Mintzberg and Waters (1983) further highlight the role for the firm's unconscious past. They view a firm's realized strategy (e.g., its SA decisions) to be a blend of rational, or at least intentional choices, and implicit or tacit forces within organizations (see also Hamel and Prahalad, 1989). The litany of biases mentioned above serves to underscore our main point here: Discretionary managerial decisions that relate to *Strategic Assets* are affected by a wide range of cognitive biases about the handling of uncertainty and complexity. This, in turn, creates sub-optimality, imperfect imitability, and organizational rents for some firms.

Conflict

Intraorganizational conflict is another serious challenge encountered by management in making SA decisions. Any change in the existing bundle of SA may benefit some employees and hurt others. Not only do complex agency problems (Jensen and Meckling, 1976; Fama and Jensen,

1983a, 1983b) exist in obtaining the necessary information and judgements concerning SA selection, but also issues of co-operation, trust, and competence must be factored into the decision of which *Resources and Capabilities* to develop and how. Allison's (1971) classic treatment of the Cuban Missile Crisis illustrates clearly the importance of organizational and political dimensions, in addition to rational ones, for setting policy.

The key point is that organizations are complex social entities with their own inertia and constraints. The issue is not simply to select the subset of *Resources and Capabilities* that is most likely to yield high rents, but to make organizational participants an integral part of such decisions. Among other things, this poses problems of nestedness; for example, SBU level choices impact divisional as well as corporate *Capabilities* and vice versa. The convenient view that organizations have carefully solved their principal-agent problems and need only select from the implicit market for *Resources and Capabilities*, which and how much of each to buy, denies the crucial role of asymmetric *Resources and Capabilities* as well as the complex decisions managers face.

In sum, as the firm's environment changes, different sets of *Strategic Assets* may have to be developed by firms. Core *Capabilities*, by definition, cannot be purchased off the shelf but require strategic visions, development time, and sustained investment. Decisions about *Strategic Assets* (e.g., the subset of *Resources and Capabilities* that bestows sustainable competitive advantage) are among the most complex that managers encounter. They are characterized by high uncertainty, complexity, and conflict, to an extent that defines optimizetion. Indeed, this lack of solvability is a necessary condition for their strategic importance and positive rent potential.

STRATEGIC ASSETS DEVELOPMENT: A MULTIDIMENSIONAL VIEW

The above analysis of *Strategic Assets* underscores the need for a multidimensional approach; one that includes internal and external elements, static and dynamic aspects, and rational as well as behavioural considerations.[18] Each perspective sheds a different light on the *Strategic Assets* challenge as captured below.

Industry Analysis excels in assessing the profit potential of various industry participants by focusing on the external competitive forces and barriers that prevail in different product/market segments. Further, it is essential in deriving a set of *Strategic Industry Factors*. It is incomplete, however, in that it treats the firm largely as a black box (i.e., a faceless, unitary actor), while de-emphasizing the role of managerial discretion. Assuming high rationality and substitutability of executive talent, industry analysis logically deduces the end-game consequences of differences in participants' initial conditions (for a particular industry structure, technology, and action space). Thus, the focus is on rent distribution in equilibrium, given initial firm asymmetries, industry structure, and known rules of the game.

The Resource View, in contrast, highlights imperfections in factor markets, resulting in systematic firm differences. Limited transferability of *Resources*, scarcity, complementarity and appropriability in turn give rise to rent opportunities. Economic rents, in this view, derive from properties unique to the firm's *Resources and Capabilities*. The focus is thus more internal and institutional, recognizing the often slow and evolutionary path by which firm-specific *Capabilities* develop (e.g., see Nelson and Winter, 1982). These *Capabilities* may include executive talent, culture and other less tangible dimensions that in standard models of rational behaviour have received limited attention.[19] Also, the exclusive focus on equilibrium and structural dimensions is absent. Instead, disequilibrium and process dynamics loom primary.

Behavioural Decision Theory (BDT) complements the resource perspective in explicitly acknowledging bounded rationality and, in particular, the crucial roles of problem framing and heuristic decision-making. Differences in decision frames and heuristics give rise to 'variable rationality' among and within players over time (see Schoemaker, 1990). A rational end-game analysis would largely ignore such factors since it generally assumes constant rationality.[20] In actuality, however, managers are hardly playing a well-defined end game. Logical consequences of moves are seldom ascertainable and equilibrium solutions are not usually transparent in complex strategy decisions. Because the rules of the game, the number of players, and the action space are seldom fixed, creative changes and innovations are permitted, which makes predictions of outcomes especially difficult.

Reliance on heuristics and on a limited repertoire of responses, punctuated by occasional bold or creative moves, introduces complexities whose net effects are hard to assess. Players generally harbour imperfect comprehension's of the deeper relationships operative in the industry or indeed, within their firm. In this view, strategy becomes partly a shot in the dark and partly an exercise in heuristic creativity aimed at overcoming biases and blind spots (Zajac and Bazerman, 1991). These biases will not be just individual or cognitive; many concern group biases (e.g., groupthink) and may be affective in nature, such as wishful thinking, dissonance reaction, etc. (see Russo and Schoemaker, 1989).

The BDT perspective is especially important in light of the pervasive *uncertainty and complexity* surrounding SA decisions. Any industry or market segment will undergo Schumpeterian shocks such that mostly equilibria (if computable at all) will have finite lives. Robust strategies thus must pay attention to disequilibrium, uncertain futures and ambiguous relationships. Without ambiguity and complexity, the SA questions would perhaps be reducible to a rational end-game analysis. In practice, however, it is about the fashioning and deployment of firm-specific *Capabilities* whose rents depend partly on unfathomable futures.

In terms of theoretical underpinnings, various attempts have been made to model the effects of uncertainty or ambiguity on individual decision making (Einhorn and Hogarth, 1986) as well as markets (Kleindorfer and Kunreuther, 1982). The dimension of complexity has yet to see significant formal treatment (although, see Rosenhead, 1980). In psychology, however, various models and techniques exist to depict how people represent complex problem situations, ranging from scripts and schema to cognitive maps (for a review see Klayman and Schoemaker, 1992). Also, numerous heuristic guidelines exist for managers on how to cope with and manage complexity, such as scenario analysis (Wack, 1985a, 1985b; Schoemaker, 1991).

Our further emphasis on *conflict and organization inertia* brings to the fore implementation and other intraorganizational problems in the development and deployment of *Strategic Assets*. The resource and behavioural perspectives refer to these organizational issues but do not develop them. Principal-agent theory provides a highly rational treatment of incentive problems, with abstract links to the origin, scope and organizational form of firms (e.g., U-vs. M-form) and scope, while placing greater emphasis on bounded rationality and internal firm complexity. Organizational theory, in contrast, has been more descriptive and process oriented in seeking to understand how firms control and co-ordinate activities. Rather than making conflict or transactions the unit of analysis, organization theory focuses on systemic aspects, in particular the interactions among such subsystems as the firm's structure, processes, rewards, culture, people and technology. These can explain firm interia and the adaptation difficulties encountered when the environment changes and managers attempt to redirect their firm's *Strategic Assets*.

CONCLUSION

We have sought to replace the strategy field's concept of Key Success Factors with the notions of: (1) *Strategic Industry Factors*, the set of *Resources and Capabilities* that has become the prime determinant of economic rents for industry participants; and (2) *Strategic Assets*, a firm level construct, referring to the set of firm specific *Resources and Capabilities* developed by management as the basis for creating and protecting their firm's competitive advantage. The rent producing capacity of these *Strategic Assets* depends, in part, on their own unique characteristics as well as on the extent to which they overlap with the industry-determined *Strategic Industry Factors*.

Building on insights from the Resource View of the firm, and Behavioural Decision Theory, we identified important theoretical features of *Strategic Assets* and the conditions under which they could produce organizational rents. The managerial difficulty of identifying, developing, and deploying an appropriate mix of SA was highlighted in the discussion. Owing to uncertainty, complexity, and conflict (both in and outside the firm), different firms will employ different *Strategic Assets*, without any one set being provably optimal or easily imitated. At best, managers can devise heuristic solutions that navigate between the numerous cognitive and affective biases characteristic of humans and organizations. We articulated a multidimensional view for the crafting of *Strategic Assets*, in relation to market-determined *Strategic Industry Factors*. Its dimensions consist of (1) industry analysis, (2) the resource perspective and (3) behavioural decision theory. The latter perspective emphasizes the pervasive uncertainty and complexity faced by managers, often resulting in sub-optimal *Strategic Assets* decisions. In this context, the role of intraorganizational conflict and inertia were identified as important barriers to implementing changes to the firm's bundle of *Strategic Assets*.

Throughout, *Strategic Assets* decisions were examined in light of resource market imperfections, bounded and variable rationality within the across firms. If optimal solutions were derivable for a firm's *Strategic Assets*, the latter would largely vanish. Barring market or cognitive imperfections, all firms would envision and pursue an optimal strategy with zero expected rents. As such, the existence of *Strategic Assets* and presence of bounded rationality are closely linked. A normative *Strategic Assets* theory that could systematically lead to the creation of sustainable rents is implausible due to competitive pressures. Our paper instead sought to develop a behavioural view of *Strategic Assets*, with limited prescriptive advice on how to target, develop and employ firm-specific *Strategic Assets*.

In concluding, it may be useful to place our view of organizational rent creation by firms within the larger framework articulated by Conner (1991). We share with the resource view, as well as the transaction cost view, an emphasis on the uniqueness and limited mobility of *Resources and Capabilities*. However, it is not market power (IO view) *per se*, or greater operating efficiency (neo-classical and Chicago school views) that produces organizational rents, although these may be consequences. In this paper uniqueness and low mobility of *Resources and Capabilities* stem from imperfect and hard to predict decisions by boundedly rational managers facing high uncertainty (à la Schumpeter), complexity, and intrafirm conflict. We thus strengthen the resource view by adding behavioural decision making biases and organizational implementation aspects as further impediments to the transferability or imitability of a firm's *Resources and Capabilities*.

NOTES

1   Lippman and Rumelt (1982) refer to this as 'causal ambiguity.'
2   Economists commonly distinguish among three types of rent: Ricardian rents are extraordinary profits earned from resources that are in fixed or limited supply. Pareto rents (or quasi rents) refer to the difference between the payments to a resource in its best and second best use. Lastly, Monopoly rents stem from collusion or government protection. Klein, Crawford and Alchian (1978) examine quasi-rents in the context of vertical integration.

3   There are numerous interpretations in the Marketing and Strategic Management literature concerning the meaning of KSF. See for example Thompson and Strickland (1990).

4   Penrose's (1959) seminal work also addresses some of these intrafirm issues.

5   See Grant (1991) for a detailed description of various types of both tangible and intangible resources of the firm.

6   The roles of factor specialization and sunk costs in a firm's ability to earn economic rents have been examined by Klein *et al.* (1978), as well as by Baumol, Panzar, and Willig (1982).

7   While it may not be possible to identify ex ante the relevant set of strategic assets, one can screen out those assets that are *not* strategic.

8   Note that we abandon from hereon the term *Key Success Factors*, because of its many possible interpretations and uses.

9   The assumption of heterogeneous firms controlling resources that are not perfectly mobile (i.e., that cannot be easily bought, sold or imitated) is essential to the existence of such an equilibrium. Lippman and Rumelt (1982) and Barney (1986a, 1986b) articulate some of the reasons for imperfect imitability. These include unique historical conditions, causal ambiguiy, and complexity. Ghemawat (1991b) refers to these conditions as intrinsic inimitability and therefore the firm's factor combinations are viewed as intrinsically heterogeneous. He suggests that less stringent conditions (e.g., imitations being costly but not infeasible) may be sufficient for sustainability. Relatedly, Peteraf (1991) equates resource heterogeneity to differential levels of factor efficiency.

10 Whereas Industrial Organization economics often looks outside the firm to explain sustained superior performance by examining, for example, various market structures, alternative regulatory settings, collusive relationships, or substitute technologies, the source of rents according to the resource perspective is internal.

11 Dierickx and Cool (1989b, 1990) have introduced the notion of complementarity in asset accumulation (or interconnectedness) which refers to economies of scope in asset accumulation. This distinction highlights the dynamic nature of asset accumulation, whereas complementarity in asset deployment is a static notion.

12 The strategic value of R&C may not lie merely in the scarcity of natural resources such as land and oil reserves, but also in the ability to deploy concurrently in multiple uses such invisible firm-specific assets as culture, reputation, and relationships with suppliers and buyers.

13 Unlike physical capital, most capabilities are enhanced with use as more experience is gained.

14 Economic rent may accrue to firms with superior or more timely heuristics, thereby capitalizing on variable as well as bounded rationality (see Schoemaker, 1990).

15 For example, when modeled as a differential game, the problem will probably not be tractable. Closed or even open-loop solutions are generally unattainable when confronted with a multiplicity of state and control variables in non-co-operative multiplayer games. An added complication in our case arises from the difficulty of specifying the game in terms of the number of players, as well as the state, action, and pay-off spaces.

16 When gambles entail well-defined probabilities, most people exhibit risk aversion (except for low probability and pure loss gambles). If probabilities are ill defined (the case of ambiguity), even greater risk-aversion is encountered due to people's dislikes to unknown risk. Most managerial decisions entail risk as well as ambiguity.

17 The predicted bias is towards risk-*seeking* for R&C that are deemed to be below some chosen reference point and towards risk-*aversion* for those that exceed this aspiration level (see Kahneman, Slovic and Tversky, 1979). Thus, unrealistic goals or ambitious targets will likely result in unduly risky R&C decisions. For additional biases and indeterminacies in risk-taking see MacCrimmon and Wehrung (1986).

18 While we hold that these dimensions need to be reflected in any comprehensive analyses of a firm's *Strategic Assets*, there may well be other relevant dimensions (e.g., ecological, sociological, political, anthropological). To integrate these additional dimensions, however, is beyond our present scope.

207

19   Some of this is changing. For instance rational models have been developed concerning the role of culture (Camerer and Vepsalainen, 1988) and reputation (Weigelt and Camerer, 1988).

20   Variable rationality refers to actors differing in the degree to which they exhibit bounded rationality. A rational end-game analysis is one in which all possible moves and counter-moves are identified and evaluated.

REFERENCES

Allison, G. (1971) *Essence of Decision: explaining the Cuban Missile Crisis*, Little, Brown, Boston, MA.

Andrews, K. R. (1971) *The Concept of Corporate Strategy*, Irwin, Homewood, IL.

Ansoff, H. I. (1965) *Corporate Strategy*, McGraw-Hill, New York.

Barnard, C. I. (1938) *The Functions of the Executive*, Harvard University Press, Cambridge, MA.

Barney, J. B. (1986a) 'Strategic factor markets: expectations, luck, and business strategy', *Management Science*, Vol. 42, pp. 1231–41.

Barney, J. B. (1986b) 'Organization culture: can it be a source of sustained competitive advantage?', *Academy of Management Review*, Vol. 11, pp. 656–65.

Barney, J. B. (1989) 'Asset stocks and sustained competitive advantage: a comment', *Management Science*, Vol. 35, pp. 1511–13.

Barney, J. B. (1991) 'Firm resources and sustained competitive advantage', *Journal of Management*, Vol. 17, No. 1, pp. 90–120.

Baumol, W. I., Panzar, J. C. and Willig, R. C. (1982) *Contestable Markets and the Theory of Industry Structure*, Harcourt Brace Jovanovitch, New York.

Camerer, C. F. (1991) 'Does strategy research need game theory?', *Strategic Management Journal*, Vol. 12, pp. 137–52.

Camerer, C. F. and Vepsalainen A. (1988) 'The economic efficiency of corporate culture', *Strategic Management Journal*, Vol. 9, pp. 115–26.

Caves, R. E. (1984) 'Economic analysis and the quest for competitive advantage', *American Economic Review*, Vol. 74, No. 2, pp. 127–32.

Coase, R. H. (1937) 'The nature of the firm', *Economica*, Vol. 4, pp. 331–51.

Cohen, M. D., March, J. G. and Olsen J. P. (1972) 'A garbage can model of organizational choice', *Administrative Science Quarterly*, Vol. 17, pp. 1–25.

Conner, K. R. (1991) 'A historical comparison of resource-based theory and five schools of thought within industrial organizational economics: do we have a new theory of the firm?', *Journal of Management*, Vol. 17, No. 1, pp. 121–54.

Cool, K. and Schendel, D. (1988) 'Performance differences among strategic group members', *Strategic Management Journal*, Vol. 9, No. 3, pp. 207–24.

De Geus, A. (1988) 'Planning as learning', *Harvard Business Review*, March–April, pp. 70–4.

De Gregori, T. R. (1987) 'Resources are not; they become: an institutional theory', *Journal of Economic Issues*, Vol. 21, pp. 1241–63.

Dierickx, I. and Cool, K. (1989a) 'Asset stock accumulation and sustainability of competitive advantage', *Management Science*, Vol. 35, pp. 1504–11.

Dierickx, I. and Cool, K. (1989b) 'Competitive strategy resource accumulation and firm performance', Mimeo, INSEAD, May.

Dierickx, I. and Cool, K. (1990) 'A resource-based perspective on competitive strategy', Mimeo, INSEAD, September.

Einhorn, H. and Hogarth, R. (1986) 'Judging probable cause', *Psychological Bulletin*, Vol. 99, pp. 3–19.

Fama, E. F. and Jensen, M. C. (1983a) 'Separation of ownership and control', *Journal of Law and Economics*, Vol. 26, p. 301.

Fama, E. F. and Jensen, M. C. (1983b) 'Agency problems and residual claims', *Journal of Law and Economics*, Vol. 26, pp. 327–49.

Fischhoff, B. and Beyth, R. (1975) 'I knew it would happen – remembered probabilities of once-future things', *Organizational Behaviour and Human Performance*, Vol. 13, pp. 1–6.

Ghemawat, P. (1986) 'Sustainable advantage', *Harvard Business Review*, Vol. 64, pp. 53–8.

Ghemawat, P. (1991a) *Commitment*, The Free Press, New York.

Ghemawat, P. (1991b) 'Resources and Strategy: an IO perspective', Mimeo, Harvard Business School, May.

Grant, R. B. (1991) 'A resource-based theory of competitive advantage: implications for strategy formulation', *California Management Review*, Vol. 33, No. 3, pp. 114–35.

Hamel, G. and Prahalad, C. K. (1989) 'Strategic intent', *Harvard Business Review*, Vol. 89, No. 3, pp. 63–76.

Hammond, K. R. (1955) 'Probabilistic functioning and the clinical method', *Psychological Review*, Vol. 62, pp. 255–62.

Hansen, G. S. and Wernerfelt, B. (1989) 'Determinants of economic and organizational factors', *Strategic Management Journal*, Vol. 10, pp. 399–411.

Hofer, C. W. and Schendel, D. (1978) *Strategy Formulation: analytical concepts*, West Publishing Company, St. Paul, MN.

Hogarth, R. M. (1987) *Judgement and Choice*, Wiley, Chichester.

Irvin, R. A. and Michaels, E. G. III (1989) 'Core skills: doing the right things right', *The McKinsey Quarterly*, Summer, pp. 4–19.

Isenberg, D. J. (1987) 'The tactics of strategic opportunism', *Harvard Business Review*, Vol. 65, No. 2, pp. 92–7.

Itami, H. (1987) *Mobilising Invisible Assets*, Harvard University Press, Boston, MA.

Jacobson, R. (1988) 'The persistence of abnormal returns', *Strategic Management Journal*, 9, pp. 41–58.

Jennings, D. L., Amabile, T. M. and Ross, L. (1982) 'Informal conversation assessment: data-based versus theory-based judgements' in D. Kahneman, P. Slovic and A. Tversky (eds), *Judgement Under Uncertainty: heuristics and biases*, Cambridge Press, Cambridge, pp. 211–30.

Jensen, M. C. and Meckling, W. (1976) 'Theory of the firm: managerial behaviour, agency costs and ownership structure', *Journal of Financial Economics*, pp. 305–60.

Kahneman, D., Slovic, P. and Tversky, A. (1979) 'Prospect theory', *Econometrica*, 47 (2), pp. 263–292.

Kahneman, D., Slovic, P. and Tversky, A. (1982) *Judgement Under Uncertainty: heuristics and biases*, Cambridge Press, Cambridge.

Klayman, J. and Ha, Y. (1987) 'Confirmation, disconfirmation and information in hypothesis testing', *Psychological Review*, 94 (2), pp. 211–28.

Klayman, J. and Schoemaker, P. J. H. (1992) 'Thinking about the future: a cognitive perspective', *Journal of Forecasting*, Vol. 30, No. 1, pp. 107–29.

Klein, B., Crawford, R. and Alchian, A. (1978) 'Vertical integration, appropriable rents, and the competitive contracting process', *Journal of Law and Economics*, Vol. 21, pp. 297–326.

Kleindorfer, P. R. and Kunreuther, H. (1982) 'Misinformation and equilibrium in insurance markets', in J. Finisinger (ed.) *Issues in Pricing and Regulation*, Lexington Books, Lexington, MA, pp. 67–90.

Langer, E. (1975) 'The illusion of control', *Journal of Personality and Social Psychology*, Vol. 32, pp. 311–28.

Lichtenstein, S., Fischhoff, B. and Phillips, L. D. (1982) 'Calibration of probabilities: the state of the art to 1990', in D. Kahneman, P. Slovic and A. Tversky (eds). *Judgement Under Uncertainty: heuristics and biases*. Cambridge Press, Cambridge, pp. 306–34.

Lindblom, C. E. (1959) 'The science of muddling through', *Public Administration Review*, Vol. 19, pp. 79–88.

Lippman, S. and Rumelt, R. (1982) 'Uncertain imitability: an analysis of interfirm difference in efficiency under competition', *Bell Journal of Economics*, pp. 418–38.

MacCrimmon, K. R. and Wehrung, D. A. (1986) *Taking Risks*, The Free Press, New York.

Mintzberg, H. (1978) 'Patterns in strategy formation', *Management Science*, Vol. 24, pp. 934–48.

Mintzberg, H. and Waters, J. A. (1983) 'The mind of the strategist(s)', in S. Srivasta (ed.), *The Executive Mind*, Jossey-Bass, San Francisco, CA, pp. 58–83.

Nelson, R. and Winter, S. (1982) *An Evolutionary Theory of Economic Change*, Harvard University Press, Cambridge, MA.

Penrose, E. T. (1959) *The Theory of Growth of the Firm*, Wiley, New York.

Peteraf, M. A. (1991) 'The cornerstone of competitive advantage: a resource-based view', Northwestern University, J. L. Kellogg Graduate School of Management, General Motors Research Center for Strategy in Management, Discussion Paper No. 90.

Porter, M. (1980) *Competitive Strategy*. The Free Press, New York.

Prahalad, C. K. and Hamel, G. (1990) 'The core competence of the corporation', *Harvard Business Review*, Vol. 68, No. 3, pp. 79–91.

Quinn, J. B. (1980) *Strategies for Change: logical incrementalism*, Irwin, Homewood, IL.

Rosenhead, J. (1980) 'Planning under uncertainty (II): a methodology for robustness analysis', *Journal of Operational Research Society*, Vol. 31, pp. 331–41.

Rumelt, R. P. (1984) 'Towards a strategic theory of the firm', in R. B. Lamb (ed.) *Competitive Strategic Management*, Prentice Hall, Engelwood Cliffs, NJ, pp. 556–70.

Rumelt, R. P. (1991) 'How much does industry matter?', *Strategic Management Journal*, Vol. 12, No. 3, pp. 167–85.

Russo, J. E. and Schoemaker, P. H. (1989) *Decision Traps: ten barriers to brilliant decision making and how to overcome them*, Doubleday, New York.

Schmalensee, R. (1985) 'Do markets differ much?', *American Economic Review*, Vol. 75, pp. 341–51.

Schoemaker, P. H. (1990) 'Strategy, complexity and economic rent', *Management Science*, Vol. 36, No. 10, pp. 1178–92.

Schoemaker, P. H. (1991) 'When and how to use scenario planning', *Journal of Forecasting*, Vol. 10, pp. 549–64.

Schoemaker, P. H. (1992a) 'Developing strategic vision: a core capabilities approach applied to Apple Computer', *Sloan Management Review*.

Schoemaker, P. H. (1992b) 'Determinants of risk-taking: behavioural and economic views', *Journal for Risk and Uncertainty*, Vol. 6, pp. 49–73.

Schumpeter, J. (1934) *The Theory of Economic Development*, Harvard University Press, Cambridge, MA.

Selznick, P. (1957) *Leadership in Administration: a sociological interpretation*, Harper and Row, New York.

Senge, P. (1990) 'The leader's new work: building learning organizations', *Sloan Management Review*, Fall, pp. 7–23.

Simon, H. A. (1979) *Models of Thought*, Yale University Press, New Haven, CT.

Stalk, G., Evans, P. and Shulman, E. (1992) 'Competing on capabilities: the new rules of corporate strategy', *Harvard Business Review*, March–April, pp. 57–69.

Teece, D. J. (1982) 'Towards an economic theory of the multiproduct firm', *Journal of Economic Behaviour and Organization*, Vol. 3, pp. 39–63.

Teece, D. J. (1986) 'Profiting from technological innovation', *Research Policy*, Vol. 15, pp. 285–305.

Teece, D. J., Pisano, G. and Shuen, A. (1990) 'Firm capabilities, resources, and the concept of strategy'. Mimeo, University of California at Berkeley, Haas School of Business, September.

Thompson, A. A. and Strickland, A. J. (1990) *Strategic Management: concepts and cases*, Irwin, Homewood, IL.

Tversky, A. and Kahneman, D. (1974) 'Judgement under uncertainty: heuristics and biases', *Science*, Vol. 185, pp. 1124–31.

Tversky, A. and Kahneman, D. (1981) 'The framing of decisions and the psychology of choice', *Science*, Vol. 211, pp. 453–8.

Vasconcellos, J. A. and Hambrick, D. C. (1989) 'Key success factors: test of a general framework in the mature industrial-product sector', *Strategic Management Journal*, Vol. 10, No. 4, pp. 367–82.

Wack, P. (1985a) 'Scenarios: uncharted waters ahead', *Harvard Business Review*, Vol. 63, No. 5, pp. 72–89.

Wack, P. (1985b) 'Scenarios: shooting the rapids', *Harvard Business Review*, Vol. 63, No. 6, pp. 139–50.

Weigelt, K. and Camerer, C. (1988) 'Reputation and corporate strategy', *Strategic Management Journal*, Vol. 9, pp. 443–54.

Wernerfelt, B. (1984) 'A resource-based view of the firm', *Strategic Management Journal*, Vol. 5, pp. 171–80.

Wernerfelt, B. (1989) 'From critical resources to corporate strategy', *Journal of General Management*, Vol. 5, pp. 171–80.

Williamson, O. (1975) *Markets and Hierarchies*, The Free Press, New York.

Zajac, E. J. and Bazerman, M. H. (1991) 'Blind spots in industry and competitor analysis', *Academy of Management Review*, Vol. 16, pp. 37–56.

12

DYNAMIC CAPABILITIES AND
STRATEGIC MANAGEMENT

David J. Teece, Gary Pisano and Amy Shuen

The dynamic capabilities framework analyzes the sources and methods of wealth creation and capture by private enterprise firms operating in environments of rapid technological change. The competitive advantage of firms is seen as resting on distinctive processes (ways of coordinating and combining), shaped by the firm's (specific) asset positions (such as the firm's portfolio of difficult-to-trade knowledge assets and complementary assets), and the evolution path(s) it has adopted or inherited. The importance of path dependencies is amplified where conditions of increasing returns exist. Whether and how a firm's competitive advantage is eroded depends on the stability of market demand, and the ease of replicability (expanding internally) and imitability (replication by competitors). If correct, the framework suggests that private wealth creation in regimes of rapid technological change depends in large measure on honing internal technological, organizational, and managerial processes inside the firm. In short, identifying new opportunities and organizing effectively and efficiently to embrace them are generally more fundamental to private wealth creation than is strategizing, if by strategizing one means engaging in business conduct that keeps competitors off balance, raises rival's costs, and excludes new entrants.

INTRODUCTION

The fundamental question in the field of strategic management is how firms achieve and sustain competitive advantage.[1] We confront this question here by developing the dynamic capabilities approach, which endeavors to analyze the sources of wealth creation and capture by firms. The development of this framework flows from a recognition by the authors that strategic theory is replete with analyses of firm-level strategies for sustaining and safeguarding extant competitive advantage, but has performed less well with respect to assisting in the understanding of how and why certain firms build competitive advantage in regimes of rapid change. Our approach is especially relevant in a Schumpeterian world of innovation-based competition, price/performance rivalry, increasing returns, and the 'creative destruction' of existing competences. The approach endeavors to explain firm-level success and failure. We are interested in both building a better theory of firm performance, as well as informing managerial practice.

In order to position our analysis in a manner that displays similarities and differences with existing approaches, we begin by briefly reviewing accepted frameworks for strategic management. We endeavor to expose implicit assumptions, and identify competitive circumstances where each paradigm might display some relative advantage as both a useful descriptive and normative theory of competitive strategy. While numerous theories have been advanced over the past two decades about the sources of competitive advantage, many cluster around just a few loosely structured frameworks or paradigms. In this paper we attempt to identify three existing paradigms and describe aspects of an emerging new paradigm that we label dynamic capabilities.

The dominant paradigm in the field during the 1980s was the competitive forces approach developed by Porter (1980). This approach, rooted in the structure–conduct–performance paradigm of industrial organization (Mason, 1949; Bain, 1959), emphasizes the actions a firm can take to create defensible positions against competitive forces. A second approach, referred to as a strategic conflict approach (e.g., Shapiro, 1989), is closely related to the first in its focus on product market imperfections, entry deterrence, and strategic interaction. The strategic conflict approach uses the tools of game theory and thus implicitly views competitive outcomes as a function of the effectiveness with which firms keep their rivals off balance through strategic investments, pricing strategies, signaling, and the control of information. Both the competitive forces and the strategic conflict approaches appear to share the view that rents flow from privileged product market positions.

Another distinct class of approaches emphasizes building competitive advantage through capturing entrepreneurial rents stemming from fundamental firm-level efficiency advantages. These approaches have their roots in a much older discussion of corporate strengths and weaknesses; they have taken on new life as evidence suggests that firms build enduring advantages only through efficiency and effectiveness, and as developments in organizational economics and the study of technological and organizational change become applied to strategy questions. One strand of this literature, often referred to as the 'resource-based perspective,' emphasizes firm-specific capabilities and assets and the existence of isolating mechanisms as the fundamental determinants of firm performance (Penrose, 1959; Rumelt, 1984; Teece, 1984; Wernerfelt, 1984).[2] This perspective recognizes but does not attempt to explain the nature of the isolating mechanisms that enable entrepreneurial rents and competitive advantage to be sustained.

Another component of the efficiency-based approach is developed in this paper. Rudimentary efforts are made to identify the dimensions of firm-specific capabilities that can be sources of advantage, and to explain how combinations of competences and resources can be developed, deployed, and protected. We refer to this as the 'dynamic capabilities' approach in order to stress exploiting existing internal and external firm-specific competences to address changing environments. Elements of the approach can be found in Schumpeter (1942), Penrose (1959), Nelson and Winter (1982), Prahalad and Hamel (1990), Teece (1976, 1986a, 1986b, 1988) and in Hayes, Wheelwright, and Clark (1988). Because this approach emphasizes the development of management capabilities, and difficult-to-imitate combinations of organizational, functional and technological skills, it integrates and draws upon research in such areas as the management of R&D, product and process development, technology transfer, intellectual property, manufacturing, human resources, and organizational learning. Because these fields are often viewed as outside the traditional boundaries of strategy, much of this research has not been incorporated into existing economic approaches to strategy issues. As a result, dynamic capabilities can be seen as an emerging and potentially integrative approach to understanding the newer sources of competitive advantage.

We suggest that the dynamic capabilities approach is promising both in terms of future research potential and as an aid to management endeavoring to gain competitive advantage in increasingly demanding environments. To illustrate the essential elements of the dynamic capabilities approach, the sections that follow compare and contrast this approach to other models of strategy. Each section highlights the strategic insights provided by each approach as well as the different competitive circumstances in which it might be most appropriate. Needless to say, these approaches are in many ways complementary and a full understanding of firm-level, competitive advantage requires an appreciation of all four approaches and more.

Models of Strategy Emphasizing the Exploitation of Market Power

Competitive forces

The dominant paradigm in strategy at least during the 1980s was the competitive forces approach. Pioneered by Porter (1980), the competitive forces approach views the essence of competitive strategy formulation as 'relating a company to its environment ... [T]he key aspect of the firm's environment is the industry or industries in which it competes.' Industry structure strongly influences the competitive rules of the game as well as the strategies potentially available to firms.

In the competitive forces model, five industry-level forces – entry barriers, threat of substitution, bargaining power of buyers, bargaining power of suppliers, and rivalry among industry incumbents – determine the inherent profit potential of an industry or subsegment of an industry. The approach can be used to help the firm find a position in an industry from which it can best defend itself against competitive forces or influence them in its favor (Porter, 1980: 4).

This 'five-forces' framework provides a systematic way of thinking about how competitive forces work at the industry level and how these forces determine the profitability of different industries and industry segments. The competitive forces framework also contains a number of underlying assumptions about the sources of competition and the nature of the strategy process. To facilitate comparisons with other approaches, we highlight several distinctive characteristics of the framework.

Economic rents in the competitive forces framework are monopoly rents (Teece, 1984). Firms in an industry earn rents when they are somehow able to impede the competitive forces (in either factor markets or product markets) which tend to drive economic returns to zero. Available strategies are described in Porter (1980). Competitive strategies are often aimed at altering the firm's position in the industry vis-à-vis competitors and suppliers. Industry structure plays a central role in determining and limiting strategic action.

Some industries or subsectors of industries become more 'attractive' because they have structural impediments to competitive forces (e.g., entry barriers) that allow firms better opportunities for creating sustainable competitive advantages. Rents are created largely at the industry or subsector level rather than at the firm level. While there is some recognition given to firm-specific assets, differences among firms relate primarily to scale. This approach to strategy reflects its incubation inside the field of industrial organization and in particular the industrial structure school of Mason and Bain[3] (Teece, 1984).

213

Strategic conflict

The publication of Carl Shapiro's 1989 article, confidently titled 'The Theory of Business Strategy,' announced the emergence of a new approach to business strategy, if not strategic management. This approach utilizes the tools of game theory to analyze the nature of competitive interaction between rival firms. The main thrust of work in this tradition is to reveal how a firm can influence the behavior and actions of rival firms and thus the market environment.[4] Examples of such moves are investment in capacity (Dixit, 1980), R&D (Gilbert and Newberry, 1982), and advertising (Schmalensee, 1983). To be effective, these strategic moves require irreversible commitments.[5] The moves in question will have no effect if they can be costlessly undone. A key idea is that by manipulating the market environment, a firm may be able to increase its profits.

This literature, together with the contestability literature (Baumol, Panzar, and Willig, 1982), has led to a greater appreciation of the role of sunk costs, as opposed to fixed costs, in determining competitive outcomes. Strategic moves can also be designed to influence rivals' behavior through signaling. Strategic signaling has been examined in a number of contexts, including predatory pricing (Kreps and Wilson, 1982a, 1982b) and limit pricing (Milgrom and Roberts, 1982a, 1982b). More recent treatments have emphasized the role of commitment and reputation (e.g., Ghemawat, 1991) and the benefits of firms simultaneously pursuing competition and cooperation[6] (Brandenburger and Nalebuff, 1995, 1996).

In many instances, game theory formalizes long-standing intuitive arguments about various types of business behavior (e.g., predatory pricing, patent races), though in some instances it has induced a substantial change in the conventional wisdom. But by rationalizing observed behavior by reference to suitably designed games, in explaining everything these models also explain nothing, as they do not generate testable predictions (Sutton, 1992). Many specific game-theoretic models admit multiple equilibria, and a wide range of choice exists as to the design of the appropriate game form to be used. Unfortunately, the results often depend on the precise specification chosen. The equilibrium in models of strategic behavior crucially depends on what one rival believes another rival will do in a particular situation. Thus the qualitative features of the results may depend on the way price competition is modeled (e.g., Bertrand or Cournot) or on the presence or absence of strategic asymmetries such as first-mover advantages. The analysis of strategic moves using game theory can be thought of as 'dynamic' in the sense that multiperiod analyses can be pursued both intuitively and formally. However, we use the term 'dynamic' in this paper in a different sense, referring to situations where there is rapid change in technology and market forces, and 'feedback' effects on firms.[7]

We have a particular view of the contexts in which the strategic conflict literature is relevant to strategic management. Firms that have a tremendous cost or other competitive advantage *vis-à-vis* their rivals ought not be transfixed by the moves and countermoves of their rivals. Their competitive fortunes will swing more on total demand conditions, not on how competitors deploy and redeploy their competitive assets. Put differently, when there are gross asymmetries in competitive advantage between firms, the results of game-theoretic analysis are likely to be obvious and uninteresting. The stronger competitor will generally advance, even if disadvantaged by certain information asymmetries. To be sure, incumbent firms can be undone by new entrants with a dramatic cost advantage, but no 'gaming' will overturn that outcome. On the other hand, if firms' competitive positions are more delicately balanced, as with Coke and Pepsi, and United Airlines and American Airlines, then strategic conflict is of interest to competitive outcomes. Needless to say, there are many such circumstances, but they are rare in industries where there is rapid technological change and fast-shifting market circumstances.

In short, where competitors do not have deep-seated competitive advantages, the moves and countermoves of competitors can often be usefully formulated in game-theoretic terms. However, we doubt that game theory can comprehensively illuminate how Chrysler should compete against Toyota and Honda, or how United Airlines can best respond to Southwest Airlines since Southwest's advantage is built on organizational attributes which United cannot readily replicate.[8] Indeed, the entrepreneurial side of strategy – how significant new rent streams are created and protected – is largely ignored by the game-theoretic approach.[9] Accordingly, we find that the approach, while important, is most relevant when competitors are closely matched[10] and the population of relevant competitors and the identity of their strategic alternatives can be readily ascertained. Nevertheless, coupled with other approaches it can sometimes yield powerful insights.

However, this research has an orientation that we are concerned about in terms of the implicit framing of strategic issues. Rents, from a game-theoretic perspective, are ultimately a result of managers' intellectual ability to 'play the game.' The adage of the strategist steeped in this approach is 'do unto others before they do unto you.' We worry that fascination with strategic moves and Machiavellian tricks will distract managers from seeking to build more enduring sources of competitive advantage. The approach unfortunately ignores competition as a process involving the development, accumulation, combination, and protection of unique skills and capabilities. Since strategic interactions are what receive focal attention, the impression one might receive from this literature is that success in the marketplace is the result of sophisticated plays and counterplays, when this is generally not the case at all.[11]

In what follows, we suggest that building a dynamic view of the business enterprise – something missing from the two approaches we have so far identified – enhances the probability of establishing an acceptable descriptive theory of strategy that can assist practitioners in the building of long-run advantage and competitive flexibility. Below, we discuss first the resource-based perspective and then an extension we call the dynamic capabilities approach.

MODELS OF STRATEGY EMPHASIZING EFFICIENCY

Resource-based perspective

The resource-based approach sees firms with superior systems and structures being profitable not because they engage in strategic investments that may deter entry and raise prices above long-run costs, but because they have markedly lower costs, or offer markedly higher quality or product performance. This approach focuses on the rents accruing to the owners of scarce firm-specific resources rather than the economic profits from product market positioning.[12] Competitive advantage lies 'upstream' of product markets and rests on the firm's idiosyncratic and difficult-to-imitate resources.[13]

One can find the resources approach suggested by the earlier preanalytic strategy literature. A leading text of the 1960s (Learned et al., 1969) noted that 'the capability of an organization is its demonstrated and potential ability to accomplish against the opposition of circumstance or competition, whatever it sets out to do. Every organization has actual and potential strengths and weaknesses; it is important to try to determine what they are and to distinguish one from the other.' Thus what a firm can do is not just a function of the opportunities it confronts; it also depends on what resources the organization can muster.

Learned et al. proposed that the real key to a company's success or even to its future development lies in its ability to find or create 'a competence that is truly distinctive.'[14] This literature also recognized the constraints on firm behavior and, in particular, noted that one should not assume that management 'can rise to any occasion.' These insights do appear to keenly anticipate the resource-based approach that has since emerged, but they did not provide a theory or systematic framework for analyzing business strategies. Indeed, Andrews (1987: 46) noted that 'much of what is intuitive in this process is yet to be identified.' Unfortunately, the academic literature on capabilities stalled for a couple of decades.

New impetus has been given to the resource-based approach by recent theoretical developments in organizational economics and in the theory of strategy, as well as by a growing body of anecdotal and empirical literature[15] that highlights the importance of firm-specific factors in explaining firm performance. Cool and Schendel (1988) have shown that there are systematic and significant performance differences among firms which belong to the same strategic group within the U.S. pharmaceutical industry. Rumelt (1991) has shown that intraindustry differences in profits are greater than interindustry differences in profits, strongly suggesting the importance of firm-specific factors and the relative unimportance of industry effects.[16] Jacobsen (1988) and Hansen and Wernerfelt (1989) made similar findings.

A comparison of the resource-based approach and the competitive forces approach (discussed earlier in the paper) in terms of their implications for the strategy process is revealing. From the first perspective, an entry decision looks roughly as follows: (1) pick an industry (based on its 'structural attractiveness'); (2) choose an entry strategy based on conjectures about competitors' rational strategies; (3) if not already possessed, acquire or otherwise obtain the requisite assets to compete in the market. From this perspective, the process of identifying and developing the requisite assets is not particularly problematic. The process involves nothing more than choosing rationally among a well-defined set of investment alternatives. If assets are not already owned, they can be bought. The resource-based perspective is strongly at odds with this conceptualization.

From the resource-based perspective, firms are heterogeneous with respect to their resources/capabilities/endowments. Further, resource endowments are 'sticky:' at least in the short run, firms are to some degree stuck with what they have and may have to live with what they lack.[17] This stickiness arises for three reasons. First, business development is viewed as an extremely complex process.[18] Quite simply, firms lack the organizational capacity to develop new competences quickly (Dierickx and Cool, 1989). Secondly, some assets are simply not readily tradeable, for example, tacit know-how (Teece, 1976, 1980) and reputation (Dierickx and Cool, 1989). Thus, resource endowments cannot equilibrate through factor input markets. Finally, even when an asset can be purchased, firms may stand to gain little by doing so. As Barney (1986) points out, unless a firm is lucky, possesses superior information, or both, the price it pays in a competitive factor market will fully capitalize the rents from the asset.

Given that in the resources perspective firms possess heterogeneous and sticky resource bundles, the entry decision process suggested by this approach is as follows: (1) identify your firm's unique resources; (2) decide in which markets those resources can earn the highest rents; and (3) decide whether the rents from those assets are most effectively utilized by (a) integrating into related market(s), (b) selling the relevant intermediate output to related firms, or (c) selling the assets themselves to a firm in related businesses (Teece, 1980, 1982).

The resource-based perspective puts both vertical integration and diversification into a new strategic light. Both can be viewed as ways of capturing rents on scarce, firm-specific assets whose services are difficult to sell in intermediate markets (Penrose, 1959; Williamson, 1975; Teece, 1980, 1982, 1986a, 1986b; Wernerfelt, 1984). Empirical work on the relationship between performance and diversification by Wernerfelt and Montgomery (1988) provides evidence for this proposition. It is evident that the resource-based perspective focuses on strategies for exploiting existing firm-specific assets.

However, the resource-based perspective also invites consideration of managerial strategies for developing new capabilities (Wernerfelt, 1984). Indeed, if control over scarce resources is the source of economic profits, then it follows that such issues as skill acquisition, the management of knowledge and know-how (Shuen, 1994), and learning become fundamental strategic issues. It is in this second dimension, encompassing skill acquisition, learning, and accumulation of organizational and intangible or 'invisible' assets (Itami and Roehl, 1987), that we believe lies the greatest potential for contributions to strategy.

The dynamic capabilities approach: overview

The global competitive battles in high-technology industries such as semiconductors, information services, and software have demonstrated the need for an expanded paradigm to understand how competitive advantage is achieved. Well-known companies like IBM, Texas Instruments, Philips, and others appear to have followed a 'resource-based strategy' of accumulating valuable technology assets, often guarded by an aggressive intellectual property stance. However, this strategy is often not enough to support a significant competitive advantage. Winners in the global marketplace have been firms that can demonstrate timely responsiveness and rapid and flexible product innovation, coupled with the management capability to effectively coordinate and redeploy internal and external competences. Not surprisingly, industry observers have remarked that companies can accumulate a large stock of valuable technology assets and still not have many useful capabilities.

We refer to this ability to achieve new forms of competitive advantage as 'dynamic capabilities' to emphasize two key aspects that were not the main focus of attention in previous strategy perspectives. The term 'dynamic' refers to the capacity to renew competences so as to achieve congruence with the changing business environment; certain innovative responses are required when time-to-market and timing are critical, the rate of technological change is rapid, and the nature of future competition and markets difficult to determine. The term 'capabilities' emphasizes the key role of strategic management in appropriately adapting, integrating, and reconfiguring internal and external organizational skills, resources, and functional competences to match the requirements of a changing environment.

One aspect of the strategic problem facing an innovating firm in a world of Schumpeterian competition is to identify difficult-to-imitate internal and external competences most likely to support valuable products and services. Thus, as argued by Dierickx and Cool (1989), choices about how much to spend (invest) on different possible areas are central to the firm's strategy. However, choices about domains of competence are influenced by past choices. At any given point in time, firms must follow a certain trajectory or path of competence development. This path not only defines what choices are open to the firm today, but it also puts bounds around what its internal repertoire is likely to be in the future. Thus, firms, at various points in time, make long-term, quasi-irreversible commitments to certain domains of competence.[19]

The notion that competitive advantage requires both the exploitation of existing internal and external firm-specific capabilities, and developing new ones is partially developed in Penrose (1959), Teece (1982), and Wernerfelt (1984). However, only recently have researchers begun to focus on the specifics of how some organizations first develop firm-specific capabilities and how they renew competences to respond to shifts in the business environment.[20] These issues are intimately tied to the firm's business processes, market positions, and expansion paths. Several writers have recently offered insights and evidence on how firms can develop their capability to adapt and even capitalize on rapidly changing environments.[21] The dynamic capabilities approach seeks to provide a coherent framework which can both integrate existing conceptual and empirical knowledge, and facilitate prescription. In doing so, it builds upon the theoretical foundations provided by Schumpeter (1934), Penrose (1959), Williamson (1975, 1985), Barney (1986), Nelson and Winter (1982), Teece (1988), and Teece et al. (1994).

Toward a Dynamic Capabilities Framework

Terminology

In order to facilitate theory development and intellectual dialogue, some acceptable definitions are desirable. We propose the following.

Factors of production

These are 'undifferentiated' inputs available in disaggregate form in factor markets. By undifferentiated we mean that they lack a firm-specific component. Land, unskilled labor, and capital are typical examples. Some factors may be available for the taking, such as public knowledge. In the language of Arrow, such resources must be 'non-fugitive.'[22] Property rights are usually well defined for factors of production.

Resources[23]

Resources are firm-specific assets that are difficult if not impossible to imitate. Trade secrets and certain specialized production facilities and engineering experience are examples. Such assets are difficult to transfer among firms because of transactions costs and transfer costs, and because the assets may contain tacit knowledge.

Organizational routines/competences

When firm-specific assets are assembled in integrated clusters spanning individuals and groups so that they enable distinctive activities to be performed, these activities constitute organizational routines and processes. Examples include quality, miniaturization, and systems integration. Such competences are typically viable across multiple product lines, and may extend outside the firm to embrace alliance partners.

Core competences

We define those competences that define a firm's fundamental business as core. Core competences must accordingly be derived by looking across the range of a firm's (and its competitors) products and services.[24] The value of core competences can be enhanced by combination with the appropriate complementary assets. The degree to which a core competence is distinctive depends on how well endowed the firm is relative to its competitors, and on how difficult it is for competitors to replicate its competences.

Dynamic capabilities

We define dynamic capabilities as the firm's ability to integrate, build, and reconfigure internal and external competences to address rapidly changing environments. Dynamic capabilities thus reflect an organization's ability to achieve new and innovative forms of competitive advantage given path dependencies and market positions (Leonard-Barton, 1992).

Products

End products are the final goods and services produced by the firm based on utilizing the competences that it possesses. The performance (price, quality, etc.) of a firm's products relative to its competitors at any point in time will depend upon its competences (which over time depend on its capabilities).

Markets and strategic capabilities

Different approaches to strategy view sources of wealth creation and the essence of the strategic problem faced by firms differently. The competitive forces framework sees the strategic problem in terms of industry structure, entry deterrence, and positioning; game-theoretic models view the strategic problem as one of interaction between rivals with certain expectations about how each other will behave;[25] resource-based perspectives have focused on the exploitation of firm-specific assets. Each approach asks different, often complementary questions. A key step in building a conceptual framework related to dynamic capabilities is to identify the foundations upon which distinctive and difficult-to-replicate advantages can be built, maintained, and enhanced.

A useful way to vector in on the strategic elements of the business enterprise is first to identify what is not strategic. To be strategic, a capability must be honed to a user need[26] (so there is a source of revenues), unique (so that the products/services produced can be priced without too much regard to competition) and difficult to replicate (so profits will not be competed away). Accordingly, any assets or entity which are homogeneous and can be bought and sold at an established price cannot be all that strategic (Barney, 1986). What is it, then, about firms which undergirds competitive advantage?

To answer this, one must first make some fundamental distinctions between markets and internal organization (firms). The essence of the firm, as Coase (1937) pointed out, is that it displaces market organization. It does so in the main because inside the firms one can organize certain types of economic activity in ways one cannot using markets. This is not only because of transaction costs, as Williamson (1975, 1985) emphasized, but also because there are many types of arrangements where injecting high-powered (market like) incentives might well be quite destructive of cooperative activity and learning.[27] Inside an organization, exchange cannot take place in the same manner that it can outside an organization, not just because it might be destructive to provide high-powered individual incentives, but because it is difficult if not impossible to tightly calibrate individual contribution to a joint effort. Hence, contrary to Arrow's (1969) view of firms as quasi markets, and the task of management to inject markets into firms, we recognize the inherent limits and possible counter-productive results of attempting to fashion firms into simply clusters of internal markets. In particular, learning and internal technology transfer may well be jeopardized.

Indeed, what is distinctive about firms is that they are domains for organizing activity in a non-market-like fashion. Accordingly, as we discuss what is distinctive about firms, we stress competences/capabilities which are ways of organizing and getting things done which cannot be accomplished merely by using the price system to coordinate activity.[28] The very essence of most capabilities/competences is that they cannot be readily assembled through markets (Teece, 1982, 1986a; Zander and Kogut, 1995). If the ability to assemble competences using markets is what is meant by the firm as a nexus of contracts (Fama, 1980), then we unequivocally state that the firm about which we theorize cannot be usefully modeled as a nexus of contracts. By 'contract' we are referring to a transaction undergirded by a legal agreement, or some other arrangement which clearly spells out rights, rewards, and responsibilities. Moreover, the firm as a nexus of contracts suggests a series of bilateral contracts orchestrated by a coordinator. Our view of the firm is that the organization takes place in a more multilateral fashion, with patterns of behavior and learning being orchestrated in a much more decentralized fashion, but with a viable headquarters operation.

The key point, however, is that the properties of internal organization cannot be replicated by a portfolio of business units amalgamated just through formal contracts as many distinctive elements of internal organization simply cannot be replicated in the market.[29] That is, entrepreneurial activity cannot lead to the immediate replication of unique organizational skills through simply entering a market and piecing the parts together overnight. Replication takes time, and the replication of best practice may be elusive. Indeed, firm capabilities need to be understood not in terms of balance sheet items, but mainly in terms of the organizational structures and managerial processes which support productive activity. By construction, the firm's balance sheet contains items that can be valued, at least at original market prices (cost). It is necessarily the case, therefore, that the balance sheet is a poor shadow of a firm's distinctive competences.[30] That which is distinctive cannot be bought and sold short of buying the firm itself, or one or more of its subunits.

There are many dimensions of the business firm that must be understood if one is to grasp firm-level distinctive competences/capabilities. In this paper we merely identify several classes of factors that will help determine a firm's distinctive competence and dynamic capabilities. We organize these in three categories: processes, positions, and paths. The essence of competences and capabilities is embedded in organizational processes of one kind or another. But the content of these processes and the opportunities they afford for developing competitive advantage at any point in time are shaped significantly by the assets the firm possesses (internal and market) and by the evolutionary path it has adopted/inherited. Hence organizational processes, shaped by the firm's asset positions and molded by its evolutionary and co-evolutionary paths, explain the essence of the firm's dynamic capabilities and its competitive advantage.

Processes, positions, and paths

We thus advance the argument that the competitive advantage of firms lies with its managerial and organizational processes, shaped by its (specific) asset position, and the paths available to it.[31] By managerial and organizational processes, we refer to the way things are done in the firm, or what might be referred to as its routines, or patterns of current practice and learning. By position we refer to its current specific endowments of technology, intellectual property, complementary assets, customer base, and its external relations with suppliers and complementors. By paths we refer to the strategic alternatives available to the firm, and the presence or absence of increasing returns and attendant path dependencies.

Our focus throughout is on asset structures for which no ready market exists, as these are the only assets of strategic interest. A final section focuses on replication and imitation, as it is these phenomena which determine how readily a competence or capability can be cloned by competitors, and therefore distinctiveness of its competences and the durability of its advantage.

The firm's processes and positions collectively encompass its competences and capabilities. A hierarchy of competences/capabilities ought to be recognized, as some competences may be on the factory floor, some in the R&D labs, some in the executive suites, and some in the way everything is integrated. A difficult-to-replicate or difficult-to-imitate competence was defined earlier as a distinctive competence. As indicated, the key feature of distinctive competence is that there is not a market for it, except possibly through the market for business units. Hence competences and capabilities are intriguing assets as they typically must be built because they cannot be bought.

Organizational and managerial processes

Organizational processes have three roles: coordination/integration (a static concept); learning (a dynamic concept); and reconfiguration (a transformational concept). We discuss each in turn.

Coordination/integration. While the price system supposedly coordinates the economy,[32] managers coordinate or integrate activity inside the firm. How efficiently and effectively internal coordination or integration is achieved is very important (Aoki, 1990).[33] Likewise for external coordination.[34] Increasingly, strategic advantage requires the integration of external activities and technologies. The growing literature on strategic alliances, the virtual corporation, and buyer-supplier relations and technology collaboration evidences the importance of external integration and sourcing.

There is some field-based empirical research that provides support for the notion that the way production is organized by management inside the firm is the source of differences in firms' competence in various domains. For example, Garvin's (1988) study of 18 room air-conditioning plants reveals that quality performance was not related to either capital investment or the degree of automation of the facilities. Instead, quality performance was driven by special organizational routines. These included routines for gathering and processing information, for linking customer experiences with engineering design choices, and for coordinating factories and component suppliers.[35] The work of Clark and Fujimoto (1991) on project development in the automobile industry also illustrates the role played by coordinative routines. Their study reveals a significant degree of variation in how different firms coordinate the various activities required to bring a new model from concept to market. These differences in coordinative routines and capabilities seem to have a significant impact on such performance variables as development cost, development lead times, and quality. Furthermore, Clark and Fujimoto tended to find significant firm-level differences in coordination routines and these differences seemed to have persisted for a long time. This suggests that routines related to coordination are firm-specific in nature.

Also, the notion that competence/capability is embedded in distinct ways of coordinating and combining helps to explain how and why seemingly minor technological changes can have devastating impacts on incumbent firms' abilities to compete in a market. Henderson and Clark (1990), for example, have shown that incumbents in the photolithographic equipment industry were sequentially devasted by seemingly minor innovations that, nevertheless, had major impacts on how systems had to be configured. They attribute these difficulties to the fact that systems-level or 'architectural' innovations often require new routines to integrate and coordinate engineering tasks. These findings and others suggest that productive systems display high interdependency, and that it may not be possible to change one level without changing others. This appears to be true with respect to the 'lean production' model (Womack *et al.*, 1991) which has now transformed the Taylor or Ford model of manufacturing organization in the automobile industry.[36] Lean production requires distinctive shop floor practices and processes as well as distinctive higher-order managerial processes. Put differently, organizational processes often display high levels of coherence, and when they do, replication may be difficult because it requires systemic changes throughout the organization and also among interorganizational linkages, which might be very hard to effectuate. Put differently, partial imitation or replication of a successful model may yield zero benefits.[37]

The notion that there is a certain rationality or coherence to processes and systems is not quite the same concept as corporate culture, as we understand the latter. Corporate culture refers to the values and beliefs that employees hold; culture can be a *de facto* governance system as it mediates the behavior of individuals and economizes on more formal administrative methods. Rationality or coherence notions are more akin to the Nelson and Winter (1982) notion of organizational routines. However, the routines concept is a little too amorphous to properly capture the congruence amongst processes and between processes and incentives that we have in mind. Consider a professional service organization like an accounting firm. If it is to have relatively high-powered incentives that reward individual performance, then it must build organizational processes that channel individual behavior; if it has weak or low-powered incentives, it must find symbolic ways to recognize the high performers, and it must use alternative methods to build effort and enthusiasm. What one may think of as styles of organization in fact contain necessary, not discretionary, elements to achieve performance.

Recognizing the congruences and complementarities among processes, and between processes and incentives, is critical to the understanding of organizational capabilities. In particular, they can help us explain why architectural and radical innovations are so often introduced into an industry by new entrants. The incumbents develop distinctive organizational processes that cannot support the new technology, despite certain overt similarities between the old and the new. The frequent failure of incumbents to introduce new technologies can thus be seen as a consequence of the mismatch that so often exists between the set of organizational processes needed to support the conventional product/service and the requirements of the new. Radical organizational reengineering will usually be required to support the new product, which may well do better embedded in a separate subsidiary where a new set of coherent organizational processes can be fashioned.[38]

Learning.　Perhaps even more important than integration is learning. Learning is a process by which repetition and experimentation enable tasks to be performed better and quicker. It also enables new production opportunities to be identified.[39] In the context of the firm, if not more generally, learning has several key characteristics. First, learning involves organizational as well as individual skills.[40] While individual skills are of relevance, their value depends upon their employment, in particular organizational settings. Learning processes are intrinsically social and collective and occur not only through the imitation and emulation of individuals, as with teacher–student or master–apprentice, but also because of joint contributions to the understanding of complex problems.[41] Learning requires common codes of communication and coordinated search procedures. Second, the organizational knowledge generated by such activity resides in new patterns of activity, in 'routines,' or a new logic of organization. As indicated earlier, routines are patterns of interactions that represent successful solutions to particular problems. These patterns of interaction are resident in group behavior, though certain subroutines may be resident in individual behavior. The concept of dynamic capabilities as a coordinative management process opens the door to the potential for interorganizational learning. Researchers (Doz and Shuen, 1990; Mody, 1993) have pointed out that collaborations and partnerships can be a vehicle for new organizational learning, helping firms to recognize dysfunctional routines, and preventing strategic blindspots.

Reconfiguration and transformation.　In rapidly changing environments, there is obviously value in the ability to sense the need to reconfigure the firm's asset structure, and to accomplish the necessary internal and external transformation (Amit and Schoemaker, 1993; Langlois, 1994). This requires constant surveillance of markets and technologies and the willingness to adopt best practice. In this regard, benchmarking is of considerable value as an organized process for accomplishing such ends (Camp, 1989). In dynamic environments, narcissistic organizations are likely to be impaired. The capacity to reconfigure and transform is itself a learned organizational skill. The more frequently practiced, the easier accomplished.

Change is costly and so firms must develop processes to minimize low pay-off change. The ability to calibrate the requirements for change and to effectuate the necessary adjustments would appear to depend on the ability to scan the environment, to evaluate markets and competitors, and to quickly accomplish reconfiguration and transformation ahead of competition. Decentralization and local autonomy assist these processes. Firms that have honed these capabilities are sometimes referred to as 'high-flex'.

Positions

The strategic posture of a firm is determined not only by its learning processes and by the coherence of its internal and external processes and incentives, but also by its specific assets. By specific assets we mean for example its specialized plant and equipment. These include its difficult-to-trade knowledge assets and assets complementary to them, as well as its reputational and relational assets. Such assets determine its competitive advantage at any point in time. We identify several illustrative classes.

Technological assets. While there is an emerging market for know-how (Teece, 1981), much technology does not enter it. This is either because the firm is unwilling to sell it[42] or because of difficulties in transacting in the market for know-how (Teece, 1980). A firm's technological assets may or may not be protected by the standard instruments of intellectual property law. Either way, the ownership protection and utilization of technological assets are clearly key differentiators among firms. Likewise for complementary assets.

Complementary assets. Technological innovations require the use of certain related assets to produce and deliver new products and services. Prior commercialization activities require and enable firms to build such complementarities (Teece, 1986b). Such capabilities and assets, while necessary for the firm's established activities, may have other uses as well. These assets typically lie downstream. New products and processes either can enhance or destroy the value of such assets (Tushman, Newman, and Romanelli, 1986). Thus the development of computers enhanced the value of IBM's direct sales force in office products, while disk brakes rendered useless much of the auto industry's investment in drum brakes.

Financial assets. In the short run, a firm's cash position and degree of leverage may have strategic implications. While there is nothing more fungible than cash, it cannot always be raised from external markets without the dissemination of considerable information to potential investors. Accordingly, what a firm can do in short order is often a function of its balance sheet. In the longer run, that ought not be so, as cash flow ought be more determinative.

Reputational assets. Firms, like individuals, have reputations. Reputations often summarize a good deal of information about firms and shape the responses of customers, suppliers, and competitors. It is sometimes difficult to disentangle reputation from the firm's current asset and market position. However, in our view, reputational assets are best viewed as an intangible asset that enables firms to achieve various goals in the market. Its main value is external, since what is critical about reputation is that it is a kind of summary statistic about the firm's current assets and position, and its likely future behavior. Because there is generally a strong asymmetry between what is known inside the firm and what is known externally, reputations may sometimes be more salient than the true state of affairs, in the sense that external actors must respond to what they know rather than what is knowable.

Structural assets.   The formal and informal structure of organizations and their external link-ages have an important bearing on the rate and direction of innovation, and how competences and capabilities co-evolve (Argyres, 1995; Teece, 1996). The degree of hierarchy and the level of vertical and lateral integration are elements of firm-specific structure. Distinctive governance modes can be recognized (e.g., multiproduct, integrated firms; high 'flex' firms; virtual corpo-rations; conglomerates), and these modes support different types of innovation to a greater or lesser degree. For instance, virtual structures work well when innovation is autonomous; inte-grated structures work better for systemic innovations.

Institutional assets.   Environments cannot be defined in terms of markets alone. While public poli-cies are usually recognized as important in constraining what firms can do, there is a tendency, par-ticularly by economists, to see these as acting through markets or through incentives. However, institutions themselves are a critical element of the business environment. Regulatory systems, as well as intellectual property regimes, tort laws, and antitrust laws, are also part of the environment. So is the system of higher education and national culture. There are significant national differences here, which is just one of the reasons geographic location matters (Nelson, 1994). Such assets may not be entirely firm specific; firms of different national and regional origin may have quite differ-ent institutional assets to call upon because their institutional/policy settings are so different.

Market (structure) assets.   Product market position matters, but it is often not at all determinative of the fundamental position of the enterprise in its external environment. Part of the problem lies in defining the market in which a firm competes in a way that gives economic meaning. More importantly, market position in regimes of rapid technological change is often extremely fragile. This is in part because time moves on a different clock in such environments.[43] Moreover, the link between market share and innovation has long been broken, if it ever existed (Teece, 1996). All of this is to suggest that product market position, while important, is too often overplayed. Strategy should be formulated with regard to the more fundamental aspects of firm performance, which we believe are rooted in competences and capabilities and shaped by positions and paths.

Organizational boundaries.   An important dimension of 'position' is the location of a firm's boundaries. Put differently, the degree of integration (vertical, lateral, and horizontal) is of quite some significance. Boundaries are not only significant with respect to the technological and complementary assets contained within, but also with respect to the nature of the coordination that can be achieved internally as compared to through markets. When specific assets or poorly protected intellectual capital are at issue, pure market arrangements expose the parties to recon-tracting hazards or appropriability hazards. In such circumstances, hierarchical control struc-tures may work better than pure arms-length contracts.[44]

Paths

Path dependencies.   Where a firm can go is a function of its current position and the paths ahead. Its current position is often shaped by the path it has traveled. In standard economics textbooks, firms have an infinite range of technologies from which they can choose and markets they can occupy. Changes in product or factor prices will be responded to instantaneously, with technologies moving in and out according to value maximization criteria. Only in the short run are irreversibilities recognized. Fixed costs – such as equipment and overheads – cause firms to price below fully amortized costs but never constrain future investment choices. 'Bygones are bygones.' Path dependencies are simply not recognized. This is a major limitation of microeconomic theory.

The notion of path dependencies recognizes that 'history matters.' Bygones are rarely bygones, despite the predictions of rational actor theory. Thus a firm's previous investments and its repertoire of routines (its 'history') constrain its future behavior.[45] This follows because learning tends to be local. That is, opportunities for learning will be 'close in' to previous activities and thus will be transaction and production specific (Teece, 1988). This is because learning is often a process of trial, feedback, and evaluation. If too many parameters are changed simultaneously, the ability of firms to conduct meaningful natural quasi experiments is attenuated. If many aspects of a firm's learning environment change simultaneously, the ability to ascertain cause–effect relationships is confounded because cognitive structures will not be formed and rates of learning diminish as a result. One implication is that many investments are much longer term than is commonly thought.

The importance of path dependencies is amplified where conditions of increasing returns to adoption exist. This is a demand-side phenomenon, and it tends to make technologies and products embodying those technologies more attractive the more they are adopted. Attractiveness flows from the greater adoption of the product amongst users, which in turn enables them to become more developed and hence more useful. Increasing returns to adoption has many sources including network externalities (Katz and Shapiro, 1985), the presence of complementary assets (Teece, 1986b) and supporting infrastructure (Nelson, 1996), learning by using (Rosenberg, 1982), and scale economies in production and distribution. Competition between and amongst technologies is shaped by increasing returns. Early leads won by good luck or special circumstances (Arthur, 1983) can become amplified by increasing returns. This is not to suggest that first movers necessarily win. Because increasing returns have multiple sources, the prior positioning of firms can affect their capacity to exploit increasing returns. Thus, in Mitchell's (1989) study of medical diagnostic imaging, firms already controlling the relevant complementary assets could in theory start last and finish first.

In the presence of increasing returns, firms can compete passively, or they may compete strategically through technology-sponsoring activities.[46] The first type of competition is not unlike biological competition amongst species, although it can be sharpened by managerial activities that enhance the performance of products and processes. The reality is that companies with the best products will not always win, as chance events may cause 'lock-in' on inferior technologies (Arthur, 1983) and may even in special cases generate switching costs for consumers. However, while switching costs may favor the incumbent, in regimes of rapid technological change switching costs can become quickly swamped by switching benefits. Put differently, new products employing different standards often appear with alacrity in market environments experiencing rapid technological change, and incumbents can be readily challenged by superior products and services that yield switching benefits. Thus the degree to which switching costs cause 'lock-in' is a function of factors such as user learning, rapidity of technological change, and the amount of ferment in the competitive environment.

Technological opportunities. The concept of path dependencies is given forward meaning through the consideration of an industry's technological opportunities. It is well recognized that how far and how fast a particular area of industrial activity can proceed is in part due to the technological opportunities that lie before it. Such opportunities are usually a lagged function of foment and diversity in basic science, and the rapidity with which new scientific breakthroughs are being made.

However, technological opportunities may not be completely exogenous to industry, not only because some firms have the capacity to engage in or at least support basic research, but also because technological opportunities are often fed by innovative activity itself. Moreover, the recognition of such opportunities is affected by the organizational structures that link the institutions engaging in basic research (primarily the university) to the business enterprise. Hence, the existence of technological opportunities can be quite firm specific.

Important for our purposes is the rate and direction in which relevant scientific frontiers are being rolled back. Firms engaging in R&D may find the path dead ahead closed off, though break-throughs in related areas may be sufficiently close to be attractive. Likewise, if the path dead ahead is extremely attractive, there may be no incentive for firms to shift the allocation of resources away from traditional pursuits. The depth and width of technological opportunities in the neighborhood of a firm's prior research activities thus are likely to impact a firm's options with respect to both the amount and level of R&D activity that it can justify. In addition, a firm's past experience conditions the alternatives management is able to perceive. Thus, not only do firms in the same industry face 'menus' with different costs associated with particular technological choices, they also are looking at menus containing different choices.[47]

Assessment

The essence of a firm's competence and dynamic capabilities is presented here as being resident in the firm's organizational processes, that are in turn shaped by the firm's assets (positions) and its evolutionary path. Its evolutionary path, despite managerial hubris that might suggest otherwise, is often rather narrow.[48] What the firm can do and where it can go are thus rather constrained by its positions and paths. Its competitors are likewise constrained. Rents (profits) thus tend to flow not just from the asset structure of the firm and, as we shall see, the degree of its imitability, but also by the firm's ability to reconfigure and transform.

The parameters we have identified for determining performance are quite different from those in the standard textbook theory of the firm, and in the competitive forces and strategic conflict approaches to the firm and to strategy.[49] Moreover, the agency theoretic view of the firm as a nexus of contracts would put no weight on processes, positions, and paths. While agency approaches to the firm may recognize that opportunism and shirking may limit what a firm can do, they do not recognize the opportunities and constraints imposed by processes, positions, and paths.

Moreover, the firm in our conceptualization is much more than the sum of its parts – or a team tied together by contracts.[50] Indeed, to some extent individuals can be moved in and out of organizations and, so long as the internal processes and structures remain in place, performance will not necessarily be impaired. A shift in the environment is a far more serious threat to the firm than is the loss of key individuals, as individuals can be replaced more readily than organizations can be transformed. Furthermore, the dynamic capabilities view of the firm would suggest that the behavior and performance of particular firms may be quite hard to replicate, even if its coherence and rationality are observable. This matter and related issues involving replication and imitation are taken up in the section that follows.

Replicability and imitability of organizational processes and positions

Thus far, we have argued that the competences and capabilities (and hence competitive advantage) of a firm rest fundamentally on processes, shaped by positions and paths. However, competences can provide competitive advantage and generate rents only if they are based on a collection of routines, skills, and complementary assets that are difficult to imitate.[51] A particular set of routines can lose their value if they support a competence which no longer matters in the marketplace, or if they can be readily replicated or emulated by competitors. Imitation occurs when firms discover and simply copy a firm's organizational routines and procedures. Emulation occurs when firms discover alternative ways of achieving the same functionality.[52]

Replication

To understand imitation, one must first understand replication. Replication involves transferring or redeploying competences from one concrete economic setting to another. Since productive knowledge is embodied, this cannot be accomplished by simply transmitting information. Only in those instances where all relevant knowledge is fully codified and understood can replication be collapsed into a simple problem of information transfer. Too often, the contextual dependence of original performance is poorly appreciated, so unless firms have replicated their systems of productive knowledge on many prior occasions, the act of replication is likely to be difficult (Teece, 1976). Indeed, replication and transfer are often impossible absent the transfer of people, though this can be minimized if investments are made to convert tacit knowledge to codified knowledge. Often, however, this is simply not possible.

In short, competences and capabilities, and the routines upon which they rest, are normally rather difficult to replicate.[53] Even understanding what all the relevant routines are that support a particular competence may not be transparent. Indeed, Lippman and Rumelt (1992) have argued that some sources of competitive advantage are so complex that the firm itself, let alone its competitors, does not understand them.[54] As Nelson and Winter (1982) and Teece (1982) have explained, many organizational routines are quite tacit in nature. Imitation can also be hindered by the fact few routines are 'stand-alone;' coherence may require that a change in one set of routines in one part of the firm (e.g., production) requires changes in some other part (e.g., R&D).

Some routines and competences seem to be attributable to local or regional forces that shape firms' capabilities at early stages in their lives. Porter (1990), for example, shows that differences in local product markets, local factor markets, and institutions play an important role in shaping competitive capabilities. Differences also exist within populations of firms from the same country. Various studies of the automobile industry, for example, show that not all Japanese automobile companies are top performers in terms of quality, productivity, or product development (see, for example, Clark and Fujimoto, 1991). The role of firm-specific history has been highlighted as a critical factor explaining such firmlevel (as opposed to regional or national-level) differences (Nelson and Winter, 1982). Replication in a different context may thus be rather difficult.

At least two types of strategic value flow from replication. One is the ability to support geographic and product line expansion. To the extent that the capabilities in question are relevant to customer needs elsewhere, replication can confer value.[55] Another is that the ability to replicate also indicates that the firm has the foundations in place for learning and improvement. Considerable empirical evidence supports the notion that the understanding of processes, both in production and in management, is the key to process improvement. In short, an organization cannot improve that which it does not understand. Deep process understanding is often required to accomplish codification. Indeed, if knowledge is highly tacit, it indicates that underlying structures are not well understood, which limits learning because scientific and engineering principles cannot be as systematically applied.[56] Instead, learning is confined to proceeding through trial and error, and the leverage that might otherwise come from the application of scientific theory is denied.

Imitation

Imitation is simply replication performed by a competitor. If self-replication is difficult, imitation is likely to be harder. In competitive markets, it is the ease of imitation that determines the sustainability of competitive advantage. Easy imitation implies the rapid dissipation of rents.

Factors that make replication difficult also make imitation difficult. Thus, the more tacit the firm's productive knowledge, the harder it is to replicate by the firm itself or its competitors. When the tacit component is high, imitation may well be impossible, absent the hiring away of key individuals and the transfers of key organization processes.

However, another set of barriers impedes imitation of certain capabilities in advanced industrial countries. This is the system of intellectual property rights, such as patents, trade secrets, and trademarks, and even trade dress.[57] Intellectual property protection is of increasing importance in the United States, as since 1982 the legal system has adopted a more pro-patent posture. Similar trends are evident outside the United States. Besides the patent system, several other factors cause there to be a difference between replication costs and imitation costs. The observability of the technology or the organization is one such important factor. Whereas vistas into product technology can be obtained through strategies such as reverse engineering, this is not the case for process technology, as a firm need not expose its process technology to the outside in order to benefit from it.[58] Firms with product technology, on the other hand, confront the unfortunate circumstances that they must expose what they have got in order to profit from the technology. Secrets are thus more protectable if there is no need to expose them in contexts where competitors can learn about them.

One should not, however, overestimate the overall importance of intellectual property protection; yet it presents a formidable imitation barrier in certain particular contexts. Intellectual property protection is not uniform across products, processes, and technologies, and is best thought of as islands in a sea of open competition. If one is not able to place the fruits of one's investment, ingenuity, or creativity on one or more of the islands, then one indeed is at sea.

We use the term appropriability regimes to describe the ease of imitation. Appropriability is a function both of the ease of replication and the efficacy of intellectual property rights as a barrier to imitation. Appropriability is strong when a technology is both inherently difficult to replicate and the intellectual property system provides legal barriers to imitation. When it is inherently easy to replicate and intellectual property protection is either unavailable or ineffectual, then appropriability is weak. Intermediate conditions also exist.

Conclusion

The four paradigms discussed above are quite different, though the first two have much in common with each other (strategizing) as do the last two (economizing). But are these paradigms complementary or competitive? According to some authors, 'the resource perspective complements the industry analysis framework' (Amit and Schoemaker, 1993: 35). While this is undoubtedly true, we think that in several important respects the perspectives are also competitive. While this should be recognized, it is not to suggest that there is only one framework that has value. Indeed, complex problems are likely to benefit from insights obtained from all of the paradigms we have identified plus more. The trick is to work out which frameworks are appropriate for the problem at hand. Slavish adherence to one class to the neglect of all others is likely to generate strategic blindspots. The tools themselves then generate strategic vulnerability. We now explore these issues further. Table 12.1 summarizes some similarities and differences.

Efficiency vs. market power

The competitive forces and strategic conflict approaches generally see profits as stemming from strategizing – that is, from limitations on competition which firms achieve through raising rivals' costs and exclusionary behavior (Teece, 1984). The competitive forces approach in particular leads one to see concentrated industries as being attractive – market positions can be shielded behind entry barriers, and rivals costs can be raised. It also suggests that the sources of competitive advantage lie at the level of the industry, or possibly groups within an industry. In text book presentations, there is almost no attention at all devoted to discovering, creating, and commercializing new sources of value.

The dynamic capabilities and resources approaches clearly have a different orientation. They see competitive advantage stemming from high-performance routines operating 'inside the firm,' shaped by processes and positions. Path dependencies (including increasing returns) and technological opportunities mark the road ahead. Because of imperfect factor markets, or more precisely the nontradability of 'soft' assets like values, culture, and organizational experience, distinctive competences and capabilities generally cannot be acquired; they must be built. This sometimes takes years – possibly decades. In some cases, as when the competence is protected by patents, replication by a competitor is ineffectual as a means to access the technology. The capabilities approach accordingly sees definite limits on strategic options, at least in the short run. Competitive success occurs in part because of policies pursued and experience and efficiency obtained in earlier periods.

Competitive success can undoubtedly flow from both strategizing and economizing,[59] but along with Williamson (1991) we believe that 'economizing is more fundamental than strategizing ... or put differently, that economy is the best strategy.'[60] Indeed, we suggest that, except in special circumstances, too much 'strategizing' can lead firms to underinvest in core competences and neglect dynamic capabilities, and thus harm long-term competitiveness.

Normative implications

The field of strategic management is avowedly normative. It seeks to guide those aspects of general management that have material effects on the survival and success of the business enterprise. Unless these various approaches differ in terms of the framework and heuristics they offer management, then the discourse we have gone through is of limited immediate value. In this paper, we have already alluded to the fact that the capabilities approach tends to steer managers toward creating distinctive and difficult-to-imitate advantages and avoiding games with customers and competitors. We now survey possible differences, recognizing that the paradigms are still in their infancy and cannot confidently support strong normative conclusions.

Unit of analysis and analytic focus

Because in the capabilities and the resources framework business opportunities flow from a firm's unique processes, strategy analysis must be situational.[61] This is also true with the strategic conflict approach. There is no algorithm for creating wealth for the entire industry.

Table 12.1 Paradigms of strategy: salient characteristics

Paradigm	Intellectual roots	Representative authors addressing strategic management questions	Nature of rents	Rationality assumptions of managers	Fundamental units of analysis	Short-run capacity for strategic reorientation	Role of industrial structure	Focal concern
(1) Attenuating competitive forces	Mason, Bain	Porter (1980)	Chamberlinean	Rational	Industries, firms, products	High	Exogenous	Structural conditions and competitor positioning
(2) Strategic conflict	Machiavelli, Schelling, Cournot, Nash, Harsanyi, Shapiro	Ghemawat (1986) Shapiro (1989) Brandenburger and Nalebuff (1995)	Chamberlinean	Hyper-rational	Firms, products	Often infinite	Endogenous	Strategic interactions
(3) Resource-based perspectives	Penrose, Selznick, Christensen, Andrews	Rumelt (1984) Chandler (1966) Wernerfelt (1984) Teece (1980, 1982)	Ricardian	Rational	Resources	Low	Endogenous	Asset fungibility
(4) Dynamic capabilities perspective	Schumpeter, Nelson, Winter, Teece	Dosi, Teece, and Winter (1989) Prahalad and Hamel (1990) Hayes and Wheelwright (1984) Dierickx and Cool (1989) Porter (1990)	Schumpeterian	Rational	Processes, positions, paths	Low	Endogenous	Asset accumulation, replicability and inimitability

Prescriptions they apply to industries or groups of firms at best suggest overall direction, and may indicate errors to be avoided. In contrast, the competitive forces approach is not particularly firm specific; it is industry and group specific.

Strategic change

The competitive forces and the strategic conflict approach, since they pay little attention to skills, know-how, and path dependency, tend to see strategic choice occurring with relative facility. The capabilities approach sees value augmenting strategic change as being difficult and costly. Moreover, it can generally only occur incrementally. Capabilities cannot easily be bought; they must be built. From the capabilities perspective, strategy involves choosing among and committing to long-term paths or trajectories of competence development.

In this regard, we speculate that the dominance of competitive forces and the strategic conflict approaches in the United States may have something to do with observed differences in strategic approaches adopted by some U.S. and some foreign firms. Hayes (1985) has noted that American companies tend to favor 'strategic leaps' while, in contrast, Japanese and German companies tend to favor incremental, but rapid, improvements.

Entry strategies

Here the resources and the capabilities approaches suggest that entry decisions must be made with reference to the competences and capabilities which new entrants have, relative to the competition. Whereas the other approaches tell you little about where to look to find likely entrants, the capabilities approach identifies likely entrants. Relatedly, whereas the entry deterrence approach suggests an unconstrained search for new business opportunities, the capabilities approach suggests that such opportunities lie close in to one's existing business. As Richard Rumelt has explained it in conversation, 'the capabilities approach suggests that if a firm looks inside itself, and at its market environment, sooner or later it will find a business opportunity.'

Entry timing

Whereas the strategic conflict approach tells little abut where to look to find likely entrants, the resources and the capabilities approach identifies likely entrants and their timing of entry. Brittain and Freeman (1980) using population ecology methodologies argued that an organization is quick to expand when there is a significant over-lap between its core capabilities and those needed to survive in a new market. Recent research (Mitchell, 1989) showed that the more industry-specialized assets or capabilities a firm possesses, the more likely it is to enter an emerging technical subfield in its industry, following a technological discontinuity. Additionally, the interaction between specialized assets such as firm-specific capabilities and rivalry had the greatest influence on entry timing.

Diversification

Related diversification—that is, diversification that builds upon or extends existing capabilities—is about the only form of diversification that a resources/capabilities framework is likely to view as meritorious (Rumelt, 1974; Teece, 1980, 1982; Teece et al., 1994). Such diversification will be justifiable when the firms' traditional markets decline.[62] The strategic conflict approach is likely to be a little more permissive; acquisitions that raise rivals' costs or enable firms to effectuate exclusive arrangements are likely to be seen as efficacious in certain circumstances.

Focus and specialization

Focus needs to be defined in terms of distinctive competences or capability, not products. Products are the manifestation of competences, as competences can be molded into a variety of products. Product market specialization and decentalization configured around product markets may cause firms to neglect the development of core competences and dynamic capabilities, to the extent to which competences require accessing assets across divisions.

The capabilities approach places emphasis on the internal processes that a firm utilizes, as well as how they are deployed and how they will evolve. The approach has the benefit of indicating that competitive advantage is not just a function of how one plays the game; it is also a function of the 'assets' one has to play with, and how these assets can be deployed and redeployed in a changing market.

Future directions

We have merely sketched an outline for a dynamic capabilities approach. Further theoretical work is needed to tighten the framework, and empirical research is critical to helping us understand how firms get to be good, how they sometimes stay that way, why and how they improve, and why they sometimes decline.[63] Researchers in the field of strategy need to join forces with researchers in the fields of innovation, manufacturing, and organizational behavior and business history if they are to unlock the riddles that lie behind corporate as well as national competitive advantage. There could hardly be a more ambitious research agenda in the social sciences today.

NOTES

1   For a review of the fundamental questions in the field of strategy, see Rumelt. Schendel, and Teece (1994).

2   Of these authors, Rumelt may have been the first to self-consciously apply a resource perspective to the field of strategy. Rumelt (1984: 561) notes that the strategic firm 'is characterized by a bundle of linked and idiosyncratic resources and resource conversion activities.' Similarly, Teece (1984: 95) notes: 'Successful firms possess one or more forms of intangible assets, such as technological or managerial know-how. Over time, these assets may expand beyond the point of profitable reinvestment in a firm's traditional market. Accordingly, the firm may consider deploying its intangible assets in different product or geographical markets, where the expected returns are higher, if efficient transfer modes exist.' Wernerfelt (1984) was early to recognize that this approach was at odds with product market approaches and might constitute a distinct paradigm of strategy.

3   In competitive environments characterized by sustainable and stable mobility and structural barriers, these forces may become the determinants of industry-level profitability. However, competitive advantage is more complex to ascertain in environments of rapid technological change where specific assets owned by heterogeneous firms can be expected to play a larger role in explaining rents.

4   The market environment is all factors that influence market outcomes (prices, quantities, profits) including the beliefs of customers and of rivals, the number of potential technologies employed, and the costs or speed with which a rival can enter the industry.

5   For an excellent discussion of committed competition in multiple contexts, see Ghemawat (1991).

6   Competition and cooperation have also been analyzed ouside of this tradition. See, for example, Teece (1992) and Link, Teece and Finan (1996).

7   Accordingly, both approaches are dynamic, but in very different senses.

8   Thus even in the air transport industry game-theoretic formulations by no means capture all the relevant dimensions of competitive rivalry. United Airlines' and United Express's difficulties in competing with Southwest Airlines because of United's inability to fully replicate Southwest's operation capabilities is documented in Gittell (1995).

9   Important exceptions can be found in Brandenburger and Nalebuff (1996) such as their emphasis on the role of complements. However, these insights do not flow uniquely from game theory and can be found in the organizational economics literature (e.g., Teece, 1986a, 1986b; de Figueiredo and Teece, 1996).

10 When closely matched in an aggregate sense, they may nevertheless display asymmetries which game theorists can analyze.

11 The strategic conflict literature also tends to focus practitioners on product market positioning rather than on developing the unique assets which make possible superior product market positions (Dierickx and Cool, 1989).

12 In the language of economics, rents flow from unique firm-specific assets that cannot readily be replicated, rather than from tactics which deter entry and keep competitors off balance. In short, rents are Ricardian.

13 Teece (1982: 46) saw the firm as having 'a variety of end products which it can produce with its organizational technology.'

14 Elsewhere Andrews (1987: 47) defined a distinctive competence as what an organization can do particularly well.

15 Studies of the automobile and other industries displayed differences in organization which often underlay differences amongst firms. See, for example, Womack, Jones, and Roos, 1991; Hayes and Clark, 1985; Barney, Spender and Reve, 1994; Clark and Fujimoto, 1991; Henderson and Cockburn, 1994; Nelson, 1991; Levinthal and Myatt, 1994.

16 Using FTC line of business data, Rumelt showed that stable industry effects account for only 8 percent of the variance in business unit returns. Furthermore, only about 40 percent of the dispersion in industry returns is due to stable industry effects.

17 In this regard, this approach has much in common with recent work on organizational ecology (e.g., Freeman and Boeker, 1984) and also on commitment (Ghemawat, 1991: 17–25).

18 Capability development, however, is not really analyzed.

19 Deciding, under significant uncertainty about future states of the world, which long-term paths to commit to and when to change paths is the central strategic problem confronting the firm. In this regard, the work of Ghemawat (1991) is highly germane to the dynamic capabilities approach to strategy.

20 See, for example, Iansiti and Clark (1994) and Henderson (1994).

21 See Hayes et al. (1988), Prahalad and Hamel (1990), Dierickx and Cool (1989), Chandler (1990), and Teece (1993).

22 Arrow (1996) defines fugitive resources as ones that can move cheaply amongst individuals and firms.

23 We do not like the term 'resource' and believe it is misleading. We prefer to use the term firm-specific asset. We use it here to try and maintain links to the literature on the resource-based approach which we believe is important.

24 Thus Eastman Kodak's core competence might be considered imaging, IBM's might be considered integrated data processing and service, and Motorola's untethered communications.

25 In sequential move games, each player looks ahead and anticipates his rival's future responses in order to reason back and decide action, i.e., look forward, reason backward.

26 Needless to say, users need not be the current customers of the enterprise. Thus a capability can be the basis for diversification into new product markets.

27 Indeed, the essence of internal organization is that it is a domain of unleveraged or low-powered incentives. By unleveraged we mean that rewards are determined at the group or organization level, not primarily at the individual level, in an effort to encourage team behavior, not individual behavior.

28 We see the problem of market contracting as a matter of coordination as much as we see it a problem of opportunism in the fact of contractual hazards. In this sense, we are consonant with both Richardson (1960) and Williamson (1975, 1985).

29 As we note in Teece *et al.* (1994), the conglomerate offers few if any efficiencies because there is little provided by the conglomerate form that shareholders cannot obtain for themselves simply by holding a diversified portfolio of stocks.

30 Owners' equity may reflect, in part, certain historic capabilities. Recently, some scholars have begun to attempt to measure organizational capability using financial statement data. See Baldwin and Clark (1991) and Lev and Sougiannis (1992).

31 We are implicitly saying that fixed assets, like plant and equipment which can be purchased off-the-shelf by all industry participants, cannot be the source of a firm's competitive advantage. Inasmuch as financial balance sheets typically reflect such assets, we point out that the assets that matter for competitive advantage are rarely reflected in the balance sheet, while those that do not are.

32 The coordinative properties of markets depend on prices being 'sufficient' upon which to base resource allocation decisions.

33 Indeed, Ronald Coase, author of the pathbreaking 1937 article 'The nature of the firm,' which focused on the costs of organizational coordination inside the firm as compared to across the market, half a century later has identified as critical the understanding of 'why the costs of organizing particular activities differs among firms' (Coase, 1988: 47). We argue that a firm's distinctive ability needs to be understood as a reflection of distinctive organizational or coordinative capabilities. This form of integration (i.e., inside business units) is different from the integration between business units; they could be viable on a stand-alone basis (external integration). For a useful taxonomy, see Iansiti and Clark (1994).

34 Shuen (1994) examines the gains and hazards of the technology make-vs.-buy decision and supplier codevelopment.

35 Garvin (1994) provides a typology of organizational processes.

36 Fujimoto (1994: 18–20) describes key elements as they existed in the Japanese auto industry as follows: 'The typical volume production system of effective Japanese makers of the 1980s (e.g., Toyota) consists of various intertwined elements that might lead to competitive advantages. Just-in-Time (JIT), Jidoka (automatic defect detection and machine stop), Total Quality Control (TQC), and continuous improvement (Kaizen) are often pointed out as its core subsystems. The elements of such a system include inventory reduction mechanisms by Kanban system; levelization of production volume and product mix (heijunka); reduction of "muda" (non-value adding activities), "mura" (uneven pace of production) and muri (excessive workload); production plans based on dealers' order volume (genyo seisan); reduction of die set-up time and lot size in stamping operation; mixed model assembly; piece-by-piece transfer of parts between machines (ikko-nagashi); flexible task assignment for volume changes and productivity improvement (shojinka); multi-task job assignment along the process flow (takotei-mochi); U-shape machine layout that facilitates flexible and multiple task assignment, on-the-spot inspection by direct workers (tsukurikomi); fool-proof prevention of defects (poka-yoke); real-time feedback of production troubles (andon); assembly line stop cord; emphasis on cleanliness, order and discipline on the shop floor (5-S); frequent revision of standard operating procedures by supervisors; quality control circles; standardized tools for quality improvement (e.g., 7 tools for QC, QC story); worker involvement in preventive maintenance (Total Productive Maintenance); low cost automation or semi-automation with just-enough functions; reduction of process steps for saving of tools and dies, and so on. The human-resource management factors that back up the

above elements include stable employment of core workers (with temporary workers in the periphery); long-term training of multi-skilled (multi-task) workers; wage system based in part on skill accumulation; internal promotion to shop floor supervisors; cooperative relationships with labor unions; inclusion of production supervisors in union members; generally egalitarian policies for corporate welfare, communication and worker motivation. Parts procurement policies are also pointed out often as a source of the competitive advantage.'

37 For a theoretical argument along these lines, see Milgrom and Roberts (1990).

38 See Abernathy and Clark (1985).

39 For a useful review and contribution, see Levitt and March (1988).

40 Levinthal and March (1993). Mahoney (1995) and Mahoney and Pandian (1992) suggest that both resources and mental models are intertwined in firm-level learning.

41 There is a large literature on learning, although only a small fraction of it deals with organizational learning. Relevant contributors include Levitt and March (1988), Argyris and Schön (1978), Levinthal and March (1981), Nelson and Winter (1982), and Leonard-Barton (1995).

42 Managers often evoke the 'crown jewels' metaphor. That is, if the technology is released, the kingdom will be lost.

43 For instance, an Internet year might well be thought of as equivalent to 10 years on many industry clocks, because as much change occurs in the Internet business in a year that occurs in say the auto industry in a decade.

44 Williamson (1996: 102–3) has observed, failures of coordination may arise because 'parties that bear a long term bilateral dependency relationship to one another must recognize that incomplete contracts require gap filling and sometimes get out of alignment. Although it is always in the collective interest of autonomous parties to fill gaps, correct errors, and affect efficient realignments, it is also the case that the distribution of the resulting gains is indeterminate. Self-interested bargaining predictably obtains. Such bargaining is itself costly. The main costs, however, are that transactions are maladapted to the environment during the bargaining interval. Also, the prospect of ex post bargaining invites ex ante prepositioning of an inefficient kind.'

45 For further development, see Bercovitz, de Figueiredo, and (Teece 1996).

46 Because of huge uncertainties, it may be extremely difficult to determine viable strategies early on. Since the rules of the game and the identity of the players will be revealed only after the market has begun to evolve, the pay-off is likely to lie with building and maintaining organizational capabilities that support flexibility. For example, Microsoft's recent about-face and vigorous pursuit of Internet business once the Net-Scape phenomenon became apparent is impressive, not so much because it perceived the need to change strategy, but because of its organizational capacity to effectuate a strategic shift.

47 This is a critical element in Nelson and Winter's (1982) view of firms and technical change.

48 We also recognize that the processes, positions, and paths of customers also matter. See our discussion above on increasing returns, including customer learning and network externalities.

49 In both the firm is still largely a black box. Certainly, little or no attention is given to processes, positions, and paths.

50 See Alchian and Demsetz (1972).

51 We call such competences distinctive. See also Dierickx and Cool (1989) for a discussion of the characteristics of assets which make them a source of rents.

52 There is ample evidence that a given type of competence (e.g., quality) can be supported by different routines and combinations of skills. For example, the Garvin (1988) and Clark and Fujimoto (1991) studies both indicate that there was no one 'formula' for achieving either high quality or high product development performance.

53 See Szulanski's (1995) discussion of the intrafirm transfer of best practice. He quotes a senior vice president of Xerox as saying 'you can see a high performance factory or office, but it just doesn't spread. I don't know why.' Szulanski also discusses the role of benchmarking in facilitating the transfer of best practice.

54 If so, it is our belief that the firm's advantage is likely to fade, as luck does run out.

55 Needless to say, there are many examples of firms replicating their capabilities inappropriately by applying extant routines to circumstances where they may not be applicable, e.g., Nestle's transfer of developed-country marketing methods for infant formula to the Third World (Hartley, 1989). A key strategic need is for firms to screen capabilities for their applicability to new environments.

56 Different approaches to learning are required depending on the depth of knowledge. Where knowledge is less articulated and structured, trial and error and learning-by-doing are necessary, whereas in mature environments where the underlying engineering science is better understood, organizations can undertake more deductive approaches or what Pisano (1994) refers to as 'learning-before-doing.'

57 Trade dress refers to the 'look and feel' of a retail establishment, e.g., the distinctive marketing and presentation style of The Nature Company.

58 An interesting but important exception to this can be found in second sourcing. In the microprocessor business, until the introduction of the 386 chip, Intel and most other merchant semi producers were encouraged by large customers like IBM to provide second sources, i.e., to license and share their proprietary process technology with competitors like AMD and NEC. The microprocessor developers did so to assure customers that they had sufficient manufacturing capability to meet demand at all times.

59 Phillips (1971) and Demsetz (1974) also made the case that market concentration resulted from the competitive success of more efficient firms, and not from entry barriers and restrictive practices.

60 We concur with Williamson that economizing and strategizing are not mutually exclusive. Strategic ploys can be used to disguise inefficiencies and to promote economizing outcomes, as with pricing with reference to learning curve costs. Our view of economizing is perhaps more expansive than Williamson's as it embraces more than efficient contract design and the minimization of transactions costs. We also address production and organizational economies, and the distinctive ways that things are accomplished inside the business enterprise.

61 On this point, the strategic conflict and the resources and capabilities are congruent. However, the aspects of 'situation' that matter are dramatically different, as described earlier in this paper.

62 Cantwell shows that the technological competence of firms persists over time, gradually evolving through firm-specific learning. He shows that technological diversification has been greater for chemicals and pharmaceuticals than for electrical and electronic-related fields, and he offers as an explanation the greater straight-ahead opportunities in electrical and electronic fields than in chemicals and pharmaceuticals. See Cantwell (1993).

63 For a gallant start, see Miyazaki (1995) and McGrath et al. (1996). Chandler's (1990) work on scale and scope, summarized in Teece (1993), provides some historical support for the capabilities approach. Other relevant studies can be found in a special issue of *Industrial and Corporate Change* 3(3), 1994, that was devoted to dynamic capabilities.

REFERENCES

Abernathy, W. J. and Clark K. (1985). 'Innovation: Mapping the winds of creative destruction', *Research Policy*, 14, pp. 3–22.

Alchian, A. A. and H. Demsetz (1972). 'Production, information costs, and economic organization', *American Economic Review*, 62, pp. 777–95.

Amit, R. and P. Schoemaker (1993). 'Strategic assets and organizational rent', *Strategic Management Journal* 14(1), pp. 33–46.

Andrews, K. (1987). *The Concept of Corporate Strategy* (3rd ed.). Dow Jones-Irwin, Homewood, IL.

Aoki, M. (1990). 'The participatory generation of information rents and the theory of the firm'. In M. Aoki, B. Gustafsson and O. E. Williamson (eds.), *The Firm as a Nexus of Treaties*. Sage, London, pp. 26–52.

Argyres, N. (1995). 'Technology strategy, governance structure and interdivisional coordination',

Journal of Economic Behavior and Organization, 28, pp. 337–58.

Argyris, C. and D. Schön (1978). *Organizational Learning*. Addison-Wesley, Reading, MA.

Arrow, K. (1969). 'The organization of economic activity: Issues pertinent to the choice of market vs. nonmarket allocation'. In *The Analysis and Evaluation of Public Expenditures: The PPB System, 1*. U.S. Joint Economic Committee, 91st Session. U.S. Government Printing Office, Washington, DC, pp. 59–73.

Arrow, K. (1996) 'Technical information and industrial structure', *Industrial and Corporate Change*, 5(2), pp. 645–52.

Arthur, W. B. (1983). 'Competing technologies and lock-in by historical events: The dynamics of allocation under increasing returns', working paper WP-83–90, International Institute for Applied Systems Analysis, Laxenburg, Austria.

Bain, J. S. (1959). *Industrial Organization*. Wiley, New York.

Baldwin, C. and K. Clark (1991). 'Capabilities and capital investment: New perspectives on capital budgeting', Harvard Business School working paper #92–004.

Barney, J. B. (1986). 'Strategic factor markets: Expectations, luck, and business strategy', *Management Science* 32(10), pp. 1231–41.

Barney, J. B., J.-C. Spender and T. Reve (1994). *Crafoord Lectures*, Vol. 6. Chartwell-Bratt, Bromley, U.K. and Lund University Press, Lund, Sweden.

Baumol, W., J. Panzar and R. Willig (1982). *Contestable Markets and the Theory of Industry Structure*. Harcourt Brace Jovanovich, New York.

Bercovitz, J. E. L., J. M. de Figueiredo and D. J. Teece (1996). 'Firm capabilities and managerial decision-making: A theory of innovation biases'. In R. Garud, P. Nayyar and Z. Shapira (eds), *Innovation: Oversights and Foresights*. Cambridge University Press, Cambridge, U.K. pp. 233–59.

Brandenburger, A. M. and B. J. Nalebuff (1996). *Co-opetition*. Doubleday, New York.

Brandenburger, A. M. and B. J. Nalebuff (1995). 'The right game: Use game theory to shape strategy', *Harvard Business Review*, 73(4), pp. 57–71.

Brittain, J. and J. Freeman (1980). 'Organizational proliferation and density-dependent selection'. In J. R. Kimberly and R. Miles (eds.), *The Organizational Life Cycle*. Jossey-Bass, San Francisco, CA, pp. 291–338.

Camp, R. (1989). *Benchmarking: The Search for Industry Best practices that Lead to Superior Performance*. Quality Press, Milwaukee, WI.

Cantwell, J. (1993). 'Corporate technological specialization in international industries'. In M. Casson and J. Creedy (eds.), *Industrial Concentration and Economic Inequality*. Edward Elgar, Aldershot, pp. 216–32.

Chandler, A. D., Jr. (1966). *Strategy and Structure*. Doubleday, Anchor Books Edition, New York.

Chandler, A. D., Jr. (1990). *Scale and Scope: The Dynamics of Industrial Competition*. Harvard University Press, Cambridge, MA.

Clark, K. and T. Fujimoto (1991). *Product Development Performance: Strategy, Organization and Management in the World Auto Industries*. Harvard Buiness School Press, Cambridge, MA.

Coase, R. (1937). 'The nature of the firm', *Economica*, 4, pp. 386–405.

Coase, R. (1988). 'Lecture on the Nature of the Firm, III', *Journal of Law, Economics and Organization*, 4, pp. 33–47.

Cool, K. and D. Schendel (1988). 'Performance differences among strategic group members', *Strategic Management Journal*, 9(3), pp. 207–23.

de Figueiredo, J. M. and D. J. Teece (1996). 'Mitigating procurement hazards in the context of innovation', *Industrial and Corporate Change*, 5(2), pp. 537–59.

Demsetz, H. (1974). 'Two systems of belief about monopoly'. In H. Goldschmid, M. Mann and J. F. Weston (eds.), *Industrial Concentration: The New Learning*. Little, Brown, Boston, MA, pp. 161–84.

Dierickx, I. and K. Cool (1989). 'Asset stock accumulation and sustainability of competitive advantage', *Management Science*, 35(12), pp. 1504–11.

Dixit, A. (1980). 'The role of investment in entry deterrence', *Economic Journal*, 90, pp. 95–106.

Dosi, G., D. J. Teece and S. Winter (1989). 'Toward a theory of corporate coherence: Preliminary remarks', unpublished paper, Center for Research in Management, University of California at Berkeley.

Doz, Y. and A. Shuen (1990). 'From intent to outcome: A process framework for partnerships', INSEAD working paper.

Fama, E. F. (1980). 'Agency problems and the theory of the firm', *Journal of Political Economy*, 88, pp. 288–307.

Freeman, J. and W. Boeker (1984). 'The ecological analysis of business strategy'. In G. Carroll and D. Vogel (eds.), *Strategy and Organization*. Pitman, Boston, MA, pp. 64–77.

Fujimoto, T. (1994). 'Reinterpreting the resource-capability view of the firm: A case of the development-production systems of the Japanese automakers', draft working paper, Faculty of Economics, University of Tokyo.

Garvin, D. (1988). *Managing Quality*. Free Press, New York.

Garvin, D. (1994). 'The processes of organization and management', Harvard Business School working paper #94–084.

Ghemawat, P. (1986). 'Sustainable advantage', *Harvard Business Review*, 64(5), pp. 53–8.

Ghemawat, P. (1991). *Commitment: The Dynamics of Strategy*. Free Press, New York.

Gilbert, R. J. and D. M. G. Newberry (1982). 'Preemptive patenting and the persistence of monopoly', *American Economic Review*, 72, pp. 514–26.

Gittell, J. H. (1995). 'Cross functional coordination, control and human resource systems: Evidence from the airline industry', unpublished Ph.D. thesis, Massachusetts Institute of Technology.

Hansen, G. S. and B. Wernerfelt (1989). 'Determinants of firm performance: The relative importance of economic and organizational factors', *Strategic Management Journal*, 10(5), pp. 399–411.

Hartley, R. F. (1989). *Marketing Mistakes*. Wiley, New York.

Hayes, R. (1985). 'Strategic planning: Forward in reverse', *Harvard Business Review*, 63(6), pp. 111–19.

Hayes, R. and K. Clark (1985). 'Exploring the sources of productivity differences at the factory level'. In K. Clark, R. H. Hayes and C. Lorenz (eds.), *The Uneasy Alliance: Managing the Productivity – Technology Dilemma*. Harvard Business School Press, Boston, MA, pp. 151–88.

Hayes, R. and S. Wheelwright (1984). *Restoring our Competitive Edge: Competing Through Manufacturing*. Wiley, New York.

Hayes, R., S. Wheelwright and K. Clark (1988). *Dynamic Manufacturing: Creating the Learning Organization*. Free Press, New York.

Henderson, R. M. (1994). 'The evolution of integrative capability: Innovation in cardiovascular drug discovery', *Industrial and Corporate Change*, 3(3), pp. 607–30.

Henderson, R. M. and K. B. Clark (1990). 'Architectural innovation: The reconfiguration of existing product technologies and the failure of established firms', *Administrative Science Quarterly*, 35, pp. 9–30.

Henderson, R. M. and I. Cockburn (1994). 'Measuring competence? Exploring firm effects in pharmaceutical research, *Strategic Management Journal*, Summer Special Issue, 15, pp. 63–84.

Iansiti, M. and K. B. Clark (1994). 'Integration and dynamic capability: Evidence from product development in automobiles and mainframe computers', *Industrial and Corporate Change*, 3(3), pp. 557–605.

Itami, H. and T. W. Roehl (1987). *Mobilizing Invisible Assets*. Harvard University Press, Cambridge, MA.

Jacobsen, R. (1988). 'The persistence of abnormal returns', *Strategic Management Journal*, 9(5), pp. 415–30.

Katz, M. and C. Shapiro (1985). 'Network externalities, competition and compatibility', *American Economic Review*, 75, pp. 424–40.

Kreps, D. M. and R. Wilson (1982a). 'Sequential equilibria', *Econometrica*, 50, pp. 863–94.

Kreps, D. M. and R. Wilson (1982b). 'Reputation and imperfect information', *Journal of Economic Theory*, 27, pp. 253–79.

Langlois, R. (1994). 'Cognition and capabilities: Opportunities seized and missed in the history of the computer industry', working paper, University of Connecticut. Presented at the conference on Technological Oversights and Foresights, Stern School of Business, New York University, 11–12 March 1994.

Learned, E., C. Christensen, K. Andrews and W. Guth (1969). *Business Policy: Text and Cases*. Irwin, Homewood, IL.

Leonard-Barton, D. (1992). 'Core capabilities and core rigidities: A paradox in managing new product development', *Strategic Management Journal*, Summer Special Issue, 13, pp. 111–25.

Leonard-Barton, D. (1995). *Wellsprings of Knowledge*. Harvard Business School Press, Boston, MA.

Lev, B. and T. Sougiannis (1992). 'The capitalization, amortization and value-relevance of R&D', unpublished manuscript, University of California, Berkeley, and University of Illinois, Urbana – Champaign.

Levinthal, D. and J. March (1981). 'A model of adaptive organizational search', *Journal of Economic Behavior and Organization*, 2, pp. 307–33.

Levinthal, D. A. and J. G. March (1993). 'The myopia of learning', *Strategic Management Journal*, Winter Special Issue, 14, pp. 95–112.

Levinthal, D. and J. Myatt (1994). 'Co-evolution of capabilities and industry: The evolution of mutual fund processing', *Strategic Management Journal*, Winter Special Issue, 15, pp. 45–62.

Levitt, B. and J. March (1988). 'Organizational learning', *Annual Review of Sociology*, 14, pp. 319–40.

Link, A. N., D. J. Teece and W. F. Finan (October 1996). 'Estimating the benefits from collaboration: The Case of SEMATECH', *Review of Industrial Organization*, 11, pp. 737–51.

Lippman, S. A. and R. P. Rumelt (1992) 'Demand uncertainty and investment in industry-specific capital', *Industrial and Corporate Change*, 1(1), pp. 235–62.

Mahoney, J. (1995). 'The management of resources and the resources of management', *Journal of Business Research*, 33(2), pp. 91–101.

Mahoney, J. T. and J. R. Pandian (1992). 'The resource-based view within the conversation of strategic management', *Strategic Management Journal*, 13(5), pp. 363–80.

Mason, E. (1949). 'The current state of the monopoly problem in the U.S.', *Harvard Law Review*, 62, pp. 1265–85.

McGrath, R. G., M.-H. Tsai, S. Venkataraman and I. C. MacMillan (1996). 'Innovation, competitive advantage and rent: A model and test', *Management Science*, 42(3), pp. 389–403.

Milgrom, P. and J. Roberts (1982a). 'Limit pricing and entry under incomplete information: An equilibrium analysis', *Econometrica*, 50, pp. 443–59.

Milgrom, P. and J. Roberts (1982b). 'Predation, reputation and entry deterrence', *Journal of Economic Theory*, 27, pp. 280–312.

Milgrom, P. and J. Roberts (1990). 'The economics of modern manufacturing: Technology, strategy, and organization', *American Economic Review*, 80(3), pp. 511–28.

Mitchell, W. (1989). 'Whether and when? Probability and timing of incumbents' entry into emerging industrial subfields', *Administrative Science Quarterly*, 34, pp. 208–30.

Miyazaki, K. (1995). *Building Competences in the Firm: Lessons from Japanese and European Optoelectronics*. St. Martins Press, New York.

Mody, A. (1993). 'Learning through alliances', *Journal of Economic Behavior and Organization*, 20(2), pp. 151–70.

Nelson, R. R. (1991). 'Why do firms differ, and how does it matter?' *Strategic Management Journal*, Winter Special Issue, 12, pp. 61–74.

Nelson, R. R. (1994). 'The co-evolution of technology, Industrial structure, and supporting institutions', *Industrial and Corporate Change*, 3(1), pp. 47–63.

Nelson, R. (1996). 'The evolution of competitive or comparative advantage: A preliminary report on a study', WP-96-21, International Institute for Applied Systems Analysis, Laxemberg, Austria.

Nelson, R. and S. Winter (1982). *An Evolutionary Theory of Economic change*. Harvard University Press, Cambridge, MA.

Penrose, E. (1959). *The Theory of the Growth of the Firm*. Basil Blackwell, London.

Phillips, A. C. (1971). *Technology and Market Structure*. Lexington Books, Toronto.

Pisano, G. (1994). 'Knowledge integration and the locus of learning: An empirical analysis of process development', *Strategic Management Journal*, Winter Special Issue, 15, pp. 85–100.

Porter, M. E. (1980). *Competitive Strategy*. Free Press, New York.

Porter, M. E. (1990). *The Competitive Advantage of Nations*. Free Press, New York.

Prahalad, C. K. and G. Hamel (1990). 'The core competence of the corporation', *Harvard Business Review*, 68(3), pp. 79–91.

Richardson, G. B. H. (1960, 1990). *Information and Investment*. Oxford University Press, New York.

Rosenberg, N. (1982). *Inside the Black Box: Technology and Economics*. Cambridge University Press, Cambridge, MA.

Rumelt, R. P. (1974). *Strategy, Structure, and Economic Performance*. Harvard University Press, Cambridge. MA.

Rumelt, R. P. (1984). 'Towards a strategic theory of the firm'. In R. B. Lamb (ed.), *Competitive Strategic Management*. Prentice-Hall, Englewood Cliffs, NJ pp. 556–70.

Rumelt, R. P. (1991). 'How much does industry matter?', *Strategic Management Journal*, 12(3), pp. 167–85.

Rumelt, R. P., D. Schendel and D. Teece (1994). *Fundamental Issues in Strategy*. Harvard Business School Press, Cambridge, MA.

Schmalensee, R. (1983). 'Advertising and entry deterence: An exploratory model', *Journal of Political Economy*, 91(4), pp. 636–53.

Schumpeter, J. A. (1934). *Theory of Economic Development*. Harvard University Press, Cambridge, MA.

Schumpeter, J. A. (1942). *Capitalism, Socialism, and Democracy*. Harper, New York.

Shapiro, C. (1989). 'The theory of business strategy', *RAND Journal of Economics*, 20(1), pp. 125–37.

Shuen, A. (1994). 'Technology sourcing and learning strategies in the semiconductor industry', unpublished Ph.D. dissertation, University of California, Berkeley.

Sutton, J. (1992). 'Implementing game theoretical models in industrial economies', In A. Del Monte (ed.), *Recent Developments in the Theory of Industrial Organization*. University of Michigan Press, Ann Arbor, MI, pp. 19–33.

Szulanski, G. (1995). 'Unpacking stickiness: An empirical investigation of the barriers to transfer best practice inside the firm', *Academy of Management Journal*, Best Papers Proceedings, pp. 437–41.

Teece, D. J. (1976). *The Multinational Corporation and the Resource Cost of International Technology Transfer*. Ballinger, Cambridge, MA.

Teece, D. J. (1980). 'Economics of scope and the scope of the enterprise', *Journal of Economic Behavior and Organization*, 1, pp. 223–47.

Teece, D. J. (1981). 'The market for know-how and the efficient international transfer of technology', *Annals of the Academy of Political and Social Science*, 158, pp. 81–96.

Teece, D. J. (1982). 'Towards an economic theory of the multiproduct firm', *Journal of Economic Behavior and Organization*, 3, pp. 39–63.

Teece, D. J. (1984). 'Economic analysis and strategic management', *California Management Review*, 26(3), pp. 87–110.

Teece, D. J. (1986a). 'Transactions cost economics and the multinational enterprise', *Journal of Economic Behavior and Organization*, 7, pp. 21–45.

Teece, D. J. (1986b). 'Profiting from technological innovation', *Research Policy*, 15(6), pp. 285–305.

Teece, D. J. (1988). 'Technological change and the nature of the firm'. In G. Dosi, C. Freeman, R. Nelson, G. Silverberg and L. Soete (eds.), *Technical Change and Economic Theory*. Pinter Publishers, New York, pp. 256–81.

Teece, D. J. (1992). 'Competition, cooperation, and innovation: Organizational arrangements for regimes of rapid technological progress', *Journal of Economic Behavior and Organization*, 18(1), pp. 1–25.

Teece, D. J. (1993). 'The dynamics of industrial capitalism: Perspectives on Alfred Chandler's *Scale and Scope* (1990)', *Journal of Economic Literature*, 31(1), pp. 199–225.

Teece, D. J. (1996) 'Firm organization, industrial structure, and technological innovation', *Journal of Economic Behavior and Organization*, 31, pp. 193–224.

Teece, D. J. and G. Pisano (1994). 'The dynamic capabilities of firms: An introduction', *Industrial and Corporate Change*, 3(3), pp. 537–56.

Teece, D. J., R. Rumelt, G. Dosi and S. Winter (1994). 'Understanding corporate coherence: Theory and evidence', *Journal of Economic Behavior and Organization*, 23, pp. 1–30.

Tushman, M. L., W. H. Newman and E. Romanelli (1986). 'Convergence and upheaval: Managing the unsteady pace of organizational evolution', *California Management Review*, 29(1), pp. 29–44.

Wernerfelt, B. (1984). 'A resource-based view of the firm', *Strategic Management Journal*, 5(2), pp. 171–80.

Wernerfelt, B. and C. Montgomery (1988). 'Tobin's Q and the importance of focus in firm performance', *American Economic Review*, 78(1), pp. 246–50.

Williamson, O. E. (1975). *Markets and Hierarchies*. Free Press, New York.

Williamson, O. E. (1985). *The Economic Institutions of Capitalism*. Free Press, New York.

Williamson, O. E. (1991). 'Strategizing, economizing, and economic organization', *Strategic Management Journal*, Winter Special Issue, 12, pp. 75–94.

Williamson, O. E. (1996) *The Mechanisms of Governance*. Oxford University Press, New York.

Womack, J., D. Jones and D. Roos (1991). *The Machine that Changed the World*. Harper-Perennial, New York.

Zander, U. and B. Kogut (1995). 'Knowledge and the speed of the transfer and imitation of organizational capabilities: An empirical test', *Organization Science*, 6(1), pp. 76–92.

Part IV

Connections between Strategy, Structure and Process

INTRODUCTION

The articles in Part IV span three types of strategy context internal to the organization. These include the design and structure of the organization; the role of organizational goals and organizational purpose; the link between corporate culture, strategic change and the cultural context in which the organization is itself embedded; and ways of incorporating knowledge management within the firm. The connections we are looking at in Part IV are those between strategy, structure, culture, change and innovation as part of the wider strategy process.

Mintzberg is concerned with the relationship between strategy and structure. As strategies evolve in response to shifting macro-environmental and competitive contexts, so the organizations through which those strategies are to be delivered must themselves evolve and change. It is unlikely that an organization structure developed under one set of conditions will be equally effective and appropriate under a different set of conditions, or if required to deliver a different type of strategy. The article by Mintzberg (Chapter 13) on the relationship between strategy and organizational structure is one of the most-quoted writings on this aspect of strategic management. In this extended chapter, Mintzberg suggests that the 'characteristics of organizations appear to fall into natural clusters, or configurations'. Mintzberg is therefore arguing beyond a simple 'contingency' approach to the strategy/structure relationship (i.e. that context will determine structure). Instead, he argues that 'no one factor – structural or situational – determines the others; rather all are often logically formed into tightly knit configurations'. He sees a convergence around six structurally distinct configurations and the situations in which they are likely to be found.

The article explains the key features of Mintzberg's influential contribution to our understanding of organization structure. He describes six basic parts of the organization, then its basic co-ordinating mechanisms (such as standardization of work processes) and the essential parameters of organizational design (such as job specialization; training and indoctrination; unit groupings and unit size, etc.). He then explains the situational factors influencing the choice of these designs (such as age and size of the organization; its technical system, environment and power structure). All these strands are pulled together to provide the six basic 'configurations'. These six represent logically consistent groupings of design parameters consistent with the situational factors facing the organization. The six configurations are: the simple structure, the machine bureaucracy, the professional bureaucracy, the divisionalized form, the adhocracy and the missionary structure. Mintzberg breaks down the elements of organization structure into their constituent parts and explains how they would combine together differently to meet different strategies and organizational objectives.

It is organizational objectives and purposes themselves that concern Campbell and Yeung in Chapter 14 and how they need to be derived from a corporate mission. The idea of a corporate mission is that it directs all the organizational elements onto a single focus. For many firms this central focus is distilled into their mission statements. For Campbell and Yeung, there must be an emotional logic, as well as a commercial logic, to placing effective mission statements in support of effective strategies. They argue that 'mission' is an intellectual concept, but that 'a sense of mission' is an emotional concept; an organization with a clear mission does not necessarily have employees with a sense of mission. Managing mission is therefore a long-term process that involves not just strategy but purpose, behaviour standards and values. Managing the relationship between mission and strategy is a social process aimed at creating emotional bonds and commitment. Mission statements should capture the vision of the organization. Campbell and Yeung believe 'that leaders will find it easier to create employees with commitment and enthusiasm if they choose a purpose aimed at a higher ideal'. Echoing Campbell and Yeung, is this comment from Senge (1990):

> Achieving return on equity does not, as a goal, mobilise the most noble forces of our soul.

Like strategy therefore, a mission contains a set of propositions that can be used to guide the policies and behaviours of an organization. By combining the business philosophy concept of a business 'mission' with a cultural view of mission (i.e. something that provides collective unity and 'glue'), mission provides a link between strategy and culture in an organization.

We return very strongly to the link between strategy and culture in Johnson's article on managing strategic change (Chapter 15). He sets out to explain successful management of strategic change as arising from a clear understanding of the links between the development of strategies in organizations and organizational culture. This is particularly important in helping to understand the frequency of obstacles and barriers to change in organizations. Strategic change must engage with the history of the organization and the political and social interests that have built up within it. Strategies thus develop through the filters of managerial experience and organizational culture. If strategic change is to occur, then these filters must be fully understood and utilized in the change process. Managerial processes that give rise to the development of strategy must be examined and understood in cultural, political and cognitive terms. To help explore this, Johnson uses the concept of the 'paradigm' (i.e. the deeper level of assumptions and beliefs that are shared by members of an organization, so that they are unconsciously taken for granted). Paradigms are cognitive structures which may be found, to a greater or lesser extent, in all firms. Paradigms are embedded in a wider cultural context which Johnson calls a 'cultural web'. This cultural web embodies the routines of organizational life between different parts of the organization and its different members. Johnson has developed a 'cultural web' framework which helps us to expose and analyse the bonds that govern life within the organization. Unless these bonds are clarified and understood, achieving change within the organization will be unlikely. That is because change is a social process and must therefore address the existing cultural and social processes at work within the organization. Indeed, it is these underlying social processes that the change must reach, if it is to be effective.

In Chapter 16, the connections are made between organization structure, dynamic capabilities and knowledge management. Sanchez argues that managing flows of knowledge and information have taken over from the more traditional management skills of managing flows of money and goods, as the main sources of potential competitive advantage. He argues that new products and new processes require new strategies. In particular, he proposes modularity in both products and organizations as the way to benefit from both available flexibility and available organizational knowledge. There is much talk about both industries and markets becoming more dynamic. Consequently, product development processes are being redesigned for speed, innovation and flexibility. Sanchez explains that this has implications for the whole organization. He calls the new type of organizational and product design 'modular' and says it has different characteristics from the more conventional organization. Modular product design explicitly minimizes interdependencies between components. At the beginning of the development process modular product architecture intentionally allows for substitution of different versions of components and for the creation of product variations with different bundles of features, functionality and performance. Thus, modular product architecture creates a flexible basic design for leveraging variations on a basic product design. Thus, flexibility is designed in at the start. This allows greater product variety, greater speed of improvement and lower overall design and production costs. However, this requires organizations to be able to manage the integration of knowledge, innovation, technology and marketing. That, in turn, requires modular or virtual organizations able to operate in these highly flexible ways in these rapidly changing markets. Rapid reconfiguration of development, production, distribution and marketing resources is needed to achieve the levels of benefit from innovation in technology development and product development. Firms increasingly need to function as open systems capable of building and leveraging knowledge throughout the organization. Furthermore three types of knowledge are explained by Sanchez: know-how, know-why and know-what. Each of these requires a different type of knowledge management by the organization. All are necessary to a network-based process. What Sanchez is explaining is that in dynamic markets, strategic management may have to shift its focus from 'managing the firm as a relatively fixed set of assets and capabilities, to designing the firm as a flexible system for co-ordinating a continuously changing mix of assets, capabilities and relationships'. Sanchez therefore has described how strategy, structure and process must combine, to put strategic flexibility into practice.

REFERENCE

Senge, P. (1990) 'The Leader's New Work: Building
  Learning Organisations,' *Sloan Management Review*,
  Vol. 32 No. 1: 7–23.

13

THE STRUCTURING OF ORGANIZATIONS

Henry Mintzberg

INTRODUCTION

[. . .]

This [reading] argues that [. . .] spans of control, types of formalization and decentralization, planning systems, and matrix structures should not be picked and chosen independently, the way a shopper picks vegetables at the market or a diner a meal at a buffet table. Rather, these and other parameters of organizational design should logically configure into internally consistent groupings. Like most phenomena – atoms, ants and stars – characteristics of organizations appear to fall into natural clusters, or configurations.

We can, in fact, go a step farther and include in these configurations not only the design parameters but also the so-called contingency factors. In other words, the organization's type of environment, its production system, even its age and its size, can in some sense be 'chosen' to achieve consistency with the elements of its structure. The important implication of this conclusion, in sharp contrast to that of contingency theory, is that organizations can select their situations in accordance with their structural designs just as much as they can select their designs in accordance with their situations. Diversified firms may divisionalize, but there is also evidence that divisionalized firms have a propensity to further diversity [. . .] Stable environments may encourage the formalization (bureaucratization) of structure, but bureaucracies also have a habit of trying to stabilize their environments. And in contrast, entrepreneurial forms, which operate in dynamic environments, need to maintain flexible structures. But such forms also seek out and try to remain in dynamic environments in which they can outmanoeuvre the bureaucracies. In other words, no one factor – structural or situational – determines the others; rather, all are often logically formed into tightly knit configurations.

When the enormous amount of research that has been done on organizational structuring is looked at in the light of this conclusion, much of its confusion falls away, and a convergence is evident around several configurations, which are distinct in their structural designs, in the situation in which they are found, and even in the periods of history in which they first developed.

To understand these configurations, we must first understand each of the elements that make them up. Accordingly, the first four sections of this [reading] discuss the basic parts of organizations, the mechanisms by which organizations co-ordinate their activities, the parameters they use to design their structures, and their contingency, or situational, factors. The final section of this reading introduces the structural configurations. [. . .]

I SIX BASIC PARTS OF THE ORGANIZATION

Different parts of the organization play different roles in the accomplishment of work and of these forms of co-ordination. Our framework introduces six basic parts of the organization, shown in Figure 13.1 and listed below:

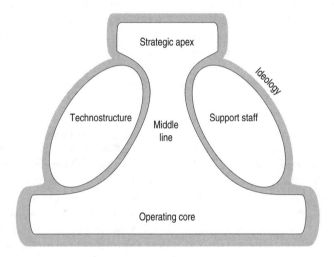

Figure 13.1 The six basic parts of the organization

1 The *operating core* is where the basic work of producing the organization's products and services gets done, where the workers assemble automobiles and the surgeons remove appendices.
2 The *strategic apex* is the home of top management, where the organization is managed from a general perspective.
3 The *middle line* comprises all those managers who stand in direct line relationships between the strategic apex and the operating core.
4 The *technostructure* includes the staff analysts who design the systems by which work processes and outputs of others in the organization are formally designed and controlled.
5 The *support staff* comprises all those specialists who provide support to the organization outside of its operating workflow – in the typical manufacturing firm, everything from the cafeteria staff and the mailroom to the public relations department and the legal counsel.
6 The *ideology* forms the sixth part, a kind of halo of beliefs and traditions that surrounds the whole organization.

II SIX BASIC CO-ORDINATING MECHANISMS

Six mechanisms of co-ordination seem to describe the fundamental ways in which organizations co-ordinate their work. Two are *ad hoc* in nature; the other four involve various forms of standardization.

1 *Mutual adjustment* achieves co-ordination of work by the simple process of informal communication. The people who do the work interact with one another to co-ordinate, much as two canoeists in the rapids adjust to one another's actions. Figure 13.2a shows mutual adjustment in terms of an arrow between two operators. Mutual adjustment is obviously used in the simplest of organizations – it is the most obvious way to co-ordinate. But, paradoxically, it is also used in the most complex, because it is the only means that can be relied upon under extremely difficult circumstances, such as trying to figure out how to put a man on the moon for the first time.

2 *Direct supervision* in which one person co-ordinates by giving orders to others, tends to come into play after a certain number of people must work together. Thus, fifteen people in a war canoe cannot co-ordinate by mutual adjustment; they need a leader who, by virtue of his instructions, co-ordinates their work, much as a football team requires a quarterback to call the plays. Figure 13.2b shows the leader as a manager with his instructions as arrows to the operators.

Co-ordination can also be achieved by *standardization* – in effect, automatically – by virtue of standards that predetermine what people do and so ensure that their work is co-ordinated. We can consider four forms – the standardization of the work processes themselves, of the outputs of the work, of the knowledge and skills that serve as inputs to the work, or of the norms that more generally guide the work.

3 *Standardization of work processes* means the specification – that is, the programming – of the content of the work directly, the procedures to be followed, as in the case of the assembly instructions that come with many children's toys. As shown in Figure 13.2c, it is typically the job of the analyst to so program the work of different people in order to co-ordinate it tightly.

4 *Standardization of outputs* means the specification not of what is to be done but of its results. In that way, the interfaces between jobs are predetermined, as when a machinist is told to drill holes in a certain place on a fender so that they will fit the bolts being welded by someone else, or a division manager is told to achieve a sales growth of 10% so that the corporation can meet some overall sales target. Again, such standards generally emanate from the analyst, as shown in Figure 13.2d.

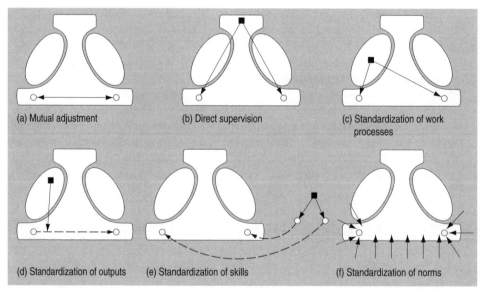

(a) Mutual adjustment

(b) Direct supervision

(c) Standardization of work processes

(d) Standardization of outputs

(e) Standardization of skills

(f) Standardization of norms

Figure 13.2   The basic mechanisms of co-ordination

5   *Standardization of skills*, as well as knowledge, is another, though looser way to achieve co-
ordination. Here, it is the worker rather than the work or the outputs that is standardized.
He or she is taught a body of knowledge and a set of skills which are subsequently applied
to the work. Such standardization typically takes place outside the organization – for example in a professional school of a university before the worker takes his or her first job – indicated in Figure 13.2e. In effect the standards do not come from the analyst; they are
internalized by the operator as inputs to the job he takes. Co-ordination is then achieved by
virtue of various operators' having learned what to expect of each other. When an anaes-
thetist and a surgeon meet in the operating room to remove an appendix, they need hardly
communicate (that is, use mutual adjustment, let along direct supervision); each knows
exactly what the other will do and can co-ordinate accordingly.
6   *Standardization of norms* (Figure 13.2f) means that the workers share a common set of beliefs
and can achieve co-ordination based on it, as implied in Figure 13.2d. For example, if every
member of a religious order shares a belief in the importance of attracting converts, then all
will work together to achieve this aim.

Bear these six co-ordinating mechanisms in mind; we shall be returning to them repeatedly.
Every organization must divide up its work among individuals (known as 'division of labour') to
get it done. These co-ordinating mechanisms as the basic means to knit together the divided
labour of the organization, serve as the most basic elements of structure – the glue that holds
the organization together.

III   THE ESSENTIAL PARAMETERS OF DESIGN

In the structuring of organizations, design means turning those knobs that influence the division
of labour and co-ordination. In this section we shall be discussing ten such knobs or 'design
parameters', which fall into four basic groups. The first deals with the design of individual positions in the organization and includes the specialization of jobs, the formalization of behaviour,
and the establishment of requirements for the training and indoctrination associated with each
job. The second concerns the designs of 'superstructure', or skeleton of the organization, and
includes the determination of the bases on which positions and units are grouped, as well as establishment of the size of units. The third deals with the design of lateral linkages to flesh out the
superstructure, and includes two design parameters called planning and control systems and liaison devices. The last concerns the design of the decision-making system in the organization and
includes the design parameters we call vertical decentralization and horizontal decentralization.

Job specialization

The first order of business in organizational design is to decide what each person will do. Key
here is the determination of how specialized each job is to be – how many distinct tasks it is to
contain – and how much control over those tasks the person who does the job should have. In
determining these aspects of job specialization, the organization designer is essentially establishing the division of labour in the organization.

Jobs that have few and 'narrow' tasks are generally referred to as *horizontally specialized*, those
with many and 'broad' ones as *horizontally enlarged*. A worker bolts on a bumper every few seconds

all day long; a maintenance man nearby is a jack-of-all-trades, shifting from one problem to another. Jobs that involve little control by those who do them – carried out without thinking how or why – are called *vertically specialized*; those which are thoroughly controlled by the worker are referred to as *vertically enlarged*. [. . .]

Jobs must often be specialized vertically because they are specialized horizontally: the work is so narrow that worker control of it would preclude the necessary co-ordination. These are generally *unskilled* jobs. On the other hand, many so-called *professional* jobs are horizontally specialized yet vertically enlarged – the worker has a narrow repertoire of programs, but because these are highly complex, he must have a good deal of control over them.

Behaviour formalization

The next issue of the design of individual positions is the determination of the extent to which the work content of tasks will be specified – in other words, the behaviour or the job 'formalized'.

Organizations formalize the behaviour of their workers in order to reduce its variability, ultimately to predict and control it. Thus behaviour formalization is also a means to achieve specialization in the vertical direction. A prime motive for formalizing behaviour is, of course, to co-ordinate work very tightly, specifically through the mechanism we have called standardization of work processes. Airline pilots, for example, cannot figure out emergency landing procedures when the need arises and then co-ordinate by mutual adjustment with the ground staff; those have to be very carefully prescribed in advance.

Organizations that rely primarily on the formalization of behaviour to achieve co-ordination are generally referred to as 'bureaucracies', a word that has become highly charged in everyday speech. We shall, however, use a neutral definition here. A structure is *bureaucratic* to the extent that it relies on standardization for co-ordination. Note that this definition includes any form of standardization, not just that of work processes. [. . .]

Training

The behaviour required of some tasks is too complex to be rationalized and then formalized directly by the analysts of the technostructure. And so the people who are to do the tasks must be extensively trained before they begin their work. In other words, they must acquire some standardized body of knowledge and set of skills. Such training can, of course, be designed in the organization itself, but more often it must take place in some formal institution (unless it must be learned under an apprenticeship system as a craft). And so this third aspect of position design entails deciding what formal training the organization will require in its different positions and then selecting the appropriately trained 'professionals' to fill them (or establishing its own training programs where it can).

We noted above that formalization and training are basically substitutes for one another. [. . .] Both are designed to program the work of the individual, but one focuses on unskilled work, while the other is oriented toward complex, professional work. And herein lies the essential difference between the two, for while one takes power from the worker and puts it into the technostructure, the other takes power from all the other parts of the organization and puts it into the hands of the professional workers themselves. In other words, professional tasks must be controlled by those who actually perform them. [. . .]

Indoctrination

Socialization refers to the process by which a new member learns the value system, the norms, and the required behaviour patterns of the society, organization, or group which he is entering [. . .] A good deal of socialization takes place informally and unofficially in the organizations, as new members interact with old. But some also takes place more formally, for the organization's own benefit, through the process known as *indoctrination*. As a parameter in the design of individual positions, indoctrination resembles training in many ways. It too takes place largely outside the job – often before it begins – and is also designed for the internalization of standards. But the standards differ. They relate not to formal bodies of knowledge and sets of skills, but to the norms of the organization itself – its values, beliefs, manners of doing things, what is generally referred to as its internal 'culture'. And because these standards are unique to each organization, indoctrination must take place within its own walls under full control of its own personnel. [. . .]

Unit grouping

Given a set of positions duly designed in terms of specialization, formalization, training, and indoctrination, the next issue in organization design relates to the establishment of a managerial 'superstructure' to knit it all together. In other words, positions are grouped into units, each under its own manager, and units clustered into ever larger units under their own managers, until the whole organization comes under a single manager – the chief executive officer at the strategic apex. Thus, a hierarchy of authority is constructed through which flows the *formal* power to control decisions and actions.

That hierarchy is generally represented by an organizational chart, what we shall call (borrowing from the French) an *organigram* [. . .] The organigram is a much maligned document, rejected by many as an inadequate picture of what really takes place in organizations. True enough, since it represents the flow of official power – formal authority – which is often superseded by informal power. Yet the organigram is inevitably the first thing asked for by anyone interested in the organization, and for good reason: like a map, it is a useful portrayal of certain surface features of the organization and their linkages. In particular, it tells at a glance how labour is divided into positions in the organization, who fills these positions, how they are grouped into units, and how formal authority flows among these units.

Two major questions arise in the design of the superstructure which are dealt with by our next two design perameters. First, on what basis are positions and units grouped into larger units, and second, what size should each of the units be?

Grouping is not simply a convenience for the sake of creating an organigram, a handy way to keep track of everyone who works for the organization. Rather, it is a fundamental way to coordinate work in the organization, for four reasons: (a) it establishes a system of common supervision among positions and units, (b) it typically requires positions and units to share common resources and (c) to be assessed on common measures of performance (i.e. output standards), and (d) as a result of the tendency to put the members of given units into close physical proximity with one another, it encourages mutual adjustment among them.

Positions and units can be grouped [. . .] by *function* (including knowledge, skill, work process work function), and by *market* (output, client, and place). In one we have grouping by *means*, by the intermediate functions the organization uses to produce or support the production of its final outputs, in the other, grouping by *ends*, by the features of the markets served by the organization – the products or services it markets, the clients it serves, the places where it serves them. [. . .]

Unit size

On the question of the size of units – historically described in terms of the 'span of control' of their managers – the classical literature was clear: [. . .] 'No supervisor can supervise directly the work of more than five or, at the most, six subordinates whose work interlocks.' Yet effective units containing dozens – sometimes even hundreds – of people or subunits have been reported. The problem as we shall see, seems to stem from the assumption in the classical literature that co-ordination was synonymous with direct supervision, in other words, that mutual adjustment and the various forms of standardization did not exist as co-ordinating mechanisms. Thus, the focus was on the span of 'control' of the manager, instead of the size of the unit, as if managerial control were the only factor in determining the size of units.

When we turn to an analysis of the co-ordinating mechanisms other than direct supervision, we get the clearest explanation of variation in unit size. Two relationships in particular explain a good deal. First the greater the use of standardization (of any kind) for co-ordination, the larger the size of the work unit. It stands to reason that the more co-ordination within a unit can be achieved by standardization – in effect, automatically, without direct managerial intervention – the less time its manager need spend on direct supervision and so the greater the number of employees that can report to him. Thus we find examples of 50 and 100 assembly line workers reporting to a single foreman; similarly, I report together with fifty colleagues directly to one dean.

The second relationship is that the greater the need for mutual adjustment, the smaller must be the size of the work unit. When tasks are rather complex yet tightly coupled, neither direct supervision nor any form of standardization suffices to effect the necessary co-ordination. The specialists who perform the various tasks must co-ordinate by virtue of informal, face-to-face communication among themselves. As we noted at the very outset of this [reading], mutual adjustment is the favoured co-ordinating mechanism for the most complex of endeavours, like putting a man on the moon for the first time. Now, what effect does reliance on mutual adjustment have on unit size? For mutual adjustment to work effectively, the work unit must be small enough to encourage convenient, frequent, and informal interaction among all its members – typically less than ten people and often of the order of five, six or seven. [. . .]

Planning and control systems

With the establishment of positions and the construction of the superstructure, we have the skeleton of the organizational structure. But the design is still not complete. We need other parameters to flesh it out, to create other kinds of linkages among the component parts. Specifically, we need planning and control systems to standardize outputs and liaison devices to encourage mutual adjustment.

The purpose of formal planning is to specify – standardize – outputs ahead of time, and the purpose of formal control is to determine later whether or not the standards have in fact been met. The two go together, like the proverbial horse and carriage. Nevertheless, we can distinguish *action planning systems* – which focus on before-the-fact determination of outputs – from *performance control systems* – which are more oriented to after-the-fact monitoring of results. [. . .]

Liaison devices

Mutual adjustment may occur naturally in the small, face-to-face work unit. But how to encourage it across units, when grouping has the known tendency to discourage *inter*unit communication even as it encourages *intraunit* communications? In the past, the resolution of this problem was left to chance. But in recent years, as it has become more and more serious, a whole series of what we shall call *liaison devices* – formal parameters of structural design – have developed to stimulate mutual adjustment across units. These, in fact, represent the most significant – development in structural design in the past fifteen or twenty years. Four are of particular importance, presented in ascending order of their capacity to encourage mutual adjustment.

- *Liaison positions* are jobs created to co-ordinate the work of two units directly, without having to pass through vertical managerial channels. They carry no formal authority *per se*; rather, those who serve in them must use their powers of persuasion, negotiation, etc. to bring the two sides together. Typical liaison positions are the purchasing engineer who sits between purchasing and engineering or the sales liaison person who mediates between the sales force and the factory.
- *Task forces and standing committees* are institutionalized forms of meetings which bring members of a number of different units together on a more intensive basis, in the first case to deal with a temporary issue, in the second, in a more permanent and regular way to discuss issues of common interest. Thus a task force may be formed of engineering, sales and production personnel to redesign a given product and then disband, while line and technocratic personnel may form a standing committee to meet weekly to plan production.
- *Integrating managers* – essentially liaison personnel with formal authority – provide for stronger co-ordination by mutual adjustment than either of the first two devices. These 'managers' are not given authority over the units they link – each of these still has its own managers. But they are given authority over something important to those units, for example, approval of certain of their decisions or control over their budgets. One example is the unit managers in the hospital, responsible for integrating the efforts of doctors, nurses, and support staff in a particular ward; another is the brand manager in a consumer goods firm who is responsible for a certain product but who must negotiate its production and marketing with different functional departments.
- *Matrix structure* carries liaison to its natural conclusion. No matter what the bases of grouping at one level in an organization, some interdependencies always remain. Functional groupings pose work-flow problems; market-based ones impede contacts among like specialists. Standardization may help, but problems often remain. As shown in Figure 13.3, we have seen three ways to deal with the 'residual interdependencies'; a different type of grouping can be used at the next level in the hierarchy; staff units can be formed next to line units to advise on the problem; or one of the liaison devices already discussed can be overlaid on the grouping. But in each case, one basis of grouping is favoured over the others. The concept of matrix structure is to balance two (or more) bases of grouping, for example functional with market (or for that matter, one kind of market with another – say, regional with product). This is done by the creation of a dual authority structure – two (or more) managers, units, or individuals are made jointly and equally responsible for the same decisions. We can distinguish a *permanent* form of matrix structure, where the units and the people in them remain more or less in place, as shown in the example of a whimsical multinational firm in Figure 13.4, and a *shifting* form, suited to project work, where the units and the people in them move around frequently. Shifting matrix structures are common in high technology industries, which group specialist in functional departments for housekeeping purposes (process interdependencies, etc.) but deploy them from various departments in project teams to do the work, as shown in Figure 13.5.

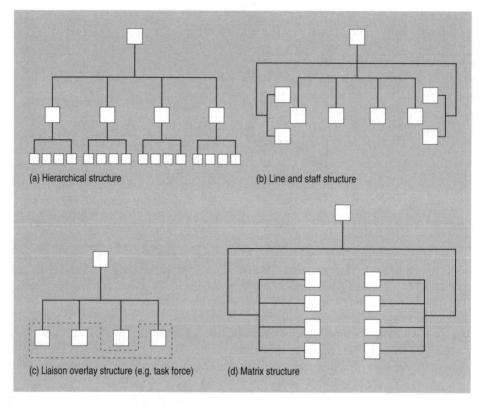

Figure 13.3   Structures to deal with residual interdependencies

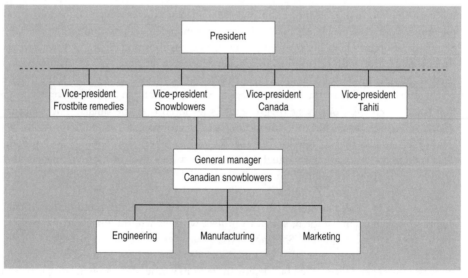

Figure 13.4   A permanent matrix structure in an international firm

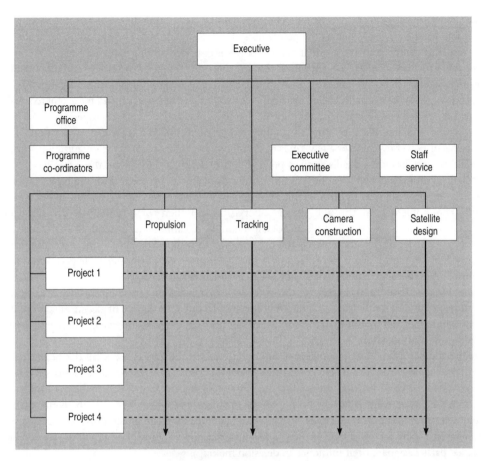

Figure 13.5 Shifting matrix structure in the NASA weather satellite program

How do these liaison devices relate to the other design parameters we have already discussed? One point seems clear. As means to encourage mutual adjustment, these are most logically used with work that is: (a) horizontally specialized, since specialization impedes natural co-ordination, (b) complex, in other words, professional, and (c) interdependent, so that co-ordination is in fact necessary. Thus, the liaison devices – especially the stronger ones, such as task forces, integrating managers and matrix structure – seem most appropriate to the second kind of professional work we discussed earlier, where the professionals must work together in small units. These liaison devices, as agents of mutual adjustment instead of standardization, are obviously associated with organic structures – indeed, in overriding formal authority or bifurcating it, they tend to destroy bureaucratic priority.

Vertical and horizontal decentralization

Finally, we come to the most extensively discussed yet least understood of the parameters of structural design, those related to *decentralization*. What does the word really mean? To some, it describes the physical location of facilities: a library is 'centralized' in one location or 'decentralized' to many. To others, it describes the delegation of formal power down the hierarchy of authority. We shall use a broader definition than the second one, but different from the first, associating the term with the sharing of decision-making power. When all the power rests at a single point in the organization, we shall call the structure centralized; to the extent that the power is dispersed among many individuals, we shall call the structure relatively decentralized. Notice that our definition of decentralization is not restricted to formal power. In fact we shall distinguish *vertical decentralization* – the delegation of *formal* power down the hierarchy to line managers – from *horizontal decentralization* – the extent to which *formal or informal* power is dispersed out of the line hierarchy to non-managers (operators, analysts, and support staffers). We also introduce another distinction: between *selective* decentralization – the dispersal of power over one or a few kinds of decisions to the same place in the organization – from *parallel* decentralization – the dispersal of power for many kinds of decisions to the same place.

Centralization has one great advantage in the organization. By keeping all the power in one place, it ensures the very tightest form of co-ordination. All the decisions are made in one head, and then implemented through direct supervision. So then why bother to decentralize? Primarily because one brain is often not big enough. It cannot understand all that must be known. Also, decentralization allows the organization to respond quickly to local conditions in many different places, and it can serve as a stimulus for motivation, since capable people require considerable room to manoeuvre if they are to perform at full capacity. [. . .]

Let us consider decentralization in terms of the six co-ordinating mechanisms because, as we shall see, each inherently leads to a different form and a different degree of decentralization. By considering them all together, in the context of our preceding discussion, we can derive six basic types of decentralization.

Direct supervision clearly constitutes full horizontal centralization, since all the power rests with the managers. In fact, it also constitutes vertical centralization since a dependence on direct supervision for co-ordination means that each manager tightly controls those below him such that all the power eventually ruses to the top of the hierarchy, where it rests in the hands of the chief executive at the strategic apex. What we call *centralization* – in effect, horizontal and vertical as well as parallel – is shown as Type I decentralization in Figure 13.6 (where the size of the shaded parts designate their influence in decision making).

The various forms of standardization can, as we have seen, lead to different degrees of decentralization. When the organization relies on the standardization of work processes for co-ordination, as we have seen, the unskilled operators and lower level line managers lose power to the managers higher up in the hierarchy and also to some extent to the analysts of the technostructure who design the systems of behaviour formalization that control others. The result is centralization in the vertical dimension, with a limited and selective degree of decentralization in the horizontal dimension (to the analysts, who control only the design of the systems of standardization). What we call *limited horizontal decentralization* (selective) is shown as Type II in Figure 13.6.

We have also seen that a reliance on standardization of output goes with the delegation of power over many decisions to the managers of market-based units. This is a form if vertical decentralization, but as we noted earlier, only a very limited form, since a few division managers can retain the lion's share of the power. Thus our Type III decentralization is referred to as *limited vertical decentralization* (parallel). (Some power is shown in the technostructure, because it is the analysts who design the planning and control systems to standardize outputs.)

Next, we have decentralization based on the two kinds of professional work. Because, as noted earlier, experts who do complex work must control it to a large degree, these represent – in contrast to our first three types – rather extensive forms of decentralization.

In the first, the standardization of skills (based on extensive training) is relied upon for co-ordination. As a result, the professionals can work rather autonomously in large units, relatively free

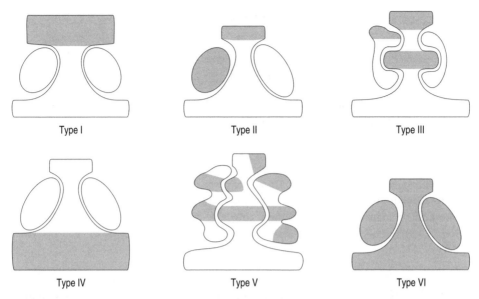

Type I

Type II

Type III

Type IV

Type V

Type VI

Figure 13.6 Six types of decentralization

of the control of line managers and in control of most of the decisions that affect their work directly. In other words, here we have an extreme form of *horizontal decentralization (parallel)*, shown as Type IV in Figure 13.6, with much of the power residing at the bottom of the hierarchy. Note that we have in Types II and IV our two kinds of bureaucracies, the first relatively centralized, the second relatively decentralized.

In the second kind of professional work, the experts work in small units and co-ordinate by mutual adjustment (encouraged by the use of the liaison devices), which gives them a good deal of power. Here we have a combination, in both cases selective, of vertical decentralization – delegation to work groups at different levels in the hierarchy – and horizontal decentralization – a varying distribution of power within each group, of managers and non-managers, with the different decisions being controlled by whoever happens to have the necessary expertise. We end up with *selective horizontal and vertical decentralization*, Type V in Figure 13.6. Note that in Types I and V we have essentially two kinds of organic structures, one based on direct supervision for co-ordination, the other on mutual adjustment.

Finally, we come to the form of decentralization dictated by a reliance on the standardization of norms for co-ordination. As noted earlier, when an organization socializes and indoctrinates its members to believe in its strong ideology, it can then allow them considerable freedom to act, since they will in fact act in accordance with the prevailing norms. The result can be the purest form of decentralization – in one sense, the most democratic form of structure. Everyone shares power more or less equally – managers, staff person, operator – hence we have just plain *decentralization*.

IV THE SITUATIONAL FACTORS

A number of contingency or situational factors influence the choice of these design parameters, and vice versa. These include the age and size of the organization; its technical system of production; various characteristics of its environment, such as stability and complexity; and its power system, for example, whether or not it is tightly controlled from the outside. Some of

257

their influences on the design parameters as found in an extensive body of research are summarized below as hypotheses.

Age and size

Five hypotheses seem to cover a good deal of the findings in the research on the effects of the age and size of the organization itself on its own structure.

H1

The older the organization, the more formalized its behaviour What we have here is the 'we've-seen-it-all-before' syndrome. As organizations age, they tend to repeat their behaviours; as a result, these become more predictable and so more amenable to formalization.

H2

The larger the organization the more formalized its behaviour Just as the older organization formalizes what it has seen before, so the larger organization formalizes what it sees often. ('Listen mister, I've heard that story at least five times today. Just fill in the form like it says.')

H3

The larger the organization, the more elaborate its structure; that is, the more specialized its tasks, the more differentiated its units, and the more developed its administrative components As organizations grow in size, they are able to specialize their tasks more finely. (The big barber-shop can afford a specialist to cut children's hair; the small one cannot.) As a result, they can also specialize – or 'differentiate' – the work of their units more extensively. This leads to greater homogeneity of work within units, but greater diversity between them, which necessitates more efforts at co-ordination. And so the larger organization tends also to enlarge its hierarchy to effect direct supervision or its technostructure to co-ordinate by standardization, or to include more liaison or integrating positions to encourage co-ordination by mutual adjustment.

H4

The larger the organization, the larger the size of its average unit This finding relates to the previous two, the size of units growing larger as organizations themselves grow larger because: (a) as behaviour becomes more formalized, and (b) as the work of each unit becomes more homogeneous, managers are able to supervise more employees.

H5

Structure reflects the age of founding of the industry This is a curious finding, but one that we shall see holds up remarkably well. Organizational structure seems to reflect not just the age of the organization itself, but the age of the industry in which it operates, no matter what its own age. Industries that predate the industrial revolution seems to favour one kind of structure, those of the age of the early railroads another, and so on. We should obviously expect different structures in different periods; the surprising thing is that these structures seem to carry through to new periods, old industries remaining relatively unaffected by innovations in structural design.

Technical system

Technical system refers to the instruments used in the operating core to produce the outputs. (This should be distinguished from 'technology' which refers to the knowledge base of the organization.) Three hypotheses are especially important here.

H6

The more regulating the technical system – that is, the more it controls the work of the operators – the more formalized the operating work and the more bureaucratic the structure of the operating core Technical systems that regulate the work of the operators – for example, mass production assembly lines – render that work highly routine and predictable, and so encourage its specialization and formalization, which in turn create the conditions for bureaucracy in the operating core.

H7

The more complex the technical system, the more elaborate the administrative structure, especially the larger and more professional the support staff, the greater the selective decentralization (to that staff), and the greater the use of liaison devices to co-ordinate the work of that staff Essentially, if an organization is to use complex machinery it must hire staff experts who can understand that machinery – who have the capability to design, select, and modify it. And then it must give them considerable power to make decisions concerning that machinery, and encourage them to use the liaison devices to ensure mutual adjustment among them.

H8

The automation of the operating core transforms a bureaucratic administrative structure into an organic one When unskilled work is co-ordinated by the standardization of work processes, we get bureaucratic structure. But it is not only the operating core that gets bureaucratized. The whole organization tends to take on characteristics of bureaucracy, because an obsessive control mentality pervades the system. But when the work of the operating core gets automated, social relationships change. Now it is machines, not people, that are regulated. So the obsession with control disappears – machines do not need to be watched over – and with it go many of the managers and analysts who were needed to control the operators. In their place come the support specialists, to look after the machinery. And they, as described in the last hypothesis, gain a good deal of power and co-ordinate by mutual adjustment. In other words, the result of automation is a reduction of line authority in favour of staff expertise and a tendency to rely less on standardization for co-ordination, more on mutual adjustment. Thus, ironically, organizations tend to get humanized by the automation of their operating work.

Environment

Environment is a catch-all term that has been used in the literature to describe the general conditions that surround an organization. We shall discuss five hypotheses here, each one dealing with a different condition.

H9

The more dynamic the environment, the more organic the structure It stands to reason that in a stable environment – when nothing changes – an organization can predict its future conditions and so, all other things being equal, can easily rely on standardization for co-ordination. But when conditions become dynamic – when sources of supply are uncertain, the need for product change frequent, labour turnover high, political conditions unstable – the organization cannot standardize, but must instead remain flexible through the use of direct supervision or mutual adjustment for co-ordination. In other words, it must have organic structure. Thus, for example, armies which tend to be highly bureaucratic institutions in peacetime, can become rather organic when engaged in highly dynamic, guerrilla-type warfare.

H10

The more complex the environment, the more decentralized the structure We saw earlier that the prime reason to decentralize a structure is that all the information needed to make decisions cannot be comprehended in one head. For example, when the operations of the organization are based on a complex body of technical knowledge (as in a hospital), then the organization must engage professionals (the physicians) and grant them a good deal of power over their own work. Note that Hypotheses 9 and 10 are independent of one another. A simple environment can be stable or dynamic (the manufacturer of dresses faces a simple environment yet cannot predict style from one season to another). A complex one likewise can be stable or dynamic (the specialist in perfected open heart surgery faces a complex task, yet knows exactly what to expect).

H11

The more diversified the organization's markets, the greater the propensity to split it into market-based units, or divisions, given favourable economies of scale When an organization can identify distinct markets – geographical regions, clients, but especially products and services – it will be predisposed to split itself into high-level units on that basis, and to give each a good deal of control over its own operations (that is, to use what we called 'limited vertical decentralization'). In simple terms, diversification breeds divisionalization. In this way, the organization can reduce the co-ordination needed across units: each has all the functions associated with its own markets. But this assumes favourable economies of scale. If the operating core cannot be divided (as in the case of an aluminium smelter), or if some critical function must be centrally co-ordinated (as in purchasing in a retail chain), then full divisionalization may simply be impossible.

H12

Extreme hostility in its environment drives any organization to centralize its structure temporarily Evidence from the social psychological laboratory suggests that when threatened by extreme hostility in its environment, the tendency for groups (and, presumably, organizations) is to centralize power, in other words, to fall back on the tightest co-ordinating mechanism they know, direct supervision. Here a central leader can ensure fast and highly co-ordinated response to the threat (at least temporarily).

H13

Disparities in the environment encourage the organization to decentralize selectively to differentiated work constellations When an organization faces very different kinds of environments – one dynamic, requiring organic structure, another stable, requiring bureaucratic structure, and so on – the natural tendency is to differentiate the structure, to create different pockets, or 'work constellations', to deal with each. Each constellation is given the power to make the decisions related to its own 'subenvironment', with the result that the structure becomes decentralized selectively.

Power

Our fourth set of situational factors relates to power. Thus impact of external control of the organization, the power needs of the members, and fashion are discussed below.

H14

The greater the external control of the organization, the more centralized and formalized its structure This important hypothesis claims that to the extent that an organization is controlled externally – for example, by a parent firm or a government – it tends to centralize power at the strategic apex and to formalize its behaviour. The reason is that the two most effective ways to control an organization from the outside are to hold its chief executive officer responsible for its actions and to impose clearly defined standards on it. Moreover, external control forces the organization to be especially careful about its actions; because it must justify its behaviours to outsiders, it tends to formalize the structure when it imposes special demands for rationalization, for example, when a parent firm insists that all its subsidiaries use a common set of purchasing procedures. The important point about this hypothesis is that the centralization of power in society – as independent organizations lose their power to larger systems – means centralization of power at the organizational level, and bureaucratization in the use of that power.

H15

The power needs of the members tend to generate structures that are excessively centralized. All members of the organization – operators, support staffers, analysts, managers – seek to enhance their own power, or at least to keep others from having power over them. But the dice are loaded in this game, the line managers and especially those at the strategic apex being favoured by the existence of an authority structure that aggregates formal power up the hierarchy of command. And so we would expect that to the extent that the members seek personal power, excessively centralized structures would tend to be the most common result.

H16

Fashion favours the structure of the day (and of the culture), sometimes even when inappropriate Ideally, the design parameters are chosen according to the dictates of age, size, technical system, and environment. In fact, however, fashion seems to play a role too, encouraging many organizations to adopt currently popular design parameters that are inappropriate for themselves. Paris has its salons of haute couture; likewise New York has its offices of 'haute structure', the consulting firms that sometimes tend to oversell the latest in structural fashion.

V   THE CONFIGURATIONS

This completes our discussion of the elements of structure. So far – and especially in our presentation of the situational factors – we have tended to look at structure the way a diner looks at a buffet table. But in fact these elements seem to cluster naturally in a certain number of ways, which we have called configurations. A number may have been evident to the reader in the discussion. In particular, we have six basic parts of the organization, six basic mechanisms of coordination, six basic types of decentralization. These in fact all fit together, to describe the essence of six basic configurations, as can be seen in Table 13.1, which also lists the design parameters and situational factors associated with each configuration.

We can explain this correspondence by considering the organization as being pulled in six different directions, one by each of its parts, as shown in Figure 13.7. When conditions favour one of these pulls over the others, a particular organization is drawn to structure itself as one of the configurations as described below.

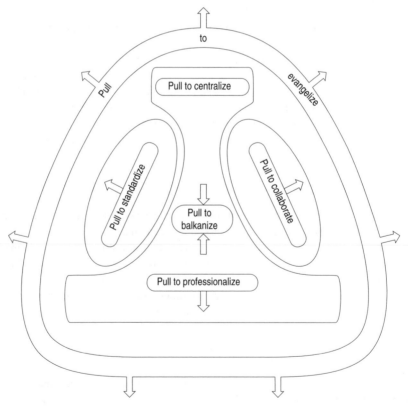

Figure 13.7   Six pulls on the organization

Table 13.1 Basic dimensions of the six configurations*

	Simple structure	*Machine bureaucracy*	*Professional bureaucracy*	*Divisionalized form*	*Adhocracy*	*Missionary*
Key co-ordinating mechanism	Direct supervision	Standardization of work	Standardization of skills	Standardization of outputs	Mutual adjustment	Standardization of norms
Key part of organization	Strategic apex	Technostructure	Operating core	Middle line	Support staff	Ideology
Design parameters:						
Specialization of jobs	Little specialization	*Much horizontal and vertical specialization*	*Much horizontal specialization*	*Some horizontal and vertical specialization* (between divisions and HQ)	*Much horizontal specialization*	Little specialization
Training	Little	Little	*Much*	Little	Much	Little
Indoctrination	Little	Little	Little	Some of divisional managers	Some	*Much*
Formalization of behaviour, bureaucratic, organic	Little formalization, *organic*	*Much formalization, bureaucratic*	Little formalization, bureaucratic	Much formalization (within divisions), bureaucratic	Little formalization, *organic*	Little formal bureaucratic
Grouping	Usually functional	*Usually functional*	Functional and market	*Market*	*Functional and market*	*Market*
Unit size	Wide	Wide at bottom narrow elsewhere	Wide at bottom, narrow elsewhere	Wide at top	*Narrow throughout*	Wide in enclaves of limited size
Planning and control systems	Little planning and control	Action planning	Little planning and control	*Much perf. control*	Limited action planning	Little planning and control

Continued

Table 13.1 Basic dimensions of the six configurations*—cont'd

	Simple structure	*Machine bureaucracy*	*Professional bureaucracy*	*Divisionalized form*	*Adhocracy*	*Missionary*
Liaison devices	Few liaison devices	Few liaison devices	Liaison devices in administration	Few liaison devices	*Many liaison devices throughout*	Few liaison devices
Decentralization	*Centralization*	*Limited horizontal decentralization*	*Horizontal decentralization*	*Limited vertical decentralization*	*Selective decentralization*	*Decentralization*
Situational factors:						
Age and size	Typically young and small (first stage)	Typically old and large (second stage)	Varies	Typically old and very large (third stage)	Often young	Typically neither very young nor very old; large only through many small enclaves
Technical system	Simple, not regulating	Regulating but not automated, not very sophisticated	Not regulating or sophisticated	Divisible, otherwise typically like Mach. Bur.	Very sophisticated, often automated, or else not regulating or sophisticated	Simple not regulating
Environment	Simple and dynamic: sometimes hostile	Simple and stable	Complex and stable	Relatively simple and stable; diversified markets (esp. products and services)	Complex and dynamic; sometimes disparate	Simple and usually stable
Power	Chief executive control: often owner-managed; not fashionable	Technocratic and external control; not fashionable	Professional operator control; fashionable	Middle line control; fashionable (esp. in industry)	Expert control: very fashionable	Ideological control; coming fashion

* Italic type within columns designates key design parameter

Figure 13.8 The simple structure

The simple structure

The name tells it all. And Figure 13.8 shows it all. The structure is simple, not much more than one large unit consisting of one or a few top managers, one of whom dominates by the pull to centralize, and a group of operators who do the basic work. Little of the behaviour in the organization is formalized and minimal use is made of planning, training, or the liaison devices. The absence of standardization means that the structure is organic and has little need for staff analysts. Likewise there are few middle line managers because so much of the co-ordination is handled at the top. Even the support staff is minimized, in order to keep the structure lean, the organization flexible.

The organization must be flexible because it operates in a dynamic environment, often by choice since that is the only place where it can outsmart the bureaucracies. But that environment must be simple, as must the production system, or else the chief executive could not for long hold on to the lion's share of the power. The organization is often young, in part because time drives it toward bureaucracy, in part because the vulnerability of simple structures causes many of them to fail. And many are often small, since size too drives the structure toward bureaucracy. Not infrequently the chief executive purposely keeps the organization small in order to retain his personal control.

The classic simple structure is of course the entrepreneurial firm, controlled tightly and personally by its owner. Sometimes, however, under the control of a very clever autocratic leader who refuses to let go of the reins, a simple structure can grow large. Sometimes under crisis conditions, large organizations also revert temporarily to simple structures to allow forceful leaders to try to save them.

The machine bureaucracy

The machine bureaucracy is the offspring of the Industrial Revolution, when jobs became highly specialized and work became highly standardized. As can be seen in Figure 13.9, in contrast to simple structure, the machine bureaucracy elaborates its administration. First, it requires a large technostructure to design and maintain its systems of standardization, notably those that formalize its behaviours and plan its actions. And by virtue of the organization's dependence on these

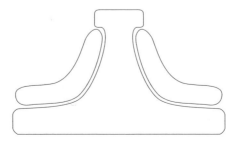

Figure 13.9 The machine bureaucracy

systems, the technostructure gains a good deal of informal power, resulting in a limited amount of horizontal decentralization, reflecting the pull to standardize. A large hierarchy of middle line managers emerges to control the highly specialized work of the operating core. But that middle line hierarchy is usually structured on a functional basis all the way up to the top, where the real power of co-ordination lies. So the structure tends to be rather centralized in the vertical sense.

To enable the top managers to maintain centralized control, both the environment and the production system of the machine bureaucracy must be fairly simple, the latter regulating the work of the operators but not itself automated. In fact, machine bureaucracies fit most naturally with mass production. Indeed it is interesting that this structure is more prevalent in industries that date back to the period from the Industrial Revolution to the early part of this century.

The professional bureaucracy

There is another bureaucratic configuration, but because this one relies on the standardization of skills rather than of work processes or outputs for its co-ordination, it emerges as dramatically different from the machine bureaucracy. Here the pull to professionalize dominates. In having to rely on trained professionals – people highly specialized, but with considerable control over their work, as in hospitals or universities – to do its operating tasks, the organization surrenders a good deal of its power not only to the professionals themselves but also to the associations and institutions that select and train them in the first place. So the structure emerges as a highly decentralized horizontally; power over many decisions, both operating and strategic, flows all the way down the hierarchy, to the professionals of the operating core.

Above the operating core we find a rather unique structure, as can be seen in Figure 13.10. There is little need for a technostructure, since the main standardization occurs as a result of training that takes place outside the organization. Because the professionals work so independently, the size of operating units can be very large, and few first line managers are needed. The support staff is typically very large too, in order to back up the high priced professionals.

Professional bureaucracy is called for whenever an organization finds itself in an environment that is stable yet complex. Complexity requires decentralization to highly trained individuals, and stability enables them to apply standardized skills and so to work with a good deal of autonomy. To ensure that autonomy, the production system must be neither highly regulating, complex, nor automated.

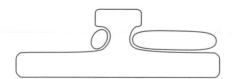

Figure 13.10   The professional bureaucracy

The divisionalized form

Like the professional bureaucracy, the divisionalized form is not so much an integrated organization as a set of rather independent entities coupled together by a loose administrative structure. But whereas those entities of the professional bureaucracy are individuals, in the divisionalized form they are units in the middle line, generally called 'divisions', exerting a dominant pull to Balkanize. The divisionalized form differs from the other four configurations in one central respect: it is not a complete structure, but a partial one superimposed on others. Each division has its own structure.

An organization divisionalizes for one reason above all, because its product lines are diversified. And that tends to happen most often in the largest and most mature organizations, the ones that have run out of opportunities – or have become bored – in their traditional markets. Such diversification encourages the organization to replace functional by market-based units, one for each distinct product line (as shown in Figure 13.11), and to grant considerable autonomy to each to run its own business. The result is a limited form of decentralization down the chain of command.

How does the central headquarters maintain a semblance of control over the divisions? Some direct supervision is used. But too much of that interferes with the necessary divisional autonomy. So the headquarters relies on performance control systems, in other words the standardization of outputs. To design these control systems, headquarters creates a small technostructure. This is shown in Figure 13.11, across from the small central support staff that headquarters sets up to provide certain services common to the divisions such as legal counsel and public relations.

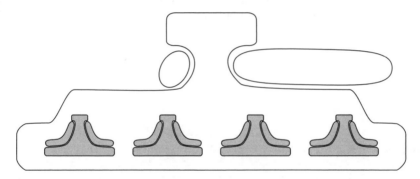

Figure 13.11 The divisionalized form

The adhocracy

None of the structures so far discussed suits the industries of our age, industries such as aerospace, petrochemicals, think tank consulting, and film making. These organizations need above all to innovate in very complex ways. The bureaucratic structures are too inflexible, and the simple structure too autocratic. These industries require 'project structures', structures that can fuse experts drawn from different specialities into smoothly functioning creative teams. That is the role of our fifth structural configuration, adhocracy, dominated by the experts' pull to collaborate.

Adhocracy is an organic structure that relies for co-ordination on mutual adjustment among its highly trained and highly specialized experts, which it encourages by the extensive use of the liaison devices – integrating managers, standing committees, and above all task forces and matrix structure. Typically the experts are grouped in functional units for housekeeping purposes but deployed in small market based project teams to do their work. To these teams, located all over the structure in accordance with the decisions to be made, is delegated power over different kinds of decisions. So the structure becomes decentralized selectively in the vertical and horizontal dimensions, that is, power is distributed unevenly, all over the structure, according to expertise and need.

All the distinctions of conventional structure disappear in the adhocracy, as can be seen in Figure 13.12. With power based on expertise, the line-staff distinction evaporates. With power distributed throughout the structure, the distinction between the strategic apex and the rest of the structure blurs.

Adhocracies are found in environments that are both complex and dynamic, because those are the ones that require sophisticated innovation, the type of innovation that calls for the co-operative efforts of many different kinds of experts. One type of adhocracy is often associated with a production system that is very complex, sometimes and so requires a highly skilled and influential support staff to design and maintain the technical system of the operating core. (The dotted lines of Figure 13.12 designate the separation of the operating core from the adhocratic administrative structure.) Here the projects take place in the administration to bring new operating facilities on line (or when a new complex is designed in a petro-chemical firm). Another type of adhocracy produces its projects directly for its clients (as in a think tank consulting firm or a manufacturer of engineering prototypes). Here, as a result, the operators also take part in the projects, bringing their expertise to bear on them; hence the operating core blends into the administrative structure (as indicated in 13.12 above the dotted line). This second type of adhocracy tends to be young on average, because with no standard products or services, many tend to fail while others escape their vulnerability by standardizing some products or services and so converting themselves to a form of bureaucracy.

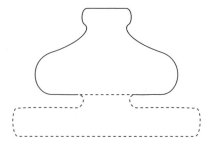

Figure 13.12   The adhocracy

The missionary

Our sixth configuration forms another rather distinct combination of the elements we have been discussing. When an organization is dominated by the pull to evangelize, its members are encouraged to pull together, and so there tends to be loose division of labour, little job specialization as well as reduction of the various forms of differentiation found in the other configurations – of the strategic apex from the rest, of staff from line or administration from operations, between operators, between divisions, and so on.

What holds the missionary together – that is, provides for its co-ordination – is the standardization of norms, the sharing of values and beliefs among all its members. And the key to ensuring this is their socialization, effected through the design parameter of indoctrination. Once the new member has been indoctrinated into the organization – once he or she identifies strongly with the common beliefs – then he or she can be given considerable freedom to make decisions. Thus the result of effective indoctrination is the most complete form of decentralization. And because other forms of co-ordination need not be relied upon, the missionary formalizes little of its behaviour as such and makes minimal use of planning and control systems. As a result, it has virtually no technostructure. Likewise, external professional training is not relied upon, because that would force the organization to surrender a certain control to external agencies.

Hence, the missionary ends up as an amorphous mass of members, with little specialization as to job, differentiation as to part, division as to status. Beyond a certain size, however, as indicated in Figure 13.13, it tends to divide itself, like the amoeba, into smaller units, best thought of as 'enclaves', with perhaps a nominal headquarters in one of the enclaves – a loose strategic apex to serve as the depository of the official manifestations of the ideology (the 'archives').

Missionaries tend not to be very young organizations – it takes time for a set of beliefs to become institutionalized as an ideology. Many missionaries do not get a chance to grow very old either (with notable exceptions, such as certain long-standing religious orders). Size, as we saw, is also not very clear-cut. On one hand, there is a clear limit to the size of each enclave; on the other hand, nothing stops the organization from spinning off enclave after enclave, since each is a rather independent entity. Neither the environment nor the technical system of the missionary can be complex, because that would require the use of highly skilled specialists, who would hold a certain power and status over others and thereby serve to differentiate the structure. Nor can the technical system be regulating, because that would lead to the formalizing of the operating work. Thus we would expect to find the simplest technical systems in missionaries, usually hardly any at all, as in religious orders or in the primitive farm co-operatives. And the environment of the missionary, in addition to being simple, can also typically be described as stable, in that the organization tends to function in a placid environment that makes few demands on it.

This completes a rather lengthy discussion of the structuring of organizations. As we have seen, what appears to be an enormously complex subject – comprising organizational parts, co-ordinating mechanisms, design parameters, and situational factors – can be made manageable by considering how all these many dimensions cluster to form distinct types of organizations. This may seem like an artificial reduction of the complexity, but in important ways it is far more realistic than trying to consider all of the permutations and combinations of these dimensions (an impossible, or at least awfully confusing task, in any event), or of giving up and dealing with this material in a fragmented way (as has been done in much of the traditional academic literature).

In fact, a good deal of experience with this 'typology' (the common label for a set of types developed logically) in both university teaching and business practice has suggested much use for it. In no way do all organizations fit one type or another. But having the set of them as a conceptual framework can help enormously to cut through, not only the complexities of structure, but of strategy and power and almost any other factor associated with organizations. [. . .]

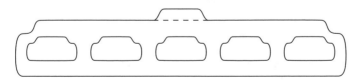

Figure 13.13   The missionary

14

CREATING A SENSE OF MISSION

Andrew Campbell and Sally Yeung

Many managers misunderstand the nature and importance of mission, while others fail to consider it at all. As far back as 1973, Peter Drucker[1] observed: 'That business purpose and business mission are so rarely given adequate thought is perhaps the most important cause of business frustration and failure'. Unfortunately, his comment is as true today as it was then.

UNDERSTANDING MISSION?

The reason for this neglect is due in part to the fact that mission is still a relatively uncharted area of management. Most management thinkers have given mission only a cursory glance, and there is little research into its nature and importance. What research there is has been devoted to analysing mission statements and attempting to develop checklists of items that should be addressed in the statement.[2] Indeed, a major problem is that mission has become a meaningless term – no two academics or managers agree on the same definition. Some speak of mission as if it is commercial evangelism, others talk about strong corporate cultures and still others talk about business definitions. Some view mission as an esoteric and somewhat irrelevant preoccupation which haunts senior managers, while others see it as the bedrock of a company's strength, identity and success – its personality and character.

Despite the diversity of opinion about mission, it is possible to distinguish two schools of thought. Broadly speaking, one approach describes mission in terms of business strategy, while the other expresses mission in terms of philosophy and ethics.

The strategy school of thought views mission primarily as a strategic tool, an intellectual discipline which defines the business's commercial rationale and target market. Mission is something that is linked to strategy but at a higher level. In this context, it is perceived as the first step in strategic management. It exists to answer two fundamental questions: 'What is our business and what should it be?' [. . .]

Recently, it has become common for companies to include a statement of what their business is in the annual report. [. . .]

The first page of the 1989 annual report of British Telecom reads: 'British Telecom's mission is to provide world class telecommunications and information products and services and to develop and exploit our networks at home and overseas'. [. . .]

In contrast, the second school of thought argues that mission is the cultural 'glue' which enables an organization to function as a collective unity. This cultural glue consists of strong

270

norms and values that influence the way in which people behave, how they work together and how they pursue the goals of the organization. This form of mission can amount to a business philosophy which helps employees to perceive and interpret events in the same way and to speak a common language. Compared to the strategic view of mission, this interpretation sees mission as capturing some of the emotional aspects of the organization. It is concerned with generating co-operation among employees through shared values and standards of behaviour.

IBM seems to subscribe to the cultural view of mission. The company describes its mission in terms of a distinct business philosophy, which in turn produces strong cultural norms and values. In his book, *A Business and its Beliefs* Thomas J. Watson Jr asserted: 'The only sacred cow in an organization should be its basic philosophy of doing business.' For IBM, 'the basic philosophy, spirit and drive of the business' lie in three concepts: respect for the individual, dedication to service and a quest for superiority in all things. The importance of other factors which contribute to commercial success, such as technological and economic resources, is 'transcended by how strongly the people in the organization believe in its basic precepts and how faithfully they carry them out'.[3]

Is it possible to reconcile these two different interpretations? Are they conflicting theories or are they simply separate parts of the same picture? We believe these theories can be synthesized into a comprehensive single description of mission. We also believe that some of the confusion over mission exists because of a failure to appreciate that it is an issue which involves both the hearts (culture) and minds (strategy) of employees. It is something which straddles the world of business and the world of the individual.

In the pages that follow we outline a framework that defines mission. The value of this framework is that it helps managers to think clearly about mission and, more importantly, it helps them to discuss mission with their colleagues. Previously, managers have had an intuitive understanding of mission. Intuition is not, however, enough. Mission needs to be managed and it can be managed better if it is clearly defined.

BUILDING A DEFINITION OF MISSION

We have developed our theory of mission both through an intellectual, top-down process and through discussions with managers and employees. Through this approach, we have tried to build an understanding of mission that is firmly grounded in the day-to-day realities of corporate life. [. . .]

We focused on managers in companies with a strong sense of purpose and a strong culture. We wanted to know why they were committed to their organizations, and if they had a sense of the company's mission. They responded by telling us about the behaviour patterns and behaviour standards in their companies.

They brimmed with stories about why their companies were special. In Marks and Spencer, a retailer known for its high quality and value for money, employees talked about quality and value. They described the high standards they demanded of themselves and their suppliers. [. . .]

At British Airways, staff spoke of the new pride and professionalism among employees as the result of the effort in the 1980s to build a service culture: 'I feel proud to work for BA', said one individual. 'People outside BA recognize the achievement, especially when they travel on the airline.'

Pride and dedication were also evident in Egon Zehnder, an executive search firm. Consultant after consultant spoke of concepts and values which the company holds dear: the primacy of the client's interest, teamwork and the 'one firm' concept. [. . .]

In these companies the commitment and enthusiasm among employees seem to come from a sense of personal attachment to the principles on which the company operates. To them mission has more to do with living out behaviour standards than with achieving goals. To the managers we spoke to, their mission appeared to be to follow the standards and behaviours their companies ask of them. [. . .]

We were hearing managers talk primarily about the standards and behaviours in their companies and why these are important to them. They gave two reasons. They are committed to the standards because, to them, they are worthwhile and elevating. They are also committed to the standards because they can see the practical good sense behind them; they can see that the standards add up to a superior business strategy.

We have attempted to make sense of these responses by developing a definition of mission. Our definition, which we have illustrated in Figure 14.1, includes four elements – purpose, strategy, behaviour standards and values. A strong mission, we believe, exists when the four elements of mission link tightly together, resonating and reinforcing each other.

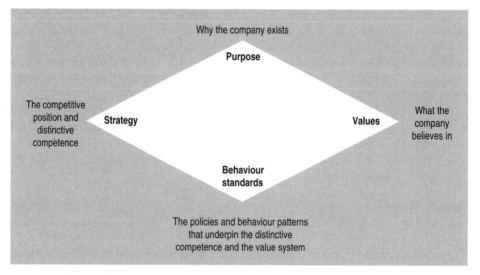

Figure 14.1 The Ashridge mission model

Purpose

What is the company for? For whose benefit is all the effort being put in? Why should a manager or an employee do more than the minimum required? For a company these questions are the equivalent of a person asking 'Why do I exist?' The questions are deeply philosophical and can lead boards of directors into heated debate. Indeed, many companies do not even attempt to reach a conclusion about the nature of their overall purpose.

However, where there does appear to be an overall idea of purpose, companies fall into three categories. First there is the company that claims to exist for the benefit of the shareholders. For these companies the purpose is to maximize wealth for the shareholders. All decisions are assessed against a yardstick of shareholder value. Hanson, a conglomerate focused on Britain and the USA, is one example. Lord Hanson repeatedly states: 'The shareholder is king.' Unlike many companies whose chairmen claim to be working primarily for the shareholders, Lord Hanson believes what he says and manages the business to that end. Hence [one Hanson] director feels quite free to say: 'All of our businesses are for sale all of the time. If anyone is prepared to pay us more than we think they are worth we will sell. We have no attachment to any individual business.'

Most managers, however, are not as single-minded as Lord Hanson. They do not believe that the company's only purpose is to create wealth for shareholders. They acknowledge the claims of other stakeholders such as customers, employees, suppliers and the community. Faced with the question, 'Is your company in business to make money for shareholders, make products for customers or provide rewarding jobs for employees?', they will answer yes to all three.

The second type of company, therefore, is one that exists to satisfy all its stakeholders. In order to articulate this broader idea of purpose many of these companies have written down their responsibility to each stakeholder group. Ciba-Geigy is an example. It has published the company's business principles under four headings – the public and the environment, customers, employees and shareholders. Under the heading of the public and the environment it has five paragraphs describing principles such as: 'We will behave as a responsible corporate member of society and will do our best to co-operate in a responsible manner with the appropriate authorities, local and national.' [. . .]

In practice it can be argued that the multiple-stakeholder view of purpose is more a matter of pragmatism than arbitrary choice. In a competitive labour market, a company which totally ignored its employees' needs would soon find its labour costs soaring as it fought to stem the tide of rising employee turnover. But what is important is the psychology of statements of purpose. Lord Hanson is saying that he is expecting his managers to put the allegiance of employees after the interests of shareholders in their list of priorities. Other companies say they have equal priority. For employees this makes them very different companies.

Managers in the third type of company are dissatisfied by a purpose solely aimed at satisfying stakeholder needs. They have sought to identify a purpose that is greater than the combined needs of the stakeholders, something to which all the stakeholders can feel proud of contributing. In short, they aim towards a higher ideal. [. . .]

At The Body Shop, a retailer of cosmetics, managers talk about 'products that don't hurt animals or the environment'. At Egon Zehnder the purpose is to be the worldwide leader in executive search. Whether these companies have an almost moral crusade, like The Body Shop, or whether they just aspire to be the best, like Egon Zehnder, they have all reached beyond the stakeholder definition of purpose. Each stakeholder, whether shareholder, employee or supplier, can feel that doing business with the company supports some higher-level goal.

We believe that leaders will find it easier to create employees with commitment and enthusiasm if they choose a purpose aimed at a higher ideal. We have met individuals committed to shareholders or to the broader definition of stakeholders, but we believe that it is harder for this commitment to grow. Purposes expressed in terms of stakeholders tend to emphasize their different selfish interests. Purposes aimed at higher ideals seek to deny these selfish interests or at least dampen their legitimacy. This makes it easier to bind the organization together.

Strategy

To achieve a purpose in competition with other organizations, there needs to be a strategy. Strategy provides the commercial logic for the company. If the purpose is to be the best, there must be a strategy explaining the principles around which the company will become the best. If the purpose is to create wealth, there must be a strategy explaining how the company will create wealth in competition with other companies.

Strategy will define the business that the company plans to hold in that business and the distinctive competence or competitive advantage that the company has or plans to create.

Egon Zehnder provides a good example of a strategy which explains how the firm will achieve its purpose. Egon Zehnder wants to be the most professional, although not necessarily the biggest, international executive search firm. Its competitive advantage comes, it believes, from the methods and systems it uses to carry out search assignments and from the 'one-firm', co-operative culture it has so carefully nurtured.

Marks and Spencer's strategy in textiles is a second example. In its clothes retailing business, Marks and Spencer seeks to offer the best value for money in the high street by providing a broad range of classic quality clothes. The company's competitive advantage comes from its dedication to quality through managing suppliers, its high levels of service, and the low overheads generated by high sales per square foot.

Behaviour standards

Purpose and strategy are empty intellectual thoughts unless they can be converted into action, into the policy and behaviour guidelines that help people to decide what to do on a day-to-day basis.

British Airways provides a good example of how the company's purpose and strategy have been successfully converted into tangible standards and actions. It promotes itself as the 'world's favourite airline' and declares as its aim, 'to be the best and most successful company in the airline industry'. The strategy to achieve this is based on providing good value for money, service that overall is superior to its competitiors and friendly, professional managers who are in tune with its staff. These strategic objectives are translated into policies and behaviour guidelines such as the need for in-flight services to be at least as good as those of competing airlines on the same route, and the requirement that managers and employees should be helpful and friendly at all times.

By translating purpose and strategy into actionable policies and standards senior managers at British Airways have dramatically changed the performance of the airline. Central to this effort was the training and behaviour change connected with the slogan 'Putting People First'. [. . .]

Egon Zehnder provides another example of the link between strategy and policies. Egon Zehnder's strategy is to be more professional than other executive search consultants. Connected with this it has a set of policies about how consultants should carry out assignments, called the 'systematic consulting approach'. One of the policies is that consultants should not take on a search assignment unless they believe it will benefit the client. Another policy is that there should be a back-up consultant for every assignment in order to ensure a quality service to the client. Supporting this systematic approach are behaviour standards about co-operation. These are ingrained into the culture rather than written on tablets of stone. An Egon Zehnder consultant willingly helps another consultant within his or her office or from other offices around the world. [. . .]

The logic for the co-operation [. . .] is a commercial logic. The firm wants to be the best. This means being better at co-operation than its competitors. As a result it needs a behaviour standard that makes sure consultants help each other. This commercial logic is the left-brain logic of the firm.

Human beings are emotional, however, and are often driven more by right-brain motives than left-brain logic. To capture the emotional energy of an organization the mission needs to provide some philosophical or moral rationale for behaviour to run alongside the commercial rationale. This brings us to the next element of our definition of mission.

Values

Values are the beliefs and moral principles that lie behind the company's culture. Values give meaning to the norms and behaviour standards in the company. [. . .]

In many organizations corporate values are not explicit and can only be understood by perceiving the philosophical rationale that lies behind management behaviour. For example, consultants in Egon Zehnder believe in co-operative behaviour because they are committed to the firm's strategy. But they also believe in co-operative behaviour because they feel that it is 'right'. Egon Zehnder people are naturally co-operative. They have been selected for that quality. They believe that people ought to be co-operative. 'It makes a nicer place to work and it suits my style', explained one consultant. 'And it's a better way to work', he added with the faintest implication of a moral judgement.

Egon Zehnder people can also be moral about certain aspects of the systematic approach. The policy of not taking on an assignment unless the consultant believes it is good for the client highlights a moral as much as a commercial rationale. Other executive search companies will take on any assignment, they argue. But Egon Zehnder puts the interests of the client first and will advise the client against an assignment even if it means lost revenues. It is a professional code of behaviour. As professionals they feel a moral duty to advise the client to do what is best for the client rather than what is best for Egon Zehnder. There is a commercial rationale for this behaviour, but the moral rationale is stronger.

[. . .]

Values can provide a rationale for behaviour that is just as strong as strategy. It is for this reason that the framework in Figure 14.1 has a diamond shape. There are two rationales that link purpose with behaviour. The commercial rationale [. . .] is about strategy and what sort of behaviour will help the company outperform competitors in its chosen arena. The emotional, moral and ethical rationale [. . .] is about values and what sort of behaviour is ethical: the right way to treat people, the right way to behave in our society.

Our definition of mission includes both these rationales linked together by a common purpose.

CREATING A STRONG MISSION

A strong mission exists when the four elements of mission reinforce each other. This is most easily perceived by looking at the links between the strategy and the value system and whether both can be acted out through the same behaviour standards. Are the important behaviour standards central to both the strategy and the value system?

In Egon Zehnder, British Airways and Hewlett-Packard they are. We looked at only one or two behaviour standards for each company, but we would find much the same reinforcement of both strategy and values if we examined other behaviour standards. Hewlett-Packard's commercial strategy depends on attracting and keeping high-quality committed employees. This means it has to demonstrate a set of values which desirable employees will find attractive. So, for example, it has an 'open door' policy that encourages dissatisfied employees to approach senior managers; a policy of high integrity and open communications with stakeholders; a belief in informality and in decentralization; a policy of promoting from within; and a commitment to teamwork. Each of these policies and behaviour standards has a rationale both in the company's strategy and in its value system. They work cumulatively to create a strong mission.

Marks and Spencer is another company where the most important behaviour standards are essential pillars of both the strategy and the value system. One of the platforms of Marks and Spencer's philosophy is good human relations. As one manager explained: 'Marcus Sieff gave many presentations both in the company and outside. But he only ever gave one speech, about good human relations.' Part of Marks and Spencer's strategy is to have employees who take more care, particularly in relation to customer service. By caring for employees, Sieff would argue, the company will create employees who will care for the company and its customers. As a result Marks and Spencer is famous for its services and support for employees, from the quality of the toilets to things like dental care. The policy of good human relations is a good standard of management behaviour referred to by one manager as 'visible management'. [. . .] Visible management requires that managers, even at the highest level, spend time visiting stores and talking to staff and customers. As one board member explained: 'In a normal week, the 12 board members will probably between them visit about 25 stores. These are not red-letter days. We will just go in and talk with some of the management, supervisors and staff. It's about getting out and listening to the organization.'

In companies like Egon Zehnder, Marks and Spencer and Hewlett-Packard, the management philosophy and value system dovetail with the strategy so that the company's policies and behaviour standards reinforce both the strategy and the philosophy. The whole has integrity. These companies have strong missions. Strong missions come, therefore, from a clear fit between the four elements in the framework.

A SENSE OF MISSION: THE EMOTIONAL BOND

A sense of mission is an emotional commitment felt by people towards the company's mission. But even in companies with very strong missions there are many people who do not feel an emotional commitment. We were told, for example, that even at the height of Hewlett-Packard's success an employee survey revealed a large minority of employees who did not have a strong belief in the capabilities of the senior management team, implying that they lacked a sense of mission.

A sense of mission occurs, we believe, when there is a match between the values of an organization and those of an individual. Because organization values are rarely explicit, the individual senses them through the company's behaviour standards. For example, if the behaviour standard is about co-operative working, the individual will be able to sense that helpfulness is valued above individual competition. If the individual has a personal value about the importance of being helpful and co-operative, then there is a values match between the individual and the organization. The greater the link between company policies and individual values, the greater the scope for the individual's sense of mission.

We see the values match (illustrated in Figure 14.2) as the most important part of a sense of mission because it is through values that individuals feel emotional about their organizations. Commitment to a company's strategy does not, on its own, constitute a sense of mission. It is not unusual for groups of managers to discuss their company's purpose and strategy and reach an intellectual agreement. However this intellectual agreement does not necessarily translate into an emotional commitment and hence the strategic plan does not get implemented. The emotional commitment comes when the individual personally identifies with the values and behaviours lying behind the plan, turning the strategy into a mission and the intellectual agreement into a sense of mission.

[. . .]

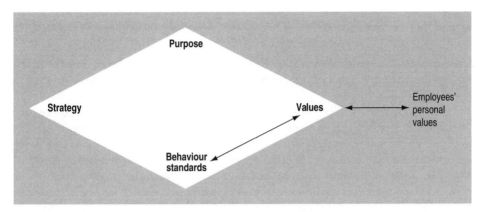

Figure 14.2 Meaning comes mainly from values

Recognizing the personal nature of a sense of mission is important because it has two implications. First, no organization can hope to have 100 per cent of its employees with a sense of mission, unless it is very small. People are too varied and have too many individual values for it to be possible for a large organization to achieve a values match for all its employees. Second, careful recruitment is essential. People's values do not change when they change companies. By recruiting people with compatible values, companies are much more likely to foster a sense of mission.

We have pointed out that even in companies with a strong mission, many people lack a sense of mission. This may be because they have few strong values and, therefore, feel very little for the company. It may also be because their values conflict with those of the company. These individuals may not be poor performers or disruptive but their motivation is more self-interested and their attitudes are likely to be more cynical. These individuals may give good service to the company but there are benefits to a company that only come through having individuals with a sense of mission.

We have defined the terms mission and sense of mission at some length and been at pains to draw a distinction between these two concepts because we believe managers are frequently confused by them.

Mission is an intellectual concept that can be analysed and discussed unemotionally. Like strategy, mission is a set of propositions that can be used to guide the policies and behaviours of a company. However, mission is a larger concept than strategy. It covers strategy and culture. The strategy element of mission legislates what is important to the commercial future of the company. The values element of mission legislates what is important to the culture of the company. When the two are in tune, reinforcing each other and bound by a common purpose, the mission is strong. When there are contradictions and inconsistencies, the mission is weak.

Sense of mission is not an intellectual concept: it is an emotional and deeply personal feeling. The individual with a sense of mission has an emotional attachment and commitment to the company, what it stands for and what it is trying to do.

A company with a clear mission does not necessarily have employees with a sense of mission. Some individuals may have a sense of mission with varying degrees of intensity. Many will not. Over time the number of employees with a sense of mission will increase as the policies of the mission become implemented and embedded in the company culture. But even a company like Hewlett-Packard, that has had a clear mission for 30 or more years, will not have more than 50 per cent of employees with what we would recognize as a sense of mission.

IMPLICATIONS OF THE MISSION MODEL

Mission thinking has implications at all levels in business as well as for those connected to business. Our greatest hope is that our research will stimulate management teams to give the subject some executive time.

First, the model states that organization values need to be compatible with employee values. This compatibility or lack of it can be analysed and measured, bringing objectivity to the discussion of culture and human resource issues. Will the member of the executive team have a values conflict with the proposed mission? Will the marketing department have a values conflict? [. . .]

Moreover, since values must be embedded in behaviour standards, values conflicts become exposed when managers or employees react to behaviour instructions. It may be hard to analyse whether the managers of the chemical laboratory believe in 'supportive management'. It is much easier to decide whether these managers are likely to implement a standard of managing by wandering around. The model's strength, therefore, is that it defines the relationship managers need to create between organization values and employee values.

Second, the model demands that strategy and values resonate and reinforce each other. It is possible to identify many values that are compatible with a particular strategy, but it is hard to analyse whether these are the right values, whether they resonate with strategy sufficiently strongly.

The mission model's emphasis on behaviour standards helps to bridge this analytical gap. By insisting that strategy and values are converted into a few behaviour standards acting as beacons of the mission, the degree of resonance between strategy and values is exposed. If it is possible to condense the mission into a few symbolically important behaviour standards, then we can be confident that the strategy and the values resonate strongly. If not, if no powerful behaviour standards can be identified, then the fault almost certainly lies in a lack of resonance between strategy and values. Further mission planning, further experimentation and further insight are needed. [. . .]

Managing mission is, therefore, a continuous, ongoing process. Few companies will be able articulate the behaviour standards that drive their mission without working at the problem over a number of years. By being clear about the need to have a mission, the need to create a relationship between strategy and values and the need to articulate behaviour standards, managers can avoid a superficial attitude to mission and continue the analysis, thinking and experimentation for long enough to develop the mission that will build a great company.

NOTES

1   Peter Drucker, *Management: tasks, responsibilities, practices*, Harper & Row, New York (1973).
2   The main academic work on the contents of mission statements has been done by Fred David and Jack Pearce (J.A. Pearce II and F.R. David, 'Corporate mission statements: the bottom line', *Academy of Management Executive*, 1 (1987); D. Cochran and F.R. David, 'The communication effectiveness of organizational mission statements', *Journal of Applied Communication Research* (1987); F.R. David, 'How companies define their mission', *Long Range Planning*, Vol. 22, No. 1 (1989).
3   Thomas J. Watson Jr. *A Business and Its Beliefs*, McGraw-Hill, New York (1963).

FURTHER READING

Campbell, A. and Towadey, K. (1990) *Mission and Business Philosophy: winning employee commitment*, Heinemann, Oxford.

Campbell, A. and Yeung, S. (1990) *Do You Need a Mission Statement?* Special Report No. 1208, The Economist Publications Management Guides, London.

15

MANAGING STRATEGIC CHANGE: STRATEGY, CULTURE AND ACTION

Gerry Johnson

One of the major problems facing senior executives is that of effect-ing significant strategic change in their organizations. This paper develops a number of explanatory frameworks which address the links between the development of strategy in organizations, dimen-sions of corporate culture and managerial action. In considering such linkages, and by illustrating them with examples from work undertaken in companies, the paper also seeks to advance our under-standing of the problems and means of managing strategic change.

A good deal has been written in the last decade about the links between organizational strategy and culture, the problems of strategic inertia in firms, and the need for managers to manage the cultural context of the organization so as to achieve strategic change and an adaptive organization to sustain the change for long term success. However much of what has been written, whilst strik-ing chords of reality for managers, is frustrating because it lacks precision in explaining links between organizational culture, strategy and managerial behaviour. This paper seeks to help rem-edy this situation. It does so by clarifying the links between the development of strategy in organ-izations and organizational culture, so as to provide quite precise frameworks and explanations by which managers can discern reasons for strategic inertia and barriers to strategic change. It goes on to consider the implications for managerial action in the process of managing strategic change. In so doing the paper builds on developing concepts and research, and also the application of tools of analysis and intervention that have been employed within companies.

EXPLAINING STRATEGY DEVELOPMENT IN ORGANIZATIONS

An incremental perspective

There are discernible patterns of strategic development in organizations. Organizations go through long periods when strategies develop incrementally; that is, decisions build one upon another, so that past decisions mould future strategy. There may occur more fundamental shifts in strategy as major readjustment of the strategic direction of the firm takes place but this is infrequent. Some writers, have argued that such incremental development in organizations is consciously and logically managed by executives as a means of coping with the complexity and uncertainty of strategy development. Managers are aware that it is not possible to 'know' about all the influences that could conceivably affect the future of the organization. They are also aware that the organization is a political entity in which trade-offs between the interests of different groups are inevitable: it is therefore not possible to arrive at an optimal goal or an optimal strategy; strategies must be compromises which allow the organization to go forward. To cope with this uncertainty and such compromise, strategies must be developed gradually so that new ideas and experiments can be tested and commitment within the organization can be achieved whilst maintaining continual, if low scale change. This is what has become known as 'logical incrementalism'.[1] It is a view of the management of strategy which is often espoused by managers themselves, although of course they may not use the same terminology.

However we need to be careful about building too much upon what managers espouse: because they espouse the idea of logical incrementalism does not necessarily mean they behave in such ways. Still less does it mean that we can confidently build guidelines about strategic management upon such views. There is no denial here that an incremental development of strategy takes place in many organizations. There are, however, other explanations as to how such patterns come about. Indeed, the whole idea of 'logical incrementalism' can be seen as a rationalization of processes which can be accounted for in quite different ways; and which shows the important links between strategy and organizational culture.

There is a good deal of difference between the rational handling of a messy organizational situation in an uncertain environmental context and the building of a strategy. The notion of strategy is to do with the long term direction of the organization and not just the response to difficulties. If some discernible patterns of strategic direction emerge in an organization then it must be because there is some guidance to that strategy. This guidance may, of course, not be explicit and conscious as is assumed in much strategic planning literature. However, strategies do not arise by pure chance. The evidence from research which has looked at the decision processes which give rise to strategic decisions and the development of strategy in organizations,[2] show that the decisions arise through the application of managerial experience as a filter of external and internal stimuli, within a politicized social setting. The 'guidance' that gives rise to strategy is, then, most likely to be to do with the taken for granted assumptions, beliefs and values that are encapsulated within the idea of managerial experience and organizational culture. The observed patterns of incremental change that occur can as readily be understood in this way.

A cultural perspective

Strategy has long been associated with logical systems of analysis and planning. However, such frameworks have been rather more based on what writers say managers *should* do rather than observations about how strategies actually come about. If managerial processes which give rise to the development of strategy are examined and understood in cultural, political and cognitive terms then it becomes clear that the strategic complexity that managers face cannot readily be analysed objectively and continually within the managerial task. Managers have a set of core beliefs and assumptions which are specific and relevant to the organization in which they work and which are learned over time. Whilst individual managers may hold quite varying sets of beliefs about many different aspects of that organizational world, there is likely to exist at some level a core set of beliefs and assumptions held relatively commonly by the managers. This has variously been called ideational culture, a mind set, an interpretative scheme, a recipe, or the term used here, a paradigm. This paradigm is essentially cultural in nature in so far as it is the 'deeper level of basic *assumptions and beliefs* that are shared by members of an organization, that operate unconsciously and define in a basic "taken for granted" fashion an organization's view of itself and its environment'.[3] It is likely to evolve over time, might embrace assumptions about the nature of the organizational environment, the managerial style in the organization, the nature of its leaders, managerial style and the operational routines seen as important to ensure the success of the organization. It may also be more easily perceived by outsiders than those inside the organization, to whom its constructs are likely to be self-evident. The paradigm is, then, a cognitive structure likely to be found to a greater or lesser extent in all firms.

It is this paradigm which, in many organizations, creates a relatively homogeneous approach to the interpretation of the complexity that the organization faces. The various and often confusing signals that the organization faces are made sense of, and are filtered, in terms of this paradigm. Moreover, since it evolves over time and is reinforced through the history and perhaps the success of the organization, it also provides a repertoire of actions and responses to the interpretations of signals, which are experienced by managers and seen by them as demonstrably relevant. It is at one and the same time, a device for interpretation and a formula for action. At its most beneficial, it encapsulates the unique or special competences and skills of that organization and therefore the bases by which the firm might expect to achieve real competitive advantage. However, it can also lead to significant strategic problems.

The paradigm as a filter

Environmental forces and organizational capabilities undoubtedly affect the performance of an organization but do not in themselves create organizational strategy: people create strategy, and one mechanism by which this occurs at the cognitive, cultural level is the paradigm. Figure 15.1 is a representation of this process. The strategies that managers advocate and those that emerge through the social and political processes previously described are typically configured within the bounds of this paradigm. Changes going on within or without the organization will affect organizational performance; however even if managers, as individuals, perceive such changes they may not necessarily acknowledge them as impinging on the strategy or performance of their organization.

The examples of this are common. Executive teams who discount competitor activity or changes in buyer behaviour as aberrations; who persist with outmoded practices or dying products, successful in the past, but now facing declining markets or competitor substitution; management teams that choose to ignore or minimize the evidence of market research, the implications of which question tried and tested ways of doing things. Any manager who has found it frustrating to use apparently objective evidence to persuade a management team of the need to change their way of thinking or their behaviour will be familiar with the problem.

The likelihood of the paradigm dominating the development of strategy and causing resistance to significant change becomes clearer when the wider cultural context in which it is embedded is considered. The paradigm is a cognitive structure or mechanism: however, this set of taken for granted assumptions and beliefs, which is more or less collectively owned, is likely to be hedged about and protected by a web of cultural artefacts. The routinized ways that members of the organization behave towards each other, and between parts of the organization; the rituals of organizational life which provide a programme for the way members respond to given situations and prescribe 'the way we do things around here'. The more formalized control systems and rewards which delineate the important areas of activity focus. The stories told which embed the present in organizational history; the type of language and expressions commonly used and

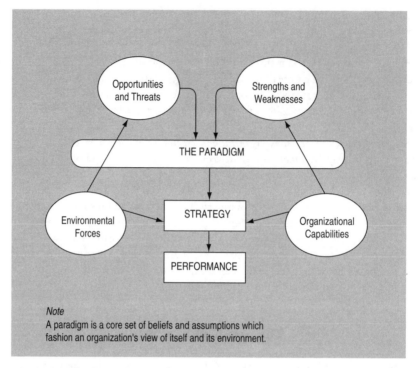

Figure 15.1 Strategy development — a cultural perspective

the organizational symbols such as logos, offices, cars and titles which become a short-hand representation of the nature of the organization. Moreover it is likely that the most powerful managerial grouping in the organization are those most closely associated with the key constructs of the paradigm. It would therefore be a mistake to conceive of the paradigm as merely a set of beliefs removed from organizational action. It lies within a cultural web which bonds it to the action of organizational life. It is therefore continually, if gradually, evolving. This notion of the paradigm and the cultural web is shown in Figure 15.2 and the company cases shown in Table 15.1.

Culture audits by managers

The cultural web itself can be used as a convenient device for a culture audit. The company cases shown in Table 15.1 are drawn up on the basis of work undertaken by managers themselves on the culture of their organizations. It is an exercise which is used frequently by the author to allow managers to 'discover' the nature of their organization in cultural terms, the way it impacts on the strategy they are following, and the difficulties of changing it.

Case A: A menswear retailer

Company A is a menswear clothing retailer. The culture audit was carried out by the managers in the mid to late 1980s. This company had a highly successful decade in the 1970s. As a menswear outfitter it had benefited from the relatively poor performance of the menswear tailors as they tried to adjust their strategies: its tried and tested down market, low price, 'reasonable

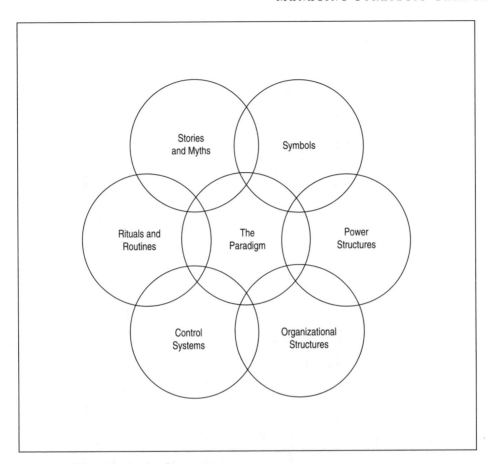

Figure 15.2 The 'cultural web' of an organization

value' merchandise offer also fitted the customer requirements of a substantial market segment at that time. However, with the revitalization of competitive retailers in the early 1980s its performance suffered badly. Attempts to shift the strategy towards a fashion offering were painfully slow in the face of a paradigm that assumed a low cost, high volume buying driven approach, heavily emphasizing sourcing from the Far East. Shops had always been seen as places to dispose of the merchandise which had been bought: there was little comprehension of marketing and the wider concepts of merchandising. Outsiders who had been brought in to effect such changes did not last for very long; and market research reports were re-interpreted to make sense in terms of the taken for granted assumptions of how to trade. Even when the managers intellectually recognized the cultural constraints under which they were labouring, the political and ritualized behaviour, controls on costs, hierarchical organization, managerial in-breeding and symbolic connections with hierarchy and the past, militated against questioning behaviour or significant changes.

Case B: A consultancy partnership

Company B is a consultancy partnership linked to an accountancy firm. Here the emphasis had always been on providing a broad general service to meet client needs in a professional manner,

Table 15.1 How managers define the cultural web – three cases

A	B	C
A menswear clothing retailer	*A consultancy partnership*	*A regional newspaper*
Paradigm	**Paradigm**	**Paradigm**
We sell to 'the working lad's market'	We are the biggest, the best, certainly the safest	We are in the newspaper business
Retailing skills (as they define them) centrally important	Client satisfaction at all costs	Our paid-for daily will always be there
Retailing is about buying: 'we sell what we buy'	Any job is worth doing – and we can do it	Readers will pay for news
Volume is vital	Professionalism is important	Advertisers need newspapers
Staff experience and loyalty important	Avoid risks	
Low cost operations (e.g. distribution channels) important	(The implication is that this consultancy is concerned to provide a very wide range of services, but is unlikely to provide services which are contentious or risky)	
A 'big-man' view of management (Note what is not here: retailing is not about shop ambience, service etc.)		
Power	**Power**	**Power**
The Chairman regarded as all powerful – 'but nicely'	Diffuse and unclear power base in a partnership structure	The parent company – a newspaper group
Divisions of power significant: the major menswear business, vs ('peripheral') businesses: head office operations vs field retail operations	However, an external power base clearly important in the parent audit firm	The autocratic CEO
Insiders with experience traditionally powerful: outsiders without company experience not powerful and do not last long		Departmental rivalry between production, commercial and editorial departments

Organization
Highly compartmentalized operations with vertical reporting relationships (e.g. buying distinct from store operations)
Every department with a Director leading to a heavy super structure
Top-down decision making with board 'fingers in every pie'
Paternalistic

Control Systems
Margin control
Long established 'proven' rigid and complex systems
Paper-based control systems

Rituals and Routines
Long established merchandise sourcing in the Far East
Induction into the company way of doing things through attrition and training: 'outsiders serve an apprenticeship until they conform'
Emphasis on pragmatic rather than analytic decisions
Lack of questioning or forcing: 'you can challenge provided I feel comfortable'
Heavy emphasis on grading systems
Promotions only within functions

Organization
The regional partnership structure of the organization giving a flat if complex matrix
Decision making through a networking system loose and flexible but based on 'who you know'

Control Systems
Emphasis on time control and utilization of consultants

Rituals and Routines
Writing and re-writing of reports – 'the product of the firm'
Partners' signatures on anything that goes to clients
Gentlemanly behaviour – particularly with clients and partners

Organization
Vertical, hierarchical system with little lateral communication and much vertical referral.
Autocratic management style

Control Systems
Emphasis on targetting and budgetting
To achieve a low cost operation

Rituals and Routines
'Slaves to time' to meet deadlines for publication
'Product' developed in hours and minutes, not days and months
Long working hours common
Ritualized executive meetings at senior level

Continued

Table 15.1 How managers define the cultural web – three cases—*Continued*

A	B	C
A menswear clothing retailer	*A consultancy partnership*	*A regional newspaper*
Stories	*Stories*	*Stories*
Big buying deals of the past	Big fee assignments	Macho personalities and behaviour
Paternalistic leaders (usually chairman) of the past	Big disasters and failures	Scoops and coverage of major events
	Stories of the dominance of the audit practice	Stories of the past
More recent 'villainous' leaders who helped cause problems	Mavericks who would not follow the systems	Major errors in print
'The Mafia' who excluded outsiders and achieved their exit		The defeat of the unions
Symbols	*Symbols*	*Symbols*
The separate Executive Directors' corridor	The partnership structure itself	Symbols of hierarchy: the MD's Jaguar; portable phones, car-parking spaces etc.
Use of initials to designate Senior Executives and 'Sir' for the Chairman	The symbols of partnership – the tea service, the office size, partners' secretaries', partners' dining rooms	The 'press'
The dining room for Directors and selected Senior Executives – but against what criteria?	One regional partnership that had always refused to integrate with other partnerships	Technical production jargon
Named and numbered car parking spaces rigidly adhered to		The street vendors

under the close scrutiny of partners. The result was a service to customers which was reliable but avoided risk; and a belief within the firm that it could turn its hand to anything. Since the 'product' was seen by many as the report at the end of the assignment, close supervision of the assignment and especially report writing was seen as essential, and was mirrored by close attention to monitoring consultancy activities, as a way of ensuring professional service, the utilization of consultants' time and the control of costs. This was supported by a super-structure of partners, many of whom were chartered accountants, whose role was not always very clear but who jealously guarded a fragmented and informal organization structure, and cultural trappings, preserving of their influence, autonomy and power. By the late 1980s, new senior partners believed that the consultancy lacked focus in the face of more targetted competitors, but it was an organization with any number of ways to frustrate the change agent.

Case C: A regional newspaper

Company C is a regional newspaper business operating in a market in which it had enjoyed long-standing dominance with its local evening newspaper. It now faced increasing competitor pressure from free newspapers and entry by competitors historically based elsewhere. Moreover a changing local population meant less traditional loyalty to the newspaper: and longer term developments of media alternatives for the public raised both strategic opportunities and possible threats. The need was for a substantial short term re-think of competitive strategy and longer term re-think of the direction of the business. Yet the culture audit undertaken by the managers revealed a taken for granted view that their paid for daily newspaper 'would always be around', and that the local community somehow needed them. Moreover the technology, structure and routines of the business did little to promote strategic thinking: the business was necessarily run on short term deadlines – hours, not days, – the 'macho' self-image of those running the business, and the vertical, hierarchical ways of doing business, prevented a free flow of ideas across management boundaries. Suggestions by some younger managers that the prime purpose of the business was to create an effective advertising medium (the main source of revenue) were set aside given the dominant belief that 'we are a *newspaper*'; a view reinforced by the symbolic significance of the presses, the associated technical jargon, street distribution system and the stories linked to news gathering and coverage.

PROBLEMS OF STRATEGIC CHANGE

If we view the process of strategic management in such ways, the phenomenon of incremental strategic development in organizations is also explained rather differently. Rather than being a logical testing out of strategies in action, *strategic management can be seen as an organizational response over time to a business environment which is essentially internally constructed rather than objectively understood.* The idea that external events have a self-evident reality is clearly not so for us as individuals: two spectators from opposing sides watching a sports event will interpret reasons for success and failure quite differently and quite partially. We should not expect it to be very different for groups of managers.

Resistance to change

This explanation of resistance to change also helps us understand how strategies come about in organizations. Faced with pressures for change, managers are likely to deal with the situation in ways which are in line with the paradigm and the cultural, social and political norms of organizational life.

This raises difficulties when managing strategic change for it may be that the action required is outside the scope of the paradigm and the constraints of the cultural web – that members of the organization would be required to change substantially their core beliefs or 'the way we do things around here'. Desirable as this may be, the evidence is that this does not occur easily. Managers are much more likely to attempt to deal with the situation by searching for what they can understand and cope with in terms of the existing paradigm. In other words, they will attempt to minimize the extent to which they are faced with ambiguity and uncertainty by looking for that which is familiar. Faced with a stimulus for action, for example declining performance, managers first seek for means of improving the implementation of existing strategy, perhaps through the tightening of controls. In effect, they will tighten up their accepted way of operating. If this is not effective, then a change of strategy may occur, but a change which is in line with the existing paradigm.

For example in the menswear clothing example (case A) the early attempts to the company to be 'more fashionable' took the form of trying to copy fashionable merchandise from UK boutiques, have it cheapened in the Far East and distributed through their low cost distribution channels in order to sell it below competitive prices. It was a merchandise and buying driven response, rather than anything to do with the expectations of customers; nor did it address the ambience of stores, the service of the staff, the behaviour of managers in Head Office, or indeed the fundamental quality of the product range. The evidence is that strategic management is, in the main, the predominant application of the familiar and that a fundamental change to the paradigm is unlikely until the attempt to reconstruct strategy in the image of the existing paradigm is demonstrably unsuccessful.

It is difficult to change aspects of the paradigm unless such changes are evolutionary. Challenges to the legitimacy of constructs within that paradigm are not only likely to be disturbing because they attack those beliefs which are central to managerial life, they will also be interpreted as threatening by political elites in the organization whose roles are likely to be closely associated with the constructs of the paradigm. Those who believe that an objective, analytical assessment of, for example, a changing environment can yield knowledge which managers should interpret intellectually and objectively, and assimilate in such a way as to change strategy, neglect the understanding that such analysis may well achieve a political rather than intellectual response and might well lead to heavy resistance. For example the change agent who attempted to introduce a revised strategy in the consultancy firm (B) was faced with resistance from some of the most senior and powerful partners trying to preserve the potential threats to partnership structure and the professional nature of the consultancy.

Strategic drift

In these circumstances it is likely that, over time, the phenomenon of 'strategic drift'[4] will occur: that is gradually, perhaps imperceptibly, the strategy of the organization will become less and less in line with the environment in which the organization operates. This may be a process which takes very many years may not be discerned by the managers until the drift becomes so marked that performance decline results. It is then that more fundamental changes in strategy are likely to occur. The reasons for this drift arise out of the explanations given above. Managers are likely to discount evidence contrary to the paradigm but readily absorb that which is in line with the paradigm. Change which is within the paradigm is therefore likely to be more comfortable. Moreover, radical challenges to the paradigm are likely to give rise to political resistance and reaction which further embeds the organization in its existing strategy: and since the organization is likely to be making changes of an incremental nature anyway, managers can point to the extent that change is occurring.

The outcome of processes of decision making of this kind is not likely to be the careful, logical, adaptive strategy making which keeps in line with environmental change. Rather it is likely to be an adaptation in line with the perceived management wisdom as enshrined in the paradigm. Nonetheless the forces in the environment will have an effect on performance. Over time this may well give rise to the sort of drift shown in Figure 15.3 (Mode 1) in which the organization's strategy gradually, if imperceptively, moves away from the environmental forces at work. This pattern of drift is made more difficult to detect and reverse because not only are changes being made in strategy – albeit within the parameters of the paradigm – but, since such changes are the application of the familiar, they may achieve some short term improvement in performance, thus tending to legitimize the action taken. As this drift becomes recognized the strategy of the organization is likely to enter a period of flux (Figure 15.3, Mode 2) in which there is no clear direction and a good deal of disquiet and counter-argument about the strategic direction of the organization. This will be likely to affect performance negatively and, perhaps, be followed by a more radical change in strategy (Figure 15.3, Mode 3).[5]

IMPLICATIONS FOR MANAGING STRATEGIC CHANGE

The main aim of discussing these links between the development of strategy, organizational culture and the social, political and symbolic behaviour of managers has been to provide explanations of the reasons for the pattern of strategic development observed in organizations, and in particular the strategic inertia and problems of managing strategic change experienced by managers. However, the explanations do help in providing some guide-lines in the management of strategic change.

Traditional planning approaches

Views on strategic management espoused by managers tend to be rooted in traditional planning models of strategy. Strategic change may be seen as equivalent to the planning of strategy implementation. Managing strategic change becomes a matter of planning how the systems and structures of the organization can be employed to achieve behaviour in line with the logic of the strategy.

The rationale for this view is clear enough, if dubious. If managers are clear about the aims and objectives of the business in the long term, and they have carried out an analysis of the factors affecting the strategy of the business, then they can make logical choices from strategic options. If the resulting decision on strategy is logical, then it is capable of being planned in detail and systematized in terms of implementation: and because it is logical and planned, it will work. The problem with this notion of planned change is that it neglects many of the processes that we have seen to be central in actual processes of strategy formulation and change: namely the socio-cultural and symbolic processes which preserve current ways of doing things; the cognitive bounds of those who take and influence decisions; and the importance of political processes, including the potential of analysis to be politically threatening. There is nothing wrong with analytic, planning approaches as *thinking* devices for strategic management: they do not, however, address the *process* of managing strategic choice or strategic change. Issues relating to the planning of strategic change need to take account of the socio-political and cultural realities of management described in this article. They also need to recognize that, certainly when it comes to major strategic change, paradigm shifts are likely to be important, and they are obviously the most difficult of all to achieve.

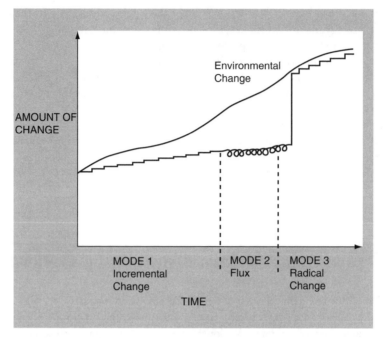

Figure 15.3 Patterns of strategic development – drift, flux and radical change

For such planning systems to be useful, there already needs to exist a climate capable of embracing and promoting strategic change: and the developments of this by managers needs to be understood and managed in ways which address the cultural constraints on strategy discussed earlier.

Managing strategic change

This article has not set out to deal primarily with mechanisms of strategic change. However, there are some guidelines on such mechanisms that are informed by the frameworks which have been discussed.

If strategy development in organizations is driven by the taken for granted assumptions that have been called the paradigm, and the aspects of organizational culture that surround and protect it, the first implication is the importance of surfacing that which is taken for granted. One way in which this might be facilitated is to undertake the sort of culture audit described above, which helps to make explicit that which is taken for granted, and to generate managerial debate about the cultural barriers to change that exist. These might be political in nature, to do with the organizational or control systems in the organization; or they may be more symbolic in nature, manifested in the stories or symbols of tradition and history that exist, or in the everyday routines that people take for granted. The important point is that such aspects of culture cannot be challenged or changed unless they are explicit and they will not necessarily become explicit through the debates on strategy that may take place within the planning agenda.

Creating a climate for change

Even where a clear direction of strategy has been established, the likelihood of achieving fundamental strategic change is low unless the climate for change exists. The acceptance of such change is likely to depend either on a widely accepted perceived need for it, or a significant trigger for change such as crisis or major threat. Such threat may typically result from a major downturn in performance, perhaps resulting from the sort of strategic drift discussed in this paper, or from major competitive moves in the market place. There is however, evidence that some chief executives 'fabricate' or 'enhance' organizational stimuli to create a climate suited to more fundamental questioning of that which is taken for granted. This may include inflating internal negative performance indicators or external threats; setting up internal devices for challenging the status quo; or visibly signalling the need for change by political manoeuvres. Such activity may take on both political and symbolic significance; for example by the removal of the 'old guard', or the visible passing over of ideas from traditional power elites; and the encouragement of 'young turks' in the organization, or the adoption of recommendations of those advocating more substantial change.

Such political activity is common but, in isolation, can be counter-productive unless members of the organization see the opportunity to contribute to organizational revitalization. Yet in many organizations hierarchical structures, autocratic leadership or unwritten rules about deference and delicacy in questioning may militate against such opportunities. Although there has been a good deal of advocacy of the need for more open 'organic management systems' to replace traditional hierarchies where change is required, senior management may still not understand the responsibility they hold as role models and builders of structures which encourage challenge and questioning.

Interventions by outsiders

Fundamental strategic change may also be associated with the intervention of 'outsiders'. By outsiders is meant those who either physically come from outside the organization, for example as a new chief executive, or those who are not, by origin or inclination, part of the mainstream culture. Such individuals bring different perspectives to the organizations, perhaps rooted in the paradigm of their previous organizational experience; they see the context of the organization afresh; and are less linked to the political systems and traditions of the organization. Yet the value of outsiders as agents of questioning and change is often overlooked in firms: non-executive directors are too infrequently encouraged to question the taken-for-granted; consultants may feel their recommendations have to be within the current paradigm in order to stand any chance of being implemented; and boards, whilst ready to condone, even encourage, strategic management development for middle or senior executives, often argue that they personally are too busy to step outside the task of running the business.

Providing signals and symbols

Managing change is often conceived by executives as control systems and structural changes; however these are typically thought of as means of monitoring change rather than signalling change. In fact they should be seen as both. For example a change in emphasis from control of costs to a emphasis on monitoring effective customer service, is not simply a means of monitoring the progress of a changed strategy, it is also a major signal of a change in corporate culture. The example can be taken further. Too few executives conceive of strategic change in terms of the symbols and routines which underpin organizational life. The executive who is planning change needs to ensure that the routines of the organization are changed in ways which affect the everyday behaviour of those in the organization. For example in the menswear retailer described earlier, it was not written plans or the words of managers that had the most significant effect on staff; it was when staff were, for example, required to wear clothes sold in the shops in which they worked that the changes became meaningful to them. As one executive put it, it was then 'they began to wear the new strategy' that had been developed.

Symbols of change are important for they signal change at the level of mundane reality for those operating in the organization. There are countless examples from changes in company logos, the expensive withdrawal from the market of old stocks, the closure of privileged dining facilities for executives, or factories associated with the traditions of a business, to changes in language and terminology employed in a firm, or changes to informal forms of address, or clothing by senior executives, to dramatic signalling of change such as the smashing of old equipment associated with the past of a business in front of the workforce.

CONCLUSIONS

This article provides a framework for the consideration of strategic management in terms of the social and cultural processes in organizations: it has proposed explanations for the strategic inertia that exists in organizations and the consequent strategic drift that can occur; and also proposed ways to consider the sorts of managerial change processes in cultural terms that can help achieve strategic change in organizations.

The core of the argument is that it is the social, political, cultural and cognitive dimensions of managerial activities which both give rise to the sort of incremental strategic change typical in organizations: but which can also be employed to galvanize more fundamental strategic change. These aspects of management are employed by managers in their everyday working lives: managers behave in ways which are political and symbolic: such approaches provide familiar, if not explicit, tools of management. Managers also recognize the powerful influence of cultural and political systems. What they lack is an explicit framework to make sense of the links between strategy, culture and managerial processes of strategic change. This paper has set out to provide this framework and thus of better considering problems and means of strategic change in such terms.

REFERENCES

(1) J. B. Quinn, *Strategies for Change: Logical Incrementalism*, Irwin (1980).

(2) P. H. Grinyer and J.-C. Spender, *Turnaround: Managerial Recipes for Strategic Success: The Fall and Rise of the Newton Chambers Group*, Associated Business Press (1979); A. M. Pettigrew, *The Awakening Giant*, Basil Blackwell (1985); G. Johnson, *Strategic Change and the Management Process*, Basil Blackwell (1987).

(3) E. H. Schein, *Organizational Culture and Leadership*, p. 6, Jossey-Bass (1986).

(4) G. Johnson, Re-thinking incrementalism, *Strategic Management Journal*, 9, 75–91 (1988).

(5) H. Mintzberg, Patterns in strategy formation, *Management Science*, pp. 934–48, May (1978).

FURTHER READING

For readers who wish to follow up the links between the processual issues raised in this paper and other concepts and techniques of strategic management, see *Exploring Corporate Strategy* by Gerry Johnson and Kevan Scholes (2nd edition), Prentice Hall (1988).

16

STRATEGIC PRODUCT CREATION: MANAGING NEW INTERACTIONS OF TECHNOLOGY, MARKETS, AND ORGANIZATIONS

Ron Sanchez

Product competition in a growing number of markets is undergoing a profound transformation. Some firms are now beginning to use new kinds of 'flexible designs' for products and organizations to pursue innovative product strategies that generate unprecedented levels of product variety and change. This article explores the ongoing changes in strategies for designing products and for organizing development processes that are driving this transformation of product competition.

Different kinds of competitive conditions require different kinds of strategies. Basic strategy concepts and derived product strategies are compared for stable, evolving, and dynamic product markets. Concepts of *modularity in products and organizations* are argued to be the core concepts driving the new kinds of product strategies now emerging in dynamic product markets. Modular product design is distinguished from traditional approaches to designing products, and the potential competitive advantages to be derived from modular product design strategies are elaborated.

Modularity in product designs allows the *decoupling* of processes for developing new products, enabling those processes to become concurrent, autonomous, and distributed and making possible the adoption of modular organization designs for product development. The 'quick-connect' electronic interfaces of shared CAD/CIM systems may allow firms to create electronically mediated product development networks that further enhance the flexibility of modular product creation processes.

Modularity in products and organizations requires new concepts for *strategically managing knowledge*. Creating modular product architectures requires an intentional and disciplined decoupling of technology development and product development. As a consequence, modular product design leads to better understanding of the state of a firm's current knowledge and makes possible more effective strategic management of new technology development. A hierarchy of organizational knowledge that distinguishes *know-how, know-why*, and *know-what* forms of knowledge is presented as a basis for developing new strategies for leveraging and controlling knowledge in product creation networks.

This article concludes by arguing that success – and perhaps even survival – in product competition will increasingly depend on more effective strategic management of product, organization, and knowledge architectures.

INTRODUCTION

It is by now 'old news' that product markets around the globe are undergoing sweeping technological transformations. During the last two decades, rapidly developing technologies have launched major global industries based on new product concepts and innovative manufacturing processes. More recently, however, there is evidence that major technological transformations now underway are taking on a new character – one that is inducing new patterns of competition in a growing number of product markets, both new and old. While many firms remain focused on applying new technologies in new products or manufacturing processes, strategic managers in some firms are discovering ways to use new technologies to create innovative linkages with other firms and with product markets. The competitive successes of these firms suggest that significant competitive advantages may now be created by developing new kinds of competences in managing flows of knowledge and information between firms and markets. In dynamic product markets where technologies and market preferences are changing rapidly, these new competences in managing flows of knowledge and information appear to have eclipsed more traditional management skills in managing flows of funds and goods as primary sources of competitive advantage. This article investigates these new competences and the ways they are being used to initiate and drive new interactions of technology, markets, and organizations in product creation processes.

The emergence of global product markets, furthermore, is increasing the potential rewards that can flow to firms with superior competences in broadly and quickly leveraging knowledge and capabilities to create new products. As customers about the globe become more sophisticated in their preferences for products, some firms are using superior abilities in creating new products to segment markets more aggressively by offering greater numbers of differentiated and improved products. In product markets as diverse as personal computers, financial services, sports and recreation equipment, college textbooks, consumer electronics, and clothing, firms with new competences in leveraging knowledge and coordinating development processes are adopting strategies of creating greater product variety and more frequently upgraded products to serve more effectively the diverse and evolving preferences of global product markets.

Firms that develop these new competences in managing product creation processes are transforming the nature of product competition in their markets, causing increasingly dynamic market conditions that are bringing traditional models for organizing and managing firms under great stress. In the most dynamic product markets, the traditional model of the firm as a standalone enterprise is now being abandoned in favor of new forms of 'virtual' or 'modular' organizations for creating and marketing products. As more firms begin to discover new ways to access and use the capabilities, knowledge, and information of many other firms in product competition, the field of strategic management itself is undergoing a veritable 'paradigm shift'. Traditional strategy concepts based on commitment to and control of production and distribution assets for serving specific market needs, for example, are becoming increasingly incongruous in product markets where changes in technologies and market preferences are accelerating. Some strategists in industry and academia are now advancing alternative strategy concepts that emphasize new competences for flexibly coordinating networks of firms in continuous processes for creating new products and, indeed, new kinds of product markets (Hamel and Heene 1994; Prahalad and Hamel 1995; Sanchez 1993, 1995a; Sanchez, *et al.*, 1996).

This article extends this initiative to reconsider the premises, objectives, and methods of strategic management in dynamic product markets. It examines new forms of product creation processes that have become drivers of the new kinds of product strategies observable in dynamic product markets. These dynamic product strategies have resulted from the insights of some managers into new ways in which technologies, markets, and organizations are now capable of interacting in product creation processes. These insights center on two key notions:

- First, *modular product architectures* create information structures that allow key product development processes to be carried out concurrently and autonomously, thereby making possible dispersed development processes that are largely self-managing. Modular product design is thus a critical new competence that enables firms to accelerate product creation processes and to access and manage an expanded network of *'modular' development organizations*.
- Second, creating modular product and organization designs requires new approaches to managing processes for creating and leveraging knowledge. Recognition of differences in the strategic values of a firm's *know-how, know-why,* and *know-what* forms of knowledge must guide the development of strategies for leveraging and controlling a firm's knowledge in product creation networks.

This discussion is developed in the following way. The underlying dynamics of technologies and market needs largely determine the nature of competition in a product market and thus the kinds of strategies that are likely to be effective at both the firm and product level. The opening discussion therefore assesses the distinctive strategic management concepts and product strategies associated with three competitive contexts characterized as stable, evolving, and dynamic product markets.

At the core of emerging product strategies for dynamic markets are concepts of modularity in products and organizations. Modular product design differs in certain fundamental respects from conventional approaches to designing products. Those differences are explained, and new forms of product creation flexibility which can be derived from strategic uses of modular product designs are identified and illustrated with examples. The use of modular product architectures as the driver of product strategies can lead to basic changes in the ways a firm directs new technology development and researches new product opportunities. Modular product architectures become, in effect, vehicles for new approaches to integrating technology strategy and marketing strategy.

Next, concepts of modularity for designing organizations are examined. Modular product architectures allow the decoupling of individual component development processes, allowing those processes to become concurrent, autonomous, and distributed – in short, modular. Thus, modularity in product designs is essential to achieving the strategic flexibility of modular organization designs. Creating electronic interfaces of shared CAD/CIM systems allows firms to 'quick-connect' with other firms in an electronically mediated product development network that can further enhance the flexibility of modular product creation organizations.

Competing with modular products and organizations also requires new concepts for strategically managing knowledge in product creation processes, which are discussed below. The knowledge structures within a firm will largely reflect the architectures of its product designs. Creating modular product architectures requires an intentional and disciplined decoupling of technology development and product development. As a consequence of this intentional decoupling, modular design leads to better identification of the state of a firm's knowledge about its product technologies and makes possible more precise and coherent management of technology development. Effectively leveraging a firm's knowledge assets and those of other organizations also requires new concepts for distinguishing and managing different kinds of knowledge. A hierarchy of knowledge that distinguishes know-how, know-why, and know-what forms of knowledge is presented as a basis for new strategies for leveraging and controlling knowledge in product creation networks.

As product markets become more dynamic, the key tasks of strategic managers begin to change fundamentally. This article concludes by arguing that success – and perhaps even survival – in dynamic product markets depend on much greater strategic management attention to creating strategic flexibilities in a firm's product, organization, and knowledge architectures.

CHANGING COMPETITIVE CONTEXTS, STRATEGY CONCEPTS, AND PRODUCT STRATEGIES

Product markets differ fundamentally in the extent to which applicable technologies and customer preferences are subject to change. The stability or instabilities of technologies and customer preferences in a product market determine the strategy concepts, product strategies, and product creation processes that are likely to be workable or effective in that competitive context. Although product markets usually defy simple classifications, it is nonetheless useful to consider how product markets with stable, evolving, or dynamic technologies and market preferences may give rise to intrinsically different strategy concepts and approaches to product competition. Table 16.1 suggests how these different competitive contexts in product markets may give rise to distinct strategy concepts, product strategies, and product creation processes.

Stable product markets

In product markets with stable technologies and market preferences, strategic management concepts are likely to reflect the emphasis of industrial organization economics on irreversible commitments to specific-use assets, control of production processes, hierarchical (vertical) integration to achieve control of production processes, and defense of established market position. Because neither market preferences for products nor technologies for creating products change significantly, product strategies focus on increasing market share by reducing costs for producing standard products and by extending control of distribution channels. Product differentiation, if attempted at all, is likely to be limited largely to non-product dimensions of the product offering, like service, warranties, and advertising. Product creation is at most episodic, and when it occurs it is likely to follow a sequential path through the functional divisions that serve the core production and distribution processes of the firm. Vendors of components and production equipment are the principal sources of innovations in products and processes.

Evolving product markets

A product market may shift to an evolving mode when either available technologies or market preferences begin to change. Although technological change can either be reflected in new

Table 16.1 Relationships between product market contexts, strategy concepts and product strategies

	Product Market Contexts		
	Stable	**Evolving**	**Dynamic**
Central Strategy Concepts	• Strategic commitment • Ownership of production assets • Hierarchical integration • Direct control of processes • Defense of market position	• Strategic change • Accumulation of resources • Partnering and alliances • Teams, process re-engineering • Create sustainable competitive advantage	• Strategic flexibility • Fixed-asset parsimony, leveraging of intellectual assets • Firm acts as 'network actuator' in development resource network • Coordination through modular product architectures • Flexible responses to changing market opportunities
Product Strategy Emphases	• Increasing market share • Increasing scale to lower costs • Low-cost production of standard products • Control of distribution channels • Infrequent redesign of standard products to lower costs	• Timing new product introductions • Timing technology transitions • Development of new product attributes and mix to suit new market demands • Distribution channel re-design • Conventional marketing research	• Speed to market • Rapid performance upgrading through improved components • Proliferation of product variety, high model turnover • Flexible distribution networks • Real-time market research
Product Creation Processes	• Vendors supply improved components, process equipment • Sequential, functional development	• Close collaboration with suppliers in development project teams • Team-based, 'over-lapping' development processes	• Multiple short-term collaborations on electronically mediated projects • Concurrent, autonomous, distributed development process

products or improved production processes, significant market change can also be driven by the evolving preferences of customers who become increasingly sophisticated in their knowledge about and use of products. As evolving technologies or market preferences induce changes in market conditions, strategy concepts focus on strategic adaptation to change, on accumulating new resources (perhaps developed through strategic alliances) useful in meeting the new competitive conditions, and on 're-engineering' business processes to adjust to new technological and market conditions. The objective of this strategic change process is to acquire the new set of capabilities needed to achieve 'sustainable competitive advantage' in the new competitive context.

Although cost advantages remain important, perceived sources of sustainable competitive advantage are likely to include capabilities that help firms differentiate products by features and performance. Product strategies become driven by forecasting changes in technologies and market preferences. Considerable emphasis will be placed on timing the adoption of new technologies and the introduction of new products that would make obsolete or 'cannibalize' current products. Product development will try to create the new product attributes and the mix of new products thought to be optimal for the new market conditions, and distribution channels may be redesigned to better match changes in product offerings.

Product creation processes become driven by marketing research into evolving customer preferences for new products. To acquire new capabilities in product or process technologies or new market knowledge, the firm may enter into long-term collaborations with other firms that have complementary capabilities in product development, manufacturing, distribution, or marketing. Increased pressure for faster development of new products that incorporate new technology or serve new customer preferences leads to adoption of multifunctional teams using over-lapping problem-solving methods for shortening and improving development processes (Clark and Fujimoto, 1991).

Dynamic product markets

Dynamic product markets result when high rates of technological change make possible accelerated evolutions of product concepts, manufacturing process capabilities, and technologies for coordinating product creation processes. In addition, as customers become more sophisticated in their abilities to identify and select products that better serve their particular needs, customer preferences become much more varied and demanding. The rising number and sophistication of customers create a positive market response to firms that offer greater product variety and more frequent introductions of better performing product models.

As firms search for ways to exploit rapid changes in technologies and market preferences, strategy concepts center on notions of *strategic flexibility* – the ability to respond advantageously and quickly to continuous change in competitive conditions. To cope with high rates of change in competitive conditions, the objective of 'managing strategic change' – that is, a transition of the firm from one technology and market context to another, as in evolving markets – is no longer adequate. Because the technological and market environment is in a high state of flux, the focus of strategic management must shift to a 'higher-order' process of redesigning the firm as a system for rapidly reconfiguring and redeploying a changing array of assets and capabilities, some of which will be within the firm, but many of which will reside in other firms (Sanchez 1993, 1994a; Sanchez and Heene 1996).

In the face of significant uncertainty about where technologies and market preferences are headed in the long term, accumulating strategic resources that will be sources of 'sustainable' competitive advantage becomes problematic, because the specific resources that will have strategic value in the future cannot be determined with precision. The resulting high risk of investing in specific-use assets leads firms to adopt a regime of fixed-asset parsimony. Instead of acquiring specific-use – and therefore *inflexible* – assets, strategic investments are increasingly channeled into building flexible intellectual assets like human capabilities and knowledge that can be leveraged in a variety of ways as market conditions change. Since no firm can identify or internalize all the intellectual and other assets that may be needed to compete effectively in the future, firms begin to develop ways of connecting with large numbers of other firms whose various capabilities may prove useful in the future. In essence, firms begin to network with other firms to improve their abilities to assemble a changing array of resource chains for creating and delivering future new products which cannot presently be defined with precision.

These tasks that strategic managers must perform in dynamic product markets represent a fundamental shift from the strategy concepts associated with evolving markets. While the concepts of strategy in evolving product markets are essentially focused on predicting and planning for market change, the extent and frequency of change in dynamic product markets are likely to defy precise prediction and planning for specific transitions. Instead, dynamic markets invite a shift in the focus of strategic management to creating new kinds of managerial and organizational competences that bring greater flexibilities to respond broadly and quickly to a range of changes in the future (Sanchez 1995a; Sanchez, *et al.*, 1996). This basic shift in the concept of strategic management is accompanied by corresponding shifts in product strategies and in processes for creating new products. Driving the new product strategies and creation processes in dynamic markets are concepts of modularity in the design of products and organizations. The next sections explore the emerging strategic use of *modularity* in product and organization designs as a new competence for achieving new levels of strategic flexibility in product competition.

Modularity in Product Designs

Most products – a great variety of assembled goods, software, and many forms of financial and service products – consist of several functions that, when combined together, provide the set of functionalities that distinguish one product from another in the eyes of customers. After defining the overall functionality desired from a new product, designers create a new product design by decomposing the overall product functionality into a set of interrelated functional components. Decomposing a product design into functional components and specifying the interfaces that define the functional relationships between those components creates a *product architecture* (Henderson and Clark 1990; Sanchez 1995a). Component interface specifications define, for example, how one component may be physically connected to another (the attachment interface), how power is to be transferred between components (the transfer interface), how signals will be exchanged between components (control and communication interfaces), the spatial location and volume a component may occupy (spatial interfaces), and various ways in which the functioning of one component may generate heat, magnetic fields, or other environmental effects that must be accommodated by other components (environmental interfaces) (Sanchez 1994b).

There are two quite different approaches to defining component interfaces in a product design, however, and the two approaches lead to fundamentally different kinds of product architectures. A modular product architecture is a relatively new – but strategically important – kind of product design that differs from 'conventional' product architectures still used in many product designs. Understanding the concept of modularity in product architecture – and its potential strategic uses in product competition – is essential to understanding the motivation behind the radical transformations of product designs and product strategies now underway in a growing number of product markets.

Conventional versus modular product design

The distinctive nature of modular product design can perhaps best be explained by contrast with the objectives and methods of conventional approaches to product design. Table 16.2 summarizes the key differences between conventional and modular approaches to defining, designing, and developing new products.

A conventional product design process typically begins with extensive marketing research that tries to determine the specific characteristics of a product that will appeal most broadly to some identified set of customers. Various statistical techniques are used in marketing research to identify the cost and performance attributes of an 'optimal' product (for a survey, see Mahajan and Wind, 1991). Once these attributes have been estimated through marketing research, the objective of product designers is to create an optimal product design that provides the desired performance attributes at the lowest possible cost or the highest possible level of performance for a given cost constraint. To do this, product designers must decide how to translate the desired set of product attributes into a product design consisting of functional components. Designing these interrelated components is a recursive process that consumes the major part of product development time. The *outcome* of a conventional, optimizing product design process is a complex product architecture that typically includes assemblies of components that have been integrated to improve performance or lower cost. Both during and after development, however, changing component designs to effect a change in the overall product design is likely to be time-consuming and costly, because changing one component design may require compensating changes in the designs of many interrelated components.

Table 16.2 Differences in product definition, design, and development in conventional versus modular product design

	Definition	*Design*	*Development*
Conventional Product Design	Attributes of 'optimal' product are determined by marketing research.	Product functionality is decomposed into components, but component interfaces are determined during component development processes.	Component designs and product architecture co-evolve in a reiterative process. Product architecture is defined in the final design for the product – i.e., as the output of the development process.
Modular Product Design	Product is conceived as a platform for leveraging product variations and improved models to serve a range of market preferences.	Modular product architecture fully specifies component interfaces at beginning of development and constrains component development.	Modular product architecture allows component development processes to be concurrent, autonomous, and distributed. Product architecture defined at outset does not change during development.

In contrast to the high degree of interdependence among component designs typical of an optimized product architecture, modular product design follows a design regime that explicitly minimizes interdependencies among component designs in a product design. Modular design accomplishes this by specifying interfaces between components to allow for *a range of variations in component designs*. Further, rather than developing a specific product architecture that represents an optimal design for a specific set of product attributes, a modular product architecture is intentionally defined *at the beginning* of a development process to allow for the substitution of different versions of components (Garud and Kumaraswamy, 1993) for the purpose of creating product variations with different bundles of functionalities, features, and performance levels. In effect, a modular product architecture creates a flexible 'platform design' for leveraging variations on a basic product design. This designed-in flexibility of a modular product architecture has several strategically important uses.

Strategic uses of modular product architectures

A modular product architecture permits changes in components that are within the range of variations allowed by its specified component interfaces. The ability to 'mix-and-match' components enables leveraging of greater product variety, speeds the introduction of improved products, *and* lowers overall design, production, and other product costs.

Greater product variety

Figure 16.1 illustrates how creating modular product architecture can permit the leveraging of a great number of product variations by mixing and matching different combinations of functional components. A modular product architecture that works in this way is the familiar desktop computer, which can be configured in a great number of variations by substituting micro-processors of different speeds, hard disk drives and memories of different capacities, and

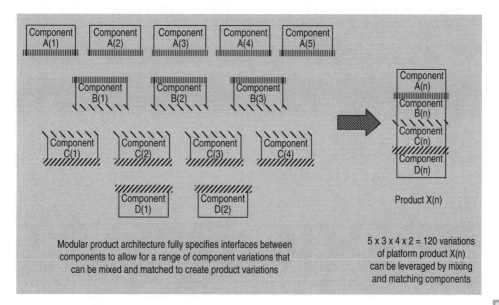

Modular product architecture fully specifies interfaces between components to allow for a range of component variations that can be mixed and matched to create product variations

5 x 3 x 4 x 2 = 120 variations of platform product X(n) can be leveraged by mixing and matching components

Figure 16.1 Modular product architecture allows leveraging of product variations

connections to a variety of monitors, printers, modems, and other devices. Of course, some of the possible combinations of components may not be very appealing or practical (for example, combining a fast microprocessor with a small memory), but among the many possible combinations are likely to be a number of component combinations that are viable product variations.

Although the use of modular product architecture to leverage many product variations from mixed-and-matched components is perhaps most readily recognizable in personal computers, further investigation shows that modular product architectures are now coming into use in a growing number of diverse product markets, as the following examples suggest:

- Automobile makers define product architectures for car models, using 'hard points' that define the interface between the car body and its mechanical components, as well as interfaces between the major mechanical components themselves. Several product model variations are then leveraged by mixing and matching body styles and major mechanical components. General Motors, for example, has established a modular product architecture for all its global automobile design projects. Future GM products must be designed using combinations of components from about 70 different body modules (hard point arrangements) and about 100 major mechanical components like engines, power trains, and suspensions (Kacher, 1994). Modular design is also being applied to major components of automobiles as well. Ford now designs families of modular engines in which different parts can be used in different combinations to give engines of different displacements, different numbers of cylinders, single or twin overhead cams, and other variations.
- Japanese consumer electronics companies often base entire product lines of stereo receivers, CD players, televisions, and other products on different mix-and-match combinations of components in a modular platform design. Sony, for example, leveraged more than 160 Walkman models for the US market in the 1980s from five modular platform designs (Sanderson and Uzumeri, 1990).
- General Electric's appliance unit creates several models of dishwashers and stoves that are differentiated primarily by offering different combinations of key components. Dishwashers are distinguished primarily by the controls contained in door panel modules, and kitchen stoves are distinguished by different cooktop modules and control panels.
- Object-oriented programming is a modular design process for software that creates applications software composed of modules of routines and data that can be mixed and matched to create new program variations to suit the needs of different users.
- The electronic funds transfer (EFT) industry has established a modular architecture for the messages that communicate various transaction requests from automated cash machines to financial institutions and back. The 128 fields available for describing transactions in the EFT standard message allow a nearly inexhaustible number of new kinds of transactions (i.e., financial service products) to be added by changing transaction codes in any of the available message fields.

Leveraging a new product variation by introducing new combinations of components also costs much less and takes much less time than creating another *de novo* product model by the conventional design process. The ability to leverage product variations from a modular product architecture relatively cheaply and quickly improves the responsiveness of a firm in differentiating products for the growing number of market segments characteristic of dynamic product markets. A firm may also use a superior ability to leverage large numbers of product variations to probe a product space to improve its knowledge of customer preferences and to proliferate product models to saturate product space in the region of most profitable demand. Sony's pattern of product introductions of its Walkman models, for example, suggests that Sony used introductions of product variations to discover customer preferences for the new product concept – and then intensified its offerings of related product models discovered to be most appreciated by consumers.

The potential to use modular product architectures to leverage product variations therefore invites the design of component 'sets' consisting of several variations of a basic component design which can then be mixed and matched in different product variations. Nippondenso Co., for example, designs a 'set' of modular radiators with various size parts that can be mixed and matched to make radiators of various capacities for use in different models in several Toyota product lines (Ward *et al.*, 1995; Whitney, 1995). If a basic modular architecture can be continued over a period of time, the various components developed for use in that architecture may be cataloged to form a 'design library' of components that are already available for use. Reusing existing components from a design library whenever possible lowers the cost and reduces the time of component development in leveraging new product variations.

Faster introductions of improved products

Modular product architectures may be designed to accommodate not only a range of presently available components, but also components that are expected to become available through technological development within the expected competitive lifetime of a given modular product design. The resulting ability to introduce components with improved performance into a modular product design (while reusing other components) enables the rapid introduction of upgraded product models as soon as improved components become available. Figure 16.2 illustrates how modular product architectures allow products to be upgraded rapidly by allowing substitution of improved components into existing product designs.

New competitive product strategies based on rapid performance improvement become possible when a firm can create a more robust modular product architecture – i.e., one that can accommodate a greater range of improved components – and can quickly develop improved components or gain early access to improved new components as soon as they become available from suppliers. Sony designed a modular product architecture for its initial M-8 HandyCam 8mm cassette video camera, for example, that enabled Sony to introduce four upgraded models within a 22-month period as quickly as it completed development of key improved components (Sanchez and Sudharshan, 1993). Similarly, Sun Microsystems uses industry standard component interfaces to define its workstation product architectures, but uses its buying power to negotiate early shipments of the newest, highest-performing components for use in upgrading the performance of its own products. Establishing a high rate of introductions of improved models creates a trajectory of rising product performance that imposes higher costs and increases competitive pressures on competitors. Fast-followers and imitators may be denied opportunities to profit from introducing 'copy-cat' products when a modular design firm can continue to introduce improved models before imitators can bring their copies of current-generation products to market (Sanchez, 1991).

Lower design, production, and other costs

Modular product design can lead to lower costs for design, manufacturing, distributing, and servicing products. Relative to creating a number of conventional product designs, creating a single modular product that allows leveraging of several product variations reduces design costs in several ways. Using some component designs in common across many models and reusing some components in successive generations of products reduces the cost of designing product variations.

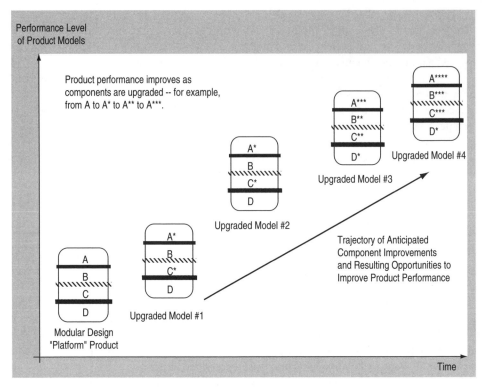

Figure 16.2 Component-based upgradeability of modular product design

When product variations can be leveraged by changing only some components, but using others in common across all or many product models, the economies of scale in manufacturing (or greater buyer power in purchasing) components used in common across product lines typically results in lower component production costs. Reuse of components in a succession of product generations also leads to greater experience in producing and using those components, which may both lower costs of production and lead to incremental design changes that improve the reliability in use of those components, reducing service and claims costs and contributing to increased customer satisfaction.

When the component variations that differentiate a product model for a given market segment can be 'contained' in a subassembly that can be added at a 'late point' in the production or distribution process, the reduced variety of parts moving through an assembly line, allows use of less costly, more efficient production lines, and the variety of components that must be inventoried can be reduced. The cooktop and control panel subassemblies that distinguish General Electric's different stove models, for example, are added in the last stage of the assembly line, so that most of the production line can be dedicated to assembling core components that are used in all GE's stove models. Hewlett-Packard has pushed the point for differentiating its ink-jet printers for local markets to its regional distribution centers around the world, where a modular power supply to suit local electrical requirements and a local language instruction manual are provided for each printer just prior to shipment to customers (Lee *et al.*, 1993). By making possible flexibilities such as these, modularity provides the 'simplicity and discipline' in product design that is necessary for manufacturing networks to become flexible and responsive in customizing products to meet diverse market demands (Collins and Schmenner, 1995).

Modularizing product designs may also lead to fundamental changes in service requirements. Canon's modularization of components in its compact personal copier design allowed Canon to introduce the concept of a cartridge component that customers can easily replace themselves, allowing Canon to overcome the barrier to entry posed by Xerox's extensive network for servicing its copiers. Makers of copiers, computers, and many other kinds of equipment are now converting to product designs with self-diagnostic capabilities and easily replaced modular components to radically reduce field service costs. Common and reused components may also reduce service costs by reducing both the variety of spare parts that must be inventoried and the training required by service staff.

Changes in new product targeting and marketing research

Changing from a conventional approach to product design to modular product design implies a major shift in both the processes of new product targeting and marketing research.

To begin a conventional optimizing design process requires a clear definition of both the desired attributes for a new product and the target cost or cost constraint for the product. In dynamic product markets in which market preferences and the means available to serve them are subject to significant change, however, precise prediction of market preferences at the completion of a product development project is likely to be impossible. The requirement of the conventional optimizing design process for a well defined development target often forces managers to base product development goals on marketing research's current 'best guess' about future market preferences, even though future market preferences cannot be reliably determined. Managers must then hope that the product being developed will appeal to actual market preferences when development is finally completed. When market preferences turn out to be different from marketing's best guess, the product optimized to a specific guess about future market preferences may prove to be inappropriate and a costly 'mistake'.

In contrast, because modular product design creates flexible platforms for leveraging product variations and upgrades capable of meeting a range of product attributes, performance levels, and costs, modular design requires as a development target only a statement of the *range of market preferences* that may need to be served in the future. Compared to the difficulty – indeed, the impossibility – of 'guessing right' about future market responses to specific product variations, managers in dynamic markets should be more capable of successfully estimating the likely range of future technological and market conditions and the corresponding range of product variations the firm should offer in the future. In essence, creating modular product architectures relieves managers of the need to make risky guesses about specific future market preferences, because modular designs provide managers with the flexibility to respond to a range of future market preferences once development is completed. Thus, the low incremental cost of leveraging product variations from modular designs not only lowers the cost of market coverage, but also lowers the costs of 'making mistakes' in testing market preferences and may therefore enable broader, accelerated learning about market preferences (Baldwin and Clark, 1994).

Because they take considerable time and may be based on rapidly obsolescing sets of consumer preferences, conventional marketing research methods may prove of limited usefulness in dynamic product markets. When a firm can use a modular product architecture to leverage product variations quickly and at low cost, however, it may begin to engage in *real-time market research* (Sanchez and Sudharshan, 1993) by introducing product variations intended to discover and serve current market preferences. Both Sony and Nike, for example, now have company-owned 'antenna shops' in trend-setting cities of the world to do real-time market research at the retail level on a stream of new modular product variations. Real-time market research driven by models leveraged from modular designs may therefore allow a firm to discover and serve many more market segments than competitors not capable of designing modular products.

As a firm uses real-time market research to learn more about market preferences, improved market knowledge may suggest the benefits of creating new 'up-market' or 'down-market' modular platform designs that are more appropriate for serving the preferences of newly discovered market segments. After leveraging over a dozen variations of its initial Walkman modular design to learn about consumer preferences, Sony subsequently developed a basic modular platform design intended to provide only the 'core' functionalities of the Walkman product concept and an expanded modular platform design intended to accommodate more features for a new range of high-end models.

MODULAR PRODUCT STRATEGIES

Integrating technology strategy and marketing strategy

Product development is essentially 'programmed innovation' – a process for applying a mix of new and existing technologies to perceived market opportunities to create new product concepts or extensions of existing product concepts. Conventional product design and development mixes processes for developing new technology and new products incorporating new technology. The time required to investigate and develop new technologies, however, typically imposes time delays and process inefficiencies on product development processes (Sanchez and Mahoney, 1995). In contrast, modular product design *intentionally decouples technology development from product development*. Fully specifying the component interfaces in a modular product architecture requires a well-developed understanding of the basic technologies used in each component and, especially, of the ways in which components interact in a product architecture. Thus, modular product architectures must be based on technologies which are well understood at the time development begins, but as a consequence the specification of component interfaces and the development of new components for a given modular design can then proceed without delays imposed by a need to resolve technological uncertainties. Incorporating new technologies into new products occurs through periodic redefinitions of product architectures, once new technologies have been developed to an adequate level of understanding about how new components based on those technologies perform and interact with other kinds of components.

Modular product design strategies based on decoupled technology and product development processes make possible new approaches to integrating technology strategy and marketing strategy (Sanchez, 1996). The decomposition of product designs into functional components whose designs are largely independent of other component designs allows a direct linking of marketing strategies to strategies for technology development *at the component level*. Components that add new features to a product or that offer improved performance in an existing product functionality can be developed in close concert with marketing efforts to probe, identify, and serve diverse market preferences for product variations incorporating those component variations. The ability of Sun Microsystems or Dell Computers to readily introduce new and improved components into their modular architecture computer systems, for example, enables those companies to directly test market reactions to new features or improved performance delivered by the various functional components of their computers. The discovery of strong customer preferences for new kinds of features or performance improvements can then direct technology development efforts to improving the components that deliver those product attributes.

The periodic redefinition of modular product architectures also provides a framework for linking longer-term technology and marketing strategies. This framework rests on the determination of which components within a modular product architecture are critical to effectively differentiating product variations for different customer preferences, and which are not. In this regard, components in a product architecture may be characterized as providing *threshold, central,* or *plus-only product attributes* (Huang 1993; Bogner and Thomas, 1996). Components that are necessary to realizing the product concept, but that are not perceived by customers as providing distinctive attributes in a product, may be thought of as providing threshold attributes of the product concept. The starter of a car, for example, is a threshold component that is unlikely ever to be a basis for differentiating a car model, but nevertheless must be present and work reliably in all car models. Components that provide central attributes differentiate a product in the eyes of customers whenever those components offer superior performance; competition in product markets therefore often emphasizes delivering superior performance in central components. Automobile engines, for example, are central or 'core' components in which differential performance levels in power and fuel consumption are generally critical in differentiating car models in all segments of the market. Components providing plus-only attributes provide features that 'delight the customer' when they are present in the product, but that do not unduly disappoint customers when they are absent. An indicator light warning a driver that a car door has not been closed completely is an example of a plus-only component.

Marketing strategy may be thought of as a process for identifying the mix of threshold, central, and plus-only product attributes that a firm ought to offer to targeted customers. When these product attributes can be delivered by components that can be mixed and matched and progressively upgraded within a modular product architecture, technology strategy and marketing strategy can be integrated through the periodic creation of new product architectures that allow for new components and new component variations. As a rule (there may of course be exceptions), technology development for providing threshold attributes can be directed at *reducing costs* for threshold components while maintaining the threshold level of performance expected by customers. Technology development for central attributes, however, may be jointly directed at advancing or developing component technologies that can *improve performance* of central components, while simultaneously trying to reduce component costs through product and process design improvements. Technology development for providing plus-only attributes may be focused on efforts to apply new and existing technologies to *creating new kinds of components* that provide new product features that enhance, but are not essential to, a basic product concept. These different marketing-driven emphases in technology strategy provide a framework for evaluating which component development activities a firm might outsource and which it may try to carry out within the firm – a key product strategy issue considered in the next section.

MODULARITY IN ORGANIZATION DESIGNS

Much has been written recently about the emergence of the 'virtual' or 'modular' organization in dynamic product markets. These innovative forms of firms have new flexibilities to quick-connect (Sanchez, 1996) with other firms in rapidly configuring a changing array of development, production, distribution, and marketing resources for pursuing a stream of new technology and market opportunities. The basic drivers of these new competitive dynamics are modularity concepts applied to organization designs as well as to product designs. This section will explain how modularity in product designs helps make possible the effective coordination of concurrent, self-managing, and distributed processes for creating new products that are the defining characteristic of the new 'modular' organizations.

Modular product designs and modular organization designs

Although organizations ostensibly design products, it can also be argued that at a more fundamental level, 'products design organizations' (Sanchez and Mahoney, 1994; 1995). In essence, the development, production, service, and other product-related tasks that are implicit in a given product design will in large measure determine the feasible designs of organizations for carrying out those tasks. In this sense, a firm's decisions about the kinds of product designs it creates may largely determine the organization structure it must adopt to develop, produce, and service those products.

Adopting modular product architectures in product creation processes has a profound, strategically significant impact on feasible organizational designs. Recall that modular product architectures define component interface specifications *before* beginning component development processes (see Table 16.2). As long as all components are designed to conform to the interface specifications that define how developed components must work together, the development process for one component will not be affected by what goes on in the processes for developing other components, Thus, specifying requirements for component interfaces before component development begins enables processes for developing components to become *decoupled* – that is, processes for developing component designs, like the modular component designs themselves, are no longer highly interdependent or 'tightly coupled' (Orton and Weick, 1990; Weick, 1976). In essence, decoupling component designs in modular product architectures intrinsically decouples processes for developing those components, allowing those processes to be carried out concurrently, autonomously, and distributively by various developers. As a result, modular product architectures make possible new product development processes that require fewer management resources, improve the speed of product development, encourage greater innovation at the component level, and allow access to an enlarged network of component development resources. All these potential benefits of modular product design may significantly increase the strategic flexibility of firms competing in dynamic product markets.

Reduced management resources

The specified component interfaces in a modular product architecture create an *information structure* that defines the required *output* of each component development process. When those interface specifications can be understood by component developers, and when the firm specifying the component interfaces can check developed components for conformance to interface specifications, modular product architectures become vehicles for *embedding coordination* of component development processes (Sanchez and Mahoney, 1995). By managing interface specifications that define the required outputs of component development processes before development begins, rather than trying to directly manage processes during component development, there is little or no need for allocation of managerial resources by the product-designing firm to supervise component development processes. Chrysler's use of 'platform' architectures ('hard points' that define interfaces between body and mechanical components) to coordinate the outputs of teams developing new car components, for example, has eliminated most of the need for managers and other employees to be involved in adjudicating component interface issues during component development. Using a modular product architecture has contributed to Chrysler's ability to develop better cars much faster – with reductions of 40 per cent or more in the number of people required for development projects (Holmes, 1995). Reductions in the management and technical staff required to develop modular products increase the flexibility of a firm to respond to a larger number of product development opportunities.

Improved speed of development

Since development of components typically consumes the major time required for overall product development, concurrent development of components for a modular product design can significantly shorten total development times and improve the speed with which a firm can bring new products to market. As part of its strategic initiative to improve speed-to-market for its new industrial automation products, GE Fanuc Automation has adopted an explicit and disciplined modular design strategy that has halved development cycle times through concurrent development of components (Sanchez and Collins, 1995). Similarly, Chrysler's use of 'platform' architectures in coordinating team development of new car designs has enabled Chrysler to achieve high levels of concurrency in developing major body and mechanical components. The average time to develop a new car at Chrysler has fallen from an average of 54 months in 1987 (before conversion to the platform team development concept) to 32 months at the end of 1995, with a further goal of reducing development time to 24 months in the next four to five years (Holmes, 1995). A faster development cycle improves the flexibility of a firm to respond quickly to new market opportunities. This time dimension of the strategic flexibility derived from modular product design can have considerable economic value when the opportunity costs of being late to market are high.

Improved ability to innovate in component development

When component development processes are co-ordinated by the product-designing firm by specifying only the interfaces to which components must conform, component development processes can be carried out autonomously by individual component developers. This autonomy may have a positive effect on development of better component-related technologies, because developers have increased freedom to innovate new component technologies and processes. Autonomous component development processes may also create development conditions conducive to greater involvement of customers and new suppliers in component development. Because decisions affecting a given component design do not involve other component development groups and can be made with reference only to that component's interface specifications, a complicated decision-making process is avoided, and customer or supplier suggestions about components can be evaluated and acted on much more readily. Boeing's modular design for aircraft, for example, facilitated the involvement of customers like United Airlines and British Airways in improving major components in the Boeing 777 (Sanchez and Mahoney, 1995). Modular component development processes may therefore improve the flexibility of a firm in gathering and incorporating new market information and new component technologies in creating new products.

Distributed product development

Fully specifying component interfaces at the outset of component development improves the ability of a product-designing firm to distribute component development tasks to groups within its own internal network of resources or to the most capable component development firms, wherever those firms may be located. In effect, fully specifying component interfaces helps to create a viable market for component development services, because the essential features of what is being contracted for are stated in full, and because making all component development processes independent of others removes what would otherwise be uncontrollable and unacceptable contingencies. When modular component specifications enable a product-designing firm to access an expanded base of component developers, the flexibility of the firm to leverage product variations is increased, because the firm can draw on more – and more diverse – component development expertise. Moreover, just as drawing on a design library of existing functional components in reusing component designs can reduce the cost and time required to develop a new product, the ability to draw on an enlarged pool of development firms who can perform well-defined development functions may reduce the time and cost of product development projects.

Electronic mediation of product creation processes

As growing use of modular product architectures leads to increased use of concurrent, distributed, and self-managing component development processes, information and telecommunications technologies are playing an important new role in linking widely dispersed product creation activities. Establishing effective electronic mediation of processes for developing, manufacturing, distributing, and marketing products requires establishing shared communications interfaces and standardizing descriptions of products, components, parts, and processes (Malone, et al., 1987). Shared CADD programs, for example, provide a common language for electronic communication between development firms. A modular product architecture provides a standardized description of individual components in a product design (the component interface specifications), allowing adequate component development task descriptions to be communicated to potential component developers over an electronic network. The combination of a shared electronic communication system and modular descriptions of components give a firm the capability to 'quick-connect' with a network of component development capabilities to assemble an electronically mediated product development process, as suggested in Figure 16.3. The 'Ford 2000' initiative for restructuring Ford's product development processes to create global platform designs, for example, is establishing a network of 7,500 CADD stations in Ford's engineering centers and at its key suppliers worldwide that can readily be reconfigured to serve changing development programs.

Electronic links now increasingly connect real-time sales of products to distribution and manufacturing processes, creating a kind of 'electronic kanban' system for driving upstream logistics and production scheduling with real-time sales data, as suggested in Figure 16.4. Wal-Mart, the world's largest retailing company, has created real-time electronic linkages between its 2,700 retail stores, its own distribution system, and its 2,500 suppliers. Wal-Mart uses real-time sales data from its stores to schedule production by suppliers and shipments of thousands of products in order to maintain stocks of the best-selling items in each of its stores. The electronic kanban concept is also being extended to the level of the individual customer, allowing 'micromarketing' of customized or personalized products. Motorola's 'Fusion' manufacturing system for pagers now allows a customer to phone in an order for a customized pager, provides automated translation of the customer's description into product specifications and bills of materials for the desired pager, schedules and manages production of the pager on a flexible assembly line, and ships the customized pager to the customer – within 24 hours (Stroebel and Johnson, 1993).

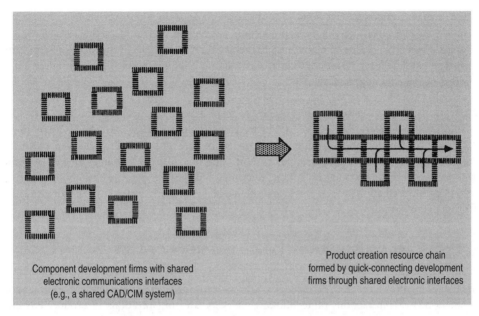

Figure 16.3 'Quick-connecting' product creation resource chains through shared electronic interfaces

Electronic kanban systems are also now being extended to directly drive product creation processes in real time. Companies like Procter & Gamble and Nike analyze real-time or 'near-time' sales data to discern patterns that suggest changing market preferences in their product markets. Nike's detection of emerging market trends stimulates the creation of new product designs whose components are produced and assembled by Nike's global network of contract manufacturers.

Firms like Ford, Motorola, and Nike are working hard to increase their already impressive abilities to use modular design and electronic linkages to establish and coordinate networks of development resources. These firms may be early examples of emerging new strategies for creating products in dynamic product markets. In contrast to traditional notions of how firms can go about developing new products, these firms appear to function as *network actuators* that:

- gather and interpret real-time market data to identify current opportunities for new products,
- define modular product architectures for leveraging large numbers of variations of a new product,

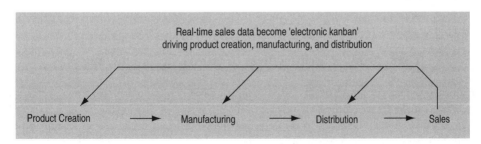

Figure 16.4 'Electronic kanban' system for driving product creation

311

- use modular component specifications and electronic linkages to establish an ability to 'quick-connect' with suppliers of development, production, distribution, and/or marketing capabilities; and
- quickly assemble chains of electronically mediated internal and external development, production, and delivery resources to create a broad and changing array of new product variations and rapidly upgraded models.

While not all product markets can be expected to reward greatly increased levels of product variety and greatly accelerated rates of product change, many product markets *are* increasingly accepting or even demanding more varied products and more rapidly improved products. Strategic managers should therefore pay careful attention to the developing abilities of some firms to use modular product design and electronic linkages to organize and coordinate new kinds of product creation processes that are capable of significantly increasing the scope and rate of product creation.

MANAGING KNOWLEDGE IN PRODUCT CREATION

Understanding how to create and manage knowledge strategically is central to the coordination of new kinds of interactions of technology, markets, and organizations in product creation processes. Strategic product creation processes in dynamic markets require new concepts for integrating and leveraging product information, market information, and the knowledge resources of the product-creating firm. These new concepts may require profound cultural and intellectual changes in most organizations, however, before they can be used effectively in managing product and market knowledge as valued corporate assets.

Management researchers are now beginning to explore basic concepts for identifying and managing organizational knowledge (Grant, 1993; Sanchez, 1995b; Wright, 1996). The following discussion examines three concepts that are key to explicitly managing knowledge as a strategic asset in product competition. First, product architectures strongly influence an organization's knowledge structures and processes. Using modular product architectures imposes a special discipline on management that may provide both stimulus and framework for improving and strategically reorienting a firm's knowledge management processes. Second, using modular design requires that learning about new technologies be decoupled from processes for developing new products. If properly managed, this decoupling can increase the effectiveness of both technology and product development processes. Third, using knowledge to greatest strategic effect in product competition requires an understanding of how a firm's knowledge can be leveraged through product creation networks without loss of strategically critical knowledge. A hierarchy of knowledge is introduced to suggest that three levels of knowledge – know-how, know-why, and know-what – must be recognized and managed strategically in network-based product creation processes.

From product architectures to knowledge architectures

Organizations that develop products often organize development and production processes in structures that closely reflect the architectures of the products they develop (Henderson and Clark, 1990). Because development and production activities are often organized into development groups focused on specific components and related technologies, the architecture of the knowledge processes and assets within a firm are likely to reflect closely the architectures of the firm's products. As a result, the component-level focus of an organization's technology development groups may act as a cognitive filter that blinds the firm to opportunities or needs to create new product architectures that meet changing market demands and incorporate new technologies.

Use of modular product design as a driver of strategic product creation processes can help to overcome this cognitive bias in development organizations. Modular design's attention to specifying and managing component interfaces, rather than specific components, shifts the focus of the modular product creating firm to the product architecture level. The focus of knowledge management processes then becomes improving a firm's 'ability to specify and control the performance characteristics' of components and subsystems of components (Venkatesan 1992). In modular product design, the performance characteristics required of components are articulated in the specifications of component interfaces that define how components will interact in a product design. In developing modular industrial automation products at GE Fanuc Automation, for example, new product architectures are elaborated through 'interface documents' that specify in detail the required performance characteristics for components within a new product architecture (Sanchez and Collins, 1995).

The requirement to fully specify component performance characteristics in creating a modular product architecture imposes a new kind of technological and design discipline on the product creation process. A development organization's knowledge about components and their interactions in a product architecture must be articulated and codified in explicit performance specifications for component interfaces. As a result, conversion from conventional product development practices to modular design has at least two strongly positive effects on an organization's ability to manage its knowledge assets strategically. Modular design forces an organization's technological knowledge about its products' constituent components and their interactions in a product design to become visible to everyone in the organization in the form of explicit component interface specifications. These specifications document the state of a firm's technical understanding about its products and in effect provide a 'balance sheet' of the firm's knowledge assets in product creation. Further, when a firm's knowledge about its products is discovered to be inadequate to fully specify some of the performance interrelationships between components in a modular product architecture, following the discipline of a modular design process helps a firm to discover the weaknesses in its technologies and product design capabilities and to identify specific areas in which it should improve its technical knowledge. Without the discipline of modular design, specific technological weaknesses within a firm are often difficult to detect, even by technical people within the firm. Unless discovered and remedied, however, areas of deficient technological understanding are likely to become persistent development bottlenecks, whether a firm simply tries to 'muddle through' traditional development processes or adopts teams using overlapping development processes.

Decoupling technology development and product development

Modular product design requires a state of technological knowledge about components and their interactions that is adequate to fully specify how components will perform and interact in a product design. As a consequence, modular product architectures must be based on technologies about which a firm has developed a high level of understanding at the time component development begins. Thus, modular design requires an *international and disciplined decoupling* of processes for developing new technology from processes for leveraging technological knowledge in developing new products (Sanchez and Mahoney, 1995). In modular design, the interactions of technology and product development are limited to periodic redefinitions of the firm's product architectures. New technology can be incorporated into new product architectures only after the firm develops high levels of understanding about that technology. Opportunities for making periodic changes in product architectures, however, provide direction to technology development activities that can be aimed at achieving improvements in future generations of the firm's products. In this regard, modular product design provides a useful framework for identifying and building new technological knowledge of strategic value to the firm.

Managing the knowledge hierarchy: know-how, know-why, and know-what

In dynamic product markets, product-creating firms increasingly function as 'open systems' (Sanchez and Heene, 1996) for building and leveraging knowledge in a network of product creation resources. Strategically managing flows of knowledge in product creation networks requires recognition of some basic differences in the kinds of knowledge a firm may have. These different kinds of knowledge reflect different levels of understanding that a firm can develop about its product creation processes. Three levels of understanding characterize three different kinds of knowledge – know-how, know-why, and know-what – within an organization (Sanchez, 1995b), as shown in Table 16.3. In different competitive contexts, each kind of knowledge may have greater or less strategic value than another and will therefore have to be managed differently to achieve greatest strategic benefit for the firm. After a brief discussion of the three kinds of organizational knowledge, the strategic management of each of the three kinds of knowledge in dynamic product markets is considered.

A firm's know-how is its 'practical understanding' about the current state of a system (Simon, 1962). Know-how enables a firm to continue performing its current operations, like running its production line, processing documents, or servicing orders for existing customers. Analogously, in terms of product knowledge, know-how is the ability to *produce* and (within some limited range) *refine* the firm's existing product designs. A firm with know-how knowledge about its products understands the way in which the parts of its current product designs fit and function together. Over time, a firm may advance its state-level of understanding through learning-by-doing, which is essentially a process of testing its current understanding by initiating or reacting to limited changes in a product design, observing the consequences, and inferring ways in which its understanding about the product should be refined in light of those consequences. Know-how level knowledge is useful in maintaining control of current product designs and production systems over some limited range of variations in internal or external conditions.

Know-why is 'theoretical understanding' of the principles governing the functioning of a system. Know-why enables a firm to change the state of a system. In terms of product knowledge, know-why is the theoretical understanding of why the parts of a given product design function together to produce the overall function of a product, and this know-why knowledge enables a

Table 16.3 Forms of knowledge: know-how, know-why, and know-what

Form of Knowledge	Level of Understanding	Capability Derived from Knowledge
Know-How	'Practical understanding' of how current products work	Enables firm to produce and refine current product designs
Know-Why	'Theoretical understanding' of why product designs work	Enables firm to adapt current designs or develop defined new products
Know-What	'Strategic understanding' of purposes to which know-why and know-how may be applied	Enables firm to imagine and define feasible new kinds of products

firm to *adapt* a product design or to *develop* a new product design to produce significant new product variations. To create a modular product architecture requires well developed know-why knowledge about components and their interactions.

Know-what is 'strategic understanding' of the purposes to which specific forms of know-why and know-how knowledge might be applied in product competition. Know-what enables managers to make conjectures about what new kinds of products a firm might develop and what the likely outcomes of specific developments might be. In essence, know-what enables managers to *imagine and define* feasible new kinds of products and new processes for developing, producing, and marketing products. Know-what knowledge requires understanding of what the firm might do with its available competences or competences it conceivably could develop.

A basic objective in strategically managing knowledge in product creation processes is to achieve the greatest advantage from leveraging the firm's knowledge, while avoiding loss of control of knowledge which brings a firm competitive advantage. To achieve the greatest leverage of its knowledge, a firm needs to articulate its useful knowledge in ways that let that knowledge be transferred to wherever it can be applied within the organization or to any other firms who can use that knowledge on behalf of the firm. In order to simultaneously leverage articulated knowledge beyond the boundaries of the firm *and* prevent the loss of control of strategically critical knowledge, managers must understand what kinds of knowledge are the sources of the firm's strategic advantages in product competition. A first step therefore is to determine the relative importance of the firm's know-how, know-why, and know-what kinds of knowledge in maintaining or creating the firm's distinctive competences in creating products. The next step in managing the firm's knowledge to greatest strategic advantage is to leverage the least strategically critical kinds of knowledge of the firm as broadly as possible, while maintaining close control within the firm of the kind of knowledge that is most critical to the firm's distinctive competences.

In dynamic product markets, a firm's most critical kind of knowledge is likely to be at the know-what and know-why levels, because the firm's ability to identify and adapt flexibly to changing technologies and market opportunities are derived from these kinds of knowledge. A firm's product creation processes in dynamic markets should therefore be organized to maintain control of those forms of knowledge. The firm may try to leverage its know-how knowledge as widely as possible, however, because sharing the firm's current know-how knowledge with other firms poses less of a threat to the firm's ability to maintain its distinctive advantages in product competition.

This strategy for knowledge management leads to a pattern of subcontracting in which a firm shares its know-how knowledge in well articulated forms that can be readily apprehended by subcontractors, while maintaining secrecy around its know-why and know-what knowledge. Boeing's current product creation processes reflect this strategy for managing knowledge strategically. Boeing transfers explicit know-how knowledge to subcontractors in the form of drawings and specifications for components for a new aircraft design, while 'hiding' the know-what knowledge that enable Boeing to identify new product opportunities and the know-why knowledge that enables Boeing to design components for new aircraft to serve those opportunities. Boeing's engineering specifications and drawings for the fabrication of a fuselage section for the 777, for example, convey the know-how needed to make the desired 777 fuselage section in a form which can be readily apprehended by subcontractors. However, the know-how provided in the design drawings and specifications reveals little or nothing of the design theory (know-why) that enabled Boeing to design the new fuselage, nor does it reveal the know-what knowledge which led Boeing to identify and define the 777 product concept as a viable application of available know-why and know-how knowledge. This strategy for managing knowledge allows Boeing to leverage its current know-how level knowledge about the 777 aircraft to access a large network of firms with capabilities in metal fabrication and component manufacture, but does not compromise Boeing's ability to maintain control of its know-why and know-what knowledge essential to maintaining its distinctive competence in defining and designing new generations of passenger aircraft.

In dynamic markets, the know-why knowledge needed to develop new kinds of components and the know-how for producing new components may reside in a large number of firms. The personal computer market, for example, has many firms competing in developing and manufacturing components like hard disk drives, memory devices, and terminals. In such markets, the most strategically important kinds of knowledge for the product-creating firm are likely to be know-what knowledge that can identify and define new products and know-why knowledge that enables the firm to create new modular product architectures. By defining the outputs of development processes to be performed by component suppliers, modular product architectures become, in effect, vehicles for leveraging the product-creating firm's know-what knowledge and product-architecture know-why knowledge to draw on the component-level know-why and production know-how of suppliers. In this process, the component interface specifications that define the required outputs of component developers' processes reveal little or nothing of the firm's know-what or product-level know-why knowledge that led to those specifications.

Managing Strategic Product Creation: Designing Products and Organizations for Strategic Flexibility

This article has suggested that increasingly dynamic product markets are being created by firms that have reconceptualized the ways in which interactions of technology, markets, and organizations can be managed in product creation processes. Fundamental to these reconceptualizations are concepts of modularity in product and organization designs. The ability to leverage product variety and change relatively quickly and inexpensively is rapidly making modular product design the new 'dominant logic' (Sanchez, 1995a) for designing products in dynamic product markets. Similarly, the ability of modular product design and electronic linkages to help firms 'quick-connect' in flexibly reconfigurable networks of development resources is rapidly making the modular organization a dominant logic for managing product creation processes.

The concepts of flexibility and modularity that characterize the new product strategies and new kinds of development organizations, however, have impacts that are reaching beyond the arena of product competition. Flexibility and modularity are becoming the central concepts in a reconceptualization of the theory of strategic management in dynamic product markets, as suggested earlier in Table 16.1. Strategic management of firms in dynamic markets is now converging to a focus on a modularity-driven strategic product creation process whose purpose is the efficient generation of significantly greater levels of product variety and change than previously witnessed in product competition. This new orientation in strategic management means that top managers must become much more directly involved in processes for designing both products and organizations that are capable of responding flexibly to rapidly changing competitive environments. This shift in strategic management focus makes at least two substantial new demands on managers who would manage strategically in dynamic product markets:

- Managerial capabilities must expand beyond the traditional skills in managing flows of financial and physical assets within a single firm to a new emphasis on skills in managing flows of intellectual assets within networks of firms.

- Because product architectures largely determine a firm's knowledge structures and feasible organizational structures and thus directly impact a firm's flexibility in dynamic competition, managers must regard decisions about a firm's product architectures as fundamental strategic issues that demand the informed participation and support of top management.

To manage the competitive uncertainties and pressures of dynamic markets, the task of strategic management must shift from a focus on managing the firm as a relatively fixed set of assets and capabilities to designing the firm as a flexible system for coordinating a continuously changing mix of assets, capabilities, and relationships in leveraging an expanded, higher-velocity stream of new products. As the diffusion of modularity concepts for designing products and organizations causes more product markets to become dynamic, competitive success will depend on greatly increased top management attention to creating strategic flexibilities in the firm's product, organization, and knowledge architectures.

REFERENCES

Baldwin, Carliss, and Kim B. Clark (1994). Modularity-in-design: An Analysis Based on the Theory of Real Options, Harvard Business School working paper, Boston, MA.

Bogner, William C, and Howard Thomas (1996). From Skills to Competences: The 'Play-out' of Resource-bundles Across Firms, in Ron Sanchez, Aimé Heene, and Howard Thomas, eds, *Dynamics of Competence-Based Competition*, Elsevier Press, Oxford.

Clark, Kim B., and Takahiro Fujimoto (1991). *Product Development Performance: Strategy, Organization, and Management in the World Auto Industry*, Harvard University Press, Boston, MA.

Collins, Robert, and Roger Schmenner (1995). Pan-European Manufacturing, *European Management Journal*, 13(3), pp. 257–68.

Garud, Raghu, and Arun Kumaraswamy (1993). Changing Competitive Dynamics in Network Industries: An Exploration of Sun Microsystems' Open Systems Strategy, *Strategic Management Journal*, 14(5), 351–69.

Grant, Robert M. (1993). Organizational Capability Within a Knowledge-based View of the Firm, School of Business Administration Working Paper Series, STRAT-2277-03-1293, Georgetown University, Washington, DC.

Hamel, Gary, and Aimé Heene (eds) (1994). *Competence-based Competition*, John Wiley, Chichester.

Henderson, Rebecca M., and Kim B. Clark (1990). Architectural Innovation: The Reconfiguration of Existing Product Technologies and the Failure of Established Firms, *Administrative Science Quarterly*, 35 (March), pp. 9–30.

Holmes, Mike (1995). 'The Utilization of CAD/CAM Technologies in the Styling Process at Chrysler,' address to Conference on Joining Information Infrastructures and Technology Management for Global Enterprises, University of Illinois, Champaign, IL, October 11.

Huang, Kathryn Sung Hom (1993). Integrating Vertical and Horizontal Dimensions in a Spatial Framework of Strategic Product Competition: An Application to the U.S. Photocopier Industry, Harvard University doctoral dissertation (Business Economics), Cambridge, MA.

Kacher, G. (1994). Spy Report: SAAB, Caddy, Sport-utes, and an Engineering Revolution, *Automobile*, September, p. 15.

Lee, H.L., C. Billington, and B. Carter (1993). Hewlett-Packard Gains Control of Inventory and Service Through Design for Localization, *Interfaces*, 23, pp. 1–11.

Mahajan, V., and J. Wind (1991). New Product Models: Practice, Shortcomings, and Desired Improvements, Report No. 91–125, Marketing Science Institute, Cambridge, MA.

Malone, Thomas J., Joanne Yates, and Robert Benjamin (1987). Electronic Markets and Electronic Hierarchies, *Communications of the ACM, T* 30(6), pp. 484–97.

Orton, J. Douglas, and Karl E. Weick (1990). Loosely Coupled Systems: A Reconceptualization, *Academy of Management Review*, 15(2), pp. 203–23.

Prahalad, C.K., and Gary Hamel (1995). *Competing for the Future*, Harvard Business School Press, Boston.

Sanchez, Ron (1991). Strategic Flexibility, Real Options, and Product-based Strategy, PhD dissertation,

Massachusetts Institute of Technology, Cambridge, MA.

Sanchez, Ron (1993). Strategic Flexibility, Firm Organization, and Managerial Work in Dynamic Markets: A Strategic Options Perspective, *Advances in Strategic Management*, 9, pp. 251–91.

Sanchez, Ron (1994a). Higher-order Organization and Commitment in Strategic Options Theory,' *Advances in Strategic Management*, 10B, pp. 299–307.

Sanchez, Ron (1994b). Towards a Science of Strategic Product Design: System Design, Component Modularity, and Product Leveraging Strategies, *Proceedings of the Second International Product Development Management Conference on New Approaches to Development and Engineering*, May 30–31, European Institute for Advanced Studies in Management, Brussels, Belgium.

Sanchez, Ron (1995a). Strategic Flexibility in Product Competition, *Strategic Management Journal*, 16 (Summer special issue), pp. 135–59.

Sanchez, Ron (1995b). Managing Articulated Knowledge in Competence-based Competition, Office of Research Working Paper #95–0131, University of Illinois, Champaign, IL.

Sanchez, Ron (1996). Integrating Technology Strategy and Marketing Strategy, in Don O'Neal and Howard Thomas, (eds), *Integrating Strategy*, John Wiley, Chichester.

Sanchez, Ron, and Robert P. Collins (1995). Competing in Modular Markets, Office of Research working, paper, University of Illinois, Champaign, IL.

Sanchez, Ron, and Aimé Heene (1996). A Systems View of the Firm in Competence-based Competition, in Ron Sanchez, Aimé Heene, and Howard Thomas, (eds), *Dynamics of Competence-Based Competition*, Elsevier Press, Oxford.

Sanchez, Ron, and Joseph T. Mahoney (1994). The Modularity Principle in Product and Organization Design, Office of Research Working Paper #94–0157, University of Illinois, Champaign, IL.

Sanchez, Ron, and Joseph T. Mahoney (1995). Modularity, Flexibility, and Knowledge Management in Product and Organization Design, Office of Research Working Paper #95–0121, University of Illinois, Champaign, IL 61820.

Sanchez, Ron, Aimé Heene, and Howard Thomas (1996). *Dynamics of Competence-Based Competition*, Elsevier Press, Oxford.

Sanchez, Ron, and D. Sudharshan (1993). Real-time Market Research, *Marketing Intelligence and Planning*, 11 (August), pp. 29–38.

Sanderson, Susan Walsh, and Vic Uzumeri (1990). Strategies for New Product Development: Design-based Incrementalism, Center for Science and Technology Policy working paper, Rensselaer Polytechnic Institute, Troy, NY.

Simon, Herbert (1962). *The Sciences of the Artificial*, MIT Press, Cambridge, MA.

Stroebel, Russ, and Andy Johnson (1993). Pocket Pagers in Lots of One, *IEEE Spectrum*, September, pp. 29–32.

Venkatesan, Ravi (1992). Strategic Sourcing: To Make or Not to Make, *Harvard Business Review*, 70 (November–December), pp. 98–107.

Ward, Allen, Jeffrey V. Liker, John J. Cristiano, and Durward K. Sobek (1995). The Second Toyota Paradox: Delaying Decisions Can Make Better Cars Faster, *Sloan Management Review*, spring issue, pp. 43–61.

Weick, Karl E. (1976). Educational Organizations as Loosely Coupled Systems, *Administrative Science Quarterly*, 21 (March), pp. 1–19.

Whitney, Daniel (1995). Nippondenso Co. Ltd.: A Case Study of Strategic Product Design,' pp. 115–51 in Jeffrey K. Liker, John E. Ettlie, and John C. Campbell, (eds), *Engineered in Japan: Japanese Technology-Management Practices*, Oxford University Press, Oxford.

Wright, Russell W. (1996). The Role of Imitable vs. Inimitable Competences in the Evolution of the Semiconductor Industry, in Ron Sanchez, Aimé Heene, and Howard Thomas, (eds), *Dynamics of Competence-Based Competition*, Elsevier Press, Oxford.

PART V

ISSUES IN CORPORATE STRATEGY

INTRODUCTION

The resource-based view of strategy covered in Part III is the basis of competence-based strategy. It marks the beginning of an evolution of strategy theories towards greater integration of positioning, resources, capabilities and learning to create a more holistic theory of the dynamics of strategy. Core competence management is not about cost-based approaches to maximizing economies of scale for individual businesses. These are a necessary but no longer distinctive source of advantage. Instead, it is about consolidating corporate-wide skills, expertise and technologies; harnessing collective learning; and co-ordinating them into multiple streams of products and services. It is concerned with the potential for synergy in corporations across portfolios of businesses and the problems of achieving its advantages in practice. It is therefore about exploiting economies of scope across the multi-business units of the corporation.

Many developments both external to the organization (such as shifting or collapsing industry boundaries) or internal (such as a focus on competencies) require radical managerial responses. The following three chapters in Part V all deal with ways of managing competencies, synergies and sources of advantage derivable from strategic thinking at a corporate, as opposed to a business unit/SBU, level. In times of internal and external turbulence, a 'wide-angle lens' is needed to manage the resulting organizational tensions: centralization combined with decentralization; control with flexibility; focus with responsiveness; standardization with adaptability; each organization attempts its own balance between these conflicting requirements. In their different ways, each of these articles is about rethinking accepted principles of management and rethinking the concept of the corporation.

The central questions in corporate strategy must surely be: does the corporate centre (i.e. the parent) add value to the individual businesses within its corporate portfolio? Why is the individual business unit better off within a corporation rather than as a stand-alone business? Is that particular corporate parent the best one for that particular business, or would that business unit be better served within the portfolio of another corporation? These and other similarly sensible basic questions about corporate strategy are asked and answered in Goold, Campbell and Alexander's article (Chapter 17). This article represents a distillation of more than ten years research on corporate-level strategy, carried out by a team at Ashridge Strategic Management Centre, led by Michael Goold and Andrew Campbell. The article is organized around a set of core issues facing multi-business corporations (i.e. those managing a number of businesses).

The concept of the corporate 'parent' is itself a helpful idea, capturing as it does certain expectations about the relationship between the business units and the corporate centre. They define a corporate parent as 'all those levels of management that are not part of customer-facing, profit-responsible business units'. A key point about corporate parents is that they swallow up costs. These costs include obvious things like corporate overheads, but also the costs to the business unit of managing its reporting relationship to the corporate parent. Are corporate parents simply an additional cost in time and resources to business units or are there ways in which parents can add genuine value? That means that corporate parents must carry out functions and activities that the businesses would be unable to afford to carry out themselves, or that they at least provide positive influences on strategic thinking. Otherwise many business units may generate better value outside the corporation. This is often the case when businesses are 'spun off' or bought out by their management. Furthermore, since merger and acquisition activity occurs frequently, and business units may be sold off to other corporations, there must be differences in the quality of corporate 'parenting' from one corporation to another, which Goold, Campbell and Alexander call 'parenting advantage'. Unfortunately, there is considerable evidence that many corporate parents, rather than adding value to the businesses in their portfolios, actually destroy value. This may be simply because central costs often creep upwards and the power relationships between the centre and the SBUs may often encourage inaccuracies in information-sharing. These phenomena seem to occur in all cultures. The issues raised, and the recommendations provided, make this a particularly thought-provoking piece of work, full of insights for managers.

Following on very closely to the issues raised by Goold, Campbell and Alexander, we come next to the classic corporate strategy issue of related versus unrelated diversification. In other words, what sorts of business portfolios should corporations seek to build, and what should be the connections between the types of business units within them? As Markides and Williamson point out in their article (Chapter 18), there have been at least thirty years of research into this issue of relatedness and the benefits of related, as opposed to unrelated, diversification. The research has come out resoundingly in favour of the benefits of related diversification. The assumption has been that related diversification allows the corporation to 'exploit the interrelationships that exist among its different businesses (SBUs) and so achieve cost and/or differentiation advantage over its rivals'. However, as Markides and Williamson argue, there is little agreement about how precisely this long-term competitive advantage is to be achieved. They explain that this may be due to two factors. First, the traditional measures of 'relatedness' (between businesses) have looked only at industry relatedness or market relatedness. Markides and Williamson suggest that the correct measure should be relatedness between strategic assets. Second, benefits of relatedness were primarily to be achieved through economies of scope (i.e. sharing a resource developed in one business, in other businesses also). Instead, Markides and Williamson argue that 'the real leverage comes from exploiting relatedness to create and accumulate *new* strategic assets more quickly and cheaply than competitors'. In other words, the real long-term benefits from related diversification should come from the speed and ability to create new assets, rather than simply from extending the use of existing ones (as with standard economies of scope). Related diversification should enable a corporation to transfer core competencies between its SBUs, in order to accelerate the speed, and lower the cost, of further asset accumulation of new strategic assets. They further argue that related firms outperform unrelated ones *only* where firms operate in portfolios of businesses that share similar market opportunities, e.g. to exploit brands; to share marketing and channel management; to build process skills in customization or in managing skilled teams.

The creation and management of strategic alliances are the final major corporate strategy issues that we address in Part V. Hitt, Ireland and Santoro (Chapter 19) give a very thorough treatment of all aspects of alliance-building. This includes alliances as part of resource and capability enhancement for the firm; alliances as social networks and generators of social capital; alliances as co-operative strategies; and alliance management itself as a strategic capability of the firm. They also look in considerable detail at the nuts and bolts of strategic alliances: alliance scope, partner selection and resource configuration, optimization and exploitation. Both small and large firms engage in strategic alliances, although large firms are likely to be involved in many alliances simultaneously. For all firms there are benefits to be gained from alliances. Such benefits would include rapid access to new technology, new markets, new knowledge or the sharing of risks. Strategic alliances can create value in three main ways: by building and enhancing resources and capabilities; by facilitating learning; and by enlarging the firm's strategic network.

Many firms, however, achieve none of these benefits. Despite the enormous popularity of strategic alliances in the global marketplace, there is also an extremely high failure rate for these collaborations. About half of all alliances fail, which suggests that managers understand them poorly. Hitt, Ireland and Santoro suggest that alliance development and management are critical capabilities that should create value and enhance the building of social networks and social capital. To achieve this, however, managers need to develop a much better understanding of alliance scope, partner selection and resource configuration, optimization and exploitation as explained here. To create value from strategic alliances requires the firm to possess the capability to effectively develop and manage such alliances.

17

CORPORATE STRATEGY AND PARENTING THEORY

Michael Goold, Andrew Campbell and Marcus Alexander

This paper provides a brief summary of what we at the Ashridge Strategic Management Centre believe we have learned about corporate strategy over the last ten years. It lays out the basis for our ideas about corporate parenting and the implications of parenting theory for management decisions. It is structured around nine propositions, each of which attempts to convey both what we have learned and why it matters. The paper concludes with our views about where future research priorities should lie.

JUSTIFYING THE PARENT

What we have learned

In multibusiness companies, the existence of a corporate parent, by which we mean all those levels of management that are not part of customer-facing, profit-responsible business units, entails costs. These costs, which include not only corporate overheads but also knock-on costs of corporate reporting in the businesses, are not balanced by any direct revenues, since the corporate parent has no external customers for its services. Furthermore, the business units often feel that they could be independently viable and, indeed, could do better without a corporate parent. This belief is given credence by the success of so many management buy-outs and spin-off companies.

The parent can therefore only justify itself if its influence leads to better performance by the businesses than they would otherwise achieve as independent, stand-alone entities. It must either carry out functions that the businesses would be unable to perform as cost-effectively for themselves or it must influence the businesses to make better decisions than they would have made on their own. In other words, the parent must add more value than cost to the businesses in the portfolio. The logic of the need to add value is now becoming more widely accepted. However, there are still relatively few companies whose corporate strategies are based on powerful and convincing sources of value creation.

Why it matters

The challenge to corporate parents to justify themselves is important because it concentrates attention on whether and how the activities of the parent do add value. Rather than assuming the existence of a corporate parent, and then asking what the businesses can do for it, it places the onus in precisely the opposite direction. Now the key question is what the parent can do for the businesses, and whether it can positively demonstrate that its undoubted costs are more than offset by tangible benefits for the businesses. For many corporate parents, this has been a new perspective, and has led to the elimination of worthless, bureaucratic routines and a sharper concentration on those things that genuinely add value.

> *Proposition: Many of the business units in multibusiness companies could be viable as stand-alone entities: To justify its existence, the corporate parent must influence the businesses collectively to perform better than they would as stand-alone entities.*

PARENTING ADVANTAGE

What we have learned

Since corporate parents exist in a competitive world, in which ownership of businesses is transferable, adding some value is not a sufficient justification for the corporate parent. Ideally, the parent must add more value than other rival parents would: otherwise all stakeholders could be made better off through a change in ownership of the businesses to a superior parent.

The force of this objective is evident when companies face the possibility of a hostile acquisition. But, even if there is no imminent threat of a take-over, the aspiration to add as much value as possible to all the businesses in the portfolio should remain the ultimate goal. Businesses whose competitors have parents that add more value are at a disadvantage, which will eventually be reflected in their results.

Why it matters

The objective of adding more value than other rival parents, which we refer to as achieving 'parenting advantage', is important because it provides a sound and powerful guiding objective for corporate strategy. All too often other objectives, such as achieving a faster rate of growth, balancing the portfolio between sectors or geographies, spreading risk, or simply survival, take precedence over parenting advantage, and lead to poor decisions. These other objectives are not in themselves wrong, but can lead corporate parents to forget that parenting advantage should be in centre stage and, hence, to take decisions that have nothing to do with added value. Parenting advantage should be the guiding criterion for corporate-level strategy, rather as competitive advantage is for business level strategy.

> *Proposition: Parent companies compete with each other for the ownership of businesses: The objective of corporate strategy should be to add more value to the businesses in the portfolio than other rival parent organisations would.*

VALUE DESTRUCTION

What we have learned

Corporate hierarchies inevitably destroy some value. Apart from the obvious issue of corporate overheads, the main problems relate to ill-judged influence from senior managers and to information filters.

Since senior corporate managers must divide their time between a number of businesses in the portfolio, they will always be less close to the affairs of each business than its own management team. Inevitably, there is a danger that their influence will be less soundly-based than the views of the managers running the businesses.

Corporate hierarchies encourage business managers to compete with each other for investment funds and for personal promotion. Business managers therefore tend to filter the information they provide to divisional and corporate management, in order to present their businesses in the most favourable light. The information on which corporate managers must base their influence and decisions tends to be systematically biased.

The corporate centre also tends to be insulated from the sort of critical examination of cost effectiveness that other parts of a company routinely receive. Processes to assess net corporate value added are seldom well-developed, and power relationships in the corporate hierarchy mean that it is hard for the businesses to express their views openly. Central costs have a tendency to creep upwards and unproductive central interference goes unchecked.

Extra costs and negative influence are therefore pervasive features in all multibusiness organisational hierarchies and can only be offset by substantial value creation in targeted areas (see proposition 5, page 329). Research with a wide cross-section of companies in the US, Europe and Asia-Pacific has provided many specific examples of the phenomenon.

Why it matters

This observation is important because it should lead corporate parents to be more disciplined. They should avoid intervening in businesses unless they have specific reasons for believing that their influence will be positive. They should avoid extending their portfolios into new businesses unless they have good grounds for believing that they will be able to add value to them. They should seriously consider demerging or spinning off businesses that do not fit well with their skills. And they should be willing to downsize or eliminate corporate functions unless they have a clear added-value role.

This perspective provides a counterweight to ill-focused and over-ambitious corporate strategies. Previously, it was too easy for corporate parents to feel that simply going through the budget or capital expenditure review process 'must be good for the businesses' or that diversifying into more glamorous or more rapidly growing sectors 'must be good for investors'. Now we know better, since we can see that good corporate strategy is as much about avoiding value destruction as it is about maximising value creation.

Proposition: All multibusiness organisations have inherent and pervasive tendencies to destroy value: Corporate strategies should recognise these tendencies and be designed to minimise value destruction as much as to maximise value creation.

LATERAL SYNERGIES

What we have learned

Since Ansoff's pioneering work on synergy, most businessmen and management thinkers have justified multibusiness companies because of the existence or potential for lateral linkages between their businesses. Managers at the centre have believed that their main role is the creation of synergy.

Our research, in contrast, has shown that parent managers are often pursuing mirages rather than real synergy opportunities, and that their interventions in the lateral relationships between businesses are often net negative rather than net positive. Furthermore, most 'synergies' are available between independent businesses. A common parent is not necessary for two or more businesses to trade with each other, form alliances or joint ventures, licence technology, share benchmarks and best practice, pool negotiating power, share services, coordinate strategies or combine to create new businesses. Only a few synergies require a common parent to be effectively implemented. We have also observed that, for many multibusiness companies, the main source of added value stems from the relationship between the centre and each business as a stand-alone entity. We have, therefore, concluded that the value potential of synergies has been systematically over-rated by managers, academics and consultants.

Why it matters

This observation is important because it should change the mindset of corporate centre managers. Instead of 'desperately seeking synergies', centre managers should be focusing their efforts only on those synergies that need central intervention. Instead of actively fostering a 'one enterprise' or 'one family' philosophy, centre managers should usually be encouraging 'market place' relationships between business units. Instead of supporting 'corporate centre creep', in which activities graduate to the centre in the name of synergy, centre managers should be vigilant in avoiding interventions unless they are clearly beneficial. This change in mindset will focus central management time on those synergies where the parent has a real role to play. It may also free time for value creating influence on businesses as stand-alone entities.

The change in mindset will also reduce the amount of value destroyed from 'contamination'. Contamination occurs when two businesses with different critical success factors are encouraged to work closely together in the name of synergy, and pollute each other's thinking and strategies. The loss of focus and muddled thinking that results can end up hurting both businesses.

Proposition: The importance of lateral synergies in creating value in multibusiness companies has been systematically overrated: Corporate parents should pay relatively more attention to other sources of value creation, in particular their ability to improve performance in each individual business as a stand-alone entity.

VALUE CREATION

What we have learned

Value creation only occurs under three conditions:

- the parent sees an opportunity for a business to improve performance and a role for the parent in helping to grasp the opportunity
- the parent has the skills, resources and other characteristics needed to fulfil the required role
- the parent has sufficient understanding of the business and sufficient discipline to avoid other value-destroying interventions.

The most successful parents concentrate their attention on a few large areas of opportunity rather than attempting to intervene more broadly: in this way they can both develop distinctive skills that are specially suitable for the opportunities they are targeting and avoid dissipating their energies on issues where their contribution will have low or negative value.

Although competitive pressures should weed out businesses that persistently underperform, opportunities for a corporate parent to add value are not uncommon. They arise when

- weaknesses in business managers are causing underperformance
- the business managers face opportunities that even a competent management team will find difficult to seize without help from the parent
- the parent possesses some special resources that open up new opportunities for the businesses.

Our emphasis is on the skills or competences of the parent and the extent to which they fit with the opportunities in the businesses. It is parenting competences or resources, what the parent can do to make a difference, that explain successful corporate strategies. The broader notion of core competences, though useful, fails to highlight the role to be played by the parent.

Why it matters

The conditions for value creation are important, because they force corporate parents to think through what major opportunities for added value lie behind the corporate strategy. If no such opportunities have been identified, the strategy is bound to be fatally flawed.

They also help corporate parents to focus their activities. By giving prominence to a few major opportunities, corporate priorities can be clarified, irrelevant or value destroying activities can be eliminated, and time and attention can be devoted to building up the competences that the parent needs most. By not trying to do everything, the parent can become specially good at doing the things that really matter.

The objective of building parenting competences that fit well with particular opportunities also gives a sharper and more practical basis for competence development at the parent level. The often fruitless quest for nebulous core competences can be replaced with a much more targeted agenda for the skills, resources and processes that the corporate parent needs most.

Lastly, an emphasis on the distinctive insights and skills possessed by the parent is valuable because it underlines how much the success of any corporate strategy depends on the experience, capabilities and attitudes of the CEO and his team. The personal views and qualities of the CEO need to be a primary criterion in selecting the corporate strategy.

> *Proposition: Value creation seldom occurs unless the corporate parent perceives a few large opportunities for business performance enhancement, and develops distinctive skills, resources and influencing processes that address these opportunities: Corporate parents should focus their efforts on building special competences that fit the particular opportunities they are targeting.*

CORPORATE CENTRES AND MANAGEMENT PROCESSES

What we have learned

The desire to follow 'best practice' in corporate processes (such as planning, capital sanctioning, performance targeting and monitoring, etc.) has resulted in several popular but ephemeral trends. Similarly, a focus on the appropriate size of the corporate centre has, at different stages, encouraged managers to increase centralisation and the staffing of functions such as corporate planning and corporate HR, or, more recently, to reduce dramatically the numbers employed in such functions.

But managers adopting the general trends and supposed best practice of the day have frequently been disappointed by the results. Furthermore, parents who appear to be successful in adding value to their businesses have processes and corporate staffing levels that are both widely different from each other and, in many cases, that are out of tune with accepted best practice at the time.

These observations have taught us that personal skills and cultural fit are the key issues; that the skills of the individuals involved and the organisational heritage in which they operate can make essentially the 'same' process either effective or ineffective. We have also learned that the opportunities to add value with a given process or level of centralisation differ depending on the specific needs of the businesses in question. A 'one size fits all' approach to designing the nature and composition of the parent is inappropriate.

Why it matters

The importance of the size, staffing and design of the corporate office is not in question, and managers devote considerable attention to it. But if corporate functions and processes are not developed as an integral part of the overall value adding corporate strategy, they may be in line with general good practice, but lead to little or no improvement in performance. Equally, it is far more important for parent managers to possess idiosyncratic skills that are suitable for the parenting opportunities they are targeting than for them to be abreast of all the currently fashionable general management trends. Worse still, changing from existing arrangements to make them fit better with general good practice may undermine value creation that is currently being achieved due to the special circumstances of the portfolio and the managers running it. Without a clear focus on selected parenting opportunities, simply going through the motions, however professionally, is as likely to destroy value as create it.

> *Proposition: Corporate centres, functions, and processes designed to achieve general best practice lack sufficient focus to achieve outstanding results: They should be designed more idiosyncratically to fit with the specific opportunities targeted by the corporate-level strategy.*

DIVERSITY

What we have learned

For many years, it has been felt that highly diverse multibusiness companies must be more difficult to manage than less diverse companies. An extensive stream of academic research has sought to examine the comparative performance of 'related' and 'unrelated' diversification strategies, where 'relatedness' was measured in terms of technologies, markets and customers.

Yet the evidence has not provided conclusive support for the intuitively appealing idea that related corporate strategies should outperform unrelated ones. And the performance of companies such as Hanson, BTR and KKR in the 1980s and of Virgin and GE in the 1990s provide specific counter-examples. 'Relatedness' seems to be neither a necessary nor a sufficient condition of a successful multibusiness strategy.

During the 1980s, a new approach to measuring diversity began to emerge. Prahalad and Bettis suggested that the mindsets and skills of the corporate team provided the constraint on how much diversity was manageable. There was a 'dominant logic' that tended to be applied across the whole portfolio, irrespective of the strategic characteristics of each business. The Ashridge Strategic Management Centre notion of 'management styles' also suggested that each corporate team had a well-defined approach that it brought to bear on all the businesses in the portfolio.

More recently, we have pushed these ideas further, arguing that diversity is best measured in terms of the differences in parenting needs and opportunities between businesses in the portfolio. Businesses with different critical success factors require parenting that is sympathetic to these differences, and businesses with different opportunities for parental value creation require different parenting skills and resources that are suitable for realising the opportunities in question. Our research has shown that successful corporate parents have portfolios of businesses that are relatively homogeneous in terms of parenting needs and opportunities, and that many corporate strategy disasters can be explained in terms of straying into businesses that turned out not to be responsive to the dominant parenting approach of the company.

These findings show why conventional measures of relatedness have proved imperfect predictors of corporate performance, since they do not focus on the fit between the businesses and the parent. The successes of the Hansons, the KKRs and the Virgins are easy to appreciate in terms of parenting opportunities and fit, but incomprehensible in terms of relatedness as conventionally defined.

Why it matters

A valid means of measuring diversity provides vital guidance to corporate parents who may have been impressed by the current vogue for 'focusing on core businesses', but are unsure how to determine which businesses should be included in the core. Now we can see that corporate parents should aim to focus their portfolios around businesses with similar parenting needs and opportunities, for which the parent either has or can build suitable parenting skills and resources. These are the businesses in which the parent is likely to be able to add the most value; we refer to them as 'heartland' businesses. To avoid excessive diversity, corporate parents should focus their portfolios on heartland businesses.

> *Proposition: Past measures of diversity based on conventional concepts of relatedness have proved unsatisfactory: To avoid excessive diversity, corporate parents should build their portfolios around businesses with similarities in terms of parenting needs and opportunities.*

STRETCH AND FIT

What we have learned

Some critics regard Ashridge Strategic Management Centre's approach to corporate strategy as too cautious. Our emphasis on the pervasiveness of value destruction, the need for a close fit between parenting capabilities and business needs, and the dangers of excessive diversification, they claim, prevents companies from seeing the potential of radical new strategies with stretching goals. And, without stretching ambitions, companies become slow moving, flabby and lacking in motivation.

We accept the need for 'stretch' as well as 'fit'. Our research supports the desirability of a continuous search for new opportunities and a commitment to refining and extending parenting skills. We recognise both the excitement of fresh challenges that cannot easily be met and the stultifying effects of an unwillingness to alter the *status quo*.

But we are also realists. We have observed how frequently corporate strategies fail because parents are overoptimistic about their ability to build new skills and understand new types of businesses. We have researched numerous diversification attempts in which there were gross underestimates of how much time and attention it would take for the parent to get to grips with the new business. As a result, we believe that much of the advice that companies receive about rejuvenation, growth ambitions, and long term survival causes managers to launch initiatives that are foolhardy rather than bold. At the least, stretch should be tempered with realism when corporate strategies are being developed, and a balance should be maintained between stretch for new opportunities and fit with the parent's existing skills.

Why it matters

A recognition that stretch should be balanced by realism is valuable. It should prevent complacency and encourage innovative ideas, while at the same time helping to eliminate many of the more extreme disasters of excessive corporate ambition (Sony in Hollywood, Exxon in office equipment, Daimler-Benz in white goods, Saatchi and Saatchi in management consulting, ...).

A company with low growth or declining core businesses faces three options. It can aggressively seek a new 'heartland' with 'platform' initiatives (investments in new or different businesses designed to speed the learning of new parenting skills). It can experiment with 'edge of heartland' investments, in the hope of evolving towards a broader heartland which offers more potential. Or it can decide to focus on its mature core and be the best in a limited field. Whereas many advisers and managers rule out the last option as defeatist, we believe it is often a reasonable choice. In a dynamic economy, new rising organisations will always be balanced with others that decline. Helping some businesses decline gracefully, without too many development attempts, may be as important as helping other businesses to broaden their portfolios and set ambitions for the next century.

Moreover, companies that do push forward into new businesses will prosper more if they choose those that are compatible with parenting skills that they have or can develop. Many parent organisations are 'stretching' their skills too far in pursuit of new opportunities, when they would do better to choose a narrower range of businesses where greater 'fit' can be created.

> *Proposition: Many corporate parents are over-ambitious about the speed with which they can build new skills and understand new types of businesses: Good corporate strategies should maintain a balance between 'stretch' for new opportunities and 'fit' with the parent's existing skills.*

BUSINESS UNIT DEFINITION AND CORPORATE STRUCTURE

What we have learned

Business units represent the basic building blocks in any multibusiness company. The boundaries around the business units

- establish what groups of activities will receive the focused attention of a single management team, and will be aggregated together for performance measurement and reporting purposes
- determine what entities will report to the corporate parent and, conversely, what entities the corporate parent will need to add value to
- establish the scope for lateral synergies by determining what activities fall within each unit, and hence what the opportunities are for units to link with each other.

Business unit definitions can either protect activities from the corporate parent's attention or expose them to it – thereby inhibiting or opening up the possibilities for the parent either to create or destroy value. Business unit definitions have a profound impact on the behaviour and aims of business managers and on the size and nature of parenting opportunities. Inappropriate business definitions lead to compromised business strategies and missed opportunities for parental value creation.

In companies with intermediate parenting levels, such as divisions, the grouping of businesses into divisions is also important. Lack of clarity on the added value role of different levels, groups and individuals within the parent leads to redundant cost, confusion, and reductions in net value creation. Where the parenting tasks are shared between different individuals, their respective responsibilities also need to be clearly defined and complementary. Getting the unit definitions and corporate structure right is an important precondition for a successful corporate strategy.

Why it matters

No-one doubts that business unit definition and corporate structure are important topics. Typically, they are high on chief executives' agendas. But a perspective on these issues that stresses value creation and the role of the parent is much less common; history, personal ambition and corporate politics often seem to be the major considerations. Instead, careful analysis of the advantages of breadth versus focus in business definition and of the impact of different structures on corporate value creation should underpin these organisational choices.

> *Proposition: Business unit boundaries and corporate reporting structures have a profound impact on both the value creation opportunities and the value destruction risks for the corporate parent: Decisions on unit definitions and corporate structures should be determined by careful analysis of their likely impact on net value creation, not by history, ambition and politics.*

FUTURE RESEARCH CHALLENGES

We see four priority areas for future research:

1. How companies can build the parenting skills that enable them to grow into new businesses.
    - By what means have corporate parents that have presided successfully over radical changes in their portfolios learnt new competencies?
    - How much time, investment and change (e.g. people change) is needed to develop a portfolio into new business areas?
    - Is it possible to distinguish in advance those new business growth ambitions that will be achievable from those that will be a bridge too far?
    - What are the chances of success with new business initiatives, and how can the odds be improved? Is it possible to identify those companies that would be better off trimming their development ambitions, breaking up or focusing more tightly?
    - Which development paths are most successful? Are there lessons to be learned from successful developers?
2. How to manage the internal and external boundaries of the corporation to create value, and in particular how to create value without full ownership.
    - How can the boundaries between business units, and between the company and third party organisations, be managed most effectively?
    - What effect do different ways of defining business units have on corporate value creation?
    - What is the impact of ownership versus joint venture versus alliance versus relational long-term contracts?
3. Better understanding of the organisation structures and capabilities needed to implement corporate strategies successfully.
    - What are the best ways to divide up tasks between different levels, groups and individuals in complex parent organisations?
    - How should corporate headquarters be designed to support the corporate strategy and to avoid being driven by empire-building or bureaucratic expansion?
    - How can the skills needed to implement a given corporate strategy be defined as fully and clearly as possible? What is the best way to develop these skills?

- What career paths best prepare a manager for a role as corporate parent? From what pools of managers should parent managers be selected and how can the quality of these pools be enhanced?

4. More precise means of measuring the net value added by the corporate parent.
   - What techniques are being used or can be developed to identify and quantify more precisely the ways in which the parent adds and subtracts value?
   - What are the best measures of value to use?

18

RELATED DIVERSIFICATION, CORE COMPETENCES AND CORPORATE PERFORMANCE

Constantinos C. Markides and Peter J. Williamson

Despite nearly 30 years of academic research on the benefits of related diversification, there is still considerable disagreement about precisely how and when diversification can be used to build long-run competitive advantage. In this paper we argue that the disagreement exists for two main reasons: (a) the traditional way of measuring relatedness between two businesses is incomplete because it ignores the 'strategic importance' and similarity of the underlying assets residing in these businesses, and (b) the way researchers have traditionally thought of relatedness is limited, primarily because it has tended to equate the benefits of relatedness with the static exploitation of economies of scope (asset amortization), thus ignoring the main contribution of related diversification to long-run, competitive advantage; namely the potential for the firm to expand its stock of strategic assets and create new ones more rapidly and at lower cost than rivals who are not diversified across related businesses. An empirical test supports our view that 'strategic' relatedness is superior to market relatedness in predicting when related diversifiers outperform unrelated ones.

A fundamental part of any firm's corporate strategy is its choice of what portfolio of businesses to compete in. According to the academic literature, this decision should reflect the 'superiority' of related diversification over unrelated diversification (e.g., Ansoff, 1965; Bettis, 1981; Lecraw, 1984; Palepu, 1985; Rumelt, 1974; Singh and Montgomery, 1987). This is because related diversification presumably allows the corporate center to exploit the interrelationships that exist among its different businesses (SBUs) and so achieve cost and/or differentiation competitive advantages over its rivals. But despite 30 years of research on the benefits of related diversification, there is still considerable disagreement about precisely how and when diversification can be used to build long-run competitive advantage (e.g., Hoskisson and Hitt, 1990; Ramanujam and Varadarajan, 1989; Reed and Luffman, 1986). In this paper we argue this disagreement exists for two main reasons:

1. Traditional measures of relatedness provide an incomplete and potentially exaggerated picture of the scope for a corporation to exploit interrelationships between its SBUs. This is because traditional measures look at relatedness only at the industry or market level. But as we explain below, the relatedness that really matters is that between 'strategic assets' (i.e., those that cannot be accessed quickly and cheaply by nondiversified competitors).[1] Therefore, to accurately measure whether two businesses are related, we need to go beyond broad definitions of relatedness that focus on market similarity; we need to look at the similarities between the underlying strategic assets of the various businesses that a company is operating in (see also Hill, 1994).

2. The way researchers have traditionally thought of relatedness is limited. This is because it has tended to equate the benefits of relatedness with the static exploitation of economies of scope. While we would not deny that economies of scope are an important short-term benefit of related diversification, we believe the real leverage comes from exploiting relatedness to create and accumulate *new* strategic assets more quickly and cheaply than competitors (rather than simply amortizing existing assets – i.e., reaping economies of scope). To predict how much a strategy of related diversification will contribute to superior, *long-run* returns it is necessary to distinguish between four types of potential advantages of related diversification.

   a. the potential to reap economies of scope across SBUs that can share the same strategic asset (such as a common distribution system);

   b. the potential to use a core competence amassed in the course of building or maintaining an existing strategic asset in one SBU to help improve the quality of an existing strategic asset in another of the corporation's SBUs (for example, what Honda learns as it gains more experience managing its existing dealer network for small cars may help it improve the management of its largely separate network for motorbikes);

   c. the potential to utilize a core competence developed through the experience of building strategic assets in existing businesses, to create a *new* strategic asset in a *new* business faster, or at lower cost (such as using the experience of building motorbike distribution to build a new, parallel distribution system for lawn mowers – which are generally sold through a different type of outlet);

   d. the potential for the process of related diversification to expand a corporation's existing pool of core competences because, as it builds strategic assets in a new business, it will learn new skills. These, in turn, that will allow it to improve the quality of its stocks of strategic assets in its existing businesses (in the course of building a new distribution system for lawn mowers, Honda may learn new skills that allow it to improve its existing distribution system for motorbikes).

We term these four potential advantages of related diversification 'asset amortization,' 'asset improvement,' 'asset creation' and 'asset fission' respectively.

We will argue that the long-run value of a related diversification lies *not so much* in the exploitation of economies of scope (asset amortization) – where the benefit is primarily short-term – but in allowing corporations to more cost efficiently expand their stocks of strategic assets. Relatedness, which opens the way for asset improvement, asset creation and asset fission, holds the key to the long-run competitive advantages of diversification.

This means that in most cases, similarities in the *processes* by which strategic assets are expanded and new strategic assets are created are more important than static similarities between the strategic assets that are the *outcome* of those processes. Firms that are diversified across a set of 'related markets' where the strategic assets are either few, or the processes required to improve and create them are context-specific cannot be expected to out-perform unrelated diversifiers.

THE MEASURE OF RELATEDNESS

The strategy of related diversification is considered superior to unrelated diversification because it allows the firm to exploit interrelationships among its different business units. Specifically, the corporate center in related diversifiers is expected to *identify* important assets residing in any one of its SBUs and then *transfer* these assets and *utilize* them in another SBU. Canon's deployment of technology from its camera SBU in developing its photocopier business is a good example.[2]

Even though the advantages of the strategy of related diversification are usually cast in terms of the cost of differentiation benefits that arise from the cross-utilization of the firm's *underlying assets*, the actual measurement of relatedness between two businesses often does not even consider the underlying assets residing in these businesses. Relatedness has been traditionally measured in two basic ways (e.g., Montgomery, 1982; Pitts and Hopkins, 1982): (i) using an objective index like the entropy index of SIC count (e.g., Caves *et al.*, 1980; Jacquemin and Berry, 1979, Palepu, 1985) which assumes that if two businesses share the same SIC they must have common input requirements and similar production/technology functions; and/or (ii) using a more subjective measure such as Rumelt's (1974) diversification categories which consider businesses as related '... when a common skill, resource, market, or purpose applies to each' (Rumelt, 1974: 29).

We do not doubt that the traditional measures could be acceptable proxies for what they are trying to measure. In fact, if these measures did not suffer from any *systematic* bias, one would consider them as a 'good enough' way to substitute for a costly and time consuming ideal measure. However, they do suffer from one systematic bias. Consider a firm using the strategy of related diversification so as to exploit the relatedness of its SBU-level assets. Suppose, however, that the SBU-level assets that the corporate center is trying to exploit are not 'strategically important' (as defined below). For example, suppose that the asset services that Firm X provides to an SBU by cross-utilizing the assets of a sister subsidiary are such that any other firm can easily purchase on the open market at close to marginal cost. In that case, even if Firm X achieves short-term competitive advantage through exploitation of economies of scope, it will not really achieve any sustainable competitive advantage *over time*; other firms will quickly achieve similar positions by purchasing similar asset services. The opportunity for a diversified firm to amortize the costs of running a trucking fleet by sharing it across two SBUs is often a case in point. If non-diversified firms could buy similar trucking services from a common carrier (which itself achieves the economies of scope across customers) at close to marginal cost, then there would be no competitive advantage to diversification even though the two markets were closely 'related' according to traditional measures like SIC similarity.

This implies that any measure of relatedness should take into consideration not only whether the underlying SBU-level assets of a firm are related, but also consider whether these assets are a potential source of competitive advantage. Even if the traditional measures of relatedness do a good job in capturing the relatedness of the underlying assets, they *consistently* ignore the evaluation of whether these assets are 'strategic' assets; and they do so because in measuring relatedness, they do not *explicitly* consider the underlying assets.

Strategic assets

To win competitive advantage in any market, a firm needs to be able to deliver a given set of customer benefits at lower costs than competitors, or provide customers with a bundle of benefits

its rivals cannot match (Porter, 1980). It can do so by harnessing the drivers of cost and differentiation in its specific industry. For example, if scale is an important driver of cost leadership then those firms that operate large-scale plants will outperform their subscale competitors. However, to effectively exploit these cost and differentiation drivers, the firm needs to access and utilize a complex set of tangible and intangible assets. For example, to reap the benefits of scale economies in production, it may require the services of tangible assets like a large-scale plant and intangible assets like the skills to manage this scale facility effectively and distributor loyalty to support a constant high volume of sales.[3]

Given that a particular set of asset stocks is necessary to allow a firm to exploit cost and differentiation advantages, the crucial question for a firm is: 'How can I access these assets?' A firm can secure these required asset services in a number of ways. It may obtain them with the *endowment* which establishes the business. A company established to exploit a proprietary technology, for example, often receives a valuable patent asset from its founder. It may *acquire* the assets on the open market, or contract directly for the services of an asset (as in the case of an equipment lease). It might access the required asset services by *sharing* the asset with a sister SBU or an alliance partner. Finally, it may *accumulate* the required asset through a process of combining tradeable inputs with existing asset stocks and learning by doing (Dierickx and Cool, 1989).

Firms that possess assets which underpin competitive advantage will earn rents (Rumelt, 1987). To the extent that competitors can identify these rent producing assets, they can decide between two alternative ways in replicating this competitive advantage: they may seek to imitate the assets through one of the four mechanisms above, or they may try to substitute them with other assets which can earn similar rents by producing equivalent or superior customer benefits. *The assets on which long-term competitive advantage critically depends (strategic assets) are, therefore, those that are imperfectly imitable and imperfectly substitutable* (Barney, 1986; Dierickx and Cool, 1989).

The importance of asset accumulation processes

The conditions above imply that assets which are readily tradeable cannot act as sources of long-term competitive advantage (Williamson, 1975). Similarly, assets which can be quickly and/or cheaply accessed through endowment, acquisition or sharing can only provide competitive advantage which is short-lived. In the long run, internal accumulation is likely to be the most significant source of imperfectly imitable and imperfectly substitutable assets. This is because most assets will be subject to erosion over time (see e.g., Eaton and Lipsey, 1980). Customer assets like brands, for example, will decay as new customers enter the market or former customers forget past experience or exit the market. The value of a stock of technical know-how will tend to erode in the face of innovation by competitors. Patents will expire. Thus, assets accessed through initial endowment or an initial asset base shared with another SBU will tend to lose their potency as sources of competitive advantage over time unless they are replenished by internal accumulation processes.

Moreover, even when an asset can be accessed through acquisition, alliance, or sharing, it is quite likely that the existing assets available will not perfectly fit the requirements of the market they will be used to serve. Existing assets generally need some adaptation to a specific market context and integration with existing asset bundles. Internal asset accumulation processes therefore play a role in molding assets which an SBU accesses externally into a competitive, market-specific bundle.

Regardless of whether the initial stock of strategic assets within an SBU is obtained by endowment or acquisition, or accessed through sharing, therefore, the long-term competitive advantage of a firm will largely depend on its ability to continuously adapt and improve its strategic assets to meet market-specific demands and to create new strategic assets that it can exploit in existing or new markets.

If these asset accumulation processes were frictionless and firms could speed them up at little cost, then it would be difficult for a firm that gained an initial advantage in respect of a set of assets (e.g., through endowment, sharing or first mover experience in a new, growing segment of the market) to maintain this lead. In practice, however, there are many impediments which prevent laggards from replicating or surpassing the asset positions of the leaders. Dierickx and Cool (1989) identify four separate categories of these impediments to asset accumulation: time compression diseconomies, asset mass efficiencies, asset interconnectedness and causal ambiguity.[4] These impediments also lie behind the concept of barriers to mobility (Caves and Porter, 1977) and Rumelt's 'isolating mechanisms' which include property rights on scarce resources, lags, information asymmetries and other sources of friction in processes of asset imitation (Rumelt, 1987).

When the process necessary to accumulate an asset suffers from one or more of these impediments, all firms will face higher costs and time delays in building it. This will restrict their ability to satisfy their market by offering the differentiation or cost advantages that the elusive asset would underpin. Impediments like time compression diseconomies, asset mass efficiencies and asset interconnectedness, however, will impose higher costs on later entrants to a business, making it more difficult for them to catch up with first movers and established firms who have had longer to accumulate nontradeable assets. Diversifiers entering a market for the first time against established firms would therefore suffer a handicap from late arrival, other things being equal.

It may be, however, that by deploying its existing core competences a diversifier can overcome some of these frictions. By drawing on its existing competence pool, such a corporation may be able to imitate valuable, nontradeable assets, or accumulate new, substitute ones, or create entirely new strategic assets more cheaply and quickly than competitors who lacked access to similar core competences: to grow new trees more rapidly and more cheaply by drawing on a common, existing root stock. Likewise, by properly deploying core competences between business units, a diversified corporation may also be able to maintain or extend its competitive advantage in its existing businesses through its ability to augment its nontradeable, market-specific assets more quickly and cheaply than its competitors. This is especially important in market environments that are undergoing significant change. Even firms with massive asset bases will lose their competitive advantage if they are unable to develop the new, strategic assets necessary to serve a changing market.

Core competences as catalysts in the 'production function' of strategic assets

If strategic assets are the imperfectly imitable, imperfectly substitutable and imperfectly tradeable assets necessary to underpin an SBU's cost or differentiation advantage in a particular market, then core competences can be viewed as the pool of experience, knowledge and systems, etc. that exist elsewhere in the same corporation which can be deployed to reduce the cost or time required either to create a new, strategic asset or expand the stock of an existing one. Competences are potential *catalysts* to the process of accumulating strategic assets. If the firm knows from past experience how to efficiently build the type of distribution network which will improve the competitiveness of its product (i.e., the 'competence' in building a suitable type of distribution network exists), then it will be able to put the necessary asset in place more quickly and cheaply than a firm which lacks this competence. Competences may also act as catalysts to the processes of adapting and integrating assets that an SBU has accessed through acquisition, alliances or sharing. Prahalad and Hamel (1990), for example, cite the case of NEC's competency in managing collaborative arrangements as an important factor in their ability to access and then internalize technological assets and skills from their alliance partners.

This catalytic role of competences in the 'production function' for building assets which are nontradeable, nonsubstitutable and difficult to accumulate is illustrated in Figure 18.1. Inputs include time, readily tradeable assets, existing nontradeable assets and the catalyst to the construction process: competences.

The obvious next question is: where can a firm get hold of the competences that would allow it to speed up its rates of asset accumulation, adaptation and integration? The first place to look is the open market. But competences themselves often have characteristics which render markets inefficient as a mechanism for exchange. Characteristics such as information impactedness and scope for opportunism make competences, like other intangible assets, difficult to sell at arms-length (Williamson, 1973; Caves, 1982, Ch. 1). This leads to excess capacity in competences which cannot be easily utilized by seeking buyers in the open market. Unique competences developed by an SBU through learning by doing therefore risk becoming 'imprisoned' in that unit, even though they could be potentially valuable catalysts to the process of asset accumulation in other businesses (Prahalad and Hamel, 1990).

Compared with the problems associated with trading competences in the open market, it is often more efficient to transfer competences between businesses using conduits *internal* to a single organization (Williamson, 1975). Such internal mechanisms include posting staff from one business unit to another, bringing together a corporate task force with individuals from a number of businesses to help solve a problem for one of them, and passing market intelligence or other information between SBUs which could act as catalysts to asset accumulation.

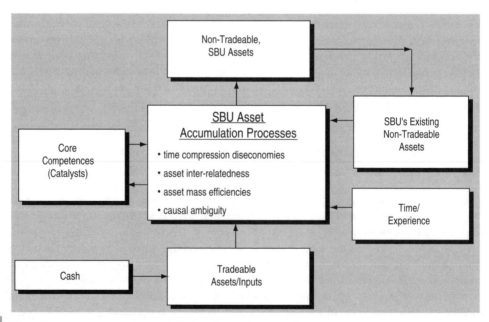

Figure 18.1 Core competences and the 'production function' for assets

Not all of the competences of a corporation which can act as catalysts in expanding the asset base of a new or existing SBU, however, will make an equal contribution to improving the competitive advantage of an SBU. Honda's competence in building networks of dealers for consumer durables may speed up the rate and improve the cost at which it can build an effective, specialized distribution network for its new lawn mower product. But if a competitor could effectively substitute this by a distribution agreement with one or two national retail chains, the Honda Corporation's competence may afford its lawn-mower SBU little or no competitive edge. Likewise, if a rival could acquire a suitable network at a competitive price, or obtain access to one through a strategic alliance, access to Honda Corporation's competence might provide its related SBU with little or no competitive advantage. In both of these cases, while the competence is both available and transferable, it does not lead to the creation of a strategic asset that is both hard to substitute and difficult to imitate.

By contrast, Honda's competence in small petrol engines may enable its lawn mower SBU to quickly and cost effectively bring a superior product to market, backed by a superior production process. If competitors had no way of matching the resulting buyer benefits, except by spending a great deal of money over a long period of time, Honda's engine design organization and the combination of its manufacturing hardware and software would represent extremely potent strategic assets for the lawn mower SBU once they were in place. So access to Honda's engine competence would be a very significant source of competitive advantage for its lawn mower SBU.

We therefore have two conditions which must be satisfied for internal transfer of competences between SBUs to create advantage for the corporation:

1. it must be more efficient to transfer the competence internally between businesses in the same group than via an external market;
2. the competence must be capable of acting as a catalyst to the creation of market-specific assets which are nontradeable, nonsubstitutable and slow or costly to accumulate, thereby acting as a source of competitive advantage for the recipient SBU.

The larger the efficiency advantage of internal transfer, and the more costly the resulting asset is to accumulate, the greater the advantage to be gained from shifting a competence from one business unit to another existing or new SBU.[5]

A DYNAMIC VIEW OF RELATEDNESS

So far we have established that an SBU's competitive advantage depends importantly on its access to strategic assets. We have also discussed how core competences can be used as catalysts in the processes of expanding an SBU's stock of strategic assets. The real, long-run benefits of relatedness should therefore lie in opening up opportunities to quickly and cheaply create and accumulate these strategic assets. It is then possible to distinguish five different types of relatedness.[6] These distinctions help pinpoint exactly when and how related diversification will lead to competitive advantage for a corporation (and when it will not).

The first category, we term 'exaggerated relatedness.' This is where the markets served by two SBUs share many similarities, but there is little potential to exploit these similarities for competitive advantage. The relatedness is 'exaggerated' in the sense that looking at the overall similarity (which traditional measures of market-relatedness tend to do, as we explain below), overstates the likelihood that a corporation will achieve superior performance by diversifying across both markets. This exaggeration may arise under any of a number of different conditions. It may be that while the diversified firm can quickly and cheaply build the asset stocks necessary to supply the market, so can any other firm, because most of these assets are easily imitable. Even if other, nondiversified firms cannot replicate the assets built by the diversifier, they may be able to substitute some other, readily available asset at no disadvantage to their competitiveness. In short, the assets that that relatedness helps a diversifier build may be *non-strategic*. A manufacturer of fashion knitwear in Europe or North America, for example, may have the competence to bring a local production facility for knitting standard, men's socks on-stream quickly and efficiently. But such a facility may prove a nonstrategic asset against competitors who rely on off-shore sourcing for this type of nontime sensitive, nonfashion product. This type of relatedness, therefore, would not create an opportunity for profitable diversification.

Similarly, exaggerated relatedness may arise when the market-specificity of the strategic assets and the competences that can help build them, are underestimated by the indicators a diversifier chooses to consider. Diversification by Levis from jeans into men's suits, for example, was recognized as a failure. The two businesses may appear highly related on many dimensions from production through to marketing and distribution, but the strategic assets and competences required to build competitive advantage turned out to be very different.

The second type of relatedness arises where the strategic assets in one SBU can be shared with another to achieve economies of scope (e.g., Porter, 1987; Teece, 1982). This type of relatedness underpins what we term 'amortization advantage,' by allowing related diversifiers to amortize the cost of an existing asset by using it to serve multiple markets. This type of relatedness can offer important, short-term advantages in the form of reduced costs and improved differentiation. But, for most corporations, diversification is a long-term step that could be costly to reverse. And simply exploiting its *existing* stock of assets (even if they are the 'right' assets) cannot be enough to create *long-term* competitive advantages (e.g., Prahalad and Hamel, 1990). The truly successful firms over the long term will be the ones that continuously *create new* strategic assets.

The third category of relatedness is where the strategic asset itself cannot be shared or transferred between two SBUs (because it is market-specific), but the competence gained in the process of building or maintaining an existing strategic asset in one SBU can be used as a catalyst to help improve the quality of an existing strategic asset in another SBU. This role of competences in asset accumulation is illustrated with the example of Canon's camera, photocopier and laser printer divisions in Figure 18.2.

Consider the position at Canon at the point where the company has successfully established itself in both the camera and photocopier businesses. Many of the strategic assets which underpin these respective SBUs cannot be shared directly. The dealer networks and component manufacturing plans are largely specific to each SBU. But in the course of its operations producing and marketing cameras, the camera division has extended this initial asset stock by a mix of learning-by-doing and further purchases of assets in the market. As a by-product of this asset accumulation process, the camera business also developed a series of competences like knowledge of how to increase the effectiveness of a dealer network, how to develop new products combining optics and electronics and how to squeeze better productivity out of high-volume assembly lines.

Because Canon is in two businesses, cameras and photocopiers, where the processes of improving dealer effectiveness, speeding up product development or improving assembly-line productivity are similar, it can improve the quality of the strategic assets in its photocopier business,

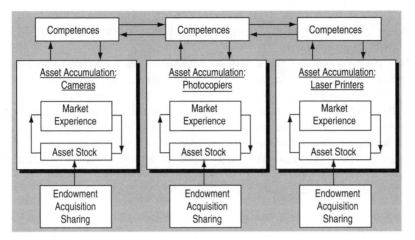

Figure 18.2 Core competences and asset accumulation at Canon

by transferring competences learned in its camera business and vice versa. This type of related-ness, similarities in the *processes* required to improve the effectiveness and efficiency of separate, market-specific stocks of strategic assets in two businesses, opens up opportunities for what we call 'asset improvement' advantages for related diversifiers.

The fourth type of relatedness emerges where there is potential to utilize a core competence developed through the experience of building strategic assets in existing businesses, to create a *new* strategic asset in a *new* business faster, or at lower cost. For example, in the course of oper-ating in the photocopier market, and building the asset base required to out-compete rivals, this SBU also accumulated its own, additional competences that the camera SBU had not developed. These may have included how to build a marketing organization targeted to business, rather than personal buyers, and how to develop and manufacture a reliable electrostatic printing engine.

When Canon diversified into laser printers, this new SBU started out with an endowment of assets, additional assets acquired in the market and arrangement to share facilities and core com-ponents. But even more important for its long-term competitiveness, the new laser printer SBU was able to draw on the competences built up by its sister businesses in cameras and photo-copiers to create new, market-specific strategic assets faster and more efficiently than its com-petitors (illustrated by the arrows pointing to the right in Figure 18.2). This kind of relatedness, where the competences amassed by existing SBUs can be deployed to speed up and reduce the cost of creating new market-specific strategic assets for the use of a new SBU, we term the 'asset creation' advantage of related diversifiers. Again, only where the processes required to build the particular strategic assets needed by the new SBU are 'related' in the sense that they can benefit from existing core competences, will this type of diversification advantage be available.

The fifth, and final, type of relatedness is where in the process of creating the new strategic assets required to support diversification into a new business (like laser printers), the corporation learns new competences that can then be used to enhance its existing SBUs. For example, in creat-ing the assets required to support the design, manufacture and service of the more sophisticated electronics demanded by the laser printer business, Canon may have developed new compe-tences that could be used to improve its photocopier business. Alternatively, by combining the competences developed in its photocopier and laser printer businesses, may have helped it to quickly and cheaply build the strategic assets required to succeed in a fourth market: that for plain paper facsimiles. This kind of advantage over single-business firms or unrelated diversifiers, we term 'asset fission' advantage.

It is these last three types of relatedness that are likely to offer the greatest advantages from related diversification over the long-run. As the label suggests, exaggerated relatedness offers little or no scope for a strategy of related diversification to deliver superior performance, despite what may be a high degree of similarity between two markets. Related diversification designed to reap economies of scope, helping to amortize existing assets, is likely to provide only ephemeral advantage. Only relatedness that allows a corporation to access asset improvement, asset creation and asset fission promises long-run competitive advantage to related diversifiers. The problem is that traditional measures of relatedness have not been designed to distinguish between these profitable and unprofitable types of diversification.

Extending traditional measures of market relatedness: Towards strategic relatedness

As we have seen above, it is not broad market-relatedness that matters. Two markets may be closely related, but if the opportunity to rapidly build assets using competences from elsewhere in the corporation does no more than generate asset stocks which others can buy or contract in at similar cost, then no competitive advantage will ensue from a strategy of diversification between them. 'Strategic relatedness' between two markets, in the sense that they value nontradeable, nonsubstitutable assets with similar production functions, is a requirement for diversification to yield supernormal profits in the long run. By failing to take into account differences in the opportunities to build strategic assets offered by different market environments, the traditional measures suffer from the 'exaggeration' problem described above. They will wrongly impute a benefit to related diversification across markets where the relatedness is primarily among nonstrategic assets.

In order to operationalize the concept of strategic relatedness, we need to develop indicators of the importance of similar types of nontradeable, nonsubstitutable and hard-to-accumulate assets in different market environments. These types of assets may be divided into five broad classes (Verdin and Williamson, 1994):

- *customer assets*, such as brand recognition, customer loyalty and installed base;
- *channel assets*, such as established channel access, distributor loyalty and pipeline stock;
- *input assets*, such as knowledge of imperfect factor markets, loyalty of suppliers and financial capacity;
- *process assets*, such as proprietary technology, product or market-specific functional experience (e.g., in marketing or production) and organizational systems;
- *market knowledge assets*, such as accumulated information on the goals and behavior of competitors, price elasticity of demand or market response to the business cycle.

Thus, if our indicator suggested that channel access and distributor relationships were likely to be very important to competitive advantage in each of two markets, we would identify them as 'strategically related' on this dimension. We would then be more confident that core competences in building networks of channel relationships would be applicable to both. If, on the other hand, the second market involved a product that was most effectively sold directly to a small number of buyers, we would class the markets as having lower strategic relatedness on the channel dimension. Although these markets may be closely related in some other way, such as use of similar raw materials, the opportunity to benefit from transfer of competences in building a third-party distribution network would not be available. Meanwhile, if all competitors could buy raw material inputs at a similar price, relatedness on the input dimension would not offer a source of competitive advantage. The relatedness between this second pair of markets would be 'non-strategic.'

We could then develop an overall picture of the degree of strategic relatedness between pairs of markets by using a portfolio of indicators, each one seeking to measure the extent to which competence in building the same class of strategic asset could add to competitive advantage in both environments. The higher the level of strategic relatedness between two markets, other things equal, the larger would be the expected gains from diversification of firms from one to the other.

We are the first to acknowledge that the structural indicators we use in the empirical investigation that follows are not direct measures of how similar the processes required to build strategic assets are between two markets. We are not able to develop a direct, quantitative measure of the degree to which core competences are transferable across SBUs serving each set of markets where our sample firms operate. However, we would contend that by going beyond the standard variables used to capture industry structure (like advertising and R&D intensity), to include indicators such as whether the product lines in each market are made-to-order or sold from stock, or how many of the product lines require after-sales service, we have taken an important step towards this goal. Specifically, we believe that our measures come closer to capturing the extent to which two markets share similar nontradeable, nonsubstitutable and imperfectly imitable assets (often intangibles), with potential to draw on the same root-stock of competences, than traditional measures (especially since these have largely ignored the distribution, marketing and service requirements as well as the need for customization during manufacture, that our measures emphasize).

In what follows, we discuss the structural indicators used for three of the main classes of strategic assets on which we have data: customer assets, channel assets, and process experience assets.

Customer asset indicators

The first set of indicators seeks to capture the fact that the nature of interactions with the customer is an important determinant of the types of assets necessary to effectively serve a market.

1. Customer concentration/fragmentation. This indicator, *FEWCUST*, measures the degree to which each manufacturer deals with few, large customers rather than interfacing with a fragmented base of accounts. *FEWCUST* is defined as the percentage of product lines for which there were less than 1000 customer accounts at the manufacturer level. If the manufacturer deals through resellers, it will reflect the number of distributor accounts which it must manage. To the extent that the manufacturer also deals direct with users, these additional accounts are also included in computing this measure.

Our objective is to capture the extent to which there is scope for manufacturers to build deep and sustained relationships with their account base: dedicating a member of sales staff to individual customers; responding to customer's specific commercial and information needs; developing proprietary IT interfaces; using consignment stocks and so on. To the extent that a corporation's portfolio of markets shares these similar sales management requirements, we would expect there to be greater opportunities for building and sharing core competences in these areas. Conversely, if a corporation's portfolio was strategically unrelated on this dimension, including a mix of businesses some with a concentrated account base and others facing account fragmentation, we would expect fewer opportunities for building and sharing core competences in sales and customer service.

2. Service requirement.   Good customer relationships (service reputation) and organizational capital (to provide quality service), both largely nontradeable assets, are likely to be more important in industries characterized by a high level of service requirement. Access to core competences in rapidly establishing an organization capable of providing quality service to the customer will offer greater advantage in such markets. To the extent that a corporation's portfolio of markets shares these similar service management requirements, we would expect there to be greater opportunities for building and sharing core competences in these areas. The service requirement in the industry is measured by the percentage of product lines requiring a 'moderate to high' degree of after sales or technical service (HSERV).

Channel asset indicators

A second class of indicators refers to the importance of imperfectly tradeable, channel-related assets as a basis for competitive advantage. Such assets are likely to be more important in industries where a large portion of the products are sold through intermediaries: opportunities for a related diversifier to share competences in delivering products, information and service to the customer will then be high.

3. Channel dependence.   Our indicator of the degree of third-party channel dependence, *CHANNEL*, is the percentage of products which pass through an intermediary before reaching the final user, rather than being sold direct to users by the manufacturer.

Distribution relationships are a critical asset in many businesses dependent on third-party channels. They are also difficult to trade on a free standing basis. Skills in building and managing distribution and dealer networks form the basis of a potentially important core competence. Where market economics dictate that that dependence on third-party channels is high, competences in dealer recruitment and overcoming 'shelf space' restrictions (Porter, 1976) will be valuable in assisting an SBU to accumulate the assets it requires to compete effectively. Strategic relatedness will also tend to be higher among markets that share similar levels of channel dependence.

Process experience asset indicators

In most industries it is important to build up relevant process experience and associated assets in order to underpin competitive advantage. We use two measures to indicate the degree of similarity between the types of process experience assets that SBUs require: the proportion of products which are made to order and the average skill level of employees.

4. Product customization (products made to order) vs. standardization.   Successful made-to-order supply depends on a variety of asset bases to facilitate two-way communication with customers, the design and management of flexible manufacturing systems, and the reduction of lead times. Efficient supply of products from stock requires a different set of tangible and intangible assets which underpin effective stock, control, demand forecasting, and batching and run-length efficiencies, etc. In both cases, nontradeable assets play a potentially important role, but the nature of the assets and the competences required to accumulate them differ. Strategic relatedness between businesses will therefore tend to be high when they share a common focus on either made-to-order production or supply from stock.

Our measure of relatedness on this dimension is the percentage of product lines supplied by the business which are made to order based on customer specifications (*TORDER*).

5. The average skill level of the labor force.   In businesses where groups of skilled staff are an important source of advantage, human capital and the associated systems to generate and manage will be even more critical to advantage than in businesses with high labor intensity, but low skill levels. Again, businesses which share the need to develop an effective base of skilled staff with experience working together will have higher strategic relatedness than a pair of businesses, one requiring highly skilled staff and the other, a base of cost effective, low skilled workers.

Our indicator, SKILL, measures the proportion of 'high-skilled' jobs in the industry as a percentage of total employment.

HYPOTHESES, DATA AND METHODOLOGY

Hypotheses

So far we have argued that the traditional way of measuring relatedness between two businesses is incomplete; to be meaningful, relatedness needs to consider: (i) the 'strategic importance' of the underlying assets of these two businesses (i.e., are these assets nontradeable and nonsubstitutable?); and (ii) whether these assets are related. Only firms that exhibit this type of 'strategic relatedness' will perform well in the long term. This implies that if we were to measure the performance of firms classified as 'related' in the traditional (Rumelt) way and again according to whether their underlying strategic assets are related, we should be able to show that the latter way of looking at relatedness is superior. Therefore:

Hypothesis 1: Related diversifiers will outperform unrelated firms only where they compete across a portfolio of markets where similar types of accumulated assets are important.

In addition, the above discussion suggests that even within the population of related-diversified firms (defined as such in the traditional way), some related firms will do better than other related firms. Specifically, those related firms that compete across a portfolio of markets where similar types of accumulated assets are important should outperform the related firms that compete in a portfolio of markets where accumulated assets are less important or the types of strategic assets required differ widely across the firm's portfolio. Therefore:

Hypothesis 2: Related firms that compete in a portfolio of markets where similar types of accumulated assets are important will outperform other related firms.

Data and methodology

To test these hypotheses, a sample of 200 firms was randomly selected from the 1981 *Fortune 500* list. The population of *Fortune 500* firms was selected for study because it contains many diversified firms. The sample firms were classified according to Rumelt's (1974) diversification categories (i.e., Single-business; Dominant-business; Related-business; and Unrelated-business), using data from the TRINET tapes as well as their annual reports. Since this is a study on diversification, the Single-business firms were excluded from the sample. Hence, the final sample consists of 164 diversified firms.

To test Hypothesis 1 we first measure relatedness in the traditional (Rumelt) way as a (0,1) dummy (*RELATED*): those firms classified as Related or Dominant take the value of 1, while firms classified as Unrelated take the value of 0. The following equation is then estimated

$$ROS_i = \alpha + \beta_i(RELATED) + \sum_{i=2}^{4}\beta_i(IND)_i + \epsilon \tag{1}$$

where *ROS* is the profitability of the sample firms, measured as return on sales, and *IND* are industry control variables. We use three standard variables to control for industry effects: R&D intensity (RDSLS), measured as the total expenditure on R&D as a percentage of sales in a given industry; advertising intensity (WXAD), measured as expenditure on media advertising as a percentage of sales in an industry; and capital intensity (CAPX), measured as capital expenditures as a percentage of sales in an industry.[7] We decided to use return on sales (ROS) rather than return on assets (ROA) as our profitability variable for a specific reason: As explained by Ravenscraft and Scherer (1987), depending on the accounting method that a firm uses to account for an acquisition (pooling of interest vs. purchase accounting), profitability measures such as ROA end up *systematically* smaller under purchase accounting than under pooling of interest accounting. To avoid this potential bias we use ROS which is not affected by the accounting policies of acquisition recording. Finally, even though it is possible that profitability affects the industry variables as much as it is affected by them, we decided to treat the system as recursive rather than endogenous because we believe that feedbacks in the system occur at sufficiently long lags to allow us to pull out individual equations for separate treatment (e.g., Cowling, 1976).

After estimating Equation (1), we replace the *RELATED* variable by our structural indicators of relatedness to reestimate the above equation, i.e.

$$ROS_i = \alpha + \sum_{i=1}^{5}\beta_i K_i + \sum_{j=1}^{3}\beta_j(IND)_j + \epsilon \tag{2}$$

where K_i are the five structural indicators described in the previous section. In order to test our hypotheses about strategic relatedness, we express each K_i as the weighted average of each structural indicator 'i' divided by the weighted variance of the indicator across the businesses in each diversified firm's portfolio (A/V).[8] The reason for this transformation is best explained by example. Suppose we have two diversified firms, Firm X has 70 percent of its sales in a business requiring a high level of after-sales service, but has diversified the remainder of its sales into businesses where the products do not require any after-sales service. The indicator HSERV will therefore have a high variance for Firm X, suggesting little scope for sharing competences in building a service network. By dividing our average indicator by this variance, we are effectively discounting for the fact that any competence Firm X has in building an after-sales service network cannot be exploited in its other businesses (it is 'imprisoned'). Compare this with Firm Y which has all of its sales in two businesses, both of which require high after-sales service. Firm Y will score in two ways on our indicator K_i (compared with Firm X). It will start out with a high weighted average on HSERV. And the fact that both its businesses share a requirement for high after-sales service means that the variance of HSERV is very low for Firm Y, so the value of its competence in building effective service networks will not be discounted as it was for the unrelated diversifier, Firm X.

To calculate the weighted average of each structural indicator we first obtained an industry breakdown of the indicator from Bailey (1975). Next, each sample firm's sales by SIC were obtained from the TRINET tapes and the percentage of the firm's sales in each SIC was calculated. The industry-weighted average of each indicator was then calculated by multiplying the share of a firm's sales in each SIC by the corresponding value of the indicator in that SIC, and adding the results.

To calculate the weighted variance of each indicator, we used the following formula:

$$\text{variance } (x) = \sum (sx^2) - \bar{x}^2$$

where $\bar{x}^2$ = weighted average of the indicator x; and s = percentage of each industry (SIC) in total sales.

A priori we would expect that the coefficient of RELATED in Equation (1) is positive and significant, consistent with previous studies on related diversification. In addition, for Hypothesis 1 to be supported we should find: (a) the R^2 of Equation (2) significantly higher than the R^2 obtained from Equation (1), implying that Equation (2) does a better job in explaining the profitability differences between Related and Unrelated firms; and (b) the coefficients of the structural indicators in Equation (2) to be positive and significant.

To test Hypothesis 2 we simply estimate Equation (2) again, but only on the subsample of firms classified as 'related' in the traditional way ($N = 109$). The hypothesis will be supported in Equation (2) does a good job (as measured by its R^2) in explaining the variability in the profitability of related firms.

Data for calculating the five structural indicators and the three industry-control variables were derived from the following sources: The variables FEWCUST, CHANNEL, HSERV and TORDER, as defined above, were drawn from a U.S. survey of marketing expenditures (Bailey, 1975); the variables ROS, CAPX and WXAD come from Compustat; RDSLS was taken from the National Science Foundation (1978); and SKILL was computed from job classifications contained in the Census of Population (1980).

RESULTS

Table 18.1 presents descriptive statistics and correlations for all the variables in the study. The low intercorrelations among these variables suggest no problems with multicollinearity. The low correlations imply that there is sufficient independent variation among the variables used in this study to allow discrete effects to be estimated.

The estimated coefficients from Equation (1) are reported in Table 18.2. Consistent with previous studies, we find that Related diversification is positively correlated with profitability. Consistent with IO theory, we also find that the proxies for industry structure (advertising, capital and R&D intensity) are also positively correlated with profitability. The equation is statistically

Table 18.1 Means, standard deviations and intercorrelations[a]

Variable	Mean	S.D.	1	2	3	4	5	6	7	8	9
1. ROS	11.904	4.69	–								
2. A/V CHANNEL	0.732	2.34	0.014	–							
3. A/V TORDER	4.321	21.65	0.128	−0.819	–						
4. A/V FEWCUST	0.66	1.42	0.145	0.245	−0.029	–					
5. A/V HSERV	0.58	1.11	−0.015	−0.309	0.126	−0.528	–				
6. A/V SKILL	220.6	375.4	0.18	−0.336	0.495	−0.051	0.217	–			
7. CAPX	6.543	3.93	0.416	−0.051	0.064	−0.197	0.038	0.101	–		
8. WXAD	3.229	2.19	0.215	0.037	−0.019	0.139	−0.096	−0.133	0.0002	–	
9. RDSLS	1.851	1.14	0.204	−0.057	0.023	−0.031	−0.108	−0.119	−0.046	0.240	–

[a]$N = 164$; Correlation coefficients greater than 0.19 are significant at $p < 0.05$, those greater than 0.25 are significant at $p < 0.01$, and those greater than 0.32 are significant at $p < 0.001$.

Table 18.2 Relatedness measured by Rumelt categories[a]

	Dependent variable = ROS81	
Variable	(A)	(B)
Constant	11.828	5.674
	(26.98)***	(6.06)***
RELATED	1.239	1.370
	(1.52)	(1.94)**
WXAD	–	0.378
		(2.55)***
RDSLS	–	0.788
		(2.72)***
CAPX	–	0.510
		(6.33)***
	N = 160	N = 159
	adj. R^2 = 0.008	adj. R^2 = 0.26
	F = 2.30	F = 15.05

[a]t-statistics reported in parentheses
*significant at the 10% level (two-tail test)
**significant at the 5% level (two-tail test)
***significant at the 1% level (two-tail test)

Table 18.3 Relatedness measured by strategic indicators

	Dependent variable = ROS81	
Variable	(A)	(B)
Constant	5.437	5.773
	(3.55)***	(1.69)*
A/V FEWCUST	0.812	0.906
	(3.13)***	(3.14)***
A/V HSERV	0.712	0.676
	(2.17)**	(1.89)*
A/V CHANNEL	0.549	0.542
	(2.24)**	(2.12)**
A/V TORDER	0.054	0.048
	(2.01)**	(1.72)*
A/V SKILL	0.002	0.002
	(2.07)	(2.12)**
WXAD	0.286**	0.165
	(2.05)**	(0.70)
RDSLS	1.04	1.178
	(3.75)***	(3.56)***
CAPX	0.556	0.572
	(7.24)***	(6.31)***
	N = 164	N = 109
	adj. R^2 = 0.36	adj. R^2 = 0.41
	F = 12.25	F = 10.13

*significant at the 10% level (two-tail test).
**significant at the 5% level (two-tail test).
***significant at the 1% level (two-tail test).

significant at the 99 percent level and and explains about 26 percent of the variation in the dependent variable.

The comparative results obtained from Equation (2) when relatedness is measured by the five strategic indicators are presented in column (A) of Table 18.3. Again, the equation is statistically significant at the 99 percent level. Two results stand out: First, the adjusted R^2 of this equation (0.36) is significantly (at the 1% level) bigger than the adjusted R^2 obtained from Equation (1). This is strong support of Hypothesis 1 in that compared with the traditional definition of relatedness, our measures of relatedness do a far superior job in explaining the variation in the dependent variable. Second, the five structural indicators that we used to capture strategic relatedness exhibit the expected sign and are statistically significant, again strongly supporting Hypothesis 1.

Our results with respect to the structural indicators imply the following:

- operating in a portfolio of markets with high service requirement (HSERV) allows the firm to benefit from customer relationship skills and accumulated competences in working with the customer and providing quality service. Other marketing competences can be most effectively developed and exploited when the firm operates in a portfolio of markets where a few large customers exist.
- when a manufacturer can operate by serving a few large accounts – FEWCUST – (i.e., its direct customers are not fragmented), it will be able to build up deep and sustained relationships with these customers, and so develop its core competences in managing sophisticated customer interfaces.
- operating in markets where products have to pass through intermediaries before reaching the final user (CHANNEL) allows the firm to build up its dealer recruitment skills and channel management competences.
- operating in markets where products are custom-made (TORDER) enables the firm to build up and exploit competences in the exchange of complex information with its customers and/or develop flexible manufacturing.
- operating in markets where labor skill is high (SKILL) allows the firm to build up competences in managing knowledge-based activities which can be transferred to other businesses. It may also help the firm improve its competences in human resource management.

These results are in general conformity with Hypothesis 1. Similarly supporting results were obtained for the second hypothesis. These results are presented in column (B) of Table 18.3 and are the estimates of Equation (2) when only the subsample of Related firms is used. The five strategic indicators are able to explain more than 41 percent of profitability differences among the population of related firms. This suggests that even within the population of related – diversified firms (defined as such in the traditional way), some related firms will do better than other related firms. Specifically, since all five of the strategic indicators come out positive and significant, we can argue that those related firms that compete across markets where certain types of assets (nontradeable, nonsubstitutable and slow and costly to accumulate) are important, outperform the related firms that compete in markets where these accumulated assets are less important.

SUMMARY AND CONCLUSIONS

In this paper, we argued that the traditional way of measuring relatedness between two businesses is incomplete because it ignores the 'strategic importance' and similarity of the underlying assets residing in these businesses. A firm may be in a set of related businesses without deriving a significant advantage from the potential links between its SBUs. Relatedness will be of little advantage when it does not assist the firm in accumulating nontradeable, nonsubstitutable assets efficiently. This, in turn, implies that it is relatedness of strategic assets between SBUs that is important, not the market-level relatedness between businesses.

But simply exploiting existing strategic assets will not create long-term competitive advantage. In a dynamic world, only firms who are able to continually build new strategic assets faster and more cheaply than their competitors will earn superior returns over the long term. Core competences have a pivotal role to play in this process. By transferring core competences between its SBUs, a corporation is able to accelerate the rate and lower the cost at which it accumulates new strategic assets. These opportunities for benefitting from core competences underpin the dynamic advantage of related diversification and define the types of relatedness that a firm should seek to exploit (asset amortization, asset improvement, asset creation and asset fission).

This analysis led us to hypothesize that 'strategic' relatedness is superior to market relatedness and that related firms outperform unrelated ones *only* in markets where accumulated assets are important. These hypotheses were supported by our empirical tests. Specifically, we found that firms operating in portfolios of businesses which shared similar opportunities to exploit brand building: marketing and channel management; and process skills in customization and management of skilled teams gained significant benefit from related diversification.

NOTES

1   It is important here to clarify the difference between 'strategic assets' and 'core competences.' Strategic assets are assets that underpin a firm's cost or differentiation advantage in a particular market and that are imperfectly imitable, imperfectly substitutable and imperfectly tradeable. These assets also tend to be market-specific. An example would be Honda's dealer network distributing and servicing its motorbikes. On the other hand, core competences are the pool of experience, knowledge and systems, etc. that exist elsewhere in the same corporation and can be deployed to reduce the cost or time required either to create a new, strategic asset or expand the stock of an existing one. Thus Honda's experience in building competitive dealer networks for a particular class of consumer durables would be an example of a core competence. Each of these networks (one for motorbikes and another for lawn mowers, for example) would be a separate strategic asset: 'different trees, sharing the same (core competence) root stock.'

2   An extension of this argument has been proposed by Hill (1988): the corporation will be in a better position to exploit the interrelationships among its businesses if it is *structured* appropriately. Hill finds that related diversifiers are better served by the CM-form organizational structure than the M-form structure.

3   See Verdin and Williamson (1994) for a fuller discussion of the link between Porter's cost and differentiation drivers and the assets on which exploitation of these drivers depend.

4   *Time compression diseconomies* are the extra cost associated with accumulating the required assets under time pressure (the cost of compressing an activity in time). For example, it may take more than twice the amount of marketing to achieve in 1 year the same level of brand awareness as an established competitor may have been able to develop over a period of 2 years (other things equal). *Asset mass efficiencies* refer to the fact that some types of assets are more costly to accumulate when the firm's existing stock of that asset is small. It is more difficult, for example, to build the customer base of a credit card when it has few existing users. *Asset interconnectedness* refers to the fact that a lack of complementary assets can often impede a firm

from accumulating an asset which it needs to successfully serve its market. *Causal ambiguity* refers to the impediment associated with the uncertainty of pinpointing which specific factors or processes are required to accumulate a required asset (the precise chain of causality is ambiguous).

5   The role of organizational structure in allowing a firm to exploit the benefits of related diversification is explored in more detail in Markides and Williamson (1993).

6   We would like to thank Gary Hamel for his contribution in the formulation of these ideas.

7   Given the multiindustry nature of the sample firms, these three variables were industry-weighted. As an example of how this was achieved, consider how we industry-weighted WXAD (a firm's *industry* advertising intensity): First, a Compustat program was used to identify all the firms assigned to each 2-digit SIC, and to calculate their advertising intensity. Then, using their sales as weights, the average advertising intensity of every SIC was estimated. Next, each *sample* firm's sales by SIC were obtained from the TRINET tapes, and the percentage of the firm's sales in each SIC was calculated. The firm's industry-weighted advertising intensity was then calculated by multiplying the share of the firm's sales in each SIC by the corresponding advertising intensity of that SIC, and adding the results.

8   We'd like to thank an anonymous reviewer for suggesting this to us.

REFERENCES

Ansoff, H. I. (1965). *Corporate Strategy*. McGraw-Hill, New York.

Bailey, E. L. (1975). *Marketing Cost Ratios of U.S. Manufacturers*. Conference Board Report No. 662. Conference Board, New York.

Barney, J. B. (October 1986). 'Strategic factor markets: Expectations, luck and business strategy', *Management Science*, 32, pp. 1231–41.

Bettis, R. A. (1981). 'Performance differences in related and unrelated diversified firms', *Strategic Management Journal*, 2(4), pp. 379–93.

Caves, R. E. (1982). *Multinational Enterprise and Economic Analysis*. Cambridge University Press, Cambridge.

Caves, R. E. and M. E. Porter (1977). 'From entry barriers to mobility barriers: Conjectural variations and contrived deterrence to new competition', *Quarterly Journal of Economics*, 91, pp. 241–62.

Caves, R. E., M. E. Porter, M. A. Spence and J. T. Scott (1980). *Competition in the Open Economy: A Model Applied to Canada*. Harvard University Press, Cambridge, MA.

Cowling, K. (1976). 'On the theoretical specification of industrial structure-performance relationships', *European Economic Review*, 8(1), pp. 1–14.

Dierickx, I. and K. Cool (December 1989). 'Asset stock accumulation and sustainability of competitive advantage', *Management Science*, 35, pp. 1504–14.

Eaton, B. and R. Lipsey (1980). 'Exit barriers are entry barriers: The durability of capital as a barrier to entry', *Bell Journal of Economics*, 11, pp. 721–9.

Hill, C. W. L. (1988). 'Internal capital market controls and financial performance in multidivisional firms', *Journal of Industrial Economics*, XXXVII(1), pp. 67–83.

Hill, C. W. L. (1994). 'Diversification and economic performance: Bring structure and corporate management back into the picture'. In R. Rumelt, D. Schendel and D. Teece (eds.), *Fundamental Issues in Strategy*. Harvard Business School Press, Boston, MA, pp. 297–321.

Hoskisson, R. E. and M. A. Hitt (1990). 'Antecedents and performance outcomes of diversification: Review and critique of theoretical perspectives', *Journal of Management*, 16, pp. 461–509.

Jacquemin, A. P. and C. H. Berry (1979). 'Entropy measure of diversification and corporate growth', *Journal of Industrial Economics*, XXVII(4), pp. 359–69.

Lecraw, D. J. (1984). 'Diversification strategy and performance', *Journal of Industrial Economics*, XXXIII (2), pp. 179–98.

Markides, C. C. and P. J. Williamson (1993). 'Corporate diversification and organizational structure: A resource-based view', Working paper, London Business School.

Montgomery, C. A. (1982). 'The measurement of firm diversification: Some new empirical evidence', *Academy of Management Journal*, 25(2), pp. 299–307.

National Science Foundation (1978). *Research and Development in Industry*, Technical Notes and Detailed Statistical Tables, Washington, DC.

Palepu, K. (1985). 'Diversification strategy, profit performance, and the entropy measure', *Strategic Management Journal*, 6(3), pp. 239–55.

Pitts, R. A. and H. D. Hopkins (1982). 'Firm diversity: Conceptualization and measurement', *Academy of Management Review*, 7(4), pp. 620–9.

Porter, M. E. (1976). *Interbrand Choice, Strategy and Bilateral Market Power*, Harvard University Press, Cambridge, MA.

Porter, M. E. (1980). *Competitive Strategy: Techniques for Analyzing Industries and Competitors*, Free Press, New York.

Porter, M. E. (May–June 1987). 'From competitive advantage to corporate strategy', *Harvard Business Review*, pp. 43–59.

Prahalad, C. K. and G. Hamel (May–June 1990). 'The core competence of the corporation', *Harvard Business Review*, pp. 71–91.

Ramanujam, V. and P. Varadarajan (1989). 'Research on corporate diversification: A synthesis', *Strategic Management Journal*, 10(6), pp. 523–51.

Ravenscraft, D. J. and F. M. Scherer (1987). *Mergers, Sell-offs and Economic Efficiency*. The Brookings Institution, Washington, DC.

Reed, R. and G. A. Luffman (1986). 'Diversification: The growing confusion', *Strategic Management Journal*, 7(1), pp. 29–35.

Rumelt, R. (1974). *Strategy, Structure and Economic Performance*. Division of Research, Harvard Business School, Cambridge, MA.

Rumelt, R. P. (1987). 'Theory, strategy and entrepreneurship'. In D. Teece (ed.), *The Competitive Challenge*. Cambridge, Ballinger, MA, pp. 137–58.

Singh, H. and C. A. Montgomery (1987). 'Corporate acquisition strategies and economic performance', *Strategic Management Journal*, 8(4), pp. 377–86.

Teece, D. J. (1982). 'Towards an economic theory of the multiproduct firm', *Journal of Economic Behavior and Organization*, 3, pp. 39–63.

U. S. Bureau of Census (1980). 'Job classification statistics', *Census of Population*, U.S. Government Printing Office, Washington, DC.

Verdin, P. J. and P. J. Williamson (1994). 'Core competences, market analysis and competitive advantage: Forging the links'. In G. Hamel and A. Heene (eds.), *Sustainable Competitive Advantage through Core Competence*. Wiley, New York.

Williamson, O. E. (May 1973). 'Markets and hierarchies: Some elementary considerations', *American Economic Review*, 63, pp. 316–25.

Williamson, O. E. (1975). *Markets and Hierarchies*. Free Press, New York.

19

DEVELOPING AND MANAGING STRATEGIC ALLIANCES, BUILDING SOCIAL CAPITAL AND CREATING VALUE

Michael A. Hitt, R. Duane Ireland and Michael D. Santoro

INTRODUCTION

Strategic alliances are cooperative arrangements between two or more firms used to improve their competitive position and performance by sharing resources (Ireland *et al.* 2002). Both tangible and intangible resources can be shared through alliances. Minimizing transaction costs and reducing technological and market uncertainties are examples of ways alliances facilitate firms' efforts to improve their competitive position and performance (Hagedoorn and Schakenraad 1994, Hitt *et al.* 2000).

In industries characterized by rapid technological change and intense global competition, a single firm rarely has the full range of resources and expertise to develop and market timely and cost effective products or new technologies (Barney 1991, Teece 1992, Zahra *et al.* 2000). In such environments, firms are motivated to cooperate with one another to access the resources necessary to develop and sustain competitive advantages (for example, to develop and market new products and technologies) (Buckley and Casson 1988, Lengnick-Hall 1992). Strategic alliances spread the risks of failure by helping each firm gain access to needed resources and technologies from its partner without incurring the high costs associated with pursuing internal initiatives alone (Pfeffer and Salancik 1978).

Alliances can provide firms with many benefits such as access to new knowledge, complementary resources, new markets and new technologies that in turn enhance the firm's ability to learn, exploit economies of scale and scope, share risks and outsource various activities along the value chain (Gulati *et al.* 2000). Consequently, strategic alliances, as a cooperative strategy, are being used with greater frequency on a global basis (Dyer *et al.* 2001, Gulati 1998, Hitt *et al.* 2003b). Indeed, evidence shows that there have been significant increases in global alliance activity since the mid-1980s, tens of thousands of strategic alliances being formed in recent years. For example, there were over 10,200 interorganizational alliances developed in 2000 alone (Schifrin 2001).

As a key strategic initiative, many large-sized firms often engage in hundreds of alliances (Ireland *et al.* 2002). Although small-sized firms do not usually have as vast an array of alliance partners as their larger-sized counterparts, small firms also engage in alliances with other organizations, especially to gain access to value-creating resources that are not in their current resource portfolio (Ireland *et al.* 2003a, Pisano 1990, Rothaermel 2001, Santoro and Chakrabarti 2001, 2002).

Strategic alliances are often a preferred growth alternative compared to acquisitions (Harrison *et al.* 2001), even in light of the evidence that roughly 50 per cent of all strategic alliances fail (Reuer 1999, Reuer *et al.* 2002, Young-Ybarra and Wiersema 1999). This rate of failure highlights the complexity and difficulty of successfully developing and managing strategic alliances. Effective alliance development and management requires several actions, including the successful coordination and integration of diverse resources and knowledge stocks across different organizations. Moreover, the mutual interdependence between alliance partners, which often manifests itself in a delicate tension between cooperation and competition, means that each party is dependent upon and vulnerable to the other (Ireland *et al.* 2002). Although more likely to create value as partners work together, managing and integrating intangible assets while engaged in alliances increases the likelihood of tension as both parties attempt to protect their critical assets from inappropriate and unwanted amounts of appropriation. The strategic alliance literature continues to grow with much of the research largely focused on the reasons for dyadic alliance formation and their outcomes (Ireland *et al.* 2002, Walker *et al.* 1997). Strategic alliances' high failure rate suggests the need for scholars and business practitioners to increase their knowledge about the successful development and management of these cooperative arrangements (Harrison *et al.* 2001, Ireland *et al.* 2002). Speaking on causes of effective alliances, Reuer (1999: 13) suggested that deriving value from alliances 'requires companies to select the right partners, develop a suitable alliance design, adapt the relationship as needed and manage the endgame successfully'. Despite recent research results (see, for example, Das and Teng 2001, Hitt *et al.* 2000, Lane and Lubatkin 1998) that address some of the issues illuminated by Reuer (1999), further work is required to enhance our understanding of this complex phenomenon.

The purpose of this chapter is to provide a conceptual framework that depicts the development and management of strategic alliances. We offer a new perspective on this important aspect of strategic alliances by introducing a conceptual model that is grounded in resource-based, social-capital and knowledge-based theories. Presented in Figure 19.1 our conceptual model depicts the development and management of strategic alliances as a key managerial activity that can be a critical capability. Herein, we argue that this critical capability is a product of alliance scope, partner selection and resource configuration, optimization and exploitation. Grounded in earlier definitions (for example, Teece *et al.* 1997), we view managers' critical capability regarding the development and management of strategic alliances as their ability to integrate, build and reconfigure organizational resources in ways required for the successful design and use of strategic alliances.

Figure 19.1 also illuminates that as a critical managerial capability, the development and management of strategic alliances has a two-way linkage with building social capital. We envision the building of social capital to result from interactions among the constructs of information sharing, trust and norms of reciprocity. Social capital is a critical component in our conceptual framework as it mediates the relationship between alliance development and management as a critical managerial capability and the subsequent creation of value. The feedback loops depicted in Figure 19.1 highlight the dynamic rather than static nature of the relationships among alliance development and management, social capital and the creation of value. The remainder of our chapter unfolds as follows. First, we discuss the importance of strategic alliance development

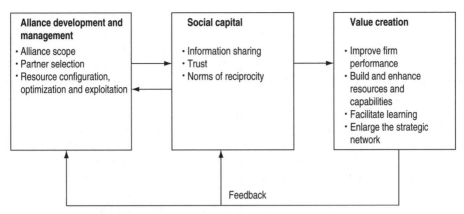

Figure 19.1 Alliance development and management, social capital and value creation

and management. We do this by describing alliance development and management's key activities (that is, alliance scope, partner selection and resource configuration, optimization and exploitation). We next describe social capital, link alliance development and management to the development of social capital and then describe social capital's mediating role in the creation of value. In the chapter's final section, we examine the implications of our proposed model for management practice and offer directions for future research that are suggested by our model.

DEVELOPING AND MANAGING STRATEGIC ALLIANCES AS A CRITICAL MANAGERIAL CAPABILITY

Firms able to develop and manage alliances in a superior manner relative to competitors can enjoy a sustainable competitive advantage, at least until others learn how to imitate the focal firm's value-creating abilities in terms of alliance development and management (Ireland *et al.* 2002). Theory supports this outcome. From transaction cost theory, for example, we know that effectively developing and managing strategic alliances can create value by reducing transaction costs (Hagedoorn and Schakenraad 1994, Hennart 1988), meaning that an effective alliance development and management alliance activity is more efficient than are market mechanisms. Likewise, from resource-based theory, we understand that developing and managing strategic alliances effectively can be a source of competitive advantage by providing partnering firms with complementary resources or expertise (Hitt *et al.* 2000, Teece 1992). While certainly important, developing and managing strategic alliances are complex activities and the managerial and subsequent organizational ability to do this successfully remains asymmetrically distributed (Ireland *et al.* 2002). As an idiosyncratic, firm-specific resource, managers able to identify and use the often intangible assetbased routines that are required for successful alliance development and management possess information that is hard for competitors to comprehend, especially if efforts were to be made to imitate them.

Following the resource-based view, resources are defined broadly as the knowledge, assets, capabilities, technologies and organizational processes that provide the basis for the firm to develop and implement strategic decisions that create value and provide competitive advantage (Barney 1991). In a more parsimonious view, resources are the tangible and intangible assets the firm controls and uses to implement a value-creating strategy (Barney 2001). A capability is a bundle of organizational resources that allows the firm to complete important tasks and create value for the firm (Hamel and Prahalad 1994, Prahalad and Hamel 1990). Moreover, a sustainable competitive advantage is created when a capability satisfies the four conditions of being (1) valuable, (2) rare, (3) difficult to imitate, and (4) non-substitutable (Barney 1991, 2001).

A managerial capability is exemplified at FedEx, where its capability of logistics management furnishes customers with on-time deliveries and provides FedEx with a competitive advantage relative to its rivals in the express package delivery business. As a second example, we note that at least historically, EDS has a competitive advantage in the information processing industry because of its ability to offer its customers seamless information through the adroit use and exploitation of a systems integration competence (Hamel and Prahalad 1994). As is true for all firms, EDS is challenged to continually upgrade its current competitive advantages while exploring for new advantages to use in the pursuit of growth and value creation.

Likewise, based on our earlier specification of managerial capability in terms of the effective development and management of strategic alliances, when this particular set of managerial skills is valuable, rare, imperfectly imitable and non-substitutable, it becomes the foundation for a sustainable competitive advantage that creates firm value. Firms, through the capabilities of their managers, possess an alliance-related competitive advantage when managers are able to develop and manage alliances in ways that are superior to how their counterparts in rival firms execute these particular managerial actions (Dyer *et al.* 2001). Conceiving this activity as a critical capability is grounded in managerial logic that, in turn, is based on a shared understanding about how the development and management of the firm's alliance portfolio should be achieved (Ireland *et al.* 2002).

As a critical capability, the firm must be proficient in three interrelated activities when concerned with the effective development and management of strategic alliances. The three closely related activities for developing and managing strategic alliances as a critical capability are: (1) defining the alliance scope, (2) selecting the right alliance partner and (3) configuring, optimizing and exploiting alliance resources. We describe each of these managerial activities in the following sections.

ALLIANCE SCOPE DEFINITION

Determining the scope of a strategic alliance is a critical first step towards effectively developing and managing strategic alliances. Because strategic alliances are complex relationships, their scope usually involves a number of dimensions. Determining the technologies to be employed and developed in an alliance, markets to be served, product categories and brands to market, boundary configurations, the governance structure to use to control the operation of the alliance and ownership of resources and assets created by the alliance, are examples of these dimensions (Ireland *et al.* 2002, Khanna 1998). Moreover, the time horizons for each of the various dimensions must be considered as well. For example, some strategic alliances, particularly those involving smaller, start-up ventures, concentrate on solving immediate problems that are affecting the firm's survival. Alternatively, partnerships involving larger, more established firms often focus on longer-term deliverables such as network building (Santoro and Chakrabarti 2001).

PARTNER SELECTION

Selecting the right alliance partner is critically important to the successful development and management of a strategic alliance. A key reason for this is that having the wrong partner could negate the achievement of potential synergies in the collaborative venture (Geringer and Herbert 1989). Locating the right or most desirable alliance partner requires substantial effort. Moreover, the search and negotiation process required to find the most desirable partner can be time consuming. Indirect experience with a potential partner informs the focal firm's understanding regarding the possible success of an alliance if it were to be formed with that particular partner. Skilled firms often rely on current partners' reputations as a basis for forming future alliances in order to reduce searching costs (Chung *et al.* 2000). Likewise, recommendations for other alliance partners from a currently valued collaborator are given great weight on the basis of reputation.

Partner firms in a strategic alliance should have compatible strategic intents and be able to offer unique resources to the alliance (Hitt *et al.* 1997). For example, Hitt *et al.* (2000) found that firms operating in developed markets and firms operating in emerging markets sought different attributes in alliance partners. The reason for this specificity was so the focal firm could maximize its learning by participating in the alliance. Moreover, firms operating in emerging markets need partners (often companies from developed markets) that are willing to share resources and help them learn. Organizations competing in emerging markets need this support primarily because of their inadequate absorptive capacities in such areas as technological knowledge and managerial capabilities (Hitt *et al.* 2000).

Smaller, lesser-known firms are often better served when they ally with larger, more experienced firms with desirable reputations. A key reason for this is that these alliance partners can help the smaller firm achieve results beyond its capabilities, market reach and reputation. Bristol-Myers Squibb, a large, experienced pharmaceutical firm, formed 56 alliances in the biopharmaceutical arena between 1985 and 2000. Many of these alliances were with young biotech firms (Gopalakrishnan *et al.* 2002). While Bristol-Myers Squibb benefited from the alliances by gaining access to their partners' technologies and technological skills, the smaller alliance partners had opportunities to gain from their larger partner's market capabilities, reputation and firm-specific capabilities. Acquisition of these skills increases the value-creating potential of the smaller firm as other large organizations consider it as a partner in future alliances.

Institutional environments are important in alliance partner selection as well because norms, rules and regulations affect managerial mindsets and strategic choices (Madhavan *et al.* 1998). Research by Hitt *et al.* (2003a) addresses this issue. These researchers found that Chinese managers' institutional environments allow them to take a long-term perspective, meaning that their focus is on the intangible assets and technological capabilities of their alliance partners. In contrast, when selecting an alliance partner, Russian managers use more short-term time horizons and concentrate instead on the financial capital and the complementary capabilities of their partners in order to address firm survival issues (Hitt *et al.* 2003a). Finally, research by Hitt *et al.* (2003c) showed that firms often value potential partners' prior experience in alliances. Their prior experience with others in an alliance provides several benefits, including information about how they interact with partners and their trustworthiness. The greater is the prior experience potential partners have with alliances, the more likely it is that they will be effective partners (Hitt *et al.* 2003c).

RESOURCE CONFIGURATION, OPTIMIZATION AND EXPLOITATION

Due to rapidly changing technologies and increased global competition, it is becoming increasingly difficult for firms to have the amount and array of resources needed to compete successfully, particularly in fast-cycle markets (Arino and de le Torre 1998, Bettis and Hitt 1995, Ireland *et al.* 2003b, Kuratko *et al.* 2001). From resource-based theory, it follows that a principal benefit of strategic alliances is gaining access to valuable resources and expertise from one's partner and jointly creating new resources (for example, new capabilities) through the alliance (Das and Teng 2002, Pisano 1990, Rothaermel 2001). Combining and leveraging unique and valuable resource combinations is a prime objective of strategic alliances, indicating that configuring, optimizing and exploiting those resources is a key component of successfully managing strategic alliances. We offer several reasons supporting the importance of these activities. First, firms must effectively configure resource bundles that cannot be perfectly imitated, exactly substituted or completely mobilized (Das and Teng 2002). Second, strategic alliances often involve a pooling of complementary resources that when optimized provide significant competitive advantages (Das and Teng 1998, Glaister and Buckley 1996). Third, alliances allow firms to get close enough to exchange, absorb and utilize tacit knowledge (Lane and Lubatkin 1998). Finally, the uncertainty and ambiguity associated with alliance resource configuration and optimization require that alliance managers have the capabilities to recognize opportunities and exploit them through the alliance's resource base (Marino 1996).

The preceding discussion illuminates how alliance development and management serve as a critical managerial capability embodying alliance scope, partner selection and resource configuration, optimization and exploitation. Furthermore, there is a two-way linkage between developing and managing strategic alliances and the building of social capital. As Figure 19.1 shows, social capital is a critical component of alliance development and management because it serves as a mediator of value creation. We discuss the two remaining components of our model; that is, social capital and value creation, and their relationship to alliance development and management in the following sections.

SOCIAL CAPITAL

Recently the concept of social capital has received attention from scholars in multiple disciplines including sociology, economics, political science, organization theory and strategic management. Social capital has been found to affect a variety of important outcomes such as children's education (Coleman 1988), career success and mobility (Burt 1992, Gabbay and Zuckerman 1998), societal productivity (Woolcock 1998, Woolcock and Narayan 2000), start-up company formation (Walker *et al.* 1997), resource exchange and innovation (Tsai and Ghoshal 1998) and interorganizational learning (Kraatz 1998).

Partly because of the scope of questions it has been used to investigate, the definitions of social capital vary considerably from this large body of social science disciplines. Baker (1990), for example, defines social capital as a resource that actors derive from specific social structures. Bourdieu and Wacquant (1992) contend that social capital is the sum of the resources that accrue to an individual or group from a network of institutionalized relationships. Knoke (1999) describes social capital as the process by which social actors create and use their network of connections within and among organizations to gain access to others' resources. Nahapiet and Ghoshal (1998: 243) define social capital as 'the sum of the actual and potential resources embedded within, available through, and derived from the network of relationships possessed by an individual or social unit'. All of these definitions suggest that social capital is a resource that helps actors gain access to resources through networks of social relationships (Ireland *et al.* 2002). Consequently, social capital is integral to alliance development and management because firms often seek to ally with other organizations having social capital as a path to use to gain access to the resource pools available in a network (or networks) of relationships (Chung *et al.* 2000).

In spite of its generally agreed upon importance, at both the individual and group levels of analysis, there are debates regarding social capital's dimensions. Nahapiet and Ghoshal (1998), for example, suggest that social capital includes a structural dimension, relational dimension and cognitive dimension. In contrast, Bourdieu (1985) identifies two critical components of social capital – the size of the network and the volume of capital possessed by network members. Coleman (1988) argues that social capital encompasses trustworthiness, information channels and norms. Similar to Coleman's (1988) framework, Woolcock (1998) contends that social capital has three dimensions to include (1) information sharing, (2) trust and (3) norms of reciprocity. Because of its richness, we used Woolcock's suggestion to examine some of the relationships depicted in Figure 19.1.

In the following sections, we describe each of these three dimensions and link social capital to alliance development and management.

Information sharing

Social capital can provide access to knowledge and enable the leveraging and exploiting of that knowledge. For example, social capital provides access to information sources, thereby contributing to the quality, relevance and timeliness of the information stream (Adler and Kwon 2002, Bolino *et al.* 2002, Nahapiet and Ghoshal 1998). Coleman (1988) suggests that information and knowledge are often costly to obtain, but social relations can offer participants with a strategic knowledge network with several potentially positive outcomes (Polodny and Stuart 1995). For example, in examining the social connections of public organizations such as the National Institute of Health and pharmaceutical firms, Cockburn and Henderson (1998) found that socially connected firms had higher research productivity. Additionally, Liebeskind, Oliver, Zucker and Brewer (1996) studied two new biotechnology firms to examine individual level exchanges of scientific knowledge and found that interpersonal relationships provided these firms with a key source of new knowledge. Based on their results, Liebeskind *et al.* (1996) argued that social network exchanges contribute to organizational learning in two important ways. First, their findings showed that each firm was able to expand the scope of its learning by developing networks of scientists from a large number of external organizations. Second, social networks allowed firms more easily to integrate externally obtained knowledge. Thus, firms with large interpersonal networks have greater access to cutting-edge scientific research and also have the means rapidly to absorb this research into their own research efforts. Kale, Sing and Perlmutter (2000) referred to these close interactions in a partnership as 'relational capital'. Among other value-creating outcomes, relational capital facilitates knowledge transfer by providing valuable avenues for gathering knowledge (Mowery *et al.* 1996).

Trust

Firms engaged in strategic alliances must be concerned about the possibility of learning races (Hamel 1991). Moreover, firms in collaborative ventures face 'relational risk' that is associated with opportunistic behaviours by partners. 'Shirking, cheating, distorting information, *appropriating resources*, and so on' [emphasis added] (Das and Teng 2001: 253) are examples of potential opportunistic behaviour. Thus, trust is critical for successful strategic alliances (Barney and Hansen 1994). An additional benefit of trust is that it reduces the costs of managing strategic alliances (Hitt *et al.* 2003b).

Trust is a complex construct that has been examined in a variety of contexts. A review of the literature, however, shows consensus on two general components of trust (Rousseau *et al.* 1998) – a willingness to be vulnerable and positive expectations. Vulnerability refers to the risk of loss should one party place its welfare in the hands of another (Barney and Hansen 1994, Mayer *et al.* 1995). Positive expectations refer to Party A's confident beliefs that Party B will behave in a manner that will benefit Party A. Herein, we use Mayer, Davis and Schoorman's (1995: 712) definition of trust as 'the willingness of a party to be vulnerable to the actions of another party based on the expectation that the other will perform a particular action important to the trustor, irrespective of the ability to monitor or control that other party'.

Following social exchange theory, trust is both a source and key component of social capital because it develops over time and is based on alliance partners' past experiences and current relationships with one another (Adler and Kwon 2002, Young-Ybarra and Wiersema 1999). Further, social capital, similar to other forms of capital that are grounded in intangible assets, constitutes an accumulated history encompassing investments in social relations and a social structure over time (Nahapiet and Ghoshal 1998). Sustaining a stable relationship over time, therefore, is important for building trust and social capital.

Strategic alliances are conduits for conveying information, including an alliance partner's organizational value-creating routines. Having access to information about potential alliance partners before actually committing to a relationship can substantially reduce the risk of an unsuccessful alliance and can serve to guide a firm's choices of future strategic ties (Gulati 1995). A firm's credibility as an alliance partner affects its trustworthiness. In turn, trustworthy firms empower their partners to accept risk and to believe that the alliance will be mutually beneficial. Thus, trust in one's partner is critical to facilitating social exchange and building social capital (Tsai and Ghoshal 1998).

Norms of reciprocity

Social capital is driven by a normative commitment for exchanges between partners (Adler and Kwon 2002, Putnam 1993). Putnam (1993: 183) clarifies this notion by suggesting that norms of reciprocity entail a commitment to the belief that 'I'll do this for you now, knowing that somewhere down the road you'll do something for me'. Consequently, the building of social capital involves expectations about future obligations and the repayment of those obligations such as between scientists from different firms working on a joint R&D project, where helping others is required for progress on the project (Nahapiet and Ghoshal 1998). Norms of reciprocity involve several facets including shared interests, common identity and shared values that together cement the bonds among alliance partners and form the basis for collective action (Adler and Kwon 2002, Nahapiet and Ghoshal 1998). As Nahapiet and Ghoshal (1998) explain, norms of reciprocity represent a commitment by actors to a social system in which the existence of such norms positively affects social exchange processes by providing the motivation and access for exchanges. Moreover, the norms of reciprocity are modified through positive exchanges to extend the circle of exchange, thereby encouraging further cooperation, increasing risk taking and building more social capital (Coleman 1988).

Merging different organizational cultures and integrating diverse skill sets to achieve an alliance's objectives is a customary hurdle. Norms of reciprocity are often the basis for obtaining cooperation in a collaborative venture with each of the parties balancing its own priorities and goals with the goals and priorities of the alliance. Adler and Kwon (2002) suggest that strong norms and beliefs create a solidarity among partners that encourages compliance and reduces the need for formal controls, especially financial controls. As a result, the emphasis in effective strategic alliances is on cooperation not competition and on strategic controls (Ireland *et al.* 2002).

To summarize, social capital results from information sharing, trust and the norms of reciprocity that are embodied within social relations. The development and management of strategic alliances as a critical managerial capability helps build social capital by providing the structure for social relations. This structure is a product of managerial efforts to facilitate social relationships between alliance partners, by framing the scope of the alliance, through attention devoted to partner selection as well as to resource configuration, optimization and exploitation. Figure 19.1 shows that the linkage between developing and managing strategic alliances and social capital is dialectical, meaning that social capital affects the firm's capability to develop and manage strategic alliances; greater social capital increases the likelihood of success in alliances (Hitt *et al.* 2003a). Successful strategic alliances, in turn, further build and fortify the firm's capability for developing and managing future alliances. Figure 19.1 shows that value is created via improved firm performance, enhanced resources and capabilities, learning and an enlarged strategic network that result from effectively developing and managing strategic alliances. Next, we discuss each of the value creation components.

Value Creation

Research shows that strategic alliances create value with positive effects on various outcome measures including stock price, firm survival, growth and innovation. The degree to which any of these outcome measures is reached is a function of the sustainability of the firm's competitive advantages (Ireland *et al.* 2003a), including those based on the development and management of strategic alliances.

Specific research findings describe the relationship between strategic alliances and firm performance. For example, McConnell and Nantell (1985) showed that equity markets reward parent companies' share prices when they announce the establishment of joint ventures. Mitchell and Singh (1996) found that alliances increased organizations' survival rates. Powell, Koput and Smith-Doerr (1996) found that companies involved in multiple strategic alliances experienced accelerated growth rates. Other studies have shown strong linkages between alliances and the level of innovation in high-tech, dynamic industries such as biotechnology (Shan *et al.* 1994) and electronics (Hagedoorn and Schakenraad 1994).

Strategic alliances create value in at least three ways, including (1) building and enhancing resources and capabilities, (2) facilitating learning and (3) enlarging the focal firm's strategic network. Below, we examine each of these sources of value creation. In the course of doing so, we suggest that the creation of value from strategic alliances is predicated on the firm having the capability effectively to develop and manage strategic alliances. In turn, this managerial capability is predicated on the firm having or owning value-creating amounts and types of social capital.

Build/enhance resources and capabilities

The underlying proposition of social capital theory is that connections among social actors provide access to resources and capabilities (Nahapiet and Ghoshal 1998) and that over time, repeated interactions between firms and their human capital reduce the relational risk that often accompanies this access (Das and Teng 2000). Strong ties between firms create social capital and unique resource portfolios that can be valuable, rare and difficult to imitate due to the exclusive nature of the inter-organizational linkages (Granovetter 1985, Gulati et al. 2000). For example, alliances created at the latter stage of a technology's development cycle (that is, exploitative alliances) often involve integrating complementary knowledge-based and property-based resources from each partner for the development, production, branding, distribution, sales and marketing of a new technology or product (Das and Teng 2000, Rothaermel 2001). The partners in these exploitative, complementary alliances often gain a new or enhanced set of resources and/or capabilities from the sharing of knowledge by partners (Glaister and Buckley 1996).

Beyond the benefits derived from integrating complementary resources and capabilities, other tangible and intangible resources can be positively affected as well. For example, alliances that merge supplementary resources and capabilities within the partnership can infuse new know-how that will prevent obsolescence and avoid a firm's core competence from becoming a core rigidity (Hamel and Prahalad 1994). As another example, a firm can gain legitimacy based on its partner's reputation and enhance its own reputation when the alliance satisfies various stakeholder needs. In sum, building social capital enhances the firm's resource inventory and set of capabilities (Ireland et al. 2003a).

Facilitate learning

Alliances provide each partner with numerous opportunities to learn. Quite simply, value is created because the participating firms in an alliance gain new knowledge (Dyer and Singh 1998); yet, what firms learn in an alliance can be quite diverse. Firms participating in an alliance will often learn something directly related to the alliance's goals and mission (for example, the development of a certain technology or product) (Santoro and Chakrabarti 2001, Santoro and Gopalakrishnan 2000). However, firms can learn other things as well. For example, firms allying in an international strategic alliance to produce a good or service may learn how to compete successfully in specific foreign markets. Or, more pointedly, firms participating in an alliance may strengthen their capability for developing and managing both current and future strategic alliances (Ireland et al. 2002).

Following the knowledge-based view, two types of knowledge, tacit knowledge and explicit knowledge, each with different characteristics, are important to firms (Grant 1996, Liebeskind 1996, Nonaka 1994, Spender 1996). Explicit knowledge can be transferred from one individual to another using some type of formal communication system. Thus, explicit knowledge is articulable or codifiable. In contrast, tacit knowledge generally cannot be formally communicated and is learned by doing (Polanyi 1966). Tacit knowledge is deeply rooted in one's experience and own mental model (Ireland et al. 2003b).

The distinction between explicit knowledge and tacit knowledge is important for two reasons. First, because it is more difficult for competitors to understand and imitate (Kogut and

Zander 1992), tacit knowledge is more valuable and more likely than explicit knowledge to lead to a sustainable competitive advantage. Inimitability is further increased when the knowledge is complex and combined with other types of knowledge in an unclear fashion; that is, there is causal ambiguity (Barney 1991, Kogut and Zander 1992). Second, and most germane in terms of learning from alliances, a number of scholars (see, for example, Kogut and Zander 1992 and Nonaka 1994) point out a critical dilemma concerning knowledge transfer; namely, that the same characteristics that make tacit knowledge difficult to imitate by competitors also make it difficult to transfer within the focal firm. Because of its value, transferring tacit knowledge in strategic alliances is a critical issue. However, the transfer of both explicit and tacit knowledge is facilitated in alliances through social capital that is based on information sharing, trust and norms of reciprocity.

Enlarge the strategic network

While strategic alliances involve dyadic relationships, firms regularly operate in and compete against strategic networks or alliance constellations of three or more firms (Das and Teng 2002, Ireland *et al.* 2002). For example, research shows that multinational firms often develop and manage relationships with a large external network of firms (Ghoshal and Bartlett 1994). Moreover, strategic networks of multiple partners include both strong ties and weak ties that together provide diversity in learning and other forms of alliance outcomes (Granovetter 1985). Based on the notion of solidarity (Adler and Kwon 2002), strategic networks gain mass and potency as bridges and bonds continue to be formed with less densely connected groups in the network and with unconnected groups outside the existing network. Similarly, as the visibility and reputation of a strategic network expands, the size of the strategic network enlarges as well. Therefore, the contribution of social capital is important because it facilitates growth of the strategic network.

Finally, as Figure 19.1 shows, we contend that a feedback dynamic exists among value creation, social capital and the capability for alliance development and management. The market power, financial wealth and reputation gains obtained from strategic alliances through enhanced resources and capabilities, new learning and an enlarged strategic network serve to fortify and renew the firm's capability and its social capital.

CONCLUSION

As Gulati *et al.* (2000: 203) note:

> the image of atomistic actors competing for profits against each other in an impersonal marketplace is increasingly inadequate in a world in which firms are embedded in networks of social, professional and exchange relationships with other organizational actors ... such networks encompass a firm's set of relationships, both horizontal and vertical, with other organizations – be they suppliers, customers, competitors, or other entities – including relationships across industries and countries.

Despite the preponderance of strategic alliances in global markets, the high failure rate for these collaborative arrangements suggests that more must be learned, particularly with respect to the effective development and management of alliances. In addressing the need for better understanding the development and management of strategic alliances, our arguments and model are consistent with the nexus of resource-based, social capital and knowledge-based theories. The intersection among these theories indicates that as a critical capability, alliance development and management routines must embody alliance scope, partner selection and resource configuration, optimization and exploitation. In doing so, the development and management of strategic alliances can become a value-creating capability integrated with the continuous building and nurturing of social capital.

The implications of our model for management practice are clear; firms must develop and maintain the knowledge and capabilities needed for successfully executing this high-level, complex activity. Or, more likely, firms must be willing to dedicate the effort and resources necessary to obtain the requisite tools through the help of external sources. Due to the importance of this management responsibility, our model implies that a dedicated alliance management role and function should be created and directed by a senior-level manager. In this manner, this important organizational function is afforded the proper status, and the executive in charge has the authority to garner the needed resources and properly leverage and institutionalize alliance development and management as a critical capability throughout the organization (Ireland *et al.* 2002). The materials presented and examined in this chapter suggest questions and issues that can be the basis of future scholarly work. First, we offer a theoretical framework that can be useful in developing specific and testable propositions about the relationships illuminated herein. In addition, our conceptual model provides direction that could be instrumental for operationalizing these constructs (that is, by detailing the dimensions of the constructs).

We believe that an initial step for future research might be to examine the direct relationships between alliance development and management and value creation with social capital as a mediator. Our suggestion that there is a two-way relationship between alliance development and management and social capital (see Figure 19.1) brings forth a second research question; namely, determining the extent to which alliance development and management and social capital are linked in a dialectical fashion. Another potentially interesting line of investigation involves the relationships among the various components for each of the constructs. For example, future research could focus on the extent to which alliance scope, partner selection and resource configuration, optimization and exploitation influence the success of alliance development and management. Likewise, future research could concentrate on investigating the role of trust in building social capital versus the roles of information sharing and the norms of reciprocity. The existence and strength of the feedback dynamic generated from the creation of value to social capital and to alliance development and management offer yet another potentially interesting area for future enquiry.

The purpose of this chapter is to contribute to our knowledge regarding the effective development and management of strategic alliances. We believe that use of the framework presented herein to specify the nature and direction of research questions has the potential to generate results that will lead to greater insights regarding strategic alliances. Achieving this outcome is desirable, in that strategic alliances are a complex, yet important phenomenon for academic researchers as well as business practitioners.

REFERENCES

Adler, P. and Kwon, S.W. (2002) 'Social capital: prospects for a new concept', *Academy of Management Review*, Vol. 27, pp. 17–40.

Arino, A. and de la Torre, J. (1998) 'Learning from failure: towards an evolutionary model of collaborative ventures', *Organization Science*, Vol. 26, pp. 306–25.

Baker, W. (1990) 'Market networks and corporate behavior', *American Journal of Sociology*, Vol. 96, pp. 589–625.

Barney, J.B. (1991) 'Firm resources and sustained competitive advantage', *Journal of Management*, Vol. 17, pp. 99–120.

Barney, J.B. (2001) 'Is the resource-based "view" a useful perspective for strategic management research? Yes.', *Academy of Management Review*, Vol. 26, pp. 41–56.

Barney, J.B. and Hansen, M. (1994) 'Trustworthiness as a source of competitive advantage', *Strategic Management Journal*, Vol. 17, pp. 151–66.

Bettis, R. and Hitt, M. (1995) 'The new competitive landscape', *Strategic Management Journal*, Vol. 16, Special Issue, pp. 7–19.

Bolino, M., Turnley, W. and Bloodgood, J. (2002) 'Citizenship behavior and the creation of social capital in organizations', *Academy of Management Review*, Vol. 27, pp. 505–22.

Bourdieu, P. (1985) 'The forms of capital', in J.G. Richardson (ed.), *Handbook of Theory and Research for the Sociology of Education*, pp. 241–58. New York: Greenwood.

Bourdieu, P. and Wacquant, L. (1992) *An Invitation to Reflexive Sociology*. Chicago: University of Chicago Press.

Buckley, P.J. and Casson, M. (1988) 'The theory of cooperation in international business', in F.J. Contractor and P. Lorange (eds), *Cooperative Strategies in International Business*, pp. 31–53. Lexington, MA: Lexington Books.

Burt, R.S. (1992) *Structural Holes: The Social Structure of Competition*. Cambridge, MA: Harvard University Press.

Chung, S., Singh, H. and Lee, K. (2000) 'Complementary assets, status similarity, and social capital as drivers of alliance formation', *Strategic Management Journal*, Vol. 21, pp. 1–22.

Cockburn, I.M. and Henderson, R.M. (1998) 'Absorptive capacity, coauthoring behavior, and the organization of research in drug discovery', *Journal of Industrial Economics*, Vol. 46, pp. 157–82.

Coleman, J.S. (1988) 'Social capital in the creation of human capital', *American Journal of Sociology*, Vol. 94, pp. 95–120.

Das, T.K. and Teng, B.S. (1998) 'Between trust and control: developing confidence in partner cooperation in alliances', *Academy of Management Review*, Vol. 23, pp. 491–512.

Das, T.K. and Teng, B.S. (2000) 'A resource-based theory of strategic alliances', *Journal of Management*, Vol. 26, pp. 31–61.

Das, T.K. and Teng, B.S. (2001) 'Trust, control, and risk in strategic alliances: an integrated framework', *Organization Studies*, Vol. 22, pp. 251–83.

Das, T.K. and Teng, B.S. (2002) 'Alliance constellations: a social exchange perspective', *Academy of Management Review*, Vol. 27, pp. 445–56.

Dyer, J.H. and Singh, H. (1998) 'The relational view: cooperative strategy and sources of competitive advantage', *Academy of Management Review*, Vol. 23, pp. 660–79.

Dyer, J.H., Kale, P. and Singh, H. (2001) 'How to make strategic alliances work', *Sloan Management Review*, Vol. 42, No. 4, pp. 37–43.

Gabbay, S. and Zuckerman, E. (1998) 'Social capital and opportunity in corporate R&D: the contingent effect of contact density on mobility expectations', *Social Science Research*, Vol. 27, pp. 189–217.

Geringer, J.M. and Herbert, L.H. (1989) 'Control and performance of international joint ventures', *Journal of International Business Studies*, Vol. 20, pp. 235–54.

Ghoshal, S. and Bartlett, C.G. (1994) 'Linking organizational contexts and managerial action: the dimensions of quality of management', *Strategic Management Journal*, Vol. 15, pp. 91–112.

Glaister, K. and Buckley, P. (1996) 'Strategic motives for international alliance formation', *Journal of Management Studies*, Vol. 33, pp. 301–32.

Gopalakrishnan, S., Santoro, M. and Scillitoe, J. (2002) 'Technological alliances in the bio-pharmaceutical arena: the relationship between alliance context and performance', paper presented at Academy of Management meetings, Denver, Colorado.

Granovetter, M.S. (1985) 'Economic action and social structure: the problem of embeddedness', *American Journal of Sociology*, Vol. 91, pp. 481–510.

Grant, R.M. (1996) 'Toward a knowledge-based theory of the firm', *Strategic Management Journal*, Vol. 17, Special Issue, Winter, pp. 109–21.

Gulati, R. (1995) 'Does familiarity breed trust? The implication of repeated ties for contractual choice in alliances', *Academy of Management Journal*, Vol. 38, pp. 85–112.

Gulati, R. (1998) 'Alliances and networks', *Strategic Management Journal*, Vol. 19, pp. 293–317.

Gulati, R., Nohria, N. and Zaheer, A. (2000) 'Strategic networks', *Strategic Management Journal*, Vol. 21, Special Issue, 203–15.

Hagedoorn, J. and Schakenraad, J. (1994) 'The effect of strategic technology alliances on company performance', *Strategic Management Journal*, Vol. 15, pp. 135–51.

Hamel, G. (1991) 'Competition for competence and inter-partner learning within international strategic alliances', *Strategic Management Journal*, Vol. 12, pp. 83–103.

Hamel, G. and Prahalad, C.K. (1994) *Competing for the Future*. Boston: Harvard Business School Press.

Harrison, J.S., Hitt, M.A., Hoskisson, R.E. and Ireland, R.D. (2001) 'Resource complementarity in business combinations: extending the logic to organizational alliances', *Journal of Management*, Vol. 27, pp. 679–90.

Hennart, J. (1988) 'A transaction costs theory of equity joint ventures', *Strategic Management Journal*, Vol. 4, pp. 361–74.

Hitt, M.A., Ahlstrom, D., Dacin, M.T., Levitas, E. and Svobodina, L. (2003a) 'The institutional effects on strategic alliance partner selection in transition economies: China versus Russia' *Organization Science*.

Hitt, M.A., Dacin, M.T., Levitas, E., Arregle, J. and Borza, A. (2000) 'Partner selection in emerging and developed market contexts: resource based and organizational learning perspectives', *Academy of Management Journal*, Vol. 43, pp. 449–67.

Hitt, M.A., Dacin, M.T., Tyler, B.B. and Park, D. (1997) 'Understanding the differences in Korean and US executives' strategic orientations', *Strategic Management Journal*, Vol. 18, pp. 159–67.

Hitt, M.A., Ireland, R.D. and Hoskisson, R.E. (2003b) *Strategic Management: competitiveness and globalization* (5th edn). Cincinnati: South-Western College Publishing.

Hitt, M.A., Keats, B.W. and Yucel, E. (2003c) 'Strategic leadership in global business organizations: building trust and social capital', in W.H. Mobley and P. Dorfman (eds), *Advances in Global Leadership*, Vol. 3. Greenwich, CT: JAI Press.

Ireland, R.D., Hitt, M.A. and Sirmon, D. (2003a) 'A model of strategic entrepreneurship: The construct and its dimensions', *Journal of Management*.

Ireland, R.D., Hitt, M.A. and Vaidyanath, D. (2002) 'Alliance management as a source of competitive advantage', *Journal of Management*, Vol. 28, pp. 413–46.

Ireland, R.D., Kuratko, D.F. and Covin, J.G. (2003b) 'Antecedents, elements, and consequences of corporate entrepreneurship strategy', working paper, University of Richmond.

Kale, P., Singh, H. and Perlmutter, H. (2000) 'Learning and protection of proprietary rights in strategic alliances: building relational capital', *Strategic Management Journal*, Vol. 21, pp. 217–37.

Khanna, T. (1998) 'The scope of alliances', *Organization Science*, Vol. 9, pp. 340–55.

Knoke, D. (1999) 'Organizational networks and corporate social capital', in R.Th.A.J. Leenders and S.M. Gabbay (eds), *Corporate Social Capital and Liability*, pp. 17–42. Boston: Kluwer.

Kogut, B. and Zander, U. (1992) 'Knowledge of the firm, combinative capabilities, and the replication of technology', *Organization Science*, Vol. 3, pp. 383–97.

Kraatz, M. (1998) 'Learning by association? Interorganizational networks and adaptation to environmental change', *Academy of Management Journal*, Vol. 41, pp. 621–43.

Kuratko, D.F., Ireland, R.D. and Hornsby, J.S. (2001) 'Improving firm performance through entrepreneurial actions: Acordia's corporate entrepreneurship strategy', *Academy of Management Executive*, Vol. 15, No. 4, pp. 60–71.

Lane, P.J. and Lubatkin, M. (1998) 'Relative absorptive capacity and interorganizational learning', *Strategic Management Journal*, Vol. 19, pp. 461–77.

Lengnick-Hall, C.A. (1992) 'Innovation and competitive advantage: what we know and what we need to learn', *Journal of Management*, Vol. 18, pp. 399–429.

Liebeskind, J.P. (1996) 'Knowledge, strategy, and the theory of the firm', *Strategic Management Journal*, Vol. 17, Special Issue, Winter, pp. 93–107.

Liebeskind, J.P., Oliver, A.L., Zucker, L. and Brewer, M. (1996) 'Social networks, learning and flexibility: sourcing scientific knowledge in new biotechnology firms', *Organization Science*, Vol. 7, pp. 428–43.

Madhavan, R., Koka, B. and Prescott, J. (1998) 'Networks in transition: How industry events (re)shape interfirm relationships', *Strategic Management Journal*, Vol. 19, pp. 439–59.

Marino, K. (1996) 'Developing consensus on firm competencies and capabilities', *Academy of Management Executive*, Vol. 10, No. 3, pp. 40–51.

Mayer, R.C., Davis, J.H. and Schoorman, F.D. (1995) 'An integrative model of organizational trust', *Academy of Management Review*, Vol. 20, pp. 709–34.

McConnell, J.J. and Nantell, T.J. (1985) 'Corporate combinations of common stock returns: the case of joint ventures', *Journal of Finance*, Vol. 40, No. 2, pp. 519–36.

Mitchell, W. and Singh, K. (1996) 'Incumbents' use of pre-entry alliances before expansion into new technical sub-fields of an industry', *Journal of Economic Behavior and Organization*, Vol. 18, pp. 347–72.

Mowery, D.L., Oxley, J.E. and Silverman, B.S. (1996) 'Strategic alliances and interfirm knowledge transfer', *Strategic Management Journal*, Vol. 17, pp. 77–91.

Nahapiet, J. and Ghoshal, S. (1998) 'Social capital, intellectual capital and the organizational advantage', *Academy of Management Review*, Vol. 23, pp. 242–66.

Nonaka, I. (1994) 'A dynamic theory of organizational knowledge creation', *Organization Science*, Vol. 5, pp. 14–37.

Pfeffer, J. and Salancik, G. (1978) *The External Control of Organizations: A resource dependence perspective.* Harper & Row: New York.

Pisano, G. (1990) 'The R&D boundaries of the firm: an empirical analysis', *Administrative Science Quarterly*, Vol. 35, pp. 153–76.

Polanyi, M. (1966) *The Tacit Dimension.* New York: Anchor Day.

Polodny, J.M. and Stuart, T.E. (1995) 'Networks, knowledge and niches: competition in the worldwide semiconductor industry', *American Journal of Sociology*, Vol. 100, pp. 1224–60.

Powell, W.W., Koput, K.W. and Smith-Doerr, L. (1996) 'Inter-organizational collaboration and the locus of innovation: networks of learning in biotechnology', *Administrative Science Quarterly*, Vol. 41, pp. 116–45.

Prahalad, C.K. and Hamel, G. (1990) 'The core competence of the corporation', *Harvard Business Review*, Vol. 68, No. 3, pp. 79–91.

Putnam, R.D. (1993) 'The prosperous community: social capital and public life', *American Prospect*, Vol. 13, pp. 35–42.

Reuer, J.J. (1999) 'Collaborative strategy: the logic of alliances', *Mastering Strategy*, October 4, 12–13.

Reuer, J.J., Singh, H. and Zollo, M. (2002) 'Post formation dynamics in strategic alliances', *Strategic Management Journal*, Vol. 23, pp. 135–51.

Rothaermel, F. (2001) 'Complementary assets, strategic alliances, and the incumbent's advantage: an empirical study of industry and firm effects on the biopharmaceutical industry', *Research Policy*, Vol. 30, pp. 1235–51.

Rousseau, D.M., Sitkin, S.B., Burt, R.S. and Camerer C. (1998) 'Not so different after all: a cross-discipline view of trust', *Academy of Management Review*, Vol. 23, pp. 405–21.

Santoro, M.D. and Chakrabarti, A.K. (2001) 'Corporate strategic objectives for establishing relationships with university research centers', *IEEE Transactions on Engineering Management*, Vol. 48, No. 2, pp. 157–63.

Santoro, M.D. and Chakrabarti, A.K. (2002) 'Firm size and technology centrality in industry-university interactions', *Research Policy*, Vol. 31, pp. 1163–80.

Santoro, M. and Gopalakrishnan, S. (2000) 'The institutionalization of knowledge transfer activities within industry-university collaborative ventures', *Journal of Engineering and Technology Management*, Vol. 17, Special Issue, pp. 299–319.

Schifrin, M. (2001) 'Partner or perish', *Forbes*, May 21, 26–8.

Shan, W., Walker, G. and Kogut, B. (1994) 'Interfirm cooperation and start up innovation in the biotechnology industry', *Strategic Management Journal*. Vol. 15, pp. 387–94.

Spender, J.-C. (1996) 'Making knowledge the basis of a dynamic theory of the firm', *Strategic Management Journal*, Vol. 17, Special Issue, Winter, pp. 45–62.

Teece, D.J. (1992) 'Competition, cooperation, and innovation', *Journal of Economic Behavior Organization*, Vol. 18, pp. 1–25.

Teece, D.J., Pisano, G. and Shuen, A. (1997) 'Dynamic capabilities and strategic management', *Strategic Management Journal*, Vol. 18, pp. 509–33.

Tsai, W. and Ghoshal, S. (1998) 'Social capital and value creation: the role of intrafirm networks', *Academy of Management Journal*, Vol. 41, pp. 464–78.

Walker, G., Kogut, B. and Shan, W. (1997) 'Social capital, structural holes and the formation of an industry network', *Organization Science*, Vol. 8, pp. 109–25.

Woolcock, M. (1998) 'Social capital and economic development: toward a theoretical synthesis and policy framework', *Theory and Society*, Vol. 27, pp. 151–208.

Woolcock, M. and Narayan, D. (2000) 'Social capital: implications for development theory, research, and policy', *World Bank Research Observer*, Vol. 15, no. 2, pp. 225–49.

Young-Ybarra, C. and Wiersema, M. (1999) 'Strategic flexibility in information technology alliances: the influence of transaction cost economies and social exchange theory', *Organization Science*, Vol. 10, pp. 439–59.

Zahra, S., Ireland, R.D. and Hitt, M.A. (2000) 'International expansion by new venture firms: international diversity, mode of market entry, technological learning, and performance', *Academy of Management Journal*, Vol. 43, pp. 925–50.

PART VI

DEVELOPING INTERNATIONAL STRATEGY

INTRODUCTION

Although many firms neither need nor want to develop international strategies, but compete mainly within their national marketplaces, they still are affected greatly by the international strategies pursued by other firms. International strategies can confer considerable benefits on the organizations that pursue them. Also, international firms or multinational corporations (MNCs), as they are more commonly known, compete within many national markets and have an effect on the competitive environment and the competitive strategies of all firms within them, local, regional or global. The articles in Part VI attempt to explain why this should be so. Chapters 20–23 all deal with ways of benefiting from the scale, scope, knowledge, innovation and learning available to MNCs. In Chapter 20, Ghoshal shows us how to apply these concepts to the evaluation of a global strategy for the corporation. In Chapter 21, Bartlett, Ghoshal and Birkinshaw show how international organization structures are evolving within an organizational form in which these resources and processes may be more effectively developed and deployed. Segal-Horn in Chapter 22, shows us their relevance and applicability to the strategies of service MNCs. In Chapter 23, Birkinshaw explores recent developments in the relationship between MNCs and their country subsidiaries. Let me present their ideas a little more fully.

Ghoshal (Chapter 20) creates a framework that can be used as a 'road map' to guide managers of multinational corporations through their choices for global strategic management. He clarifies what it means to 'manage globally' and sets out options on which decisions about global strategy should be based. Global strategy is much discussed but poorly understood. Ghoshal reminds us that corporations often 'have globalness thrust upon them' by the initiatives of competitors, and their managers may have little grasp themselves of how to manage under these particular industry conditions. His framework is simple to understand, yet a powerful aid to decision-making. He argues that the objectives of multinational corporations are three-fold: 'to achieve efficiency in its current activities; to manage the risk that it assumes in carrying out those activities; and to develop capabilities for internal learning so as to be able to innovate and adapt to future changes'. Effective global strategies enable the corporation to optimize the interactions between these strategic objectives of risk, efficiency and innovation, and the means available to multinationals for achieving those objectives. Three types of tools ('means') are available. The first is the exploitation of differences in the many national markets in which the corporation operates (e.g. time zones, currency fluctuations, specialized workforces or tax regimes). The second is scale economy benefits (e.g. an automobile MNC concentrating all world-wide gearbox production in Vietnam or a credit card company concentrating all back-office processing in India). The third is scope economy benefits (e.g. sharing a technological innovation in a product or process throughout the organization to all its subsidiaries world-wide, so that all benefit from the innovation made in one part of the organization). Managers may use Ghoshal's framework to generate a checklist of factors to consider when attempting to design and manage a global strategy for their own corporation. If managers can find no benefits for the firm available from national differences, or scale or scope economies, then they should not be intending to pursue a global strategy. There is no such thing as the best type of global strategy. Ghoshal shows clearly why instead there should be a search by each firm for the optimum balance between global integration benefits and local or national differentiation in how each firm configures its activities internationally. Ghoshal is suggesting that global strategies should be organized around the configuration of international activities and their spread across country markets, to obtain maximum benefit from each of the three sources of potential international competitive advantage.

We now move on to consideration of the organizational structures that have evolved for complex MNCs. The innovative structure for MNCs that developed beyond the more standard hierarchical or matrix M-form organizations, in the 1980s, was the transnational corporation. Bartlett, Ghoshal and Birkinshaw (Chapter 21) describe an organizational form which has evolved beyond the administrative focus of the multidivisional ('M-form'), which was designed primarily for vertical integration of vertical information-processing and decision-making. Instead, as management attention has shifted towards processes that add value (such as building capabilities), other processes have overtaken administrative functions in importance. Among these more important concerns we now include the management of flexibility, which, as we saw with Teece, Pisano and Shuen and with Sanchez, is in many ways becoming more important to organizations than management as direction and control.

Another serious concern is the management of integration and co-ordination without which economies of scope are unattainable since they need horizontal information-processing, not just vertical. Bartlett, Ghoshal and Birkinshaw also discuss what they call the management of renewal to prevent 'strategic commitment at the cost of organizational adaptability'. They emphasize the importance of an organizational context that positively reinforces the individual, without which the 'adaptability' and 'responsiveness' that are the core of the new organizational form cannot be realized. Indeed (echoing Ghoshal), they emphasize the benefits that access to a wider variety of markets and resources brings. Most of all, however, they stress the benefits of 'routinely dealing with the fast-changing, multidimensional demands and opportunities that are part of the global business environment'.

The transnational organization, and the management issues it has generated, represent an advanced form of modern corporation which has evolved to cope with uncertainty and environmental complexity. It may well be that the difficulties and challenges inherent in managing across borders is the best way of learning how to cope with the complexities facing all modern organizations. Bartlett, Ghoshal and Birkinshaw suggest a new way of thinking about large organizations, including MNCs. Instead of formal structures containing business, geographical and functional units, they see instead three core processes: the entrepreneurial process, the integration process and the renewal process. The entrepreneurial process is concerned with seeking new external opportunities. The integration process is about linking and leveraging dispersed world-wide resources and capabilities. The renewal process is about managing continuous challenge and internal revitalization. These may be used to understand any large, complex organization, although they were first developed to support the implementation of international strategies within MNCs.

Strategy research has continually been dominated by an over-emphasis on manufacturing organizations at the expense of services but Segal-Horn (Chapter 22) sets out to redress the balance. Many service industries have experienced prolonged and extreme turbulence in recent

374

years. Developed economies have become dominated by knowledge-intensive and technology-intensive industries, alongside professional and financial service firms. External developments such as technological and regulatory change have created collapsing or 'fuzzy' industry boundaries that have opened opportunities for new types of services, supported by new types of strategies, structures, systems and processes for service corporations. Segal-Horn explains how service corporations have developed asset structures, resources and potential synergies that parallel those in manufacturing corporations. Large-scale 'back-office' resources and capabilities (e.g. off-shore transaction management and data-processing by banks, airlines or insurance companies) now dominate service industries. The search for sources of advantage from 'know-how', information and knowledge management in services has created international service corporations designed to benefit from scale, scope, innovation and learning in the same ways as other types of MNCs and exactly reflecting Ghoshal's framework. She has applied Chandler's framework explaining the growth phases of MNCs to explain the rise of powerful service MNCs and service oligopolies in recent years. Service industry dynamics have changed. A shift has occurred as a result of technological development in services, making the international strategies of service MNCs asset-driven, rather than driven by the intangibles of service delivery and the service encounter.

One major recent development within international strategy has been the closer examination of the relationship between MNCs and their subsidiaries. Birkinshaw (Chapter 23) examines the issue of entrepreneurship by subsidiaries within MNCs and in particular looks at what he calls subsidiary 'initiatives', by which he means 'a discrete, proactive undertaking that advances a new way for the corporation to use or expand its resources'. Once again, we are seeing research that attempts to operationalize and apply the concept of leveraging resources, but this time within the context of MNCs. We all understand in general terms what is meant by 'leveraging resources' to achieve scale and scope benefits within large organizations, but managers have found it very difficult to implement in practice.

An obvious way for a large MNC to leverage its resource base is to derive benefit from the resources and capabilities dispersed within its subsidiary businesses around the world. Birkinshaw attempts to show to what extent such initiatives actually occur and under what circumstances. A 'subsidiary' is any operational unit controlled by the MNC and situated outside the MNC's home country. The potential value of subsidiary initiatives to MNCs is high. Many parent–subsidiary relationships treat the subsidiary as a 'semi-autonomous entity within a differentiated system', within which complete control of the subsidiary by the parent is neither possible nor desirable. There is a trade-off between control and autonomy in the parent–subsidiary relationship which must be carefully managed if useful subsidiary initiatives are to occur. Birkinshaw demonstrates that four types of subsidiary initiative can be identified: local market initiatives; internal market initiatives; global market initiatives; and hybrid initiatives. The outcomes of these initiatives are quite different. The local market initiatives lead first to enhanced service to local customers, but later develop into new business opportunities for the MNC as a whole, sometimes responsible for generating 'blockbuster' new products, from which the whole firm can learn and benefit. As Birkinshaw explains: 'without the diversity of opportunities and ideas that local market initiatives represent, the MNC's ability to adapt to changing environmental demands would be severely constrained'. Internal market initiatives lead to rationalization of activities, achieving efficiency gains throughout the whole corporation. Global market initiatives lead to the maintenance and development of a specialized corporate capability, often called 'centres of excellence' within the organization. By definition, these are perceived as having capabilities from which the parent and other subsidiaries can benefit. They, therefore, contribute to world-wide learning within the MNC. Finally, hybrid initiatives are similar in outcome to internal market initiatives in that they result in a geographically concentrated activity from which first the local market and then the larger organization benefit. This is a fascinating and very rich study of the ways in which resources and capabilities located in MNC subsidiaries can be leveraged across to provide benefits to the organization as a whole.

I would urge readers of these articles on international strategy to reflect on the extent to which they provide insight into the general strategy issues raised in earlier sections of this Reader. They address many central concerns such as strategy and structure relationships; knowledge and innovation management; corporate parenting and general corporate strategy issues; ways of managing organizational learning and how to manage resources and capabilities for the benefit of the whole organization over the longer term. It may well be that the difficulties of managing complex MNCs is laying the groundwork for the strategies of the future for other organizations.

20

GLOBAL STRATEGY: AN ORGANIZING FRAMEWORK

Sumantra Ghoshal

Global strategy has recently emerged as a popular concept among managers of multinational corporations as well as among researchers and students in the field of international management. This paper presents a conceptual framework encompassing a range of different issues relevant to global strategies. The framework provides a basis for organizing existing literature on the topic and for creating a map of the field. Such a map can be useful for teaching and also for guiding future research in this area. The article, however, is primarily directed at managers of multinational corporations, and is aimed at providing them with a basis for relating and synthesizing the different perspectives and prescriptions that are currently available for global strategic management.

MULTIPLE PERSPECTIVES, MANY PRESCRIPTIONS

This enthusiasm notwithstanding, there is a great deal of conceptual ambiguity about what a 'global' strategy really means. As pointed out by Hamel and Prahalad (1985), the distinction among a global industry, a global firm, and a global strategy is somewhat blurred in the literature. According to Hout, Porter and Rudden (1982), a global strategy is appropriate for global industries which are defined as those in which a firm's competitive position in one national market is significantly affected by its competitive position in other national markets. Such interactions between a firm's positions in different markets may arise from scale benefits or from the potential of synergies or sharing of costs and resources across markets. However, as argued by Bartlett (1985), Kogut (1984) and many others, those scale and synergy benefits may often be created by strategic actions of individual firms and may not be 'given' in any *a priori* sense. For some industries, such as aeroframes or aeroengines, the economies of scale may be large enough to make the need for global integration of activities obvious. However, in a large number of cases industries may not be born global but may have globalness thrust upon them by the entrepreneurship of a company such as Yoshida Kagyo KK (YKK) or

Procter and Gamble. In such cases the global industry – global strategy link may be more useful for *ex post* explanation of outcomes than for *ex ante* predictions or strategizing.

Further, the concept of a global strategy is not as new as some of the recent authors on the topic have assumed it to be. It was stated quite explicitly about 20 years ago by Perlmutter (1969) when he distinguished between the geocentric, polycentric and ethnocentric approaches to multinational management. The starting point for Perlmutter's categorization scheme was the world-view of a firm, which was seen as the driving force behind its management processes and the way it structured its worldwide activities (see Robinson, 1978 and Rutenberg, 1982 for detailed reviews and expositions). In much of the current literature, in contrast, the focus has been narrowed and the concept of global strategy has been linked almost exclusively with how the firm structures the flow of tasks within its worldwide value-adding system. The more integrated the flow of tasks appears to be, the more global the firm's strategy is assumed to be (e.g. Leontiades, 1984). On the one hand, this focus has led to improved understanding of the fact that different tasks offer different degrees of advantages from global integration and national differentiation and that, optimally, a firm must configure its value chain to obtain the best possible advantages from both (Porter, 1984). But, on the other hand, it has also led to certain dysfunctional simplifications. The complexities of managing large, worldwide organizations have been obscured by creating polar alternatives between centralization and decentralization, or between global and multidomestic strategies (e.g. Hout *et al.*, 1982). Complex management tasks have been seen as composites of simple global and local components. By emphasizing the importance of rationalizing the flow of components and final products within a multinational system, the importance of internal flows of people, technology, information, and values has been de-emphasized.

Differences among authors writing on the topic of global strategy are not limited to concepts and perspectives. Their prescriptions on how to manage globally have also been very different, and often contradictory.

1   Levitt (1983) has argued that effective global strategy is not a bag of many tricks but the successful practice of just one: product standardization. According to him, the core of a global strategy lies in developing a standardized product to be produced and sold the same way throughout the world.

2   According to Hout *et al.* (1982), on the other hand, effective global strategy requires the approach not of a hedgehog, who knows only one trick, but that of a fox, who knows many. Exploiting economies of scale through global volume, taking pre-emptive positions through quick and large investments, and managing interdependently to achieve synergies across different activities are, according to these authors, some of the more important moves that a winning global strategist must muster.

3   Hamel and Prahalad's (1985) prescription for a global strategy contradicts that of Levitt (1983) even more sharply. Instead of a single standardized product, they recommend a broad product portfolio, with many product varieties, so that investments on technologies and distribution channels can be shared. Cross-subsidization across products and markets, and the development of a strong worldwide distribution system, are the two moves that find the pride of place in these authors' views on how to succeed in the game of global chess.

4   If Hout *et al.*'s (1982) global strategist is the heavyweight champion who knocks out opponents with scale and pre-emptive investments, Kogut's (1985b) global strategist is the nimble-footed athlete who wins through flexibility and arbitrage. He creates options so as to turn the uncertainties of an increasingly volatile global economy to his own advantage. Multiple sourcing, production shifting to benefit from changing factor costs and exchange rates, and arbitrage to exploit imperfections in financial and information markets are, according to Kogut, some of the hallmarks of a superior global strategy.

These are only a few of the many prescriptions available to MNC managers about how to build a global strategy for their firms. All these suggestions have been derived from rich and insightful analyses of real-life situations. They are all reasonable and intuitively appealing, but their managerial implications are not easy to reconcile.

THE NEED FOR AN ORGANIZING FRAMEWORK

The difficulty for both practitioners and researchers in dealing with the small but rich literature on global strategies is that there is no organizing framework within which the different perspectives and prescriptions can be assimilated. An unfortunate fact of corporate life is that any particular strategic action is rarely an unmixed blessing. Corporate objectives are multidimensional, and often mutually contradictory. Contrary to received wisdom, it is also usually difficult to prioritize them. Actions to achieve a particular objective often impede another equally important objective. Each of these prescriptions is aimed at achieving certain objectives of a global strategy. An overall framework can be particularly useful in identifying the trade-offs between those objectives and therefore in understanding not only the benefits but also the potential costs associated with the different strategic alternatives.

The objective of this paper is to suggest such an organizing framework which may help managers and academics in formulating the various issues that arise in global strategic management. The underlying premise is that simple categorization schemes such as the distinction between global and multidomestic strategies are not very helpful in understanding the complexities of corporate-level strategy in large multinational corporations. Instead, what may be more useful is to understand what the key strategic objectives of an MNC are, and the tools that it possesses for achieving them. An integrated analysis of the different means and the different ends can help both managers and researchers in formulating, describing, classifying and analysing the content of global strategies. Besides, such a framework can relate academic research, that is often partial, to the totality of real life that managers must deal with.

THE FRAMEWORK: MAPPING MEANS AND ENDS

The proposed framework is shown in Table 20.1. While the specific construct may be new, the conceptual foundation on which it is built is derived from a synthesis of existing literature.

The basic argument is simple. The goals of a multinational – as indeed of any organization – can be classified into three broad categories. The firm must achieve efficiency in its current activities; it must manage the risks that it assumes in carrying out those activities; and it must develop internal learning capabilities so as to be able to innovate and adapt to future changes. Competitive advantage is developed by taking strategic actions that optimize the firm's achievement of these different and, at times conflicting, goals.

A multinational has three sets of tools for developing such competitive advantage. It can exploit the differences in input and output markets among the many countries in which it operates. It can benefit from scale economies in its different activities. It can also exploit synergies or economies of scope that may be available because of the diversity of its activities and organization.

The strategic task of managing globally is to use all three sources of competitive advantage to optimize efficiency, risk and learning simultaneously in a worldwide business. The key to a successful global strategy is to manage the interactions between these different goals and means.

Table 20.1 Global strategy: an organizing framework

Strategic objectives	Sources of competitive advantage		
	National differences	Scale economies	Scope economies
Achieving efficiency in current operations	Benefiting from differences in factor costs – wages and cost of capital	Expanding and exploiting potential scale economies in each activity	Sharing of investments and costs across products, markets and businesses
Managing risks	Managing different kinds of risks arising from market or policy-induced changes in comparative advantages of different countries	Balancing scale with strategic and operational flexibility	Portfolio diversification of risks and creation of options and side-bets
Innovation learning and adaptation	Learning from societal differences in organizational and managerial processes and systems	Benefiting from experience – cost reduction and innovation	Shared learning across organizational components in different products, markets or businesses

That, in essence, is the organizing framework. Viewing the tasks of global strategy this way can be helpful to both managers and academics in a number of ways. For example, it can help managers in generating a comprehensive checklist of factors and issues that must be considered in reviewing different strategic alternatives. Such a checklist can serve as a basis for mapping the overall strategies of their own companies and those of their competitors so as to understand the comparative strengths and vulnerabilities of both. Table 20.1 shows some illustrative examples of factors that must be considered while carrying out such comprehensive strategic audits. Another practical utility of the framework is that it can highlight the contradictions between the different goals and between the different means, and thereby make salient the strategic dilemmas that may otherwise get resolved through omission.

In the next two sections the framework is explained more fully by describing the two dimensions of its construct, *viz.* the strategic objectives of the firm and the sources of competitive advantage available to a multinational corporation. Subsequent sections show how selected articles contribute to the literature and fit within the overall framework. The paper concludes with a brief discussion of the trade-offs that are implicit in some of the more recent prescriptions on global strategic management.

The Goals: Strategic Objectives

Achieving efficiency

A general premise in the literature on strategic management is that the concept of strategy is relevant only when the actions of one firm can affect the actions or performance of another. Firms competing in imperfect markets earn different 'efficiency rents' from the use of their resources (Caves, 1980). The objective of strategy, given this perspective, is to enhance such efficiency rents.

Viewing a firm broadly as an input-output system, the overall efficiency of the firm can be defined as the ratio of the value of its outputs to the costs of all its inputs. It is by maximizing this ratio that the firm obtains the surplus resources required to secure its own future. Thus it differentiates its products to enhance the exchange value of its outputs, and seeks low cost factors to minimize the costs of its inputs. It also tries to enhance the efficiency of its throughput processes by achieving higher scale economies or by finding more efficient production processes.

The field of strategic management is currently dominated by this efficiency perspective. The generic strategies of Porter (1980), different versions of the portfolio model, as well as overall strategic management frameworks such as those proposed by Hofer and Schendel (1978) and Hax and Majluf (1984) are all based on the underlying notion of maximizing efficiency rents of the different resources available to the firm.

In the field of global strategy this efficiency perspective has been reflected in the widespread use of the integration-responsiveness framework originally proposed by Prahalad (1975) and subsequently developed and applied by a number of authors including Doz, Bartlett and Prahalad (1981) and Porter (1984). In essence, the framework is a conceptual lens for visualising the cost advantages of global integration of certain tasks *vis-à-vis* the differentiation benefits of responding to national differences in tastes, industry structures, distribution systems, and government regulations. As suggested by Bartlett (1985), the same framework can be used to understand differences in the benefits of integration and responsiveness at the aggregate level of industries, at the level of individual companies within an industry, or even at the level of different functions within a company (see Figure 20.1, reproduced from Bartlett, 1985). Thus the consumer electronics industry may be characterized by low differentiation benefits and high integration advantages, while the position of the packaged foods industry may be quite the opposite. In the telecommunications switching industry, in contrast, both local and global forces may be strong, while in the automobile industry both may be of moderate and comparable importance.

Within an industry (say, automobile), the strategy of one firm (such as Toyota) may be based on exploiting the advantages of global integration through centralized production and decision-making, while that of another (such as Fiat) may aim at exploiting the benefits of national differentiation by creating integrated and autonomous subsidiaries which can exploit strong links with local stake-holders to defend themselves against more efficient global competitors. Within a firm, research may offer greater efficiency benefits of integration, while sales and service may provide greater differentiation advantages. One can, as illustrated in Figure 20.1, apply the framework to even lower levels of analysis, right down to the level of individual tasks. Based on such

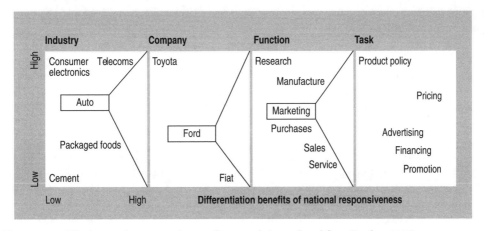

Figure 20.1   The integration–responsiveness framework (reproduced from Bartlett, 1985)

analysis, a multinational firm can determine the optimum way to configure its value chain so as to achieve the highest overall efficiency in the use of its resources (Porter, 1984).

However, while efficiency is clearly an important strategic objective, it is not the only one. As argued recently by a number of authors, the broader objective of strategic management is to create value which is determined not only by the returns that specific assets are expected to generate, but also by the risks that are assumed in the process (see Woo and Cool (1985) for a review). This leads to the second strategic objective of firms – that of managing risk.[1]

Managing risks

A multinational corporation faces many different kinds of risk, some of which are endemic to all firms and some others are unique to organizations operating across national boundaries. For analytical simplicity these different kinds of risks may be collapsed into four broad categories.

First, an MNC faces certain *macro-economic risks* which are completely outside its control. These include cataclysmic events such as wars and natural calamities, and also equilibrium-seeking or even random movements in wage rates, interest rates, exchange rates, commodity prices, and so on.

Second, the MNC faces what is usually referred to in the literature as political risks but may be more appropriately called *policy risks* to emphasize that they arise from policy actions of national governments and not from either long-term equilibrium-seeking forces of global markets, nor from short-term random fluctuations in economic variables arising out of stickiness or unpredictability of market mechanisms. The net effect of such policy actions may often be indistinguishable from the effect of macro-economic forces; for example, both may lead to changes in the exchange rate of a particular currency. But from a management perspective the two must be distinguished, since the former is uncontrollable but the latter is at least partially controllable.

Third, a firm also faces certain *competitive risks* arising from the uncertainties of competitors' responses to its own strategies (including the strategy of doing nothing and trying to maintain the status quo). While all companies face such risks to varying extents (since both monopolies and perfect competition are rare), their implications are particularly complex in the context of global strategies since the responses of competitors may take place in many different forms and in many different markets. Further, technological risk can also be considered as a part of competitive risk since a new technology can adversely affect a firm only when it is adopted by a competitor, and not otherwise.[2]

Finally, a firm also faces what may be called *resource risks*. This is the risk that the adopted strategy will require resources that the firm does not have, cannot acquire, or cannot spare. A key scarce resource for most firms is managerial talent. But resource risks can also arise from lack of appropriate technology, or even capital (if managers, for reasons of control, do not want to use capital markets, or if the market is less efficient than finance theorists would have us believe).

One important issue with regard to risks is that they change over time. Vernon (1977) has highlighted this issue in the context of policy risks, but the same is true of the others. Consider resource risks as an example. Often the strategy of a multinational will assume that appropriate resources will be acquired as the strategy unfolds. Yet the initial conditions on which the plans for ongoing resource acquistion and development have been based may change over time. Nissan, for instance, based its aggressive internationalization strategy on the expectation of developing technological, financial and managerial resources out of its home base. Changing competitive positions among local car manufacturers in Japan have affected these resource development plans of the company, and its internationalizing strategy has been threatened significantly. A more careful analysis of alternative competitive scenarios, and of their effects on the resource allocation plans of the company, may have led Nissan to either a slower pace of internationalization, or to a more aggressive process of resource acquisition at an earlier stage of implementing its strategy.

The strategic task, with regard to management of risks, is to consider these different kinds of risks *jointly* in the context of particular strategic decisions. However, not all forms of risk are strategic since some risks can be easily diversified, shifted, or shared through routine market transactions. It is only those risks which cannot be diversified through a readily available external market that are of concern at the strategic level.

As an example, consider the case of currency risks. These can be classified as contractual, semi-contractual and operating risks (Lessard and Lightstone, 1983). Contractual risks arise when a firm enters into a contract for which costs and revenues are expected to be generated in different currencies: for example a Japanese firm entering into a contract for supplying an item to be made in Japan to an American customer at a price fixed in dollars. Semi-contractual risks are assumed when a firm offers an option denominated in foreign currencies, such as a British company quoting a firm rate in guilders. Operating risks, on the other hand, refer to exchange rate-related changes in the firm's competitiveness arising out of long-term commitments of revenues or costs in different currencies. For example, to compete with a Korean firm, an American firm may set up production facilities in Singapore for supplying its customers in the United States and Europe. A gradual strengthening of the Singapore dollar, in comparison with the Korean won, can erode the overall competitiveness of the Singapore plant.

Both contractual and semi-contractual currency risks can be easily shifted or diversified, at relatively low cost, through various hedging mechanisms. If a firm does not so hedge these risks, it is essentially operating as a currency speculator and the risks must be associated with the speculation business and not to its product-market operations. Operating risks, on the other hand, cannot be hedged so easily,[3] and must be considered at the strategic rather than the operational level.

Analysis of strategic risks will have significant implications for a firm's decisions regarding the structures and locations of its cost and revenue streams. It will lead to more explicit analysis of the effects of environmental uncertainties on the configuration of its value chain. There may be a shift from ownership to rental of resources; from fixed to variable costs. Output and activity distributions may be broadened to achieve the benefits of diversification. Incrementalism and opportunism may be given greater emphasis in its strategy in comparison to pre-emptive resource commitments and long-term planning. Overall strategies may be formulated in more general flexible terms, so as to be robust to different environmental scenarios. In addition, side-bets may be laid to cover contingencies and to create strategic options which may or may not be exercised in the future (see Kogut, 1985b; Aaker and Mascarenhas, 1984; and Mascarenhas, 1982).

Innovation, learning and adaptation

Most existing theories of the multinational corporation view it as an instrument to extract additional rents from capabilities internalized by the firm (see Calvet, 1981, for a review). A firm goes abroad to make more profits by exploiting its technology, or brand name, or management capabilities in different countries around the world. It is assumed that the key competencies of the multinational always reside at the centre.

While the search for additional profits or the desire to protect existing revenues may explain why multinationals come to exist, they may not provide an equally complete explanation of why some of them continue to grow and flourish. An alternative view may well be that a key asset of the multinational is the diversity of environments in which it operates. This diversity exposes it to multiple stimuli, allows it to develop diverse capabilities, and provides it with a broader learning opportunity than is available to a purely domestic firm. The enhanced organizational learning that results from the diversity internalized by the multinational may be a key explanator of its ongoing success, while its initial stock of knowledge may well be the strength that allows it to create such organizational diversity in the first place (Bartlett and Ghoshal, 1985).

Internal diversity may lead to strategic advantages for a firm in many different ways. In an unpredictable environment it may not be possible, *ex ante*, to predict the competencies that will be required in the future. Diversity of internal capabilities, following the logic of population ecologists (e.g. Hannan and Freeman, 1977; Aldrich, 1979), will enhance the probability of the firm's survival by enhancing the chances that it will be in possession of the capabilities required to cope with an uncertain future state. Similarly, diversity of resources and competencies may also enhance the firm's ability to create joint innovations, and to exploit them in multiple locations. One example of such benefits of diversity was recently described in the *Wall Street Journal* (April 29, 1985):

> P&G [Procter and Gamble Co.] recently introduced its new Liquid Tide, but the product has a distinctly international heritage. A new ingredient that helps suspend dirt in wash water came from the company's research center near P&G's Cincinnati headquarters. But the formula for Liquid Tide's surfactants, or cleaning agents, was developed by P&G technicians in Japan. The ingredients that fight mineral salts present in hard water came from P&G's scientists in Brussels.

As discussed in the same *WSJ* article, P&G's research centre in Brussels has developed a special capability in water softening technology due, in part, to the fact that water in Europe contains more than twice the level of mineral content compared to wash water available in the United States. Similarly, surfactant technology is particularly advanced in Japan because Japanese consumers wash their clothes in colder waters compared to consumers in the US or Europe, and this makes greater demands on the cleaning ability of the surfactants. The advantage of P&G as a multinational is that it is exposed to these different operating environments and has learned, in each environment, the skills and knowledge that coping with that environment specially require. Liquid Tide is an example of the strategic advantages that accrue from such diverse learning.

The mere existence of diversity, however, does not enhance learning. It only creates the potential for learning. To exploit this potential, the organization must consider learning as an explicit objective, and must create mechanisms and systems for such learning to take place. In the absence of explicit intention and appropriate mechanisms, the learning potential may be lost. In some companies, where all organizational resources are centralized and where the national subsidiaries are seen as mere delivery pipelines to supply the organization's value-added to different countries, diverse learning may not take place either because the subsidiaries may not possess appropriate sensing, analysing and responding capabilities to learn from their local environments, or because the centralized decision processes may be insensitive to knowledge accumulated outside the corporate headquarters. Other companies, in which the subsidiaries may enjoy very high levels of local resources and autonomy, may similarly fail to exploit global learning benefits because of their inability to transfer and synthesize knowledge and expertise developed in different organizational components. Local loyalties, turf protection, and the 'not invented here' (NIH) syndrome – the three handmaidens of decentralization – may restrict internal flow of information across national boundaries which is essential for global learning to occur. In other words, both centralization and decentralization may impede learning.

THE MEANS: SOURCES OF COMPETITIVE ADVANTAGE

Most recent articles on global strategy have been aimed at identifying generic strategies (such as global cost leadership, focus or niche) and advocating particular strategic moves (such as cross-subsidy or pre-emptive investments). Underlying these concepts, however, are three fundamental tools for building global competitive advantage: exploiting differences in input and output markets in different countries, exploiting economies of scale, and exploiting economies of scope (Porter, 1985).

National differences

The comparative advantage of locations in terms of differences in factor costs is perhaps the most discussed, and also the best understood, source of competitive advantage in international business.

Different nations have different factor endowments, and in the absence of efficient markets this leads to inter-country differences in factor costs. Different activities of the firm, such as R&D, production, marketing, etc. have different factor intensities. A firm can therefore gain cost advantages by configuring its value-chain so that each activity is located in the country which has the least cost for the factor that the activity uses most intensely. This is the core concept of comparative advantage-based competitive advantage – a concept for which highly developed analytical tools are available from the discipline of international economics. Kogut (1985a) provides an excellent managerial overview of this concept.

National differences may also exist in output markets. Customer tastes and preferences may be different in different countries, as may be distribution systems, government regulations applicable to the concerned product-markets, or the effectiveness of different promotion strategies and other marketing techniques. A firm can augment the exchange value of its output by tailoring its offerings to fit the unique requirements in each national market. This, in essence, is the strategy of national differentiation, and it lies at the core of what has come to be referred to as the multidomestic approach in multinational management (Hout et al., 1982).

From a strategic perspective, however, this static and purely economic view of national differences may not be adequate. What may be more useful is to take a dynamic view of comparative advantage and to broaden the concept to include both societal and economic factors.

In the traditional economics view, comparative advantages of countries are determined by their relative factor endowments and they do not change. However, in reality one lesson of the past four decades is that comparative advantages change and a prime objective of the industrial policies of many nations is to effect such changes. Thus, for any nation, the availability and cost of capital change, as do the availability of technical manpower and the wages of skilled and unskilled labour. Such changes take place, in the long run, to accommodate different levels of economic and social performance of nations, and in the short run they occur in response to specific policies and regulations of governments.

This dynamic aspect of comparative advantages adds considerable complexity to the strategic considerations of the firm. There is a first-order effect of such changes – such as possible increases in wage rates, interest rates or currency exchange rates for particular countries that can affect future viability of a strategy that has been based on the current levels of these economic variables. There can also be a more intriguing second-order effect. If an activity is located in an economically inefficient environment, and if the firm is able to achieve a higher level of efficiency in its own operations compared to the rest of the local economy, its competitive advantage may actually increase as the local economy slips lower and lower. This is because the macro-economic variables such as wage or exchange rates may change to reflect the overall performance of the economy relative to the rest of the world and, to the extent that the firm's performance is better than this national aggregate, it may benefit from these macro-level changes (Kiechel, 1981).

Consistent with the discipline that gave birth to the concept, the usual view of comparative advantage is limited to factors that an economist admits into the production function, such as the costs of labour and capital. However, from a managerial perspective it may be more appropriate to take a broader view of societal comparative advantages to include 'all the relative advantages conferred on a society by the quality, quantity and configuration of its material, human and institutional resources, including "soft" resources such as inter-organizational linkages, the nature of its educational system, and organizational and managerial know-how' (Westney, 1985, p. 4). As argued by Westney, these 'soft' societal factors, if absorbed in the overall organizational system, can provide benefits as real to a multinational as those provided by such economic factors as cheap labour or low-cost capital.

While the concept of comparative advantage is quite clear, available evidence on its actual effect on the overall competitiveness of firms is weak and conflicting. For example, it has often been claimed that one source of competitive advantage for Japanese firms is the lower cost of capital in Japan (Hatsopoulos, 1983). However, more systematic studies have shown that there is practically no difference in the risk-adjusted cost of capital in the United States and Japan, and that capital cost advantages of Japanese firms, if any, arise from complex interactions between government subsidies and corporate ownership structures (Flaherty and Itami, 1984). Similarly, relatively low wage rates in Japan have been suggested by some authors as the primary reason for the success of Japanese companies in the US market (Itami, 1978). However, recently, companies such as Honda and Nissan have commissioned plants in the USA and have been able to retain practically the same levels of cost advantages over US manufacturers as they had for their production in Japan (Allen, 1985). Overall, there is increasing evidence that while comparative advantages of countries can provide competitive advantages to firms, the realization of such benefits is not automatic but depends on complex organizational factors and processes.

Scale economies

Scale economies, again, is a fairly well established concept, and its implications for competitive advantage are quite well understood. Micro-economic theory provides a strong theoretical and empirical basis for evaluating the effect of scale on cost reduction, and the use of scale as a competitive tool is common in practice. Its primary implication for strategy is that a firm must expand the volume of its output so as to achieve available scale benefits. Otherwise a competitor who can achieve such volume can build cost advantages, and this can lead to a vicious cycle in which the low-volume firm can progressively lose its competitive viability.

While scale, by itself, is a static concept, there may be dynamic benefits of scale through what has been variously described as the experience or learning effect. The higher volume that helps a firm to exploit scale benefits also allows it to accumulate learning, and this leads to progressive cost reduction as the firm moves down its learning curve.

The concept of the value-added chain recently popularized by Porter (1985) adds considerable richness to the analysis of scale as a source of competitive advantage. This conceptual apparatus allows a disaggregated analysis of scale benefits in different value-creating activities of the firm. The efficient scale may vary widely by activity – being higher for component production, say, than for assembly. In contrast to a unitary view of scale, this disaggregated view permits the firm to configure different elements of its value chain to attain optimum scale economies in each.

Traditionally, scale has been seen as an unmixed blessing – something that always helps and never hurts. Recently, however, many researchers have argued otherwise (e.g. Evans, 1982). It has been suggested that scale efficiencies are obtained through increased specialization and through creation of dedicated assets and systems. The same processes cause inflexibilities and limit the firm's ability to cope with change. As environmental turbulence has increased, so has the need for strategic and operational flexibility (Mascarenhas, 1982). At the extreme, this line of argument has led to predictions of a re-emergence of the craft form of production to replace the scale-dominated assembly form (Piore and Sabel, 1984). A more typical argument has been to emphasize the need to balance scale and flexibility, through the use of modern technologies such as CAD/CAM and flexible manufacturing systems (Gold, 1982).

Scope economies

Relatively speaking, the concept of scope economies is both new and not very well understood. It is based on the notion that certain economies arise from the fact that the cost of the joint production of two or more products can be less than the cost of producing them separately. Such cost reductions can take place due to many reasons – for example resources such as information or technologies, once acquired for use in producing one item, may be available costlessly for production of other items (Baumol, Panzer and Willig, 1982).

The strategic importance of scope economies arises from a diversified firm's ability to share investments and costs across the same or different value chains that competitors, not possessing such internal and external diversity, cannot. Such sharing can take place across segments, products, or markets (Porter, 1985) and may involve joint use of different kinds of assets (see Table 20.2).

A diversified firm may share physical assets such as production equipment, cash, or brand name across different businesses and markets. Flexible manufacturing systems using robots, which can be used for production of different items, is one example of how a firm can exploit such scope benefits. Cross-subsidization of markets and exploitation of a global brand name are other examples of sharing a tangible asset across different components of a firm's product and market portfolios.

A second important source of scope economies is shared external relations: with customers, suppliers, distributors, governments and other institutions. A multinational bank like Citibank can provide relatively more effective service to a multinational customer than can a bank that operates in a single country (see Terpstra, 1982). Similarly, as argued by Hamel and Prahalad (1985), companies such as Matsushita have benefited considerably from their ability to market a diverse range of products through the same distribution channel. In another variation, Japanese trading companies have expanded into new businesses to meet different requirements of their existing customers.

Finally, shared knowledge is the third important component of scope economies. The fundamental thrust of NEC's global strategy is 'C&C' – computers and communications. The company firmly believes that its even strengths in the two technologies and resulting capabilities of merging them in-house to create new products gives it a competitive edge over global giants such as IBM and AT&T, who have technological strength in only one of these two areas. Another example of the scope advantages of shared learning is the case of Liquid Tide described earlier in this paper.

Even scope economies, however, may not be costless. Different segments, products or markets of a diversified company face different environmental demands. To succeed, a firm needs to differentiate its management systems and processes so that each of its activities can develop *external consistency* with the requirements of its own environment. The search for scope economies, on the other hand, is a search for *internal consistencies* within the firm and across its different activities. The effort to create such synergies may invariably result in some compromise with the objective of external consistency in each activity.

Further, the search for internal synergies also enhances the complexities in a firm's management processes. In the extreme, such complexities can overwhelm the organization, as it did in the case of EMI, the UK-based music, electronics and leisure products company which attempted to manage its new CT scanner business within the framework of its existing organizational structure and processes (see EMI and the CT scanner, ICCH case 9–383–194). Certain parts of a company's portfolio of businesses or markets may be inherently very different from some others, and it may be best not to look for economies of scope across them. For example, in the soft drinks industry, bottling and distribution are intensely local in scope, while the tasks of creating and maintaining a brand image, or that of designing efficient bottling plants, may offer significant benefits from global integration. Carrying out both these sets of functions in-house would clearly lead to internalizing enormous differences within the company with regard to the organizing, co-ordinating, and controlling tasks. Instead of trying to cope with these complexities, Coca-Cola has externalized those functions which are purely local in scope (in all but some key strategic markets). In a variation of the same theme, IBM has 'externalized' the PC business by setting up an almost stand-alone organization, instead of trying to exploit scope benefits by integrating this business within the structure of its existing organization (for a more detailed discussion on multinational scope economies and on the conflicts between internal and external consistencies, see Lorange, Scott Morton and Ghoshal, 1986).

Table 20.2   Scope economies in product and market diversification

	Sources of scope economies	
	Product diversification	*Market diversification*
Shared physical assets	Factory automation with flexibility to produce multiple products (Ford)	Global brand name (Coca-Cola)
Shared external relations	Using common distribution channel for multiple products (Matsushita)	Servicing multi-national customers worldwide (Citibank)
Shared learning	Sharing R&D in computer and communications businesses (NEC)	Pooling knowledge developed in different markets (Procter and Gamble)

PRESCRIPTIONS IN PERSPECTIVE

Existing literature on global strategy offers analytical insights and helpful prescriptions for almost all the different issues indicated in Table 20.1. Table 20.3 shows a selective list of relevant publications, categorized on the basis of issues that, according to this author's interpretations, the pieces primarily focus on.[4]

Pigeon-holing academic contributions into different parts of a conceptual framework tends to be unfair to their authors. In highlighting what the authors focus on, such categorization often amounts to an implicit criticism for what they did not write. Besides, most publications cover a broader range of issues and ideas than can be reflected in any such categorization scheme. Table 20.3 suffers from all these deficiencies. At the same time, however, it suggests how the proposed framework can be helpful in integrating the literature and in relating the individual pieces to each other.

From parts to the whole

For managers, the advantage of such synthesis is that it allows them to combine a set of insightful but often partial analyses to address the totality of a multidimensional and complex phenomenon. Consider, for example, a topic that has been the staple for academics interested in international management: explaining and drawing normative conclusions from the global successes of many Japanese companies. Based on detailed comparisons across a set of matched pairs of US and Japanese firms. Itami concludes that the relative successes of the Japanese firms can be wholly explained as due to the advantages of lower wage rates and higher labour productivity. In the context of a specific industry, on the other hand, Toder (1978) shows that manufacturing scale is the single most important source of the Japanese competitive advantage. In the small car business, for example, the minimum efficient scale requires an annual production level of about

Table 20.3 Selected references for further reading

Strategic objectives	Sources of competitive advantage		
	National differences	*Scale economies*	*Scope economies*
Achieving efficiency in current operations	Kogut (1985a); Itami (1978); Okimoto, Sugano and Weinstein (1984)	Hout, Porter and Rudden (1982); Levitt (1983); Doz (1978); Leontiades (1984); Gluck (1983)	Hamel and Prahalad (1985); Hout, Porter and Rudden (1982); Porter (1985); Ohmae (1985)
Managing risks	Kiechel (1981); Kobrin (1982); Poynter (1985); Lessard and Lightstone (1983); Srinivasula (1981); Herring (1983)	Evans (1982); Piore and Sabel (1984); Gold (1982); Aaker and Mascarenhas (1984)	Kogut (1985b); Lorange, Scott Morton and Ghoshal (1986)
Innovation, learning and adaptation	Westney (1985); Terpstra (1977); Ronstadt and Krammer (1982)	BCG (1982); Rapp (1983)	Bartlett and Ghoshal (1985)

400,000 units. In the late 1970s no US auto manufacturer produced even 200,000 units of any sub-compact configuration vehicle, while Toyota produced around 500,000 Corollas and Nissan produced between 300,000 and 400,000 B210s per year. Toder estimates that US manufacturers suffered a cost disadvantage of between 9 and 17 per cent on account of inefficient scale alone. Add to it the effects of wage rate differentials and exchange rate movements, and Japanese success in the US auto market may not require any further explanation. Yet process-orientated scholars such as Hamel and Prahalad suggest a much more complex explanation of the Japanese tidal wave. They see it as arising out of a dynamic process of strategic evolution that exploits scope economies as a crucial weapon in the final stages. All these authors provide compelling arguments to support their own explanations, but do not consider or refute each other's hypotheses.

This multiplicity of explanations only shows the complexity of global strategic management. However, though different, these explanations and prescriptions are not always mutually exclusive. The manager's task is to find how these insights can be combined to build a multidimensional and flexible strategy that is robust to the different assumptions and explanations.

The strategic trade-offs

This, however, is not always possible because there are certain inherent contradictions between the different strategic objectives and between the different sources of competitive advantage. Consider, for instance, the popular distinction between a global and a multidomestic strategy described by Hout *et al.* (1982). A global strategy requires that the firm should carefully separate different value elements, and should locate each activity at the most efficient level of scale in the location where the activity can be carried out at the cheapest cost. Each activity should then be integrated and managed interdependently so as to exploit available scope economies. In essence, it is a strategy to maximize efficiency of current operations.

Such a strategy may, however, increase both endogenous and exogenous risks for the firm. Global scale of certain activities such as R&D and manufacturing may result in the firm's costs being concentrated in a few countries, while its revenues accrue globally, from sales in many different countries. This increases the operating exposure of the firm to the vicissitudes of exchange rate movements because of the mismatch between the currencies in which revenues are obtained and those in which costs are incurred. Similarly, the search for efficiency in a global business may lead to greater amounts of intra-company, but inter-country, flows of goods, capital, information and other resources. These flows are visible, salient and tend to attract policy interventions from different host governments. Organizationally, such an integrated system requires a high degree of co-ordination, which enhances the risks of management failures. These are lessons that many Japanese companies have learned well recently.

Similarly, consideration of the learning objective will again contradict some of the proclaimed benefits of a global strategy. The implementation of a global strategy tends to enhance the forces of centralization and to shift organizational power from the subsidiaries to the headquarters. This may result in demotivation of subsidiary managers and may erode one key asset of the MNC – the potential for learning from its many environments. The experiences of Caterpillar are a case in point. An exemplary practitioner of global strategy, Cat has recently spilled a lot of red ink on its balance sheet and lost ground steadily to its archrival, Komatsu. Many factors contributed to Caterpillar's woes, not the least of which was the inability of its centralized management processes to benefit from the experiences of its foreign subsidiaries.

On the flipside of the coin, strategies aimed at optimizing risk or learning may compromise current efficiency. Poynter (1985) has recommended 'upgrade', i.e. increasing commitment of technology and resources in subsidiaries, as a way to overcome risk of policy interventions by host governments. Kogut (1985b), Mascarenhas (1982) and many others have suggested creating strategic and operational flexibility as a mechanism for coping with macro-environmental risks. Bartlett and Ghoshal (1985) have proposed the differentiated network model of multinational organizations as a way to operationalize the benefits of global learning. All these recommendations carry certain efficiency penalties, which the authors have ignored.

Similar trade-offs exist between the different sources of competitive advantages. Trying to make the most of factor cost economies may prevent scale efficiency, and may impede benefiting from synergies across products or functions. Trying to benefit from scope through product diversification may affect scale, and so on. In effect these contradictions between the different strategic objectives, and between the different means for achieving them, lead to trade-offs between each cell in the framework and practically all others.

These trade-offs imply that to formulate and implement a global strategy, MNC managers must consider all the issues suggested in Table 20.1, and must evaluate the implications of different strategic alternatives on each of these issues. Under a particular set of circumstances a particular strategic objective may dominate and a particular source of competitive advantage may play a more important role than the others (Fayerweather, 1981). The complexity of global strategic management arises from the need to understand those situational contingencies, and to adopt a strategy after evaluating the trade-offs it implies. Existing prescriptions can sensitize MNC managers to the different factors they must consider, but cannot provide ready-made and standardized solutions for them to adopt.

CONCLUSION

This paper has proposed a framework that can help MNC managers in reviewing and analysing the strategies of their firms. It is not a blueprint for formulating strategies; it is a road map for reviewing them. Irrespective of whether strategies are analytically formulated or organizationally formed (Mintzberg, 1978), every firm has a realized strategy. To the extent that the realized strategy may differ from the intended one, managers need to review what the strategies of their firms really are. The paper suggests a scheme for such a review which can be an effective instrument for exercising strategic control.

Three arguments underlie the construct of the framework. First, in the global strategy literature, a kind of industry determinism has come to prevail not unlike the technological determinism that dominated management literature in the 1960s. The structures of industries may often have important influences on the appropriateness of corporate strategy, but they are only one of many such influences. Besides, corporate strategy may influence industry structure just as much as be influenced by it.

Second, simple schemes for categorizing strategies of firms under different labels tend to hide more than they reveal. A map for more detailed comparison of the content of strategies can be more helpful to managers in understanding and improving the competitive positions of their companies.

Third, the issues of risk and learning have not been given adequate importance in the strategy literature in general, and in the area of global strategies in particular. Both these are important strategic objectives and must be explicitly considered while evaluating or reviewing the strategic positions of companies.

The proposed framework is not a replacement of existing analytical tools but an enhancement that incorporates these beliefs. It does not present any new concepts or solutions, but only a synthesis of existing ideas and techniques. The benefit of such synthesis is that it can help managers in integrating an array of strategic moves into an overall strategic thrust by revealing the consistencies and contradictions among those moves.

For academics this brief view of the existing literature on global strategy will clearly reveal the need for more empirically grounded and systematic research to test and validate the hypotheses which currently appear in the literature as prescriptions and research conclusions. For partial analyses to lead to valid conclusions, excluded variables must be controlled for, and rival hypotheses must be considered and eliminated. The existing body of descriptive and normative research is rich enough to allow future researchers to adopt a more rigorous and systematic approach to enhance the reliability and validity of their findings and suggestions. The proposed framework, it is hoped, may be of value to some researchers in thinking about appropriate research issues and designs for furthering the field of global strategic management.

ACKNOWLEDGEMENTS

The ideas presented in this paper emerged in the course of discussions with many friends and colleagues. Don Lessard, Eleanor Westney, Bruce Kogut, Chris Bartlett and Nitin Nohria were particularly helpful. I also benefited greatly from the comments and suggestions of the two anonymous referees from the *Strategic Management Journal*.

NOTES

1 In the interest of simplicity the distinction between risk and uncertainty is ignored, as is the distinction between systematic and unsystematic risks.

2 This assumes that the firm has defined its business correctly and has identified as competitors all the firms whose offerings are aimed at meeting the same set of market needs that the firm meets.

3 Some market mechanisms such as long-term currency swaps are now available which can allow at least partial hedging of operating risks.

4 From an academic point of view, strategy of the multinational corporation is a specialized and highly applied field of study. It is built on the broader field of business policy and strategy which, in turn, rests on the foundation of a number of academic disciplines such as economics, organization theory, finance theory, operations research, etc. A number of publications in those underlying disciplines, and a significant body of research carried out in the field of strategy, in general, provide interesting insights on the different issues highlighted in Table 20.1. However, given the objective of suggesting a limited list of further readings that *managers* may find useful, such publications have not been included in Table 20.3. Further, even for the more applied and prescriptive literature on global strategy, the list is only illustrative and not exhaustive.

REFERENCES

Aaker, D.A. and Mascarenhas, B. (1984) 'The need for strategic flexibility', *Journal of Business Strategy*, Vol. 9, No. 2, pp. 74–82.

Aldrich, H.E. (1979) *Organizations and Environments*, Prentice Hall, Englewood Cliffs, NJ.

Allen, M.K. (1985) 'Japanese companies in the United States: the success of Nissan and Honda', unpublished manuscript, Sloan School of Management, MIT.

Bartlett, C.A. (1985) 'Global competition and MNC managers', ICCH Note No. 0–385–287, Harvard Business School.

Bartlett, C.A. and Ghoshal, S. (1985) 'The new global organization: differentiated roles and dispersed responsibilities', Working Paper No. 9–786–013, Harvard Business School.

Baumol, W.I., Panzer, J.C. and Willig, R.D. (1982) *Contestable Markets and the Theory of Industry Structure*, Harcourt, Brace, Jovanovich, New York.

Boston Consulting Group (1982) *Perspectives on Experience*, BCG, Boston, MA.

Calvet, A.I. (1981) 'A synthesis of foreign direct investment theories and theories of the multinational firm', *Journal of International Business Studies*, Spring/Summer, pp. 43–60.

Caves, R.F. (1980) 'Industrial organization, corporate strategy and structure', *Journal of Economic Literature*, XVIII, March 1980, pp. 64–92.

Doz, Y.I. (1978) 'Managing manufacturing rationalization within multinational companies', *Columbia Journal of World Business*, Fall, pp. 82–94.

Doz, Y.I., Bartlett, C.A. and Prahalad, C.K. (1981) 'Global competitive pressures and host country demands: managing tensions in MNCs', *California Management Review*, Spring, pp. 63–74.

Evans, J.S. (1982) *Strategic Flexibility in Business*, Report No. 678, SRI International.

Fayerweather, J. (1981) 'Four winning strategies for the international corporation', *Journal of Business Strategy*, Fall, pp. 25–36.

Flaherty, M. and Itami, H. (1984) 'Finance', in Okimoto, O.I., Sugano, T. and Weinstein, F.B. (eds), *Competitive Edge*, Stanford University Press, Stanford, CA.

Gluck, F. (1983) 'Global competition in the 1980s', *Journal of Business Strategy*, Spring, pp. 22–7.

Gold, B. (1982) 'Robotics, programmable automation and international competitiveness', *IEEE Transactions on Engineering Management*, November.

Hamel, G. and Prahalad, C.K. (1985) 'Do you really have a global strategy?' *Harvard Business Review*, July–August, pp. 139–48.

Hannan, M.P. and Freeman, J. (1977) 'The population ecology of organizations', *American Journal of Sociology*, Vol. 82, pp. 929–64.

Hatsopoulos, G.N. (1983) 'High cost of capital: handicap of American industry', Report sponsored by the American Business Conference and Thermo-Electron Corporation.

Hax, A.C. and Majluf, N.S. (1984) *Strategic Management: an integrative perspective*, Prentice-Hall, Englewood Cliffs, NJ.

Herring, R.J. (ed.) (1983) *Managing International Risk*, Cambridge University Press, Cambridge.

Hofer, C.W. and Schendel, D. (1978) *Strategy Formulation: analytical concepts*, West Publishing Co., St. Paul, MN.

Hout, T., Porter, M.E. and Rudden, E. (1982) 'How global companies win out', *Harvard Business Review*, September–October, pp. 98–108.

Itami, H. (1978) 'Japanese–U.S. comparison of managerial productivity', *Japanese Economic Studies*, Fall.

Kiechel, W. (1981) 'Playing the global game', *Fortune*, 16 November, pp. 111–26.

Kobrin, S.J. (1982) *Managing Political Risk Assessment*, University of California Press, Los Angeles.

Kogut, B. (1984) 'Normative observations on the international value-added chain and strategic groups', *Journal of International Business Studies*, Fall, pp. 151–67.

Kogut, B. (1985a) 'Designing global strategies: comparative and competitive value added chains', *Sloan Management Review*, Summer, pp. 15–28.

Kogut, B. (1985b) 'Designing global strategies: profiting from operational flexibility', *Sloan Management Review*, Fall, pp. 27–38.

Leontiades, J. (1984) 'Market share and corporate strategy in international industries', *Journal of Business Strategy*, Vol. 5, No. 4, pp. 30–7.

Lessard, D. and Lightstone, J. (1983) 'The impact of exchange rates on operating profits: new business and financial responses', mimeo, Lightstone-Lessard Associates.

Levitt, T. (1983) 'The globalization of markets', *Harvard Business Review*, May–June, pp. 92–102.

Lorange, P., Scott Morton, M.S. and Ghoshal, S. (1986) *Strategic Control*, West Publishing Co., St Paul MN.

Mascarenhas, B. (1982) 'Coping with uncertainty in international business', *Journal of International Business Studies*, Fall, pp. 87–98.

Mintzberg, H. (1978) 'Patterns in strategic formation', *Management Science*, Vol. 24, pp. 934–48.

Ohmae, K. (1985) *Triad Power: the coming shape of global competition*, The Free Press, New York.

Okimoto, D.I., Sugano, T. and Weinstein, F.B. (eds) (1984) *Competitive Edge*, Stanford University Press, Stanford, CA.

Perlmutter, H.V. (1969) 'The tortuous evolution of the multinational corporation', *Columbia Journal of World Business*, January–February, pp. 9–18.

Piore, M.J. and Sabel, C. (1984) *The Second Industrial Divide: possibilities and prospects*, Basic Books, New York.

Porter, M.E. (1980) *Competitive Strategy*, Basic Books, New York.

Porter, M.E. (1984) 'Competition in global industries: a conceptual framework', paper presented to the Colloquium in Competition in Global Industries, Harvard Business School.

Porter, M.E. (1985) *Competitive Advantage*, The Free Press, New York.

Poynter, T.A. (1985) *International Enterprises and Government Intervention*, Croom Helm, London.

Prahalad, C.K. (1975) 'The strategic process in a multinational corporation', unpublished doctoral dissertation, Graduate School of Business Administration, Harvard University.

Rapp, W.V. (1983) 'Strategy formulation and international competition', *Columbia Journal of World Business*, Summer, pp. 98–112.

Robinson, R.D. (1978) *International Business Management: a guide to decision making*, Dryden Press, Illinois.

Ronstadt, R. and Krammer, R.J. (1982) 'Getting the most out of innovations abroad', *Harvard Business Review*, March–April, pp. 94–9.

Rutenberg, D.P. (1982) *Multinational Management*, Little, Brown, Boston, MA.

Srinivasula, S. (1981) 'Strategic response to foreign exchange risks', *Columbia Journal of World Business*, Spring, pp. 13–23.

Terpstra, V. (1977) 'International product policy: the role of foreign R&D', *Columbia Journal of World Business*, Winter, pp. 24–32.

Terpstra, V. (1982) *International Dimensions of Marketing*, Kent, Boston, MA.

Toder, E.J. (1978) *Trade Policy and the US Automobile Industry*, Praeger, New York.

Vernon, R. (1977) *Storm Over the Multinationals*, Harvard University Press, Cambridge, MA.

Westney, D.E. (1985) 'International dimensions of information and communications technology', unpublished manuscript, Sloan School of Management, MIT.

Woo, C.Y. and Cool, K.O. (1985) 'The impact of strategic management of systematic risk', mimeo, Krannert Graduate School of Management, Purdue University.

21

PREPARING FOR THE FUTURE:
EVOLUTION OF THE TRANSNATIONAL

Christopher Bartlett, Sumantra Ghoshal and Julian Birkinshaw

[. . .]

since the first edition of this book was published we have repeatedly been asked both by managers and by our students 'what's next?' The model of the transnational company we have described in this book was drawn from the experiences of companies in the 1980s. How has leading-edge practice evolved since then? How must the transnational model evolve to respond to the needs of the future?

The question has been given an added urgency by the turmoil experienced by many of the world's largest MNCs over the last decade. Highly publicized problems in companies like Ford, Boeing, and Kodak – as well as the scandals that destroyed Enron and Worldcom – have led many to question the fundamental viability of companies as large, as diversified, and as geographically dispersed as these corporate behemoths. And it is not just in the United States where such problems have been emerging. In Europe, once revered names like ABB, Olivetti, and Philips have been making headlines more as problem cases than as role models. Even much admired Japanese companies such as Mazda, Yamaha, Toshiba, and the Industrial Bank of Japan have lost their lustre as deteriorating performance has led to layoffs and top-management changes.

Some critics have interpreted such turmoil in some of the largest and most visible MNCs as a sign that the era of the large worldwide companies may be over. Though many still survive and even dominate various geographic and business areas, these critics would have us believe that these are the last generation of dinosaurs still roaming the earth completely unaware of their inevitable and impending fate. The meteoric impact of simultaneous market and technological revolutions of the 1990s, they believe, will lead to the extinction of the entire population, to be replaced by more agile small companies or by a completely new genetically engineered species of 'virtual corporations.'[1]

Based on our own ongoing work in a number of companies, we believe that this news of the MNC's death is exaggerated. Indeed, our own research has indicated that it is precisely because of their experience in the international operating environment that such companies develop the best chance of surviving. Most obviously, this is due to their access to a wider scope of markets and resources and their ability to secure competitive positions and competencies unobtainable by purely domestic companies. But even more important, it is because the management in such companies gains invaluable experience in routinely dealing with the fast-changing, multidimensional demands and opportunities that are part of the global business environment. Through this experience, they develop an organizational capability that is increasingly valuable in today's complex and dynamic operating context.

In many ways, therefore, the transnational organizational and management issues we have described represent perhaps one of the most advanced forms of the modern corporation. The core management challenge in all companies is to embrace rather than to deny or minimize environmental complexity and uncertainty, and the demanding context of the transnational organization provides the ideal laboratory in which to develop such skills. In short, the challenge of managing across borders is the ideal way to develop the skills required for managing across boundaries of all kinds in the modern corporation.

In this [. . .] chapter, we examine a number of the organizational transformations currently underway in MNCs, and we describe what we see as their emerging management model – which is one possible answer to the 'what's next' question. In this process, we also suggest a new way of thinking about large companies. Instead of defining a large company in terms of a formal structure by which the overall company is divided into a series of business, geographic, and functional units, we describe it in terms of three core processes that characterize this new management approach. The entrepreneurial process drives the opportunity-seeking, externally focused ability of the organization to open new markets and create new businesses. The integration process allows it to link and leverage its dispersed worldwide resources and capabilities to build a successful company. The renewal process maintains its ability to challenge its own beliefs and practices and to continuously revitalize itself so as to develop an enduring institution. Effective management of these three processes also calls for some very different roles and tasks of frontline, middle, and top-level managers. We illustrate these organizational processes and management roles on the basis of the experiences of a number of different American, European, and Japanese companies.

THE ENTREPRENEURIAL PROCESS: SUPPORTING AND ALIGNING INITIATIVES

The traditional cross-border organization was built in a highly structured manner that allowed those at the top to coordinate and control the multifunctional, multibusiness, multinational operations. But this increasingly complex structure looks very different from the top than from the bottom (see Figure 21.1). From the top, the CEO sees order, symmetry, and uniformity – a neat instrument for step-by-step decomposition of the company's tasks and priorities. From the bottom, hapless frontline managers see a cloud of faceless controllers – a formless sponge that soaks up all their energy and time. The result, as described so colorfully by GE's Jack Welch, is 'an organization that has its face toward the CEO and its backside toward the customer.' The key assumption in these companies is that the entrepreneurial tasks would be carried out by the top management, while frontline managers would be primarily responsible for the operational implementation of top-down strategies. Such a management approach had not been a major constraint in the benevolent, high-growth environment that most companies enjoyed in the 1960s and 1970s. Throughout that period of rapid international market expansion, the opportunities for growth were enormous and the key management challenge was to allocate a company's financial resources among competing opportunities.

But in recent years market growth has slowed and, as we pointed out [. . .] the motivation for companies expanding abroad has shifted from one focused primarily on securing new markets or low-cost productive inputs, to a world-wide search for vital intelligence or scarce competencies not readily obtainable in the home market. As knowledge and specialized skills have gradually

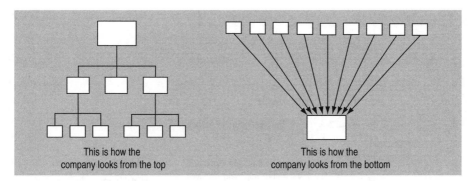

This is how the company looks from the top

This is how the company looks from the bottom

Figure 21.1 Top-down versus bottom-up view of the organization

replaced capital as the scarcest and most important source of competitive advantage, managers have become increasingly aware that, unlike money, expertise cannot be accumulated at and allocated from the top. The critical task now is to use the knowledge and insight of widely dispersed frontline managers to identify and exploit fast-moving opportunities in a rich and complex global environment. In short, the entrepreneurial function must now be focused not at the top of the hierarchy but at the bottom.

The challenge of rebuilding the initiative, creativity, and drive of those on the front lines of worldwide operations does not, however, mean that a company must now become a society of geographically spread, independent entrepreneurs held together by a top management acting as a combination of a bank and a venture fund. Instead, companies will be required to build an organization in which a well-linked entrepreneurial process will drive the company's opportunity-seeking, externally focused ability to create and exploit avenues for profitable growth wherever they may arise. It is this integrated entrepreneurial process that will bring the worldwide company advantages to the local frontline entrepreneurs and save the entrepreneurial transnational corporation from the myths of internal venturing and 'intrapreneurship' that have already proven so flawed in practice. The entrepreneurial transnational corporation will not be a hierarchical organization with fewer layers of management and a few scattered skunk works or genius awards: It will be a company built around a core entrepreneurial process that will drive everybody, and everything the company does.

The entrepreneurial process will require a close interplay among three key management roles. The frontline entrepreneurs will be the spearheads of the company, and their responsibility will be to create and pursue new growth opportunities. The coaches in senior-management positions will play a pivotal role in reviewing, developing, and supporting the frontline initiatives. Corporate leaders at the top of the organization will establish the overall strategic mission of the company that will define the boundary within which the entrepreneurial initiatives must be contained; they will also set the highly demanding performance standards that these initiatives must meet (see Figure 21.2). Just as the structural units of corporate, divisional, and operating-unit management groups were the fundamental building blocks of the hierarchical divisionalized company, the three management roles of entrepreneurs, coaches, and leaders and their interrelationships will be the core building blocks of the new entrepreneurial transnational corporation. The recent reorganization of a large American computer company provides an example of how such a management process can be structured.

Confronted with the challenge of rapidly changing customer demands and the constraints of a traditional matrix organization that impeded the company's ability to marshal its own formidable technological resources to help its customers, the company decided to restructure itself to create 'a network of entrepreneurs in a global corporation.' As described by top management, the objective

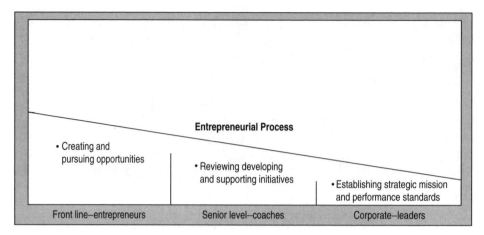

Figure 21.2   The entrepreneurial process: management roles and tasks

was to create a management approach 'which starts with opportunity and capitalizes upon the innovation, creativity, and excellence of people to secure the future of the company.' This objective was enshrined in the vision statement: to build 'a global IT service company based on people who are enthusiastic about coming to work every day knowing that they are highly valued, encouraged to grow and increase their knowledge and are individually motivated to make a positive difference.'

To achieve this vision, the company restructured itself into a large number of relatively small units, each unit being headed by a person formally designated as an entrepreneur. There were different kinds of entrepreneurial units, corresponding to different tasks such as product creation, field sales and support, or industry marketing. All shared a common mandate, however, 'to think and act as heads of companies in a networked holding.' Pursuit of opportunities was defined as their key challenge. Each entrepreneur was assured significant support and the top management collectively declared that 'everyone in the company works for the entrepreneurs.' At the same time, it was emphasized that no one could afford to own or control all the expertise, resources, or services necessary for achieving his or her objectives.

Pursuant to the reorganization, senior regional, divisional, and functional managers were relieved of their normal consolidation and control tasks and were instead regrouped as a pool of coaches. The label of coach highlighted that they should not play in the actual game. Yet the metaphor was that of a football coach who bore overall responsibility for the team's success, had the expertise to improve the players' skills, possessed the experience to guide the team's strategy, and had the authority to change players when the need arose.

In operational terms, each entrepreneur had an allotted coach to support him or her, but also a separate 'board' that has formal responsibility to 'review and question the validity of the entrepreneur's strategy and plan, provide feedback, monitor performance, encourage, stimulate, support, and, via the chairperson, propose rewards or change of the entrepreneur' (see Figure 21.3).

The coach's main task was to help the entrepreneur succeed both through personal guidance and support and also by acting as a link between the entrepreneur and all others in the company whose resources the entrepreneur might need to succeed. The board, of which the assigned coach was often the chairperson, acted in a manner not dissimilar from regular corporate boards. The chairperson was nominated by the top management and other members were selected by the entrepreneur, in consultation with the chairperson, from the company's pool of coaches. In selecting her board members, the entrepreneur looked for specific expertise and, if

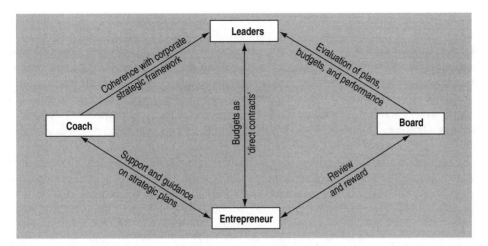

Figure 21.3   The operational structure

the desired skills are not available within the company, she could appoint outsiders such as customers, university professors, or even one of the employees from her unit.

The board was the company's key instrument for maintaining rigorous financial control. Its key tasks were to challenge the entrepreneur's plans, review her budget proposals, monitor performance against budgets, and to continuously advise top management on resource allocation decisions. Budgets were seen as sacrosanct: Once the budget was proposed and approved, the entrepreneur must achieve it, taking personal responsibility for initiating any changes that might become necessary because of unforeseen developments. But on the other side of the commitment, no one in the company could tamper with an approved budget except in response to the entrepreneur's demonstrated inability to fulfill to the contract.

Although the uniform financial control system provided rigor and discipline to the exercise of bottom-up initiative, top management of the company also recognized the need for a clear statement of strategic mission to provide direction and coherence to the entrepreneurial process. In contrast to the company's historical focus on proprietary products, the mission statement described the need for refocusing on customer service and on providing and integrating multi-vendor products and services. The simple yet unambiguous statement was explained and debated throughout the company over a six-month period to ensure not only intellectual understanding but also emotional commitment on the part of all employees.

Just the statement and its elaboration were, however, not enough. The process of discussion and debate revealed the need for establishing some clear performance standards and norms to link the mission with specific projects and plans. In response, top management articulated five key performance parameters – each clearly linked to the mission statement – and set specific overall goals against each parameter. For example, 'increase market share faster than competition' or 'profit above local competitors' was translated into tangible but differentiated objectives for the different entrepreneurial units, and approval of plans was linked to these objectives.

Whereas this is only one example of the transformation a company can go through to build the entrepreneurial process, it illustrates four key attributes that appear to be common to companies that are able to capture the creative energy of their people to develop new business opportunities.

First, they build their organizations around relatively small units. Matsushita, [. . .] has proliferated the world with its National, Panasonic, Quasar, Technic, and other branded consumer electronic products on the strength of its 'one product – one division' concept: As soon as an existing division comes out with a successful new product, it is split up as a separate division. Leading pharmaceutical company GSK (formerly Glaxo Smith Kline) has pulled apart its enormous R&D organization to create seven 'centers of excellence for drug discovery' – stand-alone units of up to 400 scientists that compete with each other for research funds. One can observe the same practice in companies as diverse as Johnson and Johnson, 3M, and Bertelsmann: To maintain the entrepreneurial spirit each unit must be restricted in size so that every member of the unit can personally know all others.

To build such small units, these companies have abandoned the notion of functionally complete 'strategic business units,' which own all key resources so as to be in full control over their performance. Instead, they have structured incomplete 'performance units' that are interdependent and must use each other's resources to achieve their own goals. The product divisions in Matsushita or Canon do not control the sales units, which are structured as separate companies, as are often the technology units. And, in contrast to the arbitrary and conflict-generating distinctions among cost centers, revenue centers, and profit centers, the performance centers are not differentiated on the basis of their activities. Whether they sell to customers, or produce for internal customers, or work to build new technologies, all performance centers are treated similarly in the planning, budgeting, and control systems.

Second, they create a multistage resource allocation process instead of up-front commitment to a clearly articulated long-term plan. Any employee can propose to start a new business at 3M and 'a single coherent sentence can often suffice as starting plan.' But, at each stage of developing the proposal, from the initial idea to product development, prototyping, technical and market testing, and commercialization, the entrepreneur must propose a specific budget and clearly quantified mileposts; all approvals are subject to satisfactory performance against the earlier commitments. As 3M managers grudgingly admit, 'We spend all our time preparing budgets, but it seems to help.'

Third, they tend to adopt a highly structured and rigorously implemented financial control system. At 3M, for example, such financial discipline is maintained through a standardized management reporting system that is applied uniformly to all operating units, who are forbidden by a central directive from creating their own systems. At the level of product families, 3,900 monthly P&L statements are generated centrally, and these are made available online to all the units within 10 days of every financial closing. Similarly, at Matsushita, a new division receives start-up capital from the corporate headquarters and loans, when justified under normal commercial conditions; it pays interest on the loans to the corporate 'bank' at regular market rates, together with 60 percent of pretax profits as dividend. Performance expectations are uniform across all divisions, regardless of the maturity of the market or the company's competitive position. If a division's operating profits fall below 4 percent of sales for two successive years, the divisional manager is replaced.

An essential corollary of such rigorous financial control is the sanctity of the budget of each entrepreneurial unit. In traditional divisionalized companies, budgets are cascaded down across each layer of the hierarchy and managers at each level are expected to achieve the aggregate budget at their level. Such an aggregation process essentially translates into sudden changes of approved budgets for certain units in response to unanticipated problems faced by other units within the administrative control of a common manager. In contrast, in companies with a firm commitment to bottom-up initiative, the budgets of the small entrepreneurial units are not changed except in response to variances in the unit's own performance. There is neither a cascading down of budget approvals nor an aggregation up of budget achievements: The budget of each unit is approved separately and its performance is monitored individually right up to top management.

And finally, all these companies have a clearly articulated and widely understood and shared definition of the 'opportunity horizon' that provides a lightning rod to channel organizational aspirations and energy into cohesive corporate development. The boundaries of the opportunity horizon tend to be precise enough to clearly rule out activities that do not support the company's strategic mission, and yet broad enough to prevent undue constraints on the creativity and opportunism of frontline managers. Without such a clearly defined strategic mission, frontline managers have no basis for selecting among the diverse opportunities they might confront and bottom-up entrepreneurship soon degenerates into a frustrating guessing game. The actual definition of the boundaries may be stated in very different terms – a strong technology focus in Canon or 3M or specific customer groups in SAS or Cartier, for example – but it provides a basis for strategic choice among different initiatives and serves as a guideline for the entrepreneurs themselves to focus their own creative energy.

THE INTEGRATION PROCESS: LINKING AND LEVERAGING COMPETENCIES

In this world of converging technologies, category management, and global competition, the entrepreneurial process alone is not sufficient. Tomorrow's successful transnational companies will also have a strong integration process to link their diverse assets and resources into corporate competencies, and to leverage these competencies in their pursuit of new opportunities. (This was at the core of the worldwide learning process discussed in [. . .].) In the absence of such an integration process, decentralized entrepreneurship may lead to some temporary performance improvement as existing slack is harnessed, but long-term development of new capabilities or businesses will be seriously impeded. Many highly decentralized companies including Matsushita have recently experienced this problem. In describing the transnational organization, we have suggested how worldwide integration can coexist with entrepreneurship at the national level, but the challenge of managing the symbiosis between entrepreneurship and integration extends beyond managing across geographic boundaries to those between the different businesses and functions of a company. The following example will illustrate how such a broader integration process can be built and managed.

Nikkei Business recently ranked Kao as the third in its list of Japan's most creative companies – well ahead of other local superstars including NEC, Toyota, Seibu, and Canon. The company had earned this distinction because of its outstanding record of introducing innovative, high-quality products to beat back not only domestic rivals such as Lion but also its giant global competitors such as Procter & Gamble (P&G) and Unilever. Technological and design innovations in Merries, Kao's brand of disposable diapers, reduced P&G's market share in Japan from nearly 90 percent to less than 10. Similarly, the introduction of Attack, Kao's condensed laundry detergent, resulted in the company's domestic market share surge from 33 to 48 percent, while that of Lion declined from 31 to 23 percent. In the 1980s, this innovative capability allowed this traditional soap company to expand successfully into personal care products where it established Sofina as the largest selling cosmetics brand in Japan, and into floppy disks in which it grew to be the second largest player in North America.

A powerful entrepreneurial process lies at the heart of Kao's innovative ability. It practices all the elements of the entrepreneurial process we have described: small functionally incomplete units driven by aggressive targets, rigorous financial discipline, a structured new product creation process, and a clear definition of its strategic mission in terms of utilizing its technological strengths to develop products with superior functionality. However, the wellspring behind this entrepreneurial process has been what Dr. Yoshio Maruta, the chairman of Kao, describes as 'biological self-control.' As the body reacts to pain by sending help from all quarters, 'if anything goes wrong in one part of the company, all other parts should know automatically and help without having to be asked.' A companywide integration process has allowed Kao to link and leverage its core competencies in research, manufacturing, and marketing not only to solve problems but also to create and exploit new opportunities. And this integration process in Kao, like the entrepreneurial process, is built on some well-defined roles, tasks, and value-added on the part of the frontline entrepreneurs, the senior-level coaches, and the corporate leaders (see Figure 21.4).

The small and relatively autonomous work units of the entrepreneurial corporation – each responsible for specific customer groups or product lines or functional competencies – create an enormous centrifugal force, which, in the absence of a countervailing centripetal force, can overwhelm the company with inconsistencies, conflicts, and fragmentation. The first task in integration, therefore, is to create a glue to hold the different parts together and to align their initiatives. A set of clear and motivating organizational values provides the basis for such normative integration, and developing, nurturing, and embedding these values become a key task of the management group we have described as corporate leaders.

The organizational processes of Kao are designed to foster the spirit of harmony and social integration based on the principle of absolute equality of human beings, individual initiative, and the rejection of authoritarianism. Free access of everyone to all information 'serves as the core value and the guiding principle of what Dr. Maruta describes as Kao's 'paperweight organization': a flat structure, with a small handle of a few senior people in the middle, in which all information is shared horizontally and not filtered vertically. 'In today's business world, information is the only source of competitive advantage,' said Dr. Maruta. 'This makes it necessary to share all information. If someone has special and crucial information that others don't have, that is against human equality, and will deprive us and the organization of real creativity and learning.' These core values of human equality and free sharing of all information are embedded throughout the organization not only through continuous articulation and emphasis by Dr. Maruta and other members of the top-management team but also through their own behaviors and through a set of institutionalized practices.

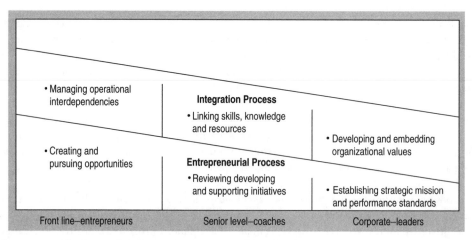

Figure 21.4   The integration process: management roles and tasks

For example, Dr. Maruta and his top-management colleagues share the 10th floor of Kao's head office building, together with a pool of secretaries. A large part of this floor is open space, with conference tables, overhead projectors, and lounging chairs spread around. This is known as 'decision space,' where all discussions with and among the top management take place. Anyone passing, including the chairman, can sit down and join in any discussion, on any topic, and they frequently do. The executive vice president in charge of a particular business or a specific territory can, therefore, be engaged in a debate on a topic that he has no formal responsibility for. The same layout and norm are duplicated in the other floors, in the laboratories, and in workshops. Workplaces look like large rooms: There are no partitions, only tables and chairs for spontaneous or planned discussions in which everyone has free access and can contribute as equals.

A biweekly Kao newspaper keeps every employee informed about competitors' moves, new product launches, overseas developments, and key meetings. Open computer-based access to company information ensures that all employees can, if they wish, retrieve data on sales records of any product from any of Kao's numerous outlets, or product development anywhere in the company. The latest findings from each of Kao's research laboratories are available for all to see, as are the details of the previous days' production and inventory at every Kao plant. 'They can even,' says Dr. Maruta, 'check up on the president's expense account.' The benefits from this open sharing of data outweigh the risk of leaks, the company believes, because, in an environment of flux, 'leaked information instantly becomes obsolete.'

Even though the corporate leaders carry the principal responsibility for developing and embedding the corporate values that provide the context for integration, it is the frontline entrepreneurs who must integrate the day-to-day activities of the company by managing the operational interdependencies across the different product, functional, and geographic units. This requires certain attitudes and some specific skills, but also some facilitating infrastructures and processes.

In Kao, information technology is a key element of the infrastructure and its own extensive value-added networks (Kao VANs) provide the anchors for operational integration. Fully integrated information systems control the flows of materials, products, and ideas from the stage of new product development, to production planning involving over 1,500 types of raw materials, to distribution of over 550 types of final products to about 300,000 retail stores.

Kao's logistics information system (LIS) links the corporate headquarters, all the factories, the independent wholesalers, and the logistics centers through a network that includes a sales planning system, an inventory control system, and an online supply system. Using LIS, each salesperson at Kao's 30 wholesalers projects sales plans on the basis of a head office campaign plan, an advertising plan, and past market trends. These are corrected and adjusted at the corporate level and provide the basis for the daily production schedules of each factory. A separate computerized ordering system, built on point-of-sales terminals installed in the retail stores and connected to LIS, allows automatic replenishment of store inventory based on the previous day's sales data.

Kao's marketing intelligence system (MIS) tracks sales by product, region, and market segment, and develops new approaches to advertising and media planning, sales promotion, market research, and statistical analysis. Another sophisticated computerized system, ECHO, codes all telephone queries and complaints about Kao's products online. Linked to MIS, ECHO is an invaluable 'window on the customer's mind' that allows the company to fine-tune formulations, labeling, and packaging and also to develop new product ideas.

These extensive IT networks provide the tools for the frontline managers in Kao to carry much of the burden of day-to-day operational coordination and integration, which, in most companies, are the key tasks of middle and senior management. But these IT networks are not seen as a replacement for face-to-face meetings. Indeed, the company has one of the most extensive systems of intrafunctional, interfunctional, and interbusiness meetings to facilitate exchange of ideas and joint development of new initiatives and projects. Top management, marketers, and research scientists meet at regular conferences. 'Open space' meetings are offered every week by different units, and people from any part of the organization can participate in such meetings.

Within the R&D organization, the wellspring of Kao's innovations, monthly conferences are hosted, in turn, by different laboratories to bring junior researchers together. Researchers can nominate themselves to attend any of these meetings; similarly, any researcher in the host laboratory is free to invite anyone he or she wishes to meet from any of Kao's several laboratories spread around the world. It is through the collaborative work triggered by such meetings that Kao developed many of its breakthrough innovations, such as a special emulsifier developed jointly by three different laboratories, which later proved to be crucial for Sofina's success. Similar processes are in place in most of the other businesses and functions, and these meetings – perhaps even more than the IT linkages – provide the means for Kao's frontline entrepreneurs to build and leverage their own lateral networks within the company.

But whereas the leaders create the context of integration and the frontline managers link and align operational activities, it is the group of coaches in senior management who serve as the engine for linking the diverse skills, expertise, and resources in different research, manufacturing, and marketing units to launch the strategic thrusts of Kao and maintain their momentum over time. If the entrepreneurs are the linchpins for the entrepreneurial process, the coaches are the pivots for the integration process.

A companywide 'total creative revolution' (TCR) project serves as the main vehicle for the senior managers in Kao to pull together teams from different parts of the company to find creative responses to emerging problems or new opportunities. TCR is the fourth phase in a two-decade-long program that started its life as an organizationwide computerization initiative (the CCR movement) and evolved into a total quality control (TQC) program, then a total cost reduction (TCR) effort. Total creative revolution – the second TCR project – was aimed at making 'innovation through collaborative learning' the centerpiece of Kao's strategic thrust through the 1990s.

According to Dr. Maruta, 'Kao must be like an educational institution – a company that has learnt how to learn.' And senior managers are formally expected to be 'the priests' – the teachers who must facilitate this process of shared learning. Thus, when a small and distant foreign subsidiary faced a problem, it was one of these constantly traveling senior managers who helped the local management team identify the appropriate expert in Japan and sponsored a task force to find a creative solution. Similarly, when some factory employees were made redundant following the installation of new equipment, one of these coaches sponsored five of them to form a team to support a factory in the United States to install and commission a plant imported from Japan. Over time, this group became a highly valued flying squad available to help new production units get over their teething troubles.

The success of Sofina was the result of a very similar process, albeit on a much larger scale. Sensing an opportunity to create a high-quality, reasonably priced range of cosmetics that would leverage Kao's technological strengths and emphasize the functionality of 'skin care' rather than 'image,' the top management of Kao presented it as a corporate challenge. To create such a product and to market it successfully, Kao would need to integrate its capabilities both within specific functions, such as diverse technologies in emulsifiers, moisturizers, and skin diagnosis lodged in different laboratories, and across functions including R&D, corporate marketing and sales, production, and market research.

Instead of trying to create one gigantic team, a few senior managers including the head of the Tokyo Research Laboratory, the director of marketing research, and a director of marketing formed themselves into a small team to coordinate the project. They created small task forces, as required, to address specific problems – such as developing a new emulsifier – but kept the lateral coordination tasks among the operating managers at the simplest possible level. When the new emulsifier created some problems of skin irritation, a different group was established to develop a moisturizer and a chemical to reduce irritation. Similarly, when the Sofina foundation cream was found to be sticky on application, they set it up as a challenge for a marketing team, who responded by positioning the product as 'the longest lasting foundation that does not disappear with perspiration,' converting the stickiness into a strength. This group of senior managers continued to play this integrating and coordinating role for over a decade, as the project evolved from its initial vision to a nationwide success.

THE RENEWAL PROCESS: MANAGING RATIONALIZATION AND REVITALIZATION

The historical management processes in large MNCs have been premised on the assumption that environmental changes will be relatively linear and incremental. The accounting, budgeting, planning, and control systems have been designed to provide order and efficiency to an essentially vertical process of managing information. The frontline units provide data. This data is analyzed by middle-level managers to create useful information. Information obtained from several different sources is combined to generate knowledge within the organization. Finally, top management absorbs and institutionalizes this knowledge to build wisdom that becomes a part of the accepted perspectives and norms within the company. In an environment of relative stability, the order and efficiency of such a linear process have allowed these companies to continuously refine their operational processes through incremental accumulation and exploitation of knowledge.

In an environment of often turbulent and unpredictable change, however, incremental operational refinement is not enough; companies now also need the ability to manage strategic renewal. They must create mechanisms in which established ways of thinking and working are continuously challenged. If the integration process links and leverages existing capabilities to defend and advance current strategies, the renewal process continuously questions those strategies and the assumptions underlying them and inspires the creation of new competencies to prepare the ground for the very different competitive battles the company is likely to confront in the future.

The renewal process is built on two symbiotic components. It consists, on the one hand, of an ongoing pressure for rationalization and restructuring of existing businesses to achieve continuous improvement of operational performance. This rationalization component aims to refine existing operations incrementally to achieve ever-improving current results. Rigorous benchmarking against best-in-class competitors provides the scorecard on concrete operational measures such as value-added per employee, contributions per unit of fixed and working capital, time to market for new products, and customer satisfaction. This process pinpoints performance gaps and focuses organizational energy on closing those gaps.

The other part of renewal is revitalization – the creation of new competencies and new businesses, the challenging and changing of existing rules of the game, and the leapfrogging of competition through quantum leaps. Driven by dreams and the power of ideas, it focuses on 'business not as usual' to create breakthroughs that would take the company to the next stages of its ambition. Revitalization may involve fast-paced, small bets to take the company into new business domains – as Canon is trying in the field of semiconductors – or big 'bet the company' moves to transform industries – as Nokia did throughout the 1990s as it led the twin technology and marketing revolutions that defined the emergence of the mobile phone industry.

As with entrepreneurship and integration, rationalization and revitalization are also often viewed in mutually exclusive terms. Managers complain of the insatiable appetite of the stock market for short-term results, which forces them to focus on rationalization rather than revitalization. Some justify poor operating results as the evidence of long-term investments. The renewal process, in contrast, emphasizes the essential symbiosis between the present and the future: There is no long-term success without short-term performance just as short-term results mean little unless they contribute to building the long-term ambition. Rationalization provides the resources needed for revitalization – not just money and people, but also legitimacy and credibility – whereas revitalization creates the hope and the energy needed for rationalization.

Amid the general bloodbath that has characterized the semiconductor business, Intel has been among the few players that have achieved steady growth together with satisfactory financial returns. While its fortunes have turned with the tide – from spectacular successes in the 1970s when it introduced, in quick succession, the 1130 DRAM, the 1702 EPROM, and the 8086 microprocessor, to heavy losses in the mid-1980s when the company was forced to exit the DRAM and SRAM businesses and cut 30 percent of its workforce, to phenomenal success again with the 80386 32-bit microprocessor in the late 1980s and the Pentium in the 1990s – Intel has so far taken most of the correct turns as it hit the forks in the road, avoiding hitting the dividers, as many of its competitors have done.

In this process, the company has continuously renewed itself, changing its products and strategies and adopting its organization and culture, to respond to the dramatic changes in its business environment. From the 'self-evident truth' that Intel was a 'jellybean' memory company, it changed itself into a logic devices company – selling boards – and then to a systems house – providing solutions in boxes. From a heritage of manufacturing inefficiency that was almost celebrated as the evidence of creativity in product development, Intel has now become cost competitive vis-à-vis its Japanese rivals. Its marketing focus has evolved too, from selling product features to OEM customers in the early 1970s, to positioning-oriented marketing in the 1980s (emphasizing compatibility with end-user standards), to full-fledged end-user marketing in the 1990s in direct partnership with the final customers of the company's microprocessors. To support these changes, Intel has also transformed its culture. From an organization of 'bright, talkative, opinionated, rude, arrogant, impatient, and very informal macho men interested only in results and not in niceties,' the company has evolved into a better balance between task focus and friendly work environment in which 'people don't have to be Milky the milk biscuit to get their work done, but then, they don't have to be Attila the Hun either,' as CEO Andy Grove colorfully put it.

Intel's ability to stay one step ahead of competition – which is all that separates the winners from the losers in the semiconductor business – has been built on some demanding roles and contributions of managers at all levels of the company (see Figure 21.5). But, if the frontline entrepreneurs drive the entrepreneurial process and the senior-level coaches anchor the integration process, it is the corporate-level leaders who inspire and energize the renewal process. It is they who create and manage the tensions between short-term performance and long-term ambition, challenging the organization continuously to higher levels of operational and strategic performance.

Until the demise of Noyce in 1990, Intel had been led by the trio of Gordon Moore as chairman, Robert Noyce as vice chairman, and Andy Grove as president, who collectively formed the company's executive committee. Of these, whereas Noyce looked after external relations, it was Moore and Grove who guided the company internally: Moore in the role of the technology

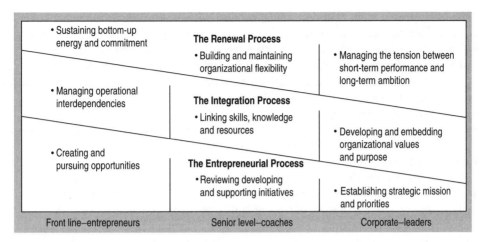

• Sustaining bottom-up energy and commitment	**The Renewal Process**	
	• Building and maintaining organizational flexibility	• Managing the tension between short-term performance and long-term ambition
• Managing operational interdependencies	**The Integration Process**	
	• Linking skills, knowledge and resources	• Developing and embedding organizational values and purpose
• Creating and pursuing opportunities	**The Entrepreneurial Process**	
	• Reviewing developing and supporting initiatives	• Establishing strategic mission and priorities
Front line—entrepreneurs	Senior level—coaches	Corporate—leaders

Figure 21.5 The renewal process: management roles and tasks

genius and architect of long-term strategy, and Grove as the detail-oriented resident pragmatist. Moore was the quiet, long-term-oriented, philosophical champion of revitalization. Grove, on the other hand, served as the vocal, aggressive, and demanding driver of rationalization.

When Motorola's competitive microprocessor gained momentum at the cost of Intel's 16-bit 8086 chip, it was Grove who initiated 'operation crush' – an 'all out combat' plan, complete with war rooms and SWAT teams, to make 8086 the industry standard. But it was Moore who built the company's long-range planning process and provided the blueprint for technological evolution – what has since come to be known as 'Moore's law.' In essence, the two divided the rationalization and revitalization components of the renewal responsibility between them in a way that was originally serendipitous but has since been institutionalized within the company as an unusual management concept: two-in-a-box. It has become normal in Intel for two executives with complementary skills to share the responsibilities of one role.

Whether through a combination of more than one person, as in the case of Andy Grove and Gordon Moore at Intel or Sochiro Honda and Takeo Fujisawa at Honda Motors, or single-handedly, as Jack Welch did so masterfully at GE, creating and managing this tension between the short term and the long term, between current performance and future ambition, between restructuring and revitalization, is a key part of the corporate leader's role in the entrepreneurial corporation. In this role, the leader is the challenger – the one who is constantly upping the ante, and creating the energy and the enthusiasm necessary for the organization to accept the perpetual stretch that such challenging implies.

Personal credibility within and outside the organization is a prerequisite for the corporate leader to play this role, but it is not enough. Charisma sustains momentum for short periods but fatigue ultimately overtakes the organization that depends on individual charisma alone for its energy. To inspire self-renewal, companies must develop an inspiring corporate ambition – a shared dream about the future and the company's role in that future – and must imbed that ambition throughout the organization. Whether the ambition focuses on something as tangible as size, as in Canon's expressed desire to be a company as big as IBM and Matsushita combined, or something less tangible, such as Intel's desire to be the best in the world, what matters is the emotional commitment the leader can build around the dream. Ultimately, it is this emotional commitment that unleashes the human energy required to sustain the organization's ability to continuously renew itself. And developing, marshaling, and leveraging this energy is key to simultaneous rationalization and revitalization, and will perhaps be the single most important challenge for the corporate leaders of the transnational companies of the future.[2]

Although the leaders must provide the challenge and the stretch necessary for organizational self-renewal, it is the coaches who must mediate the complex trade-offs that simultaneous restructuring and revitalization imply. It is they who must manage the tension between building new capabilities and stretching existing resources, and the conflict inherent in the high and unrelenting performance demands of the company. This requires enormous flexibility and an environment of mutual trust and tolerance, and creating such processes and attitudes is a key element of the coach's role.

As described by Andy Grove, in the semiconductor business 'there are the quick, and there are the dead.' In a highly volatile technological and market environment, the company has developed the ability to be very flexible in moving human resources as needs change. Levels change up or down at Intel all the time – people move in every direction, upward, sideways, or downward. Careers advance not by moving up the organization, but by individuals filling corporate needs. Official rank, decision-making authority, and remuneration – highly correlated in most companies – are treated separately at Intel and this separation among different kinds of rewards lies at the core of Intel's organizational flexibility. But such a system is also susceptible to gaming, and needs a high level of openness and transparency in decision-making processes and mutual trust and tolerance among people to be effective. Flexibility requires not only that the organization act fairly but also that it be seen to be acting fairly; creating and protecting such fairness – necessary in any winning team – is again a key task for the coaches.

Although Intel's action-oriented and direct management style, if somewhat confrontative, has evolved in Grove's mold of aggressive brilliance, it is the senior-management group heading different operating divisions and corporate functions that has embedded the norms of transparency and openness at all levels of the company. Key decisions at Intel are typically made in open meetings, all of which have preannounced agendas, and inevitably close with action plans and deadlines. During a meeting, participants are encouraged to debate the pros and cons of a subject aggressively through what is described as 'constructive confrontation.' But once something has been decided on, Intel has the philosophy of 'agree or disagree, but commit.' As a result, everyone has the opportunity to influence key decisions relevant to himself and to openly advocate their perspectives and views and is party to the final decisions, even though the decisions may not always conform to their personal preferences. The opportunity for such active participation on an equal basis in open and transparent decision processes, coupled with the norm of disciplined and fast implementation once a decision has been taken, creates the environment of trust, which, in turn, is key to the operational and strategic flexibility of the company.

The effectiveness of the renewal process ultimately depends on the ability of frontline managers to generate and maintain the energy and commitment of people within their units. The battles for efficiency and integration, for rationalization and revitalization, are ultimately fought at the level of the salesperson in the field, the operator in the plant, and the individual research scientist or engineer in the laboratory. While the energizing ambition personified by the top management and the open and transparent decision-making processes orchestrated by the senior managers provide the anchors for the grassroots-level commitment at Intel, two other elements of its organizational philosophy and practices also contribute a great deal in maintaining the enthusiasm of its frontline teams.

First, at Intel, there is not only fairness in management processes but there is also fairness in organizational outcomes. In contrast to companies that cut frontline jobs at the first sight of performance problems, Intel adopted the '125 percent solution' to deal with the industrywide recession in the early 1980s: Instead of retrenching people, all salaried workers – including the chairman – were required to work an additional 10 hours per week without additional compensation. When the recession continued in 1982, still unwilling to lay off large numbers of people, the company proposed a 10 percent pay cut on top of the 125 percent solution. As the economy pulled out of the recession, returning the company to profitability, the pay cuts were first restored in June 1983 and, by November 1983, the employees who had accepted pay cuts received special bonuses. Several years later, when the memory product bloodbath finally forced the company to reduce its workforce by 30 percent, the cuts were distributed across all levels of the company, instead of being concentrated at the lowest ranks.

Second, at Intel, it is legitimate to own up to one's personal mistakes and to change one's mind. Gordon Moore regretfully but openly acknowledges his personal role in missing the engineering workstation revolution, even though the company was among the pioneers for this opportunity. Andy Grove, the symbol of the company's confrontative, task-oriented culture, had long insisted on not having any recreation facilities in the company. 'This is not a country club. You come here to work,' he would say to all employees. But as the organization grew, and the need for supplementing the task focus with concern for a friendly work environment became manifest, he gave in and made a celebration of being beaten down. At the dedication of the new facilities, he appeared in his bathing suit and took a shower under a big banner that read, ' "There will never be any showers at Intel" – Andy Grove.' Such open acknowledgment of errors and good-hearted acceptance of alternatives one has personally opposed create an environment in which failures are tolerated and changes in strategy do not automatically create winners and losers. It is this overall environment that, in turn, co-opts the frontline managers into the corporate ambition and allows them to sustain energy and commitment at the lowest levels of the organization.

A MODEL FOR THE FUTURE

Over the last decade, many observers of large corporations have highlighted some of the vulnerabilities of the traditional company's strategy and organization described in this chapter. The specific prescriptions of needing to build entrepreneurship, integration, and renewal capabilities are also not new. Academics, consultants, and managers themselves have long recognized these needs to respond to a variety of changing environmental demands. Typically, however, these changing external demands and the consequent need for new internal capabilities have been studied in a piecemeal fashion, triggering ad hoc responses.

Facing slowing economic growth and increasingly sophisticated customer demands, companies have attempted to decentralize resources and authority to capture the creative energy and entrepreneurship of frontline managers. But prescriptions of creating and managing chaos have ignored the need for clarity of strategy and the discipline of centralized financial control to channel bottom-up energy into a coherent corporate direction. Companies that have attempted such radical decentralization without a centrally managed strategic framework have soon lost their focus and their ability to leverage resources effectively and have been forced to retreat to the known devil of their old ways.

Observing the ever-increasing pace of globalization of markets and the rising cost, complexity, and convergence of technologies, managers have recognized the need to consolidate and integrate their diverse organizational capabilities. But presented typically with examples of high-tech and highly centralized Japanese companies, they have confused capabilities with technologies, and integration with centralization. Similarly, faced with the rapid enhancement of the skills and resources of once-distant competitors and the changing norms and expectations in the many societies in which they operate, companies have realized the limits of incremental improvements and the need for dramatic change. Yet guided by prescriptions of creating dreamlike, long-term ambitions, they have allowed short-term performance to slip, thereby abandoning the long term too because of increasing resource scarcity.

In contrast to these fragmented and often contradictory prescriptions, we have presented a broad model encompassing the key capabilities we believe companies must develop to respond to the environmental demands of the 2000s. Nothing needs a theory more than practice, and the lack of an integrated theory of the new organization, we believe, has prevented companies from abandoning the old divisional model even though they have long recognized its constraints. The model of the future organization we have presented here is aimed to provide such a theory for practice.

The real challenge in building this new organization lies in the changes in management roles we have described. The metamorphosis of frontline managers – those who drive the operations in subsidiaries worldwide, for example – from being operational implementers to becoming aggressive entrepreneurs, will require some very new skills and capabilities. Similarly, the transformation of the middle-management role – global product or business managers, for instance – from that of administrative controller to that of inspiring coach will represent a traumatic change. But the management group that will be most severely challenged in the new organization will be the one currently at the top of the hierarchy – the CEO and other top-level executives. Not only will they have to change their role from that of resource allocator and political arbitrator to that of institutional leader, they will also have to create the infrastructures and the contexts necessary for the others to play the new roles demanded of them. The managers who can build the attitudes and skills appropriate for these new roles and the companies that can develop and retain such managers are likely to emerge as the future winners in the game of global competition.

NOTES

1   For one example of this line of thinking, see T.W. Malone and R.J. Laubacher, 'The Dawn of the E-lance Economy,' *Harvard Business Review*, September–October 1998, pp. 145–52.
2   For an elaboration of the importance of individual energy and focus in driving the renewal process, see S. Ghoshal and H. Bruch, "Beware the Busy Manager," *Harvard Business Review*, February 2002, pp. 63–9.

22

THE INTERNATIONALIZATION
OF SERVICE FIRMS

Susan Segal-Horn

Little of the literature in international business or global strategy addresses the service sector. Indeed, much of the research in service management suggests that services are not easily reproduced across borders and are therefore inappropriate for internationalization. This paper reviews changes in the nature of service characteristics which had led to greater international expansion by service firms. These include the increased availability of scale and scope economies in services and changed asset structures of service firms. The paper then discusses how scale and/or scope economies are differentially distributed across varying types of service businesses. As the potential for scale and scope economies affects competition in services, the result may be the creation of similar types of asset structures and similar industry dynamics to manufacturing.

INTRODUCTION

Service industries are generally regarded as possessing specific characteristics which determine the predominantly 'local' structure of service firms. These include intangibility, perishability, simultaneity of production and consumption, and buyer/supplier interaction in delivery of the service. Traditional assumptions about these service characteristics have been regarded as fundamental to the definition of what constitutes a service (Shostack, 1977; Sasser *et al.*, 1978; Normann, 1984; Daniels, 1985; Albrecht and Zemke, 1985; Heskett, 1986; Hindley *et al.*, 1987; Carlzon, 1987; Lovelock, 1988; O'Farrell and Hitchens, 1990).

This heavy emphasis on 'front-office' activities in the creation and delivery of a service means that international expansion has represented higher levels of risk and additional difficulties for service businesses compared to those faced by manufacturing businesses (Carman and Langeard, 1980) – especially, the risk of being distant from the customer interface and the problems of maintaining quality control at the point of service delivery. When combined with industry characteristics such as low entry barriers, diseconomies of scale, and close local control, these factors explain why service industries were historically defined as 'local' industries, unsuited to international expansion. However, despite these 'local' assumptions, there exists a degree of *de facto* internationalization of service firms, including multinational enterprises (MNC) and DMNC service firms.

MNCs are expected to standardize or adapt their activities at the optimum level consistent with the most advantageous international cost, scale, and market positions available to them (Hout *et al.*, 1982; Bartlett and Ghoshal, 1986, 1987, 1989; Prahalad and Doz, 1987; Kogut, 1989; Kobrin, 1991). There is a growing view that for service firms, also, MNC operations provide similar competitive opportunities to the firms that utilize them (Dunning, 1989; Enderwick, 1989). The approach taken here builds on the economic literature of the growth of the multinational enterprise (Teece, 1980, 1982; Caves, 1982; Casson, 1982; Dunning, 1981, 1985, 1989). Since industries are taken as aggregates of firms, and firms as distinctive asset structures, evidence of industry evolution can be based on the evolution of the asset structures of individual firms.

In their international expansion, service firms might be expected to seek to benefit from the same sources of potential advantage as manufacturing firms. These were collected by Ghoshal (1987) under the three headings of: national differences (e.g., to obtain beneficial factor costs or offset country-specific government policies); scale economies (e.g., to spread cost reduction and experience effects across national boundaries, to expand or exploit scale in purchasing, distribution, capital costs, and so forth) and scope economies (e.g., shared investments, knowledge, and learning across products and markets). The issue is whether such benefits from international expansion are as attainable for service firms as for manufacturing firms.

This paper argues that the sources of competitive advantage in service industries are changing. A combination of structural, market, regulatory, and technological changes has provided a shift in the balance of activities within service firms. Greater emphasis on 'back-office' activities may be lowering the levels of perceived risk, and enhancing the potential benefits, attached to international expansion of service firms.

The paper adapts, for service firms, Chandler's model (1977, 1986, 1990) of a 'logic' of manufacturing industry growth to explain the growth of service multinational enterprises. An exploration and development of this framework is used to show the potential of economies of scale and economies of scope within a variety of service firms. In addition, some initial criteria are presented for measuring scale and scope in service firms. Of particular interest are variables which drive cost for a service firm, since international expansion of a service firm should involve some efficiency advantages to justify the costs of integration of cross-border operations, compared to provision of the service by a domestic firm. An approach is suggested to understanding how economies of scale and scope actually work in service firms. These appear to be having some impact on the creation of international oligopolies in services.

THE APPLICATION OF CHANDLER'S 'LOGIC' TO SERVICES

Chandler's model, as an explanatory framework for the growth of MNE service firms, suggests a shift in the underlying 'logic' of service industry growth. It implies that the current dynamic of growth of service firms is beginning to parallel that in manufacturing.

The manufacturing 'logic'

Chandler's work (1977, 1986, 1990) addresses the circumstances under which a firm will continue to grow to maintain a position of dominance. The economic basis of Chandler's model is 'the cost advantages that scale and scope provided in technologically advanced, capital-intensive industries' (1990, p. 32). This model of the managerial enterprise was built on manufacturing industry data (e.g., oil, pharmaceuticals, agricultural machinery, steel) from which industries which remained technologically simple and labour-intensive (e.g., textiles, leather, publishing) were excluded. Chandler (1986) showed that in sectors where few large firms appeared their absence was because neither technological nor organizational innovation substantially increased minimum efficient scale. Therefore, in those industries, large plants did not offer significant cost advantages over smaller ones and 'opportunities for cost-reduction through more efficient co-ordination of high-volume throughout by managerial teams remained limited' (1986, p. 417). Hierarchies (Chandler's 'visible hand' (1977)) emerged and spread 'only in those industries or sectors whose technology and markets permitted administrative co-ordination to be more profitable than market co-ordination' (p. 11).

The structure of service industries lay outside Chandler's 'logic'. Despite considerable variance across sectors, service industries have been neither as technologically advanced nor as capital-intensive as manufacturing. They had exhibited minimum efficient scale at low levels, with significant diseconomies of scale reached at modest levels of growth. (For an example of all these industry features, see Dermine and Röller (1990) on the French mutual funds industry, where economies of both scale and scope are demonstrated for small to medium-size firms but disappear for larger firms.) The special characteristics of service businesses have also long been viewed as having an effect on both demand for, and supply of, services (Eiglier and Langeard, 1977; Lovelock and Young, 1979; Grönroos, 1982; Flipo, 1988). In particular, the interaction between buyer and supplier in the supply of the service, often known as 'the moment of truth', the point where service quality is created, (Normann, 1984; Heskett, 1986; Carlzon, 1987; Lovelock, 1988) has dominated thinking about the design and delivery of services. Received wisdom has been that services are 'different.' Thus, the growth paths of service firms have indicated a different 'logic' to manufacturing firms.

For Chandler's model of growth to now be applicable to service industries, the special characteristics of services must have diminished in significance. This paper argues that more capital-intensive asset structures and higher fixed costs have been influential in creating extranational economies of scale. This has encouraged, in turn, high levels of merger and acquisition activity in many service sectors (e.g., hotel chains, accounting and management consultancy firms, airlines, software, information services, telecommunications, financial services, and so forth). Concentration has thereby increased. Service industries are no longer fragmented industries with no clear market leaders. In many sectors, they resemble oligopolies, albeit with a long 'tail' of smaller firms co-existing as local providers in most markets. The result is a greater similarity between manufacturing and service firms.

The rest of this paper will assess the significance of greater potential for economies of scale and economies of scope on the growth strategies of service firms. The research proposition used is that:

Proposition – Where cost advantages of scale and/or scope are available, service firms are likely to internationalize.

Scale and scope in services

Any application of Chandler's 'logic' to service businesses must consider how cost advantages derived from investments in volume may yield economies of scale and scope in services. Table 22.1 lists some of the potential sources of economies of scale and economies of scope in services.

Any asset which yields scale economies can also be the basis for scope economies if it provides input into two or more processes. Economies of scope are usually defined as existing when the cost of producing two outputs jointly is less than the cost of producing each output separately (Teece, 1980, 1982). In clarifying the relationship between economies of scope and the business enterprise, Teece (1980) specified two important circumstances when integration of activities across a multiproduct firm would be needed to capture scope economies: first, where two or more products depend on the same proprietary know-how; second, when a specialized indivisible asset is a common input into two or more products. Both of these conditions are now routinely found in service enterprises.

An obvious example of the interaction between scale and scope benefits deriving from the same proprietary know-how and indivisible asset, is the central role now played by computer reservation systems (CRS) in the activities of airlines, hotel chains, car rental firms and so forth. These not only support the geographic spread of the business and the rapid processing of volumes of transactions but also provide customer databases for cross-marketing of services and the capability to design and deliver completely new services. Table 22.2 gives some illustrations of these information technology-based scale and scope benefits in three different service businesses: a financial services company (American Express), a fashion retailer (Benetton), and an airline (British Airways).

American Express is able to set and monitor service standards for fast response times for card enquiries, or to provide new and additional services such as 'free' travel arrangements or theatre

Table 22.1 Potential sources of economies of scale and scope in services

Economies of scale	Economies of scope
Geographic networks	IT/IS and shared information networks
Physical equipment	Shared learning and doing
Purchasing/supply	Product or process innovation
Marketing	Shared R&D
Logistics and distribution	Shared channels for multiple offerings
Technology/IT/IS	Shared investments and costs
Production resources	Reproduction formula for service system
Management	Range of services and service development
Organization	Complementary services
Operational support	Branding
Knowledge	International franchising
	Training
	Goodwill and corporate identity
	Culture
	Internal exploitation of economies
	Reduced transaction costs
	Common governance
	Know-how effects
	Privileged access to parent services

Source: Author's judgement and compilation from Normann (1984), Ghoshal (1987), Enderwick (1989)

Table 22.2 Some scale and scope implications of systems technology on selected service businesses

American Express	Response times
	New products
	Distribution channels
	Add-on services
Benetton	Responsive merchandising
	Inventory elimination
	Customized production
	Credit management
British Airways	Yield management
	Exclusion effect
	Vertical integration

Source: Segal-Horn (1990)

bookings for cardholders. Benetton has become renowned for its ability to replace inventory in its worldwide outlets and for using real-time information from point-of-sale systems to tailor seasonal production to demand. British Airways has developed sophisticated software to maximize yield from higher-revenue seats on all flights, a major contribution to profitability in a service business with high fixed costs.

Dunning (1989) suggests that know-how and specialized assets often combine in service firms, with knowledge featured as a special asset in services (see also Erramilli, 1990). In fact, the capability to acquire, process, and analyse information is the key asset or core competence of many services (e.g., financial, software, brokerage, and professional; also, the agency function of computerized reservation systems linking many service businesses). 'Know-how' here literally consists of the knowledge of how to combine human and physical resources to produce and process information.

Additionally, despite the traditional service industry assumptions, knowledge need not be perishable. It has a shelf life, during which time it may be repeatedly used at little or no cost (e.g., an advertisement, a software program). Many services comprise a firm-specific pool of tacit knowledge. Service firms (e.g., management consultancies and other PSFs, fast food chains hotel chains) are increasingly attempting to codify this inherited knowledge as the basis of standardization of their products, to achieve cost-reduction and increased productivity, as well as reliability of service levels. Some of the strongest brands in services are based on perceived accumulated know-how, for example, McKinsey, Reuters, Neilsen and McDonald's. The trend is for information-intensive assets to absorb heavier investment in fixed costs which in itself exerts pressure to lower unit costs by spreading output over larger markets (for scale economies) and a wider variety of products (for scope economies).

In exploring 'know-how', Teece (1982) reviews its 'fungible' character; that is, that individual and organizational knowledge represent a generalizable capability rather than necessarily referring to the particular products and services which the enterprise is currently producing (captured by Prahalad and Hamel (1990) as 'core competences'). This implies that where diversification is based on scope economies, the comparative advantage of the firm is defined in terms of capabilities rather than in terms of outputs. It therefore makes sense for service firms utilizing scope economies to manage their international expansion by means of internationalization (i.e., the internal control of co-ordination of assets and activities) rather than by market transaction. Internalization (Dunning, 1985) enables firms to bring managerial control to bear on internal capabilities, giving greater control over their realization. Thus, internalization is especially important in the growth of service firms in regard not just to efficiency, but also to the harnessing of capabilities and the management of the 'moments of truth' (Normann, 1984; Carlzon, 1987) in which the quality of service firms is experienced by their customers.

The changed services 'logic': Phase 1 – the industry evolution phase

Chandler's 'dynamic logic of growth and competition' occurs at the level of the firm and arises out of the investment and expansion decisions of the management hierarchy. Figure 22.1 is a diagrammatic representation of the path of those decisions showing the early stages of industry evolution.

Chandler's evidence explains the growth of firms to a position of dominance in their sector through the early pursuit of cost advantages derived from volume. Scale and scope are fundamentally volume and cost-driven. Chandler shows that companies which create and sustain dominant position in their industries do so by making pre-emptive investments in scale and scope which enable the firm to strongly influence the evolving structure of the industry and the bases of competition within the industry.

As shown in Figure 22.1, Phase 1 of Chandler's 'logic' consists of four sets of core investments: in volume, to achieve cost advantages of scale; in scope, to achieve consistent capacity utilization; in national, and then international, marketing and distribution networks; and in a management hierarchy to co-ordinate and allocate current and future resource utilization. Firms which moved first to make these co-ordinated sets of large investments could dominate their industries and influence their path of development, both in the short term and longer term. This is because challengers would have to match the first-mover advantages in comparable costs, build distribution and reputation to a point where the dominant incumbent could be effectively challenged, recruit teams of experienced managers, and match specialized experience curve effects.

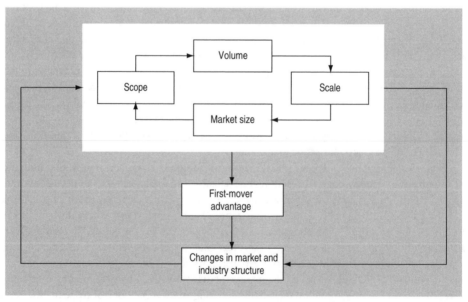

Figure 22.1 Simplified model of Chandler's dynamic of MNE growth: Phase 1

An illustration: American Express – Phase 1

An example which will be used here as an illustration of the application of this 'logic' in a service firm is American Express (Amex),[1] a financial services company in which scale and scope operate in a massive way. Over time, this company has successively made the investments in marketing, distribution, volume, product, and process outlined by Chandler for manufacturing. In so doing, it has created a world-scale service industry, which it has dominated for more than a century after its first international expansion moves.

The development of American Express involved a series of 'Phase 1' – style investments. The company was founded in New York in 1850 by Wells & Fargo, progressing rapidly from the express carriage of cash and parcels to bonded carrier of freight and finance. It handled European imports to all US Customs interior ports-of-clearance. Investments in its distribution network proceeded beyond national US coverage to the beginnings of its European network in freight forwarding. The company moved from an initial office in Liverpool, England, in 1881 to 3,000 European agencies offices in 1890. Beyond scale expansion of the network, these offices also provided considerable expansion in scope through the increased range of services offered, utilizing additional capacity in the same network of outlets. The company was already benefiting from a virtuous cycle of scale, volume, and scope effects that enabled it to advertise in brochures in Europe at this time that it could:

> pay money on Telegraphic Order, at a moment's notice, between points thousands of miles apart and sell small Drafts or Money Orders which ... can be cashed at 15,000 places.
>
> (American Express company documents, 1991)

American Express began extending its management hierarchy in Europe by beginning its own directly owned chain of European offices in 1895. The freight express business encompassed many developing financial service activities, for example, paying foreign money-order remittances from emigrants, or the commercial credit transactions begun in Rotterdam in 1907. Other major new product development initiatives included:

- Amex Express Money Order (1882)
- Amex Travellers Cheque (1891).

These provide illustrations of Chandler's proposition that incumbent first-mover advantages determine the future structure of an industry. Sale of travellers cheques unleashed demand to provide additional services to tourists, such as itineraries and tickets. A European, and eventually worldwide, travel network was established, uniquely combined with the Amex portfolio of financial products and services to create a new set of asset structures for a specialized segment of the financial services industry. The company introduced the Amex Charge Card in 1958. By the 1960s, 38,000 outlets worldwide sold American Express 'travel-related financial services' (TRS), which is still the source of 70% of the American Express Company's revenues in the 1990s.

The potential for scale and scope economies in different types of service businesses

Moving from a specific illustration of Chandler's 'logic' applied to one service company, some more general observations may be made concerning scale and scope in services.

The grid in Figure 22.2 gives a customary representation of the spread of scale and scope economies available to different types of service businesses. Examples belonging in the top right corner of the grid include financial services companies such as American Express, the major international airlines, travel firms such as Club Med, and information service firms such as Reuters and Dun & Bradstreet. The top left corner covers food retailers, where high-scale effects have arisen from electronic point-of-sale equipment and concentration of retailer buying power, combined with limited scope opportunities, although some large food multiples also trade in clothing, homewares, and even financial services such as in-house credit cards. The bottom right of the grid encompasses management consultancies or other professional service firms (PSFs) such as accountants, surveyors, civil engineers, or head-hunters. PSFs may be high on potential scope economies from assets such as shared client and project databases or shared teams of expertise across national or regional offices, but they have low potential economies of scale since these services are frequently customized, often within different national regulatory frameworks. The bottom left quadrant includes the small-scale, highly location-specific businesses typically defined as services.

Although Figure 22.2 represents the traditional view of varying types of service businesses, what is interesting from the point of view of this paper is the drift of many firms in these different sectors towards the top right of the grid. The creation via mergers (e.g., KPMG Peat Marwick, Ernst & Young, Deloitte Touche) of very large international accounting and consultancy firms, which is mirrored in other PSF sectors, is part of the search for greater efficiencies in capacity utilization of scarce resources and for productivity gains from implementation of standardized methodologies. Equally, food (e.g., Aldi) and non-food (e.g., IKEA, Toys 'R' Us) retailers have begun to operate beyond domestic boundaries (Treadgold, 1989; Segal-Horn and Davison, 1992), seeking scale benefits from volume purchasing and scope benefits from investments in information technology, logistics networks and branding. Insurance companies in Europe (e.g., Allianz of Germany, Generali of Italy, Prudential of the United Kingdom) are building cross-border opera-

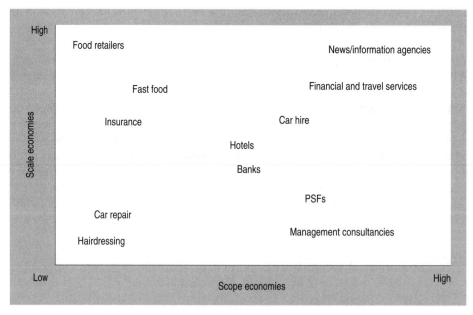

Figure 22.2 Potential for scale and scope economies in different service businesses (Source: Segal-Horn, 1992)

tions as regulatory differences become less extreme and types of distribution channels develop and converge. Finally, many erstwhile small service businesses are moving upwards on the grid, seeking volume benefits in purchasing and operations arising from specialization and standardization (e.g., Kwik-Fit Euro, which specializes in the repair of car exhausts or brakes only).

Clearly, none of these shifts would be possible without at least some perceived shift on the demand side in consumer buying behaviour. Economies of scope in services can lower transaction costs for customers. Common examples include: the effect of retailer buying power on quality and price in multiple retail chains (Segal-Horn and McGee, 1989); worldwide reservation systems of hotel chains and airlines; cheaper products in banking, insurance, and brokerage services such as travel agents or investment analysts.

Nayyar (1990) discusses the potential benefit to diversified service firms from leveraging customer relationships across service businesses. He argues that buyers of services will attempt to economize on information acquisition costs by transferring reputation effects to other services offered by a firm, thus enabling the service firm to obtain quasi-rents from firm-specific buyer-seller relationships. This research contributed to our understanding of the growing importance of the branding of services and reinforces, for services, two of the main propositions regarding the competitive advantages of MNEs. First, the ability of MNEs to create and sustain a successful brand image and its concomitant goodwill (Caves, 1982); second, the MNEs, ability to monitor quality and reduce buyer transaction costs by offering services from multiple locations (Casson, 1982).

The changed services 'logic': Phase 2 – the industry dynamics phase

Phase 2 of Chandler's model shifts from national to international growth and competition. The applicability to services of Chandler's model of MNE growth rests on the fundamental shifts that have occurred in the historically 'local', domestic and small-scale character of service businesses. There is *de facto* evidence that international chains exist in virtually all types of service businesses, even highly 'local', regulated, and culture-specific services such as education or medical services, (e.g., AMI health care group, EF language schools, international campuses trading on well-known university brand names). The documented examples of national and international concentration and competition in services include professional accountancy firms (Daniels *et al.*, 1989), financial services (Walter, 1988; Wright and Pauli, 1987), retailing (Treadgold, 1989; Segal-Horn and Davison, 1992), contracting (Enderwick, 1989), airlines (McKern, 1990; Olaisen *et al.*, 1990), and news agencies (Boyd-Barrett, 1989).

Underlying these trends is what Levitt (1986) called 'the industrialization of service'. Echoing Chandler's central themes, Levitt argues that the key point in the industrialization of service is 'volume ... sufficient to achieve efficiency, sufficient to employ systems and technologies that produce reliable, rapid and low unit cost results. That in turn requires ... managerial rationality' (Levitt, 1986, p. 61). Services can be industrialized in a variety of ways:

- by automation which substitutes machines for labour (e.g., automatic carwash, automatic toll collection, ATM cash machines, and so forth)
- by systems planning which substitutes organization or methodologies for labour (e.g., self-service shops, fast food restaurants, packaged holidays, unit trust investment schemes, mass-market insurance packages)
- by a combination of the two (e.g., extending scope in food retailing via centralized warehousing and transportation/distribution networks for chilled, fresh, or frozen foods in technically advanced temperature- and humidity-controlled trucks).

419

Such industrialization of service is based on large-scale substitution of capital for labour in services, together with a redefinition of the technology-intensiveness and sophistication of service businesses. It also assumes a market size sufficient to sustain the push for volume. The point at which a firm is likely to shift to international operations is when the domestic market provides insufficient volume to support minimum efficient scale. This may come earlier for service firms than for manufacturing firms, since for many types of services the option of exporting is not available (Carman and Langeard, 1980; Erramilli, 1990).

The changes in concentration and industrialization of services make Phase 2 of Chandler's model, relating to growth via the international expansion of scale and scope, directly applicable to this sector of the economy.

Figure 22.3 provides a more extensive representation of Chandler's complete model. Because of their investments in scale, scope, distribution and management, Chandler argues, large firms are able to build dominant positions sufficient to influence the structure, key assets, and capabilities relevant to competing in their industry. Thus, economic advantages of scale and scope lead to national and international concentration, so that competition rapidly becomes oligopolistic. Such oligopolistic competition is based more on innovation than price, although firmly rooted in continuously enhanced cost structures. Growth thus becomes a continuous search for improved quality, sourcing, distribution and marketing (especially branding and advertising), as well as new markets and lower cost. Some growth comes from acquisition, but the main emphasis for long-term growth is two-fold: first, geographic expansion into international markets in the continuous drive for increments in scale and cost advantages; second, related product markets in the pursuit of enhanced scope economies. Together these form a dynamic spiral of volume, scale, scope and cost curves, reinforced by organizational capabilities developed to cope within fierce oligopolistic competition.

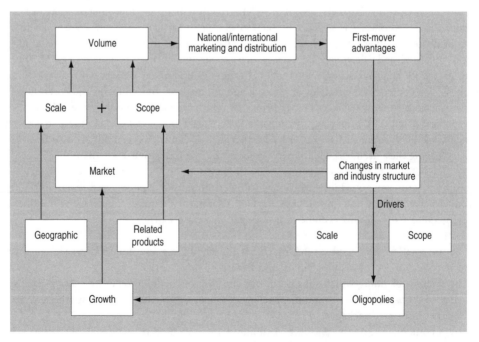

Figure 22.3 An abstract of Chandler's dynamic model of multinational growth and competition: Phase 2 (source: Segal-Horn drawing upon Chandler, 1986, 1990)

Chandler emphasizes repeatedly that the opportunity to create such first-mover investments is short-lived. The logic of sustainable international competition is to make long-term scale investments to create organizational capabilities, and then to continue to reinvest in these assets.

To demonstrate this industry concentration phase of the model, the earlier company illustration will be revisited.

An illustration: American Express – Phase 2

Many of the innovations made by American Express in new products, new markets, branding, advertising and distribution, have already been referred to above. Amex followed closely the twin routes for long-term growth described by Chandler, geographic expansion into international markets and the development of related product markets in the pursuit of enhanced scope economies. It had the earliest branded products in financial services and advertised these branded products heavily from the 1880s onwards. It invested heavily and continuously in distribution and marketing and in the extension of its network of outlets for its products and services worldwide. There was some growth via acquisition, as in the purchase of Fireman's Fund in 1968 to consolidate its move from a travel company into financial services. Amex's related product markets now cover the express business, the travel business, financial services, movement of goods, movement of people, and the flow of money. These related businesses provide scale and volume, supported by company-wide global communications, data and information systems networks, which in turn support volume, worldwide geographic coverage, and the monitoring of service quality in all outlets.

Following Chandler, Amex does not compete on price but on product innovation, market development, and levels of service. Whether its scale, scope, and cost advantages are still sufficient to fight off the current new efficient competitors in its main markets (e.g., Visa) remains to be seen. It is facing very tough competition and increasing pressure on price and margins from both trade and retail customers.

RETHINKING SERVICES

Chandler's model is of international growth and competition based on firm-specific assets. It is interesting to note that such resource-based theories of the firm are making a comeback in competitive strategy (Rumelt, 1991; Grant, 1991), balancing the industry structure-driven emphasis of strategic thinking of the 1980s. Since such assets may erode over time (Geroski and Vlassopoulos, 1991) and must be continually upgraded to sustain their advantage, it is important to review the implications of this approach to the changing nature of competition in services.

Enderwick (1989) provides insight into firm-specific advantages (FSA) and location-specific advantages (LSA) available to the services multinational enterprise. He builds on the work of Dunning (1981, 1985, 1989), and the eclectic paradigm of international production based on ownership, location, and internalization (OLI) advantages. Ownership incorporates competitive advantages; location incorporates configuration advantages; and internalization incorporates co-ordination advantages. These issues have also been conceptualized in international strategy by Porter (1986) as issues of configuration and co-ordination in the allocation of value chain activities by the firm.

Enderwick includes under FSA factors familiar from the earlier scale and scope debate in services; privileged access to assets such as goodwill and brand name, particularly important in buying decisions for services (some aspects of this were discussed above under 'know-how'); scale economies obtainable from high fixed costs and low variable costs of operation; other economies of common governance available from single hierarchical management of complementary assets; and agglomerate (scope) economies which enable incumbent firms to offer innovatory or complementary services which reinforce their competitive position. Under LSA factors, most significant is the differential between services which are location-specific because production and consumption are inseparable and therefore wide international representation is mandatory (e.g., fast food chains) and services which are tradable and therefore choice of international location results from considerations of comparative advantages (e.g., software houses).

Lastly, the internalization issue is of exceptional importance in reviewing the growth strategies of service firms and must be considered in relation to the special characteristics of service businesses discussed earlier. These characteristics have provided the rationale for one of the most influential models explaining growth paths of service firms. Carman and Langeard (1980) argue that international expansion is the most risky growth strategy for service firms, because of the 'intangibility' and 'simultaneity' characteristics of services. Carman and Langeard have particularly emphasized how the quality-control problems inherent in the daily operational detail of face-to-face service delivery are exacerbated when firms attempt to operate across national boundaries.

However, assumptions concerning the inevitability of 'intangibility' and 'simultaneity' increasingly are being eroded in the services literature. Products may be tangible or intangible or a combination of both (Levitt, 1986, p. 74). O'Farrell and Hitchens (1990) propose a 'a continuum of tangibility' as more accurate. Levitan (1985), Boddewyn et al., (1986), and Dunning (1989) distinguish pure consumer services from producer or intermediate services. Erramilli (1990) makes a distinction between 'hard' and 'soft' services. All of these authors support the separation of production and consumption in many services. For a considerable range of service businesses, therefore, one of the highest risk of international expansion is reduced.

RESOURCE EMPHASIS

The basic argument is that under changed technical and structural conditions, it becomes necessary to reconsider the definition of what constitutes a service and also to consider how firms actually design and deliver their services. One of the biggest changes in service design is reflected in the distinction between 'back-office' and 'front-office' as constituent parts of a service. 'Front-office' is that part of the service which has an interface with the customer. 'Back-office' is any part of the service delivery which may be carried out remote from the customer. Clearly different services contain differing proportions of hard or soft, tangible or intangible, elements. They will vary, therefore, in the balance of front-office to back-office capabilities required to deliver the service.

Figure 22.4 provides a simple illustration of some of these service design and reconfiguration possibilities. It reflects some of the differences in core assets and service delivery between 'hard' and 'soft' services, as well as some of the rethinking of services that has occurred. For example, the location of retail banking in the top left box reflects the capital-intensive, volume-driven transaction-processing part of retail banking operations. These activities are now usually centralized and regionalized. At the same time, the retail banks have been redesigning branch outlets to be more customer-friendly in order to cross-sell other higher-margin financial services. Software houses may sometimes appear also in the top left box if they are selling standardized rather than bespoke software packages.

However, the examples in Figure 22.4 are inevitably oversimplified (e.g., it ignores the search by PSFs for methodologies to increase productivity and margins via back-office standardization, an approach for which Arthur Andersen is well known). Consonant with Chandler's view of

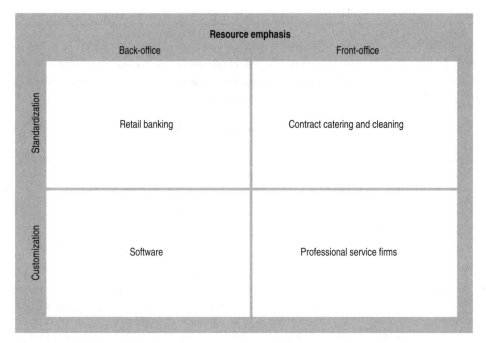

Figure 22.4   Service standardization (Source: Segal-Horn, 1992)

international growth and competition as a sustainable dynamic, it is inevitable that continuous shifts such as those between standardization and customization should result in firms continually seeking optimization of such features at the highest level of scale and cost position available to them. It is also to be expected that these positions of optimum efficiencies will be continually shifting.

In short, the continual search for optimization of OLI advantages in services, using the same models and criteria as for manufacturing firms, makes simple distinctions between product and service obsolete. Borrowing from Levitt's (1986) concept of the 'augmented' product, services increasingly cross any definition product/service boundary line whether of tangibility, perishability or simultaneity, in favour of conceptualization of 'augmented' products. Just as Levitt argues that augmented products arise in relatively mature markets or with relatively experienced or sophisticated customers, so augmented products are being developed by service firms. Many services once regarded as highly specialized (e.g., airline seats, bank accounts) have become commodities. This has exerted strong pressures on service providers to simultaneously push down costs and provide additional augmentations (e.g., better in-flight catering; longer bank opening hours). This pressure is itself contributing to the erosion of clear product-service distinctions since, increasingly, manufacturing firms are seeking product augmentation through service features (see Quinn *et al.*, 1988, 1990; Vandermerwe, 1990). Increasingly, advantage comes from exploiting the manufacturing/services interface.

THE EVOLUTION OF COMPETITION IN SERVICES

Since the Chandler growth model assumes a large enough market size to achieve benefit from scale effects, some consideration of the evolution in both markets and industry structures in services is appropriate. Much of the historic pattern of competition in services occurred within domestic market boundaries as a result of the small-scale, fragmented structure of service industries and their culture-specific patterns of demand and consumption. Under these conditions, clearly scale and volume effects will be limited. However, as has already been argued, in most service sectors restructuring has led to concentration replacing fragmentation in industry structure. In addition, some homogenization of demand in services is also observable.

Evolving patterns of demand in services

There has been a lengthy and vigorous debate about the validity of the argument that an increasing similarity exists between sets of consumers across international markets. The debate centres around the possibility of standardizing products or services for broadly defined international market segments. The belief in consumer homogeneity is controversial, since it co-exists with the view that fragmentation rather than homogenization may more appropriately describe international consumer trends. Much discussion has taken place over the opportunities for, and barriers to, such standardization (Kotler, 1985; Quelch and Hoff, 1986; Douglas and Wind, 1987; Link, 1988; Jain, 1989). It was triggered by Levitt (1983), who argued for convergence as a result of economic and cultural interdependencies across countries and markets. Levitt suggested that old-established differences in national preferences were being reduced by mass culture and communications technologies and urged companies to examine growing similarities between consumer preferences in the markets they served. Lifestyle segmentation has been around for a long time (Sheth, 1983). However, the argument for homogenization means that such segments should be defined internationally. International segmentation does not usually mean providing the same product in all countries, but offering local adaptations around a standardized core.

Well-known examples of this approach in services include the retail chain Benetton, which has built its whole strategy around the standardized 'one unit product' of casual, colour-co-ordinated leisurewear for the 18–25 age group. Although there is some adaptation of such things as colour choice for different domestic markets, consistency is maintained in product range, merchandising, store layout and design, promotion, and use of natural fabrics. Similarly, the restaurant chain Pizza Hut protects the core elements of its brand by copyrighting its individual products' brand names (such as Perfect Pizza) and operating strict specifications of product ingredients. However, the Pizza Hut concept is adapted to suit local needs by varying some elements of the menu (such as desserts), or store design, or the way in which products are served to the customer. Even McDonald's adapts its offering at the margin, for example by selling tea as well as coffee and soft drinks at its UK outlets. In other respects, its brand franchise is maintained virtually intact.

Similar, internationally standardized services would include those of American Express. This company bases much of its marketing on worldwide consistency of quality and range of services, as do the international airlines and hotel chains. International segmentation (e.g., around the business traveller) can give advantages of economies of scale, as well as branding, marketing and reputation benefits. Many services have emerged relatively recently and therefore may have the advantage in establishing cross-national segments. Credit cards, automated teller machines, airlines seats, software, and the automatic car wash, for example, have no prior patterns of usage or acculturation, thereby making them more easily acceptable across national boundaries.

However, alongside social, cultural and technological changes generating homogeneous demand for services, there are additional economic and political pressures on governments to create, or remove, regulatory barriers that can sharply divide markets. The trend is away from such barriers, however, and their removal may have a dramatic impact, as in the deregulation of international trade in financial services, or the 1970s deregulation of US airlines, also being pursued as the 'open skies' policy within [EU] airline competition policy in Europe. The Uruguay GATT round includes services and, if satisfactorily concluded, should greatly simplify many current difficulties affecting international trade in services, such as intellectual copyright protection.

This brief discussion of segmentation and regulatory issues merely indicates some of the most important enabling conditions upon which international market development for services rests. Also of relevance is the way in which the structure of service industries is evolving, often across traditional notions of industry boundaries.

Industry boundaries and firm-specific advantages in services

Reference has already been made to the contribution of fragmented industry structure to the evolution of competition in services, and to the restructuring and concentration which has been exhibited in most service sectors in recent years. Many service industries (such as travel, fast food, some financial services, information services) now meet Kobrin's (1991, p. 18) definition of a global industry, defined in terms of 'the significance of the competitive advantages of international operations' arising mainly from the structural characteristics of scale economies and technological intensity.

Even more important, service-industry growth has often been across traditional industry boundaries (e.g., retail/financial services, retail/leisure, leisure/travel, travel/hospitality, accounting/management consultancy, advertising/public relations, and so forth). This leads to the notion of increasingly 'fuzzy' industry boundaries in service, with industries most appropriately viewed not discretely but as fuzzy sets. American Express, for example, illustrates service-firm growth within a fuzzy industry set of leisure/travel/financial services. It also demonstrates that strong branding across a portfolio of related services arises precisely because Amex operates across this fuzzy set. To generalize, 'growth' for service firms may not involve a deepening of asset structure as in manufacturing companies, but a horizontal accretion of assets across different markets and different industries (i.e., scope).

The point has been made with regard to MNE activity in general (Dunning, 1989), and service MNE activity in particular (Enderwick, 1989) that the way in which firms organize their international activities may itself be a crucial competitive advantage. This is strongly reinforced in recent work by Rumelt (1991), concluding that the most important sources of long-term business rents 'are not associated with industry, but with the unique endowments, positions and strategies of individual businesses' (p. 168). While the issue of change in service-industry structure is central to any discussion of the growth of international competition in services, it therefore may be that the most important factors determining successful international expansion in services should be understood at the level of the firm. This is particularly important with regard to the managerial and organizational capabilities of the firm. The Chandler model of growth used in this paper is especially appropriate because it is a resource-based explanation of successful international competition, driven by sustained investment in the development of firm-specific asset structures.

These points may go some way toward explaining the successes and failures in international expansion undertaken by individual service firms, such as American Express in financial services or Saatchi & Saatchi in advertising.

425

The Measurement of Scale and Scope in Services

In this reassessment of the viability of international strategies for service firms, much emphasis has been placed on the attainability of scale and scope economies. Indeed, the argument can be made that if such benefits are not available for service firms, it must materially reduce the advantages which service MNEs have over local providers of that service. Because they are so important, a systematic framework for tracing the impact of scale or scope variables within the firm is needed. An initial approach to gathering sample data on a specific scale or scope variable is shown in Table 22.3.

A completed data matrix of this type should record all the value chain activities of the firm on the vertical axis. The horizontal axis should capture all resource inputs for each value activity, together with the organizational outputs arising from each input. The resource inputs are recorded at both a minimum level and an optimum level of resource provision. Minimum resources are defined as those which enable the firm to keep operational. Optimum levels of resource provision are defined as those enhancing the ability of the firm to meet its stated strategic objective. The organizational outputs are of three types: first, those that impact other elements in the value chain; second, those that affect the knowledge base of the firm; and third, those that impact the way in which the company defines demand for the service.

Table 22.3 is an illustration of part of the data matrix for an international management consultancy firm. It shows a partial value chain, covering only the activities of marketing to client (which in a service firm usually precedes 'production' i.e., delivery of the service) and R&D, which is often combined with new product development in this type of service firm. As an example of the relationship between resource inputs and outputs, Table 22.3 provides important information for the firm on such things as selection, recruitment, training, and development

Table 22.3 Partial data matrix: international management consultancy

	Inputs		Outputs		
Elements in value chain	Minimum resources	Optimum resources	Linkage to other elements in chain	Linkage to knowledge base	Impact on demand conditions
Market to clients	Informal contacts	Industry database	• Maximize repeat business	• Monitor repeat business	• Review client base
		Client database Market database Product database			
	As above	As above + consultant databases and assignment profiles, etc.	• Standardize skills and procedures	• Client profitability	• Review sector expertise
			• Optimize people quality	• Targeting expertise to opportunity	• Review style and approach to marketing
R&D and NPD			• Maximize training	• Codified knowledge 'manuals'	• Review services offered

Source: Segal-Horn (1992)

(including that of senior partners). It also indicates the back-office and front-office resource considerations in the design and delivery of its services, as well as raising many specific issues concerning the firm's products and markets.

This data matrix provides a simple route through a complex set of interrelationships. It enables variables which have significant operational impact to be distinguished from variables with a relatively trivial role, since it discloses variables which recur and can therefore be shown to have a significant impact on many outputs. This approach is also surprisingly powerful in defining and coping with many of the intangible elements of service provision.

CONCLUSION: THE FUTURE FOR SERVICES

This paper has suggested a revised competitive 'logic', explaining the internationalization of service firms. Changes in the nature of service provision which has led service companies to turn more readily to international expansion have been reviewed. It has been argued that the potential availability of a range of economies of scale and/or economies of scope will both reduce the risk, and enhance the advantages of internationalization for service firms. Sources of such scale and scope economies have been suggested, together with a framework for measuring their impact on the firm. Their potential availability across different types of service businesses has been assessed.

The basic argument is that changed technological, market, and regulatory conditions have created more favourable conditions for international expansion of many services, while the special characteristics of services have been diluted in significance. Many services contain 'hard' tangible components which are capital-intensive, amenable to separation from the point of service delivery, and responsive to standardization. In addition, core knowledge and information-based assets of service firms are codifiable and transferable across national boundaries, as is the consumer franchise from strongly branded services.

As a result of this combination of factors, service-industry dynamics are beginning to parallel those of manufacturing. Manufacturing businesses and service businesses appear to be following similar development paths, creating similar types of asset structures and competing in similar ways. Even the most distinctive characteristic of services, the criticality of the interface with the customer, is increasingly something which all types of business are now expecting to handle well. The emphasis on customer service in manufacturing and the emphasis on efficient deployment of back-office assets in services are each trying to capture the advantages the other has traditionally utilized.

NOTE

1   All information concerning American Express is taken from Annual Reports 1983, 1985, 1986, 1988, 1989, 1990; and from internal Company Reports 1990 and 1991.

REFERENCES

Albrecht, K. and Zemke, R. (1985) *Service America!*, Dow Jones-Irwin, Homewood, IL.

Bartlett, C.A. and Ghoshal, S. (1986) 'Tap your subsidiaries for global reach', *Harvard Business Review*, November–December, pp. 87–94.

Bartlett, C.A. and Ghoshal, S. (1987) 'Managing across borders', *Sloan Management Review*, Vol. 28, No. 4, pp. 7–17; Vol. 29, No. 1, pp. 43–53.

Bartlett, C.A. and Ghoshal, S. (1989) *Managing Across Borders*, Hutchinson, London.

Boddewyn, J.J., Halbrich, M.B. and Perry, A.C. (1986) 'Service multinationals: conceptualization, measurement and theory', *Journal of International Business Studies*, Vol. 16, pp. 23–35.

Boyd-Barrett, O. (1989) 'Multinational news agencies', in Enderwick, P. (ed.), *Multinational Service Firms*, Routledge, London.

Carlzon, J. (1987) *Moments of Truth*, Ballinger, Cambridge, MA.

Carman, J. and Langeard, E. (1980) 'Growth strategies for service firms', *Strategic Management Journal*, Vol. 1, pp. 7–22.

Casson, M.C. (1982) 'Transaction costs and the theory of the multinational enterprise', in Rugman, A.M. (ed.) *New Theories of the Multinational Enterprise*, St Martin's Press, New York.

Caves, R.E. (1982) *Multinational Enterprise and Economic Analysis*, Cambridge University Press, Cambridge.

Chandler, A.D. (1977) *The Visible Hand*, Harvard University Press, Cambridge, MA.

Chandler, A.D. (1986) 'The evolution of modern global competition', in Porter, M. (ed.), *Competition in Global Industries*, Harvard Business School Press, Boston, MA.

Chandler, A.D. (1990) 'The evolution of modern global competition', in Porter, M. (ed.), *Competition in Global Industries*, Harvard Business School Press, Boston, MA.

Daniels, P. (1985) *Service Industries: a geographical appraisal*, Methuen, London.

Daniels, P., Thrift, N. and Leyshon, A. (1989) 'Internationalization of professional producer services: accountancy conglomerates', in Enderwick, P. (ed.), *Multinational Service Firms*, Routledge, London.

Dermine, J. and Röller, L.H. (1990) *Economies of scale and scope in the French mutual funds industry* (Working Paper NO. 90/59/FIN) Fontainebleau: INSEAD.

Douglas, S. and Wind, Y. (1987) 'The myth of globalization', *Columbia Journal of World Business*, Vol. 22, No. 4.

Dunning, J.H. (1981) *International Production and the Multinational Enterprise*, Allen and Unwin, London.

Dunning, J.H. (ed.) (1985) *Multinational Enterprise, Economic Structure and International Competitiveness*, Wiley/IRM, Chichester.

Dunning, J.H. (1989) 'Multinational enterprises and the growth of services: some conceptual and theoretical issues', *Service Industries Journal*, Vol. 9, No. 1, pp. 5–39.

Eiglier, P. and Langeard, E. (1977) 'Le marketing des enterprises de services (Marketing in service business)', *Revue Française de Gestion*.

Enderwick, P. (1989) *Multinational Service Firms*, Routledge, London.

Erramilli, M.K. (1990) 'Entry mode choice in service industries', *International Marketing Review*, Vol. 7, No. 5, pp. 50–62.

Flipo, J.P. (1988) 'On the intangibility of services', *Service Industries Journal*, No. 8, pp. 286–98.

Geroski, P. and Vlassopoulos, T. (1991) 'The rise and fall of a market leader', *Strategic Management Journal*, Vol. 12, No. 6, pp. 467–78.

Ghoshal, S. (1987) 'Global strategy: an organizing framework', *Strategic Management Journal*, Vol. 8, No. 5, pp. 425–40.

Grant, R. (1991) 'The resource-based theory of competitive advantage: implications for strategy formulation', *California Management Review*, Vol. 33, pp. 114–35.

Grönroos, C. (1982) *Strategic Management and Marketing in the Service Sector*, Svenska Handelshögskolan, Helsinki.

Heskett, J.L. (1986) *Managing the Service Economy*, Harvard Business School Press, Boston, MA.

Hindley, B. *et al.* (1987) 'International trade in services: comments', in Giarini, O. (ed.), *The Emerging Service Economy*, Pergamon Press, Oxford.

Hout, T., Porter, M. and Rudden, E. (1982) 'How global companies win out', *Harvard Business Review*, September–October, pp. 98–108.

Jain, S. (1989) 'Standardization of international marketing strategy: some research hypotheses', *Journal of Marketing*, Vol. 53, pp. 70–9.

Kobrin, S.J. (1991) 'An empirical investigation of the determinants of global integration', *Strategic Management Journal*, Vol. 12, pp. 17–31.

Kogut, B. (1989) 'A note on global strategies', *Strategic Management Journal*, Vol. 10, pp. 383–9.

Kotler, P. (1985) *Global standardization – courting danger* (Panel Discussion 23) American Marketing Association, Washington, DC.

Levitan, S.A. (1985) 'Services and long-term structural change', *Economic Impact*.

Levitt, T. (1983) The globalization of markets. *Harvard Business Review*, May–June, pp. 92–102.

Levitt, T. (1986) *The Marketing Imagination*, The Free Press, New York.

Link, G. (1988) 'Global advertising: an update', *The Journal of Consumer Marketing*, Vol. 5, No. 2, pp. 69–74.

Lovelock, C.H. (1988) *Managing Services*, Prentice-Hall International, London.

Lovelock, C.H. and Young, R.F. (1979) 'Look to consumers to increase productivity', *Harvard Business Review*, May/June, pp. 168–78.

McKern, R.B. (1990) *Evolving strategies in the international airline industry*, Technical Report No. 77, Stanford, CA: Graduate School of Business, Stanford University.

Nayyar, P.R. (1990) 'Information asymmetries: a source of competitive advantage for diversified service firms', *Strategic Management Journal*, Vol. 11, pp. 513–19.

Normann, R. (1984) *Service Management: strategy and leadership in service businesses*, Wiley, Chichester.

O'Farrell, P.N. and Hitchens, D.M. (1990) 'Producer services and regional development: key conceptual issues of taxonomy and quality measurement', *Regional Studies*, Vol. 24, No. 2, pp. 163–71.

Olaison, J., Olsen, G., and Revang, O. (1990) *Bridges and tunnels: strategic alliances and the use of information as components of SAS strategy*, Paper presented at the SMS Annual International Conference, Stockholm.

Porter, M. (1986) *Competition in Global Industries*, Harvard Business School Press, Boston, MA.

Prahalad, C.K. and Doz, Y. (1987) *The Multinational Mission: balancing local demands and global vision*, The Free Press, New York.

Prahalad, C.K. and Hamel, G. (1990) 'The core competences of the corporation', *Harvard Business Review*, May–June, pp. 879–91.

Quelch, J.A. and Hoff, E.J. (1986) 'Customizing global marketing', *Harvard Business Review*, May–June, pp. 59–68.

Quinn, J.B., Baruch, J.J. and Paquette, P.C. (1988) 'Exploiting the manufacturing–services interface', *Sloan Management Review*, Vol. 29, No. 4, pp. 45–56.

Quinn, J.B., Doorley, T.L., and Paquette, P.C. (1990) 'Beyond products: services-based strategy', *Harvard Business Review*, May–June, pp. 58–67.

Rumelt, R.P. (1991) 'How much does industry matter?', *Strategic Management Journal*, Vol. 12, pp. 167–85.

Sasser, W.E., Wycoff, D.D. and Olsen, M. (1978) *The Management of Service Operations*, Allyn and Bacon, London.

Segal-Horn, S. (1990) 'The globalization of services', in *Proceedings of the British Academy of Management*, Chichester: Wiley.

Segal-Horn, S. (1992) *The logic of international growth for service firms*, Paper presented at the Fourth Annual Conference of British Academy of Management, Bradford, UK.

Segal-Horn, S. and Davison, H. (1992) 'Global markets, the global consumer and international retailing', *Journal of Global Marketing*, Vol. 5, No. 3, pp. 31–61.

Segal-Horn, S. and McGee, J. (1989) 'Strategies to cope with retailer buying power', in Pellegrini, L. and Reddy, S.K. (eds), *Vertical Relationships and the Distribution Trades*, Routledge, London.

Sheth, J. (1983) 'Marketing megatrends', *Journal of Consumer Marketing*, Vol. 1, pp. 5–13.

Shostack, G.L. (1977) 'Breaking free from product marketing', in Lovelock, C.H. (ed.), *Services Marketing*, Prentice Hall, Englewood Cliffs, NJ.

Teece, D. (1980) 'Economies of scope and the scope of the enterprise', *Journal of Economic Behaviour and Organization*, Vol. 1, No. 3, pp. 223–47.

Teece, D. (1982) 'Towards an economic theory of the multiproduct firm', *Journal of Economic Behaviour and Organization*, 1. Vol. 3, pp. 39–63.

Treadgold, A. (1989) 'The retail response to a changing Europe', *Marketing Research Today*, Vol. 17, No. 3, pp. 161–6.

Vandermerwe, S. (1990) 'The market power is in the services: because the value is in the results', *European Management Journal*, Vol. 8, No. 4, pp. 464–73.

Walter, I. (1988) *Global Competition in Financial Services*, Ballinger, Cambridge, MA.

Wright, R.W. and Pauli, G.A. (1987) *The Second Wave*, Waterlow, London.

23

Entrepreneurship in Multinational Corporations: The Characteristics of Subsidiary Initiatives

Julian Birkinshaw

This paper defines initiative as a key manifestation of corporate entrepreneurship, and examines the types of initiative exhibited in a sample of six subsidiaries of multinational corporations. From a detailed analysis of 39 separate initiatives, four distinct types are identified, which we refer to as 'global,' 'local,' 'internal' and 'global – internal hybrid,' to correspond to the locus of the market opportunity whence each arose. Two important conclusions are indicated. First, entrepreneurship at the subsidiary level has the potential to enhance local responsiveness, worldwide learning and global integration, a much broader role than previously envisioned. Second, the use of contextual mechanisms to create differentiated subsidiary roles has its limitations because each initiative type is facilitated in different ways.

INTRODUCTION

The ability of the large multinational corporation (MNC) to leverage the innovative and entrepreneurial potential of its dispersed assets is a fundamental strategic imperative (Bartlett and Goshal, 1989). While some studies have explicitly confronted the challenge of entrepreneurship in MNCs (e.g., Ghoshal, 1986), research has tended to focus on either the organization of the existing activities of the MNC or on corporate entrepreneurship as a generic managerial issue (Ghoshal, 1986: 6). As stated by Hedlund and Ridderstråle (1992: 5) the dominant theme in prior MNC research – particularly from a theoretical perspective – has been 'on the exploitation of givens (i.e., existing product – market combinations) rather than on the creation of novelty.' The need for research that explicitly links MNC management with studies of corporate entrepreneurship is therefore substantial.

The current paper examines initiatives in MNC subsidiaries. An *initiative* is defined here as a discrete, proactive undertaking that advances a new way for the corporation to use or expand its resources (Kanter, 1982; Miller, 1983). An initiative is essentially an entrepreneurial process, beginning with the identification of an opportunity and culminating in the commitment of resources to that opportunity. In this sense, the term is narrower than related constructs such as 'internal corporate venture' (Burgelman, 1983a) which involve both the initiative and the ongoing management of the resultant business activity. Several prior studies have used the initiative construct (e.g., Burgelman, 1991; Cohen and Machalek, 1988; Sathe, 1985).

Subsidiary is defined here to be any operational unit controlled by the MNC and situated outside the home country. This definition ensures that the artificial notion of a single parent–subsidiary relationship is avoided. The reality in most MNCs today is that subsidiaries have a multitude of linkages with other corporate entities in the home county and worldwide (Ghoshal and Bartlett, 1991), but academic research has – for the most part – continued to work on the basis of a single parent–subsidiary relationship. By working at the initiative level this study breaks new gound in that it documents activities at a sub-subsidiary unit of analysis.

Why study initiative in MNC subsidiaries rather than in the parent company? The simple answer is that despite the compelling logic for tapping into local markets through the subsidiary network (Bartlett and Ghoshal, 1986), many corporations appear to neglect the creative potential of their subsidiaries. Thus, subsidiary initiative may be a relatively rare and underresearched phenomenon but its potential value to the MNC is high. While the most common form of subsidiary initiative is probably the identification and pursuit of a new product opportunity in the local market, this paper takes the concept further by showing that three other forms of subsidiary initiative can also be identified. The paper puts forward a conceptual framework, based on the network theory of the MNC (Ghoshal and Bartlett, 1991) through which subsidiary initiative can be better understood, and then describes the results of a detailed inductive study of 39 initiatives. The major contribution of the paper is the finding that subsidiary initiative has the potential to enhance local responsiveness, worldwide learning *and* global integration, a much broader role than previously envisioned.

This paper is organized as follows. First, the literature on corporate entrepreneurship is reviewed, in broad terms and then specifically in terms of MNC subsidiary management. Second, the network theory of the MNC is used to build a conceptual framework in which three types of subsidiary initiative are identified. Each type of initiative is also identified in the extant literature. Third, the research methodology is described. Fourth, the findings from the study are discussed – this section includes the identification and description of a fourth type of initiative, and a systematic description of the salient characteristics of all four types. Finally, the implications of the study for MNC management theory and for corporate entrepreneurship are discussed.

Corporate Entrepreneurship and Initiatives

Corporate entrepreneurship is receiving increasing levels of research attention, and was the focus of a recent special issue of the *Strategic Management Journal* (Guth and Ginsberg, 1990). In broad terms, three forms of corporate entrepreneurship can be identified (Stopford and Baden-Fuller, 1994): (1) the creation of new business activities within the existing organization; (2) the transformation or renewal of existing organizations; and (3) the enterprise changing the rules of competition in its industry. The focus of this study is on the first of these forms: the creation of new business activities within the existing enterprise.

There is a broad recognition, however, that the generation of new business activities or 'new combinations' (Schumpeter, 1934) alone does not constitute entrepreneurship. A research and development group, for example, has a clear mandate to innovate, but the behavior expected of its employees falls within established norms and guidelines. Entrepreneurship suggests more: a predisposition towards proactive and risk-taking behavior (Covin and Slevin, 1991; Miller, 1983); use of resources beyond the individual's direct control (Kirzner, 1973; Stevenson and Jarillo, 1990); or a 'clear departure from existing practices' (Damanpour, 1991: 561). Kanter (1982) proposed the following distinction between 'basic' and entrepreneurial activities:

> basic accomplishments . . . are part of the assigned job and require routine and readily available means to carry them out. In contrast innovative accomplishments are strikingly entrepreneurial. They are sometimes highly problematic and generally involve acquiring and using power and influence. (1982: 97)

On the basis that within-firm corporate entrepreneurship involves a departure from existing practices or 'a *new way* for the corporation to use or expand its resources' (Kanter, 1982), the literature suggests two distinct models, which will be termed focused and dispersed corporate entrepreneurship respectively. Initiative, the focal construct in this research, is a manifestation of the dispersed approach.

Focused corporate entrepreneurship (also called corporate venturing) works on the premise that entrepreneurship and management are fundamentally different processes that require different modes of organization to occur effectively (Burns and Stalker, 1961; Galbraith, 1982; Kanter, 1985). This is typified by the New Venture Division, whose mandate is to identify and nurture new business opportunities for the corporation (Burgelman, 1983a; Kuratko, Montagno and Hornsby, 1990; Sykes, 1986). The new venture division is typically a semi-autonomous entity with little formal structure, integration across traditional functional areas, availability of 'patient money,' and management support for risk taking and creativity (Galbraith, 1982; Kanter, 1985; Kuratko et al. 1990; Quinn, 1985; Sathe, 1985). There are many examples of corporations that have pursued this approach to corporate entrepreneurship, including 3M, Kodak, and Exxon (Ginsberg and Hay, 1995; Sykes, 1986). Note that the mandate of a new venture division is fundamentally broader and more ambiguous than that of a research and development group where the set of tasks and responsibilities can be fairly narrowly defined. In Schollhammer's terms (1982), the new venture division is a case of 'incubative' entrepreneurship while the R&D group is 'administrative' entrepreneurship.

Dispersed corporate entrepreneurship (also called intrapreneurship) rests on the premise that every individual in the company has the capacity for both managerial and entrepreneurial behavior *more or less simultaneously*. Rather than hiving off separate groups or divisions to be entrepreneurial, while the rest are left to pursue the ongoing managerial tasks (Galbraith, 1982), the dispersed approach sees the development of an entrepreneurial culture or posture as the key antecedent to initiative (Covin and Slevin, 1991; Goshal and Bartlett, 1994; Kanter, 1985; Stopford and Baden-Fuller, 1994). The design of an 'organic' (Burns and Stalker, 1961) or 'integrative' (Kanter, 1985) organization creates the facilitating conditions, but entrepreneurship is actually driven by the actions of employees who – for whatever reason – choose to pursue risky or uncertain ventures 'for the good of the organization' (Barnard, 1938: 200). The challenge for corporate management is to instill the personal involvement and commitment in its employees that drives entrepreneurship (Ghoshal and Bartlett, 1994).

Dispersed corporate entrepreneurship therefore assumes a latent dual role for every employee, consisting of (a) the management of ongoing activities and (b) the identification and pursuit of new opportunities (Kirzner, 1973; Penrose, 1959; Stevenson and Jarillo, 1990). The advantage of this approach over the focused approach is that a greater diversity of opportunities will be sensed, because the entrepreneurial capability is dispersed throughout the organization, rather than restricted to a new venture division. The major disadvantage of this approach is that managerial responsibilities typically 'drive out' entrepreneurial responsibilities (Hedlund and Ridderstråle, 1992; Kanter, 1986) because they are more clearly defined and have more immediate rewards. Unless it is well managed the dispersed approach can actually inhibit entrepreneurship (Drucker, 1985).

Initiative, as used in this paper, is the primary manifestation of dispersed corporate entrepreneurship. The initiative process is bounded by the identification of an opportunity at the front end and the commitment of resources to the undertaking at the back end. Note that the long term success of the resultant business activity is a secondary issue. The entrepreneurial challenge is to move from an idea to a commitment of resources; the managerial challenge is to make the resultant business activity profitable. It is important, moreover, to recognize that the focused and dispersed approaches are complementary rather than alternative. For example, an opportunity identified in a subsidiary may be nurtured and developed in the new venture division; equally, an innovation by the new venture division may inspire further innovation by an operating division. Clinical evidence suggests that successful entrepreneurial companies such as 3M and HP do indeed exhibit both approaches (Kanter, 1985; Peters and Waterman, 1982; Pinchott, 1985).

Initiative in MNC Subsidiaries

Parent–subsidiary relationships in MNCs have been studied for many years (Martinez and Jarillo, 1989). Most early research focused narrowly on facets of the parent–subsidiary relationship such as centralization, formalization, coordination and control (Brandt and Hulbert, 1977; Cray, 1984; Hedlund, 1981; Negandhi and Baliga, 1981; Picard, 1980). More recently, new conceptualizations of the MNC such as the heterarchy (Hedlund, 1986) or the transnational corporation (Bartlett and Ghoshal, 1989) enabled a more holistic understanding of the subsidiary as a semi-autonomous entity within a differentiated system. Within this broad school of thought, two distinct views of the subsidiary can be discerned, with direct parallels to the two types of corporate entrepreneurship described in the previous section.

The first perspective viewed the subsidiary as having a 'role' in the MNC. Bartlett and Ghoshal (1986) made the observation that national subsidiaries can take one of four generic roles, based on the strategic importance of the local environment and the competence of the subsidiary. They further suggested that the MNC's structure should reflect this heterogeneity, so that certain subsidiaries receive, for example, much greater strategic autonomy than others. This study and others in the same genre (e.g., Ghoshal and Nohria, 1989; Gupta and Govindarajan, 1991; Jarillo and Martinez, 1990) shared a number of underlying characteristics: first, an implicit parent company perspective, in that subsidiaries were modeled in terms of 'relative capabilities' (vs. sister subsidiaries); second, the belief that the subsidiary's role was determined by the parent company and essentially assigned to the subsidiary in question; and third, the notion that the subsidiary's role was enacted through the definition of an appropriate set of coordination and control mechanisms (its structural context in Bower's, 1970, terms).

This model is entirely consistent with the description of focused corporate entrepreneurship above. Certain subsidiaries are given the responsibility for innovating or pursuing initiatives, while others are given implementational roles. These roles are enacted through the structural context of the MNC. As shown by Ghoshal and Bartlett (1988), autonomy, local resources, normative integration and interunit communication are associated with creation (of innovations) in subsidiaries, but negatively associated with adoption and diffusion.

The second perspective focused directly on the subsidiary level of analysis. This perspective envisioned a much greater element of strategic choice on the part of subsidiary management than the subsidiary role perspective. Thus, the subsidiary's strategy was constrained (rather than defined) by the structural context, and subsidiary managers had considerable latitude within the imposed constraints to shape a strategy as they saw fit. This body of research was predominantly Canadian, stretching back to Safarian's (1966) work on the foreign ownership of Canadian industry and with key contributions from Crookell (1986), D'Cruz (1986), Poynter and Rugman (1982) and White and Poynter (1984, 1990). In part because of the high levels of foreign ownership in Canadian industry, academic thinking has pushed towards subsidiary managers utilizing their strategic discretion rather than simply responding to parental decree. White and Poynter (1984: 69), for example, noted that subsidiary mangers 'Will have to adjust their strategies to successfully deal with changed circumstances... Through the careful development of local capabilities the subsidiary manager can contribute to the evolution of the Canadian subsidiary's strategy.' This is consistent with the dispersed approach to corporate entrepreneurship. As suggested by White and Poynter (1984) and others, creativity and innovation should be endemic to the national subsidiary as the driver of its strategy. The subsidiary has ongoing managerial responsibilities but at the same time it has the responsibility to respond to entrepreneurial opportunities as they arise.

In summary, entrepreneurship in MNC subsidiaries is a subject that has received limited research attention but that can be informed by the broader literature on corporate entrepreneurship. As with the literature on corporate entrepreneurship, the implication here is not that one model of subsidiary management is superior to the other in terms of entrepreneurial capability but that the two are complementary. In particular, proponents of the subsidiary role perspective have made the observation that complete control of the national subsidiary through contextual mechanisms is neither possible nor desirable (e.g., Prahalad and Doz, 1981). There is clearly an interesting trade-off between control and autonomy in the parent–subsidiary relationship, and the fact that subsidiary 'role' research favors control and subsidiary 'strategy' research favors autonomy is essentially a function of the opposing perspectives of parent and subsidiary managers.

CONCEPTUAL DEVELOPMENT

As defined above, an initiative is viewed as a discrete, proactive undertaking that advances a new way for the corporation to use or expand its resources. For the purposes of this research, this definition was subject to two additional constraints. First, the entrepreneurial thrust had to come from subsidiary managers, rather than those at head office. Second, the initiative had to lead to international responsibilities for the subsidiary, such as exporting intermediate products to affiliates or managing a product line on a global basis. This condition was set to exclude trivial initiatives. MNCs are becoming increasingly global in the configuration and coordination of their value-adding activities (Porter, 1986), and subsidiaries are likewise recognizing the interdependence of their activities with those of the global network. Particularly in a country such as Canada where the national market is small and the cross-border flows with the United States large, the likelihood of any new activity attracting corporate support is substantially enhanced when it has international scope.

Conceptual framework

Notwithstanding the question of personal motivation, the origin of an initiative lies in the identification of an opportunity to use or expand the corporation's resources. In Kirzner's (1973)

words, it is an 'alertness to hitherto unnoticed market opportunities' that stimulates the entrepreneur to act. In similar fashion, Stevenson and Jarillo (1990: 23) saw entrepreneurship as
'...a process by which individuals – either on their own or inside organizations – pursue opportunities without regard to the resources they currently control.'

From the perspective of the MNC subsidiary, the notion of *a market opportunity* is usually
understood in terms of its national market. The traditional role of the subsidiary was first to
adapt the MNC's technology to local tastes, and then to act as a 'global scanner,' sending signals
about changing demands back to head office (Vernon, 1966, 1979). More recently, it has been recognized that subsidiaries often have unique capabilities of their own, as well as critical links with
local customers and suppliers. In such situations, the subsidiary's ability to pursue local opportunities itself, and subsequently to exploit them on a global scale, is an important capability
(Bartlett and Ghoshal, 1986; Harrigan, 1983; Hedlund, 1986).

To view market opportunity solely in terms of the subsidiary's *local* relationships is, however,
somewhat restricting. There is a growing body of research that models the MNC as an interorganizational network (Forsgren and Johanson, 1992; Ghoshal and Bartlett, 1991), in which the
subsidiary has multiple linkages to other entities both inside and outside the formal boundaries
of the MNC. Viewed in this way, the national subsidiary sits at the interface of three 'markets:'
(1) the local market, consisting of competitors, suppliers, customers, and regulatory bodies in
the host country; (2) the internal market, which is comprised of head office operations and all
corporate-controlled affiliates worldwide; and (3) the global market, consisting of competitors,
customers and suppliers that fall outside the local and internal markets. This conceptualization
is depicted in Figure 23.1. Global market relationships, of course, do not exist in all cases, but
increasingly subsidiaries are taking on specialized roles and responsibilities within the MNC that
give them access to international customers and suppliers (Roth and Morrison, 1992). Again
using Kirzner's definition, three types of initiative are immediately suggested, namely *local market initiative, internal market initiative,* and *global market initiative.* These are defined by the locus
of the market opportunity in each case.

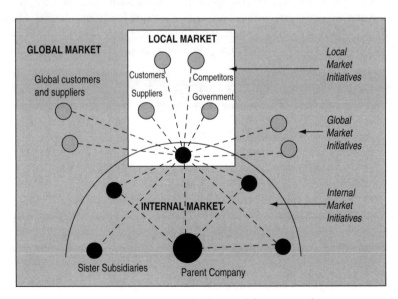

Figure 23.1 Conceptual model of the national subsidiary and three types of initiative

How much evidence is there for these types of initiative? No systematic research appears to have been done on either internal market or global market initiatives, while Ghoshal (1986) is the only detailed prior study on local market initiatives. The remainder of this section, then, will pull together the limited body of research that exists to provide a grounding for the current study. In addition to the locus of opportunity (by which the types are defined), three additional sets of characteristics will be considered: the facilitating conditions (i.e., those elements of the subsidiary's structural context that foster an environment in which initiative can occur), the intiative process; and the intended outcome. Figure 23.2 illustrates these elements. This framework is very similar to those used in several other process research studies, including Mintzberg, Raisinghani, and Theoret (1976) and Nutt (1993). Note that the relationship between these elements is not one of linear causality. Facilitating conditions and process, for example, probably interact with and reinforce one another, rather than one defining the other. Thus, the elements could best be described as configurations (Meyer, Tsui, and Hinings, 1993), which are 'tight constellations of mutually supportive elements' (Miller, 1986: 236).

Local market initiatives

There are several well-documented cases of local market initiatives in the literature: examples include Philips UK's development of Teletext technology (Bartlett and Ghoshal, 1986) and Alfa Laval U.S.'s invention of the milking machine in 1917 (Hedlund and Ridderstråle, 1992). These two cases were both inspired by local product and/or market needs and subsequently exploited on a global scale.[1]

In terms of facilitating conditions, Ghoshal's (1986) detailed study of innovation in MNCs identified local resources, local autonomy, normative integration, subsidiary–HQ communication, and intrasubsidiary communication as factors that were positively associated with the 'creation' process. No other work has systematically addressed this issue, though several Canadian studies have hinted at the conditions in which local market initiatives occur (e.g., Etemad and Dulude, 1986). Some insight into the initiative process can also be inferred from these studies. It appears to be quite protracted, involving considerable effort from subsidiary management to develop the concept in the first place, and even more effort to get it accepted in other countries. However, this is not significantly different from the generic innovation process (e.g., Howell and Higgins, 1990), or from the process that can be inferred from prior studies of global or internal market initiatives

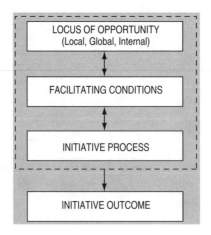

Figure 23.2 Organizing framework for process study

(see below). There is thus considerable scope for new insight in this area. Finally, the intended outcome, according to Bartlett and Ghoshal (1986), is to enhance world-wide learning.

Global market initiatives

These are driven by unmet product or market needs among *nonlocal* suppliers and customers. In theory, the subsidiary could potentially interact with any customer or supplier in the world, but evidence in the literature suggests that such initiatives probably occur as extensions to existing relationships.[2] Consider the case of Litton Systems Ltd. (Science Council of Canada, 1980). Litton developed an international business in the 1960s (through a local market initiative) around an inertial navigation system. On the basis of its worldwide customer base it then identified additional opportunities in related areas, and went on to develop products such as air traffic control systems and radar systems. These latter product introductions were global initiatives, because the locus of opportunity was outside the subsidiary's local market.

With the exception of the Science Council of Canada study, no evidence of global market initiatives was found in the literature. This is perhaps surprising, in that there are several examples of subsidiary companies taking on international product responsibilities (e.g., Hedlund, 1986; Roth and Morrison, 1992), which would naturally provide the circumstances in which global initiatives could transpire. In terms of the characteristics of global market initiatives, the Science Council of Canada suggested (a) that local autonomy, local resources and existing international responsibilities were facilitating conditions, and (b) that the intended outcome was to leverage the subsidiary's existing capabilities into related areas. However, these should be viewed as very tentative propositions because they arose from only three case studies. There was, unfortunately, no substantive insight into the initiative process, except insofar as it appeared to mirror the generic process described above.

Internal market initiatives

The concept of an internal market initiative is somewhat unusual, in that it arises through 'market opportunities' identified in the corporate system. The best way of explaining the concept is through an example: the quote below is with regard to Dow Chemical's internal market (White and Poynter, 1990: 56):

> The internal product sourcing relationship between a manufacturing plant and a commercial department can be 'challenged' at any time ... If the U.S. market for polyethylene could be sourced at lower out-of-pocket cost from a Dow Canada plant than elsewhere, that adjustment would be made.

The initiative in this case would be the Canadian plant challenging the incumbent in-house manufacturer for the rights to polyethylene production, on the basis that the incumbent was either not operating efficiently or was operating in a country where factor costs put it at a comparative disadvantage *vis-à-vis* the challenging plant. This type of initiative is thus subtly different from the other two types, because it is directed towards cost reduction rather than revenue enhancement.

The concept of an internal market, in which divisions or subsidiaries of a single company pursue competitive exchange relationships with one another, is well established in academic writing (e.g., Galunic and Eisenhardt, 1994; Halal, 1993) and is widely used in many large corporations. As before, however, the internal market *initiative* is implicit in prior research. Galunic and Eisenhardt (1994), for example, discussed competition from other subsidiaries as a stimulus for charter loss; and White and Poynter's description of the horizontal organization (above) included a clear example

437

Table 23.1 Previous research on three forms of subsidiary initiative

Locus of market opportunity (definition)	Local market initiative	Internal market initiative	Global market initiative
Facilitating factors	• Local resources, local autonomy, normative integration, sub. – HQ communication, intra-sub. communication (Ghoshal, 1986)	• Local resources, some decentralization (Galunic and Eisenhardt, 1994) • Local resources, good relations with parent (Science Council of Canada, 1980) • Horizontal network and shared decision premises (White and Poynter, 1990)	• Local resources, local autonomy, existing international responsibilities (Science Council of Canada, 1980)
Process	• No discernible difference between process models in all three types. Generic model indicates a protracted selling process by subsidiary management to parent management (Etemad and Dulude, 1986; Science Council of Canada, 1980)		
Intended outcome	• Enhance worldwide learning (Bartlett and Ghoshal, 1986) • Maximize global innovation (Harrigan, 1983)	• Efficiency of global operations and local value-added (Science Council of Canada, 1980; White and Poynter, 1990)	• Leverage existing subsidiary capabilities into related areas (Science Council of Canada, 1980)

of subsidiary initiative that was not labeled as such. The characteristics of internal market initiatives can thus be inferred from the existing literature as follows: (a) local resources, some decentralization of decision making, good relationships with the parent company and shared decision premises as facilitators of initiative; (b) an entrepreneurial selling process, again very similar to that seen in other types of initiative; and (c) efficiency in global operations and desire for local value-added as the intended outcomes. Table 23.1 represents a summary of prior research.

In conclusion, this section set forth a conceptualization of subsidiary initiative that is consistent with the emerging body of literature on interorganizational networks, but which at the same time suggests a much broader opportunity set for the subsidiary than previously thought. The three initiative types have been identified to varying degrees in the literature, so our *a priori* expectations are not sufficiently clear that research propositions can be explicated. The objective of the remainder of this paper is thus twofold: (1) to assess the validity of this conceptualization; and (2) to describe the facilitating conditions, the process, and the outcomes of the types of subsidiary initiative that are identified.

RESEARCH METHODOLOGY

Sampling methodology

438 Defining the research sample posed two methodological problems. The first problem was that many MNC subsidiaries have never undertaken initiatives, so it was necessary to identify a sample of

subsidiaries that *had* undertaken intiatives.[3] The second problem was identifying a sample of initia-tives from the sample subsidiaries. The decision was made to research the entire set of initiatives in a small number of companies, on the grounds that the quality of data was a critical element of this study. The alternative of a one company–one initiative study would also have been possible, but would have entailed very few respondents per initiative, and therefore less richness in the data. If a single initiative had been studied for each subsidiary there would have been a danger of selection bias towards the respondents' more memorable – but not necessarily representative – initiatives. A third problem was anticipated but did not materialize, namely the identification of initiatives that met the definitions posed at the outset. Kanter (1982: 99) noted that the delineation between an entrepre-neurial activity (i.e., an initiative) and a managerial activity is much easier in practice than it is in words, and this study bore out her observation. Likewise, the stated need for all initiatives to lead to international responsibilities never created any methodological problems, in that every initiative identified, even the local market type, quickly (i.e., within 24 months) led to international sales.

The following sampling methodology was adopted. Using the *Financial Post 500* index, a list of subsidiaries was drawn up with the following restrictions: (1) Canadian subsidiaries of U.S.-owned MNCs; (2) with 1992 sales revenues of greater than $200 million; and (3) participating in a global industry (Morrison, 1990). These criteria were selected on the basis that a case research design should intentionally limit the variance in the sample to make cross-case analysis mean-ingful (Parkhe, 1993; Yin, 1984). There were also strong *a priori* reasons for the size and global industry restrictions, in that the strategic imperatives for smaller subsidiaries (which may be sales-only) and subsidiaries in nonglobal industries (with limited cross-border trade flows) are not germane to the management of the mature MNC. One additional criterion was also devel-oped, namely clear evidence of initiative. By picking out those subsidiaries with an established record of success in taking the initiative or gaining international responsibilities we were able to avoid approaching companies that did not exhibit the necessary levels of entrepreneurship. Approximately 40 subsidiaries met all these criteria.

Subsidiaries from this sample were then approached on a convenience basis. Two of four initial selections agreed to participate fully. As research in these two subsidiaries progressed, additional subsidiaries were approached, and over the course of 9 months four more were added (with a further two declining to participate). The decision to stop at six sites was based on the principle of redundancy (Yin, 1984), in that no substantive additional insights appeared to be forthcoming towards the end of the study. The data collection period lasted from November 1993 to August 1994. Some basic facts about the subsidiary sample are displayed in Table 23.2.[4]

In each sample company, initiatives were identified through discussions with senior managers. The major initiatives, particularly those that had resulted in new international responsibilities, were identified immediately, but some careful investigation was required to pick out smaller or less-successful initiatives. It was only towards the end of the research that some of the more interesting failures were uncovered, presumably because respondents' comfort level with the researcher increased with time. Between 3 and 10 initiatives were identified in each company to give a total sample size of 39 initiatives (Table 23.3).

Data collection methods

The two primary sources of data were (1) semi-structured interviews with subsidiary and parent company managers, and (2) a questionnaire filled out by the key individual for each initiative.

Table 23.2 Subsidiary sample

Company	Principal industry	Approximate size (1993 revenues)	Number of interviews
A	Industrial and consumer products	$600 million[a]	22
B	Chemicals	$450 million	19
C	Computer hardware/software	$500 million	15
D	Computer hardware/software	$800 million	19
E	Industrial products	$420 million	14
F	Engineering systems	$420 million	11

[a]Figures are in Canadian dollars.

These data were complemented by business plans and other company documents, and secondary data compiled through a CD-ROM library search. Interviews followed a carefully prepared protocol, with a mixture of specific questions ('What was the proposed dollar investment in this project?') and open-ended questions ('How did this initiative arise in the first place?'). For each initiative the intention was to speak to every manager who was actively involved. Thus, between 2 and 10 managers were interviewed for each initiative. In 65 percent of cases one or more parent managers involved in the initiative were interviewed. Interviews were taped and transcribed, and notes were also taken. A total of approximately 1500 pages of data were assembled through this process.

The questionnaire was put together towards the end of the research, as a means of validating the qualitative interview findings. Questions were drawn up to measure the emerging constructs, such as the nature of the market opportunity or the level of selling by subsidiary management. Following a careful preparation process, in which four academicians and three subsidiary managers (not in the sample) provided feedback on wording and design, the questionnaire was mailed to the key respondent for each of the 39 initiatives. Thirty-five questionnaires were returned, and in the four remaining cases the questionnaire was filled in by an independent research assistant following a careful reading of the interview transcripts.[5]

Data analysis

Five constructs were measured using questionnaire data.[6] The nonparametric Kruskal–Wallis test was conducted on these measures to determine whether there were any significant differences between the means of the different initiative types. Qualitative data were analyzed using the procedures recommended by Miles and Huberman (1984), which emphasize the use of tables and diagrams for reducing and visualizing data. The analysis was undertaken by both the researchers, and discrepancies reconciled through discussion. The qualitative findings were summarized in the form of a case history, and sent to the lead respondent to verify that the case was a fair portrayal of what actually happened. Specific constructs were then abstracted from the case studies and compared to the quantitative findings. The results section (below) provides both sets of data so that the convergence between the qualitative and quantitative techniques can be judged.

RESEARCH FINDINGS

Types of subsidiary initiative

The conceptual framework suggested that three types of initiative should be identifiable, on the basis of the locus of the market opportunity (i.e., local, internal and global). This proposition

Table 23.3 Initiative sample

Sub.	Initiative	Outcome	Interviews
A	Initial proposal to manufacture in Ontario	Success	2
A	Proposal for plant extension in Manitoba	Success	2
A	Proposal to bring conversion to Ontario (a)	Failure	2
A	Proposal to bring conversion to Ontario (b)	Success	3
A	Proposal to bring finishing to Canada	Success	2
A	Proposal to consolidate production in Canada	Success	3
A	Bid for major new tape plant	Success	3
A	Restructure of sales and marketing organization	Success	8
A	Bid for plant extension	Success	5
A	New library security product	Mixed	2
B	Bid for new chemical facility in Canada	Failure	1
B	Incremental investment in Canadian plant	Success	4
B	Business management shifted to Canada	Success	5
B	Toll manufacture brought in-house	Success	7
B	Bid for new formulation of major product	Success	5
B	New dispensing product for major product	Success	2
B	Proposed technological innovation in Canada	Failure	2
C	New digital screen technology	Success	7
C	System controller product	Success	6
C	Cutting equipment innovation	Success	3
C	Electronics for defense missile	Success	3
C	Airport terminal product innovation	Success	4
C	New generation terminal product	Success	2
C	Second generation missile electronics	Failure	2
C	Communication network product	Failure	2
D	Local hardware company acquisition	Mixed	5
D	Industrial terminal product innovation	Mixed	6
D	New high-technology terminal	Success	6
D	Regional product development center	Success	10
D	Software development center	Mixed	3
D	New information protocol center	Success	3
E	Export of valve to Europe	Success	4
E	Export of switch manufacture to U.S.	Success	5
E	Rationalization of North American production	Success	10
E	Designation of two SBUs in Canada	Success	6
E	Software system for building controls	Mixed	1
F	Software/hardware system for oil flow	Success	6
F	New PC network management product	Success	5
F	Local high-tech company acquisition	Success	6

was confirmed to the extent that all three putative types were in evidence, but in addition there emerged in the course of the research a fourth type that was essentially a hybrid between the internal market and global market forms. This hybrid type took the form of subsidiary management identifying and bidding for an embryonic corporate investment. For example, in one case subsidiary management read in the corporate long-range plan that a new plant was scheduled

4 years hence. They recognized a fit with the Canadian subsidiary's capabilities so they built a case for making the investment in Canada and solicited support for their proposal at head office. In this case the initial market opportunity was identified by head office managers but subsidiary management proactively pursued it. Thus, there was a heavy element of internal selling, to persuade head office management that the subsidiary was the appropriate site for investment, but the initial market opportunity was clearly global.

The hybrid case can best be understood in terms of the locus of opportunity vs. the locus of pursuit,[7] in that its locus of opportunity was global but its locus of pursuit was internal. In all the other three forms the locus of opportunity coincided with the locus of pursuit. This state of affairs serves to underline the complexity of the subsidiary's role within the 'interorganizational network' of the MNC. Rather than just focusing on one type of market opportunity at a time, there is also the need to reconcile emerging global opportunities with internal capabilities. We might argue that this is the job of the corporate center, but the evidence shows that the proactive subsidiary can also take on parts of that role itself.

Table 23.4 lists the number of cases found of each initiative type, with a description to facilitate understanding. In terms of methodology, the fourth type (the hybrid) emerged during the data collection process. Then, during the data analysis stage each initiative was assigned by the lead researcher to one of the four types. The research assistant replicated the process, on the basis of the interview transcripts, and made the same assignment as the lead researcher in 37 of 39 cases. The remaining two were discussed and agreement was eventually reached regarding the appropriate type. Next, a discriminant analysis was undertaken on the questionnaire data, to check whether the four types could be distinguished on the basis of the 'drivers' of initiative.[8] This analysis yielded Wilk's lambdas of 0.06, 0.23 and 0.54 respectively for the three canonical discriminant functions, representing a very high level of separation between the four groups. In sum, 33 of the 39 cases were correctly classified by this procedure, or 85 percent of the total. This is an excellent result, and provides further confirmation of the validity of the typology.[9]

Table 23.4 Four types of initiative

Initiative type	Number of cases	Number of failures	Description
Local market initiative	13	2	Seek to develop a new product, market, or process through opportunities that are first identified in the subsidiary's home market
Internal market initiative	12	1	Promote the redistribution of existing corporate assets or resources such that they are more efficiently deployed. In the Canadian context the objective is typically to reconfigure a branch plant in the light of the North American Free Trade Agreement
Global market initiative	9	1	Seek to build on an existing mandate or proven capability to meet a perceived international product or market opportunity
Hybrid initiative	5	1	Seeks to attract a global investment which has already (in principle) received corporate support

Facilitators of initiative

Local market initiatives

The 13 cases of local market initiatives suggested an interesting duality to the roles of subsidiary autonomy and parent–subsidiary communication as facilitators of initiative that had not been identified before. At the formative stage autonomy had to be high and communication correspondingly low so that subsidiary resources could be applied to the opportunity without head office interference; at the more advanced stage of viability a higher level of communication and a lower level of autonomy were more appropriate, in that subsidiary management had typically to achieve sponsorship for the business in question from a U.S.-based operating division. In one case a subsidiary manager built a $20 million business from nothing in 4 years, but took a further 4 years to find a 'home' with one of the major corporate business groups. His observation was that autonomy had helped him to move quickly early on, but was a liability as he attempted to enlarge the business and integrate it into the corporate network.

In terms of resources, it become apparent in the course of the study that *proven* resources (i.e., those which were recognized by parent management) were a more important facilitator of intiative than resources *per se*.[10] However, in the specific case of local market initiatives, the sample companies only exhibited moderate levels of proven resources. Respondents commented that the subsidiary had to have sufficient experience and/or expertise to pursue opportunities as they arose, but without the high levels of proven resources that were necessary to succeed with some of the other types.

Respondents observed that *internal market initiatives* were facilitated most effectively by the credibility of the subsidiary in the eyes of the parent company, which was a function, in turn, of the subsidiary's high level of proven resources. In cases where the subsidiary had already built up a number of world product mandates through prior initiatives, subsequent initiatives progressed much more smoothly. Credibility was also a function of a high level of parent–subsidiary communication and, by the same token, a fairly low level of autonomy in that subsidiary managers had to be working very closely with their U.S. counterparts. As described by one respondent:

> It is awfully important that we have a close association [with the U.S. management]. We are talking frequently about what are the issues in their business, what are their problems, what are the opportunities that we can offer to help them solve their problems. That is important to do.

One facilitator of internal market initiatives that had not been identified in prior research was the global orientation (Perlmutter, 1969) of the senior management in the United States. Some were essentially ethnocentric in their approach, which created enormous obstacles for subsidiary management; others took a geocentric attitude which streamlined the entire process, as the following quote suggests.

> [The general manager] had a kind of 'let's do the right thing then tell everyone' attitude. Let's not be political about this, let's collaborate and do the right thing. What's right to do here is not what's right for our own camp, it's what's right for the corporation. So we got backing on this and got him interested. He then adopted it and became the overall mentor for it, and kept up the momentum.

Global market initiatives appeared to be facilitated by high autonomy, a high level of proven resources, and a correspondingly low level of parent–subsidiary communication. The importance of autonomy was underlined by one case in which the subsidiary had achieved great success in building a viable international business, but where the parent company had then curtailed its autonomy because of corporate financial difficulties. Pursuing intiatives suddenly became a time-consuming and frustrating process, as this quote suggests:

> The basic dilemma facing [the general manager of the subsidiary] is lack of investment. If he wants $100,000 to develop a product the customer is paying for he has to make a couple of visits to head office, which might take three months. By the time approval is granted, the opportunity has passed.

Proven resources here referred to a history of successful initiatives and an accumulation over time of specialized and valued capabilities. All the subsidiaries undertaking global market initiatives in this study were essentially building on existing international responsibilities or world mandates (Etemad and Dulude, 1986). With regard to parent–subsidiary communication, most respondents felt that initiative was facilitated by low levels of communication. This is not to suggest that communication is damaging, but that it is a low priority and is liable to be limited in a high-autonomy subsidiary. This quote is indicative of the level of parent–subsidiary communication that was observed:

> . . . [The head office boss] was looking at the numbers, and 'other income' was quite large. He said 'What's that?' and [his colleague] said 'that's the electronics group up in Canada.' So my head office boss called me and said, 'We don't know what you're doing up there, but keep it up.' Isn't that representative of the relationship!

Hybrid initiatives were facilitated by very similar factors to internal market initiatives. That is, the credibility of the subsidiary with head office decision-makers was felt to be critical, and this was typically a function of moderate to high levels of proven resources, strong parent–subsidiary communication and relatively low autonomy. One subsidiary president commented on the nature of the bid process in his company:

> You end up with a couple of sites that come pretty close and one that will have a minor advantage economically, but sitting in an operating committee in the States, what really swings you is the credibility of the organization that's asking for the order.

The fact that the market opportunity in the hybrid initiative was global had little bearing on the facilitating conditions, because the entire process was internal to the MNC. The evidence, in fact, suggested that hybrid initiatives required the highest level of 'selling' of all four types, which in turn necessitated a high level of ongoing parent–subsidiary communication.

Triangulation of qualitative and quantitative data

The questionnaire data that tapped into the three main constructs under discussion is displayed in Table 23.5. The nonparametric Kruskal–Wallis test was conducted to determine whether there were any significant differences between the means of the four initiative types. Despite the small sample size (between 5 and 13 observations for each type), two significant results were recorded, both consistent with the qualitative data. First, the high level of autonomy in global market initiatives was confirmed, in relation to all other types. Second, parent–subsidiary communication was different (at a marginal level of significance) across the types, with local and global initiatives

Table 23.5 Questionnaire data on initiative facilitators

	Local market initiative	Internal market initiative	Global market initiative	Global–internal hybrid initiative	Kruskal–Wallis ANOVA (F/sig.)	Pairs significantly different
Subsidiary autonomy	3.0	2.6	4.4	2.8	11.2/0.01	Global with all others
Specialized resources:						
(a) Existing international responsibilities	3.2	3.7	4.1	3.6	3.1/0.38	None
(b) Record of success with initiatives	2.9	3.8	3.4	4.0	4.3/0.23	None
Parent–sub. communication	3.1	3.9	3.0	4.2	7.4/0.06	Local and hybrid

All measures on 5-point Likert scales where 5 = high; 1 = low.

exhibiting low levels of communication and internal and hybrid initiatives exhibiting high levels. The two measures selected as proxies for proven resources (existing international responsibilities and a record of success with initiatives) were not able to distinguish between initiative types, though there was a suggestion that proven resources were slightly lower in local market initiatives. While consistent with the qualitative data, this finding is at odds with Ghoshal's (1986) observation that local innovations are associated with high levels of local resources.

Taken together, the quantitative and qualitative data provided several important new insights into the facilitators of subsidiary initiative. Internal market and hybrid initiatives exhibited a higher level of integration (in terms of parent–subsidiary communication and low autonomy) than previous studies suggested, and appeared to rely on geocentrically minded parent company managers to be successful; local market initiatives appeared to be facilitated by a careful balance between autonomy and integration; and global market initiatives were exhibited only where the subsidiary was *very* autonomous. The fact that autonomy was apparently so critical to the global market type is interesting, because *a priori* one might not expect local and global market initiatives to be significantly different. This evidence suggests that subsidiaries can not easily build world mandate businesses while at the same time remaining integrated with the rest of the corporation, but it is at odds with several studies that have suggested this is a desirable combination (e.g., Bartlett and Ghoshal, 1989; Roth and Morrison, 1992).

Initiative processes

The qualitative findings shed considerable light on the initiative process, though in broad terms they were consistent with expectations. Two distinct processes were identified: one internally focused and the other externally focused. The *internally focused* process was exhibited by internal market initiatives and hybrid initiatives, in that formal corporate approval was necessary for resources to be made available. There was therefore a high level of selling, first of all by middle-level managers to their superiors in the subsidiary, and subsequently by the top subsidiary managers to their superiors in head office. This process is encapsulated by the following quote by a middle-level manager regarding an internal market initiative:

I said really we should make a play for [this business], and started to build the argument. I sounded out the [U.S. business manager]: 'What are the possibilities here? What about running the business from Toronto? What do you think about it?' He basically thought it had merit, and he coached me. But my sales effort was not to try to convince U.S. people beyond my sphere of influence, it was really to get the people here convinced, to provide them a position that they could then embellish. So I worked with them and ultimately [the Canadian President] was the guy to say 'We would like to do this' at a very senior level in head office.

While much of the internal selling took the form of an upward progression through the hierarchy (Bower's 1970 'impetus'), there was also some evidence of horizontal selling as well. Many middle managers in the subsidiary were on global business teams, and were thus in a position to influence their head office and international peers, and subsidiary top management were typically connected into an extensive lateral network through which support for initiatives could be built. The following quote illustrates the extensive selling process undertaken by one subsidiary CEO:

First he had to get approval (for the initiative) from the operations committee, who report directly to the chairman. Then he went to the sector meetings, where you had the division VPs. There were three of them. . . . He then went to a couple of other corporate bodies, typical places where you would showcase this kind of thing – the marketing council, the technical council as well, which is a huge group of the laboratory managers. So having cascaded it down he tried to pick large bodies where he would get to the level below division VP.

The concept of a horizontal organization super-imposed on the traditional M-form has been documented by several academics (Bartlett and Ghoshal, 1993; Hedlund, 1986; White and Poynter, 1990). In terms of subsidiary initiatives, it was a valuable source of support, though typically only as a complement to the vertical chain of command through which resource allocation occurred.

Were there any differences between the observed process in internal market initiatives and hybrid initiatives? The distinguishing characteristic was the level of involvement of parent company management, in that hybrid initiatives always had parent management support in principle from the start, whereas internal market initiatives had to build their own support. This created a rather subtle difference in process: internal market initiatives were iterative, involving several rounds of credibility building with parent management and refining of proposals; hybrid initiatives were 'take-it-or-leave-it' proposals in which parent management typically had to choose between several directly competing courses of action.

The local market and global market initiatives were *externally focused*. Head office approval was typically implicit, so the majority of the effort on the part of subsidiary management was dedicated to building a viable product for local and global customers respectively. In the case of local market initiatives the subsidiary usually took responsibility for developing the concept using local development funds or bootlegged resources, without the support – and sometimes even without the knowledge – of the parent company. As stated in the previous section, approval from the parent was only sought on average several years later when the business had become viable. In the case of global market initiatives the subsidiary almost always had authority to invest in new projects within the subsidiary's existing charter (Galunic and Eisenhardt, 1994). The appropriate parent company division was kept informed of all such investments, but they did not intervene in the process. Championing was thus relegated to an internal subsidiary activity, as middle managers sought to convince the subsidiary general manager that their initiative should be pursued.

In general terms, then, the initiative process took one of two forms, neither of which corresponded precisely to the classic formulation of Bower (1970). Where resource allocation was a centralized phenomenon (i.e., with internal market and hybrid initiatives), horizontal systems complemented the vertical chain of authority as a means of building legitimacy and momentum for the initiative. Where resource allocation was decentralized, selling occurred primarily within the subsidiary and head office approval was implicit. It is not clear the extent to which this finding is specific to the sample, which was deliberately skewed to favor initiative-taking subsidiaries. Bartlett and Ghoshal (1993) observed that their 'new' organizational model, which included a very similar extension to the Bower model of resource allocation, was induced from a sample of leading-edge companies, some of which were the same as used in the current study. Thus there is some suggestion that these processes may not be representative of the population of MNCs. Future research will be necessary to examine this question.

Triangulation of qualitative and quantitative data

The questionnaire data that tapped into the two constructs under discussion are displayed in Table 23.6. The nonparametric Kruskal–Wallis test was conducted on the two internal selling measures; the approval process data were nominal so they are presented in raw form. The results provide strong support for the qualitative findings discussed above. Both local and global initiative types exhibited a lower level of internal selling than their internal and hybrid counterparts, and this difference was significant for the subsidiary president's selling activity. Equally, the approval process was predominantly implicit for the local and global types (13 out of 19 cases), and explicit for the internal and hybrid types (14 out of 15 cases). In sum, there appears to be a very clear split between the two broad processes.

Initiative outcomes

Setting aside the five that were not successful, the 34 remaining initiatives all led to increased sales, investment from head office, and new jobs. As Table 23.7 shows, however, the differences in these measures between types were mostly small. The only substantive difference, in fact, was that the internal market and hybrid initiative types both involved higher levels of capital investment

Table 23.6 Questionnaire data on initiative process

	Local market initiative	Internal market initiative	Global market initiative	Global–internal hybrid initiative	Kruskal–Wallis ANOVA (F/sig.)	Pairs significantly different
Internal selling: (a) by subsidiary management	3.6	4.1	3.3	3.8	3.9/0.27	None
(b) by subsidiary president	2.8	3.8	2.4	3.8	7.3/0.06	Local and internal; Global and internal
Nature of approval process	4 explicit 8 implicit 1 rejected	10 explicit 1 implicit 1 rejected	2 explicit 5 implicit 2 rejected	4 explicit 0 implicit 1 rejected	–	Local and global different to internal and hybrid

All measures on 5-point Likert scales (except approval process) where 5 = high; 1 = low.

Table 23.7 Initiative outcomes

	Local market initiatives	Internal market initiatives	Global market initiatives	Hybrid initiatives
Average new investment in subsidiary as a result of approval	$2.2 million	$4.8 million	$1.7 million	$8.6 million
Average new sales for subsidiary within two years	$5.2 million	$10.5 million	$7.8 million	$9.2 million
Long-term outcomes stated by respondents (subjective)	Local value-added Customer responsiveness New business for MNC	Local value-added Competitive subsidiary operations Integrated production	Specialized capability Local value-added Development of center of excellence	Local value-added Optimally located new facility

than the other two. This is presumably a function of the resource allocation system in the MNC. Where subsidiary managers had the authority to approve the initiative (as with local and global market types) they proceeded in an incremental fashion, investing relatively small sums each time. Where approval was centralized at the head office, investments were typically larger. As with the data on facilitating conditions and the initiative process, this process emphasized the similarity between the hybrid and internal market initiative types.

Qualitatively, the outcomes of the four types of initiative were markedly different. Local market initiatives led, in the first instance, to an enhanced service to local customers, but as they developed they led to new business opportunities for the MNC as a whole. Two of the 13 cases in this study became 'blockbuster' products (with revenues in 1994 of $50 million and $110 million respectively), while the rest led to niche businesses, or businesses that lasted a few years and were then phased out. Local market initiatives can therefore be viewed as enhancing worldwide learning as well, in that opportunities identified in the Canadian market were addressed and then applied in other countries. More broadly, local market initiatives are also instrumental to the imperative of corporate adaptation and renewal, in that they provide the variety that the MNC's systems can then select against (Burgelman, 1991). Without the diversity of opportunities and ideas that local market initiatives represent, the MNC's ability to adapt to changing environmental demands would be severely constrained.

Internal market initiatives, as predicted, led to a rationalization of activities between Canada and the United States, and hence a more efficient corporate system. Typically a branch plant went from producing a broad range of products for the Canadian market to one or two products on a North American or global basis. Overall volumes stayed the same (initially at least), but both U.S. and Canadian plants increased their export sales. There were also cases of rationalization in administrative functions: in one case, for example, product management was relocated to Canada to be more closely integrated with the associated manufacturing. Both outcomes are symptomatic of the shift in MNCs towards a geographical concentration of value activities (Porter, 1986).

The outcome of the global market initiatives in the study was the maintenance and development of a specialized corporate capability. That is, each initiative sought to build a new product or market around an existing business line using the distinctive capabilities resident in that subsidiary. The term 'center of excellence' was used by respondents in this regard, with the implication that the parent company and other subsidiaries also stood to benefit from those capabilities. In terms of the corporate objectives identified at the outset, then, this is another facet of worldwide learning. Tangentially, it does suggest that the concept of worldwide learning is multifaceted, with at least two separate characteristics: (1) the transfer of information about customer needs within the corporate network, as achieved through local market initiatives; and (2) the transfer of proprietary technology and other capabilities within the corporate network, as achieved through global market initiatives. Both appear to be important strategic imperatives for the MNC.

Finally, hybrid initiatives had a similar outcome to the internal market type, in that they led to a geographically concentrated value activity serving the North American or global market. The four successful cases identified in this study made use of both the comparative advantages of Canada (relative to the United States) such as cheap power and a low-cost, low-turnover workforce, and also the specialized capabilities of the subsidiary. This is a facet of the global integration imperative, but it is actually superior to the rationalization process that internal market initiatives promote because it results (in theory at least) in the positioning of the value-adding activity at the optimum global location, rather than an existing location. Table 23.8 provides a summary of the findings: it is similar in format to Table 23.1, so the findings can be easily compared to the *a priori* expectations.

DISCUSSION

MNC subsidiary management

A major contribution of this study is its documentation of an internal subsidiary phenomenon, in contrast to most previous research that has concerned itself more with aspects of the parent–subsidiary relationship. Many recent studies (Bartlett and Ghoshal, 1993; Birkinshaw, 1995; Humes, 1993; Quelch, 1992) have suggested that the parent–subsidiary relationship is multifaceted, in that it varies across business units and operates at multiple levels of management. By focusing here on the initiative as the unit of analysis the problem of defining a parent–subsidiary relationship was circumvented. Certain initiatives were found to be specific to a single plant so involved a single relationship with a U.S. manufacturing director; others involved the whole spectrum of business units and all their relationships with their U.S. counterparts. In all cases, however, it was possible to examine a generic process based around the nature of the initiative, rather than a somewhat artificial conceptualization of the parent–subsidiary relationship.

This research also embraced a broader conceptualization of subsidiary initiative than had previously been identified. Taking Ghoshal (1986) as the definitive piece of work in this area, subsidiary initiatives can be focused either on local market opportunities ('local for local innovations') or on global market opportunities ('local for global' or 'global for global' innovations). This research has shown, in addition, that initiatives can be internally focused, towards a rationalization of existing activities or the promotion of new ones. Viewed in this way, the subsidiary suddenly has the potential to enhance the local responsiveness, global integration *and* worldwide learning capabilities of the MNC. This is a significantly broader role than previous research has suggested. The implication is that the MNC that is able to harness the full entrepreneurial capabilities of its subsidiaries stands to gain competitive advantage.

Table 23.8 Summary of findings from current study

	Local market initiative	Internal market initiative	Global market initiative	Hybrid initiative
Facilitating conditions	• Low parent–sub. communication (quantitative) • High autonomy at first • Moderate proven resources (qualitative)	• High parent–sub. communication • Low autonomy • Strong proven resources, hence credibility • Geocentric perspective in parent company (all qualitative)	• High autonomy • Low parent–sub. communication (quantitative) • Strong proven resources (qualitative)	• High parent–sub. communication • Low Autonomy • Strong proven resources, hence credibility • Geocentric perspective in parent company (all qualitative)
Process	• Low to moderate internal selling • Implicit approval process[a] (qualitative and quantitative)	• High internal selling • Explicit approval process[b] (qualitative and quantitative)	• Low internal selling • Implicit approval process[a] (qualitative and quantitative)	• High internal selling • Explicit approval process[b] (qualitative and quantitative)
Intended outcome	• New business for the MNC; local opportunity leveraged worldwide (qualitative)	• Rationalization of existing activities; increased efficiency (qualitative)	• Enhancement and international leverage of an existing product line or business (qualitative)	• Optimum global siting of new value-adding activity (qualitative)

[a]The global market initiative process involved somewhat less internal selling and greater levels of implicit approval than the local market initiative process.

[b]The internal market and hybrid initiative processes differed only in subtle ways. Hybrid initiatives involved significantly earlier parent involvement than local market initiatives, but the magnitude of the investment in question coupled with the competitive nature of the bid meant that a stronger selling effort was typically observed. The internal market initiative process, by contrast, tended to be slightly more incremental in nature, often taking several years to come to fruition.

How can the subsidiary's entrepreneurial capabilities be most effectively harnessed? The first challenge is to create an appropriate structural context, that is, one that facilitates entrepreneurship. Ghoshal's (1986) research showed that *ceteris paribus* high autonomy, specialized resources, high normative integration and high interunit communication were associated with subsidiary initiative. This study suggested a more complex set of relationships. Autonomy, for example, was shown to be positively associated with local and global market initiatives and negatively associated with internal market and hybrid initiatives.[11] Likewise, the other facets of structural context actually varied between initiative types as well. The implication is that a single structural context cannot facilitate all four types of initiative. If a subsidiary is highly integrated with its parent, for example, it can easily pursue internal market and hybrid initiatives, but less easily undertake local or global market initiatives.

The implicit trade-offs that the parent company faces in shaping the subsidiary's structural context are reduced when one recognizes that the subsidiary is itself differentiated. One division of the subsidiary can be closely integrated with its parent; another may be largely autonomous. GE Canada, for example, has 11 divisions each one of which has a unique relationship to its respective parent division in the United States. Furthermore, the subsidiary's structural context and its assigned role are not cast in stone. Over time a successful initiative-taking subsidiary would expect to impact its own strategic context (Burgelman, 1983b) and hence its perceived role within the MNC. One of the subsidiaries in this study, for example, built a new business from scratch in Canada. As the division in question grew it developed an international customer base and a unique set of capabilities so that eventually it operated as a stand-alone global business. Over this period its emphasis shifted from local market initiatives to global market initiatives, and correspondingly its structural context also changed to accommodate its new role.

In sum, the idea that subsidiary roles can be differentiated through contextual mechanisms (Bartlett and Ghoshal, 1986) is a powerful one, but not without its limitations. This study has shown that context needs to be differentiated at the sub-subsidiary level (typically the division, business unit or plant) if the full scope of initiative types is to be facilitated. It has also suggested that a more dynamic approach to role and context management is appropriate, given that the subsidiary's opportunity set and internal capabilities are continually evolving.

The second challenge facing the MNC that is attempting to enhance the entrepreneurial capabilities of its subsidiaries is to develop an entrepreneurial culture, i.e., one that motivates its employees to take the initiative. The review of the corporate entrepreneurship literature identified this as a key imperative, but the current study was not able to shed light on it. By focusing on six companies that had all successfully pursued initiatives, it would be reasonable to deduce that all had relatively entrepreneurial cultures. Future research, in which a sample of initiative-taking subsidiaries is compared with a sample of noninitiative-taking subsidiaries, will be necessary to understand exactly what an entrepreneurial culture means for a MNC.

Corporate entrepreneurship

Entrepreneurship in this paper was defined as alertness to market opportunity. While this conceptualization is well accepted in the literature (Kirzner, 1973; Stevenson and Jarillo, 1990), traditional usage was extended by modeling 'market' to include entities both internal and external to the MNC. This insight, in turn, led to a recognition that there were two distinct entrepreneurial processes at work in the sample companies: (1) 'internal entrepreneurship' (internal and hybrid initiatives) in which initiatives were subject to corporate selection mechanisms such as legitimacy and approval; and (2) 'external entrepreneurship' (local and global initiatives) in which initiatives were subject to environmental selection mechanisms such as customer acceptance and survival. The concept that the corporation can create its own variation–selection–retention mechanism is, of course, not new (e.g., Burgelman, 1991), but the data in this case provided strong empirical support for what is a relatively underresearched phenomenon.

To what extent did a sample of MNC subsidiaries make this research on corporate entrepreneurship a special case? The Canadian setting is interesting (and rich in data) because the recent transition to North American Free Trade, and the perceived threat to Canadian operations, has induced many Canadian subsidiaries to actively look for ways to add value. Furthermore, the problems of building relationships and gaining credibility with decision-makers are all exacerbated by the geographical and (relatively minor) cultural distances between subsidiary and head office. In addition, the concepts of 'local' and 'global' initiative are clearly designed to apply to foreign subsidiaries and not domestic entities. Notwithstanding these facts, our position is that the subsidiary context implies a difference of degree rather than of kind. It is a small stretch (conceptually and physically) to move a subsidiary plant in London, Ontario to Buffalo, New York, so we suggest that the issues illuminated here are no less portable. While the primary focus of the research was obviously on MNC subsidiary management, the implications for corporate entrepreneurship are substantial.

CONCLUSION

The objective of this paper was to document an empirical investigation of subsidiary initiatives, and to understand them in terms of the existing theory of the MNC. The key finding was that four types of subsidiary initiative can be identified. Previous research by Ghoshal (1986) had indicated that subsidiary initiatives can be focused either on local market or global market opportunities. This research demonstrated, in addition, that initiatives can be internally focused, towards a rationalization of existing activities or towards the promotion of new ones. This finding has two implications: first, it suggests that the subsidiary has the potential to drive the local responsiveness, global integration *and* worldwide learning capabilities of the MNC, a much broader role than previously recognized; second, it indicates that the differentiation of subsidiary roles through contextual mechanisms (Bartlett and Ghoshal, 1986) has its limitations. Both of these implications are explored in the discussion.

This study had a number of limitations. First, the sample was drawn from a single country, which was appropriate given the state of knowledge about subsidiary initiatives (Parkhe, 1993; Yin, 1984) but also limiting with regard to external validity. Subsequent research in other countries and with parents of other nationalities is the important next step in building knowledge about subsidiary initiatives. Second, the sample was selected to include only those subsidiaries with some record of success with initiatives. This, again, was appropriate given the need to understand the characteristics of initiatives, but it begs the question 'What factors are responsible for promoting initiative in some subsidiaries and stifling it in others?' Now that the types of initiatives are better understood a follow-up study addressing this question can be conducted.

In terms of the methodology, three limitations were evident. The first was the challenge of collecting data on failed initiatives. For a variety of reasons managers were reluctant to dwell on their less auspicious moments, so a small number of failed initiatives may have been missed in the sample companies. This problem could potentially be mitigated by spending longer in the company, but there are clear trade-offs in terms of diminishing returns and potentially alienating time-constrained managers. A real-time study would also solve this problem, but would be very time intensive. Equally problematical were those initiatives that died out before they took off. Rather than being failures *per se*, such initiatives simply did not register as important in the minds of the respondents. Again, a real time study would be the only way to circumvent this concern. Finally, the questionnaire was deliberately short to ensure a high response rate, but this meant that one- and two-item construct measures were used. For future research greater attention needs to be given to the development of a valid and reliable measurement instrument.

Future research, then, is recommended in two directions. The first thrust should be towards a comprehensive understanding of the initiative phenomenon in other MNC settings, and in a larger sample of subsidiaries. Of interest here is not only the generalizability of the *initiative* characteristics identified in the current study, but also the characteristics of *subsidiaries* that exhibit initiatives. The second research thrust should be directed towards the personal motivation of employees to pursue initiatives. While the current study identified the intended outcomes behind initiatives, it was unable to inform the discussion of why certain individuals choose to pursue entrepreneurial opportunities while others do not. If we are to build a complete model of subsidiary initiative, the critical element may be the personal motivation and the spark of creativity that sets the whole process in motion.

NOTES

1   Note that in theory local market initiatives could remain within the local market, e.g., if a product is designed specifically for a segment of the local market. In practice, the sample used in this study exhibited no incidences of local initiatives that stayed local: all went on to become international products.

2   This point is substantiated by the body of literature on internationalization which sees international relationships growing incrementally through experience and existing contacts (e.g., Johanson and Vahlne, 1977).

3   Note that this does not impart a bias to the results: the research objective was to understand the characteristics of subsidiary initiatives, not to understand why some subsidiaries undertake them while others do not.

4   The six subsidiaries in the final sample appeared to be typical of the larger sample of 40 subsidiaries. Their average sales revenues in 1993 were $550 million compared to $440 million in the larger sample. Furthermore, informal interviews were subsequently conducted in a further 12 of the 40 companies, with qualitatively very similar findings to those reported here.

5   More specifically, the research assistant completed a questionnaire for *every* initiative (i.e., all 39) based on his reading of the transcripts. Interrater reliability for the 35 questionnaires where both the key respondent and the research assistant had completed them was 0.64 (using Cohen's kappa; Perreault and Leigh, 1989). Consistent with Nunnally (1978) this is acceptable for the early stages of a research program. It was therefore decided that the research assistant's responses were a reasonable proxy in the four cases where no response was forthcoming.

6   Questions, all on 5-point Likert scales except the last one, were as follows. AUTONOMY: (a) What level of strategic autonomy did the Canadian subsidiary have?; PROVEN RESOURCES: (a) To what extent did the subsidiary have previous international responsibilities? (b) To what extent did the subsidiary have a track record of success getting projects approved? PARENT–SUBSIDIARY COMMUNICATION: (a) What was the extent of the relationship between the parent and subsidiary management? INTERNAL SELLING: (a) What was the extent of the selling process followed by subsidiary management? (b) How active was the Canadian president's involvement in pursuing the initiative? APPROVAL: (a) What was the immediate outcome (explicit approval, implicit approval, rejection)?

7   We are indebted to an anonymous reviewer for suggesting this distinction.

8   The seven initiative drivers were: (1) desire to consolidate operations with those of the parent; (2) creation of a North American free-trade environment; (3) routine product or business upgrade on existing product; (4) business opportunity defined by a parent request for proposal; (5) a product–market opportunity arising through interaction with local customers; (6) a product–market opportunity arising through interaction with international customers; and (7) desire by subsidiary management to enhance local value-added.

9   As discriminant analysis assumes multivariate normality and equivalent variance–covariance matrices, neither of which was wholly present given the small sample size, this result should be interpreted with caution.

10   This finding is consistent with process models of strategy such as Bower (1970) in which resource allocation decisions are typically made on the basis of the individual's track record rather than on purely economic or technological arguments.

11   Qualitatively, the evidence suggested a *causal* relationship between automony and initiative in the directions indicated, though this cannot be verified with the quantitative data.

REFERENCES

Barnard, C.I. (1938). *The Functions of the Executive*. Harvard University Press, Cambridge, MA.

Bartlett, C. A. and S. Ghoshal (1986). 'Tap your subsidiaries for global reach', *Harvard Business Review*, 64(6), pp. 87–94.

Bartlett, C. A. and S. Ghoshal (1989). *Managing across Borders: The Transnational Solution*. Harvard Business School Press, Cambridge, MA.

Bartlett, C. A. and S. Ghoshal (1993). 'Beyond the M-Form: Toward a managerial theory of the firm', *Strategic Management Journal*, Winter Special Issue, 14, pp. 23–46.

Birkinshaw, J. M. (May–June 1995). 'Is the country manager an endangered species?', *International Executive*, pp. 279–302.

Bower, J. L. (1970). *Managing the Resource Allocation Process*. Irwin, Homewood, IL.

Brandt, W. K. and J. M. Hulbert (Winter 1977). 'Headquarters guidance in marketing strategy in the multinational subsidiary', *Columbia Journal of World Business*, 12, pp. 7–14.

Burgelman, R. A. (1983a). 'A process model of internal corporate venturing in the diversified major firm', *Administrative Science Quarterly*, 28, pp. 223–244.

Burgelman, R. A. (1983b). 'A model of the interaction of strategic behavior, corporate context and the concept of strategy', *Academy of Management Review*, 8(1), pp. 61–70.

Burgelman, R. A. (1991). 'Intraorganizational ecology of strategy making and organizational adaptation: Theory and field research', *Organization Science*, 2(3), pp. 239–62.

Burns, T. J. and G. Stalker (1961). *The Management of Innovation*. Tavistock Publications, London.

Cohen, L. E. and R. Machalek (1988). 'A general theory of expropriative crime: An evolutionary ecological model', *American Journal of Sociology*, 94, pp. 465–501.

Covin, J. G. and D. P. Slevin (Fall 1991). 'A conceptual model of entrepreneurship as firm behavior', *Entrepreneurship Theory and Practice*, pp. 7–25.

Cray, D. (1984). 'Control and coordination in multinational corporations', *Journal of International Business Studies*, 15(3), pp. 85–98.

Crookell, H. H. (1986). 'Specialization and international competitiveness'. In H. Etemad and L. S. Dulude (eds), *Managing the Multinational Subsidiary*. Croom Helm, London, pp. 102–111.

Damanpour, F. (1991). 'Organizational innovation: A meta-analysis of effects of determinants and moderators', *Academy of Management Journal*, 34, pp. 555–90.

D'Cruz, J. R. (1986). 'Strategic management of subsidiaries'. In H. Etemad and L. S. Dulude (eds), *Managing the Multinational Subsidiary*. Croom Helm, London, pp. 75–89.

Drucker, P. (1985). *Innovation and Entrepreneurship*. Harper & Row, New York.

Etemad, H. and L. S. Dulude (1986). *Managing the Multinational Subsidiary*. Croom Helm, London.

Forsgren, M. and J. Johanson (1992). *Managing Networks in International Business*. Gordon & Breach, Philadelphia, PA.

Galbraith, J. (Winter 1982). 'Designing the innovating organization', *Organizational Dynamics*, pp. 5–25.

Galunic, D. C. and K. M. Eisenhardt (1994). 'The evolution of intracorporate domains: Division charter losses in high-technology, multidivisional corporations', working paper, INSEAD.

Ghoshal, S. (1986). 'The Innovative Multinational: A Differentiated Network of Organizational Roles and Management Processes', unpublished doctoral dissertation, Harvard Business School.

Ghoshal, S. and C. A. Bartlett (1988). 'Creation, adoption and diffusion of innovations by subsidiaries of multinational corporations', *Journal of International Business Studies*, 19(3), pp. 365–88.

Ghoshal, S. and C. A. Bartlett (1991). 'The multinational corporation as an interorganizational network', *Academy of Management Review*, 15(4), pp. 603–25.

Ghoshal, S. and C. A. Bartlett (1994). 'Linking organizational context and managerial action: The dimensions of quality of management', *Strategic Management Journal*, Summer Special Issue, 15, pp. 91–112.

Ghoshal, S. and N. Nohria (1989). 'Internal differentiation within multinational corporations', *Strategic Management Journal*, 10(4), pp. 323–37.

Ginsberg, A. and M. Hay (1995). 'Confronting the challenges of corporate entrepreneurship: Guidelines for venture managers', *European Management Journal*, 12(4), pp. 382–9.

Gupta, A. K. and V. Govindarajan (1991). 'Knowledge flows and the structure of control within multinational corporations', *Academy of Management Review*, 16(4), pp. 768–92.

Guth, W. D. and A. Ginsberg (1990). 'Guest editors introduction: Corporate entrepreneurship', *Strategic Management Journal*, Summer Special Issue, 11, pp. 5–15.

Halal, W. E. (1993). *Internal Markets*. Wiley, New York.

Harrigan, K. R. (1983). 'Innovation within overseas subsidiaries', *Journal of Business Strategy*, pp. 47–55.

Hedlund, G. (1981). 'Autonomy of subsidiaries and formalization of headquarters–subsidiary relationships in Swedish MNCs'. In L. Otterbeck (ed.), *The Management of Headquarters–Subsidiary Relations in Multinational Corporations*. Gower Publishing, Aldershot, Hampshire, U.K., pp. 27–76.

Hedlund, G. (1986). 'The hypermodern MNC: A heterarchy? *Human Resource Management*, 25, pp. 9–36.

Hedlund, G. and J. Ridderstråle (1992). 'Towards the N-Form corporation: Exploitation and creation in the MNC', working paper, Stockholm School of Business, RP 92/15.

Howell, J. M. and C. A. Higgins (1990). 'Champions of technological innovation', *Administrative Science Quarterly*, 35, pp. 317–41.

Humes, S. (1993). *Managing the Multinational Corporation: Confronting the Global – Local Dilemma*. Prentice-Hall International, Hertfordshire.

Jarillo, J.-C. and J. I. Martinez (1990). 'Different roles for subsidiaries: The case of multinational corporations in Spain', *Strategic Management Journal*, 11(7), pp. 506–12.

Johanson, J. and J.-E. Vahlne (1977). 'The internationalization process of the firm: A model of knowledge development and increasing foreign market commitments', *Journal of International Business Studies* 1, pp. 23–32.

Kanter, R. M. (July–August 1982). 'The middle manager as innovator', *Harvard Business Review*, pp. 95–105.

Kanter, R. M. (1985). *The Change Masters*. Simon & Schuster, New York.

Kanter, R. M. (1986). 'Supporting innovation and venture development in established companies', *Journal of Business Venturing*, 1(1), pp. 47–60.

Kirzner, I. M. (1973). *Competition and Entrepreneurship*. University of Chicago Press, Chicago, IL.

Kuratko, D. F., R. V. Montagno and J. S. Hornsby (1990). 'Developing an intrapreneurial assessment instrument for an effective corporate entrepreneurial environment', *Strategic Management Journal*, Summer Special Issue, 11, pp. 49–58.

Martinez, J. I. and J.-C. Jarillo (Fall 1989). 'The evolution of research on coordination mechanisms in multinational corporations', *Journal of International Business Studies*, pp. 489–514.

Meyer, A. D., A. S. Tsui and C. R. Hinings (1993). 'Configuration approaches to organizational analysis', *Academy of Management Journal*, 36(6), pp. 1175–95.

Miles, M. B. and M. Huberman (1984). *Qualitative Data Analysis: A Sourcebook of New Methods*. Sage, Newbury Park, CA.

Miller, D. (1983). 'The correlates of entrepreneurship in three types of firms', *Management Science*, 29, pp. 770–91.

Miller, D. (1986). 'Configurations of strategy and structure', *Strategic Management Journal*, 7(3), pp. 233–49.

Mintzberg, H., D. Raisinghani and A. Theoret (1976). 'The structure of unstructured decision processes', *Administrative Science Quarterly*, 21, pp. 246–74.

455

Morrison, A. J. (1990). *Strategies in Global Industries: How U.S. Businesses Compete*. Quorum Books, Westport, CT.

Negandhi, A. R. and B. R. Baliga (1981). 'Internal functioning of American, German and Japanese multinational corporations'. In L. Otterbeck (ed.), *The Management of Headquarters–Subsidiary Relations in Multinational Corporations*. Gower Publishing, Aldershot, Hampshire, U.K., pp. 106–20.

Nunnally, J. C. (1978). *Psychometric Theory* (2nd ed.) McGraw-Hill, New York.

Nutt, P. (1993). 'The formulation processes and tactics used in organizational decision-making', *Organization Science*, 4(2), pp. 226–51.

Parkhe, A. (1993). ' "Messy" research, methodological predispositions, and theory development in international joint ventures', *Academy of Management Review*, 18(2), pp. 227–68.

Penrose, E. T. (1959). *The Theory of the Growth of the Firm*. Basil Blackwell, Oxford.

Perlmutter, H. V. (January–February 1969). 'The tortuous evolution of the multinational corporation', *Columbia Journal of World Business*, pp. 9–18.

Perreault, W. D. and L. E. Leigh (1989). 'Reliability of nominal data based on qualitative judgements', *Journal of Marketing Research*, XXVI, pp. 135–48.

Peters, T. J. and R. H. Waterman (1982). *In Search of Excellence*. Harper & Row, New York.

Picard, J. (1980). 'Organizational structures and integrative devices in European multinational corporations', *Columbia Journal of World Business*, 15, pp. 30–5.

Pinchott, G. III (1985). *Intrapreneuring*. Harper & Row, New York.

Porter, M. E. (1986). *Competition in Global Industries*. Harvard Business School Press, Boston, MA.

Poynter, T. A. and A. M. Rugman (Autumn 1982). 'World product mandates: How will multinationals respond?' *Business Quarterly*, pp. 54–61.

Prahalad, C. K. and Y. L. Doz (Summer 1981). 'An approach to Strategic Control in MNCs', *Sloan Management Review*, pp. 5–13.

Quelch, J. A. (1992). 'The new country managers', *McKinsey Quarterly*, pp. 156–165.

Quinn, J. B. (1985). 'Managing innovation: Controlled chaos', *Harvard Business Review*, 63(3), pp. 73–84.

Roth, K. and A. J. Morrison (1992). 'Implementing global strategy: Characteristics of global subsidiary mandates', *Journal of International Business Studies*, 23(4), pp. 715–36.

Safarian, A. E. (1966). *Foreign Ownership of Canadian Industry*. McGraw-Hill, Toronto.

Sathe, V. (1985). 'Managing an entrepreneurial dilemma: Nurturing entrepreneurship and control in large corporations'. In J. A. Hornaday, E. B. Shils, J. A. Timmons and K. H. Vesper (eds), *Frontiers of Entrepreneurship Research*. Babson College, Wellesley, MA, pp. 636–57.

Schollhammer, H. (1982). 'Internal corporate entrepreneurship'. In D. Sexton and K. H. Vesper (eds), *Encyclopedia of Entrepreneurship*. Prentice-Hall, Englewood Cliffs, NJ, pp. 209–23.

Schumpeter, J. A. (1934). *The Theory of Economic Development*. Harvard University Press, Cambridge, MA.

Science Council of Canada (1980). *Multinationals and Industrial Strategy: The Role of World Product Mandates*. Science Council of Canada, Supply and Services Canada, Ottawa.

Stevenson, H. H. and J.-C. Jarillo (1990). 'A paradigm of entrepreneurship: Entrepreneurial management', *Strategic Management Journal*, Summer Special Issue, 11, pp. 17–27.

Stopford, J. M. and C. W. F. Baden-Fuller (1994). 'Creating corporate entrepreneurship', *Strategic Management Journal*, 15(7), pp. 521–36.

Sykes, H. B. (1986). 'The anatomy of a corporate venturing program: Factors influencing success', *Journal of Business Venturing*, 1, pp. 275–93.

Vernon, R. (May 1966). 'International investment and international trade in the product cycle', *Quarterly Journal of Economics*, pp. 191–207.

Vernon, R. (1979). 'The product cycle hypothesis in a new international environment, *Oxford Bulletin of Economics and Statistics*', 41, pp. 255–67.

White, R. E. and T. A. Poynter (Summer 1984). 'Strategies for foreign-owned subsidiaries in Canada', *Business Quarterly*, pp. 59–69.

White, R. E. and T. A. Poynter (Autumn 1990). 'Achieving worldwide advantage with the horizontal organization', *Business Quarterly*, pp. 55–60.

Yin, R. K. (1984). *Case Study Research*. Sage, Beverly Hills, CA.

PART VII

POSTSCRIPT

INTRODUCTION

Strategy as a subject does not have clear boundaries. It has to generate theory capable of informing practice in dynamic rather than static contexts. We have looked at and discussed a variety of strategy research, together with the development of new theory for emergent organizational issues. These have included: ethics in strategy, corporate social responsibility, knowledge-based organization structures, structures for managing innovation and learning, and strategies and structures to enable positive corporate parenting both in MNCs and in other organisations. We have argued that strategy is context- and culture-specific, usually contingent to be effective and that many organizations now operate as part of larger networks of resources and capabilities. That may be as buyer, supplier, competitor, complementor (other firms from which customers buy complementary products and services) or alliance partner, both across corporations and across geographic boundaries.

The final three chapters in Part VII complete our look at strategy by critically discussing some of the assumptions built into traditional strategic thinking. We do this not in a negative way but because it is important always to ask questions about the ideas and concepts within the strategy mainstream. We will look in turn at failure, at chaos, and finally at the lack of self-criticism within mainstream strategy itself.

The sub-title of Miller's article says it all (Chapter 24): 'How Exceptional Companies Bring about their Own Downfall'. He calls this 'The Icarus Paradox' after the boy Icarus, in Greek mythology, who flew too high. As Icarus flew closer to the sun, his wings, made of wax, melted and let him fall into the sea and drown. So it happens also with many great companies. The paradox is that their strengths become their weaknesses: what had been confidence turns into complacency; the search for growth turns into a never-ending spiral of unrelated acquisition, and so on. Flexibility becomes rigidity, and, in exactly the ways that Johnson's cultural web helps us to understand, rituals and routines replace innovation. Miller uses some wonderfully evocative phrases to capture this paradox:

> organizations turn into their 'evil twins' – extreme versions or caricatures of their former selves.

He is explaining that success can lead to failure, because the very characteristics that contributed to the success, are the ones that trap the firm in decline and failure. Miller suggests many ways that organizations can combat this strategic myopia or tunnel vision. He especially champions the need for self-reflection to help managers think deeply about the direction of their organization. He talks of 'mirrors' that managers can develop to aid this self-reflection and intelligence-gathering to become less self-centred. This is a very important lesson to learn at the end of a book about strategy. Too often, ideas and frameworks seem to imply only recipes for success. Instead, Miller warns us that:

> all leaders must operate with the firm assumption that one day they will have to go to war with the past.

Although chaos theory and complexity theory were briefly mentioned in the Introduction as part of the recent new dimensions of strategic thinking, only now are we about to discuss them further. Pascale (Chapter 25) has written extensively about organizations as 'complex adaptive systems' from which four principles emerge. First, for complex adaptive systems, equilibrium is a precursor to death. Second, they exhibit a capacity for self-organization (arising from clusters of intelligence) and for emergent complexity (generated by the propensity of simple structures to generate infinite variety). The analogy he uses for this phenomenon is to think of life on earth as an example of emergent and escalating complexity in action. Third, they tend to move towards chaos when given complex tasks, but this 'bounded instability' is conducive to evolution. Fourth, one cannot direct a living system, one can only disturb it. They, therefore, have *weak links between cause and effect*. It is that final characteristic that most people think of first in relation to complexity theory; that single causes may have multiple and unpredictable effects, (as with the global consequences of butterfly wings beating quietly in Amazonian rainforests).

So what has this to do with strategy? Pascale explains that nothing novel can emerge from systems with high degrees of order and stability (e.g. regulated industries). Similarly, completely chaotic systems are too formless to survive (e.g. a stampede). It is at the boundary between rigidity and total random-ness that regeneration and renewal can occur. Miller tells us that within living systems there is only a weak connection between cause and effect. That is surely familiar to every manager whose strategic implementation plan just does not seem to have worked quite as intended. This also reflects Mintzberg's unrealized strategies. What Pascale is trying to tell us is that as strategists we must never assume that a particular input will directly lead to a particular output. Organizations and the people within them are complex adaptive systems embedded around each other. The potential for chaos and complexity is immense, but the potential for adaptation and renewal is also immense. Pascale recom-mends that managers, as strategic leaders, need to start letting go of many of the old controls on which they have traditionally depended, even though they have never really worked.

> What you don't realize until you do it [let go] is that you may, in fact, have more controls but in a different fashion. You get more feedback than before, you learn more than before, you know more through your own people what's going on in the marketplace.

Jones (Chapter 26) closes our review of current strategic thinking with a critical discussion of ideas and approaches within strategy. He suggests that the discipline of strategy fulfils a managerial need for legitimacy, by providing seemingly rational and objective criteria for their exercise of the power of decision-making in corporations. He aims to encourage a healthy debate about strategy and to help us to challenge our own ideas and assumptions on many issues within strategy. He reviews many schools of strategic management thinking, beyond the four major schools described by Whittington and those mentioned in the Introduction. Jones contrasts their assumptions and prescriptions in some detail. It is possible that strategies are 'not chosen; they are programmed', since they are the way in which managers 'try to simplify and order' a complex world. Strategic planning and strategy reviews, offer comforting ritual that Jones describes as 'managerial security blankets in a hostile world'.

Particularly useful are Jones' discussions of what is wrong with strategy. He presents some of the problems that arise from the assumptions that strategy makes. These include the fact that an increasing amount of management education does not automatically lead to improved eco-nomic performance; and the difficulties that academics and managers have in valuing equally the practical or experiential, and the theoretical. He also provides a stimulating analogy of strategy with drama: each has two 'audiences': those who study it, and those who perform or do it. Strategy is largely a 'performance' art. It matters how well it is performed and its performance has serious widespread consequences for all our lives.

I have a genuine hope that the concepts, ideas and intellectual challenges contained in these articles will, at the very least, bring your strategy ideas up-to-date. At best, however, these read-ings should encourage you to review your own style of strategic thinking and find it enriched.

24

The Icarus Paradox: How Exceptional Companies Bring about their Own Downfall

Danny Miller

The fabled Icarus of Greek mythology is said to have flown so high, so close to the sun, that his artificial wax wings melted and he plunged to his death in the Aegean Sea. The power of Icarus's wings gave rise to the abandon that so doomed him. The paradox, of course, is that his greatest asset led to his demise. And that same paradox applies to many outstanding companies: their victories and their strengths so often seduce them into the excesses that cause their downfall. Success leads to specialization and exaggeration, to confidence and complacency, to dogma and ritual. This general tendency, its causes, and how to manage it are what this article is all about.

It is ironic that many of the most dramatically successful organizations are so prone to failure. The histories of outstanding companies demonstrate this time and again. In fact, it appears that when taken to excess the same things that drive success – focused, tried-and-true strategies, confident leadership, galvanized corporate cultures, and especially the interplay of all these elements – also cause decline. Robust, superior organizations evolve into flawed purebreds; they move from rich character to exaggerated caricature as all subtlety, all nuance, is gradually lost.

Many outstanding organizations follow such paths of deadly momentum – time-bomb trajectories of attitudes, policies, and events that lead to falling sales, plummeting profits, even bankruptcy. These companies extend and amplify the strategies to which they credit their success. Productive attention to detail, for instance, turns into an obsession with minutiae; rewarding innovation escalates into gratuitous invention; and measured growth becomes unbridled expansion. In contrast, activities that were merely de-emphasized – not viewed as integral to the recipe for success – are virtually extinguished. Modest marketing deteriorates into lackluster promotion and inadequate distribution; tolerable engineering becomes shoddy design. The result: strategies become less balanced. They center more and more around a single core strength that is amplified unduly while other aspects are forgotten almost entirely. Such changes are not limited to strategy. The heroes who shaped the winning formula gain adulation and absolute authority, while others drop to third-class citizenship. An increasingly monolithic culture impels firms to focus on an ever smaller set of considerations and to rally around a narrowing path to victory. Reporting relationships, roles, programs, decision-making processes – even target markets – come to reflect and serve the central strategy and nothing else. And policies are converted into rigid laws and rituals by avidly embraced credos and ideologies. By then, organizational learning has ceased, tunnel vision rules, and flexibility is lost.

This riches-to-rags scenario seduces some of our most acclaimed corporations; and in our research on outstanding companies we have found four principal examples of it, four very common 'trajectories' of decline (see Figure 24.1).

Types :	CRAFTSMAN	FOCUSING →	TINKERER
Strategy :	Quality leadership		Technical tinkering
Goals :	Quality		Perfection
Culture :	Engineering		Technocracy
Structure :	Orderly		Rigid
Types :	BUILDER	VENTURING →	IMPERIALIST
Strategy :	Building		Overexpansion
Goals :	Growth		Grandeur
Culture :	Entrepreneurial		Gamesman
Structure :	Divisionalized		Fractured
Types :	PIONEER	INVENTING →	ESCAPIST
Strategy :	Innovation		Hi-tech escapism
Goals :	Science-for-society		Technical utopia
Culture :	R&D		Think tank
Structure :	Organic		Chaotic
Types :	SALESMEN	DECOUPLING →	DRIFTER
Strategy :	Brilliant marketing		Bland proliferation
Goals :	Market-share		Quarterly numbers
Culture :	Organization man		Insipid and political
Structure :	Modestly decentralized		Oppressively bureaucratic

Figure 24.1 The four trajectories

The focusing trajectory takes punctilious, quality-driven CRAFTSMEN organizations with their masterful engineers and airtight operations, and turns them into rigidly controlled, detail-obsessed TINKERERS – firms whose insular, technocratic monocultures alienate customers with perfect, but irrelevant, offerings.

The venturing trajectory converts growth-driven, entrepreneurial BUILDERS – companies managed by imaginative leaders and creative planning and financial staffs – into impulsive, greedy IMPERIALISTS who severely overtax their resources by expanding helter-skelter into businesses they know nothing about.

The inventing trajectory takes PIONEERS with unexcelled R&D departments, flexible think tank operations, and state-of-the-art products, and transforms them into utopian ESCAPISTS run by a cult of chaos-loving scientists who squander resources in the pursuit of hopelessly grand and futuristic inventions.

Finally, the decoupling trajectory transforms SALESMEN – organizations with unparalleled marketing skills, prominent brand names, and broad markets – into aimless, bureaucratic DRIFTERS whose sales fetish obscures design issues, and who produce a stale and disjointed line of 'me too' offerings.

These four illustrative trajectories have trapped many of the firms we studied, including IBM, Polaroid, Procter & Gamble, Texas Instruments, ITT, Chrysler, Dome Petroleum, Apple Computer, A&P, General Motors, Sears, Digital Equipment, Caterpillar Tractor, Montgomery Ward, Eastern Airlines, Litton Industries, and Disney.

A CASE HISTORY

The glorious but ultimately tragic history of ITT demonstrates well the course of the venturing trajectory. Harold Geneen was a manager's manager, a universally acclaimed financial wizard of unsurpassed energy, and the CEO and grand inquisitor of the diversified mega-conglomerate ITT. It was Geneen, the entrepreneurial accountant, who took a ragtag set of stale, mostly European telecommunications operations and forged them into a cohesive corporate entity. With his accountant's scalpel, he weeded out weak operations; and with his entrepreneur's wand he revived the most promising ones. He installed state-of-the-art management information systems to monitor the burgeoning businesses on an ongoing basis. And he built a head office corps of young managers to help him control his growing empire and identify opportunities for creative diversification.

At first, this diversification paid off handsomely as it so aptly exploited the financial, organizational, and turnaround talents of Geneen and his crack staff. Many acquisitions were purchased at bargain prices and most beautifully complemented ITT's existing operations. Moreover, a divisional structure in which managers were responsible for the profitability of their units provided incentive for local initiative. Geneen's legendary control and information systems – with frequent appraisal meetings and divisional accountants reporting directly to the head office – ensured that most problems would be detected early and corrected.

Unfortunately, ITT's success at diversification and controlled decentralization led to too much more of the same. Their skills at acquisition and control made Geneen and his staff ever more confident that they could master complexity. So diversification went from a selective tactic to an ingrained strategy to a fanatical religion; decentralization and head office control were transformed from managerial tools into an all-consuming, lock-step way of life. The corporate culture worshipped growth, and it celebrated, lavishly paid, and quickly promoted only those who could attain it. The venturing trajectory had gotten under way, and the momentum behind it was awesome.

To achieve rapid growth, Geneen pursued ever more ambitious acquisitions that were further afield from existing operations. From 1967 to 1970, just six of ITT's larger acquisitions – Sheraton, Levitt, Rayonier, Continental Baking, Grinnell and Canteen – brought in combined sales of $1.8 billion; a seventh, Hartford Fire, one of the largest property and casualty insurers in the U.S., was about to be added. Loads of debt had to be issued to fund these acquisitions. In less than 10 years, Geneen the imperialist bought a staggering 100 companies, a proliferation so vast it exceeded the complexity and scope of many nation states – 250 profit centers in all were set up. Geneen, quite simply, had created the biggest conglomerate on earth, encompassing 375,000 employees in 80 countries by 1977.

Even Geneen and his sophisticated staff troops, with all their mastery of detail and their status as information system gurus, could not manage, control, or even understand so vast an empire. But they tried, meddling in the details of their divisions, and pressing home the need to meet abstract and often irrelevant financial standards. Political games took place in which head office controllers would try to impress Geneen by making the divisions look bad. Divisional executives, in turn, would try to fool the controllers. It got to where more than 75 percent of divisional managers' schedules were taken up preparing budgets and going to meetings at the head office, leaving them little time to direct their own units.

This obsession with acquisitions and financial control detracted from the substance of divisional strategies. The product lines of many units were neglected and became stale. Return on capital fell, and by the late 1970s many of the divisions were experiencing major operating problems. A subsequent CEO, Rand Araskog, had to sell off more than 100 units in an attempt to revive the company, which shrunk the workforce by more than 60 percent. The great ITT had become a flabby agglomeration of gangrenous parts.

The general pattern is clear. Over time, ITT's success – or more specifically, its managers' reactions to success – caused it to amplify its winning strategy and to forget about everything else. It moved from sensible and measured expansion to prolific and groundless diversification; from sound accounting and financial control to oppressive dominance by head office hit men; and from invigorating divisionalization to destructive factionalism. The substance of basic businesses – their product lines and markets – was lost in a sea of financial abstractions. By concentrating exclusively upon what it did best, ITT pushed strategies, cultures, and structures to dangerous extremes, and failed to develop in other areas. Greatness had paved the way to excess and decline as ITT the BUILDER became ITT the IMPERIALIST.

CONFIGURATION AND MOMENTUM

The example of ITT reveals two notions that surfaced again and again when we looked at outstanding companies. We call these notions configuration and momentum.

Outstanding corporations are a bit like beautiful poems or sonatas – their parts or elements fit together harmoniously to express a theme. They are perhaps even more akin to living systems whose organs are intimately linked and tightly coordinated. Although organizations are less unified than organisms, they too constitute configurations: complex, evolving systems of mutually supportive elements organized around stable central themes. We found that once a theme emerges – a core mission or a central strategy, for example – a whole slew of routines, policies, tasks, and structures develop to implement and reinforce it. It is like seeding a crystal in a super-saturated solution: once a thematic particle is dropped into solution, the crystal begins to form naturally around it. Themes may derive from leaders' visions, the values and concerns of powerful departments, even common industry practices.

ITT's configuration, like all others, had a central theme and a 'cast of players' – human, ideological, strategic, and structural – that completed the scenario. The theme was 'rapid growth through expansion'; the cast of players included an entrepreneurial, ambitious CEO with a strategy of diversification and acquisition, a powerful financial staff who dominated because they could best implement this strategy, elaborate information systems and sophisticated controls, and even decentralized profit centers that infused expertise into the far-flung divisions amassed by diversification. All these 'players' complemented each other and were essential to the enactment of the play. And as with all configurations, the parts only make sense with reference to the whole BUILDER constellation.

Our research uncovered a number of exceptionally common but quite different configurations associated with stellar performance: BUILDERS, CRAFTSMEN, PIONEERS, and SALESMEN, each subject to its own evolutionary trajectory.

Our second finding showed that organizations keep extending their themes and configurations until something earthshaking stops them: a process we call momentum. Firms perpetuate and amplify one particular motif above all others as they suppress its variants. They choose one set of goals, values, and champions and focus more and more tightly around them. The powerful get more powerful; others become disenfranchised as firms move first toward consistency, and then toward obsession and excess. Organizations turn into their 'evil twins' – extreme versions or caricatures of their former selves.

Once ITT began to diversify, for example, it accelerated its policy because it seemed successful; because it was very much in line with the dreams and visions of what leaders and their powerful financial staffs wanted; and because it was undergirded by a vast set of policies and programs. Similarly, having implemented their financial control systems, ITT continued to hone and develop them. After all, these systems were demanded by the expanding and diverse operations; they were favored by the growing staff of accountants; and they were the only way top managers could exert control over existing operations and still have time to scout out new acquisitions.

Momentum is also contagious and leads to a vicious cycle of escalation. As diversification increased at ITT, so did the size of the head office staff and the time spent on divisional meetings. The staff's role was to generate still more attractive candidates for diversification, and that's what they did. Diversification increased still further, requiring even larger legions of accountants and financial staff. And so the spiral continued. In short, momentum, by extending the BUILDER configuration, led to the dangerous excesses of IMPERIALISM.

Outstanding organization, it seems, extend their orientations until they reach dangerous extremes; their momentum issues in common trajectories of decline. And because successful types differ so much from one another, so will their trajectories.

THE TRAJECTORIES

Our four trajectories emerged in a study we conducted of outstanding companies. Our earlier research identified four very common, wonderfully coherent configurations possessing powerful strategic advantages. We studied the long-term evolution of outstanding firms conforming to each of these types by tracking them for many years. The types are described in Figures 24.1 and 24.2.

CRAFTSMEN, BUILDERS, PIONEERS, and SALESMEN were all susceptible to their own trajectories, and firms of a given type followed remarkably parallel paths, albeit at differing speeds. For purposes of simple comparison, our four strategies are classified in Figure 24.3 along two dimensions: scope is the range of products and target markets; change is the variability of methods and offerings. Excellent businesses are driven toward extremes along both of these dimensions (among others). Take scope. Firms that excel by focusing on one product or on a precisely targeted market ultimately come to rely on too narrow a set of customers, products, and issues. Conversely, firms that thrive by aggressively diversifying often become too

	CRAFTSMEN	BUILDERS
Strategies	Quality Leadership	Expansion Diversification Acquisition
Product-Market Scope	Focused	Broad
Strategic Change	Stable	Dynamic
Key Goals	Quality	Growth
Dominant Depts	Operation, Production, & Engineering	Planning & Control; Finance
Structure	Bureaucracy; Many controls	Divisional Profit Centers
Trajectory	Focusing	Venturing
Destination	TINKERER	IMPERIALIST
	PIONEERS	SALESMEN
Strategies	Differentiation via Innovation	Marketing Differentiation
Product-Market Scope	Focused	Broad
Strategic Change	Dynamic	Stable
Key Goals	Technical Progress	Market share
Dominant Depts	R&D	Marketing
Structure	Organic, Flexible	Divisional Bureaucracy
Trajectory	Inventing	Decoupling
Destination	ESCAPIST	DRIFTER

Figure 24.2 The configurations compared

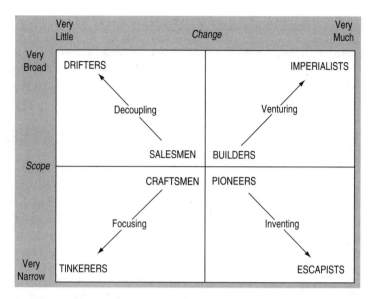

Figure 24.3 The configurations and trajectories arrayed

complex, fragmented, and thinly spread to be effective. The same tendencies apply to strategic change as dynamic firms move toward hyperactivity, and conservative ones inch toward stagnation.

CRAFTSMEN TO TINKERERS: THE FOCUSING TRAJECTORY

Digital Equipment Corporation made the highest quality computers in the world. Founder Ken Olsen and his brilliant team of design engineers invented the minicomputer, a cheaper, more flexible alternative to its mainframe cousins. Olsen and his staff honed their minis until they absolutely could not be beat for quality and durability. Their VAX series gave birth to an industry legend in reliability, and the profits poured in.

But DEC turned into an engineering monoculture. Its engineers became idols, while its marketers and accountants were barely tolerated. Component specs and design standards were all managers understood. In fact, technological fine-tuning became such an all-consuming obsession that customers' needs for smaller machines, more economical products, and more user-friendly systems were ignored. The DEC PC, for example, bombed because it was so out of sync with the budgets, preferences, and shopping habits of potential users. Performance began to slip.

CRAFTSMEN are passionate about doing one thing incredibly well: Their leaders insist on producing the best products for the market, their engineers lose sleep over micrometers, and their quality control staff rules with an iron and unforgiving hand. Details count. Quality is the primary source of corporate pride; it gets rewarded and recognized and is by far the paramount competitive advantage. Indeed, it is what the whole corporate culture is based on. Shoddiness is a capital offense. (There is also a cost leader variant of the CRAFTSMAN.)

But in becoming TINKERERS, many CRAFTSMEN become parodies of themselves. They get so wrapped up in tiny technical details that they forget the purpose of quality is to attract

467

and satisfy buyers. Products become over-engineered but also over-priced; durable, but stale. Yesterday's excellent designs become today's sacrosanct anachronisms. And an ascendant engineering monoculture so engrosses itself in the minutiae of design and manufacture that it loses sight of the customer. Before long, marketing and R&D become the dull stepchildren, departments to be seen but not heard. Unfortunately, the bureaucratic strictures that grew up to enforce quality end up perpetuating the past and suppressing initiative.

BUILDERS TO IMPERIALISTS: THE VENTURING TRAJECTORY

Charles 'Tex' Thornton was a young Texas entrepreneur when he expanded a tiny microwave company into Litton Industries, one of the most successful high technology conglomerates of the 1960s. Sales mushroomed from $3 million to $1.8 billion in 12 years. By making selective and related acquisitions, Litton achieved an explosive rate of growth. Its excellent track record helped the company amass the resources needed to accelerate expansion still further.

But Litton began to stray too far from familiar areas, buying larger and more troubled firms in industries it barely understood. Administrative officers and control systems became overtaxed, debt became unwieldy, and a wide range of problems sprang up in the proliferating divisions. The downward spiral at Litton was no less dramatic than its ascent.

BUILDERS are growth-driven, entrepreneurial companies with a zeal for expansion, merger, and acquisition. They are dominated by aggressive managers with ambitious goals, immense energy, and an uncanny knack for spotting lucrative niches of the market. These leaders have the promotional skills to raise capital, the imagination and initiative to exploit magnificent growth opportunities, and the courage to take substantial risks. They are also master controllers who craft acute, sensitive information and incentive systems to rein in their burgeoning operations.

But many BUILDERS become IMPERIALISTS, addicted to careless expansion and greedy acquisition. In the headlong rush for growth they assume hair-raising risks, decimate resources, and incur scads of debt. They bite off more than they can chew, buying sick companies in businesses they do not understand. Structures and control systems become hopelessly overburdened. And a dominant culture of financial, legal, and accounting specialists further rivets managerial attention on expansion and diversification, while stealing time away from the production, marketing, and R&D matters that so desperately need to be addressed.

PIONEERS TO ESCAPISTS: THE INVENTING TRAJECTORY

By the mid-1960s, Control Data Corporation of Minneapolis had become the paramount designer of supercomputers. Chief engineer Seymour Cray, the preeminent genius in a field of masters, had several times fulfilled his ambition to build the world's most powerful computer. He secluded himself in his lab in Chippewa Falls, working closely with a small and trusted band of brilliant designers. Cray's state-of-the-art 6600 supercomputer was so advanced it caused wholesale firing at IBM, whose engineers had been taken completely off guard by their diminutive competitor.

CDC's early successes emboldened it to undertake new computer development projects that were increasingly futuristic, complex, and expensive. Substantial lead times, major investments, and high risks were entailed, and many bugs had to be purged from the systems. Long delays in delivery occurred and costs mushroomed. Science and invention had triumphed over an understanding of competition, customers, and production and capital requirements.

PIONEERS are R&D stars. Their chief goal is to be the first out with new products and new technology. Consistently at the vanguard of their industry, PIONEERS are, above all, inventors. Their major strengths are the scientific and technological capacities that reside within their brilliant R&D departments. Typically, PIONEERS are run by missionary leaders-in-lab-coats: PhDs with a desire to change the world. These executives assemble and empower superb research and design teams, and create a fertile, flexible structure for them to work in that promotes intensive collaboration and the free play of ideas.

Unfortunately, many PIONEERS get carried away by their coups of invention and become ESCAPISTS – firms in hot pursuit of technological nirvana. They introduce impractical, futuristic products that are too far ahead of their time, too expensive to develop, and too costly to buy. They also become their own toughest competitors, antiquating prematurely many of their offerings. Worse, marketing and production come to be viewed as necessary evils, and clients as unsophisticated nuisances. ESCAPISTS, it seems, become victims of a utopian culture forged by their domineering R&D wunderkinder. Their goals, which soar to hopelessly lofty heights, are expressed in technological terms, rather than market or economic terms. And their loose "adhocracy" structures might suffice to organize a few engineers working in a basement, but only serve to breed chaos in complex organizations.

SALESMEN TO DRIFTERS: THE DECOUPLING TRAJECTORY

Lynn Townsend ascended to the presidency of Chrysler at the youthful age of 42. He was known to be a financial wizard and a master marketer. 'Sales aren't just made; sales are pushed,' Townsend would say. In his first five years as president, he doubled Chrysler's US market share and tripled its international one. He also conceived the five-year, 50,000-mile warranty. But Townsend made very few radical changes in Chrysler's products. Mostly he just marketed aggressively with forceful selling and promotion, and sporty styling.

Chrysler's success with its image-over-substance strategy resulted in increasing neglect of engineering and production. It prompted a proliferation of new models that could capitalize on the marketing program. But this made operations very complex and uneconomical. It also contributed to remote management-by-numbers, bureaucracy, and turf battles. Soon strategies lost focus and direction, and profits began to plummet.

SALESMEN are marketers *par excellence*. That is their core strength. Using intensive advertising, attractive styling and packaging, attentive service, and penetrating distribution channels, they create and nurture high-profile brand names that make them major players within their industries. To place managers in especially close contact with their broad markets, SALESMEN are partitioned into manageable profit centers, each one of which is responsible for a major product line.

Unfortunately, SALESMEN tend to become unresponsive DRIFTERS. They begin to substitute packaging, advertising, and aggressive distribution for good design and competent manufacturing. Managers begin to believe they can sell anything as they concoct a mushrooming proliferation of bland, copycat offerings. This growing diversity of product lines and divisions makes it tough for top managers to master the substance of all their businesses. So they rely increasingly on elaborate bureaucracy to replace the hands-on management of products and manufacturing. Gradually DRIFTERS become unwieldy, sluggish behemoths whose turf battles and factionalism impede adaptation. In scenarios that come straight from Kafka, the simplest problems take months, even years to address. Ultimately, the leader is decoupled from his company, the company from its market, and product lines and divisions from each other.

FORCES TO WATCH

In considering these four trajectories, you might want to keep in mind some of the 'subtexts': the hidden causes at work behind the scenes that drive every one of them.

Sources of momentum

Leadership Traps. Failure teaches leaders valuable lessons, but good results only reinforce their preconceptions and tether them more firmly to their 'tried and true' recipes. Success also makes managers overconfident, more prone to excess and neglect, and more given to shaping strategies to reflect their own preferences rather than those of the customers. Some leaders may even be spoilt by success – taking too much to heart their litany of conquests and the praise of their idolizing subordinates. They become conceited and obstinate, resenting challenges and ultimately isolating themselves from reality.

Monolithic Cultures and Skills. The culture of the exceptional organization often becomes dominated by a few star departments and their ideologies. For example, because CRAFTSMEN see quality as the source of success, the engineering departments who create it and are its guarantors acquire ever more influence. This erodes the prominence of other departments and concerns, making the corporate culture more monolithic, more intolerant, and more avid in its pursuit of one single goal.

To make matters worse, attractive rewards pull talented managers toward rich, dominant departments, and bleed them away from less august units. The organization's skill set soon becomes spotty and unbalanced, compromising versatility and the capacity for reorientation.

Power and Politics. Dominant managers and departments resist redirecting the strategies and policies that have given them so much power. Change, they reason, would erode their status, their resources, and their influence over rival executives and departments. The powerful, then, are more likely to reinforce and amplify prevailing strategies than to change them.

Structural Memories. Organizations, like people, have memories. They implement successful strategies using systems, routines, and programs. The more established and successful the strategy, the more deeply embedded it will be in such programs, and the more it will be implemented routinely, automatically, and unquestioningly. Indeed, even the premises for decision making – the cues that elicit attention and the standards used to evaluate events and actions – will be controlled by routines. Yesterday's programs will shape today's perceptions and give rise to tomorrow's actions. Again, continuity triumphs.

Configuration and momentum

The qualities of leadership, culture, skills, power, and structure are by no means independent. They configure and interact to play out a central theme. Over time, organizations gradually adhere more consistently to that theme – so much so that an adaptable, intelligent company can turn into a specialized, monolithic machine.

Take the PIONEER. Successful innovations reward and empower their creators, who will recruit and promote in their own images. The resulting horde of 'R&D types' then set up the flexible structures and design projects they find so invigorating. This further encourages innovation and the search for clients who value it. Meanwhile, other departments begin to lose influence and resources, and their skills diminish. So cultures become monolithic, strategies more focused, skills more uneven and specialized, and blind spots more common. The firm has embarked on the inventing trajectory.

'Chain reactions' such as this make an organization more focused and cohesive. At first, this greatly benefits the firm. But ultimately, concentration becomes obsession. All prominent features become exaggerated, while everything else – auxiliary skills, supplementary values, essential substrategies, and constructive debate – vanishes.

THE PARADOX OF ICARUS

This brings us to the Icarus paradox that traps so many outstanding firms: Overconfident, complacent executives extend the very factors that contributed to success to the point where they cause decline. There are really two aspects to the paradox. The first is that success can lead to failure. It may engender overconfidence, carelessness, and other bad habits that produce excesses in strategies, leadership, culture, and structures. Icarus flew so well that he got cocky and overambitious.

The second aspect of the paradox is that many of the preceding causes of decline – galvanized cultures, efficient routines and programs, and orchestrated configurations – were also initially the causes of success. Or conversely, the very causes of success, when extended, may become the causes of failure. It is simply a case of 'too much of a good thing.' For example, a focused strategy can produce wonderful competitive advantages as it mobilizes resources so efficiently; but when taken too far, it becomes narrow obsession. Favoring certain departments and skills creates distinctive competencies and galvanizes effort, but it can also produce intolerant monocultures. Programs and routines promote efficiency and simplify coordination, but they can also blind managers and mire the organization in its past. Above all, cohesive, orchestrated configurations are indispensable for companies to operate effectively, but they also create myopia. Icarus's wings and his courage were strengths, but when pushed to the limit they became deadly. Unfortunately, it is very hard sometimes to distinguish between the focus, harmony, and passionate dedication necessary for outstanding performance, and the excesses and extremes that lead to decline.

COMBATING THE PERILS OF SUCCESS

It is time now to turn from problems to cures – to suggest ways of avoiding the trajectories, of fending off the myopia induced by cohesive configurations. We will describe the 'mirrors' managers can develop: the capacities for self-reflection and intelligence gathering that may help guard against excess and irrelevance.

Managers must confront a poignant paradox: Excellence demands focus, dedication, and cohesive configuration. But these are precisely the things that give rise to momentum, narrowness, complacency, and excess. So what to do?

Some successful organizations have adopted a few potentially powerful methods for avoiding problems. They:

- build thematic, cohesive configurations; but they also
- encourage their managers to reflect broadly and deeply about the direction of the company.

In other words, they act telescopically, but reflect using mirrors. Moreover, they:

- scan widely and monitor performance assiduously; and,
- where possible, they temporarily de-couple renewal activities from established operations, at least for a while.

Thematic configurations

It is tempting to use the sources of momentum discussed above to derive the prescriptions for avoidance. Are world-views too confining? Then dismantle them. Are cultures too monolithic? Then open them up. Are configurations too cohesive to allow meaningful adaptation? Then throw them into question, inject noise into the system, and make disruptive changes. Unfortunately, employing these remedies too freely might destroy the concentration and synergy so necessary for success.

In humans, greatness demands dedication and focus – a 'living on the edge' quality. Prodigies in the arts are not known for their well-rounded lives. Brilliant scientists and entrepreneurs give up much of their family life. And superb college athletes are too preoccupied with training to excel at their studies. To do anything really well requires giving some things up. Because there is within us all only so much talent and energy, it must be focused for maximum effect.

The same logic holds for organizations. Concentration and synergy – not middle-of-the-road flexibility – are the hallmarks of greatness. Successful organizations zealously align their strategies, structures, and cultures around a central theme to create powerful, cohesive, brilliantly orchestrated configurations.

Conversely, middle-of-the-road strategies may be anathema to competitive advantage – the jack-of-all-trades is too often master of none. The same is true of culture and structure. Equality among marketing, production, and R&D departments might slow down decision making and prevent a coherent strategic theme from emerging. Similarly, organizational cultures that nurture too many dissidents might be stymied by conflict.

Managers, therefore, should reap the benefits of a well-tuned configuration without regret. They should take care not to kill their competitive edge by prematurely watering things down, introducing too much noise into the system, or permitting too many discordant practices.

I wish to amend Peters and Waterman's thesis: It is not just the pieces of a configuration – closeness to customers, innovation, high quality, differentiated products, loose-tight structures, or skunkworks – that create excellence. Stardom is attained also through configuration, the way the pieces fit together – their complementarily, their organization. To achieve success, form or configuration must animate and orchestrate the substance of individual elements.

Liberating self-reflection

Unfortunately, configuration and synergy are usually attained at the cost of myopia. Stellar performers view the world through narrowing telescopes. One point of view takes over; one set of assumptions comes to dominate. The result is complacency and overconfidence.

The only way to avoid myopia and the resulting excesses of the trajectories is for managers to reflect on their own basic assumptions about customers, competitors, and what they deem good or bad about strategy, structure, and culture. They must search for the underlying values, presumptions, and attributions that drive their organization. Only after they become conscious of the various inbred premises for action can they begin to question them.

Managers need to buy mirrors. They have to engage in more self-reflection and be less self-centered. They must audit themselves and solicit the views of objective third parties to discover their own blind spots. They can start by asking themselves the following questions:

1. What kinds of customers do we prefer? Why?
2. What assumptions are we making about our customers and competitors? How have our views of clients changed in the last few years?
3. Which aspects of strategy have not changed in many years? Why?
4. To whom do we pay the most attention, both inside and outside the organization? Whom do we ignore and why?
5. What are our most cherished goals and values? How have they evolved?
6. Which of our strengths are declining? Which are on the rise?
7. How will we find out if our strategies are wrong? How quickly?
8. Which departments and types of employees do we treasure and reward the most? Why?
9. What biases might filter our views? Who might tell us about these biases?
10. How do others in the industry see us?

It might be useful for managers individually to answer these deliberately general questions, to then circulate their written responses to colleagues, and finally, to come together to frankly discuss the answers.

Gathering information

Self-knowledge cannot be attained in a vacuum. Many of the best sources of such knowledge can be found outside the organization. To discover whether momentum is driving organizations toward dangerous excesses, managers must test their assumptions against reality – against evolving customer needs, new technologies, and competitive threats.

The whole point of gathering information is to create uneasiness, to combat complacency. Information must serve as the clarion call that awakens a somnolent system, the brakes that slow down a runaway trajectory. Combined with self-knowledge, it can prevent many of the excesess that have plagued our firms. What follows are some general maxims for corporate information gathering, written in the more lively prescriptive tone.

Dedication and Commitment. Information gathering should not be viewed as a routine accounting function; it is the sentinel that guards the fort. Gather and analyze information as if your company's life depends on it. It often does. Look at what happened to Sears when it ignored K mart and Wal-Mart, or to Caterpillar when it missed the shift away from heavy equipment.

Managers at many levels and from a variety of departments must religiously watch and analyze their customers, suppliers, and competitors. Such devotion may take lots of time and money, but it is usually worth it. Xerox, for example, trained 200 of its most astute line managers to look diligently and systematically for any changes in its rivals' pricing, products, and technologies.

Counterintuitive Scanning. Look for trends in soft data you do not normally think are of central importance, then try to interpret them in a manner least favorable to the company. For example, SALESMEN should supplement the sales and market reports to which they are so addicted with indicators of product quality and manufacturing efficiency. CRAFTSMEN should listen to what customers are saying about their products as well as looking at cost figures. PIONEERS should cost out their innovation projects and try to establish how well their competitors are doing with much less advanced offerings. Finally, BUILDERS should look for which operations to sell, what to cut back on, and how to get more out of existing operations.

Getting Through to the Top. Make sure information goes to the powerful and is gathered by the bold. Don't ever shoot a messenger. Get people at high levels involved in the collection and analysis of information – like the executives at Apple who listen in on customer complaint lines both to find out what is wrong with their products and to see how those complaints are being addressed. Members of the board must also play a role in monitoring performance. Because they have the power to make a difference, they should become as familiar as possible with products and markets.

Keep the game honest and reliable by using multiple sources of information. Leaders such as President Franklin Roosevelt would make themselves very well informed about an issue using one set of sources before they were formally briefed by another. They would then make their expertise obvious during the briefing, exuding an aura of super-competence that would discourage any subsequent attempts at concealment.

Sources of Good Information: Operations. If you are a senior manager in particular, make sure you tour your operations. You could pretend to be a customer or try to buy your own products or services incognito. Talk to lots of employees at all levels. Get your teenage nephew hired and listen to his reports. Find out what people in plants, warehouses, and branches are saying. Sam Walton of the super successful Wal-Mart stores visited every one of his 700 stores every year, hitchhiked with Wal-Mart trucks across the country, and frequented distribution centers to chat with the rank and file. Peters and Austin (1985) call this 'management by wandering around' (MBWA). It keeps managers in touch with 'the first vibrations of the new.'

Sources of Good Information: Customers. Visit customers and have them visit you. Work on some projects together, and benefit from their free advice. Find out what they need, like, and dislike. Allergan, a successful subsidiary of drug giant SmithKline Beckman, supplied ointments for ophthalmology patients such as contact lens users. In discussions with consumers – with whom most drug companies never deal directly – they heard repeated complaints about dry, itchy eyes, a problem never detailed in formal prescriptions compiled in their data bank. This qualitative symptom was the source of one of Allergan's most successful new products (Peters and Austin 1985).

Sources of Good Information: Competitors. Find out how the firm stacks up against its competitors in the minds of industry financial analysts. Buy and benchmark rivals' products. Determine what customers think of the competition's offerings and what new products your rivals are introducing. Discover how well competitors are faring with their new products. Xerox purchased the machines of rivals such as Canon and tore them apart to discover how to economize on or improve their own offerings (Dumaine 1988). The powerful Komatsu, once an upstart Japanese heavy equipment manufacturer, eventually overtook rival Caterpillar by benchmarking Cat's machines and finding ways to produce equivalent quality at a fraction of the cost.

Sources of Good Information: Performance Trends. A static statistic tells us much less than a trend, so monitor everything over time. Plot graphs of information so that trends become apparent. For example, try to determine what is happening to the prices, margins, and growth rates of your various products, to their market share, and to your outlets according to geographic region and store type. Creative aggregation and disaggregation of information is critical. For example, to find out where to expand, monitor results by region; to find out what kinds of new products to introduce, look at your lines on a product by product basis.

Go Beyond the Formal Information System. Things change, but formal information systems reflect only the kind of news – mostly quantitative – that was important yesterday. Many acute challenges will not be captured. So use these systems creatively and go beyond them. Look for 'unobtrusive indicators' of potential problems by finding out such things as:

Which offices make the most photocopies, write the longest and the most memos, and order the most stationery per capita? (Is this the locus of too much bureaucracy or overstaffing?)

How many days are salespeople out of the office? Are they traveling more? What percentage of calls are made to new clients? Is this increasing or decreasing? (Are we reaching out or closing up?)

Which departments have the highest absentee rates? The most turnover? The greatest loss of highly rated employees? The smallest loss of poorly rated employees?

From which departments are all (or none) of the promotions coming? What is the background and profile of those promoted, those left behind, and those leaving the firm? (What kind of culture do we have? What are its values?)

Almost everything done in an organization leaves traces of information. These potential 'watch-dogs' should be tapped regularly.

Pattern Recognition. Use your ability to recognize patterns to discover what the mountain of data is saying. Are ominous trends developing that have a common and dangerous cause? Are symptoms intensifying? Is there a vicious cycle that explains this? Ask which configuration is emerging, which trajectory applies. Generate questions that would complete the picture and gather new data accordingly.

Enlist managers from the different functions in these tasks of probing and interpretation. Meet with them regularly, not to plug numbers into a pro forma budget, but solely to spot important threats and opportunities. This is the only way of finding out when it is time to change. No bells will ring when that happens. There are no hard and fast rules. It is all a matter of judgment. The only imperative is that all leaders must operate with the firm assumption that one day they will have to go to war with the past.

Learning and innovating at the boundaries

Concentrated, orchestrated configurations produce wonderful results but can slow learning and renewal. One way for a large organization to have its cake and eat it too is to establish small independent units to experiment and do new things outside of – that is, without disturbing the configuration of existing operations. Firms might, for example, set up small-scale development teams that have the flexibility to get things done quickly and economically. Companies such as 3M give such teams much independence but limited resources, killing projects that remain unsuccessful after five years or so. Hewlett Packard's small, agile teams collectively introduced products at the rate of eight per week in the mid-1980s. Some items went from conception to debugged prototype in just 17 weeks.

Many Japanese companies also use such small development teams to increase the number of new product experiments. These teams always work outside the normal structure. They are populated by young turks with tremendous energy (the average age at Honda was 27), and are fast tracks for advancement. Most teams fail, but the ones that succeed go on to become very significant business units.

In his monumental *A Study of History*, Arnold Toynbee has painstakingly traced the rise and fall of 21 civilizations. All of these once great cultures, except perhaps our own, have collapsed or stagnated. Toynbee argued that their declines came not from natural disasters or barbarian invasions, but from internal rigidity, complacency, and oppression. He saw that some of the very institutions and practices responsible for ascendance ultimately evolved into the perverse idolatries that caused decline: 'When the road to destruction has perforce to be trodden on the quest of life, it is perhaps no wonder that the quest should often end in disaster.'

Organizations too are built into greatness and then launched toward decline by similar factors: focused strategies, galvanized cultures, specialized skills, efficient programs, and the harmonious configuration of all these things. When used with intelligence and sensitivity, these factors can make for tremendous success. But when taken to extremes, they spawn disaster. Ironically, success itself often induces the myopia and carelessness that lead to such excesses. It turns inspired innovation into blind invention, acute controls into imprisoning regulations, cohesive cultures into monolithic cabals. In the process, rich, nuanced firms become distended caricatures of their former selves, transformed from intelligent, adaptive systems into programmed, insular machines.

Paradoxically, the power of a tool increases both its potential benefits and its dangers. Icarus could not have flown without the wings so deftly crafted by his loving father Daedalus; but at the same time the wings placed a terrible onus upon Icarus's mastery and his discipline. Similarly, focused cultures and strategies and orchestrated configurations contribute mightily to outstanding performance. But they carry with them daunting risks of rigidity and isolation. To compound the problem, it is terribly hard to distinguish between the concentration needed for success and the narrowness that guarantees irrelevance. Managers of thriving organizations must forever remain alert to such 'perils of excellence.'

REFERENCES

Brain Dumaine, 'Corporate Spies Snoop to Conquer,' *Fortune*, November 7, 1988, pp. 68–76.

Tom Peters and Nancy Austin, 'A Passion for Excellence,' *Fortune*, May 13, 1985, pp. 16, 20.

Arnold Toynbee, *A Study of History* London: Oxford University Press, 1947.

25

SURFING THE EDGE OF CHAOS

Richard T. Pascale

Every decade or two during the past one hundred years, a point of inflection has occurred in management thinking. These breakthroughs are akin to the S-curves of technology that characterize the life cycle of many industrial and consumer products: Introduction → Acceleration → Acceptance → Maturity. Each big idea catches hold slowly. Yet, within a relatively short time, the new approach becomes so widely accepted that it is difficult even for old-timers to reconstruct how the world looked before.

The decade following World War II gave birth to the 'strategic era.' While the tenets of military strategy had been evolving for centuries, the link to commercial enterprise was tenuous. Before the late 1940s, most companies adhered to the tenet 'make a little, sell a little, make a little more.' After the war, faculty at the Harvard Business School (soon joined by swelling ranks of consultants) began to take the discipline of strategy seriously. By the late 1970s, the array of strategic concepts (SWOT analysis, the five forces framework, experience curves, strategic portfolios, the concept of competitive advantage) had become standard ordnance in the management arsenal. Today, a mere twenty years later, a grasp of these concepts is presumed as a threshold of management literacy. They have become so familiar that it is hard to imagine a world without them.

It is useful to step back and reflect on the scientific underpinnings to this legacy. Eric Beinhocker writes:

> The early micro-economists copied the mathematics of mid-nineteenth century physics equation by equation. ['Atoms'] became the individual, 'force' became the economists' notion of 'marginal utility' (or demand), 'kinetic energy' became total expenditure. All of this was synthesized into a coherent theory by Alfred Marshall – known as the theory of industrial organization.[1]

Marshall's work and its underpinnings in nineteenth century physics exert a huge influence on strategic thinking to this day. From our concept of strategy to our efforts at organizational renewal, the deep logic is based on assumptions of deterministic cause and effect (i.e., a billiard ball model of how competitors will respond to a strategic challenge or how employees will behave under a new incentive scheme). And all of this, consistent with Newton's initial conceptions, is assumed to take place in a world where time, space (i.e., a particular industry structure or definition of a market), and dynamic equilibrium are accepted as reasonable underpinnings for the formulation of executive action. That's where the trouble begins. Marshall's equilibrium model offered appropriate approximations for the dominant sectors of agriculture and manufacturing of his era and are still useful in many situations. But these constructs run into difficulty in the far from equilibrium conditions found in today's service, technology, or communications-intensive businesses. When new entrants such as Nokia, Amazon.com, Dell Computer, or CNN invade a market, they succeed despite what traditional strategic thinkers would write off as a long shot.

During the 1980s and 1990s, performance improvement (e.g., total quality management, *kaizen*, just-in-time, reengineering) succeeded the strategic era. It, too, has followed the S-curve trajectory. Now, as it trails off, an uneasiness is stirring, a feeling that 'something more' is required. In particular, disquiet has arisen over the rapidly rising fatality rates of major companies. Organizations cannot win by cost reduction alone and cannot invent appropriate strategic responses fast enough to stay abreast of nimble rivals. Many are exhausted by the pace of change, and their harried attempts to execute new initiatives fall short of expectations.

The next point of inflection is about to unfold. To succeed, the next big idea must address the biggest challenge facing corporations today – namely, to dramatically improve the hit rate of strategic initiatives and attain the level of renewal necessary for successful execution. As in the previous eras, we can expect that the next big idea will at first seem strange and inaccessible.

Here's the good news. For well over a decade, the hard sciences have made enormous strides in understanding and describing how the living world works. Scientists use the term 'complex adaptive systems' ('complexity' for short) to label these theories. To be sure, the new theories do not explain everything. But the work has identified principles that apply to many living things – amoebae and ant colonies, beehives and bond traders, ecologies and economies, you and me.

For an entity to qualify as a complex adaptive system, it must meet four tests. *First*, it must be comprised of many agents acting in parallel. It is not hierarchically controlled. *Second*, it continuously shuffles these building blocks and generates multiple levels of organization and structure. *Third*, it is subject to the second law of thermodynamics, exhibiting entropy and winding down over time unless replenished with energy. In this sense, complex adaptive systems are vulnerable to death. *Fourth*, a distinguishing characteristic, all complex adaptive systems exhibit a capacity for pattern recognition and employ this to anticipate the future and learn to recognize the anticipation of seasonal change.

Many systems are complex but not adaptive (i.e., they meet some of the above conditions, but not all). If sand is gradually piled on a table, it will slide off in patterns. If a wave in a stream is disturbed, it will repair itself once the obstruction is removed. But neither of these complex systems anticipates and learns. Only living systems cope with their environment with a predictive model that anticipates and pro-acts. Thus, when the worldwide community of strep bacteria mutates to circumvent the threat of the latest antibiotic (as it does rather reliably within three years), it is reaffirming its membership in the club of complexity.

Work on complexity originated during the mid-1980s at New Mexico's Santa Fe Institute. A group of distinguished scientists with backgrounds in particle physics, microbiology, archaeology, astrophysics, paleontology, zoology, botany, and economics were drawn together by similar questions.[2] A series of symposia, underwritten by the Carnegie Foundation, revealed that all the assembled disciplines shared, at their core, building blocks composed of many agents. These might be molecules, neurons, a species, customers, members of a social system, or networks of corporations. Further, these fundamental systems were continually organizing and reorganizing themselves, all flourishing in a boundary between rigidity and randomness and all occasionally forming larger structures through the clash of natural accommodation and competition. Molecules form cells; neurons cluster into neural networks (or brains); species form ecosystems; individuals form tribes or societies; consumers and corporations form economies. These self-organizing structures give rise to emergent behavior (an example of which is the process whereby pre-biotic chemicals combined to form the extraordinary diversity of life on earth). Complexity science informs us about organization, stability, and change in social and natural systems. 'Unlike the earlier advances in hard science,' writes economist Alex Trosiglio, 'complexity deals with a world that is far from equilibrium, and is creative and evolving in ways that we cannot hope to predict. It points to fundamental limits to our ability to understand, control, and manage the world, and the need for us to accept unpredictability and change.'[3]

The science of complexity has yielded four bedrock principles relevant to the new strategic work:

1. Complex adaptive systems are at risk when in equilibrium. Equilibrium is a precursor to death.[4]
2. Complex adaptive systems exhibit the capacity of self-organization and emergent complexity.[5] Self-organization arises from intelligence in the remote clusters (or 'nodes') within a network. Emergent complexity is generated by the propensity of simple structures to generate novel patterns, infinite variety, and often, a sum that is greater than the parts. (Again, the escalating complexity of life on earth is an example.)
3. Complex adaptive systems tend to move toward the edge of chaos when provoked by a complex task.[6] Bounded instability is more conducive to evolution than either stable equilibrium or explosive instability. (For example, fire has been found to be a critical factor in regenerating healthy forests and prairies.) One important corollary to this principle is that a complex adaptive system, once having reached a temporary 'peak' in its fitness landscape (e.g., a company during a golden era), must then 'go down to go up' (i.e., moving from one peak to a still higher peak requires it to traverse the valleys of the fitness landscape). In cybernetic terms, the organism must be pulled by competitive pressures far enough out of its usual arrangements before it can create substantially different forms and arrive at a more evolved basin of attraction.
4. One cannot direct a living system, only disturb it.[7] Complex adaptive systems are characterized by weak cause-and-effect linkages. Phase transitions occur in the realm where one relatively small and isolated variation can produce huge effects. Alternatively, large changes may have little effect. (This phenomenon is common in the information industry. Massive efforts to promote a superior operating system may come to naught, whereas a series of serendipitous events may establish an inferior operating system – such as MS-DOS – as the industry standard.)

Is complexity just interesting science, or does it represent something of great importance in thinking about strategic work? As these illustrations suggest, treating organizations as complex adaptive systems provides useful insight into the nature of strategic work. In the following pages, I will (1) briefly describe how the four bedrock principles of complexity occur in nature, and (2) demonstrate how they can be applied in a managerial context. In particular, I use the efforts underway at Royal Dutch/Shell to describe an extensive and pragmatic test of these ideas.

The successes at Shell and other companies described here might be achieved with a more traditional mind-set (in much the same way as Newton's laws can be used to explain the mechanics of matter on earth with sufficient accuracy so as to not require the General Theory of Relativity). But the contribution of scientific insight is much more than descriptions of increasing accuracy. Deep theories reveal previously unsuspected aspects of reality that we don't see (the curvature of space-time in the case of relativity theory) and thereby alter the fabric of reality. This is the context for an article on complexity science and strategy. Complexity makes the

479

strategic challenge more understandable and the task of strategic renewal more accessible. In short, this is not a polemic against the traditional strategic approach, but an argument for broadening it.

STABLE EQUILIBRIUM EQUALS DEATH

An obscure but important law of cybernetics, the law of requisite variety, states: For any system to survive, it must cultivate variety in its internal controls. If it fails to do so internally, it will fail to cope with variety successfully when it comes from an external source.[8] Here, in the mundane prose of a cybernetic axiom, is the rationale for bounded instability.

A perverse example of this axiom in action was driven home by the devastating fires that wiped out 25 percent of Yellowstone National Park in 1992. For decades, the National Park Service had *imposed* equilibrium on the forest by extinguishing fires whenever they appeared. Gradually, the forest floor became littered with a thick layer of debris. When a lightening strike and ill-timed winds created a conflagration that could not be contained, this carpet of dry material burned longer and hotter than normal. By suppressing natural fires for close to 100 years, the park service had prevented the forest floor from being cleansed in a natural rhythm. Now a century's accumulation of deadfall generated extreme temperatures. The fire incinerated large trees and the living components of top soil that would otherwise have survived. This is the price of enforced equilibrium.

The seductive pull of equilibrium poses a constant danger to successful established companies. Jim Cannavino, a former IBM senior executive, provides an anecdote that speaks to the hazards of resisting change. In 1993, Cannavino was asked by IBM's new CEO. Lou Gerstner, to take a hard look at the strategic planning process. Why had IBM so badly missed the mark? Cannavino dutifully examined the work product – library shelves filled with blue binders containing twenty years of forecasts, trends, and strategic analysis. 'It all could be distilled down to one sentence,' he recounts. ' "We saw it coming" – PC open architecture, networking intelligence in microprocessors, higher margins in software and services than hardware; it was all there. So I looked at the operating plans. How did they reflect the shifts the strategists had projected? These blue volumes (three times as voluminous as the strategic plans) could also be summarized in one sentence: "Nothing changed." And the final dose of arsenic to this diet of cyanide was the year-end financial reconciliation process. When we rolled up the sector submissions into totals for the corporation, the growth opportunities never quite covered the erosion of market share. This shortfall, of course, was the tip of an iceberg that would one day upend our strategy and our primary product – the IBM 360 mainframe. But facing these fundamental trends would have precipitated a great deal of turmoil and instability. Instead, year after year, a few of our most senior leaders went behind closed doors and raised prices.'[9]

While equilibrium endangers living systems, it often wears the disguise of an attribute. Equilibrium is concealed inside strong values or a coherent, close-knit social system, or within a company's well-synchronized operating system (often referred to as 'organizational fit'). Vision, values, and organizational fit are double-edged swords.

Species are inherently drawn toward the seeming oasis of stability and equilibrium – and the further they drift toward this destination, the less likely they are to adapt successfully when change is necessary. So why don't all species drift into the thrall of equilibrium and die off? Two forces thwart equilibrium and promote instability: (1) the threat of death, and (2) the promise of sex.

The Darwinian process, called 'selection pressures' by natural scientists, imposes harsh con-

sequences on species entrapped in equilibrium. Most species, when challenged to adapt too far from their origins, are unable to do so and gradually disappear. But from the vantage point of the larger ecological community, selection pressures enforce an ecological upgrade, insofar as mutations that survive offer a better fit with the new environment. Natural selection exerts itself most aggressively during periods of radical change. Few readers will have difficulty identifying these forces at work in industry today. There are no safe havens. From toothpaste to camcorders, pharmaceuticals to office supplies, bookstores to booster rockets for space payloads, soap to software, it's a Darwinian jungle out there, and it's not getting easier.

As a rule, a species becomes more vulnerable as it becomes more genetically homogeneous. Nature hedges against this condition through the reproductive process. Of the several means of reproduction that have evolved on the planet, sex is best. It is decisively superior to parthenogenesis (the process by which most plants, worms, and a few mammals conceive offspring through self-induced combination of identical genetic material).

Sexual reproduction maximizes diversity. Chromosome combinations are randomly matched in variant pairings, thereby generating more permutations and variety in offspring. Oxford's evolutionary theorist, William Hamilton, explains why this benefits a species. Enemies (i.e., harmful diseases and parasites) find it harder to adapt to the diverse attributes of a population generated by sexual reproduction than to the comparative uniformity of one produced by parthenogenesis.[10]

How does this relate to organizations? In organizations, people are the chromosomes, the genetic material that can create variety. When management thinker Gary Hamel was asked if he thought IBM had a chance of leading the next stage of the information revolution, he replied: 'I'd need to know how many of IBM's top 100 executives had grown up on the west coast of America where the future of the computer industry is being created and how many were under forty years of age. If a quarter or a third of the senior group were both under forty and possessed a west coast perspective, IBM has a chance.'[11]

Here's the rub: The 'exchanges of DNA' attempted within social systems are not nearly as reliable as those driven by the mechanics of reproductive chemistry. True, organizations can hire from the outside, bring seniors into frequent contact with iconoclasts from the ranks, or confront engineers and designers with disgruntled customers. But the enemy of these methods is, of course, the existing social order, which, like the body's immune defense system, seeks to neutralize, isolate, or destroy foreign invaders. 'Antibodies' in the form of social norms, corporate values, and orthodox beliefs nullify the advantages of diversity. An executive team may include divergent interests, only to engage in stereotyped listening (e.g., 'There goes Techie again') or freeze iconoclasts out of important informal discussions. If authentic diversity is sought, all executives, in particular the seniors, must be more seeker than guru.

Disturbing equilibrium at Shell

In 1996, Steve Miller, age fifty-one, became a member of Shell's committee of managing directors – the five senior leaders who develop objectives and long-term plans for Royal Dutch/Shell.[12] The group found itself captive to its hundred-year-old history. The numbing effects of tradition – a staggering $130 billion in annual revenues, 105,000 predominantly long-tenured employees, and global operations – left Shell vulnerable. While profits continued to flow, fissures were forming beneath the surface.

Miller was appointed group managing director of Shell's worldwide oil products business (known as 'Downstream'), which accounts for $40 billion of revenues within the Shell Group. During the previous two years, the company had been engaged in a program to 'transform' the organization. Yet the regimen of massive reorganization, traumatic downsizing, and senior management workshops accomplished little. Shell's earnings, while solid, were disappointing to financial analysts who expected more from the industry's largest competitor. Employees registered wide-spread resignation and cynicism. And the operating units at the 'coal face' (Shell's term for its front-line activities within the 130 countries where Downstream does business) saw little more than business as usual.

For Steve Miller, Shell's impenetrable culture was worrisome. The Downstream business accounted for 37 percent of Shell's assets. Among the businesses in the Shell Group's portfolio, Downstream faced the gravest competitive threats. From 1992 to 1995, a full 50 percent of Shell's retail revenues in France fell victim to the onslaught of the European hypermarkets: a similar pattern was emerging in the United Kingdom. Elsewhere in the world, new competitors, global customers, and more savvy national oil companies were demanding a radically different approach to the marketplace. Having observed Shell's previous transformation efforts. Miller was convinced that it was essential to reach around the resistant bureaucracy and involve the front lines of the organization, a formidable task given the sheer size of the operation. In addition to Downstream's 61,000 full-time employees, Shell's 47,000 filling stations employed hundreds of thousands, mostly part-time attendants and catered to more than 10 million customers every day. In the language of complexity, Miller believed it necessary to tap the emergent properties of Shell's enormous distribution system and shift the locus of strategic initiative to the front lines. He saw this system as a fertile organism that needed encouragement to, in his words, 'send green shoots forth.'

In an effort to gain the organization's attention (i.e., disturb equilibrium), beginning in mid-1996, Miller reallocated more than 50 percent of his calendar to work directly with front-line personnel. Miller states:

> Our Downstream business transformation program had bogged down largely because of the impasse between headquarters and the operating companies, Shell's term for its highly independent country operations. The balance of power between headquarters and field, honed during a period of relative equilibrium, had ground to a stalemate. But the forces for continuing in the old way were enormous and extended throughout the organization. We were overseeing the most decentralized operation in the world, with country chief executives that had, since the 1950s, enjoyed enormous autonomy. This had been part of our success formula. Yet we were encountering a set of daunting competitive threats that transcended national boundaries. Global customers – like British Airways or Daimler Benz – wanted to deal with one Shell contact, not with a different Shell representative in every country in which they operate. We had huge overcapacity in refining, but each country CEO (motivated to maximize his own P&L) resisted the consolidation of refining capacity. These problems begged for a new strategic approach in which the task at the top was to provide the framework and then unleash the regional and local levels to find a path that was best for their market and the corporation as a whole

Shell had tried to rationalize its assets through a well-engineered strategic response: directives were issued by the top and driven through the organization. But country heads successfully thwarted consolidation under the banner of host-country objections to the threatened closing of their dedicated refining capacity. Miller continues:

> We were equally unsuccessful at igniting a more imaginative approach toward the marketplace. It was like the old game of telephone that we used to play when we were kids: you'd whisper a mes-

sage to the person next to you, and it goes around the circle. By the time you get to the last person, it bears almost no resemblance to the message you started with. Apply that to the 61,000 people in the Downstream business across the globe, and I knew our strategic aspirations could never penetrate through to the marketplace. The linkages between directives given and actions taken are too problematic.

What made sense to Miller was to fundamentally alter the conversation and unleash the emergent possibilities. Midway through the process, Miller became acquainted with core principles of living systems and adopted them as a framework to provide his organization with a context for renewal.

Miller's reports in the operating companies were saying. 'Centralization will only bog us down.' 'They were partly right,' he acknowledges.

These are big companies. Some earn several hundreds of millions a year in net income. But the alternative wasn't centralization – it was a radical change in the responsiveness of the Downstream business to the dynamics of the marketplace – from top to bottom such that we could come together in appropriate groups, solve problems, and operate in a manner which transcended the old headquarters versus field schism. What initially seemed like a huge conflict has gradually melted away, I believe, because we stopped treating the Downstream business like a machine to be driven and began to regard it as a living system that needed to evolve.

Miller's solution was to cut through the organization's layers and barriers, put senior management in direct contact with the people at the grassroots level, foster strategic initiatives, create a new sense of urgency, and overwhelm the old order. The first wave of initiatives spawned other initiatives. In Malaysia, for example. Miller's pilot efforts with four initiative teams (called 'action labs') have proliferated to forty. He states:

It worked because the people at the coal face usually know what's going on. They see the competitive threats and our inadequate response every day. Once you give them the context, they can do a better job of spotting opportunities and stepping up to decisions. In less than two years, we've seen astonishing progress in our retail business in some twenty-five countries. This represents around 85 percent of our retail sales volume, and we have now begun to use this approach in our service organizations and lubricant business. Results? By the end of 1997. Shell's operations in France had regained initiative and achieved double-digit growth and double-digit return on capital. Market share was increasing after years of decline.

Austria went from a probable exit candidate to a highly profitable operation. Overall, Shell gained in brand-share preference throughout Europe and ranked first in share among other major oil companies. By the close of 1998, approximately 10,000 Downstream employees have been involved in this effort with audited results (directly attributed to the program) exceeding a $300 million contribution to Shell's bottom line.

Self-Organization and Emergent Complexity

Santa Fe Institute's Stuart Kauffman is a geneticist. His lifetime fascination has been with the ordered process by which a fertilized egg unfolds into a new-born infant and later into an adult. Earlier Nobel Prize-winning work on genetic circuits had shown that every cell contains a number of 'regulatory' genes that act as switches to turn one another on and off. Modern computers use sequential instructions, whereas the genetic system exercises most of its instructions simultaneously. For decades, scientists have sought to discover the governing mechanism that causes this simultaneous, nonlinear system to settle down and replicate a species.[13]

Kauffman built a simple simulation of a genetic system. His array of 100 light bulbs looked like a Las Vegas marquee. Since regulatory genes cause the cells (like bulbs) to turn on or off, Kauffman arranged for his bulbs to do just that, each independently of the other. His hypothesis was that no governing mechanism existed; rather, random and independent behavior would settle into patterns – a view that was far from self-evident. The possible combinations in Kauffman's arrangement of blinking lights was two (i.e., on and off), multiplied by itself 100 times (i.e., almost one million, trillion, trillion possibilities!).

When Kauffman switched the system on, the result was astonishing. Instead of patterns of infinite variety, the system always settled down within a few minutes to a few more or less orderly states. The implications of Kauffman's work are far-reaching. Theorists had been searching for the sequence of primordial events that could have produced the first DNA – the building block of life. Kauffman asked instead, 'What if life was not just standing around and waiting until DNA happened? What if all those amino acids and sugars and gasses and solar energy were each just doing their thing like the billboard of lights?' If the conditions in primordial soup were right, it wouldn't take a miracle (like a million decks of cards falling from a balcony and all coming up aces) for DNA to randomly turn up. Rather, the compounds in the soup could have formed a coherent, self-reinforcing web of reactions and these, in turn, generated the more complex patterns of DNA.[14]

Emergent complexity is driven by a few simple patterns that combine to generate infinite variety. For example, simulations have shown that a three-pronged 'crow's foot' pattern, if combined in various ways, perfectly replicates the foliage patterns of every fern on earth. Similar phenomena hold true in business. John Kao, a specialist in creativity, has observed how one simple creative breakthrough can evoke a cascade of increasing complexity.[15] 'Simple' inventions such as the wheel, printing press, or transistor lead to 'complex' offshoots such as automobiles, cellular phones, electronic publishing, and computing.

The phenomenon of emergence arises from the way simple patterns combine. Mathematics has coined the term 'fractals' to describe a set of simple equations that combine to form endless diversity.[16] Fractal mathematics has given us valuable insight into how nature creates the shapes we observe. Mountains, rivers, coastline vegetation, lungs, and circulatory systems are fractal, replicating a dominant pattern at several smaller levels of scale. Fractals, in effect, act like genetic algorithms enabling a species to efficiently replicate essential functions.

One consequence of emerging complexity is that you cannot see the end from the beginning. While many can readily acknowledge nature's propensity to self-organize and generate more complex levels, it is less comforting to put oneself at the mercy of this process with the foreknowledge that we cannot predict the shape that the future will take. Emerging complexity creates not one future but many.

Self-organization and emergence at Shell

Building on (1) the principles of complexity, (2) the fractal-like properties of a business model developed by Columbia University's Larry Seldon,[17] and (3) a second fractal-like process, the action labs, Steve Miller and his colleagues at Shell tapped into the intelligence in the trenches and channeled it into a tailored marketplace response.[18]

Miller states:

> We needed a vehicle to give us an energy transfusion and remind us that we could play at a far more
> competitive level. The properties of self-organization and emergence make intuitive sense to me.
> The question was how to release them. Seldon's model gave us a sharp-edged tool to identify cus-
> tomer needs and markets and to develop our value proposition. This, in effect, gave our troops the
> 'ammunition' to shoot with – analytical distinctions to make the business case. Shell has always been
> a wholesaler. Yet the forecourt of every service station is an artery for commerce that any retailer
> would envy. Our task was to tap the potential of that real estate, and we needed both the insight and
> the initiatives of our front-line troops to pull it off. For a company as large as Shell, leadership can't
> drive these answers down from the top. We needed to tap into ideas that were out there in the ranks
> – latent but ready to bear fruit if given encouragement.

At first glance, Shell's methods look pedestrian. Miller began bringing six- to eight-person teams
from a half-dozen operating companies from around the world into 'retailing boot camps.' The
first five-day workshop introduced tools for identifying and exploiting market opportunities. It
also included a dose of the leadership skills necessary to enroll others back home. Participants
returned ready to apply the tools to achieve breakthroughs such as doubling net income in filling stations on the major north-south highways of Malaysia or tripling market share of bottled
gas in South Africa. As part of the discipline of the model, every intention (e.g., 'to lower fuel
delivery costs') was translated into 'key business activities' (or KBAs). As the first group went
home, six more teams would rotate in. During the next sixty days, the first group of teams used
the analytical tools to sample customers, identify segments, and develop a value proposition. The
group would then return to the workshop for a 'peer challenge' – tough give-and-take exchanges
with other teams. Then it would go back again for another sixty days to perfect a business plan.
At the close of the third workshop, each action lab spent three hours in the 'fishbowl' with Miller
and several of his direct reports, reviewing business plans, while the other teams observed the
proceedings. At the close of each session, plans were approved, rejected, amended. Financial
commitments were made in exchange for promised results. (The latter were incorporated in the
country's operating goals for the year.) Then the teams went back to the field for another sixty
days to put their ideas into action and returned for a followup session.

Miller continues:

> Week after week, team after team, my six direct reports and I and our internal coaches reached out
> and worked directly with a diverse crosssection of customers, dealers, shop stewards, and young and
> mid-level professionals. And it worked. Operating company CEOs, historically leery of any 'help'
> from headquarters, saw their people return energized and armed with solid plans to beat the com-
> petition. The grassroots employees who participated in the program got to touch and feel the new
> Shell – a far more informal, give-and-take culture. The conversation down in the ranks of the organ-
> ization began to change. Guerrilla leaders, historically resigned to Shell's conventional way of doing
> things, stepped forward to champion ingenious marketplace innovations (such as the Coca-Cola
> Challenge in Malaysia – a free Coke to any service-station customer who is not offered the full menu
> of forecourt services. It sounds trivial, but it increased volume by 15 percent). Many, if not most, of
> the ideas come from the lower ranks of our company who are in direct contact with the customer.
> Best of all, we learned together. I can't overstate how infectious the optimism and energy of these
> committed employees was for the many managers above them. In a curious way, these front-line
> employees taught us to believe in ourselves again.

As executives move up in organizations, they become removed from the work that goes on in
the fields. Directives from the top become increasingly abstract as executives tend to rely on

mechanical cause-and-effect linkages to drive the business: strategic guidelines, head-count controls, operational expense targets, pay-for-performance incentives, and so forth. These are the tie rods and pistons of 'social engineering' – the old model of change. Complexity theory does not discard these useful devices but it starts from a different place. The living-systems approach begins with a focus on the intelligence in the nodes. It seeks to ferret out what this network sees, what stresses it is undergoing, and what is needed to unleash its potential. Other support elements (e.g., controls and rewards) are orchestrated to draw on this potential rather than to drive down solutions from above.

Miller was pioneering a very different model from what had always prevailed at Shell. His 'design for emergence' generated hundreds of informal connections between headquarters and the field, resembling the parallel networks of the nervous system to the brain. It contrasted with the historical model of mechanical linkages analogous to those that transfer the energy from the engine in a car through a drive train to the tires that perform the 'work.'

EDGE OF CHAOS

Nothing novel can emerge from systems with high degrees of order and stability – for example, crystals, incestuous communities, or regulated industries. On the other hand, complete chaotic systems, such as stampedes, riots, rage, or the early years of the French Revolution, are too formless to coalesce. Generative complexity takes place in the boundary between rigidity and randomness.

Historically,[19] science viewed 'change' as moving from one equilibrium state (water) to another (ice). Newtonian understandings could not cope with the random, near-chaotic messiness of the actual transition itself. Ecologists and economists similarly favored equilibrium conditions because neither observation nor modeling techniques could handle transition states. The relatively inexpensive computational power of modern computers has changed all that. Nonequilibrium and nonlinear simulations are now possible. These developments, along with the study of complexity, have enabled us to better understand the dynamics of 'messiness.'

Phase transitions occur in the realm near chaos where a relatively small and isolated variation can produce huge effects. Consider the example of lasers: while only a complex system and not an adaptive one, the infusion of energy into plasma excites a jumble of photons. The more the energy, the more jumbled they become. Still more and the seething mass is transformed into the coherent light of a laser beam. What drives this transition, and how can we orchestrate it? Two determinants – (1) a precise tension between amplifying and damping feedback, and (2) (unique to mankind) the application of mindfulness and intention – are akin to rudder and sail when surfing near the edge of chaos.

Two factors determine the level of excitation in a system. In cybernetics, they are known as amplifying (positive) and damping (negative) feedback.[20] Damping feedback operates like a thermostat, which keeps temperatures within boundaries with a thermocouple that continually says 'too hot, too cold.' Amplifying feedback happens when a microphone gets too close to a loudspeaker. The signal is amplified until it oscillates to a piercing shriek. Living systems thrive when these mechanisms are in tension.

Getting the tension right is the hard part. Business obituaries abound with examples of one or the other of these feedback systems gone amok. IT&T under Harold Geneen or Sunbeam under 'Chainsaw' Al Dunlap thrive briefly under stringent damping controls, then fade away owing to the loss of imagination and creative energy. At the opposite end, Value Jet thrives in an amplifying phase, adds more planes, departures, and staff without corresponding attention to the damping loop (operational controls, safety, reliability, and service standards).

Psychologists tell us that pain can cause us to change, and this is most likely to occur when we recontextualize pain as the means by which significant learning occurs. When the great Austro-American economist Joseph Schumpeter described the essence of free-market economies as 'creative destruction,' it could be interpreted as a characterization of the hazards near the edge of chaos. Enduring competitive advantage entails disrupting what has been done in the past and creating a new future.

Hewlett-Packard's printer business was one of the most successful in its portfolio. Observing a downward spiral of margins as many 'me too' printers entered the market, HP reinvented its offering. Today, HP's printers are the 'free razor blade' – the loss leader in a very different strategy. To maintain scale, HP abandoned its high-cost distribution system with a dedicated sales force, opting instead for mass channels, partnering, and outsourcing to lower manufacturing costs. To protect margins, it targeted its forty biggest corporate customers and formed a partnership to deliver global business printing solutions – whether through low-cost, on-premise equipment, or networked technology. States Tim Mannon, president of HP's printer division: 'The biggest single threat to our business today is staying with a previously successful business model one year too long.'[21]

Shaping the edge of chaos at Shell

Shell moved to the edge of chaos with a multi-pronged design that intensified stress on all members of the Shell system.[22] First, as noted, Miller and his top team performed major surgery on their calendars and reallocated approximately half their time to teaching and coaching wave after wave of country teams. When the lowest levels of an organization were being trained, coached, and evaluated by those at the very top, it both inspired – and stressed – everyone in the system (including mid-level bosses who were not present). Second, the design, as we have seen, sent teams back to collect real data for three periods of sixty days (interspersed with additional workshop sessions). Pressure to succeed and long hours both during the workshops and back in the country (where these individuals continued to carry their regular duties along with project work) achieved the cultural 'unfreezing' effects. Participants were resocialized into a more direct, informal, and less hierarchical way of working.

Miller states:

> One of the most important innovations in changing all of us was the fishbowl. The name describes what it is: I and a number of my management team sit in the middle of a room with one action lab in the center with us. The other team members listen from the outer circle. Everyone is watching as the group in the hot seat talks about what they're going to do and what they need from me and my colleagues to be able to do it. That may not sound revolutionary – but in our culture, it was very unusual for anyone lower in the organization to talk this directly to a managing director and his reports.
>
> In the fishbowl, the pressure is on to measure up. The truth is, the pressure is on me and my colleagues. The first time we're not consistent, we're dead meat. If a team brings in a plan that's really a bunch of crap, we've got to be able to call it a bunch of crap. If we cover for people or praise everyone, what do we say when someone brings in an excellent plan? That kind of straight talk is another big culture change for Shell.
>
> The whole process creates complete transparency between the people at the coal face and me and my top management team. At the end, these folks go back home and say, 'I just cut a deal with the

managing director and his team to do these things.' It creates a personal connection, and it changes how we talk with each other and how we work with each other. After that, I can call up those folks anywhere in the world and talk in a very direct way because of this personal connectedness. It has completely changed the dynamics of our operations.

DISTURBING A LIVING SYSTEM

An important and distinct property of living systems is the tenuous connection between cause and effect. As most seasoned managers know, the best-laid plans are often perverted through self-interest, misinterpretation, or lack of necessary skills to reach the intended goal.

Consider the war of attrition waged by ranchers and the U.S. Fish and Wildlife Service to 'control' the coyote. A cumulative total of $3 billion (in 1997 dollars) has been spent during the past 100 years to underwrite bounty hunters, field a sophisticated array of traps, introduce novel morsels of poisoned bait, and interject genetic technology (to limit fertility of females) – all with the aim of protecting sheep and cattle ranchers from these wily predators. Result? When white men first appeared in significant numbers west of the Mississippi in the early 1800s, coyotes were found in twelve western states and never seen east of the Mississippi. However, as a direct result of the aggressive programs to eliminate the coyote, the modern day coyote is 20 percent larger and significantly smarter than his predecessor. The coyote is now found in forty-nine of the fifty states – including suburbs of New York City and Los Angeles. How could this occur? Human intervention so threatened the coyote's survival that a significant number fled into Canada where they bred with the larger Canadian wolf. Still later, these visitors migrated south (and further north to Alaska) and, over the decades, bred with (and increased the size of) the U.S. population. The same threats to survival that had driven some coyotes into Canada drove others to adapt to climates as varied as Florida and New Hampshire. Finally, the persistent efforts to trap or hunt or poison the coyote heightened selection pressures. The survivors were extremely streetwise and wary of human contact. Once alerted by a few fatalities among their brethern, coyotes are usually able to sniff out man's latest stratagem to do them harm.

As the tale of the coyote suggests, living systems are difficult to direct because of these weak cause-and-effect linkages. The best laid efforts by man to intervene in a system, to do it harm, or even to replicate it artificially almost always miss the mark. The strategic intentions of governments in Japan, Taiwan, and Germany to replicate Silicon Valley provide one example. The cause-and-effect formula seemed simple: (1) identify a region with major universities with strong departments in such fields as microelectronics, genetics, and nuclear medicine and having a geography with climate and amenities suitable to attract professionals, and (2) invest to stimulate a self-reinforcing community of interests. But these and many similar efforts have never quite reached a critical mass. The cause-and-effect relationships proved unclear.[23] A lot depends on chance. One is wiser to acknowledge the broad possibilities that flow from weak cause-and-effect linkages and the need to consider the second- and third-order effects of any bold intervention one is about to undertake.

Disturbing a complex system at Shell

In today's fast-changing environment, Shell's Steve Miller dismisses the company's old traditional approach as mechanistic. 'Top-down strategies don't win ballgames,' he states. 'Experimentation, rapid learning, and seizing the momentum of success is the better approach.'[24]

Miller observes:

We need a different definition of strategy and a different approach to generating it. In the past, strategy was the exclusive domain of top management. Today, if you're going to have a successful company, you have to recognize that the top can't possibly have all the answers. The leaders provide the vision and are the context setters. But the actual solutions about how best to meet the challenges of the moment, those thousands of strategic challenges encountered every day, have to be made by the people closest to the action – the people at the coal face.

Change your approach to strategy, and you change the way a company runs. The leader becomes a context setter, the designer of a learning experience – not an authority figure with solutions. Once the folks at the grassroots realize they own the problem, they also discover that they can help create and own the answers, and they get after it very quickly, very aggressively, and very creatively, with a lot more ideas than the old-style strategic direction could ever have prescribed from headquarters.

A program like this is a high-risk proposition, because it goes counter to the way most senior executives spend their time. I spend 50 percent to 60 percent of my time at this, and there is no direct guarantee that what I'm doing is going make something happen down the line. It's like becoming the helmsman of a big ship when you've grown up behind the steering wheel of a car. This approach isn't about me. It's about rigorous, well-taught marketing concepts, combined with a strong process design, that enable front-line employees to think like businesspeople. Top executives and front-line employees learn to work together in partnership.

People want to evaluate this against the old way, which gives you the illusion of 'making things happen.' I encountered lots of thinly veiled skepticism: 'Did your net income change from last quarter because of this change process?' These challenges create anxiety. The temptation, of course, is to reimpose your directives and controls even though we had an abundance of proof that this would not work. Instead, top executives and lower-level employees learn to work together in partnership. The grassroots approach to strategy development and implementation doesn't happen overnight. But it does happen. People always want results yesterday. But the process and behavior that drive authentic strategic change aren't like that.

There's another kind of risk to the leaders of a strategic inquiry of this kind – the risk of exposure. You're working very closely and intensely with all levels of staff, and they get to assess and evaluate you directly. Before, you were remote from them; now, you're very accessible. If that evaluation comes up negative, you've got a big-time problem.

Finally, the scariest part is letting go. You don't have the same kind of control that traditional leadership is used to. What you don't realize until you do it is that you may, in fact, have more controls but in a different fashion. You get more feedback than before, you learn more than before, you know more through your own people about what's going on in the marketplace and with customers than before. But you still have to let go of the old sense of control.

Miller's words testify to his reconciliation with the weak cause-and-effect linkages that exist in a living system. When strategic work is accomplished through a 'design for emergence,' it never assumes that a particular input will produce a particular output. It is more akin to the study of subatomic particles in a bubble chamber. The experimenter's design creates probabilistic occurrences that take place within the domain of focus. Period. Greater precision is neither sought nor possible.

REFERENCES

1. E.D. Beinhocker, 'Strategy at the Edge of Chaos.' *McKinsey Quarterly*, number 1. 1997, p. 25.

2. For an entertaining treatment of this inquiry, see: M.M. Waldrop. *Complexity* (New York: Simon & Schuster, 1992).

3. A. Trosiglio, 'Managing Complexity' (unpublished working paper, June 1995), p. 3: and D. Deutsch. *The Fabric of Reality* (New York: Penguin, 1997), pp. 3–21.

4. See S. Kauffman, *At Home in the Universe* (New York: Oxford University Press, 1995), p. 21; and G. Hamel and C.K. Prahalad, 'Strategic Intent,' *Harvard Business Review*, volume 67. May-June 1989, pp. 63–76.

5. See Kauffman (1995), p. 205; and J.H. Holland, *Hidden Order* (Reading, Massachusetts: Addison-Wesley, 1995), p. 3.

6. See Kauffman (1995), p. 230: and M. Gell-Mann. *The Quark and the Jaguar* (New York: Freeman, 1994), p. 249.

7. See Gell-Mann (1994), pp. 238–9; and Holland (1995), pp. 38–9 and p. 5.

8. W. Ashby, *An Introduction to Cybernetics* (New York: Wiley, 1956).

9. R. Pascale, interviews with James Cannavino, May 1996.

10. See Gell-Mann (1994), p. 64 and p. 253; and S.J. Gould. *Full House* (New York: Crown Publishing, 1996), p. 138.

11. G. Hamel, 'Strategy as Revolution,' *Harvard Business Review*, vol. 74, July-August 1996, pp. 69–82.

12. Information and quotations in this section are drawn from: R. Pascale, interviews with Steve Miller, London. The Hague, and Houston, October 1997 through February 1998.

13. Kauffman (1995), pp. 80–6.

14. Waldrop (1992), p. 110.

15. J. Kao, *Jamming: The Art and Discipline of Business Creativity* (New York: HarperCollins, 1997).

16. I. Marshall and D. Zohar, *Who's Afraid of Schrodinger's Cat?* (New York, Morrow, 1997), p. 16, p. 19. pp. 153–8.

17. Seldon's work is unpublished. He considers it proprietary and solely for consulting purposes.

18. Information and quotations in this section are drawn from: R. Pascale, interviews with Steve Miller, London, The Hague, and Houston, October 1997 through February 1998.

19. Gell-Mann (1994), pp. 228–30.

20. Waldrop (1992), pp. 138–9.

21. R. Hof, 'Hewlett Packard,' *Business Week*, 13 February 1995, p. 67.

22. Information and quotations in this section are drawn from: R. Pascale, interviews with Steve Miller, London. The Hague, and Houston, October 1997 through February 1998.

23. A. Saxenian, 'Lessons from Silicon Valley,' *Technology Review*, vol. 97. no. 5. July 1994, pp. 42–5.

24. Information and quotations in this section are drawn from: R. Pascale, interviews with Steve Miller, London, The Hague, and Houston, October 1997 through February 1998.

26

PERSPECTIVES ON STRATEGY

Geoff Jones

INTRODUCTION

This chapter is primarily concerned with strategy as a management discipline, what it consists of, what its roots are, what its critics say about it and how it changes. Understanding these things can help us come to our own view and be clearer about what we can and cannot reasonably expect strategy to be able to *do* for us, regardless of the claims made for it by its proponents.

We shall be considering a range of different approaches to strategy in an attempt both to demonstrate its diversity and to highlight some of its dominant assumptions. It is clear that there is no one 'theory' of strategy, or even one definition, but there is what might be considered to be a 'mainstream' of writers and approaches, and certainly many different ideas about what is important in strategy and how strategy research should be conducted. The historic dominance of North American or at least Anglo-American academics, writers and consultants in strategy, with their distinctive concerns and research traditions, has been an important aspect of strategy affecting its global relevance.

Also, because the boundaries of strategy are permeable, there are a number of perspectives, including 'critical' perspectives, which are not part of the mainstream, yet which might become so, or have some influence on how the discipline will change in the future. Here is where some of the biggest challenges to the dominant paradigm(s) may come from. Some of these perspectives will be discussed in this chapter. However, the aim is not to write a compendium but to illustrate the range and scope of the alternatives on offer and place the latest writings on strategy in broader sets of ideas. What might be called the rhetoric of strategy – its persuasive power – is strong, and it is important to be appreciative of its strengths but also to be able to see where they originate, what assumptions they depend on and how they are constructed. One way of doing this is to contrast them with some other management perspectives which are at present not well represented within the discipline.

I begin with a general discussion about the role of different perspectives in strategy and some of the assumptions which underlie them. This is followed by an introduction to some of the ways in which strategy has been divided up into different 'schools'. Problems with these categorizations lead me to consider some perspectives which are more critical of the role of strategy in organizations and of some of its (often undeclared) assumptions. We then introduce some of the less considered approaches to strategy, such as the 'dramaturgical' or 'enactment' approaches which are probably outside the strategy mainstream but which nevertheless are influential in other areas of management and organization studies. We conclude with some brief suggestions about how managers in particular can arrive at their own choices.

PERSPECTIVES ON STRATEGY AND STRATEGY IN PERSPECTIVE

In the period since the end of the Second World War, the discipline of strategy or strategic management has become one of the most powerful elements in the discourse and practice of management. Evidence for this simple statement could no doubt be gathered in many different ways; for example, through surveys of managers and academics, by noting the existence and success of learned journals such as the *Strategic Management Journal*, by analysing the number of books, articles and other media dealing with strategy or strategic issues and so on.

For most readers of this chapter, however, I suspect that no such empirical justification is necessary: strategy self-evidently *is* important. Indeed, one of the ways in which it has achieved its success in becoming such a major part of the management field has been by steadily reinforcing the rough equivalence of 'strategic' and 'important' in the English language. This equivalence gives the management discipline of strategy great power. When any rival formulation of management problems comes along to claim and demand attention, whether it originates in academic research programmes, from accounts of managers' experience or from translation from other fields such as politics or computer science, strategy can immediately make its own claim to appropriate the new ideas, because if they are as important as their proponents say, they must, by definition, be *strategic*, and hence potentially a legitimate part of the domain of strategy. Thus strategy continues to incorporate the best ideas and as it does so it can attract more researchers and fund more research; and so its own power increases along with the knowledge it generates.

In management there can arguably be no more important questions than 'why does this organization exist and what is it trying to achieve?', 'what activities should it undertake?', 'how big should it be?', 'how can it achieve its objectives?' and so on. Strategy claims to be the discipline which deals with these kinds of question. And today we regard these questions as fundamental. Yet in the sociology of knowledge, the kind of questions posed are usually more important than the answers given (Zan, 1995). And the questions strategy poses have not always been conceived in the way we now regard as self-evident, and certainly they have not always been answered in the way we choose to answer them today. The latter may not surprise us if we believe in scientific and academic progress – we simply 'know' more now than we did – but the former perhaps ought to be more persuasive in alerting us to the historical contingency of strategy as a discipline, and that, in turn, should sensitize us to the need to understand the different perspectives and conditions of possibility contained in the dynamics of the discipline today.

Business strategy[1], whether traced from its presumed ancestry in ancient Greece or China (e.g. Ansoff, 1965; Bracker, 1980), from developments in the mid-nineteenth century in North America (Chandler, 1962, 1977; Hoskin, 1990; Hoskin, Macve and Stone, 1997), from the evolution of the 'policy' concept (e.g. Sloan, 1963) or to the industrial economics of the post-World War II era (Rumelt *et al.*, 1991), is easily shown to be made up of a wide range of elements. It does not have an 'essence', either in content or method, which is applicable for all time and circumstances. It changes and transforms itself. Yet if we read a book or article about strategy, what is striking about it is its self-confidence, its apparent certainty that the current view is the best view available, that its methods of analysis are capable of being brought to bear on any 'strategic' management issue and that this knowledge is clearly superior to its historical predecessors. And unlike other parts of the social sciences or humanities, the challenge of contemporaneous multiple perspectives seems to be relatively ignored in favour of declaiming the merits of the latest approach (for example, the current prominence of the resource-based view of strategy – see e.g. Grant, 1995).

That is not to say that strategy academics are unaware of different views or unwilling to debate them: there have been some celebrated public disagreements. But as a discipline, like many in management, largely composed of bits of others, there is a rather keen awareness of boundaries, of what is and what is not 'strategy', even if the precise definition is hard to ascertain. There is a certain attempt to promote the discipline and qualify the epithet of 'strategist' (Alvesson and Willmott, 1996: 133). This commitment to the discipline tends to obscure some of the assumptions and effects of strategy. Let me start with some widely used yet often undeclared or unexamined assumptions which underpin many writings and courses on strategy.

ASSUMPTIONS AND PREFERENCES IN STRATEGY

It is clear that the style adopted by writers on strategy does not always present any approach or set of ideas uncritically. Many of the models and concepts on offer are qualified in some way so that the reader can form a balanced view of their strengths and weaknesses. Yet it is also clear that particular writers believe that, for example, the resource-based view of strategy has a greater claim on legitimacy and utility than some other views (for example, that organizations should primarily consider and attempt to enter more attractive industries). Also, a number of strategy concepts are underpinned by further concepts which may not always be fully scrutinized. There are various reasons for this in addition to the desire of the writers to legitimize their discipline – for example, you have to start somewhere, with some common understandings, and not need to do a course in philosophy first.

So when considering some of the approaches presented in writings on strategy, I suggest that there are a number of common yet disputable values and assumptions underlying them. These may be summarized as follows:

- The approach is analytical and realistic; that is, it presumes there is some 'reality' 'out there' which can be apprehended and understood with sensitive enough research and conceptual frameworks. Yet there is also recognition of the value of experience and meaning, for example in paradigms and institutions.
- It postulates 'bounded' actors who nevertheless will be 'rational' if 'allowed' to be.
- It stresses the interconnectedness of all elements in the discussion, and implies that these connections can be articulated, mapped in some way and manipulated.
- It conceives of the possibility and desirability of an optimal balance of stakeholder interests while recognizing inevitable imbalances of power.
- It suggests that managers have power to act and change things for the better in accordance with some collective agreement on what 'better' is.
- It is 'positivist' in the sense of claiming (perhaps implicitly) that the knowledge we have now is superior to the knowledge possessed by our predecessors. The present is seen to have emerged from the past in accordance with certain rules (for example, that changes in 'environments' lead to changes in 'organizations') which we believe exist even if we only dimly comprehend them. So it is determinist also, even though we recognize that rationality is bounded.

Many of these assumptions may strike you as being pretty reasonable – even as being 'common sense' (although the strategy material on paradigms (e.g. Johnson, 1987) should alert us to the dangers of taking common sense for granted). But many writers have come to challenge some or all these 'taken-for-granted' assumptions over the last twenty years or so. Later we will consider some of these. First, though, we will look at some of the ways in which strategists have attempted to classify and categorize their own discipline.

APPROACHES TO STRATEGY

A good place to start a review of approaches to strategy is to refer to Richard Whittington's well-regarded and accessible text *What is Strategy and Does it Matter?* (Whittington, 1993). Commenting that there is a fundamental implausibility in the claims made by books on strategy to disclose the 'secrets' of strategy for £25 when top managers are paid so much, he organizes his discussion and theories of strategy into four broad groupings which differ in two fundamental respects: the extent to which organizations seek either profit-maximizing or pluralist outcomes, and the extent to which strategy is deliberately planned rather than emerging incrementally, accidentally or through a more or less muddled and uncertain process. This allows many of the key thinkers in strategy to be located in relation to each other, as in Figure 26.1. The approaches can be roughly characterized as follows:

Classical – Stresses rationality and analysis.

Evolutionary – Stresses the unpredictability of the environment which makes irrelevant much of what is traditionally regarded as strategic analysis. It is analogous to the biological 'survival of the fittest' model.

Processual – A pragmatic view of strategy: the world and our knowledge are imperfect, so organizations have to take account of this in their strategic processes.

Systemic – stresses the importance and, to an extent, the uniqueness of social systems within which diverse attitudes to, and conceptualizations about, strategic issues occur. Strategy will thus, in part, reflect the social system in which it occurs.

Although certain writers can be 'placed' in certain 'schools', it is unlikely that any particular view of strategy can be confined entirely within that school, or, indeed that the writings of any particular writer over a long career can be easily classified. It seems even more unlikely that anyone ever set out to be included in any particular category or school. So Whittington's categories are useful primarily as an heuristic device – a way of clarifying or categorizing a complex set of issues. Some people will find his categories too neat and simplistic – for example, categorizing both the Classical and Evolutionary schools as profit-maximizing underrates the Evolutionary approach's emphasis on survival.

There are even simpler ways to categorize approaches to strategy. One common way of dividing up strategy is between the *strategic choice* and *ecological* approaches. Whittington's Classical, Processual and Systemic approaches all in their various ways presume that strategists can make choices which influence outcomes. The ecological approach, on the other hand, tends to see strategists as virtually powerless in the face of uncontrollable, and in many ways unknowable, forces (arising from uncertainty and complexity). Hence, Whittington's Evolutionary category might be considered 'anti-strategy'. But even this distinction is open to challenge: some strategists, particularly those heavily influenced by economics, tend to see macro-economic forces in a similar way to the ecologists, but still believe in strategic choice. They place emphasis on the short-lived nature of advantage and the beneficial effects of this (Rumelt *et al.*, 1991).

In contrast to Whittington's four approaches, there are more elaborate categorizations available, for example, Mintzberg's ten 'schools of strategic thought':

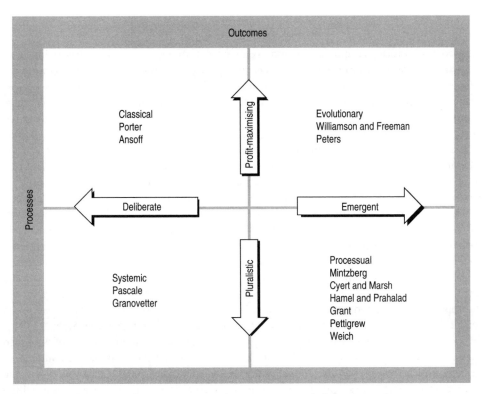

Figure 26.1 Whittington's four generic approaches to strategy with illustrative authors

- design
- planning
- positioning
- entrepreneurial
- cognitive
- learning
- political
- cultural
- environmental
- configurational.

(Mintzberg, 1990a)

These schools have been found to differ significantly in the language and concepts they use (Crouch and Basch, 1996) and thus may be genuinely distinctive and incompatible approaches. This possibility ties in well with some of the more critical approaches to strategy (especially strategy as drama and the linguistic aspects of strategy) discussed below.

One important distinction which Whittington's classification draws out is the difference between the Classicists' and the Processualists' attitudes to research and the development of theories of strategy. Classicists stress rational and deliberate processes. This is based on certain commitments to the rules and procedures of science as the only means by which valid and reliable knowledge can be obtained. Their characteristic way of proceeding is to conduct detailed analytical research in an attempt to deduce rules and laws which will work in all (or most) circumstances. The human subject with its vagaries and inconsistencies tends to assume a more subordinate role – unless in the role of strategist, of course!

By contrast, Processual approaches tend to emphasize learning as a means of developing ideas; in particular, learning from experience rather than purely from research. Even this ignores the influential contribution of other modes of learning such as *action research* (Peters and Robinson, 1984). Although it is difficult to criticize the idea of learning as being a 'good thing', learning approaches are not without their difficulties, many of which are recognized by their advocates. Levinthal and March (1993), for example, highlight some of the important limitations of learning processes. They draw attention to the difficulties of coping with confusing experience and the dilemmas involved in deciding whether to explore new knowledge areas or to exploit current competencies. They argue that organizations suffer from three kinds of 'learning myopia': the tendencies to overlook distant times, distant places and failures. For example, strategies which permit survival in the short term may be incompatible with long-run success. Strategies for individual parts of an organization may be incompatible with strategies for the whole. Confidence in control may lead to expectations about outcomes before consequences are observed and interpreted. All this leads to an overinvestment in the exploitation of current capabilities at the expense of exploration of new knowledge. Levinthal and March conclude that expectations about what learning can achieve should be more restrained. This debate between 'science' and 'learning' was the topic of a celebrated exchange between Mintzberg and Ansoff (Mintzberg, 1990b, 1991; Ansoff, 1991) representing the Processual and Classical schools of strategy respectively.

The more conventional view of how strategy develops relies on a careful analysis of published studies. For example, Eisenhardt and Zbaracki (1992) reviewed the 'dominant paradigms' of strategy, which they viewed as rationality and bounded validity, politics and power and the 'garbage can' model of strategic choice. They examined the theory and empirical support within each paradigm and concluded that the empirical evidence showed:

1   that strategic decision-makers are boundedly rational
2   that power wins battles of choice, and
3   that chance matters.

But they also argued that 'these paradigms rest on unrealistic assumptions and tired controversies which are no longer very controversial'. A new research agenda in strategy might involve 'creating a more realistic view of strategic decision-making by opening up our conceptions of cognition and conflict to include insight, intuition, emotion and conflict resolution ... [and] emphasizing normative implications'.

So even a view that strategy develops from empirical studies concludes that something may be wrong with the underlying assumptions in the research itself. To assume, therefore, that strategy develops in any particular way – especially a 'scientific' way – is itself an assumption.

There are other approaches which move beyond the categories presented here; for example, some researchers attempt to deal with problems of uncertainty, complexity and non-linearity through theories of *complex adaptive systems* (Stacey, 1995). This approach embraces complexity and 'chaos theory' in an attempt to overcome some of the problems with deterministic approaches. It attempts to model uncertainty and complexity through simulations of randomly formed informal networks. This moves beyond the categories used by Whittington.

These various approaches may influence the kinds of strategy which organizations pursue. Classical approaches stress rationality and clarity and hence are likely to lead to highly analytic and deliberate styles of strategy based in a few expert hands. By contrast, Processual approaches are more likely to recognize a range of factors and inputs leading to a range of outcomes, many of which will be unintentional. This is more likely to involve a wider set of people and to emphasize *learning and bargaining* rather than analysis as the means by which strategic insight is acquired, with *incrementalism* as the typical strategic process.

The Systemic approach draws attention to the effect of local cultures and attitudes, and the Anglo-American roots of strategy itself. It is likely to lead to an interest in different styles of strategy in different cultures and hence to understanding and working with these differences rather than the 'one style fits all' approach characteristic of Classicists. This approach pays attention to differences (in things such as values and governments) and developing strategy accordingly. One rather surprising aspect of Whittington's assessment of this approach is that he seems to regard it as being essentially *deliberate*: there seems to be no particular reason why an emergent stance cannot be adopted here also, or that it might incorporate a Processual outlook.

Another factor not considered by Whittington is the effect of the kind of organization being managed and its type of ownership. For example, small firms are likely to have little or no effect on the environments in which they operate. Also, they may not need to persuade stock markets and analysts that they conform to 'accepted' practices. The Classical rational planning approach, irrespective of its validity otherwise, would just be a waste of time for such an organization.

WHAT'S WRONG WITH STRATEGY?

Most management researchers, although disagreeing with each other about various things (such as dominant theories and methods), do share certain assumptions, particularly generally positive views about the value of strategy and management. These views are not, however, necessarily shared by all researchers, particularly those from the social sciences. Unlike the management researchers, who focus on the actions of managers (often with a view to developing ways of producing 'better' management), many social scientists tend to see management as a wider social phenomenon whose benefits should not be automatically assumed and which is suffering from a range of problems which cast doubt on the bases of management research traditionally underpinning strategy. Some of these problems are:

- The rise of management and in the number of managers does not correspond with cycles of economic prosperity.
- Increasing the amount of management education does not seem to lead automatically to improved economic performance.
- 'Managerialism' is becoming so widespread and influential we find it hard to think of anything except in terms of managing it – our families, our relationships, our time, the environment, etc.
- The world is now seen by some to be too complex and uncertain to be 'managed' in the sense that we ordinarily understand the term (i.e. that managerial actions lead to desired effects and *only* those effects).
- There is a long tradition of valuing the practical and experiential and a distrust of the 'theoretical'.
- There is doubt about whether management practices and meanings can be generalized globally because of fundamental cultural differences. Therefore the idea of management as a science (in the traditional understanding of 'science') is challenged (French and Grey, 1996).

Strategy, because of its claims to be an inclusive and important management discipline, has attracted criticism. This criticism focuses in particular on the *power effects* of strategy and strategic discourse, which I shall discuss next.

Critical Approaches

Despite its apparently long history, business strategy has only recently become a subject of its own, and a very powerful one at that (Hoskin, Macve and Stone, 1997). Why is this and what are the consequences? Critics of strategy cite its tendency:

> ...to abstract the politics of strategic decision-making from the wider historical and social contexts of managerial action. Insufficient account is taken of how managers are positioned by historical forces to assume and maintain a monopoly of strategic decision-making responsibility... [t]here is little consideration of how managerial values are laden with ideological assumptions about the 'facts' of strategic management. Corporate strategies are rarely assessed in terms of their wider impact on society.
>
> (Alvesson and Willmott, 1996: 132)

This argument draws attention to the position and power of the strategist and the consequences of (usually) his actions. It also considers exactly how this power is 'manufactured' – how we come to accept the language of strategy as being 'common sense' and thus accept the power of its speakers as inevitable and deserved. Knights and Morgan (1991) have focused on how strategy has come to be so influential.

They first draw attention to the way in which strategy entered the business field, which they argue was the result of US domination of managerial discourse and the changes which affected US corporations in the post-Second World War period. These changes have three notable features:

1 the gradual restructuring of ownership patterns and the institutional separation of ownership from managerial control which began in the US in the inter-war period (though it had occurred earlier in the UK)
2 changes in international market conditions which gave the USA a stewardship role in the world economy through its multinational corporations
3 changes in the organizational form of these companies, in particular the rise of the multidivisional form, which led to changes in the means of controlling them.

These control requirements led to an opportunity to develop a 'discursive space' which military strategy (with its emphasis on controlling far-flung units through its utilization of communications technology and surveillance techniques, and the prestige acquired through success in war) was able to fill. Academics such as Ansoff (1965) began to articulate the need for corporate strategy. Specialist business practitioners also begin to emerge. Knights and Morgan draw attention to the ways in which, as more and more people come to be involved, it becomes more difficult to think of any alternative. But not everyone is swept along by the power of the discourse. Managers who favour a more instinctive entrepreneurial approach, as well as staff at the lower levels of the organization, are likely to resist, rather than regard strategy as inevitable.

Knights and Morgan identify seven reasons why the discourse of corporate strategy came to be dominant. These are:

1 It provides managers with a rationalization of their successes and failures.
2 It sustains and enhances the prerogatives of management and negates alternative perspectives on organizations.
3 It generates a sense of personal and organizational security for managers.

4 It reflects and sustains a strong sense of gendered masculinity for male management.
5 It demonstrates managerial 'rationality' to colleagues, customers, competitors, govern-ment and other significant people in the environment, who are likely to be looking for such signals.
6 It facilitates and legitimizes the exercise of power.
7 It creates a language and practice which enables organizational members to construct an identity for themselves.

Clearly, these kinds of explanation for the development of strategy are far from Ansoff's con-ception of the 'facts' determining strategy. But what they provide is an explanation which regards the power effects of strategy as being more related to the interests of the people involved than a neutral and objective view of a truth which has become apparent through rigorous and disinterested research techniques.

Knights and Morgan then conduct their own analysis of the assumptions which they say underpin strategy. These are as follows:

• It is characteristic of strategy that everything is explicable in the end. There is nothing in principle which is unknowable.
• Managers are credentialled experts with the ability to both define the problems the organi-zation faces and the solutions it needs to adopt.
• Managers can create a sense of comfort that their destiny is in their own hands.
• Strategic discourse and practice both reflects and reproduces what may be termed a 'mas-culist conception of power' (Brittan, 1989).
• The construction of managers as competent strategists becomes crucial in coping with the insecurity and the proliferation of information.

These ideas in fact echo some of the Processual school. For example, Pettigrew (1985) draws attention to the construction of power through the creation of expertise. What is different about Knights and Morgan's critique is that it regards the way in which we perceive our roles as man-agers or customers or strategists as also being the product of these power relations. In other words, the occupation and power of a 'strategist' is a socially constructed, not a natural phenomenon, and depends on there being certain spaces, discourses and power relations avail-able before it can come into existence. Therefore:

> Strategy does not simply respond to pre-existing problems. In the process of its formulation, strat-egy is actively involved in the constitution, or re-definition, of problems in advance of offering itself as a solution to them.
>
> (Knights and Morgan, 1991: 270)

This discussion may have taken us a long way from the usual discussions found in strategy textbooks. But it is important to appreciate that much debate about strategy – even where there are strong opposing views such as those of Mintzberg and Ansoff – is conducted by 'insiders', those who already accept the boundaries and subject matter of strategy as largely given. What the critical approach does for us, at the very least, is to sensitize us to the existence of a range of views which do not necessarily regard strategy as an inevitable and desirable phenomenon.

What we have discussed is a range of different perceptions of strategy which in turn seem to embody a whole range of different assumptions about human attitudes and behaviour in organizations. 499

The distinctions between Whittington's Classical and Processual schools, the debate between Mintzberg and Ansoff, the critical views of Knights and Morgan, all challenge the idea that strategy is an unambiguously rational activity. The Processualists cast doubt on the feasibility or desirability of the planned, 'rational' approach; the critical theorists draw attention to the role of 'interests' in the development of strategy. The significance of management gurus (Huczynski, 1993) draws attention to another way of looking at strategists – as secular priests or witchdoctors. This suggests a number of different ways of regarding strategy *in terms of* rationality and interests.

One way of conceptualizing this (Thomas, 1993) proposes a framework based on two main dimensions: rationality and sectionalism. Rationality can be divided into the objective (demonstrated through the application of scientific procedures) and the subjective rationality of actions.

Sectionalism contrasts management action as oriented towards 'unitary' ends (in accordance with the interests of all an organization's stakeholders) with that pursued for 'sectional' ends (the interests of specific groups such as shareholders). The resulting matrix (Figure 26.2) defines a conceptual space within which theories of management can be located. This framework would depict Whittington's Classical school as a rational profession and his Processual school as being more concerned with politics. But in addition, we can also include approaches critical of strategy such as those which view strategy as an agency of capitalism, or of a subjectively rational but objectively irrational practice akin to magic or religion.

This framework allows a different set of concerns from Whittington's about management and strategy to be taken into account. We shall now consider some of these perspectives.

Strategy as Drama

Moving towards an outlook which is less analytical than much of mainstream strategic thinking, this section will consider some different emphases which are emerging in the strategy literature. There is an analogy between strategy and drama which leads us to a view of strategy as 'dialogue and doing'. Finally, we consider briefly a kind of criticism which is growing, often under the slippery label of postmodernism, which looks even more carefully than we have so far done at the ways in which management and strategy language and text are constructed.

The discussion in the previous paragraph has drawn attention away from seeing strategy as representing our best interpretation of 'the facts' to seeing it more as a matter of style rather than content. One metaphor which captures this outlook is given by Mockler (1994). In contrast to the 'management guru as witch doctor' (Cleverly, 1971; Clark and Salaman, 1996) he suggests that we need not worry too much about the range of theories and approaches we have been discussing. Mockler claims that strategy is analogous to the field of drama and dramatic literature. Like drama, it has two 'audiences': those who study it as literature and those who perform it. In strategy, the academic or observer perspective prevails despite strategy being largely a performance art acted out by managers. Like strategy, there are many 'schools' of drama – Classical Greek and Roman, sixteenth- and seventeenth-century Elizabethan and Jacobean, seventeenth-century Classical French and so on – which have close ties with the country and era in which they were written, the dramatic genre and author, and other contextual aspects. Drama has a number of factors which separate it from other arts and which allow it to be interpreted in a range of different cultures and situations.

Strategy may also have some common elements which transcend situational context. But in strategy, comparatively little attention is given to the contextual factors themselves. This view directs our attention to three things:

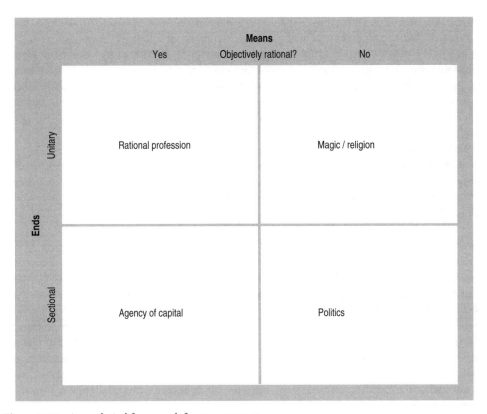

Figure 26.2 An analytical framework for management

- The futility of trying to decide which general approach to strategy is 'best', because the ideas themselves are not directly comparable to each other. Your view of strategy depends on a whole range of factors to do with you, your stakeholders, the situation, its history and so on. Strategy is judgemental, and therefore uncertain and prone to error.
- That the question of what is 'best' is meaningless since different views can happily co-exist – people just find some kinds of drama / strategy more appealing to their experience and expectations than others. If it 'works' for you – it works.
- Finally, there can be a set of concepts which can be applied to different dramatic situations, whether in the theatre or in organizations, which establish the language in which debates and evaluations can be conducted, yet which do not permit participants to establish privileged positions, because the concepts can be applied to and support many different positions. It is because of these differences that learning can occur, but only if we are sensitive to them and reflective about our own attitude towards them.

THE SOCIAL CONSTRUCTION OF STRATEGY

It is only a short step from seeing strategy as drama to seeing strategy as 'talk' – as a kind of legitimate cultural communication which is actually 'made up' (invented or enacted) in the organizational setting, which makes the participants feel 'in touch', and maybe able to achieve some of the benefits they seek (of being secure, in control, or simply having a role to play). In an article entitled 'Strategy through dialogue and doing', Pye (1995) argues that managing is about dialogue and action – that is, 'through listening and talking, creating, shaping and sharing meaning, things are made to happen and managing is said to have taken place. If, in this process, it is helpful to call this strategic decision-making, so be it. But this should be recognized as a *communicative device* rather than a canon of business: indeed, any search for the principles is ... elusive.'

Weick (1990) sees culture as about sharing certain things. But he points out that sharing can mean either to divide and distribute or to hold things in common. He thinks that we need to refine this and to see sharing as both process and outcome. We need to get away from seeing things in 'I'm right and everybody else is wrong' terms, and more in terms of 'I don't know, let's see...'. The subjects of Pye's study – senior executives from a range of industries such as textile manufacturing, banking, engineering, retailing and conglomerates – practised this kind of orientation. Their readings of situations, their grounding in the language and traditions of the organization differ, yet their ability to craft new languages and meanings, and to maintain relationships through talking and communicating, is what underpins their success – nothing about understanding the principles of strategy. Indeed, Pye goes further and detects a kind of 'halo effect' surrounding senior executives – that is, a tendency on the part of subordinates to *assume* that their discussions with their seniors were based on some set of rules or logic, and to assume that they did not have access to these. Yet Pye argues that it does not matter what these rules are or whether they exist at all, because they are irrelevant to the enactment of management and strategy. People behave *as though* there were principles of management, even though no one can be sure what they are. Yet management 'happens' or is enacted in the talk and transactions between people.

You may recall the story recounted by Weick (1990) of the Hungarian soldiers marooned high in the Alpine snows, who despaired until one of them found a map in his pocket. The soldiers confidently marched down the mountain to safety and only discovered when they got back that the map was of the Pyrenees. This is part of what Pye is saying: strategy may happen *despite* rather than because of the formulations of strategists and gurus. It may not matter whether what they say is 'true' or not. It seems to be more important that we believe that *someone* knows what to do (back to the view of strategists as organizational witch doctors) – but even this may not be what determines whether strategy is successful or not. What matters is the 'talk' and how it is conducted and enacted, and how people interpret and apply what is said in their day-to-day situations – not in the boardroom or the strategy seminars. Strategy is achieved through dialogue and doing.

This seems to sum up much of the world of managing, whether it is called strategic decision-making, executive process, managing or communicating – a search for rules to describe something that is little more than a communicative device. As Pye says, 'every means of appreciating it hinges on dialogue – listening and talking – and *things* may be talked up or down, round or about, over or through. And, ultimately, *things* may be talked out, subsequently to be replaced by different talk. But in this way, *things* are made to happen'. Here we are returning to some themes of management and strategy as symbolic action, as having a value and meaning independent of the facts and theories offered by academics. This approach overcomes some of the problems of strategy in organizations, because an emphasis on constructed meanings applies to all kinds of social interaction, not just to those specialist activities which are undertaken in the kinds of organization included in strategy. It argues that there is no difference between the substantive and the symbolic because all behaviour is symbolic and socially constructed. This line of thought has strong roots in the social sciences (Berger and Luckmann, 1966). There seems no reason why it should not be applied equally to strategy, as Pye suggests.

POSTMODERNISM AND STRATEGY

The debate about strategy and management as 'dialogue' is not the most extreme departure from the more usual ideas about what strategy is. In recent years, a more radical critique of managerial discourses has been developed, drawing from developments in the social sciences and the humanities, and based not on concepts of interests but on linguistic analysis. This approach, still very much a minority interest, considers management disciplines as purely *textual* phenomena – that is, concerned with the relationship between language and thought. As we have seen, there is a range of views on how management or strategy ideas come to be adopted. We have considered a continuum from the 'scientific' at one end, through a behavioural or processual set of views, to views which stress the importance of power and interests, and others which regard the existence of management principles as incidental to the enactment of management and strategy.

The final position I want to consider is what is often controversially labelled a 'postmodern' approach to management and strategy (Cooper and Burrell, 1988). What this concentrates on is not how power or principles come to dominate what is regarded as legitimate management discourse, but how certain assumptions and relations are built into the very language itself that we use to express ourselves. Proponents of postmodernism, such as the French philosopher Derrida (1978), argue that we must attempt to analyse the way in which texts and languages themselves are constructed if we are to understand why our world is the way it seems. This method of analysis, known as *deconstruction*, places at least as much emphasis on what is *not* said as what is said. It is argued that the *presence* of something in a text simultaneously constructs an *absence* of something else, and that attending to these absences will illuminate a lot of our textual practices and hence what we regard as our 'common sense'. Postmodernists go further and argue that there is no *necessary* relationship between our texts and the world 'out there' that can be satisfactorily established: our texts are simply a set of arbitrary signs that only have meaning because we treat them as though they were meaningful. The goal of deconstruction is to expose the inherent contradictions which reside in any text.

This is not the place to explore these ideas in any depth – the postmodernist position is virtually the opposite of that taken in any writing on strategy. It is mentioned here because there seems to be a growing doubt in some quarters about whether the 'science' of management is at all capable of dealing with the issues it claims to be able to, and this has prompted some academics to analyse management from a postmodern perspective (Burrell, 1992). To give some idea of what these writers are interested in, we need to consider some of the ways in which the *concept* of strategy is constructed.

Let us start with a general set of comments. In order for managers to manage we rely on our mutual understanding of certain concepts such as 'organization', 'environment' and 'network'. Most of the time, we do not bother to subject these concepts to any detailed scrutiny unless we want to elaborate them in some way.

There are some other assumptions implicit in these ordinary but unexamined words in strategy and other management fields which may be more problematic than you might think. This is because we are accustomed to their use and may not realize that they are part of our 'paradigm', or way of thinking about these things.

'Environment' is a good example of a concept which seems self-evident to us and which we presume has always existed. But people have only very recently (in historical terms) conceptualized their surroundings in terms of an 'environment'. Does that mean that people have always had an 'environment' even if they did not conceptualize it as such? We tend to think that they did – because we believe in the 'reality' of the concept and its analytical usefulness. Yet 'environment' presupposes something which by definition is *not* environment. Similarly, if we think of an organization, we think also of something which is *not* the organization. These alternations can reveal a lot about the assumptions inherent in the concept itself. This line of thought involves us in questioning the validity (and in some contexts the ethics) of imposing our 'version' of reality on to people who do not share it, arguing that we can only make sense of people's behaviour (and hence formulate programmes of action, such as strategy, which are useful to *us*) if we understand the concepts and categories of thought which were (or are) meaningful to *them*.

Like environment, 'strategy' also has a very recent history in its application to business as against its long use in military discourse. The term is traditionally believed to have its roots in economics and game theory in the post-Second World War period but not to have been widely used in a business context until the 1960s. This ought to make us think about the role that strategy played in the success of organizations before they had things they called strategies. Did, therefore, DuPont or General Motors in the early twentieth century succeed without having any strategy? Or did they have strategies but call them something else?

Strategists tend to make two kinds of responses to these questions. They are likely to argue either:

(a) that the environment (that word again) we exist in today is different from earlier times in particular ways (more uncertainty, complexity, turbulence, rapid change, etc.) which now make strategy vital where it may not have been in the past; or

(b) businesses *did* have strategy in the past in the sense of having purposes, goals, intentions or whatever; they just did not have the benefit of the modern conceptions of it which we have acquired through our research and experience.

In both cases, the modern conception of strategy remains intact and unchallenged. But strategy also has power as a rhetorical device to mobilize support for a particular way of looking at strategic problems (Eccles and Nohria, 1992) and to influence the language in organizational debates. Postmodernists would draw attention to the way in which texts on strategy were constructed regardless of any 'empirical' relationships between the signifier (the language) and the signified (the object being referred to).

So when we 'talk strategy' we should be aware that we are constructing a certain view of the world, mainly in terms of what interests us as strategists; and this construction may not accord with the constructions which non-strategists put on the aspects of the situation which concern them most. The language game itself is one of the areas where power relations are played out.

This general attempt to examine some of the implications of the language and concepts of strategy should facilitate more awareness of a strategist's perspective being a *particular* perspective which might not be shared.

The range of perspectives presented in this chapter is summarized in Figure 26.3 which presents them in terms of their authors' perceptions of the desirability of rationality in management, as defined by Thomas (1993) in Figure 26.2.

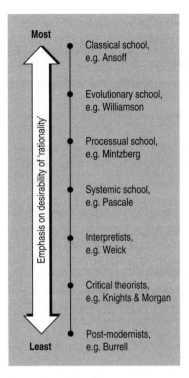

Figure 26.3 The rationality continuum for approaches to strategy

WHAT TO DO: THE FOUR FACES OF PRAGMATISM

Given the doubts about, but accepting the continuing demand for, the kinds of offering academics and strategy gurus make available, what should the manager do? Managers need to make up their own minds about how good and how useful is the material they are being offered. The uncritical adoption of the latest management nostrums ('flavour of the month management') has been shown to be harmful to US business over the last 30 years (Locke, 1996). Nohria and Berkley (1994) argue that 'the widespread adoption of trendy management techniques during the 1980s allowed managers to rely on ready-made answers instead of searching for creative solutions'. They call for a 'return to pragmatism' which explicitly recognizes the uncertainties inherent in the managerial environment and the ways in which managers actually try to make sense of it.

To do this, they borrow a well-known concept from anthropology, that of the *bricoleur* ('handyman' in English – but the French connotation is that of an improviser, using anything appropriate for the task). The suggestion is that managers should be *bricoleurs* when it comes to management ideas – taking bits and pieces that seem useful to them and welding them into a set of perhaps imperfect tools for the task in hand. Inevitably, as with much management writing, there are some 'guiding principles' (but only four) as follows:

505

The four faces of pragmatism

- *Sensitivity to context* – Being able to judge the parameters of a particular situation and decide what ideas and actions will work in that context.
- *Willingness to make do* – Experimenting with and using available resources and material to find workable solutions.
- *Focus on outcomes* – Being concerned with getting results, but not being too 'hung-up' on how to get them.
- *Openness to uncertainty* – Recognizing the impossibility of being able to anticipate all circumstances and thereby being required to act out of ignorance.

(Adapted from Nohria and Berkley, 1994)

So we need to consider our own particular 'portfolios' of meaningful concepts, and, given the diversity of approaches this is bound to contain, how we come to accept such a plurality of incongruent actions or techniques in strategy yet remain able to communicate and act effectively. This 'neo-pragmatism' will not be compatible with all the approaches discussed in this chapter, but it probably is compatible with those perspectives which remain convinced that strategy, however defined and with whatever qualification, is an activity worth pursuing.

CONCLUSION

In this chapter, we have taken a journey around the borders of the 'field' of strategy and have occasionally gone through the gate into the world outside and looked back. The aim of this exercise is to assert that no body of knowledge is discrete and sacrosanct, or 'knows all the answers' – even to problems it has itself defined. There is a wide range of approaches to strategy, some of which do not even share basic assumptions. There are some views which are critical of its power, or sceptical about its legitimacy. We need to understand these differences but not be overwhelmed by them. Incompatible approaches can still be melded together in a practical situation even if the mix is likely to vary from one set of problems to another.

The pragmatic model of the conceptual *bricoleur*/handyman and the significance of dialogue and communication in constructing individual strategy models allows us to construct perspectives with which we can be comfortable *and* which also seem to work for us. What is most important is that to achieve this insight it is necessary to have gone through a learning process, and in particular to 'learn how to learn'. Here we return to the propositions put forward at the beginning of the chapter about strategy incorporating ideas from elsewhere, which is one of the key capabilities stressed by the resource-based view of strategy (Grant, 1995). With this capability of learning we might associate the capabilities of choosing and acting, and this chapter has, through its presentation of the wide range of perspectives on strategy which are available, attempted to provide a wider range to choose from than usual. I hope and expect that this will mean that what I have called mainstream strategy becomes in the future a broader rather than narrower discipline and activity than it seems to be at present.

NOTE

1   Within the field of strategic management, 'business strategy' is a discrete specialism of its own concerned with strategy at the level of the business unit as against, say, corporate strategy. But I use the term here simply to differentiate the use of strategy in a business management rather than a military context. The term 'strategic management' which used to denote this distinction is giving way to a more generic use of the term 'strategy' for business or non-military application, yet which excludes certain aspects of strategy in its modern military usage.

REFERENCES

Alvesson, M. and Willmott, H. (1996) *Making Sense of Management: a critical introduction*, Sage, London.

Ansoff, H.I. (1965) *Corporate Strategy*, McGraw-Hill, New York.

Ansoff, H.I. (1991) 'Critique of Henry Mintzberg's "The design school: reconsidering the basic premises of strategic management" ', *Strategic Management Journal*, Vol. 12, pp. 449–61.

Berger, P. and Luckmann, T. (1966) *The Social Construction of Reality*, Penguin, Harmondsworth.

Bracker, J. (1980) 'The historical development of the strategic management concept', *Academy of Management Review*, Vol. 5, pp. 219–24.

Brittan, A. (1989) *Masculinity and Power*, Blackwell, Oxford.

Burrell, G. (1992) 'Back to the future', in Reed, M. and Hughes, M. (eds) *Rethinking Organization*, Sage, London.

Chandler, A. (1962) *Strategy and Structure: chapters in the history of American enterprise*, MIT Press, Cambridge, MA.

Chandler, A. (1977) *The Visible Hand: the managerial revolution in American business*, Harvard University Press, Cambridge, MA.

Clark, T. and Salaman, G. (1996) 'The management guru as organizational witchdoctor', *Organization* Vol. 3, No. 1, pp. 85–107.

Cleverly, G. (1971) *Managers and Magic*, Longman, London.

Cooper, R. and Burrell, G. (1988) 'Modernism, postmodernism and organizational analysis: an introduction', *Organization Studies*, Vol. 9, No. 1, pp. 91–112.

Crouch, A. and Basch, J. (1996) 'The structure of strategic thinking: a lexical and content analysis', Paper presented to the second International Conference on *Organizational Discourse: Talk, Text and Tropes*, London, July.

Derrida, J. (1978) *Writing and Difference*, Routledge, London.

Eccles, R. and Nohria, N. (1992) *Beyond the Hype: rediscovering the essence of management*, Harvard Business School Press, Cambridge, MA.

Eisenhardt, K. and Zbaracki, M. (1992) 'Strategic decision making', *Strategic Management Journal*, Vol. 13, pp. 17–37.

French, R. and Grey, C. (eds) (1996) *Rethinking Management Education*, Sage, London.

Grant, R. (1995) *Contemporary Strategy Analysis*, Blackwell, Oxford.

Hoskin, K. (1990) 'Using history to understand theory: a reconceptualization of the historical genesis of "strategy" ', Paper presented to the EIASM workshop on *Strategy, Accounting and Control*, Venice.

Hoskin, K., Macve, R. and Stone, J. (1997) 'The historical genesis of modern business and military strategy: 1850–1950', Proceedings of the fifth *Interdisciplinary Perspectives on Accounting Conference*, University of Manchester.

Huczynski, A. (1993) *Management Gurus: what makes them and how to become one*, London, Routledge.

Johnson, G. (1987) *Strategic Change and the Management Process*, Blackwell, Oxford.

Knights, D. and Morgan, G. (1991) 'Corporate strategy, organizations and subjectivity: a critique', *Organizational Studies*, Vol. 12, No. 2, pp. 251–73.

Levinthal, D.A. and March, J.G. (1993) 'The myopia of learning', *Strategic Management Journal*, Vol. 14, pp. 95–112.

Locke, R. (1996) *The Collapse of the American Management Technique*, Oxford University Press, Oxford.

Mintzberg, H. (1990a) 'Strategy formation: schools of thought', in Fredrickson, J. (ed.) *Perspectives on Strategic Management*, Harper Business, New York.

Mintzberg, H. (1990b) 'The design school: reconsidering the basic premises of strategic management', *Strategic Management Journal*, Vol. 11, No. 3, pp. 171–96.

Mintzberg, H. (1991) 'Learning 1, Planning 0, Reply to Igor Ansoff', *Strategic Management Journal*, Vol. 12, p. 462.

Mockler, R. (1994) 'Strategic management research and teaching', *Management Learning*, Vol. 25, No. 3, pp. 371–85.

Nohria, N. and Berkley, J.D. (1994) 'Whatever happened to the "take-charge" manager?', *Harvard Business Review*, January–February, pp. 128–37.

Peters, M. and Robinson, V. (1984) 'The origins and status of action research', *Journal of Applied Behavioural Science*, Vol. 20, pp. 113–24.

Pettigrew, A. (1985) *The Awakening Giant*, Blackwell, Oxford.

Pye, A. (1995) 'Strategy through dialogue and doing', *Management Learning*, Vol. 26, No. 4, pp. 445–62.

Rumelt, R., Schendel, D. and Teece, D. (1991) 'Strategic management and economics', *Strategic Management Journal* Vol. 12, pp. 5–29.

Sloan, A. (1963) *My Years with General Motors*, Sedgewick and Jackson, London.

Stacey, R.D. (1995) 'The science of complexity: an alternative perspective for strategic change processes', *Strategic Management Journal*, Vol. 16, pp. 477–95.

Thomas, A.B. (1993) *Controversies in Management*, Routledge, London.

Weick, K. (1990) 'Cartographic myths in organizations', in Huff, A. (ed.) *Mapping Strategic Thought*, Wiley, London.

Whittington, R. (1993) *What is Strategy and Does it Matter?*, Routledge, London.

Zan, L. (1995) 'Interactionism and systemic view in the strategic approach', *Advances in Strategic Management*, Vol. 12, pp. 261–83.

INDEX

Note: 'n.' after a page reference indicates the number of a note on that page.